D1250627

EFFECTIVE MANAGERIAL COMMUNICATION

Robert W. Rasberry
Southern Methodist University

Laura Lemoine Lindsay
Louisiana State University

Wadsworth Publishing Company
A Division of Wadsworth, Inc.
Belmont, California

Business Communications Editor: Kathy Shields
Editorial Assistant: Tamara Huggins
Production Editor: Merrill Peterson
Designer: John Edeen
Print Buyer: Barbara Britton
Copy Editor: Vicki Nelson
Illustrator: Boston Graphics
Cover Design: Image House
Compositor: G&S Typesetters, Inc.
Printer: Arcata Graphics/Fairfield

This book is printed on acid-free recycled paper.

International Thomson Publishing
The trademark ITP is used under license.

Printed in the United States of America

2 3 4 5 6 7 8 9 10—98 97 96 95 94

Library of Congress Cataloging-in-Publication Data

Rasberry, Robert W.
Effective managerial communication / Robert W. Rasberry, Laura Lindsay. — 2nd ed.
p. cm.
Includes index.
ISBN 0-534-21468-1
1. Communication in management. 2. Business communication.
I. Lindsay, Laura. II. Title.
HD30.3.R37 1993
658.4'5—dc20 93-2578

Dedication

To *Jenni, Paul Michael,* and *John Robert,* whose love, support, and encouragement made the long hours of this writing much shorter. R.W. R.

To *Ashley* and *Wendell,* in loving appreciation of their enthusiasm, encouragement, and inspiration. L.L.L.

CONTENTS

PREFACE

The Importance of Communication

Communication is one of the most important tools in a businessperson's arsenal—it is the means by which all organizational activity is managed. With both a well-designed communication plan and effective communication skills, a manager can be highly successful.

Proof of the importance of effective communication emerges from interviews with numerous employees in various business settings. When the authors of this book asked employees what they most liked about their bosses, the most common responses referred to communication situations. The following are some examples: "I like my manager because he listens to me." "Anytime I have a problem I can go and talk to my boss." "Staff meetings are a joy because of the positive communication climate." "My employer is a fantastic communicator. I can listen to her speak for five minutes in the morning, and I'm on a 'high' all day long." "My manager not only tells me clearly what he wants me to do, he also instills in me a belief that I can do it."

The Plan of the Book

The topic of this book is communication as it applies to management within an organizational setting. We realize that not all readers are or will be managers; however, everyone in business, even those in staff positions, must perform various managing tasks, and to do this effectively requires communication skills. Furthermore, managers agree that their job is made easier when those they supervise understand the role that managers must occupy. A basic understanding of the principles and techniques of good communication will improve the process among all participants. This book is designed to help the reader develop three essential types of communication skills: *technical skills,* or the process and techniques of communication in the work environment; *human skills,* or how to communicate interpersonally on the job; and *conceptual skills,* or the ability to communicate effective decisions designed to accomplish organizational goals.

The techniques and principles of organizational communication are conveyed through our experience in the field. We have examined communication from advisory roles in actual business practice, from managerial roles in public and private settings, and from consulting roles that range from needs assessment to training and program evaluation. We feel this array of experience gives us a perspective of communication as an event within an organization that few other business communication authors have. Thus, we feel this textbook will be unique in meeting the needs of those who anticipate a future in the business world—especially those who believe they will one day be managing other people.

The book contains five major parts, each of which begins with a review of the forthcoming chapters and insights into the philosophy of the material. Each chapter starts with an introductory situation and concludes with a summary. Following the summary are a list of key words, a group of review questions, and a variety of exercises that students can perform alone after completing the chapter or in groups in the classroom.

New to this edition is an emphasis on two important areas: global management and ethics. Each chapter presents a "global perspective" report and an ethics case that relate to the chapter content.

Part 1 examines communication as a management process. The roles that managers play and the skills that they need are discussed. Next we introduce a theoretical yet practical model of communication that will be applied throughout the book. The elements that go into communication are defined within the framework of the model. Central to this model is the role communication plays in the lives of managers. We then describe the many ways businesspeople communicate formally and informally in organizations. We describe how the culture, climate, networks, and channels of communication either facilitate or deter understanding.

Part 2 describes four potential hurdles that can limit the development of effective communication skills: perception, language, nonverbal behavior, and listening. This section focuses on perception and its impact on the way people understand and communicate with other people. Words mean different things to different people. Thus, knowledge of language and comprehension of language barriers help cultivate common understanding and avoid misunderstandings with other people.

With a model of the way in which communication works and an awareness of four key barriers that can minimize effective communication, the reader is ready to examine the two major communication skills that are most used in business. Part 3 contains four chapters that cover the areas of speaking and writing. Chapter 8 describes a seven-part process of making oral presentations that looks at ways to answer initial questions, arrange material visually, package supporting material, use technology effectively, construct the presentation, practice giving it, and deliver the actual performance.

Chapter 9 concentrates on letters and memos and the three primary formats: direct, indirect, and persuasive. Chapter 10 contrasts formal reports with the new inverted writing style. Chapter 11 examines the important process of editing.

Making use of the material in the first eleven chapters, Part 4 demonstrates the importance of effective communication, comprehension of potential communication barriers, and development of particular communication skills as significant factors in establishing effective management.

In Chapters 12 through 17, six communicative strategies are explored. These are teamwork and leadership, problem resolution, managing conflict, making meetings work, conducting interviews, and managing change.

Part 5 consists of only one chapter, but it is one of the most important sections of the book. By interlacing every chapter and concept detailed in the preceding chapters, the Overview of Chapters presents an overview of the entire text. It concludes that a clear knowledge and understanding of the communication process and potential communication problems, coupled with practiced communication skills, will enable a person to become an effective communicator in business.

Six appendices follow the main text. Appendix A gives an overview of three ethical theories that can be used to analyze the short ethics cases that are found in each chapter. The theories are utilitarian, social contract, and pluralism (or duty-based ethics). Appendix B presents the outlines of eight sample presentations, each with a different pattern of organization, thus providing a variety of types of verbal supporting material. Appendix C contains the pages and format of a formal report. In Appendix D are two additional formal reports, both on the Knight Foundation Commission on Intercollegiate Athletics. Appendix E contains the answers to the exercises in Chapter 11. Finally, Appendix F presents a longer, more comprehensive case, "The Space Shuttle *Challenger* Disaster."

Suggestions to the Student

It is our hope and belief that mastery of the material presented in this text will lead to the development of effective communication skills. To enhance the success with which this task is accomplished, we offer some ideas on how to approach this book. Following these suggestions while you are reading this book will make your job easier and more efficient and will improve your retention of the material.

First, *preview* the entire book by looking at its various parts: the title page, contents, body of the text, appendices, and index.

Second, when a chapter is assigned, quickly *skim* each page of it before you start reading. Start with the chapter title, and then look at the number of pages in the chapter. Next, go through the chapter and note the main headings and subheadings in order to form a mental outline of the chapter. Look at all the figures and illustrations; doing this will help improve your ability to relate these items to the text when you read it in detail. Read the chapter summary in its entirety, and note important words that are briefly described. Ask yourself how these words fit into the organization plan that you have been building in your mind. If you have some confusion about the chapter outline, skim quickly through the chapter again and reread the summary.

Third, *review* the list of key words and the review questions at the end of the chapter. Seeing the words before reading the text will reinforce the words and their definitions as you read the chapter. Treat the review questions in the same way. If a review question requires that a concept, definition, or idea be stated in a brief and clear manner, look for that information as you read. Avoid reading the *exercise* questions because some of these questions give answers to quizzes presented within the chapter. Reading the exercises before reading the text will detract from the learning that you will experience later.

Fourth, *read* the chapter in its entirety. As you read, remember to relate the concepts and ideas to the mental outline that you developed during the skimming stage. Note the important items that you will want to talk about in the classroom. After you have read the chapter, answer the discussion questions and complete the exercises.

We wish you enjoyable reading, and we hope this book will help you to understand communication theory and to apply communication skills effectively as an employee and as a manager. If you have comments or feedback about this text, the authors would enjoy talking with you. Especially welcome are real-life examples and cases that could be incorporated into future editions. Please address your thoughts to: Dr. Robert W. Rasberry, Cox School of Business, Southern Methodist University, Dallas, Texas 75275.

Our Thanks

Writing a book is a tremendous undertaking. Although we are responsible for the contents and design of the material, we acknowledge that without the help of others the book would have been much more difficult to complete.

We would like to thank our families for the steady support, encouragement, and especially "alone time" that they gave us. To Jenni, Paul Michael, John Robert, Ashley, and Wendell, our special love and thanks.

A number of individuals contributed to the writing of the text. The manuscript was read and edited by Tim Riggins, Sally Rawlings, Kim Feil, Connie Johnson, Alan Tompkins, David Radman, Don Nichols, Kirk Blankenship, John Grinaldi, and Sarah Sams. Thank you all. On this second edition Frances Roper and Eric Johnson gave hours of time and valuable input and ideas.

We would also like to thank the following reviewers of this new edition for their time and significant comments: Karon L. Tomerlin, Southwest Missouri State University; Chase De Long, Brigham Young University, Hawaii; Paula R. Kaiser, University of North Carolina at Greensboro; Vera Hummel, Wayne State College; Richard Immenhausen, College of the Desert; Robert L. Kemp, University of Iowa; Retha H. Kilpatrick, Western Carolina University; Valerie E. Mock, Georgia State University; Marc H. Goldberg, Portland State University.

Robert W. Rasberry
Laura Lemoine Lindsay

ABOUT THE AUTHORS

ROBERT W. RASBERRY, Ph.D. (University of Kansas), has been teaching in the Edwin L. Cox School of Business at Southern Methodist University in Dallas, Texas, since 1974. He is the Director of Communication Services and is a professor of organizational behavior. His major areas of research and teaching include communication skills, management, and corporate social responsibility—especially as it relates to ethics. Bob has written over 25 articles and professional papers. In addition to being a coauthor of this text, he is the author of *The "Technique" of Political Lying* and the coauthor of *Power Talk: How to Win Your Audience.* He is also the coauthor of another Wadsworth book, *Advanced Business Communication.* He has extensive training and consulting experience. Since the early 1970s he has participated in over 300 middle-management and executive-level seminars. His client list numbers over 50 organizations and associations, among them IBM, Oryx Energy, the United States Chamber of Commerce, Mobil Exploration, Tandem Computers, Rockwell International, and AT & T.

LAURA LEMOINE LINDSAY, Ph.D. (Louisiana State University), has been Associate Vice Chancellor of Academic Affairs at Louisiana State University since November 1984. Previously she was dean of the Junior Division. She is a graduate of the Harvard Management Development program, the Council for a Better Louisiana Leadership program, and the Baton Rouge Chamber of Commerce Leadership program. Her experience includes acting as supervising lecturer and director of the Comprehensive Public Training Program, a managerial and career enrichment program at LSU, for Louisiana state employees. She has taught oral and written organizational communication skills, personnel management, public speaking, group discussion, problem solving, conflict resolution, mediation, time management, counseling and discipline, interpersonal communication, and broadcasting. She has designed core curricula and training manuals, coordinated communication programs on the graduate and undergraduate levels, and conducted over 250 training programs for the public and private sector. Among her clients are the U.S. Civil Service Commission, the Ethyl Corporation, and Gulf States Utilities.

PART 1

EFFECTIVE COMMUNICATION AS A MANAGEMENT PROCESS

Managers are involved in a variety of roles in the workplace. These roles require effective skills. The ability to master these skills requires effective communication ability. Consequently, employers look for strong communication skills in the new employees they hire.

A *model of communication* is introduced in Chapter 1, and it will be used throughout the book. This model presents both theoretical and practical approaches to the way that managers can increase their effectiveness by improving the way they communicate with others.

Chapter 2 starts by describing the importance of organizational culture. The culture is impacted by the *formal communication* in an organization. This is the horizontal and vertical flow of information. This flow helps determine the structure that an organization designs. Recent improvements in technology have altered the flow of communication and consequently the structural designs of organizations.

Chapter 3 presents a look at the *informal flow* of communication both inside and outside the organization. This informal process is also called the rumor mill or grapevine. The communication climate is the key to defining how well information is conveyed in an organization. The climate is impacted by the quantity and quality of communication in the organization and the channels that carry it. This chapter also describes informal networks that are created when communication flows frequently between certain people. To improve communication in the organization, a variety of auditing tools, including the Malcolm Baldrige National Quality Award, are available.

CHAPTER 1

THE ROLE OF COMMUNICATION IN MANAGEMENT

It is Tuesday, 8:00 A.M., and Sue has a project due for her company's president Friday morning. She realizes that John has some information that she must have to complete the job and finds him at the coffee pot. She asks, "John, will you give me the information on the Smither's budget by Thursday?"

John responds, "Sorry, Sue, I can't get that to you by Thursday. Would Monday be all right?"

The verbal messages in this scenario are brief, but the information relayed is important to the people involved. Sue needs help from John. Is his response a refusal? a delaying tactic? an indication of a bigger problem? What Sue and John communicate and how they communicate it influences their behavior and, in turn, the resolution of their problem.

Our ability to develop and use effective communication skills is demonstrated when we visit with colleagues, purchase equipment, or operate a computer terminal. In the organization, communication skills have special importance. The complexity and dynamics of even a small organization involve the recording, storage, dissemination, and evaluation of ideas, information, directions, policies, and rules to accomplish specific goals. To this mix must be added human capabilities and experiences, modern technology, the explosion of current knowledge, and the movement from international to global communication networks. Effective communication must exist if complex organizations are to be productive.

The communication demands placed on today's manager are growing. A quick glance at a series of courses offered in continuing education programs for adults reveals that 75 to 80 percent of those courses deal with communication: They teach participants how to read, write, communicate with computer operators, resolve conflict, upgrade interpersonal skills, learn group leadership skills, develop total quality management skills, learn computer software packages, develop presentational speaking skills, coach and counsel, and train for television appearances.

To engage in each one of these activities, a manager must master specific roles and skills. In addition, a manager must know what form of communication to use in a given situation. Since the goals of management are accomplished through the worker, it is the manager's job to communicate the goals of the organization to the worker in the form of coordinated tasks and to eliminate barriers or problems that might prevent goal attainment.

The Job of Being a Manager

A manager is involved in a variety of roles that require the mastering of several specific skills.

Managerial Roles

According to Henry Mintzberg, there are ten different roles in which a manager is involved. Figure 1.1 shows how these ten roles fall into three categories: interpersonal, informational, and decisional. Some managers do not perform each role. Some perform a combination of the roles. Although the roles

Interpersonal Roles	*Activities*
Figurehead	—Handles symbolic and ceremonial tasks
Liaison	—Builds internal and external information networks
Leader	—Directs and coordinates the group's goals
Informational Roles	*Activities*
Monitor	—Seeks, receives, and sifts information
Disseminator	—Distributes information to others
Spokesperson	—Provides information to many outside the organization through speeches, reports, and television
Decisional Roles	*Activities*
Entrepreneur	—Identifies and starts needed projects and programs
Disturbance handler	—Solves conflicts between individuals and departments
Negotiator	—Represents the company or department in bargaining
Resource allocator	—Decides who gets what resources and how much they will receive

FIGURE 1.1 Mintzberg's Managerial Roles
Source: Marshall Sashkin and William C. Morris, *Experiencing Management,* (Adapted from pp. 2–3) © 1987 Addison-Wesley Publishing Company. Reprinted by permission.

are described seperately, in reality they are highly integrated. Also, the outcome of these roles varies according to a manager's place in the organizational structure (first-line management, middle management, or executive-level management).[1]

Management Skills

Since a manager's job can be described through a variety of specific roles, a manager must have developed skills to complete the roles effectively. Robert Katz has identified three basic types of skills that managers need: technical, human, and conceptual.[2]

Technical skill is the means by which the worker accomplishes a specialized activity and may include methods, processes, techniques, and procedures. For example, technical skills set apart the electrical engineer from the mechanical engineer.

Human skill is the ability to work interpersonally with other group members. Human skills include self-knowledge, communication, motivation, and understanding. A doctor's ability to relate to patients is often referred to as the doctor's bedside manner; it is recognized as an essential ingredient of effective medicine. Managers too must develop human skills.

Conceptual skill may be defined as the ability to identify and analyze problems and implement effective decisions. Conceptual skills include perceptual, creative, coordination, and integration skills that help lead the organization toward a common goal.

The ability to communicate requires a mastery of each of Katz's skill areas. Technical skill is important for managerial success, but human and conceptual skills are essential.

Management Level	Balance of the Three Skills
Executive	Conceptual skills
Middle management	Human relations skills
Supervisory	Technical skills

FIGURE 1.2 Katz's Three Managerial Skills
Source: Marshall Sashkin and William C. Morris, *Experiencing Management,* (Adapted from pp. 2–3) © 1987 Addison-Wesley Publishing Company. Reprinted by permission.

Figure 1.2 describes the balance among the three skills. First-line supervisors need a tremendous amount of technical skills and a lot of human relations skills. They do not need a great deal of conceptual skill, however. At the top management level this requirement is reversed.

Communication Skills

The ability to master each of the three skill levels requires communication skills. Mintzberg, in developing his ten managerial roles, assumed that at the minimum managers would have written, oral, and nonverbal communication skills. Hellriegel and Slocum describe how important these communication skills are for university students who will become managers.

> Because managers spend a large portion of their time communicating, recruiters look for people who can communicate effectively. A common complaint is that professional programs in universities spend too much time developing students' technical skills and not enough time developing their communication skills. In fact, the importance of good communication skills cannot be stressed enough. At a time when organizations increasingly expect employees to work with minimal supervision and to show more initiative, competent communication skills are becoming a must.[3]

Managers in the Year 2000

Managers today find the world is shrinking and becoming one interdependent marketplace. Globalization of business is a reality. Computerization and telecommunications allow a manager to be everywhere at once. As you read through this book, you will discover how managers apply their skills in the marketplace. But you will also discover that change is occurring rapidly and the skills demanded today may be obsolete tomorrow. Figure 1.3 shows the predicted results of a major study, *Workforce 2000,* conducted by the Hudson Institute and the U.S. Department of Labor.

The study shows that new workers entering the work force between now and the year 2000 will be much different from those employed today. Diversity will be the norm with nonwhites, women, and immigrants making up more than five-sixths of the net additions. When the report was published in 1987, those same groups made up half of the work force. Added to the diversity of the work force will be rapid changes in the nature of the job market. The fastest-growing jobs will be in professional, technical, and sales fields. These will require the highest education and skill levels. "Of the fastest-growing job categories, all but one, service occupations, require more than the median level of education [13.5] for all jobs. Of those growing more slowly than average, not one requires more than the median education."[4]

Figure 1.3 shows that "when jobs are given numerical ratings according to the math, language, and reasoning skills they require, only twenty-seven percent of all new jobs fall into the lowest two skill categories, while 40 per-

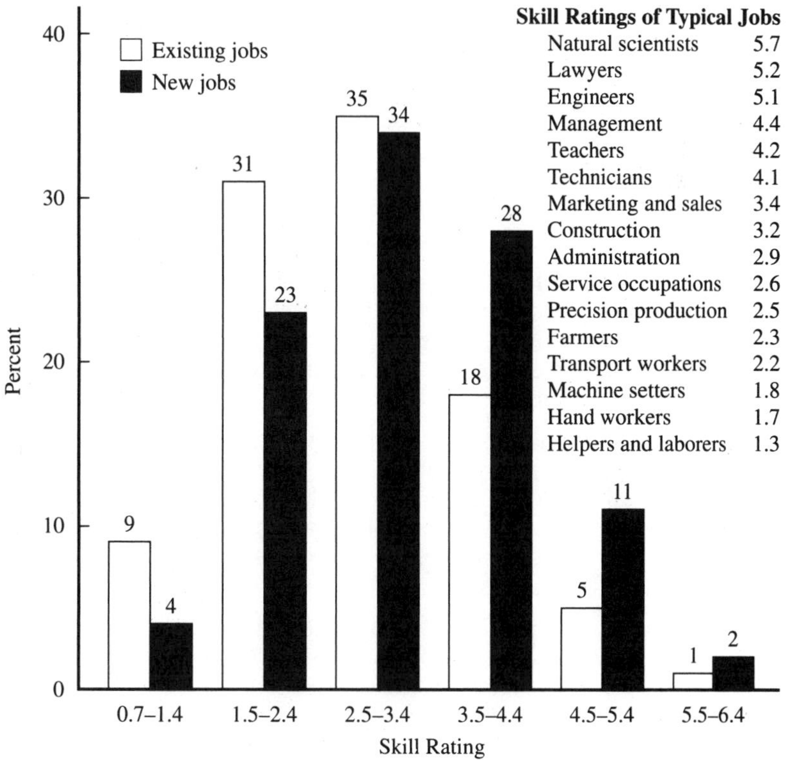

FIGURE 1.3 Changing Job Skills
Source: *Workforce 2000: Work and Workers for the Twenty-first Century* (Indianapolis: Hudson Institute and the U.S. Department of Labor, June 1987), p. 100.

cent of current jobs require these limited skills. By contrast, 41 percent of new jobs are in the three highest skill groups, compared to only 24 percent of current jobs."[5]

As the following story describes, the world of the twenty-first-century manager will be much different than the world of today's manager.

A Day in the Life of Tomorrow's Manager[6]

6:10 A.M. The year is 2010 and another Monday morning has begun for Peter Smith. The marketing vice-president for a home-appliance division of a major U.S. manufacturer is awakened by his computer alarm. He saunters to his terminal to check the weather outlook in Madrid, where he'll fly late tonight, and to send an electronic voice message to a supplier in Thailand.

7:20 A.M. Mr. Smith and his wife, who heads her own architecture firm, organize the home front before darting to the supertrain. They leave instructions for their personal computer to call the home-cleaning service as well as a gourmet carryout service that will prepare dinner for eight guests Saturday. And they quickly go over the day's schedules for their three- and six-year-old daughters with their nanny.

On the train during a speedy 20-minute commute from their suburb to Manhattan, Mr. Smith checks his electronic mailbox and also reads his favorite trade magazine via his laptop computer.

8:15 A.M. In his high-tech office that doubles as a conference room, Mr. Smith reviews the day's schedule with his executive assistant (traditional secretaries vanished a decade earlier). Then it's on to his first meeting: a conference via video screen between his division's chief production manager in Cincinnati and a supplier near Munich.

The supplier tells them she can deliver a critical component for a new appliance at a 10 percent cost saving if they grab it within a week. Mr. Smith and the production manager quickly concur that it's a good deal. While they'll have to change production schedules immediately, they'll be able to snare a new customer who has been balking about price.

10:30 A.M. At a staff meeting, Mr. Smith finds himself refereeing between two subordinates who disagree vehemently on how to promote a new appliance. One, an Asian manager, suggests that a fresh campaign begin much sooner than initially envisioned. The other, a European, wants to hold off until results of a test market are received later that week.

Mr. Smith quickly realizes this is a cultural, not strategic, clash, pitting a let's-do-it-now, analyze-it-later approach against a more cautious style. He makes both parties aware they're not really far apart and the European manager agrees to move swiftly.

(continued)

12:30 P.M. Lunch is in Mr. Smith's office today, giving him time to take a video lesson in conversational Chinese. He already speaks Spanish fluently, learned during a work stint in Argentina, and wants to master at least two more languages. After 20 minutes, though, he decides to go to his computer to check his company's latest political-risk assessment on Spain, where recent student unrest has erupted into riots. The report tells him that the disturbances aren't anti-American, but he decides to have a bodyguard meet him at the Madrid airport anyway.

2:20 P.M. Two of Mr. Smith's top lieutenants complain that they and others on his staff feel a recent bonus payment for a successful project wasn't divided equitably. Bluntly, they note that while Mr. Smith received a hefty $20,000 bonus, his fifteen-member staff had to split $5,000, and they threaten to defect. He quickly calls his boss, who says he'll think about increasing the bonus for staff members.

4 P.M. Mr. Smith learns from the field that a large retail customer has been approached by a foreign competitor promising to supply him quickly with a best-selling appliance. After conferring with his division's production managers, he phones the customer and suggests that his company could supply the same product but with three slightly different custom designs. They arrange a meeting later in the week.

6 P.M. Before heading to the airport, Mr. Smith uses his video phone to give his daughters a good-night kiss and to talk about the next day's schedule with his wife. Learning that she must take an unexpected trip herself the next evening, he promises to catch the SuperConcorde home in time to put the kids to sleep himself.

RESEARCH ON COMMUNICATION SKILLS

The last thirty years of research have shown repeatedly that communication skills are of primary importance to business graduates. In 1959, two simultaneous studies sponsored by the Ford and Carnegie foundations made a tremendous impact on business education and research. These studies declared that the educational objective of business education in colleges and universities should be to prepare students for personally fruitful and socially useful careers in business and related types of activity. They argued that business students must be able to assimilate and apply specific knowledge in areas of finance, accounting, and economics based on a broad educational background in nonprofessional areas. Complementary skill areas that were recommended for study included problem solving, organizing, maintaining interpersonal relationships, and communicating. Those influential in business school education felt that these skills should be acquired in appropriate disciplines in a standard sequence of study.

A decade later, Clark surveyed the importance of communication skills in private and governmental organizations. She found that business school graduates lacked sufficient preparation in oral communication.[7] Ranked high in importance by business people were (1) effective interviewing, (2) giving oral orders and instruction, (3) telephoning, (4) listening, and (5) leading informal conferences. Formal speech making was ranked lower in importance.

Although a variety of studies conducted in the 1960s through the 1980s have supported the need for more communication training, a study by Penrose found that "The more specific and traditional . . . topics of business writing and business speaking remained fairly consistently in the top half of the list of twelve abilities."[8] At one conference on career communication, representatives from a variety of professions responded to the question, "What speech communication competencies are required in your business, industry, agency, or profession?"[9] They agreed on the need for such competencies as the ability to:

- Facilitate small group discussions in an organization in order to accomplish an assigned task in a cooperative spirit.
- Interview an individual in order to determine whether he or she has the capabilities necessary to advance with the company.
- Solve problems and make decisions using a variety of strategies and evaluate the effectiveness of a decision.
- Use public relations in order to maximize credibility between the organization and the public sector.
- Apply good listening skills.
- Use persuasion effectively with clients or employees to inform, convince, or accomplish a course of action.
- Motivate employees to accomplish the objectives of the organization.
- Resolve conflict within the organization.
- Speak effectively.
- Utilize a team approach to problem solving and goal achievement by building productive relationships among members of the organization.
- Ask questions that elicit the information that the organization needs in order to function well.

Understanding which communication skills are needed by managers requires an understanding of how communication occurs in an organization and which key theories of management have made those skills necessary.

In 1986, the Carnegie Foundation for the Advancement of Teaching issued a report, *College: The Undergraduate Experience in America.* In it the foundation called for a severe overhaul of undergraduate education. Supporting the critical need for communication skills improvement, the report recommended that all college seniors write a senior thesis and defend it orally in a seminar with classmates. In acknowledging the moral decline of society, the report also urged that students' majors be broadened to require a study of the history of and the ethical questions about their chosen field.[10]

In 1990, the American Society for Training and Development (ASTD) surveyed its members who are training practitioners, managers, administrators, educators, and human resource developers. They arrived at sixteen skills that employers say are basic to success in the workplace. "The foundation skill upon which all other skills are based is learning to learn. Technical competence requires reading, writing and computation. Skills that enable people to communicate effectively on the job are oral communication and listening."[11]

Added to the need for improving communication skills and incorporating ethical training is the new requirement for global understanding. Claire Gaudiani, president of Connecticut College, addressed this issue.

> Right now the United States of America needs a generation of citizens entering all professions who are prepared to operate in the international arena, even if they never leave their hometown. They will be in a position to interact in a multinational, multicultural environment through telecommunications and through travel, which will become increasingly important. . . . In order for Americans to operate effectively in a global environment, they have to understand the tensions in a foreign country. . . . This need in the nation is going to cause liberal education to broaden its scope, to stretch, not to transform its values, but to stretch them out to face this challenge.[12]

Key Theories of Management

Since the turn of the twentieth century much discussion and controversy have focused on the issue of how to manage an organization. "Management" style affects our productivity, employers, leaders, foes, or the success of a family: It molds society. While we recognize its importance, we find it difficult to define the essential features of management. Its history is vague.

While principles of management existed in early civilizations, little was written describing them for succeeding generations. Because one civilization failed to learn from the successes and failures of others, continual relearning of principles was required to reach specific management goals.

Not until the end of the nineteenth century was management recognized as a science. Standards of production were subjectively established, with persuasion and coercion the prime motivators and decisions based on experience and intuition. Since that time several key theories of management have been developed. Each of the theories revolves around a particular way of viewing an organization, its people, and, ultimately, communication.

Classical Management Theory

Managers established standards of production subjectively until the end of the nineteenth century. At that time, Frederick W. Taylor began to espouse a philosophy of work. His approach, labeled *scientific management,* focused on the systematic observations of production and shop operations. His definition of management, widely accepted today, is the process of getting things done by others, either independently or in groups.[13]

Taylor's two essential elements of scientific management were *cooperation* and *scientific knowledge.* He employed many mechanisms to accomplish these ends, including time study, functional foremanship, standardization of tools and implements, differential rates, and modern costs systems.[14]

Making a contribution at the same time was Henri Fayol, a managing director of a French industrial and mining company. Fayol was the first to advocate management as a body of knowledge that could be taught. He defined its functions as (1) forecasting and planning, (2) organizing, (3) commanding, (4) controlling, and (5) coordinating. Of these five functions, *planning* was the most important.

Other writers also had an impact on the classical school and the development of scientific management. Frank and Lillian Gilbreth focused on the human side of management and used time and motion studies. They believed there was *one best way* to work, and they analyzed jobs to determine the most efficient movements for performing a particular task based on the standardization of tools and processes, the study of motion, the impact of fatigue, and the skill of the worker. They contributed to the current ideas of job simplification, work standards, and incentive wage plans.[15]

Inherent in all three of these contributions are the ideas that (1) there is a human side of management, (2) management and labor must cooperate, and (3) communication is an important tool. Fayol noted in his writings the difference between oral and written communications, the importance of explaining complicated problems, and the need to give instructions face to face. Taylor recognized the importance of providing recognition and rewards to keep the "human machine" running. And in his studies of time and motion, Frank Gilbreth emphasized studying the impact of fatigue and skill on performance. Lillian Gilbreth never wavered in her belief that the worker needed attention and recognition.

New methods of communicating with workers evolved. Rather than the directive or authoritarian approach, theorists espoused cooperation between worker and management. Greater emphasis was placed on new forms of communicating: on recognition, evaluation, explanation, and information gathering. As the classical approach to management became more widely accepted, however, a new theory, which emphasized the human factor, emerged.

Human Relations Theory

Mary Parker Follett made major contributions to shifting management focus from the scientific approach to the human relations approach. She criticized the "old fashioned theory of leadership" professed by psychologists of the day and proposed that leaders should possess a thorough knowledge of their industries and the ability to remember that different situations call for different leaders. She also felt that managers should be able to grasp complex situations, organize work groups, find creative solutions, direct management power, and develop leadership skills in employees.[16] Follett's writings in the area of coordination are filled with practical ideas and examples and remain relevant today. She set forth three principles of coordination in business:

1. *Using integration* and finding alternatives that all employees can live with, as opposed to compromise or domination by managers as a method of working out differences.
2. *Cross-functioning,* or the manager's ability to confer and solve problems at various levels of the organization instead of being limited to upward and downward communication.
3. *Sharing collective responsibility,* or the ability to integrate knowledge and experience in order to produce effectively.

The human relations school was primarily interested in experimenting with working conditions and people. One of the most famous series of these experiments was conducted by Elton Mayo at the Hawthorne Plant of the Western Electric Company in the Chicago area. Mayo found that productivity seemed to be affected more by attitudes and feelings than by job conditions and environment. He observed that *informal systems* within the organization determined employee output. The importance of *social networks* surfaced as well as the role of formal horizontal communication and employee-oriented management.

The human relations movement encouraged recognition of employees' needs such as first-name status with all coworkers, employee parties, suggestion boxes, and benefit packages. Increasing employee involvement in this type of program often led to happy employees but, since these were superficial advances, led also to unproductive work forces.

The findings of proponents of the human relations school have been enhanced by the work of Douglas McGregor. In the 1950s he began to explore leadership and the way that employees respond to their superiors' actions and developed a theory of the X and Y style of management that is now considered a classic. He looked at earlier, classical schools of management thought and described, in his theory X, how those managers viewed employees. In theory Y, McGregor elaborated on his earlier theory X contentions and established a foundation for furthering the examination of human behavior in management.[17]

Theory X

1. People don't like work. They are inherently lazy, will avoid work if they can, and usually work for the basics of life: food, shelter, and clothing.
2. Because of their dislike for work, people must be forced to work or, at the very least, coerced. Consequently, they must be directed, controlled, and monitored closely.
3. People don't like responsibility unless forced to take it. By keeping employees anxious about their security, they can be induced to take responsibility and work toward organizational goals.

Theory Y

1. Work is as natural as play or rest.
2. Exercising external controls and threats is not the only way to direct people. Managers can help employees exercise self-direction and self-control and still accomplish organizational goals.
3. Commitment to objectives is directly related to the rewards associated with their achievement.
4. Under the proper work conditions the average person learns to accept and seek responsibility.
5. Most employees, not just a few, can exercise a high degree of imagination, ingenuity, and creativity in solving organizational problems.
6. Under the conditions of modern industrial life, the intellectual potentials of the average worker are only partially utilized.

Systems Theory

An organization is affected by many interrelated influences: environment, customers, competitors, labor organizations, government, suppliers of available resources, and employee interaction. Each interrelates with others and contributes to the overall purpose of the organization. The systems theory of management emphasizes these interrelationships and views the organization as a set of subsystems.

Organizational systems are either *open* or *closed.* An open system interacts with its environment, while a closed system functions without environmental interaction. Few systems have no interaction with the environment. A computer, for example, can perform a series of very complex functions but requires interaction with the programmer before it can perform those functions. The organizational system is influenced by several factors: input, output, and feedback (see Figure 1.4).

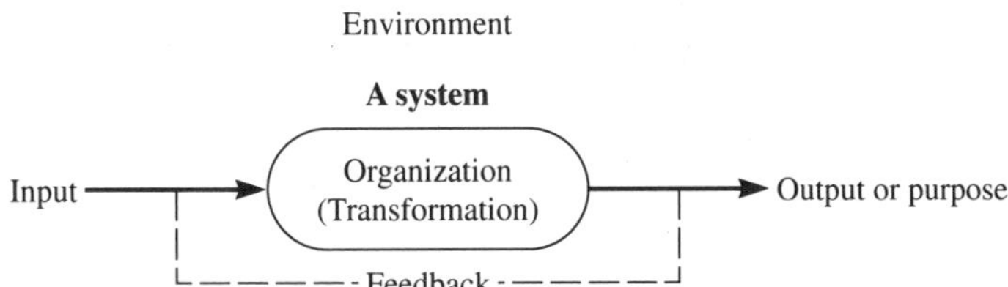

FIGURE 1.4 A Systems Theory Model

Input

Input can be money, raw materials, information, data from opinion polls, or economic conditions. The primary functions of input are to determine the characteristics of the environment, identify trouble spots that might affect organizational output, reflect the organization as others see it, provide information for effective decision making, and improve output. Input is then analyzed and evaluated to determine if current organizational procedures should be altered.

Transformation

The organization consists of a complex network of subsystems that transforms inputs into outputs, and the organizational design plays an integral part in the logic of the network that results in tangible outputs. Compared to the smaller U.S. Senate, the House of Representatives' sheer size vastly increases the complexity of its communication channels. The number of House contacts necessary to gain support on an issue affects both the form of a representative's message and its content.

Output

Organizational output occurs in the form of products, public relations, information, and public service. Although the primary forms of output are products and face-to-face communication, other types of output implement telephone messages, public appearances, letters, and the mass media.

Feedback

The final element of the systems model is feedback. Once decisions are made and the organization transforms input into output, consumers react to the finished product. Their reactions are feedback for the organization, and that feedback occurs in several forms: Product consumption may increase or decrease; survey results may uncover product weaknesses or strengths; complaints, lawsuits, or letters of support may become organizational barometers of success. Feedback allows the organization to evaluate its output.

The systems theory emphasizes interrelationships among workers and managers, the environment and technology, input and output, consumers and competitors. Because it functions in a dynamic environment, an effective organization seeks to maintain a balance between input and output. Few organizational systems can operate without interacting with the environment. Systems theory does not attempt to evaluate the interrelationships between environment, specific organizational structure, and job functions.

Contingency Theory

Early management studies searched for universal answers that could be applied to any organization's problems. Eventually, however, researchers realized that various factors like the environment, organizational setting,

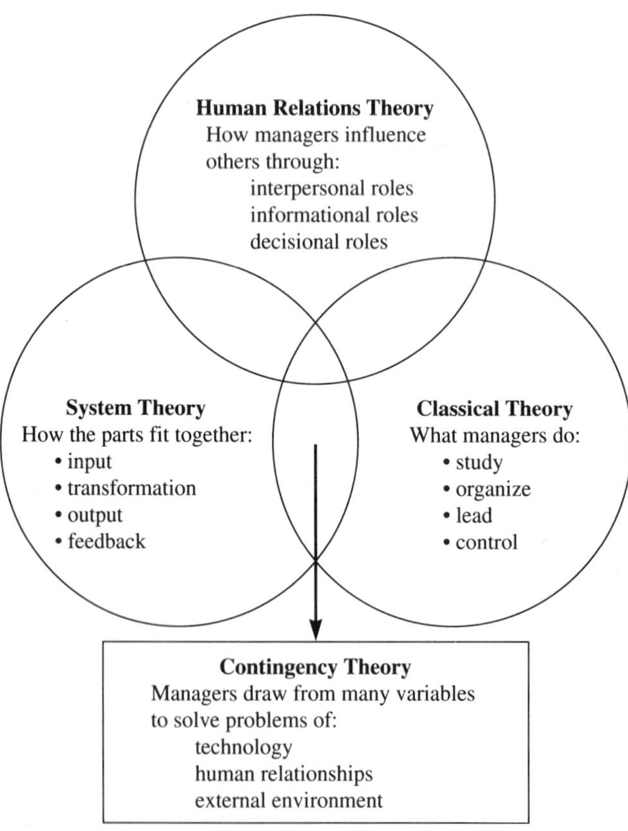

FIGURE 1.5 Converging of Different Management Theories
Source: Adapted from Don Hellriegel and John Slocum, *Management, Sixth Edition,* © 1992 Addison-Wesley Publishing Company. Reprinted by permission.

and behavior of employees made all-inclusive solutions impossible. What worked for an organization at one location would not work for the same organization at another location. In fact, most situations and outcomes are *contingent* upon influence by several variables.[18] The contingency theory is especially popular in examining motivation, leadership, and organizational structure. Moorehead and Griffin cite an example of how theories of managing must often change.

> When Jim Treybig founded Tandem Computers, he used an open, laid-back management style. His office was always accessible, and he paid little attention to what others were doing. Tandem grew rapidly, but eventually problems set in. Profits started to drop, and a financial scandal occurred. Treybig soon realized that his relaxed approach would not work in a larger, more formal organization. Consequently, he developed a more formalized control process and adopted a clearer hierarchy. As a result, Tandem regained its lost effectiveness. Treybig learned the hard way that what works in one situation (for example, a new, small company) will not necessarily work in another (a larger, more established firm).[19]

The contingency theory allows managers to use the other three management theories in whole or in parts, independently or collectively, as needed to resolve problems. Figure 1.5 describes how the various theories all influence one another in practice. Using the method requires the development of conceptual skills that allow adequate researching and creativity to determine the best solution.

Managerial Communication

For a manager to perform effectively the tasks required in the various management models, and especially to implement decisions, strong interpersonal and communication skills are vital.

The Elements of Communication

Communication can be defined as sorting, selecting, forming, and transmitting symbols between people to create meaning; it can best be understood by examining its elements. Two common elements are necessary in every communication situation: a source and a receiver. In the opening scenario of this chapter, as John listens to Sue, he sees and hears her message. Likewise, as Sue is talking, she sees and hears John's reactions. To understand the communication process better, we can examine this situation and identify its elements:

> It is Tuesday, 8:00 A.M., and Sue finds John at the coffee pot. She wants to convince John to give her information and sends the message, "John, will you give me the information on the Smither's budget by Thursday?"

Source. Sue is the source since she initiated a message, a complex process that includes several steps: (1) A stimulus creates a thought and a desire to communicate; (2) these thoughts are encoded into a message; and (3) they are transmitted through a channel to John.

Encoding. Sue's central nervous system ordered her to select symbols to form the sounds and actions that convey her message.

The message. The message includes everything that conveys meaning to the listener. With Sue, this includes words, facial expression, vocal expression, and appearance. Contrast her message by considering the following possibilities:

1. With hands on hips, in a stern tone and with a serious expression, Sue demands, "John, will you give me the information on the Smither's budget by Thursday?"
2. Holding papers in disarray and dropping some, Sue stoops to pick them up, appears embarrassed, and uses a hesitant, questioning tone: "John, will you give me the information on the Smither's budget by Thursday?"

In these two situations, Sue vocalizes her message differently and thereby conveys different meanings to her listener.

Transmission. Sue's message is sent into the environment and is made available to John. Her brain orders her muscles to react, and they produce sounds, gestures, and movement.

Channel. The channel is the means chosen to convey the message. Sue could have chosen a variety of modes of transmitting her message, such as a letter or telephone call, but she selected face-to-face interaction.

Receiver. John's response depends on a number of factors: the fidelity or acuteness of his senses, his competing needs, the environment, his understanding of the message, and his knowledge of Sue. Let's continue our scenario:

> John is pretty busy. Besides, Sue has had a recent promotion for which John was also considered, and she has a number of new responsibilities and tasks. To John, she appears nervous, disorganized, and less relaxed and informal than she used to be. John decides that Thursday is too soon to give her the information she wants and asks for a later date. He responds, "Sorry, Sue, I can't get that to you by Thursday. Would Monday be all right?"

John's response to Sue's message provided feedback. He decoded and interpreted Sue's message and then encoded his response, which acted as feedback for Sue.

Decoding. To decode a message, the receiver must determine the meaning of the symbols used by the sender. When John said, "I can't get that to you by Thursday," did he mean (1) it was physically impossible, (2) he had other priorities, or (3) he didn't want to?

Interpreting. When John interpreted Sue's message, he put it through his mental filter. At that point his knowledge, attitudes, experience, culture, and the social system interacted to help him give meaning to the message. John interpreted Sue's message on the basis of his previous experiences with Sue. For instance, if Sue consistently asked for work before she needed it, his action might be to purposely delay this job. If she is usually late with projects, he may suggest alternatives or decide not to get involved. After interpreting her message, John decided to give Sue the information but to ask for a few extra days to prepare it. When we filter a message, applying our knowledge and experience, we give a thinking response. John reacted to Sue's request only after he considered his knowledge of Sue and his own personal needs.

Feedback. Feedback is the response of the receiver that can be perceived by the sender as a new stimulus. John's response to Sue gave her feedback that might require her to alter her plans for preparing the report unless she can manage to find the information sooner. John's vocal tone, expression, and appearance during their encounter enhanced the feedback concerning her message.

Using feedback properly has become the subject of many treatises on improving message accuracy. Berlo discusses its usefulness in his text, *The Process of Communication,* and gives the following examples:

> Advertisers control the reasons given to the public for buying this or that product. But the consumer affects the advertiser—through feedback. If the public buys more (positive feedback), the advertiser keeps his messages. If the public quits buying the product (negative feedback), the advertiser then changes his messages—or the stockholders get a new advertising manager.[20]

As the exchange process continues, numerous opportunities arise for miscommunication. The speaker's purpose may not be clear, his or her attitude may be condescending, the words selected may be too technical, background noise may interfere with the listener's ability to hear, or divergent backgrounds and interests may cause misinterpretation of the speaker's message by the listener. These aspects of communication may be mapped and objectively analyzed, and it is in the interests of more effective management to do so. In the words of Wendell Johnson:

> The ability to respond to and with symbols may be the single most important attribute of great administrators. . . . Mr. A talking to Mr. B is a deceptively simple affair, and we take it for granted to a fantastic and tragic degree. . . . We have yet to learn how to use the wonders of speaking and listening.[21]

Characteristics of Communication

Several fundamental characteristics are inherent to communication: Communication is dynamic, irreversible, proactive, interactive, and contextual.[22] Because of the nature of these characteristics, they are difficult to depict in model form. Nevertheless, our model must accommodate them.

Communication is dynamic. When you speak to another person, you engage in an activity that involves ongoing behavioral changes. From the moment you utter the first word of a sentence, this continuous series of changes begins and may include varying facial expressions, body movement, gestures, or eye movement. More than likely, you will join together a series of words to form one or more sentences. Once you finish speaking, your listener begins to respond using a series of gestures, movements, or spoken words. Responses to a message may occur weeks, months, or even years after the sender originates the message. Communication is dynamic as it evolves through an ongoing process.

Communication is irreversible. Have you ever said something you wished you could take back? Communication, once it begins, cannot be reversed. You may amplify, modify, apologize, or attempt to explain something, but you cannot take it back; you can only go forward.

Communication is proactive. Communication involves the total person. How we select words or react to another's words will be affected by our uniqueness. All that we have learned and experienced helps us select the words, movements, and vocal patterns that communicate our messages. These factors become part of how we analyze the message and how it affects our behavior.

Communication is interactive. Communication also involves two or more parties. When two people communicate, they symbolically link their behavior, and this interaction conveys meaning from one person to another.

Communication is contextual. Communication does not occur in a void. Taking notes at a high-level meeting or talking to a client over the telephone are behaviors that are affected by the environment. A person taking notes may be surrounded by eager and attentive employees or be distracted by interruptions or arguments. Relaxed or harried, the climate alters people's reactions to message importance.

A Managerial Communication Model

Given the above elements and characteristics of communication, we can now develop a model that fits interpersonal and organizational settings (see Figure 1.6). One disadvantage of a model is that it depicts a process as if it were static. During communication, everything is in constant motion—the events in the environment, relationships, time, and the situation. We even receive and decode messages at the same time we are encoding and sending other messages. Imagine a situation where a worker is explaining a problem

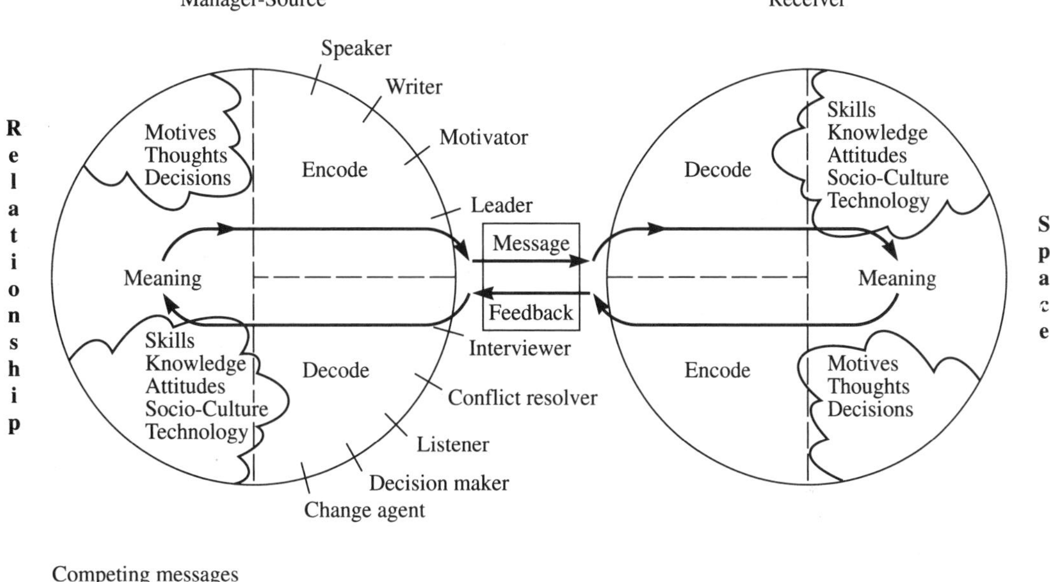

FIGURE 1.6 A Model for Effective Managerial Communication

to a supervisor only to catch nonverbal signs of inattention and lack of interest. The boss proceeds to shuffle papers, look up a telephone number, and check the time while the worker is talking. A very clear message is sent: "I'm too busy to bother with this right now!" The sender and receiver are communicating simultaneously.

If it were possible to do so within a textbook, everything in this model would appear in constant motion: the arrows would move to indicate the constant selection, decoding, and interpreting of stimuli from the environment; stimuli would constantly change and interrupt or compete with the message; even the shape of the environment, source, and receiver would change to demonstrate growth and development. Time, space, and the receiver form a communication set and can affect interaction in a variety of ways, as will be demonstrated in the following chapters of this book.

While the sender and receiver are represented in our model by two circles, remember that within each of them many factors interact to affect the accuracy of the message: communication skills, knowledge, attitudes, and position within the sociocultural system.[23]

Factors That Affect the Accuracy of the Message

Communicators have varying *skills* as writers, speakers, readers, listeners, thinkers, and problem solvers. These skills affect their abilities to analyze motives, mediate conflict, act as change agents, and be leaders or decision makers because they affect their ability to encode the message.

The *knowledge* that communicators have about subject matter affects the content of the message. If a person does not understand what he or she is talking about, the message may be distorted before it reaches the listener. Conversely, when the communicator is well informed, he or she must be careful to avoid using highly technical language that might not be understood by the receiver.

Attitudes—or the way that a person tends to respond to situations, ideas, values, objects or people—may prevent us from speaking to someone we feel hostile toward and again may distort our message.[24] In an organization, people form attitudes toward their jobs, bosses, and coworkers and react positively or negatively toward them. A boss who repeatedly encounters problems with an employee may avoid the employee. The reaction may become so intense that the employee's office is physically "out of sight."

Sociocultural backgrounds also affect the communicators in the model. A person's role, group associations, functions, and prestige determine many aspects of both sending and receiving the message, which is why retailers usually survey potential social and cultural needs of an area before marketing a product.

Finally, technological skills impact both the content of the message and the relationships between the people sending and receiving messages. Improvements in this area allow messages to be sent around the world in seconds and people to interact in billion-dollar transactions without even meeting.

These factors act on the source and receiver to increase or decrease the accuracy of the message. Without communication skills, knowledge about the subject matter, consideration of the receiver's attitude, or understanding of the receiver's place in the sociocultural system, the source is at an immediate disadvantage and will more than likely initiate message distortion during the encoding stage of the communication process.

Factors within the source and receiver affect the message intrapersonally—how it is interpreted in our minds—and the relationship between the source and receiver affects the message interpersonally. Wilbur Schramm stressed that the essence of communication is getting the sender and receiver "in tune" for a message.[25] The accumulated experience of the sender is present during each interaction. Unless there is an overlap between the experiences of the sender and those of the receiver (that is, unless they speak the same language), communication is limited, if not almost impossible. Neither party can send or receive an understandable message. Conversely, the more experiences they hold in common, the greater their ability to communicate the fully intended meaning of the message.

Finally, the intrapersonal and interpersonal factors interact to affect how the source and receiver perceive the message. Both parties will select the parts of the message that reinforce their experiences and relationship.

The Organizational Environment

The model depicts a sender and receiver in an organizational environment in which there are many competing sources and receivers. Messages are continually sent to us, whether we are convening in meetings, receiving memoranda, letters, and reports, hearing directives, or participating in interviews. Our physical space, the timing of the message, the particular situation, and the surrounding activity or noise all affect the way we perceive, decode, and interpret the intended message.

The Process

Although the communication process is continual, the model depicts the process beginning at the point when something in the environment gains our attention and acts as a stimulus. The nervous system transmits the stimuli to the brain, which decodes the message and assigns meaning to it based on personal experiences. We then encode our thoughts into words and actions, so that the message again becomes part of the environment.

A receiver hears, sees, tastes, smells, or touches parts of our message. Depending on the fidelity of the receiver's senses and predispositions (alertness, attention, interest), he or she will transmit the message through sensory receptors to the brain. The receiver decodes and interprets the message and then sends a response in the form of feedback.

Feedback informs the sender how the message is being interpreted—for example, a frown on the forehead of the listener, a letter to the editor, or the applause of an audience. We even get feedback to our own messages. We can correct misspellings, modify style, and correct typing errors. A person playing a video game receives immediate feedback in the form of a visual message whenever he or she makes an error in timing or judgment: The video "player" may disappear, explode, or in some way lose ground.

At each stage in this communication process some distortion takes place. The receiver may have a hearing or sight impairment; perhaps someone or something blocks vision so that the receiver cannot see the sender's facial expressions. The receiver may minimize or disregard the sender's actions or use technical words that the sender does not understand during the feedback stage. Given the seven stages at which communication can be distorted by either the sender or receiver, it is no wonder that communication is difficult: Distortion can occur when the participant (1) selects stimuli from the environment, (2) experiences sensory receptors and nervous system fidelity or infidelity, (3) decodes the message, (4) assigns meaning, (5) encodes the response, (6) transmits the message, or (7) is interfered with by factors in the environment.

ETHICS: RIGHT OR WRONG?

The Libeled Ex-Worker

On February 26, 1991, Don Hagler was stopped by a guard at a Procter & Gamble Company manufacturing plant in Dallas, Texas. The guard found a telephone stuffed in a bag that Hagler was carrying. After a brief investigation by management, the warehouse employee of forty-one years was fired the next Monday. A notice was placed on the plant bulletin board accusing Hagler of theft.

In May 1991, two months after he was fired for allegedly stealing the phone, Don Hagler sued Procter & Gamble for libel. Sadly he commented, "In forty-one years there I had an unprecedented record. More than once I went beyond the call of duty."[27] At his trial Hagler said he had purchased the phone for cash because his supervisor had asked him to buy it for the office a year earlier. However, he had never asked for reimbursement because he had lost the receipt. Hagler said his supervisor later acknowledged that he had indeed purchased the phone and it was not company property. A coworker also testified that she had gone to an AT&T telephone store with Hagler and had watched him pay for the phone with money from his pocket. At the trial Hagler's supervisor said he never told Hagler the phone was his and that he could take it off the company property.

Mr. Hagler, sixty-one years of age, was unable to find employment after being fired. He testified that he had applied for over 100 jobs and had always been rejected when the potential employer learned of his firing. Hagler's doctor testified that Hagler had suffered high blood pressure and severe stress following the dismissal.

Case Questions

1. Is there a question of ethics in this case? If so, what is it?
2. What role did communication play in this case?
3. If you were on the jury, what verdict would you submit for Don Hagler?
4. What ethical theory would you use in making your decision?

Despite these distortions, at least four conditions can be identified as conducive to successful communication:[26]

1. The message must be easily perceived or made "available." We must be loud enough, clear enough, visible enough, and so forth. This means that we must time, place, and equip our messages with cues that will appeal to the listener.

2. We must be sure that we are speaking a "language" that the other person understands. Our message must be consistent with the other person's

experiences. We will reject their message if we don't understand the words or if they do not fit in with our knowledge, experience, needs, or interests.

3. People act because of needs, and their actions are directed toward goals that satisfy those needs. A person's message is more likely to be accepted and understood if it considers the other person's needs.

4. Response to communication is often made within groups. The response must be approved by the group and will succeed if it fits accepted behaviors.

Communicating effectively as a manager takes more than making a good impression and knowing the mechanics of the job. It requires understanding multiple forces: The manager's message must be easily perceived and consistent with the receiver's experiences, needs, drives, attitudes, and organizational or group relationships.

Communication in the Global Arena

In the 1960s, Marshall McLuhan introduced the notion of a "global village." He believed the world would soon be interconnected through electronic communication. In *Understanding Media* he described how a planetary communication network "would make of the entire globe, and of the human family, a single consciousness."[28] Though so far McLuhan's predictions have not come true, the world has been tremendously impacted by technological improvements in global communication. Howard H. Frederick describes this impact.

> In some ways, McLuhan was right. Today's informed citizen daily consumes news of student demonstrations for democracy in China and Burma, of oil production in the Middle East, and of natural disasters in Asia. In no other age have we been so preoccupied with what is happening in other parts of the globe.
>
> . . . To be sure, there is a growing web of information and communication networks throughout the globe that connects far-flung places in a way unheard of even in McLuhan's time. But huge stretches of territory are not interconnected, and many of those information and communication networks carry content that is a far cry from the enlightened messages that would lead to the general "cosmic consciousness" McLuhan predicted.[29]

The reference to global communication is important. International communication means communication between and among people in nation-states. Global communication goes beyond the boundaries of countries, and it more fully emphasizes communication between and among peoples.

In McLuhan's day, politicians and business leaders used shuttle diplomacy as a way of communicating messages quickly between leaders who resided in different countries. Henry Kissinger used this method as he traveled by airplane back and forth between Israel and Egypt, several times each day, while serving as Secretary of State under President Richard Nixon. Shuttle diplomacy today is a very time-consuming and dated way of sending and receiving messages. Now messages are encrypted and communicated globally via satellites, optical fibers, or microwave radio.

Global Communication Technology

Several entire generations of technology have evolved in a handful of years. Even radio and electrical transferal of information is now often at risk. The United States found during the Persian Gulf War that radio waves can be jammed, electrical signals can be affected by magnetic interference, and telephone cables can be cut. Light waves are more secure than radio waves. Figure 1.7 shows how oceanic telephone cables connect the world through

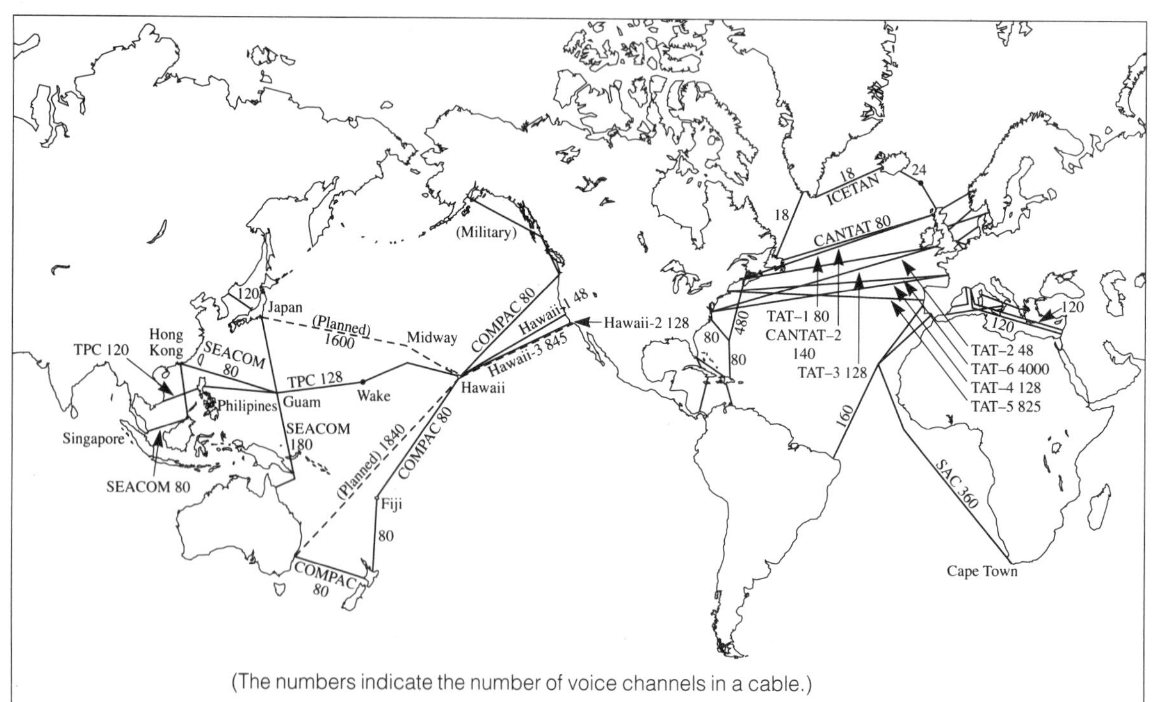

(The numbers indicate the number of voice channels in a cable.)

FIGURE 1.7 Oceanic Telephone Cables
Source: The map, "Oceanic Telephone Cables" from Howard H. Frederick, *Global Communication & International Relations,* Wadsworth, 1993, p. 95. Reprinted with permission, Wadsworth Publishing Co.

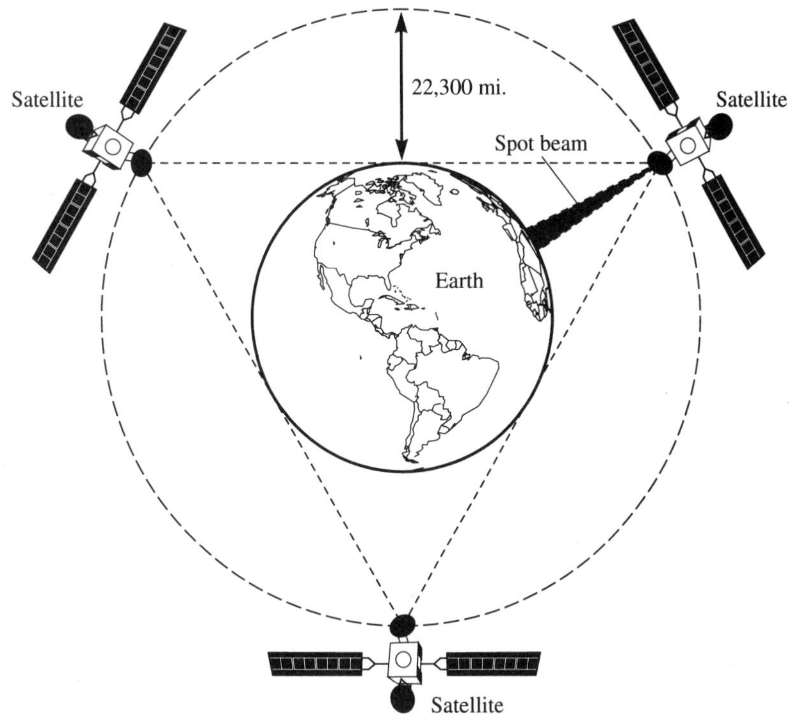

FIGURE 1.8 Satellite Global Coverage
Source: From Sidney W. Head and Christopher H. Sterling, *Broadcasting in America,* 4th ed. (Boston: Houghton Mifflin, 1982), p. 89.

voice channels. Figure 1.8 shows how three communication satellites, positioned at equidistant points on a circle above the earth's equator, can also carry communication to the entire globe.

Global Telecommunication

Cable News Network faced a problem when the Romanians staged a coup in December 1989. The country's telecommunications system was so antiquated CNN reporters could not send home beepers or voice-over commentaries on the telephone lines.

But the network owned a satellite telephone, which allows the user to dial up a land line anywhere in the world using a satellite link. The network sent a staffer with the telephone, which fits into a standard size suitcase, to Frankfurt,

> Germany. He rented a van and drove to Bulgaria, where he picked up a hitchhiker to guide him through the serpentine mountain passes. The next morning CNN was one of the first American news teams to file live reports from the balcony of a Bucharest hotel.
>
> "We bought our satellite telephone because we needed instantaneous responsiveness," says Leon Harris, a CNN executive responsible for satellites and circuits.[30]

Global telecommunication is the transmitting of electrical signals over great distances at a very fast speed. Both satellite and fiber optic cables are critical to the growing global business demands. The CNN example shows how satellite transmission provided instantaneous responsiveness. DGL Publishing found that a U.S. Sprint–installed fiber optic cable to Russia allowed them to establish a joint venture with Interfax Ltd., the only Russian independent news agency. DGL prepares its news during the day and loads it into a fax machine at the end of every business day. At 3 A.M. the following morning, the material is sent by fax to customers in the United States, France, and Germany. When the customers arrive at the office, the information is waiting for them.[31]

Richard Fisher, president of Fisher Capital Management, describes the global changes in his business that were brought on by improved communication technology.

> "A decision maker can be anywhere he wants to be." I live in Dallas. I manage $350 million for 60 clients spread across the globe from the United Arab Emirates to Santo Domingo to Tokyo, and in the United States from Boston to San Francisco and from Detroit in the north to Miami in the south. I buy and sell U.S. securities, German securities, Dutch securities and so on, and safe-keep them in London.
>
> I have only nine employees, five of whom are clerical workers. Yet, thanks to the microchip, I am able to communicate with my clients and operate in the New York, London, Frankfurt or Tokyo markets in real time, 24 hours a day. And given the miracle of air transportation, I can visit with any of my clients in the companies I invest in in a day's time.[32]

Information technology drives much of today's business transformation. Improved technology has lowered the once-high prices of telecommunications services to an affordable range enjoyed by many small businesses. International call minutes mirror the rapid increase of international business transactions. In 1984, Americans made 3.1 billion calls abroad. In 1990, the total had moved to 8.2 billion. AT&T estimated that in 1993 the total would be almost 11 billion calls abroad.[33] But managers should not focus merely on delivering more information. They should seek to deliver quality information and build strong relationships through communication.

Transforming Global Relationships

Although changes in information technology have increased both the frequency of interaction and the amount of information that is sent, a byproduct of the process is the changing of global relationships. As *Los Angeles Times* writer Michael Schrage comments, "technology isn't just a medium of information but a medium for *relationships.* Information matters, but it's the relationships—the formal and informal networks of people—that really govern how the organization runs and how value is created."[34] Companies that spend more time generating data and less time in employee and customer interaction will quickly decline in quality and revenue.

American Airlines' Sabre system serves as an excellent example of the data versus relationship return. Sabre allows American to track and coordinate hundreds of thousands of data pieces each day. It is the leading information management system in the airline industry. But American never saw the system as merely a way of processing information. It realized that the true value of Sabre lies in allowing "American to create a whole new set of relationships with its customers. Travel agents and regular customers could link up with the airline in previously unimagined ways. A business person on the go could craft an entire itinerary from a payphone anywhere in the U.S. By creating the new 'relationships infrastructure,' American could track demand patterns and alter its schedules accordingly."[35]

Transforming Global Boundaries

Just as improved technology has allowed businesses to build new relationships with employees and customers, that same improved technology has made the world a single market. Harlan Cleveland, president of the World Academy of Art and Science and former U.S. assistant secretary of state for international organizations, put it this way:

> What made the world an increasingly single market was not trade, aid or alliances. . . . What happened was that, with the help of computers and reliable telecommunications, capital (because it is a form of information) could flow faster and more freely than goods.
>
> The diagnosis is now plain. The information revolution has stormed the ramparts of the nation-state, and most of our favorite economic theories—capitalist as well as Marxist—have been trampled in the rush.[36]

As boundaries have fallen, three regional trade blocs have been established and are exerting power: North America, the European Community (EC), and the Pacific Rim. The North American region is made up of the United States, Canada, and Mexico and has 5 percent of the world's population. The European Community is a combination of twelve countries in

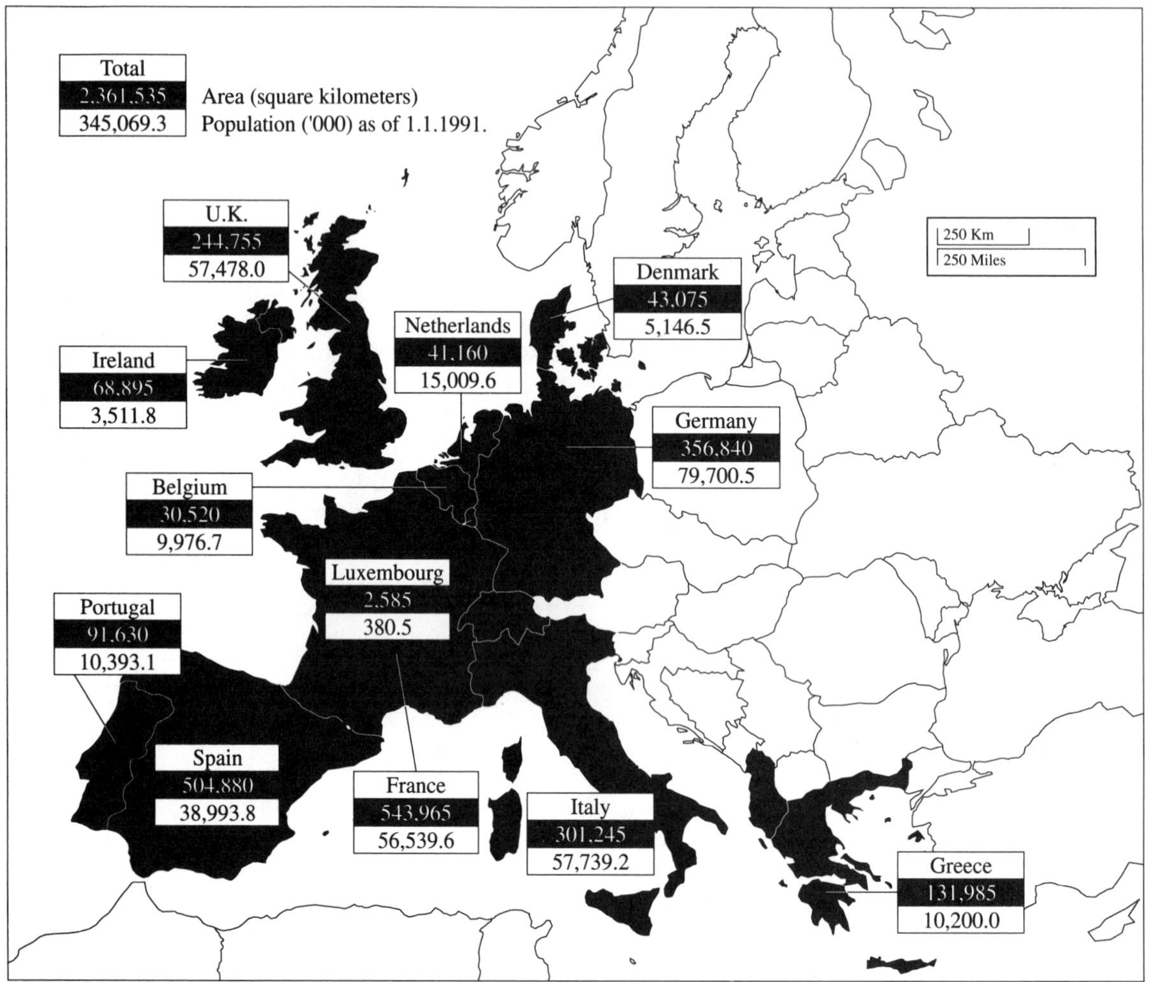

FIGURE 1.9 The New European Community Nations

Western Europe and jointly has 6 percent of the world's population. (The twelve countries with total area and population are listed in Figure 1.9.) The third region, the Pacific Rim, consists of Japan, South Korea, Taiwan, Hong Kong, and Singapore. Only 4 percent of the world's population live in that portion of Asia. Although these three regions make up only 15 percent of the world's population, together they control 72 percent of the world's "wealth" as it is measured in traditional gross domestic product (GDP) terms.[37]

With the emergence of these three economic regions, some second-tier nations in Africa, Latin America, South Asia, and the former Soviet Union face being left out of world economic developments. The three economic

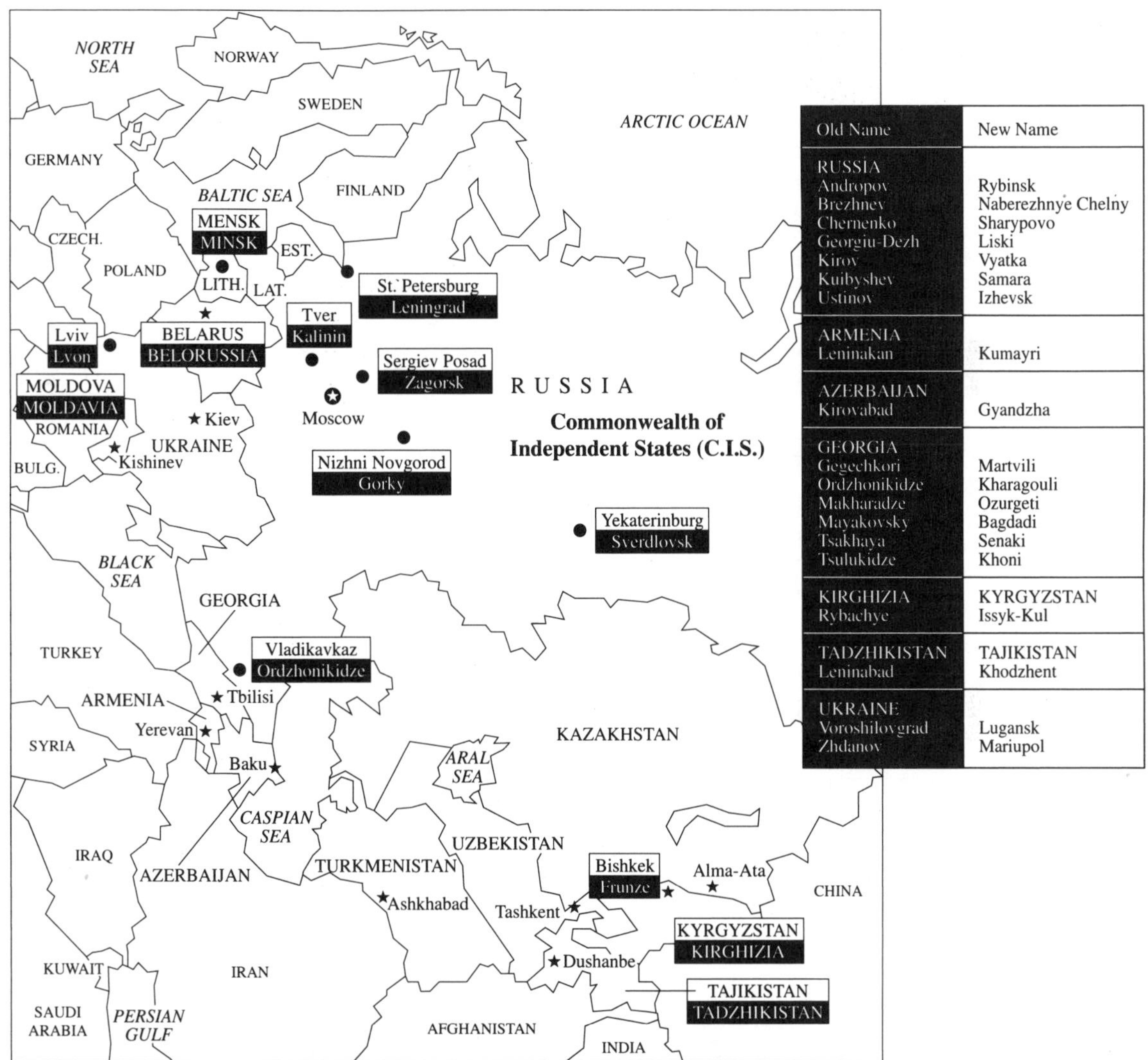

Old Name	New Name
RUSSIA	
Andropov	Rybinsk
Brezhnev	Naberezhnye Chelny
Chernenko	Sharypovo
Georgiu-Dezh	Liski
Kirov	Vyatka
Kuibyshev	Samara
Ustinov	Izhevsk
ARMENIA	
Leninakan	Kumayri
AZERBAIJAN	
Kirovabad	Gyandzha
GEORGIA	
Gegechkori	Martvili
Ordzhonikidze	Kharagouli
Makharadze	Ozurgeti
Mayakovsky	Bagdadi
Tsakhaya	Senaki
Tsulukidze	Khoni
KIRGHIZIA	KYRGYZSTAN
Rybachye	Issyk-Kul
TADZHIKISTAN	TAJIKISTAN
Leninabad	Khodzhent
UKRAINE	
Voroshilovgrad	Lugansk
Zhdanov	Mariupol

FIGURE 1.10 Name Changes in Former Soviet Union States

regions also present a challenge for most multinational corporations, who "must establish a presence in each of the three regions if they want to take full advantage of growth potential. They can no longer stay at home and expect potential customers from other regions to need them so badly that they will come calling."[38]

While global boundaries are changing rapidly, so too are national names. Figure 1.10 shows how many of the former Soviet Union states that have gained their independence have also changed their names. Some are returning to traditional national place names that they had before communism made sweeping name changes.

Changing national boundaries have brought with them confusion about nation and product identity. Today it is not easy to identify products and the countries in which they are made. Table 1.1 lists twelve items. Test your knowledge of where the items are made by checking country of origin against product.

TABLE 1.1 Product/Country Identity

Item	U.S.A.	Japan	England	Mexico	Other
Haagen-Dazs					
Firestone tires					
Holiday Inn					
Sony television					
Atari video					
Canon cameras					
Kodak film					
Magnavox television					
Dodge Colt cars					
Honda Prelude cars					
Nike athletic shoes					
Nestlé chocolate bars					

Answers: Haagen-Dazs (U.S.A.); Firestone tires (Japan, division of Bridgeport); Holiday Inn (Great Britain); Sony television sets (Japan); Atari video games (U.S.A.); Canon cameras (Japan); Kodak film (U.S.A.); Magnavox television (U.S.A. and Mexico); Dodge Colt cars (Japan); Honda Prelude cars (Japan); Nike athletic shoes (several countries); Nestlé chocolate bars (U.S.A.). Source: *USA Today* (March 9, 1992).

The Hazards of Doing Business Abroad

The reality of the world today is that no executive or organization can be isolated from the effects of globalization. There is no strictly domestic business. Regardless of where a company is based, or whatever product it makes or service it provides, competition is pushing that company to think globally. This movement into the global marketplace is often one that is not voluntarily taken.

Arco Chemical is a typical example. Largely owned by Atlantic Richfield Company, this well-established chemical organization was forced into going global. A few years ago, an exclusive agreement with the big three auto makers allowed the company to sell its engineering resins, made under the Dylark trademark, to the domestic auto industry. Things changed when Arco started facing increasingly stiff competition from abroad, as well as from traditional U.S. competitors like Dow Chemical. German companies Bayer and BASF, the French company Rhone Poulenc, and the British maker ICI suddenly acquired U.S. positions. To keep its auto contracts, Arco had to scramble quickly into the global market. According to a company spokesperson, "Today we deal with Nissan, Toyota, Honda, Renault, Peugeot and Volkswagen. . . . We're dealing with Nissan and Toyota in Japan and in the U.S. We're dealing with Ford and General Motors in the U.S. and in Europe. . . . Arco has to be able to deliver a product anywhere in the world or else lose the business."[39]

If competition is too strong and the cost of such a move too great, the answer is sometimes found in forming a joint venture. Most large companies prefer to operate alone overseas, but that is seldom practical. A joint venture is fast, cheap, and the least risky way to become involved worldwide. But the small risk can turn into a nightmare when the company loses a certain amount of control of its production, processes, and administration. Union Carbide found out the high cost of joint venture after its plant explosion in Bhopal, India in 1984.

Unforeseen political events can also pose a formidable risk for the joint venture. Following the Beijing Tiananmen Square demonstrations in 1989, Arco experienced interrupted shipments of styrene, the main ingredient in many of the company's major products. "The inability of Western companies to get supplies into China caused a glut in the market and a worldwide drop in prices. Partly as a result, Arco's 1989 earnings fell from year-earlier levels, to $405 million from $494 million. Revenue declined slightly, to $2.66 billion from $2.7 billion."[40]

SUMMARY

A manager is involved in a variety of roles that require mastering different skills. Henry Mintzberg identified three categories of managerial roles: interpersonal, informational, and decisional. Robert Katz added to Mintzberg's work by identifying three skill areas that must be developed for a manager to complete the roles effectively: technical, human relations, and conceptual. Central to the second and third areas is the ability to communicate.

Communication is so important in business that even the definition of an organization requires that goals be accomplished by a cooperative effort through the use of communication. The *type* of communication used may vary according to the managerial theory used within a given context, but communication itself will be the foundation for practicing any and all theories.

The key management theories are classical management theory, human relations theory, systems theory, and contingency theory. Many variables, from context to culture, may determine which theory will be most effective in practice. The most important variable is communication style, and some styles may be more successful than others within the practice of a given management theory.

Common elements can be identified in any communication situation. The source or sender is stimulated by some need, motive, or drive to send a message to a receiver. The source must encode the message by sorting and selecting symbols through a channel such as a face-to-face encounter, written message, or telephone call. The receiver decodes the meaning of the symbols used by the sender and interprets the message. Knowledge, attitudes, experience, sociocultural background, and technology act as a filter in giving meaning to the message. Finally, the receiver responds to the message and thereby provides feedback to the sender.

During the past few decades, the world has become interconnected through a web of information and communication networks. Today global communication has become a concern of managers in both large and small companies. The technology of light waves, telephone cables, and communication satellites allows information to be transmitted over great distances at a very quick speed. A manager in the year 2000 will be able to communicate as easily 10,000 miles away as she can to a colleague in the office next to hers. Learning to use new communication availability is a task that the effective manager must learn quickly.

KEY WORDS

channel
classical management
communication
conceptual skills
contingency theory
decisional roles
decode
encode
feedback
global
global telecommunication
human relations skills
human relations theory
informational role
interpersonal role
managerial roles
message
noise
organization
organizational structure
receiver
sociocultural system
source
systems theory
technical skills
theory X
theory Y
transmission

DISCUSSION QUESTIONS

1. What are the ten managerial roles that Henry Mintzberg identified? How many of these roles require communication from the manager?
2. Name Robert Katz's three basic types of management skills. How does communication differ in each type of skill?
3. What are the key theories of management, and how do they view communication?
4. Using one of these key theories, describe an organization to which you belong.
5. How can communication knowledge and skill help you be a more effective organizational person?
6. What is the difference between the human relations approach and the classical approach to management? How does communication differ in each approach?
7. How does the contingency theory of management relate to the other three theories?
8. Describe how a prominent politician uses television as a communication channel. What does he or she understand (or fail to understand) about the nature of communication?
9. What characteristics of the receiver/decoder should the sender consider? Why?
10. Give an example of interpersonal communication in the business environment.
11. Describe a recent situation in which you had

difficulty communicating with another person. At which stage of the communication process did a breakdown occur? Why?

12. Why is communication at the supervisory level complex? Give an example, and design a model to amplify your discussion.
13. How has technology impacted a manager's global communication?

EXERCISES

1. As you read the section of this chapter that describes the communication skills that employers look for when they hire individuals, you undoubtedly thought about your skills and qualifications. In the space provided below make a quick inventory of your communication skills. Which skills do you feel are adequate at the present time to help you qualify for the business world? Which do you need to improve?

   My communication skills that are sufficient:

   My communication skills that need improving:

   After you identify the skills that need improvement, look through the contents of this book. Make special note of the chapters that cover these areas. Write a contract with yourself that highlights some things that you can do during the course of this semester or year, with the exception of reading the chapter or the book, that will help you improve those skills. If you have trouble deciding which methods you should use outside your classroom, consult with your instructor about possibilities.

   Things I will do to improve my skills:

2. In reading through the Key Theories of Management section of this chapter you probably remembered managers or supervisors whom you have known or observed who had characteristics described in the theories. Make a list of these characteristics so that you can discuss them in class.
3. Record your communication activities for one day by tabulating in 15-minute intervals the number of times you speak, listen, read, or write. When you have completed your record, calculate the percentage of time you spent in each communication activity.
4. Select a word that has special meaning for you, such as a technical term, the name of a pet or friend, or a word from a song. Ask several people what the word means to them. You might ask them to describe their feelings about the word. How did their responses differ?
5. Analyze a communication situation in which you participated. Identify the elements. What did you know about the receiver that affected

your message? What did the receiver know about you that affected his or her response to your message? How would you alter your message for another receiver?

6. Observe a communication situation and analyze the behaviors of the source and receiver. How did vocal patterns, body movement, gestures, facial expression, and context affect the message?
7. Using ten lines one inch in length, make two different drawings. Without showing the first drawing and giving only oral instructions, ask a friend to draw it. Do not allow questions. Repeat this exercise with the second drawing but allow questions. Which drawing was more accurate? Why? How does this exercise relate to the manager's role in the organization?
8. Pick a large corporation that you know has operations abroad. Go to the library and find as much information as you can about how that organization operates globally. Share your information with your class.

REFERENCES

1. Henry Mintzberg, *The Nature of Managerial Work* (New York: Harper & Row, 1973).
2. Robert L. Katz, "Skills of an Effective Administrator," *Harvard Business Review* (January/February 1955), pp. 33–42.
3. Don Hellriegel and John W. Slocum, Jr., *Management,* 6th ed. (Reading, Mass.: Addison-Wesley, 1992), p. 26.
4. *Workforce 2000: Work and Workers for the Twenty-First Century* (Indianapolis: Hudson Institute and U.S. Department of Labor, June 1987), xxi.
5. Ibid.
6. Carol Hymowitz, "Day in the Life of Tomorrow's Manager," reprinted by permission of *Wall Street Journal,* © (1989) Dow Jones & Company, Inc. All rights reserved worldwide March 20, 1989, p. B1.
7. Kathryn Bullington Clark, "Oral Business Communication Needs as a Basis for Improving College Courses," Ph.D. dissertation, University of Michigan, 1968.
8. John M. Penrose, "Survey of the Perceived Importance of Business Communication and Other Business-Related Abilities," *Journal of Business Communication,* 13:2 (Winter 1976), p. 23.
9. Diane Lockwood and Sara Boatman, "Marketability: Who Needs Us and What Can We Do for Them?," unpublished paper presented at Central States Speech Association Convention, Kansas City, 1975, pp. 2–7.
10. "Report Assails Colleges: Carnegie Foundation Urges Massive Reform," *Dallas Morning News,* November 2, 1986, p. 49D.
11. Joyce Lain Kennedy, "Learning Basic Skills Can Lead to Success in the Workplace," *Dallas Morning News,* September 9, 1990, p. 1D.
12. Connie Pryzant, "Educator Assesses Evolving Role of Colleges," *Dallas Morning News,* April 17, 1989.
13. Claude S. George, Jr., *The History of Management Thought* (Englewood Cliffs, N.J.: Prentice Hall, 1960), p. 138.
14. Ibid.
15. Frank B. Gilbreth, "Science in Management for the One Best Way to Do Work," in Harwood F. Merrill, ed., *Classics in Management* (New York: American Management Association, 1960), pp. 245–91.
16. M. P. Follett, *Freedom and Co-ordination* (London: Management Publications Trust, Ltd., 1949), pp. 61–76.
17. Douglas McGregor, *The Human Side of Enterprise* (New York: McGraw-Hill, 1960).
18. Fremont Kast and James Rosenzweig, eds., *Contingency Views of Organizations and Management* (Chicago: SRA, 1973).
19. Gregory Moorhead and Ricky W. Griffin, *Organizational Behavior,* 3rd ed. (Boston: Houghton Mifflin, 1992).
20. David K. Berlo, *The Process of Communication* (New York: Holt, Rinehart and Winston, 1960), pp. 113–14.
21. Wendell Johnson, "The Fateful Process of Mr. A. Talking to Mr. B.," *Harvard Business Review,* 31 (Jan./Feb. 1953), pp. 49–56.
22. C. David Mortenson, *Communication: The Study of Human Interaction* (New York: McGraw-Hill, 1972), pp. 13–21.
23. Berlo, *Process of Communication,* pp. 113–14.
24. Winston L. Brembeck and William S. Howell, *Persuasion: A Means of Social Influence,* 2nd ed. (Englewood Cliffs, N.J.: Prentice-Hall, 1976), p. 84.
25. Wilbur Schramm, "The Nature of Communication Between Humans," *The Process and Effects of Mass Communication* (Urbana, IL: University of Illinois Press, 1972), pp. 7–53.
26. Ibid.
27. Anne Belli, "Jury Finds Firm Libeled Ex-Worker,

Owes $15 Million," *Dallas Morning News,* April 24, 1993, p. 31A.

28. Marshall McLuhan, *Understanding Media: The Extensions of Man* (New York: New American Library, 1964), p. 67.
29. Howard H. Frederick, *Global Communication and International Relations.* (Belmont, Calif.: Wadsworth, 1993), pp. 119–120.
30. Beth Ellyn Rosenthal, "Global Telecommunications/91," *International Business* (November 1991), p. 109.
31. Ibid.
32. Richard Fisher, "A Business Person Now Can Be Everywhere At Once," *Dallas Morning News,* January 20, 1991, p. 9J.
33. Rosenthal, "Global Telecommunications," p. 109.
34. Michael Schrage, "In Information Technology, the Key Is Good Relationships," *Wall Street Journal,* March 19, 1990.
35. Ibid.
36. Harlan Cleveland, "The End of Geography?" *International Business* (November 1991), p. 78.
37. Wilford H. Welch, "Engines of Global Economy," *International Business* (November 1991), p. 79.
38. Ibid.
39. Bernard Wysocki, Jr., "Chemical Reaction: Both Risks and Rewards," *Wall Street Journal,* September 21, 1990, p. R4.
40. Ibid.

CHAPTER 2

THE ROLE OF FORMAL COMMUNICATION IN THE ORGANIZATIONAL SETTING

When you walk through the gates at Walt Disney World, you immediately understand why it is the world's most popular tourist attraction. From the beautifully landscaped Mickey Mouse to the exciting rides, the great food, and the courteous personnel, the focus is on making "you," the guest, happy. It works so well that people return again and again to experience the magic. Why? Disney management credits the success to proper "imagineering" (imagination plus engineering). Organizational behavior experts contribute the success to Disney's culture, organizational structure, and first-rate communication. In the next few pages you will read more about this excellent organization.

Organizational Culture

Every organization has a *culture.* Whether it is weak and fragmented, or strong and cohesive, the culture has an extremely powerful and pervasive effect on an organization. Culture plays a critical role in determining the success or failure of an organization and its communication.

You have undoubtedly studied cultures in your history and sociology classes. In society a "culture" denotes a set of shared values, beliefs, mores, customs, and behavioral patterns that can be identified with a certain population or community. Like the larger society, organizations have sets of values that are expressed in practices and institutions. Like society, these cultures promote maturity, communication, health, and successful accomplishment of goals.[1]

Just like societies, business cultures vary greatly. "A company's culture goes deeper than the spoken or written word, most often expressing itself in tacit understandings and shared expectations."[2]

Madelyn Jennings, senior vice president of personnel at the Gannett Company, put it like this: "Culture is not an it—it's an us. For most employees, a job is not a job, it's a way of life, and their company's culture can rightly or wrongly shape that life. In other words, culture is what's sane, according to your company's definitions. It helps employees make sense of events and symbols."[3] It is what William Whyte, in his classic *The Organization Man,* called the "unique spirit" of the organization.

It is critical that effective managers gain a solid understanding of their organization's culture. Such an understanding is a power lever for guiding employee behavior. It is also vital in establishing successful communication.

Characteristics of A Successful Organization's Culture

As we examine the culture of successful organizations, several characteristics can be identified.

1. *An overall philosophy prevails.* The organization has a vision for itself, its product, and its service. This vision is transmitted into a mission, which is accomplished by meeting goals and objectives. The company's philosophy explains this process. In strong companies a consensus on philosophy, goals, and objectives is evident. People understand what is important, and they work together for a common cause. Resources support the company's objectives, and overall teamwork exists.

2. *Norms, values, and standards are understood and shared.* This encompasses the "do's" and "don'ts" for the company and its people. Individ-

uals who do not accept the norms and values eventually leave the company. Those who follow them closely stay and are rewarded. Performance standards play an important role because people see how things are measured in terms of quality, quantity, cost, and time. In successful firms standards are engrained in the culture and communicated throughout the company.[4]

3. *Common rites and rituals are practiced.* Deal and Kennedy write in their classic work on organizational culture: "Without expressive events, any culture will die. In the absence of ceremony or ritual, important values have no impact."[5] Rituals reinforce an organization's values and standards. When employees accomplish a goal or standard that is valued, they should be recognized.

A national paint manufacturer signals the receipt of a large order by ringing a bell on the production floor. At Frito-Lay a new employee in the marketing department can expect to work alongside a route salesperson delivering potato chips to local grocery racks. Rituals and rites focus on elements like promotions, transfers, training programs, achievements, and retirement. They are practiced through articles in the company paper, special acknowledgments in meetings, and employee-of-the-month awards.

4. *Stories and myths describe the company.* Often the stories are simple and even relate to the original founder. James Cash Penney entered the retail business in the early 1900s with the formation of the Golden Rule Store. His philosophy, to treat the customer right, which was accepted and practiced by his employees, revolved around a single principle: "Does our action square with what is just and right?" Today many stories and myths of the founder still circulate with the J. C. Penney organization. The heart of its ethics policy is still the "golden rule."

5. *A special feeling or climate exists.* This is conveyed through interpersonal interaction and physical layouts and arrangements. As we will see in Chapter 6, the physical arrangement of open or closed offices enhances or inhibits employee communication. Interaction is also affected by the structure of a company.

6. *There is a concern for people.* Though all organizations claim to be concerned for employees and customers, truly successful cultures display a genuine heartfelt concern in their policies and actions. This may be expressed in common ways, like communicating a "thank you" for a job well done, or in uncommon ways, like cutting employee hours across the ranks to avoid layoffs during down times.

7. *Open communication prevails.* Of all the components of organizational culture, communication is the most critical. All the other factors depend upon the ability to get a message across. In weak-cultured organizations, like the military, the emphasis is on formalized downward communication. People are talked at instead of talked with. In healthy and strong-cultured companies, communication is open, free, spontaneous, adequate, and full of feedback.[6]

8. *Excitement, pride, and commitment are apparent.* One word that

describes the excitement of strong cultural organizations is "fun." People really enjoy working there. They take pride in their organization and the job they do. They believe in the vision and goals of the company. The values of the organization are their values. They are committed to helping the organization achieve its highest end, the accomplishment of its mission.

How do these characteristics apply to Disney World? This organization is an excellent example of a large, diverse entity that is held together by certain binding concepts and values. The Disney philosophy is well known by every employee. It is simply, "to satisfy the guests." Anyone who visits the property knows the organization accomplishes its purpose. Even though an organizational hierarchy exists, each cast member, including C.E.O. Michael Eisner, communicates on a first-name basis. This adds to the Disney value of "family" caring for each other.

A wonderful feeling of excitement prevails as employees become involved in the process of helping the guests have fun. Each new employee attends Disney University, which serves as an organizational rite of passage. There they learn the Disney history and philosophy. Job titles reflect the Disney concept of leading employees and guests to thoughts of a grander world. Disney World, consequently, has no waiters, waitresses, bellhops, security guards, janitors, busboys, or dishwashers. Instead, they are cast members—hosts and hostesses for dining, food preparation, food service, custodian services, and security. Prospective "cast members" audition for their "roles" and are chosen by "directors" who decide in what way each "actor" can best please the "guests and visitors." Norms and values are constantly apparent. All cast members must adhere to strict grooming standards (no facial hair for men, minimal makeup for women). Because employees are "on stage" anytime a guest is present, they pick up, clean up, and correct any aspect of their job, or another's, that they see is out of order. They never let the guests see them angry, frustrated, or under stress. The "show biz" theme means the roles are played consistently.

Overriding this application process is the value of clean, wholesome family entertainment. Stories and myths are at the center of the Disney culture. Cartoon characters that span decades become the drawing card of the theme park. Stories of Mickey Mouse, the Mouseketeers, and other characters abound. They become the glue that pulls all the parts of this "magical" organization together.[7]

Communication is at the center of Disney's success. It is described in a formula that incorporates other aspects of the organization's culture: Training + Communication + Care = Pride. "By carefully training and developing cast members, by making all cast communications timely and effective, and by encouraging a friendly and caring work environment, Disney creates a strong sense of pride in each cast member, which in turn inspires him or her to give first-rate service to all Disney guests."[8] The following story by Blocklyn discusses this dynamic communication process.

The Medium Is the Message

The cast communications department at Disney World is quick to make two points: (1) Disney essentially views itself as a communications company, and (2) it believes that over 90 percent of all organizational problems stem from a lack of communication. For these reasons, Disney places great emphasis on three kinds of communication: from management to cast member, from cast member to guest, and from cast member to management.

When communicating with cast members, management has four major goals: (1) to impart the company's objectives, (2) to reinforce the company's traditions and values, (3) to create a legacy for employees, and (4) to impart information. Doug Cody, senior representative of cast communications, sums up the management-to-cast communication philosophy this way: "Relevant information in an effective medium on a timely basis gives employees pride, morale, and a sense of belonging."

Disney attempts to fulfill this philosophy through four "communications strategies": environmental communications, audiovisual presentations, print communications, and personal contact. Environmental communications include bulletin and communications boards; audiovisual presentations involve executive and stockholders' updates and use of the Cast Communications Network (Disney's cast television network). Some of the more important examples of print communications are policy manuals and brochures, weekly division newsletters and *Eyes & Ears* (a company-wide weekly newsletter). Major types of communication by personal contact include management forums, focus groups, and the basic "hands-on" approach of "management by walking around."

"Management makes a point of listening to the cast," says Heather Eberhart of human resources development. Communication from cast to management may be either quantitative or qualitative. The primary quantitative communication is the employee opinion poll, which consists of both multiple-choice and essay questions and provides management with concrete data on employee reaction to a variety of topics. The most important kinds of qualitative cast-to-management communication include focus groups, exit interviews, and the "I Have an Idea" Program, in which cast members can win up to $10,000 for submitting original creative ideas to management.

In addition to management-to-cast and cast-to-management communication, there is also communication from guest to cast and from cast to guest. Forms of guest-to-cast communication include guest letters and surveys and the "guest comment report" form, on which guests have the opportunity to provide their reactions to their experiences at Disney World. From Disney's viewpoint, cast-to-guest communication is simply the daily, ongoing cast practice of providing gracious courtesy, hospitality, and a "good show" to Disney guests. "The guest may not always be right," explains Dave Venables, manager of guest relations, "but the guest's *perception* is right from his or her point of view."[9]

The Clash of Different Cultures

As the globalization of business continues, more non-American companies will establish plants in the United States. In the early 1990s, Japanese manufacturers far outranked other countries. It is estimated that by the year 2000 over 840,000 Americans will be working for Japanese companies. In 1992, Japan's investment approached $85 billion. Much of that money revitalized American industry in the industrial heartland (Ohio, Michigan, Illinois, Indiana, Kentucky, and Tennessee). The *Wall Street Journal* reported in 1991 that the Japanese investment included "39 steel mills, nine rubber and tire factories, seven auto-assembly plants and 250 auto-parts suppliers."[10] Their presence is also felt across the United States.

Although this investment has been an economic lifesaver for industry in that area, the joining of America and Japanese management and employees is not without its problems. Initially the idea was to create a new industrial culture by combining the concept of quality and teamwork to produce a substantial profit. "The idea of a corporation treating its employees as members of a family, of engaging them in the *process* of production instead of just in the technique, of training them to do a variety of skilled jobs and then allowing them to work in a team that allotted its own tasks sounded good. It still does."[11]

But in most factories the marriage is far from happy. In general the problem is the "dissonance between two cultures." According to Lehmann-Haupt, it starts with basic differences between the races. "On the one hand, the Japanese are a homogeneous island people, conditioned by crowded living to fit their wishes to the mass. In contrast, the Americans are a people with strong social currents of self-gratification, individualism and competitiveness."[12]

In most instances the "teamwork" concept is popular. At Setex, a Japanese-American joint venture that manufactures car seats, team members rotate jobs every two hours and move through a series of eighteen job rotations in a few days. But the Japanese desire for high productivity requires demands, like long hours of overtime and little warning that it will be required. As one Toyota employee states, "There's a good deal of overtime, and they're expected to be there no matter what."[13]

One of the greatest sources of difficulty between the Japanese and American managers is communication. American managers often feel they must fight to gain Japanese attention. There was a belief that the Japanese did not want their input in the decision-making process; they only wanted to tell them how to implement the decision that had been made. At Setex there were often American-Japanese staff meetings followed by a Japanese-only meeting.[14]

Language barriers also present problems. At a Honda plant an American manager often resented "the fax machines that transmitted messages in a language he couldn't understand."[15] At Southland Corporation (the 7-Eleven Company) in Dallas, an account manager, following his company's purchase by the

Japanese, was given an assignment to design a company retreat. When he set up the golf roster, each foursome had two Americans and two Japanese. He thought that would encourage collegiality. When the concept was reviewed by top management, it came back rearranged to accommodate all Japanese foursomes and all American foursomes.[16]

An example from a Fujitsu plant in Richardson, Texas, however, points out a success in merging two cultures. Dr. Steven Miller, an American, became plant manager in 1991. To prepare for his job, he spent three years in Oyama, Japan working for Fujitsu. At Carnegie-Mellon he studied how to implement state-of-the-art factory systems. When he graduated, he decided he wanted to apply his talent in an American and Japanese venture. His mission was to find a leading Japanese electronics company where he could be trained, become a trusted manager and, eventually become an executive. He believed that over a twenty- or thirty-year span, he could help to bridge gaps in understanding. He summed this up by saying: "Learning the Japanese language was the most difficult task. [At first] I was discouraged by how little Japanese I could assimilate each day." But Miller found his Japanese tutors to be very patient and complete in their training. That gave him a glimpse into how the steadiness of the Japanese culture translates into the manufacturing process. "The consistency of purpose and execution," Miller concludes, "is a very powerful kind of thing."[17] Miller's training abroad has helped him successfully blend the two cultures here in America.

Organizational Structure

Organizational cultures evolve to meet different goals and missions. In this evolution the organizational structure also changes. The structure of an organization profoundly impacts its internal communication. When an organization is founded, the owners and managers design a structure that allows the company goals to be met in an effective and productive manner. According to White and Bednar, the structure of an organization accomplishes four distinct functions. It (1) divides work logically among individuals and organizational subunits (work teams, departments, etc.), (2) recombines or coordinates the activities of those units to accomplish organizational objectives, (3) distributes formal power (authority) to direct or coordinate work, and (4) establishes channels of communication.[18]

An organization's *structure* is the formal pattern of authority relationships that exists between all of its parts. The structure is usually described by an organizational chart. The chart does not diagram formal communication flow, but it does indicate who may or may not communicate with whom.

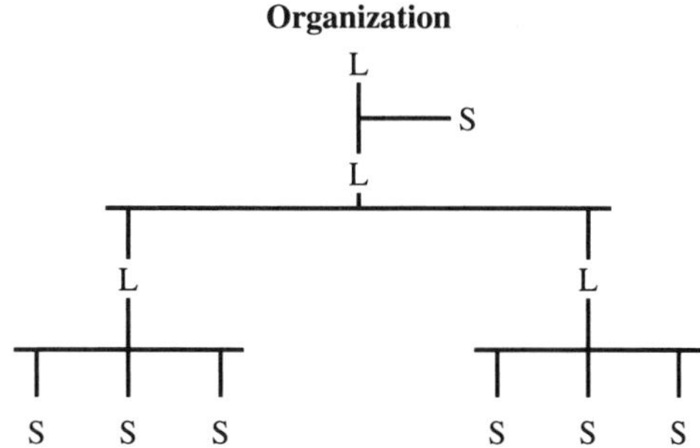

FIGURE 2.1 Line (L) and Staff (S) Positions in an Organization

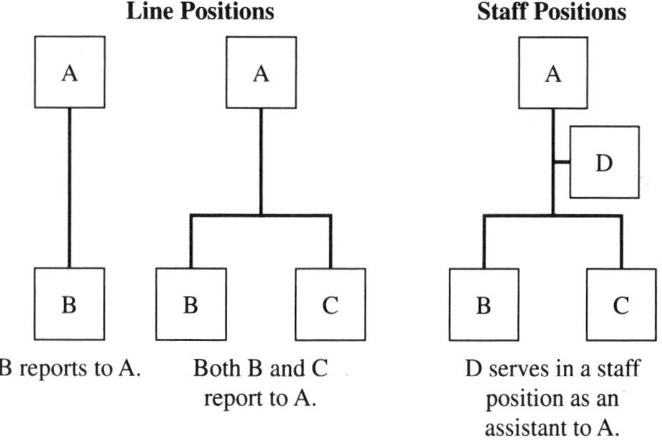

FIGURE 2.2 Communication Through Line and Staff Positions

In early classical theory, organizational charts took the form of a pyramid. The structure included line and staff positions (see Figure 2.1). *Line positions* (L) carry authority and responsibility over personnel and serve the direct flow of formal organizational communications. *Staff positions* (S) assist or advise the line organization. Staff members rarely have authority or responsibility over other members of the organization. They can, however, achieve some power due to their positions in the organization. For example, an assistant to a divisional director might assume some of the director's power.

The fewer the number of employees working for a manager, the greater the control he or she can have over them. The number of subordinates

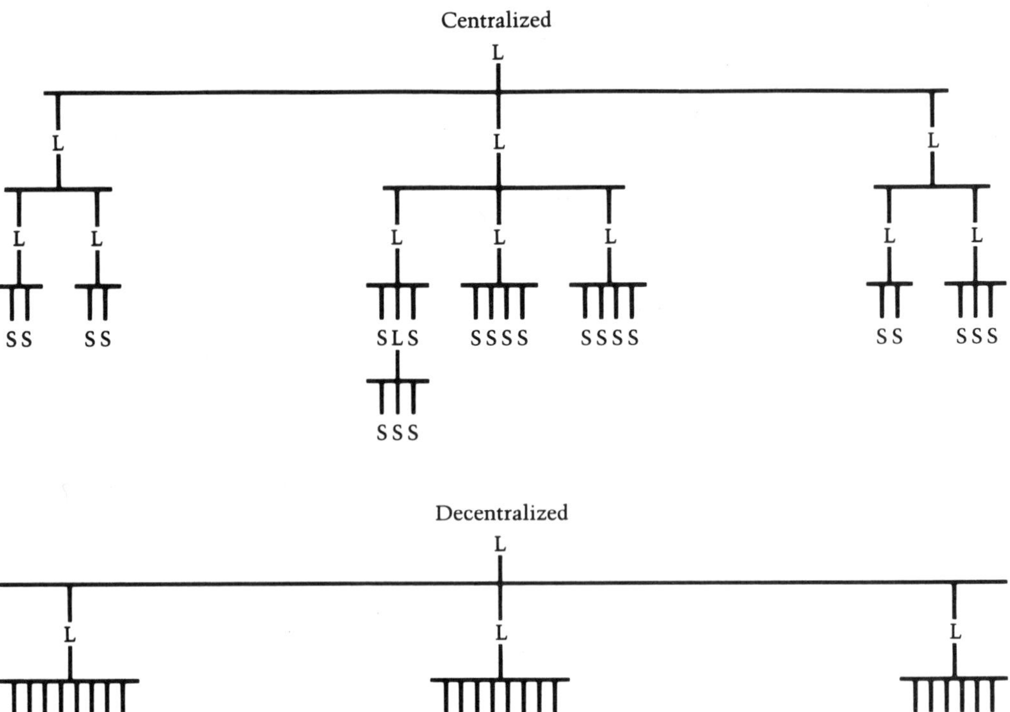

FIGURE 2.3 Comparison of a Tall Organization with a Flat Organization

assigned to a manager affects the shape of the organization (see Figure 2.3). If *span of control* is limited to two or three employees, the organization will be tall. If, however, the manager has a span of control of five to fifteen subordinates, the organization will be flat.

Span of control within an organization also determines whether centralized or decentralized decision making will be used. With a narrow span of control, decisions can be made quickly because fewer people are involved. Participative decision making, however, can lead to higher morale and is facilitated by a flat, decentralized organization.

The shape of the organization influences personal dynamics, especially communication, within the organization. A tall organization will have more levels through which communication must pass. These multiple levels increase the possibility of distortion but, nevertheless, result in the manager's exerting greater control over employees. The flat organization, in contrast, reduces the number of levels through which communication must flow. It also limits the manager's opportunities to have one-to-one contact with employees and increases the amount of communication that the manager must handle.

Communication occurs differently as a result of position in the hierarchy. For example, as Baron and Greenberg point out, "persons at higher levels tend to be called by their titles (e.g., "President Davis") and are usually addressed in a formal manner. Such individuals may also communicate their higher positions by virtue of the way they dress (e.g., formal as opposed to informal attire) and by the size and location of their offices in the corporate complex."[19]

Another aspect of management theory is the *division of labor*, the object of which is to produce greater quantity and better-quality output. Labor can be divided according to either the nature of the work and its corresponding responsibility (*functional* division of labor) or the authority of the person involved (*scalar*). Often an organization combines both forms. For example, scalar division related to the allocation of authority in an organization would include the board of directors, president, vice-president, directors, and department heads. Functional divisions might include engineering staff, clerical staff, janitorial staff, and administrative personnel.

Japanese Management Contribution

Since the late 1970s, management theorists have developed new theories that enhance all the earlier ones and especially affect the human side of management. Theory Z is the name associated with the best of the Japanese management styles viable in the United States. It assumes that people who engage in socioeconomic activity are tied together by a variety of bonds and that a culture is established where individuals cooperate to reach common goals.

As the level of productivity in the United States falls and that of Japan increases, theorists examine and compare the organizational and management concepts of both countries. Most would agree that U.S. managers have been less than totally successful, whereas Japanese managers have made great headway. Although it will be years before a final assessment can be made of how well theory Z can be applied to U.S. organizations, management theorists have discovered eight areas in which the Japanese have been successful:[20]

1. *Organizational direction.* Organizations in the United States have long had clearly defined goals and objectives, but in their Japanese counterparts, the philosophy and values of the organization are clearly stated, understood, and shared by all employees. This creates commitment and cohesion. Top management shares information about all parts of the organization with

all employees so that all have a "big picture" of the direction that they and the company are taking.

2. *Rational process.* Managers take a systematic and objective approach that emphasizes planning and problem solving. They make decisions based on plenty of information, accountability of employees, and careful monitoring and evaluating of work progress.

3. *Adaptability and innovativeness.* The organization anticipates change and is sensitive to internal and environmental needs and trends. Instead of the short-range perspective that many U.S. companies tend to have, the Japanese perspective is both short and long range. Management seeks to be tolerant of unknown possibilities, flexible in examining them, versatile in its approaches to problem solving, and always open to new ideas.

4. *Resource allocation.* Instead of placing the greatest emphasis on financial results, the Japanese focus on human resource management. The Japanese organizations seek generalists, not specialists, and make use of each employee's full range of expertise and capabilities. When new skills are needed, training is provided. The reward system is based on achievement and competence.

5. *Distribution of authority.* Participation and input into decision making are not based on position or status but on competence and knowledge of information that can be shared. This means that the lowest-level employee is invited to the highest-level meetings if he or she has information that can be used by others. The Japanese system of supervision operates on delegating not only assignments but authority and responsibility as well.

6. *Organizational climate.* The Japanese atmosphere is conducive to productiveness because management communicates a sense of respect for employees and interest in their well-being. This, in turn, generates in employees a trust of management. Status barriers like dress and office locations are not used, and the superior/subordinate relationships are based on the informal power of mutual respect.

7. *Structure.* The Japanese organizational chart is not the chart well known in the United States. It is a structure that is integrated, flexible, and either temporary or permanent. It often incorporates small groups that have overlapping membership for greater information sharing.

8. *Communication.* Management listens to employees, and information successfully flows upward, downward, and horizontally. Communication is open, direct, and accurate.

In the late 1980s and early 1990s the Total Quality Management movement in the U.S. grew out of Theory Z learning. This movement stressed awareness of quality as an important element in competitiveness, the need to measure carefully between what is desired and what is produced, the ability to quickly make production changes that will turn mistakes into successes, and the necessity of shared communication and efforts in producing a quality product.

RECENT DESIGN CHANGES IN AMERICAN ORGANIZATIONAL STRUCTURE

Some organizations have determined that their growth over the past few years has occurred randomly rather than with tailored design. This realization started during a major economic recession in the late 1980s and early 1990s. Consequently, whole layers of line managers and many staff departments were reduced or eliminated, making the organizations leaner and flatter.[21] Such changes are reflected in new organizational charts.

One new organizational chart was introduced by Frances Hesselbein, former executive director of the Girl Scouts of the United States and now president and chief executive officer of the Peter E. Drucker Foundation for Nonprofit Management. Her theory of an effective organizational chart looks more like a wheel than a pyramid. Positioned at the center is the chief executive officer (CEO), with four to six executives connected in a circle. Additional teams flow outward from the circle.

According to Hesselbein, "you are able to eliminate 'up' and 'down' from your vocabulary. . . . It really helps the CEO in job enrichment and job retention."[22] The structure makes team management and task forces inevitable. Communication is emphasized and departmental boundaries and status distinctions are deemphasized. The staff can be moved easily into interdepartmental task forces because the system is flexible and responsive.

Hesselbein stresses that her preferred organizational structure would not work for everyone. The circular approach is a natural way for her to work simply because it gives a sense of ownership to all concerned. The structure facilitates the involvement of every person in the company.[23] An example of this structure is shown in Figure 2.4, the organizational chart of the Mobile, Alabama Chamber of Commerce. This not-for-profit organization relies on the involvement of its dues-paying membership for all its goal achievement. A *systems concept* structure was chosen to generate the greatest member involvement and to reduce the number of meetings and work hours needed to accomplish the Chamber's objectives and yearly work program.

Seven *councils* are designed to develop the Chamber objectives. *Members* are appointed to councils of their choice. The Chamber president appoints a chairperson to each council. This person then becomes a chamber vice-president and a member of the executive committee. The function of each council is to collect ideas from the membership and then to keep the membership informed regarding the council's work. Within each council a group of members make up the *council coordinating committee.* This committee coordinates the activities of all committees of the council and then reviews, studies, and considers the new projects received from the council. Finally, the Chamber president appoints members to *action committees,* where the Chamber projects are completed.

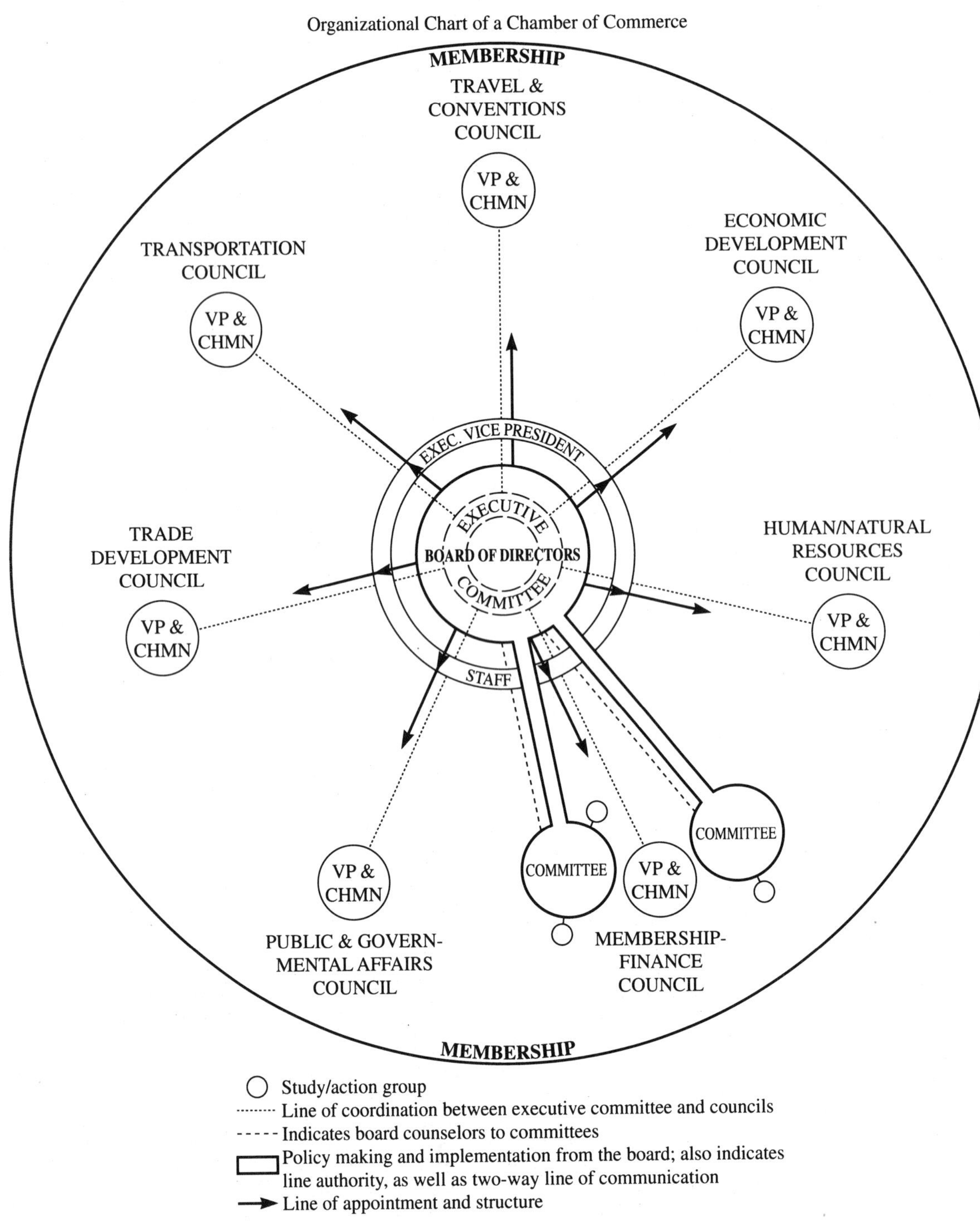

FIGURE 2.4 Systems Concept Organization Structure
©1971, Mobile Area Chamber of Commerce. Used with permission.

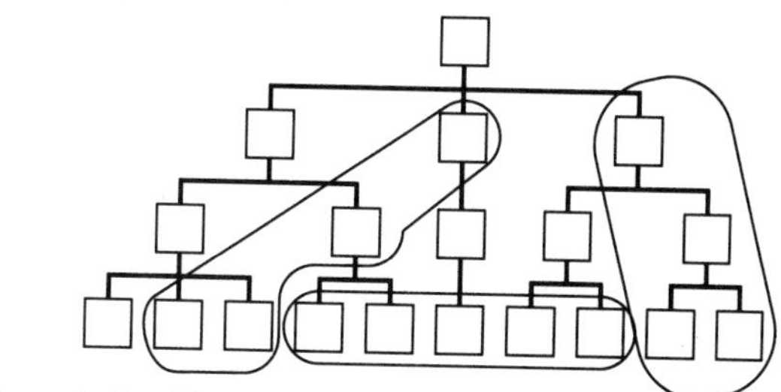

Frame A: Troublesome team concept in structures

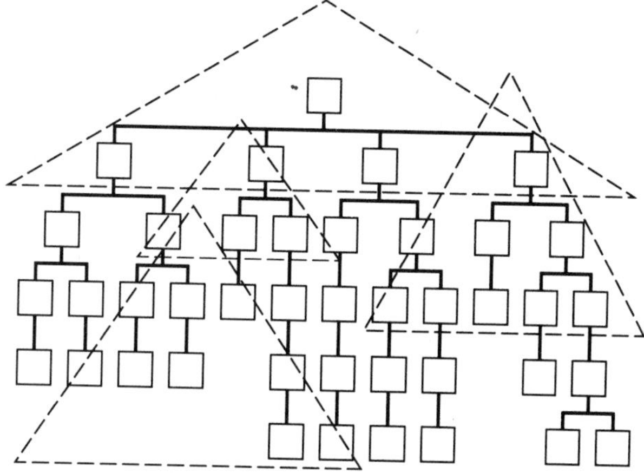

Frame B: Overlapping teams

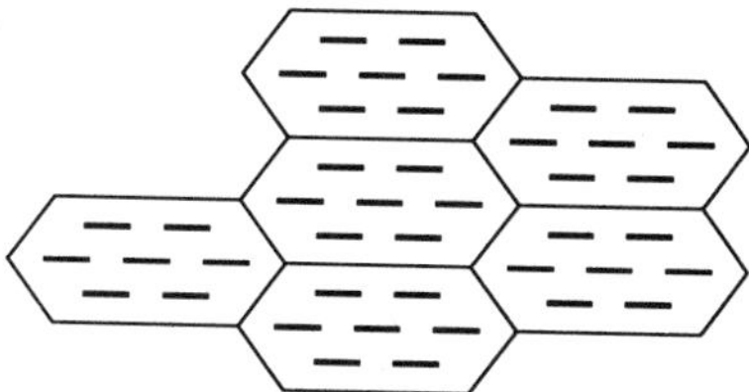

Frame C: "Team blocks"

FIGURE 2.5 New Organizational Structure Designs

While Hesselbein's organizational structure and that of the Mobile Chamber is designed for not-for-profit organizations, examples from for-profit corporations show that they too can benefit from structural changes. In some major organizations like Motorola, Chrysler, General Electric, AT&T, and Xerox, the vertical hierarchy is out and "small business units," "empowered workers," and "customer-driven processes" are in. Organizations that use a horizontal structure allow workers to be grouped for special projects, thus cutting out layers of management. As Frame A in Figure 2.5

shows, creating work teams is difficult to do in the traditional organizational structure. Consequently, organizations are forming the work teams first and then creating the new overall organizational structure. Frame B shows one possibility: Small pyramids of teams overlap, with each team leader positioned on the next higher team. Frame C displays "team blocks" listing the name of each team member.

At Chrysler, designers, engineers, and manufacturers now cooperate to build specific vehicles. . . . One goal is to encourage workers to make more decisions, saving time and money and responding better to the marketplace.[24]

A variety of descriptive names have become associated with the organizational structure changes: *business process redesign, process reengineering, revamping, organizational architecture, implementing,* and *horizontal organization.*

Even as the movement to restructure organizations is underway, the majority of both for-profit and not-for-profit organizations still have a rather traditional shape. As we describe the movement of communication within business, we will refer to both the "traditional" and "restructured" organization.

Overhauling Xerox

The jargon has changed at Xerox Corporation. Gone are the "assembly lines" and "corner offices." In are terms like "empowered workers" and "focus factories." In other words "the organizational architecture has shifted from 'functional' to 'customer-driven' in new divisions with 'end-to-end' responsibility for products."[25]

Since 1959, the old Xerox pyramid placed a chairman at the top, had layers of management, and the factory workers were at the bottom. The company operations were grouped into four gigantic functional units: manufacturing and development, research, marketing, and finance. Top management made nearly all decisions for the entire company. Now, as Figure 2.6 shows, there are nine Xerox divisions, each resembling an independent business within a larger company.

In 1992 Xerox trimmed layers of management. Now three markets exist: copier, printer, and software and services. Each market has three divisions. The nine divisions have twenty-three business units where decisions are made about what machines to build, how they should be built, and where the materials should be obtained.

The old company president has been replaced by a six-person corporate office. Throughout the company the emphasis is on efficiency. In the old Xerox a simple decision like the color of a machine button went almost to the top of the hierarchy. Orders then descended from the top

(continued)

Xerox Corp.'s new structure consists of nine product divisions in three categories, ranging in size from a start-up to an $8 billion office-copier unit.

COPIERS

- **Office Document Products**
  Familiar light-lens office copy machines, plain-paper fax machines
- **Personal Document Products**
  Desktop copiers for consumers and small businesses
- **Document Production Systems**
  High-end business copiers and printers, including full-color digital copiers

PRINTERS

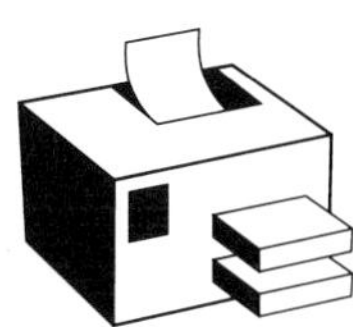

- **Printing Systems**
  High-speed laser printers usually found in corporate data centers
- **Office Document Systems**
  Individual and work-group printers, including full-color digital models
- **Xerox Engineering Systems**
  Large-format copiers and plotters for architects and engineers

SOFTWARE AND SERVICES

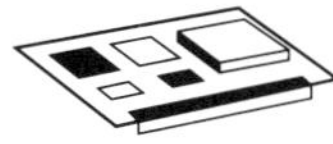

- **Xsoft**
  Software products for managing documents
- **Xerox Business Services**
  Provides copying services at customer offices or off-site centers
- **Advance Office Document Services**
  Start-up operation to develop products linking paper and electronic documents

FIGURE 2.6 The New Xerox
Source: Adopted from "Xerox Overload Puts Power Back In Hands of Workers," *Dallas Morning News*, January 2, 1993, p. 6F. Reprinted with permission of the *Dallas Morning News*.

of the pyramid and new decisions moved from the bottom back up. Now all major decisions are made within the business units. Overall, the company is beginning to see creative thinking, quick decision making, and increased efficiency.[26]

FORMAL COMMUNICATION FLOW

Communication flows in three directions within the traditional organization: downward, upward, and horizontally. The nature and form of the specific communication depends upon the individuals and their jobs in the organization.

Downward Communication

Messages and information sent from top management to subordinates comprise the downward flow. On traditional organizational charts the flow normally follows the formal lines of authority downward from position to position. On the restructured chart the flow often bypasses the lines of authority.

The downward flow is the strongest of the three directions. Management has the power to put messages in motion and start them on their downward journey. Yet messages are sometimes not received, arrive distorted, arrive too late, or are not sent at all.

When asked to define the objective of business communication within their organization, most managers respond with, "keeping employees informed on issues that pertain to our company." With such a system in place, management can spell out company objectives, change employee attitudes, mold opinions, help adjustments to change, and diminish employee fears and suspicions. A study by the consulting firm of Towers, Perrin, Forster & Crosby (TPF&C) indicates the many things that employees want to hear from their company:

> The kinds of things that modern, multi-faceted people want to know about reflect an awareness that they and their jobs are parts of larger things. They want to know how their firm is doing financially; what profits mean and how they relate to the economy as a whole; why layoffs occur; what their organization's product or service means to consumers, the environment, and the economy; what the firm is doing about equal treatment for different age, sex, and racial groups; how pay is determined; why improved productivity is important to them; and how to respond when their firm is attacked by outsiders.
>
> If the information supplied by the organization is unsatisfactory in quality, amount, or timeliness, today's employees will find out what they want to know from other sources: the grapevine, the union, the mass media. Then they'll act in one or more of their guises. They may buy more stock, or sell what they have; they may buy a case of the company's product, or boycott it; they may write letters to the editor supporting the firm's position on public issues, or call for a government takeover; they may dismiss a union organization attempt, or they may sign the organization card and return it promptly to the union. But they *will* act, and management's communications philosophy and expertise will have a lot to do with the way they act.[27]

According to Katz and Kahn, downward communication in an organization usually encompasses the following:

1. Job descriptions and instruction regarding specific employee tasks and methodology.
2. Policy rationale that explains why and how the tasks fit the company's overall objectives.
3. Straight information on the company's past, present, and future along with explanations about policies, practices, and procedures.
4. Job performance evaluations that focus on how well a person is doing the job.
5. Company ideology designed to make employees respect, support, and work for continued company and product success.[28]

Reasons for Poor Downward Communication

There are five common reasons for poor downward communication.

Growth causes isolation. Many companies at their start-up are small enough for face-to-face contact between management and subordinates. With growth, however, more formal lines become established, and soon individuals isolate themselves. Messages go to the wrong people, are late in being sent, and sometimes are not sent at all.

Clearly defined objectives are missing. Management is sometimes confused about information that it thinks that subordinates need and want to know. This confusion is seldom audited or clarified by useful communication. Most companies constantly update both long-term and short-term goals, yet they pay little attention to clarifying their objectives about how to communicate these goals, useful information, and important issues to all people in the company.

Management never audits present communication techniques. Habits are established when people communicate in the same way for long periods of time. Management may never audit its style of communicating with subordinates and so will never learn whether its communication is received, is understandable, or is adequate and timely. An electronic mail message may be automatically issued when a face-to-face conversation would be more appropriate.

Confusion arises over who is responsible for communicating. Top-level management may feel that middle-level or first-line supervisors should be responsible for issuing certain information, while those in lower positions may feel that it is top-level management's responsibility to communicate downward to all the employees.

Segregation exists between supervisory and nonsupervisory personnel. Unspoken norms can segregate management and nonmanagement personnel. This usually starts when management is held responsible for making decisions that affect the entire organization. A nonparticipatory management style may isolate management from the wants and needs of subordinates.

As the formal leader of an organization, the chief executive officer is responsible for making sure that the internal communication lines are open and working. Another report by TPF&C indicates that the problems of poor downward communication often start with the person at the top of the organizational chart—the chief executive officer.

- CEOs usually have limited direct, personal contact with employees of their organizations; generally, they communicate regularly only with those who report directly to them.
- Although CEOs and top managers usually blame breakdowns in downward communications on middle managers and/or supervisors, the problems usually start—through distortion, delay, omission of information—at the higher levels and mushroom at each successively lower level.
- CEOs, top managers, and middle managers usually acknowledge a need for improved downward communication to employees, but they are not usually as aware as first-line supervisors of how inadequate communication to employees often is.
- CEOs believe that upward communication from their top managers is good but emphasize that too many problems are withheld from them until situations reach the "disaster" stage.
- CEOs generally consider the communication of hard facts, particularly financial information, and the creation of a favorable public image to be their most important and attainable communications goals. Most haven't thought much about a philosophy or a set of objectives for employee communications.
- Upward communication to the CEO level tends to be most effective when managers at each organizational level are held responsible for effective communications performance.[29]

The same TPF&C report reveals that the most credible source of information within an organization is the organization's lowest-ranking employee. The report cites examples of the different perceptions between management and employees:

Management says:	1. We are concerned about employees.
Employees say:	1. Management couldn't care less.
Management says:	2. Our employees believe us.
Employees say:	2. We don't believe a word they say.
Management says:	3. Profits haven't been high enough to warrant any unnecessary frills.
Employees say:	3. This outfit is really swimming in dollars. The president makes $300,000 a year, and we just built a lush headquarters building.[30]

When employees of an organization hold such beliefs, the programs of pay, benefits, and communications do not work. The burden of the problem's solution must be placed on the CEO and top management:

> Employees at all levels want to hear from you. They want to hear your views, hopes, and aspirations, just as much as they want you to hear theirs. Employee communication really is *everyone's* job—but the tone and substance of that communication must come from the top.[31]

Methods for Improving the Downward Flow

There are three ways in which favorable downward communication can be implemented. First is the establishment of *objectives* for both the intended message that a manager wishes to communicate and the overall flow of communication downward within the organization. Second, the *content* of the message is important. Chase lists six content qualities of a manager's message:

> 1. *It must be accurate.* That is, the message must be a true report, be it good or bad concerning information about the company. . . .
> 2. *It must be both definite and specific in meaning.* . . .
> 3. *It must be forceful,* i.e., the message must be stated in a way to show that management carries a firm conviction for any actions taken which may affect the company. . . .
> 4. *It must suit the occasion and must be receiver oriented.* The message must be stated in such a way that subordinates will have no trouble understanding how it directly affects them. . . .
> 5. *It should not contain complexities, but be stated as simply as possible.* The contents of the message should be transmitted in such a way that the recipient will understand and be able to grasp it quickly. . . .
> 6. *Finally, it should contain no hidden meaning.* A message may have one meaning under certain circumstances and another under different circumstances.[32]

The third way in which favorable downward communication can be implemented is careful choice of the *technique* by which the message is sent. Is individual face-to-face contact better than small group meetings, telephone conversations, electronic mail, or written forms? Successful organizations use a variety of methods. Executives at Tandem Computers, for example, "hold monthly teleconferences with their employees (600 hours worth in 1985 alone), and in-person discussions and a monthly newsletter are used to keep employees up to date on General Motors' activities in its Packard Electric plant in Mississippi." The effect of the improved communication is improved productivity and reduced turnover.[33]

Another exciting example of excellent downward communication, in which an organization uses topical, relevant information that is highly creative, is Allie's from the files of TPF&C.

Management does have a responsibility for keeping employees informed on issues, for building pride in the organization and its products, and for gaining employee acceptance and support of organization policies and goals. This downward flow of communication is nevertheless only one-third of the communication needs that a manager must oversee and nurture. To complete the

Allie's

A major U.S. hotel company created "Allie's," a new family restaurant chain. Management wanted the service level at Allie's to be as high as it was in the famous hotel. They had some problems, however. Turnover in the restaurant industry was high, and motivating short-term employees to maintain top-level service standards was hard. Added to this was a language problem. "Front-of-the-house" restaurant employees were typically English-speaking college students. The "back-of-the-house" kitchen workers were Spanish speaking.

Allie's designed an excellent profit-sharing plan, but few employees seemed to care since they wouldn't be around long enough to participate. So management, in its desire to show concern for all employees, created the "square deal" package. This was a takeoff of the "square meal" that Allie's customers received. The package consisted of a cash bonus plan that paid out quarterly and let employees earn paid time off. This benefit was unheard of for hourly restaurant workers.

Finally, the biggest job was determining how to communicate the program to employees. Since management knew that its employees were not inclined to read company literature, a new plan was required. Innovation took over and a four-part communication effort was created with:

- A humorous, light-on-detail video designed to provide an overview of the square deal.
- A promotional wheel in the shape of a fancy cake succinctly described what employees had to do to earn a bonus.
- Newsletters for managers explaining their own bonus plan in more detail.
- All materials produced in Spanish as well as English.[34]

This unique approach was very successful and could be copied by other firms that have lots of part-time employees.

organizational communication loop, upward and horizontal flows must also be established and working.

Upward Communication

Bruce Harriman, a former vice-president of New England Telephone, makes an interesting point contrasting downward and upward communication:

> Communications in a hierarchical society or organization work according to the principle that governs gravity. Downward communications are usually

> better than anyone realizes and frequently more accurate than those at higher levels want them to be. Conversely, upward communications have to be pumped and piped, with a minimum of filters, in order to be effective.[35]

Upward communication flows from subordinates to superiors. In a study of seventy-five companies in the United States and Canada, Harriman found the following disappointing information about upward communication: "We encountered no experts, studies, or programs on upward communication. Most corporate communications programs dealt with downward communications, and the few that were aimed upward were individual techniques, such as employee suggestion plans, methods for answering questions, or ways of letting off steam."[36]

Curley explains the importance of establishing an "upward" communication loop in management:

> An effective business communication program is not only one which "speaks," but also one which "listens." . . . [I]t has a two-way orientation. Employee publications, defined procedures, speeches to the work force, orientations and effective day-to-day work direction can handle the "speak" half of the communication loop; but how about the "listen" half of the loop? Is it really necessary? If so, how can it be accomplished? The "listen" dimension takes on considerable importance if the organization wants the loyalty and complete support of its people.[37]

Reasons for Poor Upward Communication

Size and complexity of an organization. The larger the organization, the more common the barriers to upward flows of communication. This is especially true at the ground-floor levels of the organization.

Unrealistic assumptions. Often, assumptions about the organization, employees, and the in-place communication process create enormous problems. Eisenmann and Hughes comment on this factor:

> We often send messages out through the organization with the assumption that all people are listening and understanding exactly the way we intended. Many managers presume their communiques are penetrating the minds of their employees but never bother to check. In reality, there is often a serious gap between the message sent and the one received. The amount of time and money spent on employee communications, directed from management to the people, generally exceeds tenfold the amount spent on listening to people and getting feedback about the effectiveness of the management process as perceived by the members of the organization.[38]

Filtering and distortion. Each step in the upward flow of communication within an organization allows for a filtering and consequential distortion of messages. Such filtering easily occurs when management perceives that everything is positive but in reality there is tremendous employee unrest.

Fear in the Cockpit

The dynamics between pilots and copilots of commercial airliners are a perfect example of the problem of poor upward communication. Too many times copilots are reluctant to assert themselves clearly to pilots when they fear an error is being made. Norms in the cockpit dictate that a senior person should not be contradicted, and so copilots are frequently much too polite to do so. Unfortunately, some fatal accidents have been directly attributed to such failures of upward communication in the cockpit. One well-known case is the 1982 Air Florida accident in which cockpit voice recordings revealed that the copilot's warnings to the pilot were too subtle to avoid the crash in which seventy-eight persons lost their lives after the plane struck a bridge in Washington, D.C.[39]

Fear of presenting bad news. In some companies middle management has learned to respond promptly and effectively to actions they perceive to be of personal interest to top management. Sometimes this is inadvertent; sometimes it is self-serving. There is a tendency to delay sending bad news in hope that the problem will be resolved or eliminated before those above must be told or involved.

Step-loss sequence. As information flows upward from one level to the next, meaning is distorted and filtered intentionally and unintentionally. This is partly due to limited knowledge of the total organization and its specific problems. Added to this are managers who are fearful of having subordinates receive credit for ideas and accomplishments that could make the manager look weak, unproductive, or uncreative.

Superior-subordinate relationship. Three factors discourage upward communication in the superior/subordinate relationship:

1. *When relationships between superiors and subordinates are not compatible* neither person takes the time to truly know the other and to communicate openly. They allow misperceptions to occur, and these later develop into conflicts that are unresolved. DuBrin contends that subordinates usually place the responsibility for developing the needed relationships on the managers. But he believes the subordinate is ultimately responsible for the growth of this important fit. He offers four suggestions that can help subordinates solidify relationships.
    a. *Understand your boss's goals* and then determine how you can help your boss accomplish her objectives. Sometimes these are clear, other times they may be obscure. They are determined by thought-out communication.
    b. *Support your boss* by helping her solve problems, realize mistakes,

and discover new methods for accomplishing things, and by not talking about her behind her back.

c. *Help your boss succeed* by putting excellence into every part of your job. Finish deadlines ahead of time and go beyond the stated expectations of your work. Realize that you are a team and that the other's winning accomplishments will also make you a winner.

d. *Reward your boss* just as you want to be rewarded yourself. Write notes of appreciation. Tell top management how great your manager is. Realize that when a compliment is given to your boss, it is also given to you.[40]

2. *Fear of punishment* can cause subordinates to conceal or distort their feelings, important information, or disclosure of problems and potential solutions. Gemmill comments on the ramifications of this action:

> Decisions by subordinates not to disclose such information results in a superior being unaware of how his actions affect them. This lack of feedback may prevent him from changing his managerial style or from correcting misconceptions on their part. Similarly, he is put in a position where he is unable to share knowledge with them that might lead to improvements in their performance. Perhaps most important, however, from a manager's perspective is that this lack of communication may cut him off from some essential information.[41]

3. *Belief that emotions should not be displayed* can cause a subordinate to hold back feelings, opinions, and matters that he or she would otherwise like to talk over with a superior. If such emotions are aired, the person expressing them will probably experience some feelings of guilt and anxiety about the superior's perception of his or her strength and ability to do the job.

Bottlenecks. Several types of bottlenecks to the effective flow of information have been discovered:

1. *The gatekeeper* is usually the second in command (see Figure 2.7). This person can be a secretary or administrative assistant. They filter the

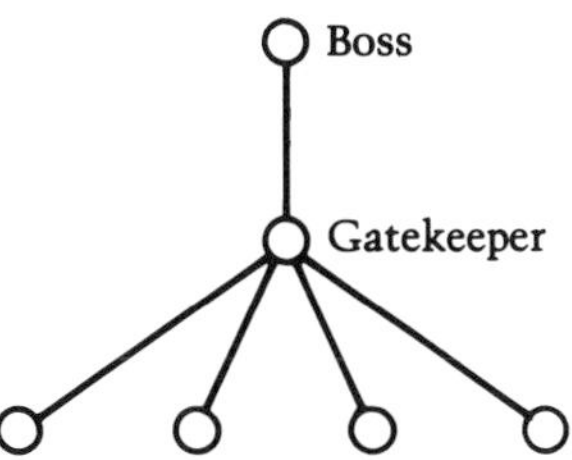

FIGURE 2.7 The Gatekeeper

information they receive and pass on only what they think their superior should know. In the illustration the subordinates have to trust the gatekeeper to pass their information upward.

2. *The status seeker* hordes information that he or she receives and uses it for personal benefit. This person is fearful that divulging it would make others his or her equal.

3. *The promotion rival* keeps information that could help others receive faster advancement in the organization.

4. *The department competitor* wants his or her work group to look better and be more productive than other departments. Consequently he or she withholds information that might help other departments.

Ice jams. The blockage problems in the upward communication flow have also been referred to as an ice jam:

> What can be done about the blockages? Not a great deal, unless the main effort to break up the ice jam comes from the same source that started it.
>
> The breaking of the jam can be accomplished by some or all of the following techniques: empathetic listening, question-and-answer columns in employee publications, small group meetings, suggestion systems, real "open door" policies, ombudsman programs, participative decision making, attitude surveys, and communication audits. The common denominator among all of these should be a managerial attitude that is *actively* cognizant and supportive of employees' innate desire to know, to participate, to understand, and to contribute.[42]

According to a study by Elizabeth and Francis Jennings, the basic remedy for unfreezing the flow requires a manager to gain insight into his or her own thoughts and feelings before attempting to gain insight into an employee's thoughts and feelings:

> It may be that the executive does not understand his function; it may be that he fears the responsibilities he has assumed, that he does not value people and so misuses them, that he is afraid he will lose his power, that he needs training—but any of these statements can be reduced to this: he is unaware of himself. If the executive were aware of himself in relation to others, he would make an attempt to alter his behavior.[43]

Methods for Improving Poor Upward Communication

While each company must determine the best upward communication techniques that can be implemented to meet employee needs, several suggested methods are used today:[44]

1. *Small group meetings* are conducted periodically so that employees can ask for information and their supervisor can provide it.
2. *Operational reviews* occur when managers visit the work stations of the people they manage and review problems and hindrances for successful completion of the work.

3. *Suggestion boxes* are found in many companies and ideas are forwarded to the appropriate persons.
4. *In-company educational courses* are often designed where written assignments allow employees to express their thoughts and ideas to instructors, who then channel them to appropriate top-level officials.
5. *Task teams* consist of nonmanagement personnel who serve on panels to identify problems and possible solutions. This information is then forwarded to management for responses.
6. *Employee annual meetings* resemble stockholder meetings where top management solicits and answers questions asked by company employees.
7. *Junior boards of directors* are made up of several middle managers and subordinates who develop policy recommendations that are presented to the corporate board.
8. *Corps of counselors or ombudsmen* are often located throughout an organization and are accessible to employees as liaisons.
9. *Subordinates are included in management meetings* when information is needed that only a specialist might have. Those subordinates should be included in management meetings to answer questions and serve as resources.
10. *Subordinates make presentations to top management* and describe the responsibilities of their jobs.
11. *Employee audits* reveal how employees feel about their jobs and the company.

Horizontal Communication

Communication in a lateral or diagonal manner within the charted organization is referred to as *horizontal* (see Figure 2.8). This is the most frequent flow of communication because individuals at the same level talk to each other constantly about work-related events, management, and personal matters. Lewis estimates that two-thirds of the organizational communication flow is horizontal.[45]

Work-related communication revolves around formal tasks and goals that are vital to the organization. The personal, informal communication is

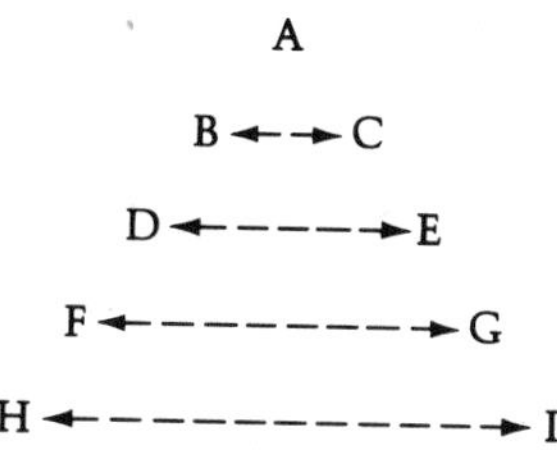

FIGURE 2.8 Horizontal Communication Distance in an Organization

Professor Richard L. Simpson, a sociologist at the University of North Carolina, conducted a survey of eight supervisors in the spinning department of a synthetic textile mill in order to test the hypothesis that "work-related communications between officials are more often vertical than horizontal."

The method employed by the researcher was a structured but open-ended interview procedure. The question put to the supervisors was: "About how often do you talk with——on business? Don't include times when you just say hello or pass the time of day; just the contacts needed to get your work done. . . . What kinds of things do you talk about with him?" Some of the findings and interpretations were:

The contacts of the three men at the higher levels—A, B-1, and B-2 (see Figure 2.9)—were overwhelmingly vertical, but they could hardly have been otherwise. A, being the only man at his level, could not possibly have any horizontal contacts. B-1 and B-2 could communicate horizontally only with each other, but they could communicate downward with several foremen and upward with A. They seldom had to communicate with each other, since the work relations between their sections were coordinated mainly through horizontal contact between their subordinates. . . .

On the C-foreman level most contacts were horizontal except those of C-3. . . . Three of these five foremen—C-1, C-2, and C-5—had markedly fewer vertical and more horizontal contacts than would have occurred on the chance expectations that every man communicates equally with every other man. The contacts of C-4 were mainly horizontal, in

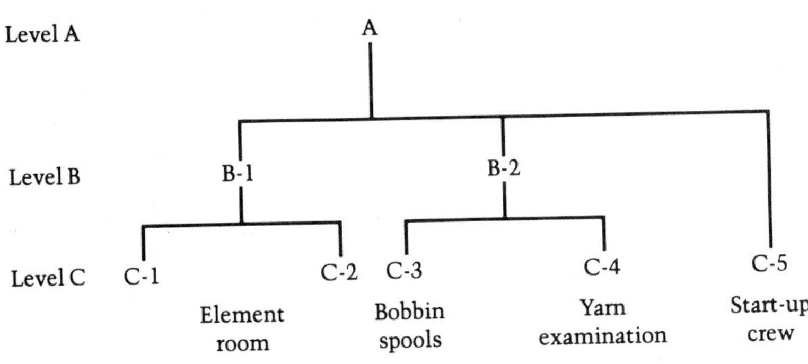

FIGURE 2.9 Organization Chart of Spinning Department Supervisors
Source: R. L. Simpson, "Vertical and Horizontal Communication in Formal Organizations," *Administrative Science Quarterly*, 4, 2 (September 1959), pp. 188–196. Used by permission.

(continued)

> about the same proportion as would be expected on the basis of chance. . . .
>
> The preponderance of horizontal communications reported by four of the five first-line foremen (level C) is understandable if we examine the content of the communications they reported. Very few communications involved the issuing of commands or the reporting of results—the standard types of vertical communications. Most contacts of men at level C involved either (1) joint problem-solving or (2) coordination of work flow between sections. These were mainly horizontal communications. . . .
>
> It is noteworthy that they (the level-C men) worked out these problems without consulting or informing their superior.
>
> The findings neither confirmed nor rejected the hypothesis but led to a modified hypothesis:
>
> Mechanization reduces the need for close supervision (vertical communication), since instead of the foreman the machines set the work pace; but automation (i.e., extreme mechanization) increases the need for vertical communication, to deal with the frequent and serious machine breakdowns.

part of the social/emotional needs that all people must maintain while working closely together for long periods of time.

The shape of the pyramid organizational structure symbolizes that employees at the bottom have a greater need for information and a wider gap to fill than those at the top. Henri Fayol described this in his bridge for horizontal communication. We can also see the wasted time and energy if H had to communicate to G or I but had to go up through the different levels and then have the message go back down from A through G before the sending was complete.

When the types of messages passed among individuals on this plane are task related, they encompass ways to coordinate work, solve problems, share information, and resolve conflicts, and they cover such areas as production, sales, personnel, purchasing, and finance. Kelley describes a study of a textile mill where supervisor communication patterns were influenced by technology.[46]

The horizontal flow also is a place where subordinates evaluate their superiors in areas of skill, attitudes, values, personality, problem solving, planning, and organizing. Messages transmitted at this level are important to a supervisor because they serve as feedback on how well he or she is managing. The information, however, is rarely given in person and is usually transmitted through the grapevine.

Reasons for Poor Horizontal Communication

Departmentalization is the biggest barrier to horizontal communication. There are increased numbers of people and messages to deal with on this plane. Employees compete for resources, positions, and recognition. Departmental rivalries can develop. Vibrations from the created friction can be felt even at the top of the organization as departments strive to meet their own goals, regardless of the impact on other departments or on the whole organization.

Personality clashes and conflicts between employees are common and are more often felt in the horizontal flow of messages. These clashes and conflicts may be the result of suppressed facts, of one person's possession of material that another person needs, or of one person's general dislike for another.

Methods for Improving Horizontal Communication

1. *Construct realistic organization charts.* The organizational chart that shows both the formal and informal structure can enhance the flow of communication. True authority relationships should also be noted. This saves guesswork on the part of employees.

2. *Individual job descriptions should be accurate.* Each employee should know precisely what he or she is to do and how it is to be done. Such descriptions should also list the authority that is delegated to each employee and supervisor and the vertical and horizontal channels of communication that should be followed.

3. *Organize and utilize interdepartmental projects.* Individuals in groupings and departments should communicate before their communication is sent to others. Such projects cut down on interdepartmental competition and open the flow of communication within the entire organization.

4. *Encourage regular meetings and communication.* If departments and divisions within an organization establish regular times for meetings, there is less use of the grapevine and a greater sense of organizational loyalty. While it is not practical to demand that each subordinate communicate regularly with every other subordinate, it is vital that access to other employees be available and that needed communication be adequate.

5. *Model proper communication usage.* As Strickland and his colleagues describe, several skills can be taught:

> Conflict management is certainly a valuable one. Considerable time and energy can be wasted through conflicts which are not resolved effectively. If managers and supervisors can model effective conflict resolution, subordinates can pick it up without much difficulty.
>
> In addition, managers and supervisors can teach subordinates management skills, planning skills, and so on. The point to remember is that subordinates learn the most from you by what is demonstrated in addition to what is said. Consistent good modeling is the best way to teach skills of any kind.[47]

THE IMPACT OF INFORMATION TECHNOLOGY ON THE ORGANIZATIONAL STRUCTURE

In the past three decades, giant strides have been made in the average businessperson's ability to send and receive messages. This started with the creation of companies like Federal Express, whose long-distance delivery process improved upon the federal postal system's speed and service. But more important are the devices that have grown out of computer technology: electronic mail, voice mail, facsimile, cellular telephones, and paging. As a radio commercial states, "staying in touch has never been so easy."

H. Mitchell Watson, Jr., chief executive officer of ROLM Company, a telecommunications organization jointly owned by IBM and Siemens, believes that the most effective companies of the future will be those who make use of cutting-edge technology. "The key is to provide people with the flexibility to get information, to pass on that information, and to communicate when it's convenient for them. I believe the companies destined to be the most successful in the '90s are those that weave communications right into the fabric of their business."[48]

While technology has impacted business communication in a variety of ways, this section will concentrate only on computer-based communication and how it affects individuals in the organizational structure.

Computer networks cut across organizational boundaries in both technical and social ways and alter the formal flow of communication. They have helped produce tremendous change in organizations. Technically computer communication has six important characteristics.

1. *Computer communication cuts across time boundaries.* Employees determine when in their work day they will use computer communication. Electronic mail can be sent at the convenience of the sender and read at the convenience of the receiver. Some employees respond to received messages as they would to telephone calls. Other employees schedule certain times of the day to read and respond to electronic requests. The frustration of trying to reach someone by telephone or having to return calls only to play telephone-tag is eliminated.

2. *Computer communication cuts across geographical boundaries.* Messages can be sent to a colleague down the hall or a customer in another country. Lawyers in England fax documents to India for word processing. When finished, those documents are express-mailed back to England. The speed of getting information to the preparer, along with cheap labor, makes the process economical.

Employees who have computers with modems can generate and receive information at their home, in their car, or in hotel rooms while traveling.

3. *Multiple messages are sent simultaneously.* Instead of preparing and sending individual memos or making separate telephone calls, employees can use computers to send messages to one person or a thousand people automatically and within a few seconds. Each will receive his own copy, and each can respond back to the sender.

4. *Computer messages avoid the bottleneck gap.* Since employees on line usually send and receive their own messages, information sent by computer avoids the filters and bottlenecks found in traditional spoken and written communication.

5. *Computer messages allow employees to avoid paperwork collections.* Messages are sent and received on computer terminals. Unless a hard paper copy is desired and printed, the entire transaction takes place electronically. The majority of messages are never printed on paper.

6. *Computer communication leads to the creation of special information networks.* A good example of such a network comes from the defense field. Several years ago the Department of Defense built a large computer network, the ARPANET, to link computers at selected sites. Soon the use was not computer to computer but researcher to researcher. The ARPANET helped create communities of researchers who exchanged reports, ideas, computer programs, gossip, and travel plans.[49]

Though the technical characteristics of computer communication are important to consider in examining organizational structures, two social characteristics are just as vital.

1. *The tone of a message is absent.* In interpersonal conversations a speaker can use verbal and nonverbal expression to emphasize words and feelings. With computer communication there is no way to link the content or tone of messages to the sender's or receiver's responses. Consequently the evaluation of a message is based on the content alone.

2. *The absence of personal information about the sender and receiver strips much of a message's power.* In face-to-face interaction the person with the most power often talks the most. When communication takes place on computers, the senders and receivers have basic identifying factors like names, dates, and writing styles. Absent is information related to "job, title, status, departmental affiliation, gender, race, appearance, and demeanor. . . . Missing also is information about the person's background, personality, style, and intention."[50]

Kiesler describes the impact of this absence. "When social definitions are weak or nonexistent, communication becomes unregulated. People are less bound by convention, less influenced by status, and unconcerned with making a good appearance. Their behavior becomes more extreme, impulsive, and self-centered. They become, in a sense, freer people."[51] Computer communication has become a tremendous success in a very short time period. It has helped to alter the structure of organizations and the way people communicate. But along with the success there are also problems.

1. *Retrieving the information is often difficult.* Messages that can travel around the world in seconds can remain in office computers for days if not retrieved. For example, traveling managers may have to call one number for voice mail, log on to a computer for electronic mail, and then call a secretary for faxed messages. Perfected technology will tie all these channels together and allow each to be checked with one call. "With these new systems, executives calling in to their voice box for recorded messages can also learn that a computer message, or electronic mail, is waiting, and in some cases have a synthesized computer voice read it over the phone. Other systems now appearing allow people to punch a telephone keypad to have faxes that arrive at their offices forwarded to a fax machine at their locations. And pagers can relay voice and electronic mail messages instantly."[52] As Figure 2.10 shows, basic computers and voice mail systems are evolving into office communication hubs.

2. *There is potential for overload.* Another down side of improved computer communication is information overload. Recently a software engineer at Digital Equipment Corporation returned to his office after a three-week assignment. To his horror, over 1,000 electronic messages were awaiting him. The engineer's computer, however, helped him solve his dilemma. Coded to identify the message's sender, the computer sorted all communiques. "Messages from the company president . . . [went] into a high-priority electronic file, while announcements about cafeteria hours went to the bottom. Other messages [were] killed outright. One person sends nothing but annoying jokes. Those trifles are not deleted upon arrival."[53]

Just as having too little information causes problems, having too much can also be detrimental. According to Kiesler, "having too much information can mean costly attention to things that don't need it. Because computer networks reach so many people, so fast, the information effects are magnified."[54]

3. *Information is often sent to people who do not need it.* Computer networks can have long automatic distribution lists. Often people receive information when they do not want it or have no use for it.

4. *Information may produce unwanted results.* Because of the vast quantity and power of information produced in computer networks, organizational goals may be undesirably altered. A few years ago, the Kansas City Police Department used a central computer at their headquarters to send information on suspects, stolen cars, and criminal records to officers in the field. The goal was to make each officer more efficient. Soon the police chief lamented that his officers had become too efficient in enforcing minor offenses—spotting unregistered vehicles and parking-ticket offenders—and had neglected other more important work. Others noted that the computer information had led to many false arrests and had helped to clog the courts with traffic offenders.[55]

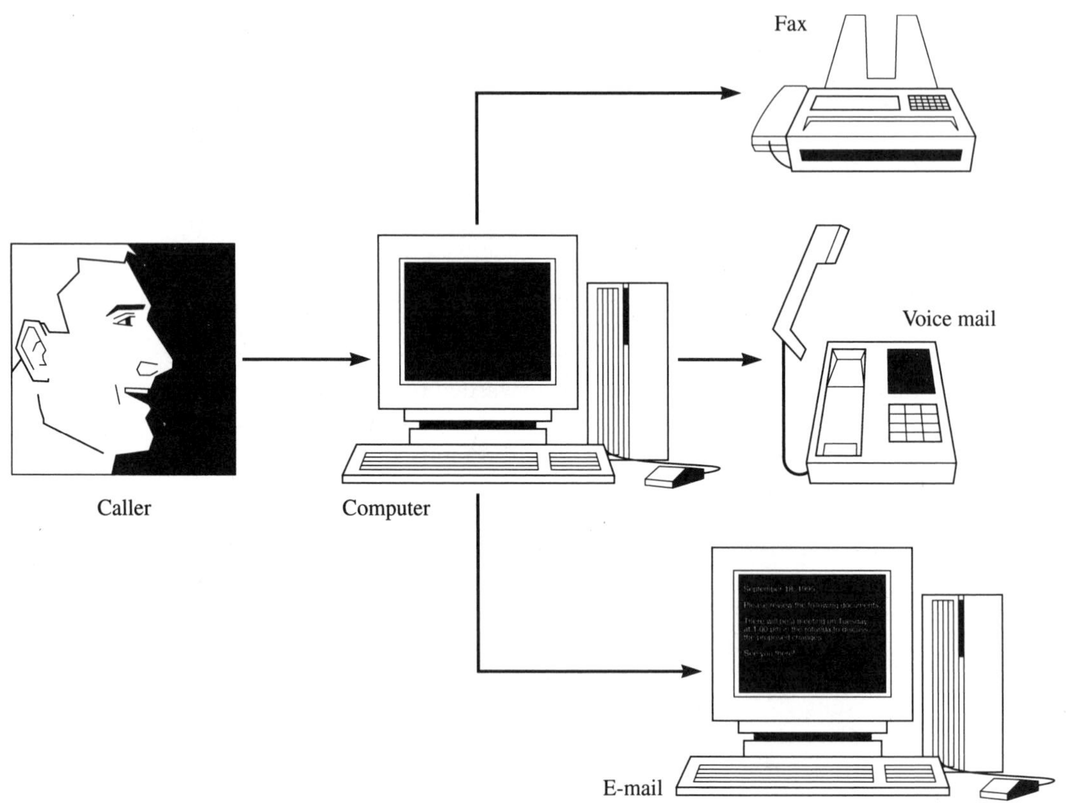

FIGURE 2.10 Office Communication Hubs

5. *Computer communication can cause the grapevine to flourish.* Computer networks are often full of nonbusiness-related topics. But even when the topics are business related, the electronic collection of messages can equal that of the oral grapevine. IBM has found this to be true on several occasions. In the mid-1980s, the employee network carried so many complaints about company policy that the network was tagged with the name GRIPENET. In 1991, an IBM employee network also made the headlines. The *Wall Street Journal* reported that the remarks indicated such bad morale problems that they were closed down after just a few days. One participant complained about the 35 percent raise that the IBM chairman had received. Another reported that even with the large employee discount, employees could buy IBM clones cheaper than they could buy the company's machines. The publicity over the reported information caused then chairman John Akers to say that "his employees spend too much time around the water cooler and too little worrying about their jobs."[56]

ETHICS: RIGHT OR WRONG?

The Sears Automotive Scandal

In the late 1800s, Sears, Roebuck was one of the most exciting retailers in the United States. Its main customers were midwestern farmers who used the Sears mail order catalog to purchase products. In the 1920s, the company accurately predicted the population shift from rural to urban centers. The emphasis on mail order business shifted to city retail centers.

As the company grew, management took on a typical pyramid design. At the retail level, department managers and clerks worked in harmony selling Sears brand products. Culturally, Sears was "a great place to work." The employee profit-sharing program motivated management and salespeople alike to please customers and retain their business.

In the 1960s and 1970s, Sears, like other retailers, found itself in an identity crisis. New retailers emerged, introducing sleekly designed stores and cutting-edge technology. They helped the consumer to develop an image of Sears as old-fashioned, bureaucratic, and unresponsive. Sears's advertising and marketing appeals did little to change that image. In 1978, they announced their philosophy, "We are not a store for the whimsical or the affluent. We are not an exciting store. We are not a store that anticipates. We reflect the world of Middle America."[57]

Trying desperately to keep Middle America's business did not work. In 1991, Sears learned that it had slipped from being the nation's largest retailer to third largest, outranked by Wal-Mart and K-Mart. By this time it had become evident to consumers and financial analysts that Sears was in trouble and had internal management problems. The pleasant salespeople had disappeared. A retail-satisfaction survey by Frequency Marketing ranked Sears at the bottom of most service categories. "In terms of a pleasant shopping experience, consumers ranked Sears 35th of 39 retailers. Nordstrom was No 1 . . . for friendly employees, Sears was 32 of 39; for speedy service, Sears ranked 31."[58]

In an attempt to boost company sales, Edward A. Brennan, company chairman, implemented a new pay structure in 1990 for employees who earned commissions on their sales. From the chairman's suite to the sales floor, the overall thrust was on profits. The new emphasis placed quotas on the numbers of items that had to be sold and services that had to be performed hourly and daily. A thirty-year Sears appliance salesman stated that he had received over a dozen letters from his department manager in a two-year period. Each letter stated that he could expect to be fired if he failed to increase the number of maintenance agreements that he sold. The salesman transferred the pressure that management placed on him to the customer. He said, "An unhappy salesman who figures he's been shafted is going to shaft someone else."

In 1990, departments throughout the stores established new programs designed to generate more profits. The Sears Auto Centers implemented a new pay structure with an incentive system based on the number of parts and services sold. Sears had 868 auto repair shops located around the country, seventy-two of which were in California. The automotive unit accounted for $2.8 billion of Sears's $31.4 billion in 1991 retailing revenues. The commissioned pay structure instructed employees to sell a certain number of repairs or services per eight-hour shift and to sell a specified number of shock absorbers or struts every working hour. Sears rewarded employees with commissions, bonuses, free trips for top sellers, and the assurance of keeping their jobs.

Commissions and quotas are a routine part of the retail business, but top managers who became overzealous in pushing sales performance failed to perform the proper management checks designed to ensure that "overselling" did not take place. This omission came to light on June 11, 1992, when the California Department of Consumer Affairs publicly announced its desire to revoke Sears's state license to operate its seventy-two California car centers. They alleged that Sears performed "unnecessary" service and repairs on its customers' automobiles.

In December 1990, after complaints against the retailer had jumped by 29 percent, the state of California started its investigation of the Sears Automotive Centers. The Consumer Affairs Agency found that Sears charged an average of $235 for unnecessary repairs. Following California's action, the states of Florida, Illinois, New York, and New Jersey also contemplated charges.

Sears responded to the allegations by saying that its compensation system conformed to industry standards, its sales goals were reasonable, and that it emphasized outstanding service, not revenues. The company denied any wrongdoing but admitted that the compensation program and sales goals could have created a communication climate in which mistakes could occur. Chairman Brennan claimed the mistakes were isolated incidents and not intentional fraud on the part of Sears. Soon after, however, Sears went back to an hourly pay system for auto service technicians, based on customer satisfaction.

On September 2, 1992, Sears agreed to pay $8 million to resolve the California complaints. The settlement included paying the state of California $3.5 million for investigative costs and establishing a $1.5 million auto-repair training program. Also, over 900,000 coupons for $50 would be offered to consumers who purchased and had installed selected Sears automotive products or services between August 1, 1990 and January 31, 1992. In addition, Sears agreed to retain an independent organization that would conduct shopping audits at the auto centers to ensure that overselling did not reoccur.

Acting quickly to stop the erosion of customer trust, the company ran TV and print ads apologizing for the car repair overcharges and explaining the new pay structure. The ads cost Sears $27 million. But according to one customer service consultant, the cost was necessary: "The scandal made people doubt every department at Sears . . . Whatever smaller complaints there were before, now consumers think of Sears, and think of the editorial cartoon showing a shopper chased by a Sears salesman armed with a big screw."[59]

Case Questions

1. Is there a question of ethics in this case?
2. How did the organizational structure influence the problem?
3. How could better formal communication have prevented this problem?
4. Will the informal communication structure help or hinder the rebuilding of customer trust in the Sears Automotive Centers' behavior?
5. Was the solution to the case a fitting way to resolve an ethics issue?

SUMMARY

A study of communication in organizations must first examine the characteristics of their culture, structure, and formal communication flow as well as the impact of information technology.

Every organization has a culture. Cultures in excellent organizations are characterized by eight factors: a prevailing philosophy, shared norms, practiced values and standards, practiced rites and rituals, circulating stories, an interaction climate, a concern for people, open communication, and visible excitement, pride, and commitment. In this chapter the culture of Walt Disney World was highlighted and matched with these eight characteristics.

The structure of an organization also impacts communication. Traditionally, organizational structures have taken a pyramid design showing line (authority and responsibility) and staff (assist and advise) positions. In recent years, design changes have taken place in many organizations. Such changes have served to impact the traditional "up" and "down" flow of communication.

Even with changing structure, the communication mindset of many managers still reflects a formal communication flow. This flow was examined in three directions: downward, upward, and horizontal. Downward communication flows from management to subordinates. Upward communication flows from subordinates to superiors. Horizontal communication normally occurs between individuals at the same level.

Information technology has impacted greatly the organization person's ability to communicate. Computer networks cut across the traditional organizational structure to control time of information sending and receiving, cut across geographical boundaries, avoid bottlenecks, and eliminate paperwork. This technological revolution is seen in the rise of computers, facsimile, voice mail, and electronic mail.

KEY WORDS

bottleneck
computer networks
departmentalization
division of labor
downward communication
electronic mail
facsimile
filtering
formal communication flow
horizontal communication
ice jam
information technology
line position
organizational culture
organizational structure
span of control
staff position
total quality management
upward communication
voice mail

Review Questions

1. Name and describe the eight characteristics of an organizational culture.
2. What distinct functions does an organization structure accomplish?
3. What are the differences between line and staff positions?
4. How do recent design changes impact organizational structure?
5. What are the precise differences among the three formal ways that communication flows in an organization?
6. What are some specific reasons for poor downward flow?
7. What are four ways that the downward communication flow can be improved?
8. Cite six reasons for a poor upward communication flow.
9. What are some ways that upward flow can be improved?
10. Name two reasons for poor horizontal communication flow.
11. Cite five ways to improve the horizontal flow.
12. Describe several ways that information technology has impacted organizational structure.

Exercises

1. The following statements pertain to your personal use of the upward, downward, and horizontal communication flow as a manager. If you have had, or now have, supervisory experience, respond to the statements from that framework. If you have never had a supervisory job, respond from the position of what you think should be done to correct the communication problems. After you have written your solutions, look up the suggested solutions. The numbers in parentheses indicate the suggested solutions.

Upward Communication

a. Your communication does not inspire your superior's confidence in you as a communicator. (1)
b. You do not receive the desired results from your writing. (1)
c. You have difficulty getting your messages to the right person. (2)
d. Your superiors seem to not have the time to listen to you. (3)
e. Your superior does not respond to your written memos until it is too late for effective action. (3)
f. You are often confused about which communication method to use. (4)

Horizontal Communication

g. Those on your horizontal level do not have confidence in your communication. (1)
h. Those you communicate with receive so much communication that yours does not receive needed attention. (1)
i. People misunderstand your communications. (1)
j. You are often puzzled about which communication method to use. (4)
k. Those on your level question your authority to issue communications. (7)

Downward Communication

l. Your written communications are often ignored and do not produce the desired action. (1)
m. Your communications are often resented. (1)
n. The accuracy of your statements is often doubted. (1)
o. Your subordinates feel that your position on issues is on the other side of the fence. (1)
p. You are often confused over which communication method to use. (4)
q. Rumors and information leaks affect the results of your communication. (5)
r. You have trouble reaching every person you wish to communicate with. (6)

Possible Solutions to the Communication Flow Statements

The following possible solutions address some common managerial communication problems. The number before each response corresponds with the number following each statement above. One solution may be applicable to several problems.

1. Work on improving your communication techniques. Plan your meetings and organize your thoughts ahead of time. Make sure that written communications are accurate, are presented in a timely manner, are concise, and communicate your exact message. Be sure that messages do not leave out necessary information.
2. Make sure that your messages are directed to the specific person you wish to reach. If that person does not receive your message, find out why. Perhaps someone is blocking the reception. Is there a person who is intercepting messages between you and the intended person? If it is important for this interceptor to have the information, send it to him or her first. Stress the importance of the date and when the message must be received. If blockages continue to occur, carry the message to the intended person.
3. Perhaps you have sent too many messages or have not stressed when you need a reply. Perhaps the person is busy and has not had an opportunity to read your message and respond. Try setting up a few minutes when you can see the person. Also try developing the message in a form that can be responded to in short written answers. Follow-up memos may also be advantageous, but be careful not to offend.
4. Consider the objective of your communication. What do you wish to accomplish? Do you want to share information, instruct, issue a directive, or receive a response? After you decide your objective, make decisions about how to accomplish it. A directive might be best received with a memo or on a bulletin board or may be mailed to each person. Instruction or transfer of certain types of information may be more easily exchanged at a meeting.
5. Find out if there is a definite leakage. A leak may indicate that you need to send additional information to your subordinates. Instruct them to disregard unofficial messages that do not come from you or another authorized source.
6. Be sure that a summary of each meeting is prepared and distributed. Have a routing slip designed that each person can initial when he or she receives your information.
7. Attach an informal note explaining why you issued the communication.

REFERENCES

1. George A. Steiner and John F. Steiner, *Business, Government and Society* (New York: McGraw-Hill, 1991), p. 613.
2. Lawrence Schein, "A Manager's Guide to Corporate Culture" research report no. 926 (New York: The Conference Board, 1989), vii.
3. Madelyn Jennings, *Human Resource Management News,* February 15, 1986, p. 2. Quoted in Schein, "Manager's Guide," p. 2.
4. Cass Bettinger, "Use Corporate Culture to Trigger High Performance," *Journal of Business Strategy* (March/April, 1989), p. 39.
5. Terrence E. Deal and Allan A. Kennedy, *Corporate Cultures* (Reading, Mass.: Addison-Wesley, 1982), p. 63.
6. Bettinger, "Use Corporate Culture," p. 40.
7. Ronald Grover, "Disney's Magic." *Business Week* (March 9, 1987), pp. 62–69; Christopher Knowlton, "How Disney Keeps the Magic Going," *Fortune* (December 4, 1989), pp. 111–16; Stephen Koepp, "Do You Believe in Magic?" *Time* (April 25, 1988), pp. 66–73; Charles Leerhsen, "How Disney Does It," *Newsweek* (April 3, 1989), pp. 48–54.
8. Paul L. Blocklyn, "Making Magic: The Disney Approach to People Management," *Personnel* (December 1988), p. 29.
9. Ibid., p. 32.
10. Thomas F. O'Boyle. "Under Japanese Bosses, Americans Find Work Both Better and Worse," *Wall Street Journal,* November 27, 1991, p. 1A.
11. Christopher Lehmann-Haupt, "Synergy Gone Awry: Mazda in Michigan," *The New York Times,* August 6, 1990, p. C14.
12. Ibid.
13. O'Boyle, "Under Japanese Bosses," p. 1A.
14. Ibid, 5A.
15. Ibid.
16. Personal interview with Dan Pinkley, manager of

Video and Media, Southland Corporation, January 9, 1993.

17. Tom Steinert-Threkeld, "Fujitsu Executive Will Meld Two Cultures at Richardson Plant," *Dallas Morning News*, December 16, 1990, p. 1H.
18. Donald D. White and David A. Bednar, *Organizational Behavior*, 2nd ed. (Boston: Allyn & Bacon, 1991), p. 431.
19. Robert A. Baron and Jerald Greenberg, *Behavior in Organizations*, 3rd ed. (Boston: Allyn & Bacon, 1990), pp. 343–44.
20. Ibid., p. 344. Taken from Walter Kiechell, III, "No Word from on High," *Fortune* (January 6, 1986), pp. 19, 26.
21. J. Byrne, "Caught in the Middle," *Business Week* (September 1988), pp. 80–85; J. Main, "The Winning Organization," *Fortune* (September 1988), pp. 50–52.
22. Diane Kunde, "Showing Her Promise," *Dallas Morning News* (March 12, 1991), p. 10.
23. Ibid.
24. "Corporations Evolve to Compete in '90s," *Dallas Morning News* (January 2, 1993), p. 2F.
25. Adapted from "Xerox Overhaul Puts Power Back in Hands of Workers," *Dallas Morning News*, January 2, 1993, p. 6F.
26. Ibid.
27. "Face Values," *Communications & Management* (Spring 1975), p. 2 (a publication printed by Towers, Perrin, Forster, and Crosby, New York). Reprinted by permission.
28. Daniel Katz and Robert Kahn, *The Social Psychology of Organizations* (New York: John Wiley & Sons, 1966), pp. 239–43.
29. "The Cheese Stands Alone," *Communications & Management* (Winter 1974), pp. 1–2 (a publication printed by Towers, Perrin, Forster, and Crosby). Reprinted by permission.
30. *Ibid.*, p. 3.
31. *Ibid.*, p. 4.
32. Andrew B. Chase, Jr., "How to Make Downward Communication Work," *Personnel Journal* (June 1970), pp. 480–81.
33. Baron and Greenberg, from Kiechell, "No Word from on High," pp. 19, 26.
34. "Allie's Gives Its Workforce a 'Square Deal,'" *Communication Management Issues* (a publication printed by Towers, Perrin, Forster, and Crosby, April 1991), p. 8.
35. Bruce Harriman, "Up and Down the Communication Ladder," *Harvard Business Review* (Sept./Oct. 1974), p. 97.
36. *Ibid.*, p. 97.
37. Douglas G. Curley, "The Other Half of Employee Communication," *Personnel Administrator* (July 1979), p. 29.
38. Charles W. Eisenmann and Charles L. Hughes, "Have Your People Talked to You Lately—Candidly?" *Personnel Administrator* (October 1975), p. 13.
39. Baron and Greenberg, p. 345, taken from H. C. Foushee, "Dyads and Triads at 35,000 Feet," *American Psychologist* (August 1984), pp. 885–93.
40. Andrew J. DuBrin, *Winning Office Politics* (New York: Prentice-Hall, 1990).
41. Gary Gemmill, "Managing Upward Communication," *Personnel Journal* (Feb. 1970), p. 107.
42. "Fear and Trembling in the Workplace," *Communications & Management* (Fall 1973), p. 2 (a publication printed by Towers, Perrin, Forster, and Crosby).
43. Elizabeth Jennings and Francis Jennings, "Making Human Relations Work," *Harvard Business Review Supplement* (1970), p. 66.
44. Driver, "Opening the Channels," pp. 26–29; John B. McMaster, "Getting the Word to the Top," *Management Review* (Feb. 1979), pp. 64–65.
45. Philip Lewis, *Organizational Communications*, 2nd ed. (Columbus, Ohio: Grid), p. 68. Reprinted by permission.
46. Joe Kelly, *Organizational Behavior: An Existential-Systems Approach*, rev. ed. (Homewood, Ill.: Irwin, 1974), pp. 616–17. A case condensed from R. L. Simpson, "Vertical and Horizontal Communication in Formal Organizations," *Administrative Science Quarterly* (September 1959), pp. 188–96.
47. Ben Strickland, John Arnn, and Edna Harper, "Communicating to Motivate: How Good Are You?" *Magazine of Bank Administration* (March 1980), p. 39.
48. H. Mitchell Watson, Jr., "I Want That Information Now," *Management Digest* (July 15, 1991), p. 4.
49. Sara Kiesler, "The Hidden Messages in Computer Networks," *Harvard Business Review* (January-February 1986), p. 47.
50. Ibid., p. 48.
51. Ibid.
52. Andrew Pollack, "Any Messages? Now Get Them All," *The New York Times* (June 12, 1991).
53. Ibid.
54. Kiesler, "Hidden Messages," p. 47.
55. Daniel Goleman, "The Electronic Rorschach," *Psychology Today* (February 1983), p. 38.
56. Paul B. Carroll, "Computers Indicate Mood at Big Blue Is Practically Indigo," *Wall Street Journal*, August 7, 1991.
57. Lewis, *Organizational Communications*, p. 69.
58. Peter Drucker, *Management: Tasks, Responsibilities, Practices* (New York: Harper & Row, 1974), p. 124.
59. Mike Flanagon, "Ear-Catching Rumors," *Dallas Morning News* (October 15, 1986), p. 1C.

CHAPTER 3

The Role of Informal Communication in the Organizational Setting

In August 1991, unfounded rumors about the insolvency of Citibank in Hong Kong led to a two-day run on the bank. The rumor linked Citibank to the scandal-ridden Bank of Credit and Commerce International (BCCI). An unknown party sent hundreds of faxes warning customers and others alike that the bank was financially unsafe and would collapse soon. Citibank successfully responded to the crisis by faxing messages to its branches throughout the world and assuring its employees and depositors that the bank was indeed sound.[1]

Chapter 2 described the *formal* flow of communication within organizations. This flow moves in both the horizontal and vertical dimensions. This chapter will describe the *informal* flow of communication both inside and outside the organization.

Informal Communication Flow

Formal communication within an organization is supplemented by an astonishing variety of off-the-record information. Some say that these unsanctioned communications start in the rumor mill, which implies that rumors, or gossip (which is unconfirmed and generally not based on knowledge), is processed like grain in a mill on a regular basis. Does this occur?

The Grapevine

According to Lewis, "Managers should be aware . . . that a number of organization studies show that almost five out of every six messages are carried by the grapevine instead of the official organization channels."[2]

The *grapevine* is "an unofficial, confidential, person-to-person chain of verbal communication."[3] The term originated during the Civil War when telegraph lines were hung from trees and resembled grapevines. The messages sent over them were usually garbled, and so all rumors were said to be from the grapevine. Rumors, according to Allport and Postman, "are unverified bits of information from uncertain origins . . . specific propositions for belief, passed along from person to person, usually by word of mouth, without secure standards of evidence being present."[4]

According to Keith Davis, however, whose research has given us much of the knowledge that we currently have on the corporate grapevine, the grapevine is "a natural, normal part of a company's total communications system and is no more evil in itself than pain or the weather. It is also a significant force within the work group, helping to build teamwork, motivate people, and create corporate identity."[5]

Facts About Rumors and the Grapevine

1. *Rumors increase during times of conflict, crisis, and catastrophe.* This increase is a result of people's efforts to make sense out of disorder. Many rumors are associated with wars, economic and political crises, and natural disasters. Koening states that "such rumors give legitimacy to any sense of hostility, fear and suspicion. . . . To some suffering from such paranoia, a conspiracy rumor can indicate that their fears are well-founded, and a contamination rumor can demonstrate their conviction that one cannot trust anybody."[6]

2. *The grapevine spreads information faster than most formal systems.* With the help of the grapevine, messages can be received before they are formally issued or even prepared. The fast pace is uncanny, as the following example shows:

> One company . . . signed its labor contract at 11:00 P.M. and had to keep its publications staff busy all night in order to have a suitable bulletin ready for

> employees arriving at work the following morning. It was the only way that the company could match the grapevine's speed and forestall undesirable rumors about the agreement.[7]

3. *The grapevine can complement the formal flow of communication.* Both the formal and informal flows of communication allow information to be sent and received in ways that meet the needs of all employees.

4. *The grapevine can destroy the effectiveness of the formal system.* If employees elect to use the grapevine because they distrust formal channels or because they believe that their message will not be conveyed accurately or the receiver will not listen, the formal system will eventually be rendered inoperative.

5. *The grapevine does not follow the official channels.* While the formal communication flow significantly follows the organizational chart and the chain of command, the grapevine does not follow official channels. As Korda states:

> There are various ways in which news, or rumor, travels. It works something like a river system: there is invariably a headwater of mysterious origin, then a mainstream from which tributaries branch off to every department. Once you have traced the main river to its source, it is perfectly possible to pick up whatever news you want from the tributaries—the water is the same.[8]

Informal Communication Chains

Like the river, the grapevine is considerably more flexible in the paths it takes than the formal flow. In his research Davis found four paths for informal communication (see Figure 3-1).

The single-strand chain. In this chain **A** talks to **B**, who then tells **C**, who tells **D**, and finally each person in the system hears the message. Most people picture this type of chain when they think of how the grapevine distorts and filters information beyond the point of being recognizable. Indeed, the statement that **K** will receive will probably be completely different from that started by **A**.

The gossip chain. Here **A** shares the message with everyone available. The length of the lines, however, will vary. This indicates the degree of trust, gullibility, or interest on the part of either **A** or the various receivers. If **A** believes **C** wants more explanation of the story than **B**, **A** will spend more time giving **C** the story or will add more to the story.

The probability chain. Because of the law of probability it is conceivable that when **A** tells **F** and **D**, they will then pass the message on to a select group. Organizations often use this method to test the response of employees regarding new policies or changes the company may contemplate making. Knowing that several individuals will hear and respond, they can then wait for an indication of how best to proceed.

The cluster chain. This chain contains a degree of surety that the proba-

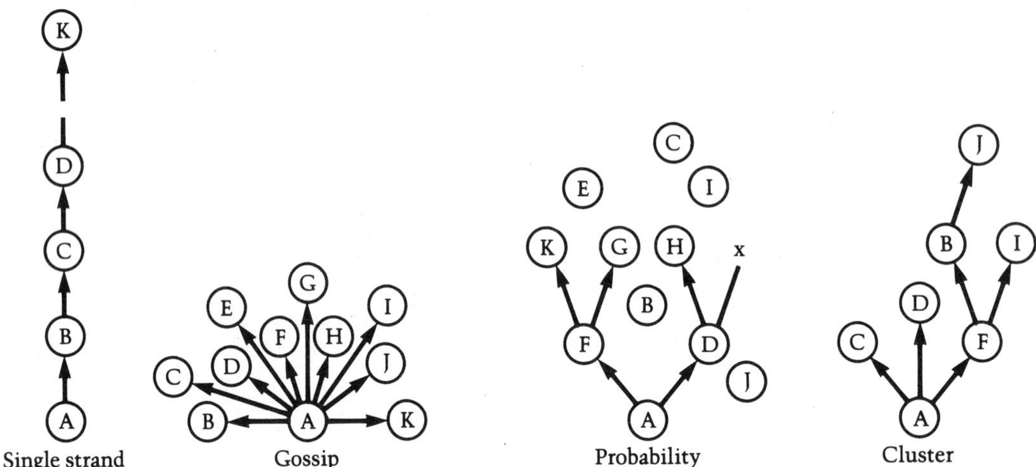

FIGURE 3.1 Four Paths of Informal Communication
Source: Adapted from Keith Davis, "Management Communication and the Grapevine," *Harvard Business Review* (January/February, 1953), p. 46. Reprinted by permission.

bility chain does not have. **A** tells two or three select individuals who in turn tell others. According to Davis's research, this chain is probably the most used in organizations. Here a company can use the grapevine in a productive way. A supervisor can plant a rumor to person **A**, knowing that **A** takes coffee breaks and eats lunch with **C**, **D**, and **F**. Since **F** carpools with **B** and **I**, they will usually be told as the message is discharged throughout the cluster.

In each of the chains and clusters, research shows that isolated or less popular members of groups are often motivated to spread stories that can draw attention to themselves. According to Koening, "people who understand the dynamics and motivations of the rumor process are far less likely to become involved in irresponsible and destructive hearsay and more likely to develop a critical mind-set toward rumors. . . . If people learn to be critical of the content of any message, and to question the motivations of a message-bearer, they are less likely to be a listener and transmitter of false stories."[9]

Methods for Controlling Rumors and the Grapevine Influence

In seeking to make the organizational communication system as effective as possible, a manager can adopt several strategies to combat the grapevine influence:

1. *Do nothing.* Many companies that fall prey to rumors prefer to do nothing in hopes that the rumor will eventually "burn itself out." Even public relations experts prefer this approach because antirumor campaigns can add fuel to the fire and give a company undeserved negative press. Their assumption is often correct. Many people do not hear of a rumor until it is publicized through an antirumor campaign.

2. *Control openness.* Since the grapevine often flourishes because employees feel they cannot exchange information freely, seek to destroy the ice jam in the formal flow of communication. This will lessen employees' reliance on the grapevine. Some managers try to control the grapevine by being "completely open" about problems or situations the company is encountering. This is not always practical. If information cannot be shared until tough decisions are made or remedies are found, be honest about it. This may not cut the amount of talk in the grapevine, but it is better than indiscriminate sharing that can increase employee speculation.

3. *Limit the attempt to seek subversion.* A company can often successfully fight a rumor by disproving it and turning it back on itself. But the task is also time consuming, and obvious fighting tends to give more credence to the rumors.

4. *Tell the truth as soon as possible.* Davis found that the greatest spread of all information occurs immediately after it is known and that more people feed the grapevine when their friends and work associates are involved.[10] For this reason, on matters of firings, promotions, layoffs, and so forth, employees need to know the true story as quickly as possible. If they don't receive it from the company, they will fill in the gaps with rumors.

In the early 1990s, a rumor surfaced in the financial world that Equitable Life Assurance Company, the nation's third largest insurer, was going bankrupt. The rumor was false, but Equitable executives immediately launched a major effort to kill the story. They issued memos to employees, letters to customers, and statements to the media. They even had the New York State Insurance Department certify that the company was healthy. The impact of such a rumor can be disastrous. DeFrancisci Machine Corporation, in Queens, New York, is a small pasta-making machine company. They were in the process of transferring $390,000 of their retirement fund money to Equitable when they heard the rumor. They stopped all transfers until Equitable sent its people to assure them that the story was nonsense.

5. *Effective formal communication systems, good subordinate/superior relationships, and a healthy climate prevent the grapevine's destructive tendencies.* The supervisor must get to know his or her employees and understand their needs and problems, their attitudes and values, and their perceptions of the company and job. If a supervisor sees gaps in what employees want and need to know, and in what they are receiving, he or she should move quickly to supply the information.

If you question why the grapevine flourishes, examine the communication that takes place within your own office. Davis found that the relation-

1. To stop employee morale from slipping and keep the rumor from spreading outside the company, send out a memo dispelling it. Write the memo in a conversational tone, not stiff bureaucratese, which turns people off and inspires distrust.

2. If that doesn't work, get middle managers to call staff meetings and counteract the talk. Don't use high-ranking corporate officers whom the workers don't know and maybe don't trust.

3. The rumor has spread to the outside world? Open up a press offensive right away. Don't wait for the gossip to keep circulating unanswered. Issue a statement by the CEO discounting it. Company public relations officers should follow up by calling reporters individually.

4. The rumor still breathes? Take out a newspaper ad denying it. But don't make the ad too rah-rah. Self-promotion makes people skeptical. Just lay out your case, using facts and figures.

FIGURE 3.2 Four Ways to Quash an Untrue Rumor
Source: Irv Schenkler, in Larry Light, "Killing a Rumor Before It Kills a Company," p. 23. *Business Week* (December 24, 1990), p. 23. Reprinted from December 24, 1990 issue of Business Week by special permission, copyright © 1990 by McGraw-Hill, Inc.

ship between secretary and boss is a major indicator of the extent of fuel for the grapevine: "The secretary plays a key role as liaison agent in the grapevine. Since she processes her boss's correspondence, greets visitors, makes appointments, and often acts as her employer's confidante, she is strategically located as a communication center in the work system and is the one most likely to feed the grapevine."[11]

6. *Educate employees to the deleterious effects of the grapevine.* You can maximize the potential benefits of the grapevine and minimize its deleterious effects by educating employees to the care and cultivation of the grapevine. Freeman describes the process taken by Xerox:

a. *Begin by setting up a one-day workshop* consisting of 10 to 12 first- and second-line managers from different work units. These are the people furthest away from "what's really happening," yet usually the first called upon to validate or debunk information.
b. *Use an external resource as a workshop leader* to minimize the appearance that the workshop is just another attempt by "management" to control the news.

c. *Start off by acknowledging the existence* of the grapevine. Review both its positive and negative effects. Explain its function and purpose.
d. *Develop examples of grapevine use and abuse* in the organization. Have specific instances available as case study material for initial review. Then undertake a workshop exercise that assures that each individual describes personally how he has used the system.
e. *Establish an action plan* that will allow these managers to communicate about the grapevine with their people on the job. Particular attention should be given to techniques that will allow the grapevine to function in a controlled, constructive fashion.[12]

Professor Irv Schenkler of New York University's Stern School of Business has developed an entire program designed to zap rumors and save businesses. As Figure 3.2 shows, the program starts internally by sending memos to employees. It ends externally, if necessary, by running ads in newspapers and magazines.[13]

The Destructiveness of Rumors

In 1979, a rumor involving the Procter and Gamble (P&G) logo started. It still prevails today, though to a much lesser degree, and has impacted the image of P&G in a variety of ways.

The original logo, which was registered in 1882, featured thirteen stars representing the thirteen original colonies and a sorcerer's head in the shape of a crescent moon. Used as early as 1837, it was printed on crates so that customers who could not read would be able to identify the P&G brand. Rumors began that when the stars were connected to one another, they formed the numbers 666, a symbol for the biblical Antichrist. Additional false rumors stated that the insignia connected P&G to the Church of Satan.

One of the first rumors, which started around 1981, claimed that the president of P&G had appeared on the Merv Griffin show and had announced that P&G had contributed 20 percent of its earnings to the Church of Satan. Spreading into the Midwest and southern United States, ministers used church newsletters to call for a boycott of P&G products. These stories tainted P&G's name and affected its financial strength.

(continued)

(continued)

FIGURE 3.3 Procter & Gamble's Evolving Logo
Source: "P&G Cuts Moon Man's Controversial Locks," *USA Today*, July 11, 1991.

For several years the rumor lay dormant. Then, on March 26, 1990, the *Wall Street Journal* reported that the stories had resurfaced in the Midwest and South. "Totally ludicrous is what company officials say about the rumors," the *Journal* reported. But they have unleashed a team of public affairs, legal and security officials to track down the rumor's sources. P&G is sending its 'truth packets' to scores of churches, schools, newspapers and radio stations in those states. They include letters from evangelists Billy Graham and Jerry Falwell, both of whom deem P&G wholesome. And there are letters from producers of the Phil Donahue and Merv Griffin shows, who verify that no one from P&G has appeared to announce any joint ventures with the devil."[14]

What were the results? Millions dismissed the rumors immediately. But P&G has found that some retailers have turned away representatives, delivery trucks have been vandalized, their toll-free hotline has been swamped with up to 200 calls a day, and legal costs have soared. "P&G has filed a dozen lawsuits and won all of them, including judgments against a minister, a school teacher and others found to be spreading the tales. More lawsuits could follow: 'We will take whatever steps are necessary to put this to rest,' says a P&G spokeswoman."[15] In July 1991, P&G made changes to its logo, shown in Figure 3.3. According to a company spokesman, the changes were "evolutionary, not revolutionary. . . . We were looking to develop corporate identity symbols that would translate to consumers around the world."[16]

Perhaps the greatest harm, which cannot adequately be measured, is that done to P&G's name. Once it is entrenched, even a false and disproven rumor is very difficult to eradicate completely.

The Success of Rumors

USF&G Corporation, a New York Stock Exchange company operating in the continental United States, was founded in the late 1800s and is one of the few insurance companies to survive the Great Depression. Steeped in the corporate culture of USF&G was a great sense of pride that the company had never reduced its workforce through layoffs. In 1984, the entire insurance industry was faced with record underwriting losses. USF&G attempted to develop a program to reduce operating expenses through the use of a program called "Model Branch Office."

The model branch office (MBO) concept was developed by a task force of five branch managers who supervised the operation of five of the smaller USF&G offices. The concept was initially presented to employees as a mechanism to improve efficiency and to increase uniformity among USF&G's fifty-nine branch offices.

The entire plan was kept secret from employees and was disclosed confidentially, in stages, to the underwriting managers. Managers, under threat of termination, could not disclose any of the MBO information to their subordinates. The plan was so secret that outside typing services were employed to type all correspondence relating to it.

Though branch managers were not aware of it, the MBO concept was in fact a mechanism for layoffs with very specific compensation packages attached. The layoffs were to be announced simultaneously across the country on Friday, March 1, 1985, and would have become effective immediately. Despite the threat of firing, word of the pending layoffs leaked in February and spread rapidly through the fifty-nine branch offices. Management responded just as rapidly. The planned layoffs were quickly scrapped and never spoken of again.

ETHICS: RIGHT OR WRONG?

Rumor Control: Cellular Phones and Brain Cancer

In 1992, Xerox's executive vice-president Vittorio Cassoni died six weeks after being diagnosed with brain cancer. On January 20, 1993, TLC Beatrice International Holdings disclosed that its chairman, chief executive, and principal shareholder, Reginald Lewis, had also died of complications brought on by brain cancer. On that same day, Tenneco CEO Michael Walsh received the bad news that he, too, had a brain tumor. When asked about the similarity of these occurrences, Naomi Berkowitz of the American Brain Tumor Association commented that "brain tumors do not discriminate'' and the disclosures about the executives were ''just coincidence and happenstance.''[17]

One week following Lewis's death and Walsh's disclosure, speculation about the cause quickly erupted into a nationwide panic among cellular owners: ''Cellular phones cause brain cancer!'' On Cable News Network's *Larry King Live* show, several cellular phone users claimed they or their relatives had developed brain cancer as a result of using the phones. David Reynard of St. Petersburg, Florida revealed that he had filed a lawsuit alleging that his wife had died of brain cancer obtained by using her cellular phone.[18]

On the day following King's show, investors dumped more than $40 million in cellular phone stock. Big financial losses were experienced by McCaw Cellular, Contel Cellular, Vanguard Cellular, and Motorola. Analysts reported that ''fear of the unknown'' was hurting the stock price. ''Most investors are not doctors, they're not engineers. So from an investor's standpoint the controversy comes down to the fact that nobody has conclusive evidence one way or the other.''[19]

Quickly the industry responded with a full-blown spin-control campaign. McCaw Cellular, first to respond to the allegations, offered its 2 million customers a chance to swap their pocket-size cellular phones for bulkier mobile phones or car phones. Mobile phones and car phones are powered by antennas in boxlike receivers or on a car's window or trunk. The cellular phone uses low-wattage transmitters in the antennas of the phones that are held up to the caller's head and next to the ear while in use. McCaw also offered to keep the cellular phone numbers of its canceling customers active for three months free of charge in case they wanted to ''wait the scare out.''[20]

Sensing a crisis of confidence, the Cellular Telecommunications Industry Association (CTIA) sent letters to the Food and Drug Administration, the Federal Communications Commission, and the Environmental Protection Agency. The CTIA asked the agencies to supervise the formation of a panel of experts who would conduct new research into cellular phones, promising to pick up the cost of the research (expected to be over $1 million).[21] ''We recognize,'' the association acknowledged, ''that some may find industry-sponsored research is suspect. Therefore, we are asking the federal government to appoint a blue-ribbon panel to review the methodology and findings of this research.''[22]

Diana McElfresh, executive director of the Electromagnetic Energy Policy Alliance, stated that it was important that conclusions be based on scientific knowledge and analysis and not on scare tactics or speculation: ''The scientific facts are clear: 40 years of sound research incorporating thousands of studies supports the safe use of radio frequency in telecommunications today. Nothing has happened to place this conclusion in doubt.''[23]

In the research cited by McElfresh, which took place in the 1970s, walkie-talkies were taped to the heads of pigs with electronic devices implanted in their brains. The purpose was to see if electromagnetic energy from the walkie-talkies could penetrate the pigs' skulls. The transmitting power used was 6 watts, the maximum power level of a cellular phone. In those studies radiation failed to penetrate the skull.[24]

Dr. Stephen Cleary, a biophysicist at the Medical College of Virginia, disagrees with these findings and contends that there is ample room for caution. "There certainly is (electromagnetic) penetration, there is no question about that. I think there is no question there is absorbed power in the brain tissue. It's not all going to be absorbed by the skull. A major question is what exactly are the cellular phones putting out and where is it being absorbed and what is being absorbed?"[25]

Patrick Dreysse of Johns Hopkins University School of Public Health supports Cleary. "We do know that brain cancer is going up. But is holding a radio transmitter to your head enough to cause it? Not enough is known, but there's enough concern to warrant the research necessary to answer the question."[26] Charisse Y. Russell, owner of the Telephone Warehouse in Lewisville, Texas, offers a further interesting thought: "The studies on cellular usage did not envision people making one-or two-hour telephone calls, with usage of more than 1,000 minutes a month common. The studies were geared toward the idea that calls would be short."[27]

Craig McCaw, CEO of McCaw Cellular, says he is stunned at how the words of two or three alleged victims have been taken at face value by the public. "I think this is the greatest unjustified stampede in history. . . . I've been using two-way phones all my life and I've only gotten smarter every year. I like to say my health's gotten better since I've used a cellular phone."[28]

Case Questions

1. Is there an ethical issue in this case? If so, what is it?
2. Do you believe the cellular industry conducted sufficient research before releasing cellular phones to the marketplace?
3. Should the Cellular Telecommunications Industry Association sponsor the new research being conducted?
4. From a social responsibility position, was the cellular phone companies' response to the panic adequate? Explain.

THE ORGANIZATIONAL CLIMATE

As we saw in Chapter 2, Disney World is famous for its nurturing culture. The company believes communication is the key to its success in meeting the expectations of both its employees and customers. While a company's culture reflects those expectations, its *organizational climate* gives a measure of whether employees' expectations are actually being met. Goldhaber connects the two factors in this way: "Typically, if employees' views are consistent with the organization's culture, then the climate will be positive. If there is a wide disparity between the culture and employees' values, the climate will be negative. Climate is often short term and may depend upon current management of an organization, but culture is usually long term, rooted in deeply held values and often very hard to change."[29]

The structure that an organization establishes helps it to meet its goals productively. Those goals are accomplished by employees who have been directed and motivated by management. The climate of understanding required for successful direction and motivation is best achieved through a solid two-way communication policy that is developed and supported by top management.

In the typical organization, communication occurs in a variety of oral, written, and nonverbal ways: daily meetings, face-to-face conversations, voice and electronic mail, sales forecast discussions, fax-printed manuals and documents, letters, reports, and telephone conversations. Even titles, signs, and office locations communicate messages.

The Communication Climate

According to research, a company's *communication climate* is primarily the perception employees have of "messages and message-related events that occur in the organization, along with the quantity and quality of those messages and the relationships of the people sending and receiving them."[30] The communication climate is the degree to which the system allows and encourages a free flow of ideas and information between employees. You can test the climate in your organization by answering the following questions. The answers you give will help you determine whether the climate is healthy or unhealthy:

1. Do you generally get enough information from the other people at work (including superiors, subordinates, and peers) to do your job properly?
2. Do you generally get more information than you need to do your job?
3. Does the information usually come when you need it, not when it's too late to be fully useful to you?
4. Is information generally clear, relevant, accurate, and consistent?
5. As a rule, do you know where to turn for information?
6. Can you get information from other people easily, without having to press them for it?
7. Do other people at work usually give you information directly and officially, or "through the grapevine"?[31]

There are three key components to a healthy climate: the *quantity* of the information shared between employees, the *quality* of the content, which determines how well it accomplishes the purpose, and the number and nature of *channels* available for relaying information.

Quantity of Information

The climate is usually considered favorable if the quantity of information is adequate for people to perform their jobs with sufficient knowledge, understanding, and confidence.

Too little information exchanged between employees can be frustrating and confusing and can lead to errors and incomplete results, which, in turn, can generate mistrust of superiors and colleagues who one feels are sending nonverbal messages by withholding information. If this occurs between departments, it produces feelings of isolation and generally leads to an "us against them" rivalry. In areas of production and finance the lack of information leads to extremely costly errors.

Too much information is also a problem. If needed but given in abundance, it produces feelings of mental overload. If the abundance is delivered sparingly instead of evenly it contributes to the same feelings of overload. If the information arrives in the form of company propaganda, it can tarnish an employee's perception of the company and make him or her wonder why the organization is "wasting" so much money.

Exchanging information too late can create costly errors, require work to be redone, is frustrating to the receiver, and can tarnish the sender's credibility. If this is a habitual problem, the receiver, who needs the information, may alter work behavior to the point that other individuals and departments are affected and the entire organization suffers.

Quality of Information

Sources of quality information can be found from the top to the bottom of an organization. From an employee's perspective, however, the most important sources of information are the following: subordinates, colleagues, immediate supervisor, top management, middle management, department meetings, and the grapevine.

Channels of Information

Information is exchanged in organizations through two channels: vertical (downward and upward) and horizontal (from side to side, peer to peer, and department to department). Two requirements must be met for channels to successfully support the quantity and quality of information needed in a thriving organization: They exist where they are needed and necessary; employees who need to use them have easy access to them.[32] Employees who need information or want to send information but cannot find channels through which to do so become threatened and fearful, lack trust, and look to others (often inappropriate people or the grapevine) for help.

Effective channels of communication that exist directly between individuals are called *formal channels,* as opposed to the indirect, underground, *informal grapevine.*

Communication Networks

As we have seen, the formal flow of vertical communication within an organization moves both horizontally and vertically, downward and upward. Informal communication occurs through a variety of grapevines. Both formal and informal communication come together in organizations by establishing communication networks. Such networks tend to look formal in appearance because of respected usage. They are also informal in that communication flow can quickly change their shape and composition.

Networks form because employees have a critical need for information. When the formal communication flow does not produce the needed messages, employees search out the easiest, most direct, and most believable sources. Sometimes this requires that they search upward, other times downward, and often from side to side for their desired information. Unlike the available formal directions, communication networks depend on personalities and the working conditions of small groups for their existence.

An example of how a communication network develops within an organization structure is found in Figure 3.4. This figure indicates several things. First, people search out the individuals they can get information from. Second, even though they may be prominently listed on the organization chart, some people are isolated from information in the system. Positions 2, 3, and 13 indicate isolates. Isolates may lack information, be shy, or may not be liked by colleagues within the organization. Positions 4 and 13 indicate that one half of a major division in an organization has little communication with other individuals. Third, competition, bottlenecking, status seeking, and bridge building occur in this communication network. Person 9 appears to not communicate well with his colleagues (6, 7 and 8). He uses the person in position 11 for obtaining needed information which is then passed on to position 10 (who does not communicate well with the person in position 11). Position 6 serves as a bottleneck or conveyer for the President (1) by channeling communication from positions 7, 8, 9, 10, 11 and 14. While the President will learn things about positions 7, 8, 9, 10 and 11, he must realize the information has been filtered and presented by position 6 in a subjective manner.

DiSalvo and colleagues referred to these clusters as *communication loops:*

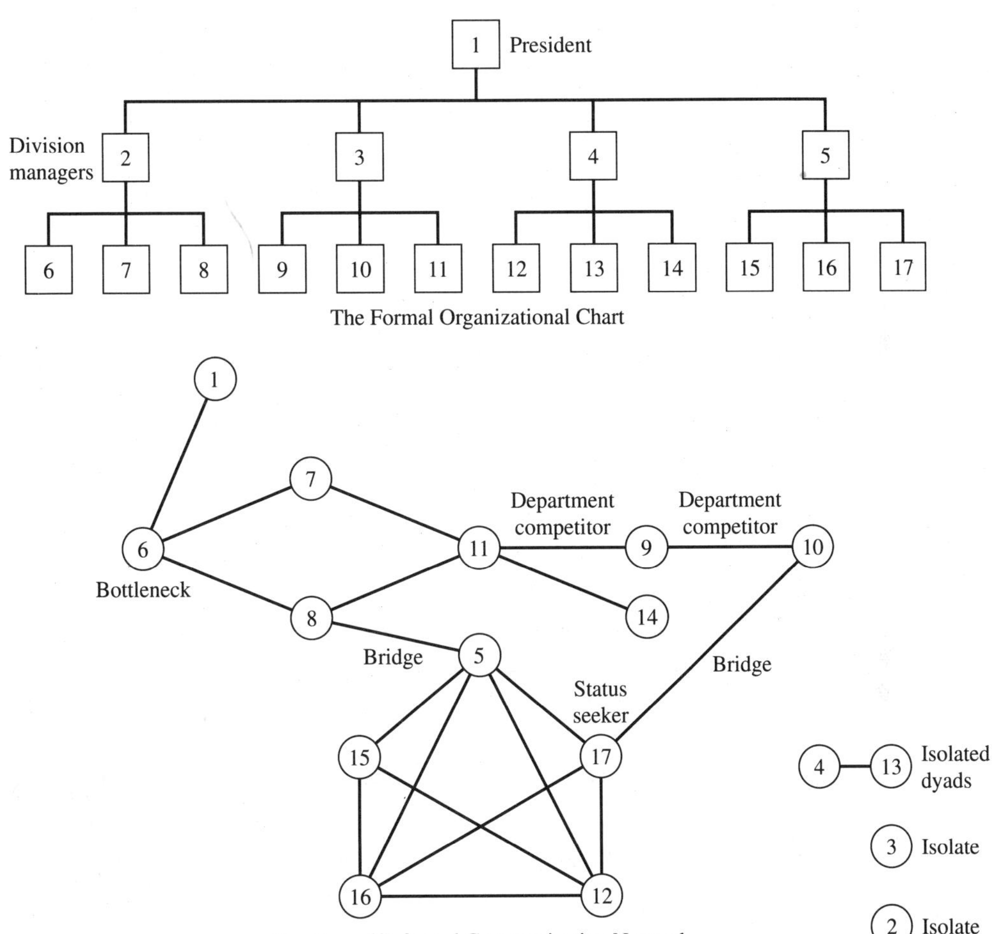

FIGURE 3.4 Comparison of the Formal Organizational Chart and the Formal/ Informal Communication Network

When we talk about communication loops existing in the organization, we are talking about people being linked together in permanent or temporary loops as the organization works toward achieving multiple goals. Many times the effectiveness and efficiency of a loop will be determined by the people that make up the loop."[33] Katz and Kahn developed five characteristics of communication loops:[34]

1. *Size.* The size of a loop is determined by the number of people in an organization, the amount of distance between people, and, most important, by the

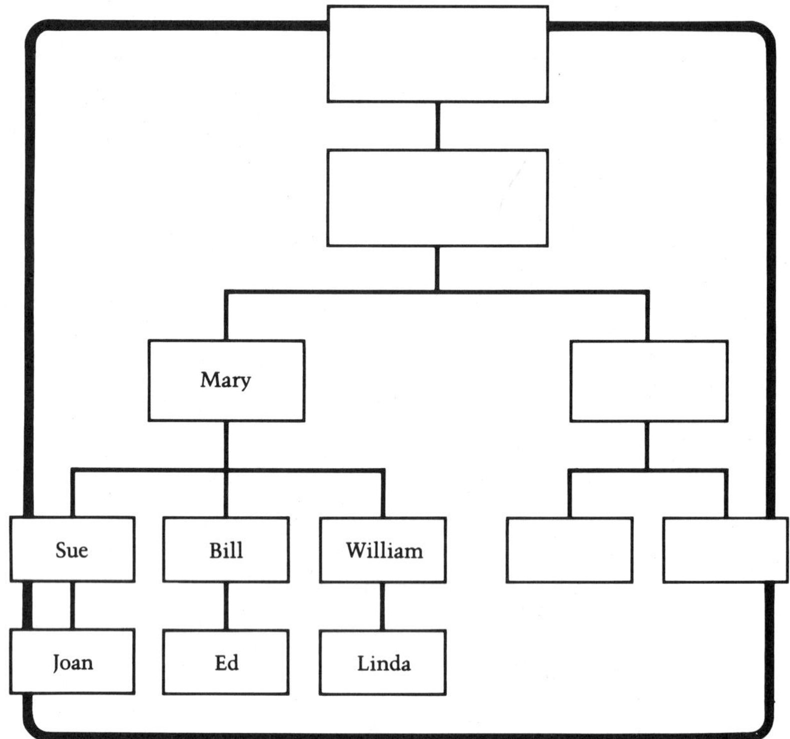

FIGURE 3.5 A Communication Loop Within the Organizational Chart

number of individuals who need to receive and pass particular types of information. According to DiSalvo, "many [loops] are operating simultaneously, some operate continually, and others operate at different times throughout the work day. The makeup, size, and shape of the communication loop depends on the task at hand and the employees involved in the task."[35] Managers sometimes can perceive incorrectly the "real" communication loop. In Figure 3.5 Mary never gets her message either to Ed or to Linda. The reason? Bill forgets to tell Ed, and William thinks Linda doesn't really need the information.

2. *Transmission technique.* When messages are passed between people, the information is either echoed or modified as it passes through the loop. In the *echo approach* the same message is given to each person; these messages can be notices on bulletin boards, printed policy statements, reports, memos, etc. In the *modified approach* information is changed somewhat as it is given, usually verbally, to different individuals: "What typically happens is that as the message passes through the multiple links in the loop, through different people, the

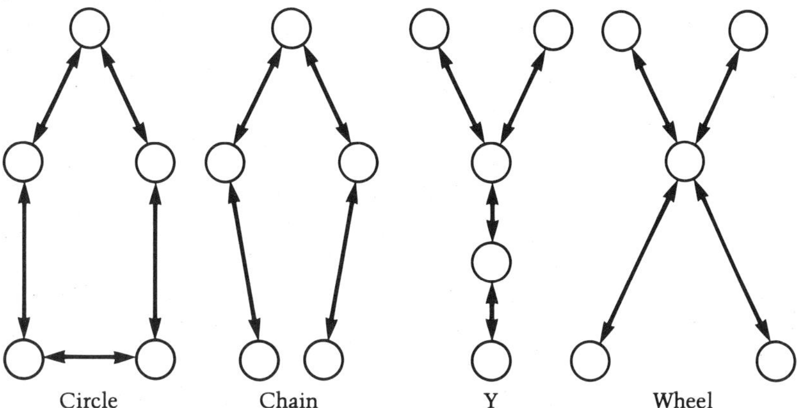

FIGURE 3.6 Types of Communication Loops

message changes so that when it reaches its destination, it is no longer the 'same' message that was sent."[36]

3. *Immediate or delayed closure.* Immediate closure occurs when a message is sent but the process for providing feedback is closed or blocked immediately after the message is delivered. For instance, Mary calls Sue at 4:50 P.M. with a question about dates for a new promotion campaign. By the time Sue checks with Joan and calls Mary back, it is 5:10 P.M. Unfortunately, Mary's secretary has left for the day, and she transferred Mary's phone to another desk so that her boss would not be disturbed as she finished her day's work. Delayed closure would occur if Mary calls Sue and asks her to check the dates. She tells Sue that she will stay and wait for her answer. The feedback loop is open, but closure of the message is delayed until Mary receives her answer.

4. *Efficiency and satisfaction.* Research on communication loops has tended to examine the various effects of freedom and restrictions on an employee's ability to freely communicate. In a classic study Leavitt tested four loops: circle, chain, Y, and wheel (see Figure 3.6). By making certain adjustments these loops can be rearranged to fit a typical organization chart. What did Leavitt find? (1) The *wheel* loop was the most efficient in terms of fewest errors and fewest messages needed to accomplish a task; (2) the *circle* had the highest level of job satisfaction, followed by the chain, the Y, and the wheel. Leavitt found two extremes between the circle and wheel: The circle is active, leaderless, unorganized, and erratic, and yet in it a deep cohesion exists among members; the wheel has a distinct leader, is well organized and less erratic, but its members are unsatisfied.[37]

The circle can be expanded to an all-channel model that allows two-way communication to flow between each person within the loop (see Figure 3.7). Great-

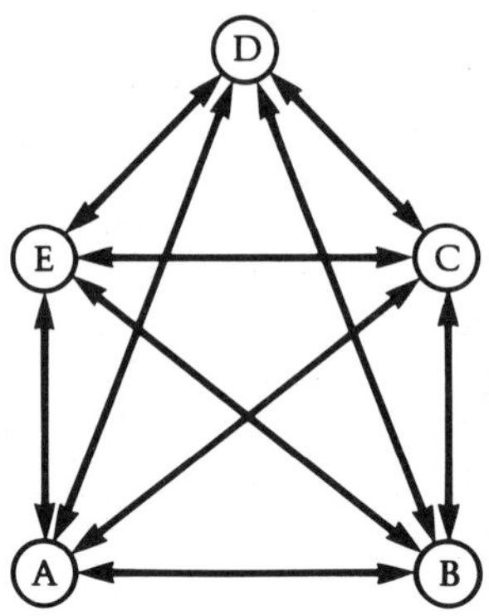

FIGURE 3.7 All-Channel Network

TABLE 3.1 Communication and Organizational Structure

Characteristic	Circle	Chain	Wheel	All-Channel
Speed	slow	fast	very fast	slow/fast
Accuracy	poor	good	good	poor/excellent
Morale	high	low	very low	very high
Leadership stability	none	marked	very pronounced	none
Organization	unstable	emerging stability	very stable	unstable
Flexibility	high	low	low	high

Source: Adapted from Philip Lewis, *Organizational Communications,* 2nd ed. (Columbus, Ohio: Grid, 1975), p. 86.

est satisfaction is found between employees in this type of loop, and a strong leader generally must emerge to orchestrate a free-for-all communication flow into a dynamic, purposeful, task-accomplishing process. Without this direction the communication is overcomplete, and a great deal of time is wasted.

5. *Matching and mismatching.* Hierarchical levels within organizations are shaped by the tasks that must be completed and the skills and personalities of persons within the organizations. The formal vertical and horizontal channels of communication that were examined at the beginning of this chapter allow information to be communicated to the right people at the right time. Ideally people receive the precise information they need, when they need it, and they do not receive information that is not needed. Communication loops, however, may or may not fit the ideal. If they fit, a match is declared. If they do not, a mismatch occurs. Findings from most of the research on communication networks and loops are summarized in Table 3.1.

Communication Through Global Networks

In the past few years, emerging global patterns of production and trade have created global value-added networks. This means that as products or services move from one location to another, changes made to those products have the effect of adding to the products or services. Communication is a critical ingredient within the networks. Operating consistency is necessary, and glitches and delays must be avoided, or the entire global chain can stop. As Professor William H. Davidson of the University of Southern California testifies, "effective global operations must be built on a firm platform of communication, operating, and logistic systems."[38] Three examples prove the need for effective communication within these global networks.

American Standard, producer of bathroom fixtures found in homes and offices, has a network that stretches around the world. Its products are designed at a company design center in Italy. The designs are then sent to the company's CAD/CAM unit in Germany. Final design specifications are forwarded to the master mold facility in France. When construction of the molds is complete, the master molds are shipped to a manufacturing plant in Germany, Korea, or Mexico. Finished products are then shipped to the local sales market.

VLS Technologies, a custom computer chip maker in Milpitas, California, also uses a global network for design and production of its products. Chips are designed at a division in North America, Asia, or Europe, or at a customer's location any place in the world. Once design is completed, the specifications are sent back to Milpitas by an electronic data communications system, where the photo masks are then produced. The masks are shipped to Japan for wafer etching. The completed wafers are sent to Korea for dicing and mounting. The chips are assembled in Malaysia and sent from there to customers throughout the world.

Service organizations also utilize value-added networking. Tickets from all American Airlines' flights are sent to a flight operations office in the Caribbean. There data are taken from each ticket and entered into the company's data base.

Although these global networks operate much like communication networks inside an organization, they require that the staff in each country or location practice common and consistent operating standards that the company has developed and maintained. According to Davidson, the best way to assure this consistency is "to utilize precisely the same product codes, formulations, processes, databases, forms, formats, software and equipment in all locations. . . . Many firms use translators to convert information, but not from one language to another so much as from one operating environment to another. They exist to convert a request into something their operating systems can respond to. In effect, they translate the customer's or partner's request into local dialect."[39]

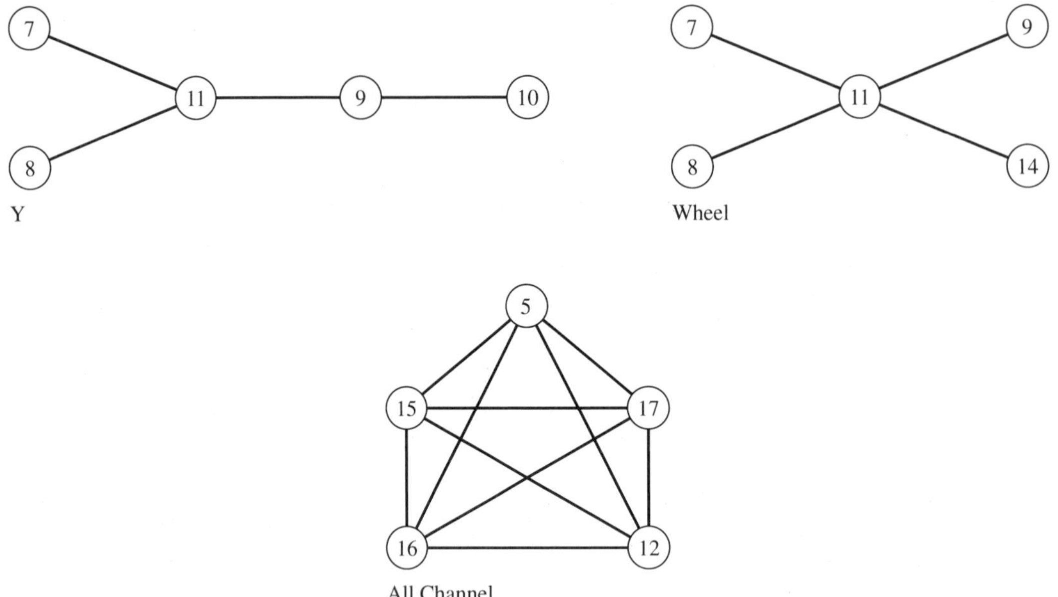

FIGURE 3.8 Communication Loops in Figure 3.4

Going back to the formal chart in Figure 3.4, we now see that within the formal/informal communication network three different communication loops can be seen. Figure 3.8 displays these loops.

Auditing Organization Communication

In Chapter 2 and thus far in Chapter 3, we have seen that the communication desired by management and the communication that actually exists within an organization are often two different things. When management senses that communication problems exist, a thorough examination of the process is in order. Numerous studies show that senior management often incorrectly assumes that it knows what employees want and need to know and hear; they also show that it does not know what employees actually hear. Organizations, and especially organization consultants, have developed several tools for locating the weaknesses in communication systems and for prescribing corrective action.

Employee Surveys

Specifically designed and sharply focused surveys can tell management a great deal about employees' attitudes regarding an existing communication system. Many companies use the survey as the starting point for diagnosing improvement processes. The best surveys allow employees to explain such things as how much information they receive and how much they need.

Generally, such surveys are followed by small group meetings where employees talk freely and honestly about how they perceive needed changes. A company should use objective interviewers and often employ out-of-company consultants. Employee comments are then analyzed and weighted for intensity before being summarized to both employees and management. Surveys also give valuable demographic information based on sex, age, loop location, job responsibilities, pay categories, and so forth.

Gildea and Emanuel found that the initial survey provides a good tool for maintaining long-term two-way communication:

> The initial survey, in fact, provides a model mechanism for maintaining two-way communications over the long term. A survey conducted to include employee group discussions can be logically followed with periodic small group meetings. These provide for effective and ongoing upward communication of employee suggestions for improving productivity. Employees' suggestions should, of course, be acted upon, with feedback—positive or negative—provided to the appropriate employee(s). We have observed that most employees want to know management's reaction to their proposals and why they will or will not be adopted; simply rewarding employees with cash for suggestions is a short-lived motivator.
>
> Employee participation through two-way communications discourages the belief that management's ideas are dominating the program or that management has a free hand to manipulate measurement standards. Another formal survey at the end of the time frame initially established by management can provide data to be compared with the findings of the first survey.[40]

Communication Audits

An audit is something like a physical checkup. Properly handled, it can provide an organization with valuable information about the health of its internal communication. Three audit techniques are currently in use: OCD, ECCO, and ICA.

The OCD Audit

The *Organizational Communication Development (OCD) Audit* system was developed by Osmo Wiio at the Helsinki Research Institute in the early 1970s and is used extensively in Europe. OCD implements an attitudinal and perceptual questionnaire and then statistically evaluates that questionnaire to see if the results correspond with norms from the test bank. The advantages of this tool are that it is inexpensive, easy to administer, brief, and provides quickly obtainable results. Its disadvantage is that the test norms for the data bank are based on twenty-four Finnish organizations and may not be equally valid for other cultures.

ECCO Analysis

The *Episodic Communication Channels in Organization (ECCO)* analysis was designed by Keith Davis in 1952. The tool was created to map communication networks, measure rates of communication flow, indicate redundancy, and pinpoint distortion of messages. This tool is fast, convenient, reliable, and inexpensive. It deals with concrete messages rather than perceptions or attitudes. It has limited use in large organizations, however, since answers assume that a respondent knows everyone in the organization.

The ICA Audit

The *International Communication Association (ICA) audit* was established in the early 1970s by a professional society composed of communication researchers, practitioners, and teachers. Considered to be the most complete auditing system available, the tool incorporates substantial research and documentation. Because of the nature of its design and its completeness, the focus of this chapter will be on the ICA audit.

Gerald Goldhaber, one of the audit's developers, states that the overall objective of the ICA evaluation is to determine the effectiveness of the organization's communication system and to make recommendations for its improvement. The audit is capable of identifying source, quality, extent, and type of communication.[41] A full ICA audit gives the surveyed organization several usable items. Falcione describes these:

1. An organizational profile of perceptions of communication events, practices, and relationships, analyzed according to demographics such as age, sex, education, supervisory status, division, and department.
2. A map of the operational communication network for rumors, social messages, and job-related information.
3. Summaries of successful and unsuccessful communication experiences related to communication problems and strengths.
4. A profile of actual communication behaviors that allows comparisons between actual and perceived communication behaviors relative to message sources, receivers, topics, channels, length of time, and qualities.
5. A set of recommendations indicating which attitudes, behaviors, and practices should be continued, added, changed, or eliminated.
6. Personnel in the organization are made familiar with the audit instruments and procedure, thereby helping the organization take the major initiative in conducting future audits itself.

7. Future access to the ICA data bank, allowing the organization to compare the results of present and future audits with those of similar organizations.
8. Benchmarks on communication behaviors, perceptions, and practices provided to managers for pre- and post-measurement comparisons that can be used to diagnose organizational change and development activities.[42]

The ICA audit uses a standardized system of five instruments and incorporates both computer analysis and feedback methods. In addition, the ICA data bank can be tapped for comparisons among communication systems of various organizations. The audit's five measuring tools are the questionnaire survey, interviews, network analysis, diary of specific communication activities (conversations, phone calls, meetings, and written materials) for a given period, and a description of critical communication episodes that represent typical incidents occurring in the organization.[43]

The Questionnaire Survey

The full ICA survey is broken into eight sections with 122 questions and twelve demographic items. Additional "specific questions" can be added by the organization. Questions are worded so that respondents can indicate their perception of *how communication currently exists* as well as *how they would ideally like it.* The eight sections are: (1) receiving information from others, (2) sending information to others, (3) follow-up on information sent and received, (4) sources of information, (5) quality of information from key sources, (6) channels of communication, (7) communication relationships, and (8) organizational outcomes. Table 3.2 gives two samples from a survey questionnaire.

Interviews

Two interview formats are used. The first format has open-ended questions like these: describe how you actually receive information; describe the channels through which you typically receive information; describe your communication relationship with your immediate supervisor, colleagues, and top management. The second format is used as a follow-up for questioning specific findings revealed on other audit tools. The interviews are usually conducted confidentially and are often taped for later review.

Network Analysis

Respondents use this tool to indicate the extent of their typical communication with other people both inside and outside their work units. The results are computer scored and indicate the networks and loops for both formal and informal information. Table 3.3 gives an example of how this tool could have been used to examine the extent of communication between the individuals in the example on page 101.

TABLE 3.2 Sample Segment from a Survey Questionnaire

Receiving Information from Others

	Amount of Information I Receive Now					**Amount of Information I Want to Receive**				
	Very little	Little	Some	Great	Very great	Very little	Little	Some	Great	Very great
1. Progress on my job	1	2	3	4	5	1	2	3	4	5
2. My job requirements	1	2	3	4	5	1	2	3	4	5
3. Organizational policies	1	2	3	4	5	1	2	3	4	5
4. Changes affecting my job	1	2	3	4	5	1	2	3	4	5
5. News from other departments	1	2	3	4	5	1	2	3	4	5
6. Mistakes and failures of our organization	1	2	3	4	5	1	2	3	4	5
7. How I am being judged	1	2	3	4	5	1	2	3	4	5
8. How my job-related problems are being handled	1	2	3	4	5	1	2	3	4	5
9. How decision are made that affect my job	1	2	3	4	5	1	2	3	4	5
10. What competitors are doing	1	2	3	4	5	1	2	3	4	5
11. The results of my work	1	2	3	4	5	1	2	3	4	5
12. Financial success of my company	1	2	3	4	5	1	2	3	4	5
13. From formal channels	1	2	3	4	5	1	2	3	4	5
14. From the grapevine	1	2	3	4	5	1	2	3	4	5
Other ______ ______ ______ (write here)										

Sending Information to Others

	Amount of Information I Send Now					**Amount of Information I Want to Send Now**				
15. Suggestions for improving my job	1	2	3	4	5	1	2	3	4	5
16. Reports of my job activity and progress	1	2	3	4	5	1	2	3	4	5
17. Complaints about my job and/or working conditions	1	2	3	4	5	1	2	3	4	5
18. My suggestions about job-related problems	1	2	3	4	5	1	2	3	4	5
19. Personal problems	1	2	3	4	5	1	2	3	4	5
20. Requests for information I need to do my job	1	2	3	4	5	1	2	3	4	5
21. My evaluation of the performance of supervisors	1	2	3	4	5	1	2	3	4	5
22. My evaluation of the performance of coworkers	1	2	3	4	5	1	2	3	4	5

TABLE 3.3 Sample Page from a Communications Network Analysis

During a Typical Work Week, I Usually Communicate with the Following People:

	Name	About Job-Related Matters	About Non-job-Related Incidental Matters	About Organizational Rumors
1.	Mary	______ 1 2 3 4 5*	______ 1 2 3 4 5	______ 1 2 3 4 5
2.	Sue	______ 1 2 3 4 5	______ 1 2 3 4 5	______ 1 2 3 4 5
3.	Bill	______ 1 2 3 4 5	______ 1 2 3 4 5	______ 1 2 3 4 5
4.	William	______ 1 2 3 4 5	______ 1 2 3 4 5	______ 1 2 3 4 5
5.	Joan	______ 1 2 3 4 5	______ 1 2 3 4 5	______ 1 2 3 4 5
6.	Ed	______ 1 2 3 4 5	______ 1 2 3 4 5	______ 1 2 3 4 5
7.	Linda	______ 1 2 3 4 5	______ 1 2 3 4 5	______ 1 2 3 4 5
8.	______	______ 1 2 3 4 5	______ 1 2 3 4 5	______ 1 2 3 4 5
9.	______	______ 1 2 3 4 5	______ 1 2 3 4 5	______ 1 2 3 4 5
10.	______	______ 1 2 3 4 5	______ 1 2 3 4 5	______ 1 2 3 4 5
11.	______	______ 1 2 3 4 5	______ 1 2 3 4 5	______ 1 2 3 4 5
12.	______	______ 1 2 3 4 5	______ 1 2 3 4 5	______ 1 2 3 4 5
13.	______	______ 1 2 3 4 5	______ 1 2 3 4 5	______ 1 2 3 4 5
14.	______	______ 1 2 3 4 5	______ 1 2 3 4 5	______ 1 2 3 4 5
15.	______	______ 1 2 3 4 5	______ 1 2 3 4 5	______ 1 2 3 4 5
16.	______	______ 1 2 3 4 5	______ 1 2 3 4 5	______ 1 2 3 4 5
17.	______	______ 1 2 3 4 5	______ 1 2 3 4 5	______ 1 2 3 4 5
18.	______	______ 1 2 3 4 5	______ 1 2 3 4 5	______ 1 2 3 4 5
19.	______	______ 1 2 3 4 5	______ 1 2 3 4 5	______ 1 2 3 4 5
20.	______	______ 1 2 3 4 5	______ 1 2 3 4 5	______ 1 2 3 4 5
21.	______	______ 1 2 3 4 5	______ 1 2 3 4 5	______ 1 2 3 4 5
22.	______	______ 1 2 3 4 5	______ 1 2 3 4 5	______ 1 2 3 4 5
23.	______	______ 1 2 3 4 5	______ 1 2 3 4 5	______ 1 2 3 4 5
24.	______	______ 1 2 3 4 5	______ 1 2 3 4 5	______ 1 2 3 4 5
25.	______	______ 1 2 3 4 5	______ 1 2 3 4 5	______ 1 2 3 4 5

* *Remember:* 1 = not at all important; 2 = somewhat important; 3 = fairly important; 4 = very important; 5 = extremely important. In the space to the left of each column, place an estimate of the number of times communication with that person occurs each week.

Communication Diary

Each participant is asked to keep a diary of each communication activity for a one-week period. The person records activities like phone calls, meetings, conversations, and sending and receiving written and electronic mail messages. These data are also computer scored to show linkage to others inside and outside the organization. This tool is also helpful in improving time management.

Communication Experiences

Respondents describe critical communication episodes that are representative of both successful and unsuccessful communication experiences in their organization. The results are used to evaluate why a given work area is experiencing effective or ineffective communication and at what level the impact is occurring. The results usually help clarify facts found through other tools.

The Postaudit Feedback

The time, money, and energy spent on an ICA audit are wasted if the findings are not used correctly. Only when feedback is given to all concerned can effective changes be made. The feedback delivery process is critical. Deciding who will receive it, how it will be delivered, and what data will be given are all questions that management and possible outside consultants must answer.

Several types of feedback sessions can be used. Falcione highlights five types.[44]

1. *Family group survey feedback* sessions include both supervisors and employees who work together within a formal unit. Often a consultant conducts this meeting and facilitates the top-down communication of feedback and the conversations that follow.
2. *Subordinate group* sessions provide communication flow from the bottom up. Here subordinates receive feedback before the managers. This grouping is most appropriate when subordinates are experiencing anxiety.
3. *Peer group intergroup* feedback sessions start with manager and subordinate work groups that meet and analyze the data separately with their peers. The groups are then brought together to share and work on strategies for change.
4. *Intergroup feedback* sessions assemble different work groups to exchange the audit feedback. A consultant is usually involved to facilitate the process.
5. *Ad hoc collaterial groups* exchange feedback in a large session or in multiple sessions. Small groups are formed to work on specific issues that surfaced in the audit. Consultants or management then determine the needed change and the steps of implementation.

The Baldrige Award as a Communication Audit Tool

In 1987, the Malcolm Baldrige National Quality Award was established by an act of Congress. The purpose was "to stimulate American companies to improve quality and productivity." Since then, hundreds of U.S. companies have adopted the award's guidelines as their "standard for management excellence." The guidelines are based on "total quality management" principles which were designed for manufacturing companies. Over the years organizations have found that these principles are applicable to any business because they define the critical role of communication in a quality organization. Consequently, managers can use the Baldrige guidelines as a set of standards for measuring excellence in communication in their own organizations. According to Skutski, "the first lesson to be drawn from the guidelines is that communication, like quality itself, is an all-pervasive *management* process that impacts the effectiveness of each and every facet of the organization."[45]

The Baldrige guidelines divide the total quality process into seven categories that are subdivided into a total of twenty-eight items (see box). No outright "communication" category exists, but in these guidelines "communication is viewed as a *horizontal* management discipline, not as a vertical departmentalized function. Communication is the 'glue' that holds all other facets of a total quality culture together."[46]

According to a study by Skutski & Associates, a Pittsburgh-based public relations firm, about 400 of the 1,000 possible points in the Baldrige guidelines are impacted by communications, and most of these points are contained in ten of the subcategories. Skutski calls these categories the "vital few" areas in which communications can have the greatest impact in the total quality management process. According to Baldrige Award winners and members of the Baldrige Board of Examiners, the first of the seven categories, "leadership," is where "communicators can have the greatest impact, even though, from a sheer 'points' perspective, 'customer satisfaction' can have three times the impact."[47] The key communication subcategories are as follows.[48]

1. *Encouraging employee involvement and empowerment.* This is the area in which communication within the organization can have the greatest impact. Here managers must describe the methods used by the organization to create and sustain the involvement of its employees in total quality. Communication lies at the heart of this endeavor. The Baldrige guidelines describe several ways in which this area can be analyzed.

The Seven Malcolm Baldrige Award Categories

1. Leadership — 90 points

Examines senior executives' *personal* leadership and involvement in creating and sustaining a customer focus and clear and visible quality values. Also looks at how the quality values are integrated into the

(continued)

(continued)

company's management system and how they are reflected in the manner in which the company addresses its public responsibilities.

2. Information and Analysis — 80 points

Examines the scope, validity, analysis, management, and use of data and information to drive quality excellence and improve competitive performance. Also examined is the adequacy of the company data, information, and analysis system to support improvement of the company's customer focus, products, services, and internal operations.

3. Strategic Quality Planning — 60 points

Analyzes the company's planning process and how all key quality requirements are integrated into overall business planning. Also examined are the company's short- and longer-term plans and how quality and performance requirements are deployed to all work units.

4. Human Resource Development and Management — 150 points

Examines the key elements of how the company develops and realizes the full potential of the workforce to pursue its quality and performance objectives. Also examined are the company's efforts to build and maintain an environment for quality excellence conducive to full participation and personal and organizational growth.

5. Management of Process Quality — 150 points

Analyzes the systematic processes the company uses to pursue ever-higher quality and company performance. Examined are the key elements of process management, including design, management of process quality for all work units and suppliers, systematic quality improvement, and quality assessment.

6. Quality and Operational Results — 180 points

Looks at the company's quality levels and improvement trends in quality, company operational performance, and supplier quality. Also examined are current quality and performance levels relative to those of competitors.

7. Customer Focus and Satisfaction — 300 points

Examines the company's relationships with customers and its knowledge of customer requirements and of the key quality factors that determine marketplace competitiveness. Also examined are the company's methods to determine customer satisfaction, current trends, and levels of satisfaction as well as these results relative to competitors.

4.2 Employee Involvement

(40 pts.)
Describe the means available for all employees to contribute effectively to meeting the company's quality and performance objectives; summarize trends in involvement.

AREAS TO ADDRESS

a. management practices and specific mechanisms the company uses to promote employee contributions, individually and in groups, to quality and company performance objectives. Describe how and how quickly the company gives feedback to contributors.
b. company actions to increase employee empowerment, responsibility, and innovation. Briefly summarize principal goals for all categories of employees, based upon the most important requirements for each category.
c. key methods and key indicators the company uses to evaluate and improve the extent and effectiveness of involvement of all categories and types of employees
d. trends in percent involvement for each category of employee. Use the most important indicator(s) of effective employee involvement for each category.

Note: *Different involvement goals and indicators may be set for different categories of employees, depending on company needs and on the types of responsibilities of each employee category.*

2. *Proactive management of customer relationships.* This subcategory demands that management must have a proactive method of gathering feedback from its customers and that the information received must be used to constantly improve customer relations. As the summary of the seven categories indicates, the need for extensive, quantitative customer-based research is vital.

7.1. Customer Relationship Management

(65 pts.)
Describe how the company provides effective management of its relationships with its customers and uses information gained from customers to improve customer relationship management strategies and practices.

AREAS TO ADDRESS

a. how the company determines the most important factors in maintaining and building relationships with customers and develops strategies and plans to address them. Describe these factors and how the strategies take into account: fulfillment of basic customer needs in the relationship; opportunities to enhance the relationships; provision of information to customers to ensure the proper setting of expectations regarding products, services, and relationships; and roles of all customer-contact employees, their technology needs, and their logistics support.
b. how the company provides information and easy access to enable customers to seek assistance, to comment, and to complain. Describe types of contact and how easy access is maintained for each type.
c. follow-up with customers on products, services, and recent transactions to help build relationships and to seek feedback for improvement
d. how service standards that define reliability, responsiveness, and effective-

ness of customer-contact employees' interactions with customers are set. Describe how standards requirements are deployed to other company units that support customer-contact employees, how the overall performance of the service standards system is monitored, and how it is improved using customer information.

e. how the company ensures that formal and informal complaints and feedback received by all company units are aggregated for overall evaluation and use throughout the company. Describe how the company ensures that complaints and problems are resolved promptly and effectively.

f. how the following are addressed for customer-contact employees: (1) selection factors; (2) career path; (3) special training to include: knowledge of products and services; listening to customers; soliciting comments from customers; how to anticipate and handle problems or failures ("recovery"); skills in customer retention; and how to manage expectations; (4) empowerment and decision-making; (5) attitude and morale determination; (6) recognition and reward; and (7) attrition

g. how the company evaluates and improves its customer relationship management practices. Describe key indicators used in evaluations and how evaluations lead to improvements, such as in strategy, training, technology, and service standards.

3. *Determining customer requirements.* This subcategory examines how the organization gathers information about the current and future needs of its customers. Once the information is received, it must then be communicated to managers and employees.

7.6 Future Requirements and Expectations of Customers

(35 pts.)
Describe how the company determines future requirements and expectations of customers.

AREAS TO ADDRESS

a. how the company addresses future requirements and expectations of customers. Describe: (1) the time horizon for the determination; (2) how data from current customers are projected; (3) how customers of competitors and other potential customers are considered; and (4) how important technological, competitive, societal, economic, and demographic factors and trends that may bear upon customer requirements and expectations are considered.

b. how the company projects key product and service features and the relative importance of these features to customers and potential customers. Describe how potential market segments and customer groups are considered. Include considerations that address new product/service lines as well as current products and services.

c. how the company evaluates and improves its processes for determining future requirements and expectations of customers. Describe how the improvement process considers new market opportunities and extension of the time horizon for the determination of customer requirements and expectations.

4. *Benchmarking companywide and function-by-function performance against competitive and best-in-the-field measures.* Surveying customer needs is not enough. Many companies research customer needs but fail to determine how their response to meeting the needs compares to the "best-in-the-field" practices. Through communicating with other companies and comparing practices, they learn how to raise their standards to a world-class level.

7.5 Customer Satisfaction Comparison

(75 pts.)
Compare the company's customer satisfaction results with those of competitors.

AREAS TO ADDRESS

a. trends and current levels in indicators of customer satisfaction relative to that for competitors, based upon methods described in Item 7.3. Segment by customer group, as appropriate.
b. trends in gaining or losing customers, or customer accounts, to competitors
c. trends in gaining or losing market share to competitors

Note: *Competitors include domestic and international ones in the company's markets, both domestic and international.*

5. *Providing counsel and support to executive management.* This is the first subcategory in the Baldrige listing. It examines how communication is used by the "senior executive leadership" to support the total quality endeavor. Managers must communicate with employees about goals, plans, and company progress. They must also recognize and praise employee performance. In return, employees must be free to communicate to top management about the quality process.

1.1 Senior Executive Leadership

(45 pts.)
Describe the senior executives' leadership, personal involvement, and visibility in developing and maintaining a customer focus and an environment for quality excellence.

AREAS TO ADDRESS

a. senior executives' leadership, personal involvement, and visibility in quality-related activities of the company. Include: (1) reinforcing a customer focus; (2) creating quality values and setting expectations; (3) planning and reviewing progress toward quality and performance objectives; (4) recognizing employee contributions; and (5) communicating quality values outside the company
b. brief summary of the company's quality values and how the values serve as a basis for consistent communication within and outside the company
c. personal actions of senior executives to regularly demonstrate, communicate, and reinforce the company's customer orientation and quality values through all levels of management and supervision
d. how senior executives evaluate and improve the effectiveness of their personal leadership and involvement

Notes:
(1) *The term "senior executives" refers to the highest-ranking official of the organization applying for the Award and those reporting directly to that official.*
(2) *Activities of senior executives might also include leading and/or receiving training, benchmarking, customer visits, and mentoring other executives, managers, and supervisors.*
(3) *Communication outside the company might involve: national, state, and community groups; trade, business, and professional organizations; and education, health care, government, and standards groups. It might also involve the company's stockholders and board of directors.*

6. *Counseling management and developing public responsibility plans.* This area addresses how well the organization listens to and communicates with its external stakeholders. Groups that fall within this arena include the community, the government, industry groups, trade associations, and educational groups.

1.3 Public Responsibility

(20 pts.)
Describe how the company includes its responsibilities to the public for health, safety, environmental protection, and ethical business practices in its quality policies and improvement activities, and how it provides leadership in external groups.

AREAS TO ADDRESS

a. how the company includes its public responsibilities, such as business ethics, public health and safety, environmental protection, and waste management in its quality policies and practices. For each area *relevant and important* to the company's business, briefly summarize: (1) how potential risks are identified, analyzed, and minimized; (2) principal quality improvement goals and how they are set; (3) principal improvement methods; (4) principal quality indicators used in each area; and (5) how and how often progress is reviewed.
b. how the company promotes quality awareness and sharing with external groups

7. *Recognizing employees for their quality contributions.* While other areas touch on recognizing employee performance, this subcategory analyzes exactly what a company does to measure, recognize, and reward the quality performance of individuals and teams.

4.4 Employee Performance and Recognition

(25 pts.)
Describe how the company's employee performance, recognition, promotion,

AREAS TO ADDRESS

a. how the company's performance, recognition, promotion, compensation, reward, and feedback approaches for individuals and groups, including managers, support the company's quality and performance objectives. Address: (1) how the approaches ensure that quality is reinforced relative to compensation, reward, and feedback processes support the attainment of the company's quality and performance objectives.

short-term financial considerations; and (2) how employees contribute to the company's performance and recognition approaches.

b. trends in reward and recognition, by employee category, for contributions to the company's quality and performance objectives

c. key methods and key indicators the company uses to evaluate and improve its performance and recognition processes. Describe how the evaluation takes into account cooperation, participation by all categories and types of employees, and employee satisfaction.

8. *Promoting and supporting the quality education process.* The Total Quality Management movement believes that proper training is the primary energy that will continually allow an organization to advance. This subcategory examines how a company listens to and communicates with its employees through training methods.

4.3 Employee Education and Training

(40 pts.)
Describe how the company determines what quality and related education and training is needed by employees and how the company utilizes the knowledge and skills acquired; summarize the types of quality and related education and training received by employees in all categories.

AREAS TO ADDRESS

a. (1) how the company determines needs for the types and amounts of quality and related education and training to be received by all categories and types of employees. Address: (a) relevance of education and training to company plans; (b) needs of individual employees; and (c) all work units having access to skills in problem analysis, problem solving, and process simplification; (2) methods for the delivery of education and training; and (3) how the company ensures on-the-job use and reinforcement of knowledge and skills.

b. summary and trends in quality and related education and training received by employees. The summary and trends should address: (1) quality orientation by new employees; (2) percent of employees receiving quality and related education and training in each employee category annually; (3) average hours of quality education and training per employee annually; (4) percent of current employees who have received quality and related education and training; and (5) percent of employees who have received education and training in specialized areas such as design quality, statistical, and other quantitative problem-solving methods.

c. key methods and key indicators the company uses to evaluate and improve the effectiveness of its quality and related education and training for all categories and types of employees. Describe how the indicators take into account: (1) education and training delivery effectiveness; (2) on-the-job performance improvement; and (3) employee growth.

Note: *Quality and related education and training address the knowledge and skills employees need to meet their objectives as part of the company's quality and performance plans. This may include quality awareness, leadership, problem solving, meeting customer requirements, process analysis, process simplifi-*

cation, waste reduction, cycle time reduction, and other training that affects employee effectiveness and efficiency.

9. *Establishing and promoting companywide quality values.* Quality companies establish quality values and communicate those values to their employees. This subcategory examines how this communication process occurs, from creation to continued efforts throughout the organizational structure.

1.2 Management for Quality

(25 pts.)
Describe how the company's customer focus and quality values are integrated into day-to-day leadership, management, and supervision of all company units.

AREAS TO ADDRESS

a. how the company's customer focus and quality values are translated into requirements for all levels of management and supervision. Include principal roles and responsibilities of each level: (1) within their units; and (2) cooperation with other units.
b. how the company's organizational structure is analyzed to ensure that it most effectively and efficiently serves the accomplishment of the company's customer, quality, innovation, and cycle time objectives. Describe indicators, benchmarks, or other bases for evaluating and improving organizational structure.
c. types, frequency, and content of reviews of company and work unit quality plans and performance. Describe types of actions taken to assist units which are not performing according to plans.
d. key methods and key indicators the company uses to evaluate and improve awareness and integration of quality values at all levels of management and supervision

10. *Facilitating the total quality planning process.* A quality organization develops a strategic plan for accomplishing its mission. This subcategory examines how that strategic plan is structured and managed. The publication of an annual quality plan serves as a major communication device, forcing the organization to articulate its vision, goals, and quality plans. Every Baldrige Award winner has such a plan that is shared with each of its employees.

3.1 Strategic Quality and Company Performance Planning Process

(35 pts.)
Describe the company's strategic planning process for the short term (1–2

AREAS TO ADDRESS

a. how the company develops plans and strategies for the short term and longer term. Describe data and analysis results used in developing business plans and priorities, and how they consider: (1) customer requirements and the expected evolution of these requirements; (2) projections of the competitive years) and longer term (3 years or more) for quality and customer satisfaction leadership. Include how this process integrates quality and company performance requirements and how plans are deployed.

environment; (3) risks: financial, market, and societal; (4) company capabilities, including research and development to address key new requirements or technology leadership opportunity; and (5) supplier capabilities.

b. how plans are implemented. Describe: (1) the method the company uses to deploy overall plan requirements to all work units and to suppliers, and how it ensures alignment of work unit activities; and (2) how resources are committed to meet the plan requirements.

c. how the company evaluates and improves its planning process, including improvements in: (1) determining company quality and overall performance requirements; (2) deployment of requirements to work units; and (3) input from all levels of the company

SUMMARY

The quality and success of organizations depend to a great extent upon effective management of the communication process. In this chapter we have seen that the informal communication flow, or the organizational grapevine, can enhance or hurt corporate effectiveness. Through the use of informal communication chains, managers can predict the extent of the rumor process. Six methods for controlling rumors or the grapevine were given.

The quality of an organization's climate is influenced by the quantity and quality of information that is available and used, and by the formal and informal channels of information through which communication takes place. These formal channels develop into networks known as communication loops.

To keep the organizational communication healthy and to ensure that networks operate at top efficiency, employee surveys and communication audits are often used. Three primary audit systems were described: the OCD, the ECCO, and the ICA audits. The ICA audit is the one most often used in the United States. In addition, the popular Malcolm Baldrige National Quality Award guidelines can also be used as a tool to analyze organizational communication.

KEY WORDS

cluster chain mismatching
communication audit
communication climate
communication loop
communication network
ECCO audit
global networks
gossip chain
horizontal flow
grapevine
ICA audit
informal communication chain
informal communication flow
information channel
information quality
information quantity
informative network
integrative network
innovative network
OCD audit
Malcolm Baldrige National Quality Award
organizational climate
probability chain
regulative network
rumor
single strand chain
vertical flow

REVIEW QUESTIONS

1. What is the common name for the informal communication flow of information in business?
2. Draw out and explain the four informal communication chains.
3. What are some ways to control the grapevine influence?
4. Give some examples of both the positive and destructive effects of rumors.
5. What is the communication climate in an organization, and what three factors of information can be analyzed in determining this climate?
6. What are communication networks or communication loops?
7. What are global networks?
8. Describe the five tools that can be used in the ICA communication audit.
9. How does a communication audit differ from an employee survey?
10. Describe how the Malcolm Baldrige Award criteria can be put to use as a communication audit tool in organizations.

EXERCISES

1. Pick a rumor that you have heard within the past few weeks about an organization. Go to a library and see what kind of information you can find that will tell you whether the rumor was true or false. Share the information with some of your colleagues.
2. Call the company you were researching in question 1. Talk to the public relations employees and ask them the methods they used in fighting the rumors.
3. Pick a current group in which you are actively involved. Describe its communication climate by using the information in this chapter.
4. Using the same group described in question 3, what communication network patterns do you find? Draw the networks in relation to the overall organizational chart.
5. Using the material on communication audits presented in this chapter, describe ways that communication within the group you picked for questions 3 and 4 can be analyzed.
6. Read the following story about organizational communication, and then answer the questions that relate the story to this chapter. Discuss the story and your answers with fellow classmates.
   a. What type of organizational communication process does this story fit?
   b. How do you think that the notice of the shutdown/layoff left the company so fast?
   c. What methods would you have used if you were Oliver Manzini, or an executive of his company, to ensure that a rumor of this type would not circulate?
   d. What would you do now?

Don't Let the Grapevine Trip You Up

As Oliver Manzini drove home, he was deep in thought about the news he had heard that day and what he was going to do about it. Because the government space program was being phased out, Manzini's company had lost a major contract—one that had called for the production of integrated circuits for computers.

(continued)

But things were not as bad as they had seemed at first because the marketing department had anticipated the loss more than a year before. To head off the bad effects of a drop in sales, the sales manager had contracted with two major computer manufacturers to provide the two with the same integrated circuits, only slightly modified, that the company had been supplying to the government. The modification required a change in two machines that were used in producing the circuits, and so the machines would have to be shut down for two weeks while the maintenance department made the necessary adjustments. During the shutdown, thirty workers—all of them under Manzini's supervision—would have to be temporarily laid off.

As he approached his house, Manzini was pondering the best approach for telling his subordinates about the change so that they would understand and accept the layoff as well as possible. He knew that if the employees were not properly informed, rumors would circulate, and the situation could turn into a real problem.

As Manzini entered the house, his wife hurried to greet him. "Oh, honey," she said. "I just heard. It's so terrible! Will it affect you?" Manzini ran through several events of that day to try to figure out what his wife was talking about but finally had to ask her to explain.

"I'm talking about the big layoff," she said. "Jane heard about it at the beauty parlor and called me right away. She was so worried that they would let you go. It's all over town now that your company has lost all of its government contracts and will have to close down most of its operations at that plant. The way you looked when you came up the walk, I just knew you had been laid off." [49]

REFERENCES

1. "Hong Kong Officials Move to Restore Confidence After Runs on Two Banks," *Wall Street Journal*, August 12, 1991, p. A8.
2. Philip Lewis, *Organizational Communications*, 2nd ed. (Columbus, Ohio: Grid), p. 68.
3. Peter Drucker, *Management Tasks, Responsibilities, Practices* (New York: Harper & Row, 1974), p. 124.
4. Mike Flanagan, "Ear-Catching Rumors," *Dallas Morning News*, October 15, 1986, p. 1c.
5. Keith Davis, "The Care and Cultivation of the Corporate Grapevine," *Dun's* (July 1973), p. 44.
6. Frederick Koenig, *Rumor in the Marketplace: The Social Psychology of Commercial Hearsay* (Boston: Auburn House, 1985).
7. Davis, "Corporate Grapevine," p. 46.
8. Michael Korda, *Power: How to Get It, How to Use It* (New York: Ballantine Books, 1975), p. 104.
9. Koenig, *Rumor in the Marketplace.*
10. Davis, "Corporate Grapevine," p. 46.
11. Ibid., p. 47.
12. Jefferson Freeman, "The Grapevine: Bane or Boon?" *Xerox Xchange*, 2 (1975), p. 2.
13. Larry Light, "Killing a Rumor Before It Kills a Company," *Business Week* (December 24, 1990), p. 23.
14. Alecia Swasy, "P&G Once Again Has Devil of a Time with Firm's Logo," *Wall Street Journal*, March 26, 1990.
15. Ibid.

16. Kevin Maney, "P&G Cuts Moon Man's Controversial Locks," *USA Today*, July 11, 1991.
17. Blair S. Walker, "Another CEO Discloses Brain Cancer," *USA Today* (January 21, 1993), p. 1B.
18. Dan Dorfman, "Pro: More Trouble on Line for Cellular Stocks," *USA Today*, February 1, 1993, p. 5B.
19. Blair S. Walker, "Cellular Firms Grapple with Cancer Scare," *USA Today*, February 1, 1993, pp. 1–2B.
20. John Schneidawind, "Executive Battles Storm over Cellular Phones," *USA Today*, February 2, 1993, p. 4B.
21. John J. Keller, "Cellular Industry Group Acts to Avert Crisis by Research Into Phones' Safety," *Wall Street Journal*, February 1, 1993.
22. Walker, "Cellular Firms Grapple," p. 1B.
23. Ibid., p. 2B.
24. Ibid.
25. Ibid.
26. Tim Friend, "Investigating Cellular Phones and Cancer Link," *USA Today*, February 2, 1993, p. 1A.
27. Terry Maxon, "Cancer Scare Doesn't Dent Phone Sales," *Dallas Morning News*, February 2, 1993, p. 8D.
28. Schneidawind, "Executive Battles Storm."
29. Gerald M. Goldhaber, *Organizational Communication*, 5th ed. (Dubuque, Iowa: Wm. C. Brown, 1990), p. 71.
30. Ibid.
31. Corwin P. King, "Keep Your Communication Climate Healthy," *Personnel Journal* (April 1978), p. 204.
32. Ibid., p. 206.
33. Vincent DiSalvo with Craig Monroe and Benjamin Morse, *Business and Professional Communication* (Columbus, Ohio: Charles E. Merrill, 1977), p. 252.
34. Daniel Katz and Robert Kahn, *The Social Psychology of Organizations* (New York: John Wiley & Sons, 1966), p. 240.
35. DiSalvo, *Business and Professional Communication*, p. 254.
36. Ibid., p. 255.
37. Harold J. Leavitt, "Some Effects of Certain Communication Patterns," *Journal of Abnormal and Social Psychology* (January 1951), p. 46.
38. William H. Davidson, "Making Globalization Networks Work For You," *World Trade* (February/March 1990), p. 68.
39. Ibid.
40. Joyce Asher Gildea and Myron Emanuel, "Internal Communications: The Impact on Productivity," *Public Relations Journal* (February 1980), p. 12. Copyright 1980.
41. Gerald M. Goldhaber and Donald P. Rogers, *Auditing Organizational Communication Systems: The ICA Communication Audit* (Dubuque, Iowa: Kendall/Hunt, 1979), p. 8.
42. Raymond L. Falcione, "Auditing Organizational Communication," *The Handbook of Executive Communication* (Homewood, Illinois: Dow Jones-Irwin, 1986), pp. 778–79.
43. Goldhaber and Rogers, *Auditing Organizational Communication Systems*, pp. 9–19.
44. Falcione, "Auditing Organizational Communication," pp. 790–92.
45. Karl J. Skutski, "Conducting a Total Quality Communications Audit," *Public Relations Journal* (April 1992), pp. 29–32.
46. Ibid., p. 29.
47. Ibid.
48. The description for each of the ten subcategories is taken directly from the "1992 Award Criteria: Malcolm Baldrige National Quality Award." The 34-page booklet is available from the U.S. Department of Commerce, Technology Administration, National Institute of Standards and Technology, Gaithersburg, Maryland.
49. Jack Danner, "Don't Let the Grapevine Trip You Up," *Supervisory Management* (November 1972), pp. 2–3.

PART 2

POTENTIAL BARRIERS TO AN EFFECTIVE COMMUNICATION PROCESS

Four major elements can limit the development of effective managerial communication skills: people, language, nonverbal behavior, and listening techniques. These elements are examined in the next four chapters.

Chapter 4 focuses on *perception,* or the filter through which we take in stimuli and understand the world. The way that we perceive people is the starting point for how we communicate with others.

Language is the theme of Chapter 5. Humans are unique because they can use symbols, or words that represent items and events within society. Symbols, however, can become a barrier to effective communication among people who do not share a common understanding.

Chapter 6 looks at how *nonverbal* behavior can either augment or contradict what is spoken. Three important nonverbal areas of environmental, social, and physical communication are discussed. In Chapter 7 we discover the difference between hearing and *listening.* Unless managers develop good listening skills, they may hear what is being said, yet never fully understand.

CHAPTER 4

PERCEPTION AS A POTENTIAL COMMUNICATION BARRIER

Before a recent football season started at Southern Methodist University, a story circulated about a walk-on hopeful fresh out of a local Dallas high school. The young man was making his first visit to the athletic department's impressive weight room and was eager to make a good impression on his potential coaches. He was appalled when he glanced about and saw what he later called "huge dudes lifting houses, trucks, and trees" and at the same time heard them talking nonchalantly about their physical prowess. The young man feared that he would be killed during the first day of scrimmage. Bravely he sauntered over to one of the bulging-bicepped bragging behemoths and asked, "Are you guys upperclassmen at SMU, or are you walk-ons like me?" The giant replied that he was neither: "I play for the Oilers, that fellow is with the Rams, and those two are with the Dolphins." The young man's sigh was heard by everyone in the room, including the pros using the facilities to get in shape before reporting to their pro football camps.

PERCEPTION DEFINED

Perhaps you have never felt as that young man did, that you were a midget in the land of giants. All of us, however, have had similar problems. We have had people evaluate, judge, and mistakenly think things about us and consequently communicate to us in error. Likewise, we have been guilty of the same type of behavior. Perception is the process of gaining insight and knowledge about the world through any of our senses, especially through seeing and hearing.

As shown by the model presented in Chapter 1, communication is the process of sharing ideas, information, and knowledge. When one person wishes to share an idea with another, he or she formulates ideas into words or symbols that the other person can attach meaning to and understand. In this formulation process we use references that are constructed from past events, experiences, expectations, and current motivational states. When a receiver sees or hears the message, he or she relies on a particular frame of reference for decoding and understanding. But instead of responding to the stimulus, the person processes the information cognitively and then reacts to his or her interpretation rather than to the event itself. The more similar the frames of reference and the interpretation between people, the easier it is to communicate.

In business this perceptual process is critical. As a manager, you must hire new employees. How do you choose the right person out of the pool of applicants? Clearly, perception plays an important role as you evaluate qualifications, interpersonal skills, and general appearance. When you question an employee about reported behavioral actions, you listen to the explanation while your mind is also working through an interpretation of the person's nonverbal response.

Misunderstandings often occur in communication. Sometimes the perception process is responsible for the misunderstanding. For that reason understanding perceptual behavior can be an important hurdle to effective communication. This chapter describes ways that perceptual problems can be resolved. It starts by examining the categories of perception types—how perception varies among different types of people—and then moves on to look at the problems involved in how people perceive other people—the effects of perceptual errors. Since human behavior lies at the heart of how people get along with others, the chapter looks at how attitudes and values influence the stages of perceptual development that people pass through. Finally, the chapter focuses on methods that can be used to correct perceptually based problems, moving from self-examination to disclosure of information to others. Leaders exert a tremendous amount of influence by their expectations of subordinates. The Pygmalion effect says that the subordinate fits the role he or she is expected to play.

First Impressions Become Lasting Impressions

When we first see other people or hear their voices, our minds create mental impressions based on the verbal and nonverbal signals that we gather. If we do not have access to additional information, the initial impression often becomes the lasting impression. Communications consultant Roger Ailes tells us that when we send those same signals, we have just a few seconds to make the right first impression. The signals that we send to others tell them whether we are confident, comfortable, sincere, and even trustworthy. "In business, those crucial first seven seconds can decide whether you will win that new account, get financing, or succeed in a tense negotiation."[1] We can better control those precious seconds if we have thought through what we want to say, have practiced how we want to respond, and then allow our full presence (body and voice) to communicate our intended message.

Jan Carlzon, president of Scandinavian Airlines Systems (SAS), relates the importance of this initial impression to his company. He refers to the "moment of truth" when customers first encounter an SAS employee and immediately perceive whether that employee is going to meet or not meet their needs and expectations. Regardless of whether the need is actually met, Carlzon states, a customer often returns or does not return based on that initial moment:

> Last year, each of our 10 million customers came in contact with approximately five SAS employees, and this contact lasted an average of 15 seconds each time. . . . Thus SAS is "created" in the minds of our customers 50 million times a year, 15 seconds at a time. Those 50 million "moments of truth" are the moments that ultimately determine whether SAS will succeed or fail as a company. They are the moments when we must prove to our customers that SAS is their best alternative.[2]

Perception Problems in Information Processing

We gather information about the world by looking at and observing things around us. All too often characteristics or facts about objects are inferred based on mere visual or tactile exploration. Although we take information from things that we can see, we also infer and use information based on what we can't see but assume to know. Using this type of information can lead to problems for four reasons.

Multiple Levels of Meaning

An object like a tree, a car, or a building is visible to the naked eye, yet each of these is composed of certain elements that can't be seen. While the outer layer is observable, the layer beneath the surface can be detected only with x-rays, a microscope, or a scanning device. When seen with such an aid, the object takes on new shapes and colors. Yet a level exists beyond the observational powers of such sensing devices, and this level also can convey new meaning and definition to the object. Some technical jobs require such minute internal understanding of objects. As large high-rise buildings are built, they must appear sound to the outward eye and must pass stress tests to indicate internal soundness. Following a May 1979 crash of a DC-10 plane in Chicago, the Federal Aviation Administration ordered a close inspection of all DC-10 engine mounts. Special scanning devices revealed hairline cracks invisible to the unaided eye on several engine mounts of planes that were in use. The mounts were immediately replaced and further accidents were prevented.

Indirect Gathering of Information

By observing the world, we gain knowledge on a daily basis. Yet most of our knowledge comes from television, radio, magazine, and newspaper accounts in which others interpret the world for us. Wars that involve hundreds of thousands of people and negotiations that involve only three or four are both reported in short one- to three-minute editions on radio and television and a few short columns in newspapers. Often the communicated words and the pose of the picture selected to support a reporter's words are staged by the communicator so that the reader or viewer will perceive and accept the message as reality.

Distortion

The oldest and most complete study of perception was conducted in the early 1900s by individuals who held that the world we perceive is a composite of simple and elementary experiences or sensations and the memory of past sensations in various combinations. The school of structural perception used a variety of figures to show that people receive meaning in several ways when they view objects. A typical example is Figure 4.1, in which some immediately see a vase, others the profile of two face-to-face people. In Figure 4.2 many see a sad old woman, yet others see a very beautiful young lady with a large head covering.

Look at Figure 4.3. Are the lines the same length? In almost all cases people answer *no.* However, when told that these lines represent two telephone poles that are standing in the desert the answers quickly change from an emphatic *no* to *maybe* or *probably* and even *yes.*

Figure 4.4 is similar. Are the lines parallel? Again, most people answer no, but when told that the lines represent the rails of a railroad track that are receding into the distance, most agree that they could be parallel.

FIGURE 4.1

FIGURE 4.2

FIGURE 4.3

FIGURE 4.4

Today perception is studied within the schools of behaviorism, gestalt psychology, and functionalism. Structuralism remains important, however, because most of the knowledge about perception has been discovered through the structuralist approach.

Varying Perceptions

One reason that problems and conflicts arise in the area of perception and how it affects human communication is that people see different things in the objects they view. The Peanuts cartoon illustrates this point.

Source: © 1960 by United Feature Syndicate, Inc. PEANUTS reprinted by permission of UFS, Inc.

Research on Person Perception

Research in the area of human perception has uncovered much about what goes on during personal interactions. For instance, the way we perceive others guides our behavior toward them. Some dispositions or states are more important than others (such as warm versus cold or loud versus soft). Just as in perception of things, much of how we perceive people is the result of inference or analogy instead of facts. We often share similar experiences and consequently can make what we hope are accurate predictions ("because of . . . therefore"). While this type of inference can accurately give us some information about others, it fails to account for factors such as the transitory moods or thought processes of others, especially if we have not had the same experiences that others have had.

Most research on human perception has centered on the sources of information available to the perceiving party. These sources are external to the beholder and include factors like feelings, attributes, and intentions. We use common characteristics, cultural differences, and social pressures in the process of gathering information. Our world takes on the framework of reality because others share our views and give us feedback on the accuracy of our reality.

Examine the photo. What is happening in the crowd? Describe what you see to others in your class. How does their perception differ from yours?
Photo by Mikkel Aaland.

How the Person Perception Process Works

1. *Physical proximity.* When we can be close to and interact with others, we formulate a first impression—a mental image drawn with certain attributes and qualities attached to the image. In developing impressions, we usually group or stereotype people into categories as a result of reactions or a transfer of thoughts, such as "You remind me of. . . ." The result of the first impression can take such forms as disillusionment, liking, disliking, or desire to increase or decrease interaction. Generally, similarity encourages interaction, and differences discourage it.

2. *Self-esteem.* The perception process continues and takes on a different twist as we react to others and how they seem to perceive us. We seem to be more attracted to those whom we perceive to *agree* with our perception of ourselves and others.

3. *Rewards and costs.* Further interaction usually takes place only when one or both individuals perceive it to be worthwhile.

4. *Discrepancies.* When discrepancies occur between self-image and how one is viewed by others, information gathering is affected and further interaction can be threatened. Future contact will be limited unless the wrong information is cleared up or the impressions are balanced.

5. *Perceived intent.* Generally, people can forgive and forget if they feel another's behavior was not intentional.

6. *Accurate perceptions.* As we get closer to interpreting correctly the information we perceive about others, our relationships grow. When that occurs, people become better managers, the workforce is more productive, and all involved are rewarded.

Stages of Development

A frame of reference is as necessary for perceiving people as it is for perceiving things. As the six requirements above illustrate, trouble arises when the symbolic realities of two people are different. This occurs because each individual's frame of reference is a direct result of major influences in several areas of life: family, social interaction, politics, geography, life expectancy/lifestyle, work, communication/media, music/dance/books, and travel.

Psychologists tell us that we pass through distinct developmental stages from infancy through maturity and later life. While the ages of these stages vary according to the various researchers, they normally cover the following ranges:

1. Infancy and early childhood (birth to 6 years)
2. Middle childhood (6–12 years)
3. Adolescence (12–18 years)
4. Young adulthood (18–35 years)
5. Middle age (35–60 years)
6. Retirement (60–70 years)
7. Older life (70+ years)

Certain developmental tasks must be learned at every stage, but the most important stages for tasks dealing with "people perception" occur during the middle childhood and adolescence periods. Starting around years 4 and 5, we observe and imitate the activities of adults. As we move into the school years, we start modeling heroes, observing from our peers, and making decisions that will serve as the foundation for the rest of our life. This foundation is a set of operating values and attitudes that governs our behavior and shapes our view of the world around us. By the time we become adults, we are so locked into that foundation that our attitudes and values seldom change during the rest of our life, except for "significant emotional events."[3] Such events can be the death of a parent or friend, financial failure, foreign travel, the reading of a book, or a personal experience. Whatever the event, it makes a lasting impact on our lives. The charts that follow show some of the developmental tasks that are established during those formative years.

Middle childhood (6–12 years)

- Building attitudes about oneself
- Getting along with playmates
- Developing fundamental skills in reading, writing, and calculating
- Building conscience, morality, and a set of values
- Developing attitudes toward social groups and institutions

Adolescence (12–18 years)

- Developing intellectual skills needed for social relationships
- Achieving socially responsible behavior
- Selecting and preparing for life's occupation
- Refining and aligning conscious values for one's place in the world

The Programming Makes the Difference

We are programmed with certain attitudes and values, and our foundation serves as a filter through which we see and evaluate people and things. One way to examine this foundation is to look carefully at the decade in which segments of the American public received its programming. This examination of decades is important because each period has unique events, individuals, and philosophical thoughts that cause people to think and behave in particular ways. When two people, representing two different decades, communicate regarding issues that reveal their attitudes or values, true differences become apparent. Table 4.1 (pages 126–129) outlines some of the influencing factors for the past seven decades. Starting with the 1920s and running through the early 1990s, the chart shows the current age of a person programmed during that decade.

Results of the Programming

People think differently as a result of their programming. For example, Ed Bush is president of a small town bank. Ed's bank has many services for its customers. Over the past few years he has noticed a real age difference in certain customers' participation in the bank's programs. Older customers, those in their seventies, keep their money fairly liquid. Most put large sums in savings accounts, government bonds, and certificates of deposit. When Ed pushes them to take more risks in their investment program in order to make higher gains, most do not listen. Ed believes that several have money buried around their houses. Regarding their ultraconservative behavior, they comment, "You never know when another depression can hit. I'm going to be

TABLE 4.1 Major Influencers of Attitudes and Values[4]

Decade: Age in 1992:	1920s (63–72)	1930s (53–62)	1940s (43–52)	1950s (33–42)
Family	Close families the basic social/economic unit Women were 23 percent of work force	Every member contributed to welfare of family during Depression	Women were 26 percent of workforce (40) Rosie the Riveter hit 37 percent (42) Baby boom (46)	Members started spending more time with peers
Social Influence	Beginning of Flapper age (20) Scopes trial on evolution (25) Stock market crash (29)	Great Depression (30) 1,300 banks closed in first months of Depression (30) Social Security start (36) Works Progress Administration (WPA)	Nylons replaced silk stockings (40) Nation/economy focused on war (41–45) Young girls called Bobby Soxers (42) WPA stopped (42) Religion in school violates first amendment (45)	Juvenile delinquency problem (54) School racial segregation unconstitutional (54) Voting Rights Bill (57)
Politics	Nineteenth Amendment (women's right to vote) passed (20)	Roosevelt and the New Deal (33)	Pearl Harbor (41) War with Japan, Germany, Italy (41) U.S. savings bonds (41) Atomic bomb on Japan (45)	Korean War (51–53)
Geography	First Time in U.S. history that urban population exceeded rural, although agrarian community still thrived			
Life Expectancy/ Lifestyle	U.S. life expectancy 54 (20) 60 percent in U.S. with income $2,000 or less (bare minimum to survive)		U.S. life expectancy 64 (40)	Middle class more affluent Prosperity, productivity, distribution jobs (50)

1960s (23–32)	1970s (13–22)	1980s (10+)	1990s (Less than 10)
43 percent of households with only one working spouse 48 percent married women work (68)	More divorces than marriages ½ eligible females work, 20 percent in blue-collar jobs (78) 58 percent of women with schoolchildren work (78) *Roe v. Wade* legalizes abortions (73)	Divorce hits high of 5.3 per 1,000 (81) Nuclear family (working husband, housekeeping wife, 2 children) is 7 percent More singles, marriage postponed, childbearing delayed to late 30s	No children in 51 percent of households (91) Divorce lowers to 4.7 per 1,000 (90)
Racism concern (63)/ sexism concern (69) Crime rate doubled Ecology concern (62) First U.S. astronaut (62)/ moon walk (69) Public school prayer unconstitutional (63) President Johnson's Great Society program (65) Use of LSD/marijuana (66) Civil rights legislation (66) Medicare for aged (66) Campus revolts (68) Hippies, liberal sex views	450 colleges/universities closed by students (70) Kent State deaths (70) 18-year-olds vote (71) Long hair worn in revolt, later became style Switch to sexism/racism concern Environment issues more important than civil rights (73)	Greed decade "Yuppies" Self-help groups (82) Status symbols: Rolex, BMW, Corona, Club Med Concern with ageism Television evangelists: Roberts, Baker and Swaggart scandals (87–88) Space Shuttle *Challenger* explodes (86) Stock Market plunged 508 points (87) Hostile takeovers	Seniors' communities Junk bond king Michael Milken sentenced to 10 years (90) Reemphasis on environmentalism New spirit of "volunteerism" Demise of communist party except in China/ Cuba (91) Collapse of Soviet Union (91) European Common Market (92) New focus on Sexual Harrassment Japan world leader in manufacturing (mid-90s)
Bay of Pigs (61)/Cuban missile crisis (62) President Kennedy assassinated (63) Troops in Vietnam increase from 200,000 to 475,000 (67) Martin Luther King and Robert Kennedy assassinated (68)	Environmental Protection Agency established (70) Illegal corporate contributions to Nixon election campaign Watergate (72–74) Vietnam War ends (73) Nixon resigns (74) Bicentennial celebration (76)	First female VP candidate (84) Oliver North and Iran-Contra affair Foreign investment in U.S. is $200 billion (88) National debt hits $2 trillion (86) Sandra O'Connor Supreme Court Justice (81)	Persian Gulf War (91) Record Federal debt of $3.6 trillion (92) Repair of savings and loan collapse Looming crisis in banks and insurance companies
Western states population boom; California had 6.9 million in 60, 16 million in 61, most populous state in 64	More in U.S. move to South and West Celebrate geographic diversity ("I love NY")	Few farms, each farmer produces for 75 people Decentralization of people from city to small towns Berlin Wall falls (89)	Shift to "globalization" era (90) Reunification of Germany (90)
Retirement villages start, first in Sun City, Arizona (60) Physical fitness program started by President Kennedy (61), ¼ population exercises First heart transplant (67)	Fast food	Life expectancy 74+ Half U.S. population regularly exercising (82) More wine consumed than hard liquor (80) 500 U.S. companies directed fitness programs AIDS epidemic	Health-conscious foods/ exercise "Daddy Track" considered Baby boomers turn 40

TABLE 4.1 Continued

Decade: Age in 1992:	1920s (63–72)	1930s (53–62)	1940s (43–52)	1950s (33–42)
Work	Henry Ford introduced 8-hour day, 5-day week (26)	Unemployment at 13 million (32)	40-hour work week (40) Worker's compensation laws (48)	17 percent had information processing/distribution jobs (50) More white-collar jobs than blue-collar (56) End of industrial era (56–57)
Communication/ Media	30 radio stations, 60,000 radio sets in the U.S. (22) 2.5 million radios in U.S. (24); 7.3 million by 1927		30 million radios (40) Television sets sold in U.S. (47) 38 U.S. magazines with circulation of over 1 million (47) 2,079 radio stations, 76 million radio sets (48)	First commercial color television telecast (51) Coast-to-coast dial telephone service, nonoperator assisted (51) Three of five homes have a television set (54) *I Love Lucy* favorite television show (54) Sputnik marked globalization of information revolution (57)
Music/Dance/ Books	"Look for the Silver Lining" (20) The Charleston (23)	"Brother Can You Spare a Dime?" (32) *Gone with the Wind* (36)	"This is My Country" (40) "Remember Pearl Harbor" (41) The jitterbug (43)	190 million recordings sold in U.S. (51) "Hello, Young Lovers" (51) Elvis hits it big (56)
Travel	Federal Highway Act passed for improving highways (21)	1 of every 4.9 Americans owned auto (30) Streamlined trains (34)	Public gasoline rationing (42)	Interstate highway construction started (56) 70 million cars (59)

1960s (23–32)	**1970s (13–22)**	**1980s (10+)**	**1990s (Less than 10)**
Theory Y style of management introduced Congress passed "equal pay for equal work, regardless of sex" bill (63) Mass use of calculators "Big-is-better" philosophy Bigness in companies, 4 or 5 in each field produce 80 percent of goods IBM Selectric typewriter (61)	Unemployment hit 30-year high at 8 percent (75) Quality consciousness Multinationals making drastic changes in big corporations Productivity starts decline (73) First personal computer, Apple II (77)	Participatory decision making/equality/delegation Generalist instead of specialist Work at home IBM personal computer (81) 13 percent of labor in manufacturing, 60 percent information processing, 3 percent farmers (82) 75 percent of all jobs involve computers Savings and loan bankruptcy	Downsizing/contract labor Total Quality Management Middle-manager elimination (90–92) Cultural diversity increases Growing pool of older workers Sexual harassment focus Nonprofit/public sector jobs desirable
Kennedy/Nixon television debates (60) *N.Y. Times* best paper in U.S. (61) Lee Harvey Oswald shot on nationwide television (63)	Televised Watergate hearings (73–74) CB radio craze (76) Decline of radio and television audience starts (77) Big papers/magazines dying; small thriving *Roots* (77)	Cable television, video games, allow viewer participation Montgomery Ward drops catalogue (85) *MASH* ends (83) MTV	ABC, CBS, NBC continue to lose viewers CNN becomes official world TV station (91) *The Civil War* documentary (90) Sears drops catalog (93)
The Twist Beatles popular (64) Hard rock music Woodstock (69) *Games People Play* (69)	"Bridge over Troubled Waters" (70) *Rocky* (75) *Saturday Night Fever* (78) Punk rock	"We Are The World" (85) Boy George, Cyndi Lauper, Madonna, Prince *One-Minute Manager, In Search of Excellence, The Road Less Traveled*	Art censorship wars (90) Milli Vanilli charged with plagiarism (90) 2 Live Crew, M.C. Hammer, Garth Brooks Stephen Hawking, *A Brief History of Time*
	Smaller cars Gasoline exceeded $1.00 per gallon	City-to-country shift made possible by highways, mass transit	Increased ride-share Growth of mass transit Segments of inner-cities becoming walking malls

Depression of the 1930s. For those people who lived through, and were programmed by, the events of the 1930s, the possibility of another depression is very real. No amount of information or persuasive talk by others can change their minds. Contrast that older group with those who are in their twenties today. They were programmed in the 1980s, when economic risk taking was high. Ed worries about some customers in that category because he knows they have borrowed money to invest in get-rich-quick schemes. Many in that group are living today on what they hope to earn tomorrow.

People behave differently as a result of their programming. In the 1920s there were economic reasons for women to stay at home and be housewives. Many were uneducated and lacked business skills, especially management skills. Consequently, women comprised only 23 percent of the workforce and worked at jobs that primarily required few skills. During World War II women were needed in the workforce because most men were in military service. Since the 1960s, many women have received the same education as their male counterparts, have proved themselves in the work world, and want the opportunity to reap the benefits of their education and ability.

One of the most pressing conflicts in the workforce of the 1990s is created by biases that exist against women in top-level management positions. Some men who received their programming in the 1920s and 1930s still believe that a woman's place is in the home and in the kitchen. Only a "significant emotional event" of seeing a truly capable woman manager can change their behavior; sadly enough, their biases often prevent this from occurring.

People view work differently as a result of their programming. Employees programmed during the 1920s to 1940s were introduced to the eight-hour/five-day a week work schedule. As unions gained power, the schedules and specification of work became more firmly established. Most people during this period tended to work best in routine, scheduled types of jobs. Contrast this to the currently growing popularity of flex-time, nontraditional work schedules, and at-home work in the "electronic cottage." The people programmed for this type of work are motivated by jobs that provide latitude in time, space, and working conditions and would be frustrated in an old-style work environment.

People even display different purchasing behaviors as a result of their programming. A midwestern pork sausage manufacturer surveyed his purchasing audience and found that most grew up in the 1930s to 1950s. Those individuals had been served pork sausage by their parents, and so they included it in their own diets. The manufacturer found that younger buyers preferred other meat products. Such information helped him design a new marketing strategy and create new products attractive to the younger purchaser.

By learning to understand programming categories that workers, buyers, and the general public fall into, we come closer to removing the perception barrier that impedes management communications.

Categories of Perception Types

The influencing factors give us a framework for viewing our world. Because each decade has different influencers, and because young people are collectively programming at the same time, it is possible to identify three categories of perception types. As we apply the individual factors to the business world, we can better understand the range of behavior exhibited there today.

The traditional employee/manager grew up during the 1920–1940 period. This was a time when manufacturing was thriving, people struggled for survival, and determination and perseverance were encouraged. World War I and the Depression impacted every life. People did not complain or give up, they pulled together to form organizational structures. The culture of those organizations developed like families. The company was respected and in turn respected hard-working employees. Since the company represented security, drastic changes of policy and process were generally discouraged. A work ethic of superior performance was the norm. The golden rule ("Do unto others as you wanted them to do to you") was strictly observed.

Traditional managers' leadership is task directed, authoritarian, and "talk-down" in style. They like working in groups and attending meetings. Because of the hard times in which they were programmed, these people often behave in a stoic, tough, aloof, and emotionless way. Today this manager is often in a CEO or top management position. He is generally a male because few females rose to management in the earlier work world. This category of manager, if successful, has learned to allow for changes within the organization and his own personal life. Some have retired and are even finding their way back into the workplace in consulting and even entry-level service jobs. They are excellent in face-to-face interactions with customers. Employers like them because they are loyal, motivated, and dependable and have established work habits. But younger managers often have difficulty in relating to them and in giving them instructions.[5]

The baby boomer employee/manager represents a pool of 75 million people born between 1946 and 1964. As the children of the original 1950s "organization man," they were raised in traditional families and still retain a traditional value base. Today they are moving gradually into the boardrooms and top management positions of corporate America. They are loyal in the same ways their fathers were loyal, and they often work in the same organizations. But they identify more with the work they do than with the company they work for.

Raised during times of unprecedented economic prosperity, they carry high materialistic expectations for their own lives. Because of technological advancements, media exposure, and global travel, they have refined tastes and a sophisticated world view. They are offended by second-rate products and experiences. Education has been the key to their success, and they see future changes in business and the world as depending upon indispensable information. This is the first group in the workforce where a high school education is the norm and a college education is expected. Most have self-starting qualities that make them suited to the flatter management structures of the 1990s and an environment of rapid change.

People in this category possess a sense of specialness. They desire to be treated as individuals and find it a little more difficult to be team players than managers in the traditional category. They are uncomfortable with evaluation and feedback on how they should change. These managers are now learning a different management style than that used by traditionalists. Japan's consensus decision making has had an impact on American business, and U.S. managers are learning to listen to employees, and to serve as resources, and teachers rather than as just supervisors. They are stressing self-supervision and are creating an office climate in which employees feel comfortable sharing their ideas.[6]

Time is the most valued resource of the baby boomers. They believe careers should not interfere with their personal time, and they try to seek a definite balance between work and other life demands. They promote shorter meeting times and expect each meeting to teach them something new. They are evenly split on technological advancement. While they see a definite advantage to computerization, many do not use computers and do not intend to become computer literate. They tolerate changes like teleconferencing but prefer to meet face to face and get to know other people as individuals.[7]

The twentysomething employee/manager was born between 1965 and 1980 and represents the age range 18–25. While the baby boomers are confident risk takers who thrive on change, people in the youngest of our three categories are called the "unsure" generation. They desire to avoid risk, pain, and rapid change. They also have trouble making decisions. They are the best educated generation in history, but rather than having a love for learning they see a college degree as necessary for survival. Education is a means to an end for them. They represent a generation that learns most of its facts about the world from television, not from reading. They are comfortable with computers and other forms of technology because they grew up with high-tech toys.

Statistically, the twentysomethings represent a fraction of the size of the baby boomer generation. They are the first generation to be raised in the households of divorced single parents and step-parents. They had fewer brothers and sisters, and fewer playmates. They "crave" entertainment and have been accustomed to entertaining themselves, especially with television and electronic games. Consequently, their attention spans are short.

This group views society and global events as "out of control," and they see few solvable issues. They feel the opposing tugs of making money and contributing to society. While money is important as an indicator of performance, materialism is not valued. The true desire of this group is not to change things, but to fix things. Many find their employment in public ser-

> **Shinjinrui: Japan's New Generation**
>
> America is not the only country where values are changing. In Japan the attitudes of young people in their twenties are so profoundly different than those held by their traditional elders that the young call themselves *shinjinrui,* or the new race. The post–World War II generation's values of "service to country first, company second, family third and self last" are no longer honored. For the new generation, individualism takes first place. Surveys show the young Japanese believe that obtaining individual fulfillment is more important than making a "contribution to society." Fewer place their work as the centerpoint of their lives. Industrial manufacturing jobs have lost favor. In their place is the luring work of medicine, banking, and hotels. Finally, the stable concept of lifetime employment has lost its lure. A recent survey by the Japanese government found that "only 29 percent of Japanese 20 to 29 years old plan to stick with one company throughout their working lives, in contrast to 70 percent of Japanese aged 55 and older."[8]

vice jobs and nonprofit organizations. The American dream, they are finding, is much tougher to realize than they anticipated. They know "fast money" is not available and their generation is experiencing the first decline in income since the 1980s. Economically, they are having a hard time making it on their own. Many continue to live at home following college graduation and the acquiring of the first job.

One key word that describes this generation is "cautious." They are cautiously postponing marriage because it could end in divorce. They are often cautious about relationships because they could get hurt emotionally. They are cautious about getting a job because it may not be the "right one." They are cautious about a career because they could end up "burned out."

When they do enter the work world, they want constant reviews, performance evaluations and feedback from their managers. Because they desire approval for each step in the job, they often prefer short tasks with observable results. They tend to be polite and courteous, which are traits needed in the service sector. Yet they value leisure more than career, they refuse overtime, and often do not want the undesirable hours of service organizations.[9]

People Wear Different Hats

Even when we understand how another person's programming has developed, another perceptual problem can arise because we usually know our coworkers in only one role or facet of their lives. When we examine the different hats they wear, or the other roles they play in their lives, we find more than just the one-sided personality from which we formulate our impressions.

Bill Tucker worked in the commercial loans department of a bank. Frank Wills, a colleague of Bill's, worked in the same department. They had worked together for four years and often ate lunch together. Bill thought he knew Frank well. One Saturday the bank sponsored a picnic for its employees, and both Bill and Frank attended with their families. There Bill saw a part of Frank that he had never seen before: This normally good-natured person was overbearing with his wife and children and even snapped at Bill during a conversation.

If you could see Frank Wills, you would draw an immediate impression about him. You have probably conjured up a picture of Frank, but your perception of the man is only a part of the person that he is and the many roles that he plays. All his roles are influenced directly or indirectly by his earlier programming. The social, environmental, and political conditions under which he lives and works also influence his personality and behavior. As we list Frank's many roles, try to develop a clear mental picture of the different requirements of each role.

At work he is an *employee* for the company, a *boss* to his secretary and

A Case of Mistaken Perception

For ten years Al Gibson was a successful marketing director for a firm in Boston. Approached by a headhunter about a comparable position in St. Louis with a substantial raise and plenty of talented people, he jumped at the chance.

Self-confident and challenged, Al was determined to make an immediate impact during his first week at the new company. As he made the rounds and met his subordinates, he quickly perceived their polite and gentle manner. He concluded on the spot that they needed to become more aggressive and to demonstrate that they could be highly productive.

Al planned and executed his first-quarter strategy. He set high standards for himself and his staff. He coached his colleagues, encouraged them, critiqued their sales methods, and shared with them proven theories of marketing. At the end of the first quarter, Al was incredulous when he was informed that his subordinates and peers hated him. They did not like his style. They did not like his aggressiveness. They saw him as intimidating, demanding, and uncooperative.

Al wondered what he should do. He asked himself, "How can I be so misunderstood?" His conclusion only compounded his initial perceptual error. "These polite, low-key Midwesterners obviously feel threatened by my competence and drive," Al decided. "They're out to get me."[13]

staff, and a *service representative* to his depositors. At home he is a *husband* to his wife, a *father* to his children, a *son* to his parents, and a *brother* to his sister. When he relaxes, he is a *viewer* of the local television stations, a *fan* of his local baseball team, and a *subscriber* to magazine publishers. He is an *appointment* to his barber, a *patient* for his doctor, and a *policy holder* for the insurance company. At church he is a *teacher* to the class and a *member* of the congregation. Frank wears a different hat for each of the above roles; he also behaves differently in each role. Misunderstandings can occur when we know people in one role but observe them in a completely different role. We need to prevent initial impressions from becoming lasting impressions. Managers must constantly allow for a personal latitude that gives them freedom to change impressions as they gain new information about others.

Effective managers not only allow for the differences in people; they seek out the differences. As you read the case on p. 134, consider the different ways in which Al Gibson perceives his subordinates and, in turn, is perceived by them.

THE EFFECTS OF PERCEPTUAL ERRORS

Regardless of how hard we try to understand each other and communicate effectively, we often do not see the world in the same way. Perception is a subjective experience, and a variety of errors can occur.

Stereotyping results when we oversimplify differences in people and attribute categorical traits to them. Once in place, these attributed characteristics are persistent over time and resist change. They are often destructive in nature and ignore the uniqueness and individuality of a person or group. Typical stereotypes might include: "Private college students are snobbish," "Women managers are emotional," and "Lawyers are unethical."

Three primary types of stereotyping—age, race, and gender—occur in the organizational world. A study by Rosen and Jerdee identified six commonly held stereotypes about older, more traditional employees. They are thought to be (1) more resistant to organizational change, (2) less creative, (3) less likely to take calculated risks, (4) less physically able, (5) less desirous to learn new methods, and (6) less capable of learning new skills.[10] As we saw earlier, the most successful members of our first category have learned how to allow for organizational and personal change. While research has disproven most sexist stereotypes about gender differences, men and women are still described differently. Men are perceived as more assertive, active, objective, rational, and competent than women. Women are perceived as more passive, emotional, submissive, and sensitive.[11]

Denial is a behavior by which we try to protect ourselves from people, situations, and ideas that threaten our security. People quickly perceive what is supportive and tend to shut out what is personally threatening or culturally unacceptable. In the past few years, as companies have "downsized," employees have felt the sting of layoffs. In many instances the organizations have communicated their intent months in advance, have established outplacement programs, and have given those losing their jobs several months to prepare. Still, when the axe finally falls, many employees are absolutely stunned. In conversations they express how they never thought they would be the ones to go. For those many months they were perceptually receiving a different message than the one their company was actually sending.

The *halo effect* is the positive perception of certain characteristics or traits of an individual influencing the way people see other characteristics of that person. For example, the Big Six accounting firms usually solicit top grade-point-average (GPA) accounting majors for employment interviews. If the firm hired a candidate solely on the basis of that 4.0 GPA, however, they could regret it later. The high GPA does indicate academic excellence, but it tells the firm little about the student's interpersonal and leadership skills.

The halo effect can be either positive or negative. Steers gives an excellent example of how the halo effect made its way into the performance appraisal system at General Motors.

> A former GM executive claims that so much emphasis was placed on cost cutting in the company that other important areas of managerial accountability went almost unnoticed in evaluations. For instance, the Tarrytown, New York, assembly division once had the dubious distinction of producing the poorest-quality cars of all 22 U.S. GM plants. During this time, some trucks were so poorly built that dealers refused to accept them. Even so, the plant had the lowest manufacturing costs in GM. As a result, the plant manager at Tarrytown received one of the largest bonuses of all the assembly divisions while building the worst cars in the company. Clearly, the manager's evaluation concerning costs overshadowed considerations of product quality.[12]

Projection occurs when people project their own feelings, motives, or desires into their perception of other people. A manager obsessed by quality control may come to believe that no one else shares a desire for total quality. In reality, employees may truly have a desire to produce a quality product but may lack the necessary equipment. Projection often occurs because a person fails to recognize his or her own personal traits but projects them to others. For example, a hypercritical person may not see himself as such but may perceive others as overly critical of him. Emotional biases enter into perceptual projection. Feelings of love, fear, anger, hate, distrust, or even uncertainty can influence how we perceive another person. This is often revealed when an employee makes highly subjective statements about others: "My boss is sexist," "That manager is biased," "That supervisor is always unfair." While each of these statements could represent a truth, it could also in reality be disclosing information about the employee's own feelings.

The Right Person for the Right Overseas Assignment

In the 1990s, American firms are finding a great demand for qualified international personnel, but a shortage of those who are truly the "right people for the right assignments." When asked if they would consider international work in the future, most college graduates answer with a resounding *yes*. But as they later face the basic question of "Why do you want to go overseas?" many find that their answers do not satisfy their employer. Although the pay is higher overseas and the opportunity for travel is exciting, there are also several drawbacks and companies must try and perceive which employee is right for each job.

For years, an overseas assignment was the dead-end detour for those on a traditional career track. They were left for years in an outpost with little communication with the home office and their colleagues. Infrequent return trips made their adjustment back home very difficult at the end of their assignment. Today, with globalization as a key motivator, many large corporations are making an international assignment a requirement for a rising manager's career. Technology now allows almost daily communication with the home base. Frequent home trips and an attractive job assignment when they return also makes an overseas assignment easier than in the past. Still, poor education facilities for children, lack of job and career opportunities for a spouse, and often inadequate medical facilities can be drawbacks for some considering a move.

Matching the right person for the right overseas assignment is important for both the company and the candidate. From the company's position, an overseas move is costly. Consulting firm Booz, Allen & Hamilton estimates that the cost of picking the wrong person for the assignment starts at $250,000. This is for items such as out-of-pocket expenses, loss of productivity overseas, delay in opening new markets, damage to the company's image, and the cost of finding a new position when the person returns home. In fields like manufacturing, the cost could be in the millions if manufacturing and marketing are delayed for several months.

From the candidate's position, the correct match is also critical. Stability is an important characteristic for all overseas employees. If bad relationships on the job or at home lead the candidate to seek an escape, the international job will often end up being twice as stressful. Research shows little difference in the overseas success rate between singles and married employees. Singles are often younger, with fewer relationship ties, and they fill positions as engineers, salespeople, and lower-level technicians. Seasoned senior management candidates are usually married with children. Since potential problems can develop outside the manager's job area, interviews are usually conducted with spouses and children. Some of the most successful candidates are "empty nesters." These are usually senior managers with grown children and a spouse who is excited about an overseas transfer.

Many global companies use initial screening tools to get past first perceptions and to help both management and the candidates understand a candidate's cross-cultural adaptivity. One of the most popular instruments is the *Overseas Assignment Inventory* (OAI), administered by Moran, Stahl & Boyer in New York City. The OAI measures attitudes and characteristics of successful international executives by monitoring fifteen predictors. The results are then compared to a database average compiled by over 10,000 previous testtakers. This test and others serve as a first-step screening device.

The fifteen OAI predictors are:

1. *Motivation.* What is the strong and sustaining reason for wanting to go overseas?
2. *Expectations.* Is the person realistic about life and work in the country?
3. *Open-mindedness.* Is the person receptive and not threatened by ideas and beliefs that are different?
4. *Respect for others' beliefs.* Is the person nonjudgmental of other people's religious and political beliefs?
5. *Trust in people.* Can the person convey and encourage mutual trust among coworkers and associates?
6. *Tolerance.* Can the person tolerate different and possibly less comfortable living conditions and lifestyles?
7. *Personal control.* Does the person control, shape, or direct her life, or does she feel helpless in change situations?
8. *Flexibility.* Is the person willing to receive and accept feedback from others regarding different approaches to problem solving?
9. *Patience.* Can the person remain patient with different forms of business protocol?
10. *Adaptability.* Can the person socialize easily with new people in unfamiliar settings?
11. *Self-confidence/initiative.* Is the person a self-starter?
12. *Sense of humor.* Can the person laugh at himself and others?
13. *Interpersonal interest.* Does the person possess good cross-cultural "people" skills?
14. *Interpersonal harmony.* Is the person empathic and accepting of others who are culturally different?
15. *Spouse/family communication.* Is the relationship between couples and families healthy or troubled?

Steps that companies take in preparing selected candidates for an overseas assignment include: cultural and language training to help them understand and communicate with people in the new country, complete physicals to ensure that hard-to-treat medical problems do not exist, and an on-site preview to actually see where they will live and work. Total success is never guaranteed until an employee lands in a country, starts working there, is productive for the company, and enjoys the assignment. Smart companies recognize that a strong preparation helps both the candidate and the company perceive the assignment accurately.[14]

Methods for Correcting Perception-Based Problems

Perceptual behavior problems must be understood before managers can become effective communicators. This section discusses five major ways to correct perception-based problems. First, we must examine ourselves and how we feel about our self-image. Second, we must go through a period of self-discovery to see ourselves clearly and not in light of how we wished we were. Third, we must learn to share what we think and feel with others through self-disclosure. Fourth, we must realize the perceptual dimensions that exist when we communicate with others. Fifth, we can help others change by becoming a "positive Pygmalion."

The Self-Concept

Research conducted on self-perception reveals several interesting findings:

1. *The self is a product of interaction.* Need satisfaction is fulfilled in a developmental process.
2. *The self is unique—one of a kind.* Just as no two sets of fingerprints are identical, each individual is unique in a variety of physiological and psychological ways.
3. *The self is composed of attitudes that determine action within society.*
4. *The self grows in stages.*
5. *The self needs favorable regard.* Since we are products of interaction, we need to be seen and treated respectfully.
6. *The self prefers reciprocal behavior.* We respond best to others when we feel positive reciprocation.

At work, the growth of manager-peer-subordinate relationships is initially determined by our perceptive impression of others and their impression of us. At the core of the perceptive process, however, is our view of ourselves. We all are able to recognize certain things about ourselves, but some managers have delved more deeply than others into self-analysis.

The concept of self is fundamental in every interpersonal relationship, every social interaction, and every working atmosphere. In the business world, a healthy concept of self is essential. Success at each level of the organization—no matter how high one climbs—is based on a belief in the self that breeds confidence and determination. It is the start of self-assertiveness that enables communication, personal growth, and improved self-image to occur.

As managers, we must also build the self-concepts of our subordinates. This takes place as we set up strong communication channels, establish caring relationships, and empower people under us to make decisions themselves. The following example describes how one manager's self-concept had fully developed into what the company needed.

Alexander's Big Decision

Alexander was manager of a Pizza Hut in Moscow, Russia, when the attempted *coup d'etat,* aimed at overthrowing Soviet Union President Mikhail Gorbachev, took place in August 1991. The rebellious leaders had President Gorbachev under house arrest. There were tanks and soldiers in the streets of Moscow, and most residents were inside their houses fearing for their lives. Boris Yeltsin and a group of faithful cabinet leaders were determined to not let the government be overthrown. They were cloistered in the Parliament building for several days. As food ran out, one individual called the local Pizza Hut and ordered 300 pizzas to be delivered to the Parliament building. At first Alexander thought it was a prank. But after talking to the official, he realized the order was for real. His mind quickly calculated . . . "Should I fill the order or not? If Yeltsin loses the standoff, the opposition might think I was a Yeltsin supporter." This was the biggest decision that Alexander had ever had to make in the short history of Moscow's Pizza Hut. For an order that large, and under those circumstances, a young manager might call his superior for an approval. But Alexander's regional manager lived in London. So Alexander did what any empowered manager who had a big order would do . . . he started to work. Three hours later, he was maneuvering his van between tanks and artillery guns to deliver 300 hot pizzas. After the coup attempt was successfully ended, Alexander received a call from one of Yeltsin's leaders. He simply said, "Thank you for what you did for us that night. We will not forget it!" [15]

Self-Discovery

Understanding and controlling our perceptive behavior is a major step in learning to communicate effectively, and it requires that we gain a better understanding of our self-concept. We do this by examining three different aspects of who we are.

The me that I know. This is the image of ourselves that we derive from all the information (both positive and negative) that we accumulate from the world around us. For a manager, it is the accumulation of her technical knowledge, her supervisory experience from other jobs, feedback that she has received about her behavior, and other forms of information. For relationships to grow effectively between a manager and a subordinate, both parties need to be capable of perceiving themselves realistically. Managers with healthy self-images do not harbor fears, resentments, or other "not OK" feelings that they project on peers, subordinates, and customers. Instead, they are able to admit to those people that they have both strengths and weaknesses. They can admit it if they do not have an immediate answer to a problem.

The Different Supervisory Styles of Maria and Elise

Maria and Elise are supervisors for a microprocessor production plant. Both started as supervisors five months ago and have ten employees reporting to them. While their jobs and responsibilities are similar, their management styles are drastically different.

Maria knows each of her subordinates on an individual basis. She prides herself in talking or checking with them every two or three days. She is always available for discussing problems and seeks to help her workers find solutions that fit both the job and their personalities. During the past five months, Maria has promoted two people out of her department because the employees developed their skills to the point where they also became supervisors. An additional person moved laterally to another position that required someone who enjoyed working with minute parts. Maria was able to help the company fill the spot because of her in-depth discussions with her people about things that came easily for them.

To an observer, Maria's department might seem unorganized. People talk and laugh, work at a seemingly casual pace, design their own work style, and come and go as they please. But Maria's department almost doubles its production quota on a weekly basis, and its quality control inspection reveals only a 1 percent defect ratio.

Elise's department is different. An observer might see little talking, people continually working, and the entire group starting and stopping for breaks and lunch at the same time. The department is a perfect example of rigid control. Elise prescribes for her workers the method of production and the quota that must be met. Her department meets its quota, but in five months has never surpassed the required goal. No workers have been promoted, although five have quit the company and two were fired.

As you can imagine, morale is extremely low in Elise's department. Perhaps one person's statement about Elise best sums how her people see her: "She could not care less about me as a person. There are a lot of things my colleagues and I could tell her about doing this job better, and our department would be more productive, but she doesn't want to sit and listen to us. She sees us at things, not as people."

The me that I wish I were. All of us have areas of our lives where we wish we were different. For some it may be the fantasy of being a movie star or the chief executive officer of an organization; for others it can be an unclear goal. Those types of images are healthy parts of our daydreams. For other people, "the me I wish I were" is an unhealthy, "not-OK" position from which they combat the world.

The me that I want others to see. Occasionally "the me that I know," and "the me that I wish I were" become mingled to the point of becoming "the me that I want others to know." This may be the calm, cool, and collected image of a speaker making a presentation to a large group. On the outside the smile and mannerisms say, "Nothing ruffles my feathers," but on the inside the person is slowly falling apart.

Some people project such good images of themselves to others that the real person is never displayed or known. On one end of the continuum, this position is effective and a part of the manager's public and professional appearance. Control to the extreme, however, hides characteristics about the real person inside that we fear to let others know.

Self-Disclosure

One of the best ways to achieve self-discovery, and to help others learn about us, is to practice self-disclosure. Since communication is a two-way process, information must travel between both senders and receivers.

The *Johari window,* conceived by Joseph Luft and Harry Ingham, examines different areas of life and people's awareness of them.[16] The window is like a large framed picture of you. Inside is everything there is to know about yourself: wants, needs, likes, dislikes, goals, fears, and so on (Figure 4.5). The frame can be divided into vertical and horizontal halves. The vertical halves contain what is known and not known to each person. The horizontal halves contain what others know about us and what they do not know. When the vertical and horizontal halves are overlaid, we have the Johari window. The four quadrants are displayed in Figure 4.6.

Quadrant 1 is the open area in a manager's life that is known to her and also to others. It is a public area where questions can be asked freely and answers given unthreateningly. This area concerns attitudes, feelings, and behavior that the manager understands and that colleagues, subordinates, customers and the public see and interpret.

Quadrant 2 is the blind area of her life. Here others see and know things about her that she does not know about herself. A simple example might be

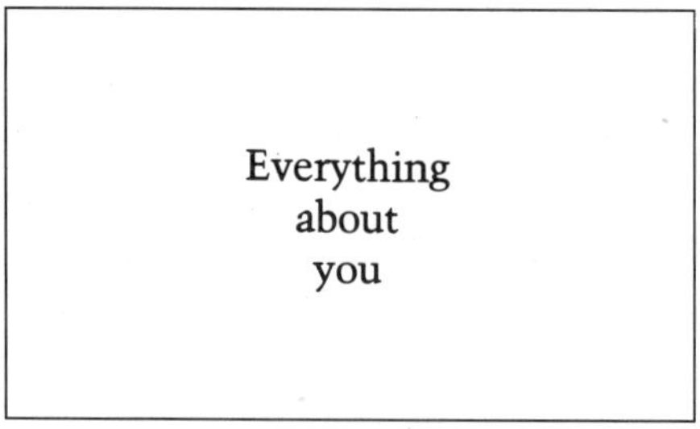

Everything about you

FIGURE 4.5 Undivided Johari Window

	Known to self	Not known to self
Known to others	1 Open	2 Blind
Not known to others	3 Hidden	4 Unknown

FIGURE 4.6 The Johari Window with Quadrants
From *Group Processes: An Introduction to Group Dynamics* by Joseph Luft, by permission of Mayfield Publishing Company. Copyright © 1984, 1970, and 1963 by Joseph Luft.

nervous habits. Others see them, yet she never realized they exist. A more complex example might be attitudes, biases, anger, and fears that she has toward people or events. Others observe these attitudes in her behavior, but she easily ignores them.

Quadrant 3 is the hidden area and contains those secret thoughts, fears, desires, and motives that she has and realizes but conceals from others.

Quadrant 4 is the unknown area that is full of deeply hidden and programmed attitudes and knowledge. She is often motivated to behave in certain ways where unknown responses prevail, yet she is uncertain why she behaves as she does. As information within this area becomes known, she then understands her thoughts and behavior.

Figure 4.7 shows the Johari window for two individuals. Which one tends to share more personal information? If these two people shared a relationship, their communication patterns would probably lead to problems and conflicts. Since A has a large open area and a very small unknown area, we can infer that he has done some introspective examining of his life and talked a lot about himself with others. We call such talk *disclosure.* As he shared information with others, they told him things.

Figure 4.7 shows the Johari window for Maria and Elise. Can you guess from the diagram which one is Elise? Elise is in the B position, and the diagram shows why her relationships with her subordinates lead to problems and conflicts. People like Maria (A) have large open areas and very small unknown areas. We can infer from their openness that they have done some introspective examining of their life and have talked to lots of people about themselves. We call such talk *disclosure.* As Maria has shared information with her peers and subordinates, they have told her things that she was blind to before. As she grew comfortable in her relationships, she found there was

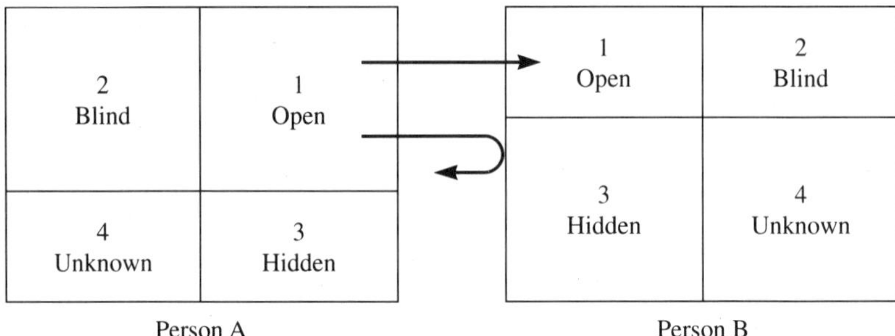

FIGURE 4.7 Johari Window for Two Individuals

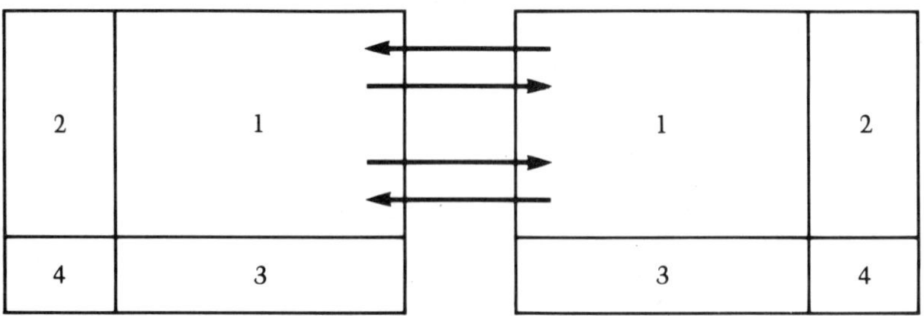

FIGURE 4.8 Communication Growth in the Johari Framework

less and less that she felt she had to hide from people. Consequently, her unknown area has grown smaller and smaller. As this has occurred, her self-concept has improved, her subordinates have grown more secure about their relationship with Maria, and in turn their individual self-concepts have also grown.

Elise has real fears about life, and especially about her ability to manage other people. She is hesitant to share some of these fears (hidden area). Consequently, her unknown area is large. When Elise communicates with her subordinates who have larger open areas, their overall range is limited. The subordinates soon feel unfulfilled because their communication is ignored and unanswered.

Several possibilities exist for Elise and her department members: (1) They can settle on simple communication in a limited scope; (2) they can feel unfulfilled and stop talking; (3) they can become more open with each other, share more information, learn more about themselves and the other, and let their relationship grow. If a commitment to growth is made, the potential for a large open area exists with all people. Figure 4.8 depicts the outcome.

In this situation it was lucky for Elise that her supervisor observed the problems and called her in for a conference. In the course of the conversation, she learned of Elise's hidden feelings about herself, her job, and her subordinates. The manager worked with Elise and helped her see herself better, gave her some useful tools, and promised to work with her in establishing some new goals for her department. Within two months, Elise had changed tremendously and so had the morale in her department. Suddenly output quotas were being exceeded on a regular basis.

Three Perceptual Dimensions of Each Person

Information about self-concepts and perceptions of other people is collected from three distinct perceptual dimensions that exist for each person involved in the communication act. Since communication involves two people and each person has three dimensions, six dimensions are involved each time two people communicate:

- My perception of me
- My perception of you
- My perception of how you are perceiving me
- Your perception of you
- Your perception of me
- Your perception of how I am perceiving you

Why is the uniqueness of the person important in business? Many would say that it is not, and others feel that business must minimize the differences among people, especially in their styles of work, and try to have everyone look and act alike. Japanese management style, however, suggests that this misconception is partially responsible for the recent low rate of productivity in the United States. Americans have specialized jobs, while typical Japanese employees tend to be generalists. In the United States, job specialization and specific job descriptions have limited potential employee performance.

Because the workplace is filled with people from all avenues of life, managers must understand that their programming and life experiences make each person unique. What is a wise decision for one individual may be foolish for another. One author expressed it this way:

> I act in a way that is *cautious* to me, but *cowardly* to you.
> You act in a way that is *courageous* to you, but *foolhardy* to me.
> She sees herself as *vivacious,* but he sees her as *superficial.*
> He sees himself as *friendly,* she sees him as *seductive.*
> She sees herself as *reserved,* he sees her as *haughty and aloof.*
> He sees himself as *gallant,* she sees him as *phony.*
> She sees herself as *feminine,* he sees her as *helpless and dependent.*
> He sees himself as *masculine,* she sees him as *overbearing and dominating.*[17]

A Short but Shaggy Morality Story About Suggestion

Back when Robert T. Hill was employed at Pennsylvania State University, a graduate instructor in the education of exceptional children asked him to approve production of a highly unstructured instructional videotape. "I went into my development act," recalls Hill, who currently is training manager at Poppin Fresh Pies, Inc., Minneapolis. "I tried to pry behavioral objectives and a content outline out of him. All he would say, however, is that he wanted to bring an eight-year-old child into the studio and tape some activities. Although this sort of unstructured program is the instructional television producer's nightmare, I finally relented and we taped a program of a young boy playing with some toys and taking a psychological word test."

A few months later, Hill happened to meet the instructor and asked him if he was using the videotape. The instructor said he was and had been very pleased with the results.

"How do you use it?" Hill asked. "Well," he said, "I have two classes of graduate students with a good background in psychology. I show one class the tape and tell them that they will be observing a child with a genius-level IQ and that they should write down the characteristics that demonstrate this. I show the same videotape to the other class and tell them that the kid is mentally retarded and that they should write down the characteristics he displays that indicate this. Every time I do it, I get what is a normal young boy written up as either a genius or a retarded child. I then tell them the truth and hope they profit from the experience."

The uniqueness in people makes them real people who have value: They are not mechanisms that can be manipulated and treated without respect, nor are they embodiments of concepts or definitions. For many years business has spent enormous amounts of money on its machines but ignored its most valuable resource—its people. Current management theorists exhort managers to "prize the human resource."

Psychologists have long known that much of what people are is a direct result of the influence of others. Children model their behavior on that of parents and peers. Workers follow the examples of mentors and prodigies. Managers and supervisors can have an extraordinary amount of influence on the people they lead. This influence phenomenon is called *the self-fulfilling prophecy*, or the *Pygmalion effect*, which means that the prediction or expectation of an event can actually cause it to happen. People can become what other people expect them to be.

In Greek mythology, Pygmalion was a King of Cyprus who carved an ivory statue of the ideal woman and then fell in love with his beautiful creation. Aphrodite interceded and brought the statue to life for him. In modern times the playwright George Bernard Shaw used the concept in his play, *Pygmalion,* which was made into the musical comedy *My Fair Lady.* In these plays and in the myth, one person, with desire and patience, transformed the behavior of another. Professor Henry Higgins proved it was possible through hard work and positive expectations to change Eliza Doolittle from a rumpled, impolite, and loud flower girl into a gentle, soft-spoken, and attractive lady.

Becoming a Positive Pygmalion

While research on the Pygmalion effect has been instrumental in helping managers develop staff members, the initial tests on the effect were conducted in the educational system. Rosenthal and Jacobson told a group of teachers that tests showed that certain of their elementary students were "intellectual bloomers."[18] In reality the children labeled "bloomers" were picked randomly. When retested after eight months, the so-called bloomers had improved in overall IQ by four points over other children in the teachers' classrooms. Controls showed that there was no difference in the amount of time the teachers spent with the regular and bloomer children, nor did the type of classroom make a difference in the test scores. The important denominator was the *quality* of the interaction between the teacher and the students. When questioned about their impression of the students, they stated that those designated as bloomers were smarter, more appealing, more affectionate, and adjusted better and more quickly than other students. Those not classified as bloomers were seen as less bright, less interesting, less affectionate; they also were said not to adjust as well. A teacher's expectations of his or her students is a key factor in their growth and success.

Principles of the Pygmalion Effect

1. Employees act as they believe they are expected to act.
2. A manager's treatment of each employee is influenced by what the manager expects of the employee.
3. If a manager's expectations are high, productivity will likely be high.
4. If a manager's expectations are low, output will likely be low.
5. A subordinate's performance rises or falls to meet a manager's expectations.

In business the same principle applies. A manager's expectations of his or her subordinates is a key factor in the growth and success of the organization, the employees, and management. Just as Professor Higgins did in the play *Pygmalion,* many managers play Pygmalion-like roles in developing successful and productive subordinates and encouraging their growth.

J. Sterling Livingston introduced the business community to the Pygmalion effect in a 1969 *Harvard Business Review* article in which he recounted the story of a Metropolitan Life Insurance Company district office. In that office, management grouped superior salesmen with highly productive assistant managers. That group became known as the "super staff." Average salesmen were grouped with average assistant managers, and low producers were grouped with low assistant managers. The superior and poor groups both performed according to management's expectation. The superior staff exceeded their production quota; the lower group's performance rate was lower than expected, and its attrition rate higher. The real change occurred with the "average" group. According to Livingston:

> Although the district manager expected only average performance from this group, its productivity increased significantly. This was because the assistant manager in charge of the group refused to believe that he was less capable than the manager of the "super-staff" or that the agents in the top group had any greater ability than the agents in his group. He insisted in discussions with his agents that every man in the middle group had greater potential than the men in the "super-staff," lacking only their years of experience in selling insurance. He stimulated his agents to accept the challenge of out-performing the "super-staff." As a result, in each year the middle group increased its productivity by a higher percentage than the "super-staff" did.[19]

The assistant manager became a positive Pygmalion, and his expectations of his staff produced an effective change in their behavior. But what about the poor producers? The unsuccessful salesmen had low self-images and sought to prevent further damage to their egos by avoiding situations where potential failure was possible. They made fewer calls and avoided trying to "close" sales where rejection might result: "Low expectations and damaged egos lead them to behave in a manner that increases the probability of failure, thereby fulfilling their manager's expectations."[20]

Livingston explains how the pattern of failure leads to a self-fulfilling prophecy:

> Not long ago, I studied the effectiveness of branch bank managers at a West Coast bank with over 500 branches. The managers who had their lending authority reduced because of high rates of loss became progressively less effective. To prevent further loss of authority, they turned to making only "safe" loans. This action resulted in losses of business to competing banks and a relative decline in both deposits and profits at their branches. Then, to reverse the decline in deposits and earnings, they often "reached" for loans and became almost irrational in their acceptance of questionable credit risks. Their actions were not so much a matter of poor judgment as an expression of their willingness to take desperate risks in the hope of being able to avoid further damage to their egos and to their careers.
>
> Thus, in response to the low expectations of their supervisors, who had reduced their lending authority, they behaved in a manner that led to larger credit losses.

They appeared to do what they believed they were expected to do, and their supervisors' expectations became self-fulfilling prophecies.[21]

Managers communicate both high and low expectations to their subordinates and do so through both verbal and nonverbal behavior. Even unintentional feelings are transmitted through facial expressions, eye contact (or lack of eye contact), tone of voice, physical touch, and body posture. In fact, the importance of the message is not so much in what is said as it is in how it is conveyed. Indifferent, "cold," or noncommital behavior by managers communicates low expectations and leads to low performance. Although most managers want to communicate positively, they are generally most effective in communicating low expectations.

While the Pygmalion effect occurs both positively and negatively at all levels of the organization, studies show that young workers who are new to a job are the ones most influenced by the process because they are eagerly ready to develop in the direction of an organization's expectations. Their first supervisor is likely to be the most influential person in their careers. Although the Pygmalion process can have positive application to all individuals in the organization, older employees with seniority often possess a hardened self-image, see themselves in light of their career record, and have set expectations and perceptions of management.

Receiving Verbal Praise

As one employee stated, "I never hear from my boss until I do something wrong, and then I really catch it." Ken Blanchard talks in his *One Minute Manager* books about managers who behave in that way. Those managers take potentially high-achieving employees and turn them into discouraged losers. In the first book of the series, Spencer Johnson shares three secrets of highly successful managers: one-minute goal setting, one-minute praising, and one-minute reprimands. He has found that most managers avoid the second stage of praising but are expert at reprimanding.[22] True praising takes place at many steps along the road to completing a project. A recent survey shows that the field of work greatly determines the likelihood of receiving praise.

TABLE 4.2 Frequency of Praise, by Field (percent)

	Professional	Sales	Assembly Line	Clerical
Verbal praise	57	20	40	60
Nothing	24	11	45	28
Bonus	10	21	12	7
Written note	10	6	2	6

Source: Adapted from "USA Today Poll: Looking at Your Jobs," *USA Today* (June 15, 1987), p. 2A.

ETHICS: RIGHT OR WRONG?

The Colombian Petrochemical Executive

Alberto Diaz doesn't look like a drug smuggler or terrorist. A petrochemical company executive who lives in South America, he has business degrees from both Harvard and Wharton. One thing about Mr. Diaz, however, encourages a questionable perception. That one thing is his Colombian passport. Because of his Colombian nationality, Mr. Diaz has been scrutinized by customs and immigration agents in airports on three continents. He has been interrogated in Tokyo, strip-searched for cocaine in Miami, and pulled over for questioning in Zurich, Switzerland.

Mr. Diaz represents thousands of modern-day travelers whose passports automatically trigger suspicion when they are outside their native country. He states, "My passport has become a symbol of a nation's crimes. Everywhere I travel, it casts doubt on me." In New York City federal agents treated him with disdain. "They saw my passport and started questioning me with an air of disgust. They poked around in my bags and examined my electric razor. I said, 'What are you doing? I didn't come here to offend you, and anyway, I'm leaving the country now!' "

From what does such action stem? The countries of Colombia, Peru, and Bolivia produce nearly all of the world's cocaine. On some days as many as twelve people, all from Andean countries, are arrested at Miami International Airport on suspicion of drug smuggling or money laundering. The same ritual occurs in Mexico, Italy, England, and around the world.

One U.S. Customs Service spokesman had the following to say: "Here in the southeast United States, Colombia is without a doubt a source country for illegal drugs. And because of that, individuals who are traveling from Colombia are scrutinized to a higher degree. We are very sensitive to being perceived as discriminatory toward any nationality or ethnic group, and because of that we take great efforts to make sure that we are not."

Mr. Diaz, however, would question the accuracy of that statement. Recently, as he arrived at the Miami airport, he overheard a uniformed agent say: "The little Colombians are arriving. We better search all the bags because certainly they have cocaine." The woman ahead of him heard the comment also, and it made her anxious. The agent said, "You look very nervous, do you have anything to declare?" They inspected her suitcase, hand luggage, and pocketbook, but they let her go when they found nothing. As Mr. Diaz stepped up, the agent could see that he was angry. The agent said, "You don't have to come here if you don't want to." Diaz retorted, "I suggest you go to Louisiana and Texas and talk to them. I'm purchasing over $5 million in equipment and engineering, and I understand they are currently in a recession." After the search, the agent let him pass.[23]

Case Questions

1. How does the concept of perception relate to this case?
2. What is the ethical issue in this case?
3. What ethical theory would you use to argue this case? Why?
4. What possible solutions are available for solving the case?
5. Which solution is the best?
6. If you were Alberto Diaz's manager, what would your instruction be?
7. If you were a manager of U.S. Customs and Immigration agents, what would you tell them?

Summary

Understanding perceptual behavior is the first step on the way to becoming an effective communicator. Because perception is defined as the way we take in information about our world, and because each person gathers information differently, problems arise in the way each individual perceives things and other people. Many of the differences among people can be explained by the programming that occurs during formative stages of childhood and adolescence. Other differences occur because wants and needs vary from person to person. Self-discovery and self-disclosure represent an effective way to correct perception-based problems. The Pygmalion effect, or self-fulfilling prophecy, can condition people to behave the way they are expected to, either positively or negatively.

Key Words

baby boomer employee/manager
cognitive dissonance
defensiveness
distorted information
halo effect
Johari window
levels of perception
lifestyle development
perception
projection
Pygmalion effect/self-fulfilling prophecy
self-concept
self-disclosure
self-discovery
stereotyping
traditional employee/manager
twentysomething employee/manager

Review Questions

1. Describe perception, and relate your description to a real-life situation (for example, you developed a first impression about someone but later changed it).
2. Clarify how Jan Carlzon's "moment of truth" ties in with a customer's perception of an employee.
3. Describe the four main problems that occur in perception, and use examples from your own life to illustrate. These may be instances when you allowed your perceptions to be guided by information given by others, or other examples.
4. What are the six items that explain "person perception"?
5. Describe how your attitudes and value system were shaped as a result of early programming events.
6. As a result of value programming, each individual is "different." Describe the variety of ways in which difference occurs.

7. Name and describe the three categories of perception types.
8. What are the three primary effects of perceptual errors?
9. List several ways in which negative or erroneous perceptions of others can be changed. Cite examples of times you have taken some of these steps in repairing relationships with others. Cite examples of times others have done the same with you.
10. What are the different indicators that have been proven to help determine who should receive overseas assignments?
11. Describe the Johari window and its four quadrants. Relate the window to relationships in your life at the present time. How would you like to see the quadrants changed?
12. Describe the principles of the Pygmalion effect. Has anyone acted as a Pygmalion for you? Describe that person's characteristics.

EXERCISES

1. Here's a nonthreatening exercise that can show you and your classmates how first impressions are formulated, how accurate they are, and how, with additional information, they can be changed. Team up with a classmate you have never met or talked with, and find a quiet place where you both can work. Complete the following first impression questionnaire. As you look at each other, write down answers about the other that you imagine to be true. Do not talk with your partner until you both have answered all questions. After you have finished writing, share your answers, and find out which person gave the most accurate responses.

First Impression Questionnaire

a. What is your partner's name? ____________
____

b. What city do you think he or she is from? ____________

c. What kind of car (specifically) do you think he or she drives? ____________

d. Is he or she married? ______ engaged? ______

e. How many children does he or she have? ____

f. What political party does he or she support?
____
____

g. What kind of music on tape or album do you think he or she would buy? ____________

h. What book (specifically) do you think he or she is now reading? ____________

i. What is his or her main hobby? ____________

j. What athletic activity do you think he or she enjoys? ____________

k. What does he or she enjoy doing in free time? ____________

l. What subject area do you think he or she is majoring in? ____________

m. What kind of job do you think he or she wants or has? ____________

n. What three adjectives would define how he or she feels right now? ____________

o. What three adjectives would best describe his or her personality? ____________

p. How many of the above questions did you answer correctly? ____________

2. First impressions either become lasting impressions or change as more information is gathered. On the following questionnaire, write the initials of people that you know who fit each category. Next to their initials, write words that describe the image you have of these people. You may want to do this exercise in small groups and share your impressions with others. It is not necessary to use names.

	Person's Initials	Person's Image to You
a. A person you really like who is the same age and sex as you		
b. A person you really like who is the same age but opposite sex as you		
c. A person you dislike		
d. Someone who openly accepts others		
e. Someone who rejects others		
f. A teacher you like		
g. A teacher you dislike		
h. A successful person		
i. An unsuccessful person		
j. An ethical person		
k. An unethical person		

3. Between the time you read this chapter and meet for your next class, note the different roles that you play and the specific expectations that people have of you as you play those roles. Use the following space to record your findings, and report them to class.

   a.

   b. Form a small group to talk about people who have been positive Pygmalions in your life. Use your answers to the following to help begin the discussion: "I have done my best work for teachers who ______________________."

4. In the space provided, draw two Johari windows. In the one above, draw quadrants that represent how you feel about your relationship with someone close to you (a friend, parent, etc.). In the one below, draw quadrants that represent how you think that they feel about their present relationship with you. Do the two windows match? How are they different? If a difference exists, should you and how can you make adjustments?

   a.

   b.

REFERENCES

1. Roger Ailes, "The First Seven Seconds," *Success* (November 1988), p. 18.
2. Jan Carlzon, "Moments of Truth," *Success* (May 1987), p. 40.
3. The term *significant emotional event* is used by Morris Massey in his video program, "What You Are Is Where You Were When." Those interested in additional research and investigation into the area of attitude and value programming can benefit from a reading of Massey's book, *The People Puzzle: Understanding Yourself and Others* (Reston, VA: Reston Publishing, 1979).
4. Demographic information used in these charts was pulled from several sources. The most valuable were Paul C. Murphy, *What's Happened . . . Since 1776* (Oklahoma City: Journal Record Publishing, 1980); John Naisbitt, *Megatrends* (New York: Warner Book, 1982); Alvan Toffler, *The Third Wave* (New York: William Morrow, 1980); David Wallechinsky and Irving Wallace, *The People's Almanac* (Garden City, N.Y.: Doubleday, 1975); *Chronicle of America* (Mount Kisco, NY: Chronicle Publications, 1989).
5. James S. Hirsch, "Older Workers Chafe Under Young Managers," *Wall Street Journal,* February 26, 1990, p. B1.
6. "Hard-Nosed Bosses Are on the Way Out," *USA Today,* February 13, 1991, p. 11A.
7. Dave Migdal, "Make Room for the Boomers," *Meetings and Conventions* (March 1990), pp. 26–32.
8. Adapted from: "Japan's New Face," *Inc* (October 1990), p. 106.
9. David M. Gross and Sophfronia Scott, "Proceeding with Caution," *Time* (July 16, 1990), pp. 56–62.
10. B. Rosen and T. Jerdee, "Influence of Sex-Role Stereotype on Personnel Decisions," *Journal of Applied Psychology,* 59 (1974), pp. 9–14.
11. J. E. Parson, T. Adler and J. L. Meese, "Sex Differences in Achievement: A Test of Alternative Theories," *Journal of Personality and Social Psychology,* 46 (1984), pp. 26–43.
12. Richard M. Steers, *Introduction to Organizational Behavior,* 4th ed. (New York: HarperCollins, 1991), pp. 184–85. As adapted from Patrick Wright, *On a Clear Day You Can See General Motors* (New York: Avon Books, 1979).
13. Adapted from Val J. Arnold, "The Six Types of Abrasive Managers," *National Business Employment Weekly* (December 27, 1987), p. 35.
14. Adapted from William Lobdell, "Who's Right for an Overseas Position?" *World Trade* (April/May 1990), pp. 20, 23–24, 26.
15. Story told by Roger A. Enrico, former chairman and CEO of Frito-Lay, Inc., at the undergraduate graduation ceremony, Cox School of Business, Southern Methodist University, Dallas, Texas, May 16, 1992.
16. Joseph Luft, *Group Processes: An Introduction to Group Dynamics* (Palo Alto, Calif.: Mayfield, 1984), pp. 11–12.
17. John Stewart, *Bridges Not Walls: A Book About Interpersonal Communication* (Reading, Mass.: Addison-Wesley, 1977), p. 209.
18. Robert Rosenthal's work on the Pygmalion effect is found in two separate publications: Robert Rosenthal, "The Pygmalion Effect Lives," *Psychology Today* (September 1973), and Robert Rosenthal and Lenore Jacobson, *Pygmalion in the Classroom* (New York: Holt, Rinehart and Winston, 1968).
19. J. Sterling Livingston, "Pygmalion in Management," *Harvard Business Review* (July/Aug. 1969), pp. 82–83.
20. Ibid., p. 83.
21. Ibid., pp. 83–84.
22. Ken Blanchard and Spencer Johnson, *The One-Minute Manager* (New York: Morrow, 1982).
23. Adapted from David L. Marcus, "Passport Pariahs," *Dallas Morning News,* November 19, 1991.

CHAPTER 5

Word Usage as a Potential Language Barrier

John Hancock was giving a speech outside Faneuil Hall in Boston. He had spent weeks preparing it and had high hopes of rousing the patriots' ire. A group of British soldiers stationed in Boston passed by as Hancock was speaking. Disapproving of the speech, they shouted "Fie, fie!" in defiance. But the Bostonians, who drop the *r* in their accent, thought that the soldiers were yelling "Fire, fire!" The patriots disbanded, the fire department rushed to the scene, and John Hancock's speech went—as it were—up in smoke!

As we read in the last chapter, the communicator's cognitive view of the world before, during, and after the act of communication influences what is communicated. People never come into direct contact with total reality because everything they experience is filtered through their nervous system. Word usage, like other experiences, influences meaning and consequently communication. As we will find in this chapter, language barriers must be overcome before we can achieve effective communication.

SOCIAL SEMANTICS DEFINED

Language—and its effect on perception, communication patterns, and interpersonal behavior—is an important facet of effective communication. Social semantics—as this field is called—evolved from research in four disciplines: science, linguistics, psychology, and sociology. *Science* contributed knowledge of the biological stimulus-response process and the physical sciences; *linguistics* contributed knowledge of how symbols are used as patterns of thought for languages; *psychology,* the mental process of using symbols; and *sociology,* the relationships between groups of people.

S. I. Hayakawa, long considered the contemporary father of general semantics, explains the field:

> The general semanticist . . . deals not only with words, assertions, and their referents in nature, but also with their effects on human behavior. For a general semanticist, communication is not merely words in proper order properly inflected (as for the grammarian) or assertions in proper relation to referents (as for the semanticist), but all these together, with the chain of "fact to nervous system to language to nervous system to action."[1]

Social semantics derived its conceptual core from general semantics and added relevant materials on the social consequences of semantic habits, particularly as those habits are displayed in human interaction. Social semantics also influences managerial behavior, and certain semantic tools are available for managers to use.

The word *semantics* comes from the Greek word *semantikos,* which means *significant.* Today it is defined as the study of meanings between *symbols* (words, signals, and so forth) and the objects that they refer to, or the *referents.* The term *general semantics* was coined in the early 1930s by Alfred Korzybski, whose major work was *Science and Sanity: An Introduction to Non-Aristotelian Systems and General Semantics.* Korzybski studied cognitive perception and in doing so explored new territory. The work of those he gathered around him (Wendell Johnson, Irving J. Lee, Stuart Chase, and

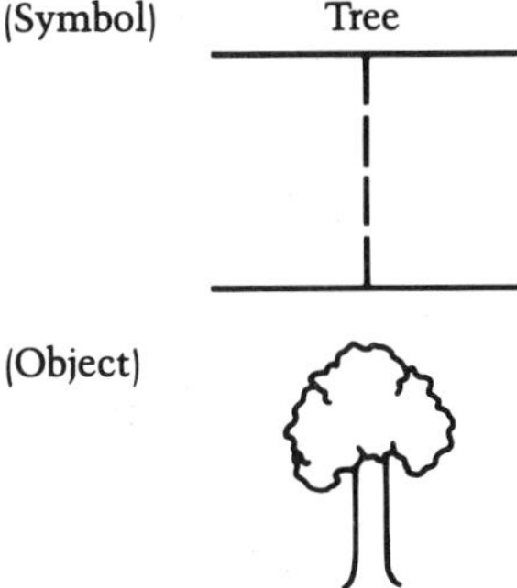

FIGURE 5.1 The Symbol and Its Referent

S. I. Hayakawa) has greatly advanced this field of study. Hayakawa and his writings, particularly his influential book *Language in Thought and Action,* gave the field credibility and introduced practical tools that are taught and used today.

The entire study of semantics is based on a relationship between a symbol and its referent (see Figure 5.1). The referent is the object, and the symbol is the word that represents the object. A gap always exists between the world of reality and the world of symbols. Before we can understand that gap, we must learn more about symbols.

The Symbol-Using Process

Human communication occurs in two ways: verbally and nonverbally. Nonverbal communication includes environmental signals, social symbols, human gestures, and signs that are used in the transfer of message and meaning. We examine the area of nonverbal communication in Chapter 6.

A profound difference is found between the use of *symbols* and *signs.* The human use of signs is evidence of the first manifestation of the mind. This is the beginning of intelligence and mentality, since signs are learned by trial and error. Animal mentality is built on sign usage because a sign is something to act on—a means to command action. Signs stand in a one-to-one relationship with an experience.

Animals have evolved in stature by using signs as signals. When their environments are small (a dog in a backyard), the learning is limited. When the environments are large (eagle on a mountaintop), the variety of available signals increases. Learning also increases as a result of long experience and reactions to many signs.

The uniqueness and superiority of human beings over other animals are attributed to their wider range of signals, greater power in integrating reflexes, and quicker learning by trial and error. Most of all, humans have the ability to use signs to indicate things and to represent them. With people, signs do not announce things; they are reminders. They serve not as vicarious stimuli to action but as references to things removed; they serve as symbols.

Signs do not limit people to using them in the here and now. They serve as symbols for the past, present, and future of something. A wet street is a *sign of rain,* the patter on the roof is a sign that *it is raining,* greenness of vegetation means that *it has rained.* These are all natural signs. The development of language documents a gradual accumulation and elaboration of verbal symbols.

The human mind can be compared to a telephone exchange. Messages can be relayed, answered by proxy, stored if the line is busy, sent over lines that didn't exist when first used, and even jotted down and kept if no desired recall number is given. Words are the plug put into the superswitch board that connects impressions of ideas, information already stored, and the total functioning of the entire system. Sometimes these lines become crossed in humorous or even disastrous ways.

A significant difference between humans and other animals is that humans can survive because they can think. Animals learn to respond to signs, but only humans can use symbols. Through the use of symbols (or the word-using communication skill process), people can learn from the past, adapt themselves to new and changing conditions, learn new skills, and create the type of living environment that they want. The symbol-using process makes us human.

In her autobiography, Helen Keller describes the point when she became "fully human." Born blind and deaf, she communicated as a child through grunts, groans, and growls. She had used signs, had formed associations, and had learned to identify people and places. But sign learning was finally eclipsed by the miracle of symbols and a word. The months of teaching paid off one day with the help of her tutor, Anne Sullivan.

As they walked down the path toward the well-house together, someone was drawing water. Anne placed Helen's hand under the waterspout. As the cool stream of water gushed over Helen's hand, Anne spelled into the other hand the word *water,* first slowly, then rapidly. Somehow the mystery of language was revealed to Helen. She understood that *w-a-t-e-r* meant the wonderful cool something that was flowing over her hand. Helen left the well-house eager to learn. Everything had a name, and each led her to a new thought and understanding.

Helen Keller's experience shows the difference between *signs* and *symbols.* Signs are things to act on; symbols are instruments of thought. *W-a-t-e-r* was a sign that previously could be acted on. But as a word it became an object that could be communicated, remembered, and referred to at a later date.

Aristotelian Logic

General semanticists started their study of language and meaning by rejecting three premises of Aristotle's framework on thought. Aristotle used a certain technique of definition—classification—that has three parts: identity, excluded middle, and contradiction. When Aristotle used his classification premise, he placed people in categories and grouped all people together. General semanticists classify by operational definition on a one-to-one basis, which makes classification more accurate.

1. *Law of identity.* According to Aristotle, "A is A." In application this could be stated, "Grass is green," or "Henry is dumb." But when we attempt to analyze what *dumb* means, we suddenly realize that we are referring to Henry's behavior. Consequently, Henry is not dumb; he does dumb things.
2. *Law of the excluded middle.* Aristotle stated this in a right or wrong, one or the other, dichotomy: "A is B or not B." Statements are often made in good/bad or true/false terms. For instance, some feel a person is either a conservative or a liberal, motivated or unmotivated. The world is not this black and white; it contains shades of gray.
3. *Law of contradiction.* This is stated as "A is not A." Things cannot be "good and bad" or "right and wrong" at the same time. Is the water hot or cold? If it is one, it cannot be the other. For Aristotle, language defined the world and the way of thinking. Our language influences our thinking and defines our world.

Linguists have shown that language is more than vocabulary and terminology or a way of identifying something as one thing or another. It reflects culture and gives insights into the world. Languages are different; they are not synonymous. A person who learns a language also absorbs certain predispositions of the culture that produced the language and certain ideas that can be verbalized. Each language has symbols that have been derived for its vocabulary. When people speak two or more languages, they therefore can experience more than one view of the world. Semanticists have established three basic steps for drawing order into the communication process:

1. Establish facts and characteristics of life of which communicators are aware.
2. Be aware of the language habits that represent reality inadequately.
3. Find specific, usable, and teachable devices that can make language habits produce a proper evaluation of what is being discussed.

Social semanticists have examined the way that language symbols are used and, as a result, have discovered several "bad" language habits. These habits have been analyzed and systematized along with techniques and devices for correcting them. Also, these bad language habits can be used to evaluate how we communicate with others.

Words as Symbols

The symbols most used by humans are words. Words serve as pointers, indicators, and representatives of things in the world. Communicating messages requires that we implement several different characteristics of words.

Basic Characteristics of Words

One word can have several meanings. There would be fewer communication problems if each word that we used had only one meaning, but that is not the case. The examples below give us ten different meanings for the word *case:*

1. Harold has a *case* of mononucleosis. (occurrence of disease)
2. The *case* Dr. Jones is working on concerns a small boy. (a client)
3. State the *case* for increasing corporate taxation. (a set of reasons for or against an action or thing)
4. Sue's a real *case.* (a peculiar or eccentric person)
5. Type the letter with upper *case* characters. (style of type)
6. The thieves *cased* the store before the break-in. (planned observation)
7. The engine is housed in the metal *casing.* (a cover or framework)
8. Please put the books in their proper book*case.* (wooden or metal structure)
9. I and you, respectively, are in the nominative and objective *case* in "I like you." (a linguistic pattern)
10. Please take the papers out of my brief*case.* (a carrying object)

One meaning can have two or more words. The cultural and social sources of language make it possible for one symbol to have more than one word that can describe it. Inuits have several words for that cold, wet substance that English-speaking people call snow. They use distinctive terms for falling snow, snow on the ground, snowdrifts, and so forth.

Ordinary conversations in business reflect that different people using different words can end up with the same meaning. Take the example of the manager speaking to a subordinate, "We're heading into system one. We have to have the design work and the infrastructural people aren't ready. I'm holding my breath until we get these two pages in to see what kind of linkages are being developed." While a third person might not understand this conversation, the meaning was clear to both of the individuals since they were intricately involved in the context.

As we will see in Chapter 7, a listener often has to go past the words of a conversation to decipher the intended meaning. An example comes from a Transportation Research Board meeting on airport capacity. The following are the actual words of one speaker: "Capacity is when, when we talk about capacity, capacity refers to a certain level of service. Capacity deterioration is when—capacity deterioration, as time goes by, has a time element."[2] What do you think listeners made of this statement?

Words sometimes have no meaning. While it doesn't often occur, a word can be coined before it has a verified referent in the outside world. Pluto, the ninth and farthest planet from the sun, was named before it was ever seen. Astronomers knew it was there because only the presence of another planet in that part of the solar system could provide an explanation for the orbits of other heavenly bodies.

There are technical and nontechnical words. According to Don Fabun, "There are believed to be 600,000 words in the English language today. The number is constantly growing, as we add new human experiences to be reported upon . . . or as we coin new expressions to describe present experiences. . . . The number of words . . . that an educated adult uses in daily conversation is about 2,000. Of these, the 500 most frequently used have 14,000 dictionary definitions."[3]

Technical words tend to have restricted and limited usage. Take, for example, the technical term *sodium chloride.* The definition of this technical term leaves little room for confusion. It is a colorless or white crystalline compound. But its nontechnical name, salt, can have many uses and meanings.

Words have regional meanings and usages. People who travel from place to place in the United States and around the world become accustomed to the different regional meanings and usages of words. In England a *tonic* is a bottle of pop and a *soft drink* is mineral water. In the United States we might use the words *pop* or *soft drink* for a refreshment or call it by its brand name. If you order a *soda* in New York, you'll get a soft drink, but in Ohio you would get an ice cream soda. The Amish refer to vacations by saying, "He's on his free and his free is almost all." In the North, candy on a stick is a *lollipop,* but in the South it's a *sucker.* At some hotels people want to carry your *suitcase,* or *grip,* which also is the term used to describe a person who handles sound equipment in movie productions.

Regionalisms have their original roots in the many local and social dialects of early British English. Founders of each American colony usually came from the same part of Great Britain and the same social class. Those adults and their children spoke a language that had the specific intonation and syntax of their native region. American speech in the original areas of colonization—New England, the central Atlantic states, the mid-Atlantic states, and the South—maintain many of these deviations. The West is a combination of the other four, with distinct variations still noticeable. One linguist expressed it this way, "Flying across [the United States], you can see variations in plowing patterns—spiral plowing, straight furrows. . . . Language is as regionally bound as these things."[4]

Here is a good example of the impact of regional influence on language. New Englanders call a freshwater stream a brook or river, and occasionally a creek (rhymes with *freak*). Many people in the North or Northwest refer to a freshwater stream as a creek (rhymes with *trick*), whereas in Indiana and Kentucky it is a branch. Louisianians label such bodies of water with the

Do We Speak the Same Language?
by Stanley Marcus

Every business or industry has its own language called trade jargon. The medical profession calls an emergency a "stat," and a journalist calls a typewritten page a "take." Usually, jargon is harmless enough, but in some cases it creates unnecessary confusion.

Outside the retail trade, for example, most people consider any large store that sells a wide variety of durable merchandise to be a department store. Not so. Large stores such as Neiman Marcus, I. Magnin and Saks Fifth Avenue, although they sell items from designer dresses to gourmet chocolates, are known in the trade as "specialty stores." The Limited and The Gap are classified as specialty "shops." To be department stores, they would also have to carry appliances and furniture, pots and pans.

Sears, J. C. Penney and Montgomery Ward stock the same classifications of merchandise as do the department stores, but they are known as "mass merchants." Some other large national chains such as K-Mart and Woolco are called "discounters." For clarification, I might suggest that specialty stores are apt to give the best service and best-edited selections; department stores, more amplified stocks; mass merchants, even fuller stocks, particularly in hard goods and in basic soft goods; and the discounters, the lowest prices, with a minimum of service.

Source: Reprinted from the *Dallas Morning News*, November 27, 1990.

French word *bayou*, and Southwesterners commonly use the Spanish word *arroyo*.[5]

An American businessman found that mistranslations can be very embarrassing. Shopping at Harrod's in London to purchase some casual clothing, he went to the men's furnishings department and "informed the salesman that he wished to purchase some clothing suitable for relaxing. Say, some casual sports pants, a matching vest, and for fun, a nice pair of suspenders." When the salesman returned he carried a pair of men's underpants, an undershirt, and a woman's garter belt.[6]

Though variations in vocabulary can be amusing, regional differences in pronunciation and syntax are not always accepted in the U.S. business world. The norm today is what we hear on the national news programs. This "standard broadcaster's language" has fixed grammatical rules that are taught by most English teachers and a correct pronunciation intoned over the national broadcast media. Small variations exist, but conformity has its rewards . . . especially if a manager has to communicate with employees from all over the world.

Words reflect the culture of an organization. Over many years a jargon language develops within many companies. Sometimes words are designed by managers as a method of linking members together and even describing their rank and status. At International Business Machines Corp. (IBM), a "hipo" is a fast-track employee with high potential; an "alpo" is an employee with low potential. At Disney World, jargon abounds and fits smoothly into the image of the theme-park's service. Employees are "on stage" while they are working and "backstage" before and after work and during their break time. A "bad Mickey" can be any negative action like trash on the sidewalk. A "good Mickey" is used as a means of encouragement for positive action. Loyal employees of McDonald's are said to have "ketchup in their veins," while a happy employee at Eastman Kodak would say that she worked for "the great yellow father."[7]

Words can carry the mission of doublespeak. The National Council of Teachers of English created the word *doublespeak* a few years ago for language that only pretends to communicate but in reality bamboozles, befuddles, and obfuscates true meaning. Their 1991 Doublespeak Award was given to the U.S. Department of Defense for its wording of events in the Persian Gulf war. The war was referred to as an "armed situation" instead of a war. U.S. bombing attacks against Iraq were "efforts," the airplanes were "weapons systems" or "force packages." Bombing missions were "sorties," pilots were "visiting a site," the buildings were "hard targets," and the people were "soft targets." The bombs, instead of killing, "degraded, neutralized, attrited, suppressed, eliminated, cleansed, sanitized, impacted, or took out targets." "Servicing the target" was killing the enemy, but ordinary people who were killed unintentionally were "collateral damage."[8]

The second-place award went to U.S. Representative Newt Gingrich, a Georgia Republican who headed a group of office-holding Republicans that printed *Language: A Key Mechanism of Control.* The publication advised Republicans to use "optimistic, positive governing words to characterize the Republican vision—words such as 'environment, peace, freedom, fair, flag, family and humane.'" For opponents the publication advised the use of words like "betray, sick, pathetic, lie, liberal, hypocrisy, permissive attitude and self-serving."[9]

Words carry emotional meaning. When words stir emotions, the logical thought process stops and the subjective emotional process takes over. Biases develop, and often the true meaning of words can never be known. While doublespeak often seems designed to prevent true communication, there are instances where it can remove some of the emotional sting from the action it symbolizes.

During the economic recession of 1992, corporate wordsmiths attempted to design positive words for rather depressing events—people losing their jobs. Companies recognized that the words like *discharged, fired,* and *terminated* were simplistic expressions of a complex process. The word *fired* implied that a person lost a job because of his or her poor performance. A *layoff* legally and psychologically implied a short-term condition. There was no single word describing those taking voluntary early retirement or severance offers. Instead of using negative words, companies coined the terms *rightsizing, downsizing, reshaping, repositioning, deselection process, reducing head count, reducing duplication,* and *focused reduction.*

The best companies communicate what they are doing in simple terms. The worst companies use trite expressions and euphemisms to describe their actions. One company talked about "reshaping" the organization and predicted that a "reduction in head count" might be a result. Top management stressed that reshaping did not always mean layoffs. Two days later, however, they "restructured" and several hundred employees lost their jobs.[10]

Sometimes companies and people use the wrong words, activating strong emotions in the receivers. Such an event occurred in 1988 when the Sony Corporation issued the Sony SLV-50 VCR as its entree into the VHS-format VCR market. The instruction manual gave "December 7, 1988" as the example to explain how the machine's date functions worked. That same date was also used in several drawings in the manual, including one that showed how to set the machine's timer. The date symbolically carried tremendous emotional messages to many Americans when they saw it. It was on December 7, 1941, that Japan bombed Pearl Harbor. While Sony apologized publically for the mistake, the emotional message reinforced a negative perception of Japan for many Americans.[11]

Words in Transition

Words are added. In this age of rapid change, new words are added on a regular basis. Each edition of *Webster's New World Dictionary* contains some 250 to 300 new words that are added to our language. While several find their way into dictionaries, some drop out, others change meaning.

Words are deleted. Some words remain in the dictionary even though they are rapidly becoming obsolete. One such word is *bamboozle,* meaning to deceive or cheat by trickery. The word began more than 200 years ago as a slang word and then became an informal word. It probably will be dropped soon because most people twenty years old and younger don't know its meaning. To linguistic purists the dropping of a word or the change in its meaning is regrettable, but language is in a constant state of flux: To think that words are static is like saying that life cannot change.

Words change meaning. As society changes, the words it uses and the meanings of words also change. The word *dynamite* has long been listed in the dictionary as a noun and defined in terms of a power explosion caused by compositions of chemicals and absorbant materials. But a few years ago the meaning expanded to be used as a slang adjective, as in "That was a dynamite presentation." Other terms like *genetic engineering, information processing,* and *citizen's band* are combinations of words that mean more than the sum of their parts.

Words as Barriers to Communication

Social semanticists have examined a variety of language problems and have devised solutions that make communication easier.

Allness

Chapter 4 noted that people perceive only a portion of what is going on in the world. Noted semanticists Irving J. Lee and Laura L. Lee used a diagram (see Figure 5.2) to illustrate how little of the available world we select and how much is omitted. The large circle contains everything that is available to discuss about any subject; the small circle contains the limited details that are selected for discussion. Whenever we talk, we always omit more than we can say. We also have the option of making factual statements or inferential statements.

The Vocabulary of the Computer

Nowhere is the example of words in transition as obvious as in the computer industry. As Devern Perry has noted, "The personal computer has added more new words and definitions to the English language than any other single invention in modern times. As new computer-related products were marketed, common words often seemed inappropriate to vendors and publicists; thus new words and terms were coined. Many of these words became part of computer users' everyday vocabularies. . . . others became common in everyday usage."[12]

Perry was so intrigued by this changing word usage that he conducted a study of computer-related words and whether they had entries in the ninth edition of *Webster's New Collegiate Dictionary* (1988). His survey of press releases and product announcements of computer-related companies produced a total of 887 unique words and terms that are associated with the computer. He found the following results:

- Only 182 of the words were in the dictionary with a computer-related definition.
- Another 108 words were in the dictionary without a specific computer-related definition. However, the definition was similar enough that the word could be defined with a computer-related meaning.
- Another 168 words were in the dictionary but did not carry a specific or similar computer-related definition or meaning.
- Of the 887 words, 429 did not have a dictionary entry.

Perry's findings indicate clearly the problems that we have in business when words are added, deleted or have their meanings changed. Of

(*continued*)

(continued)

the 887 words that Perry found, 597 (67.3 percent) are used regularly in computer-related product announcements and press releases, yet they carry no current dictionary definition. The following list provides examples from all four categories of his study.[13]

Dictionary Words with Computer Definitions	Dictionary Words with Definition Similar to a Computer Definition	Dictionary Words with No Computer Definition	Words with No Dictionary Entry
alphanumeric	adaptor	application	ANSI
ASCII	analog	archival	ATM
baud	component	backup	auto-configuration
coax	dedicated	benchmark	batch printing
compiler	driver	boot	baud rate
cursor	enhanced	bulletin board	boot up
debugging	execute	chip	CAD
down loading	glitches	compact	CD-ROM
electronic mail	icon	configured	command keys
encrypts	kerning	debugging	copy-protected
font	merges	default	data files
hardcopy	module	desktop	desktop publishing
input	overridden	digital	DIR
K (kilobytes)	parallel	download	disk drive
LCD	parameters	escape	DOS
menu	programmer	execution	fault tolerance
modem	query	footprint	file manager
mouse	remote	format	hard drive
on-line	security	header	high resolution
peripheral	start-up	host	hypercard
readout	super-conductors	keypad	laptop
scroll	tutorial	laser	log on
sort	upgrade	mailbox	motherboard
stored	user	node	online
		plot	

When people forget about the selection process, and that certain things are always omitted, they have what semanticists call "allness illness." These people think it is possible to know and say everything about something. Comments that reflect this position are "It all happened because . . ."; "The problem with that is . . ."; "I'll tell you exactly what is wrong. . . ." People

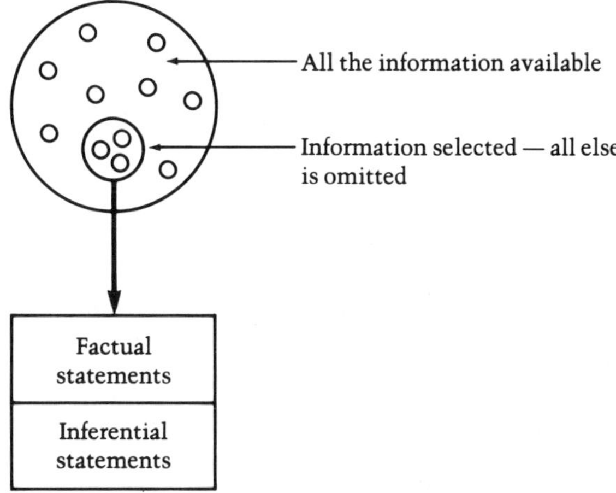

FIGURE 5.2 Selective Perception
Source: Irving J. Lee and Laura L. Lee, *Handling Barriers in Communication* (New York: Harper & Row, 1968), p. 136. Copyright © 1956, 1957 by Laura L. Lee. Used by permission of Harper & Row, Publishers, Inc.

who have the allness illness are intolerant of others' viewpoints; they think they know all there is to know about something; they ignore information that could change an outcome; they judge people by one small action or a particular event; and they will not listen to additional information that others want to give.

An example occurred in a recent factory accident in which four eyewitnesses saw an employee fall off a two-story scaffold. Each witness reported "factual" detail about the incident, yet all four gave different accounts. Even firsthand observation doesn't allow us to see and know *all* that there is to know. Statements that include the word *all* can often be wrong: "All minority members are lazy"; "All Southerners are rednecks"; "All managers cover their own hides before helping their subordinates."

People with allness problems tend to be close minded. Their use of language has locked them into a mindset that excludes and never considers many possibilities. Fish in marine life exhibits and elephants in circuses are programmed to be close minded. Humans often allow themselves to be programmed in the same way. A large fish in a natural environment eats small fish. But in commercial exhibits these fish are trained with a clear piece of glass between themselves and the small fish. When they attempt to eat the smaller fish they hit the glass and soon give up trying. Soon afterward they can be placed in the same aquarium with the smaller fish, and the earlier programming will prohibit their eating the small ones.

"Clean Up the Mess"

Cecil Mead was working hard at his station in the machine shop when his supervisor, Ed Jones, turned the corner and asked him to "clean up the area." "I'm trying to finish this piston job." "Finish it when you clean up," Ed said.

Thirty minutes later Ed came hurrying up to Cecil as he was cleaning grease off a machine. "What do you think you're doing, Mead?" "I'm doing what you told me—cleaning up." "My gosh, delivery is waiting for the piston to be bored, and you're wiping grease off that machine." "You told me to clean up this whole area," justified Cecil. "I only meant for you to sweep up some of the filings from the middle of the floor. I didn't say the 'whole' area. You could have swept up in a couple of minutes."

The Word Is Not the Thing

Semanticists use the word *bypassing* to distinguish miscommunication patterns that occur when senders and receivers miss each other with the meaning of words they use. Supervisors and subordinates can use the same words, but the intent of their communication can fail because they each attribute different meanings to the specific words. This was disastrously displayed in 1969 when four English Royal Air Force jets were involved in an accident. As the four pilots flew in formation, the rear pilot noticed a fire in the plane in front of him. He radioed, "You are on fire—eject!" Two of the first three pilots immediately ejected, and their planes crashed. Only one of the planes was on fire.

The problems in these examples occurred because the individuals involved thought that they knew what common words meant. They didn't stop to question whether the other person's meaning was different from their own.

The fallacy is, "Words have meaning." When a word leaves its symbolic use, it serves as the object. But words are not the object. Managers must remember that people have meanings; words don't. People use words in an attempt to convey ideas between themselves. Words are different than the things they represent; they are only symbols, arbitrarily chosen to stand in reference for certain things. Words are the product of our experiences (that's why the first automobile was called a "horseless carriage").

Managers can resolve the bypassing problem by concentrating on the person instead of the words, asking people what they mean when their statements are not completely clear, and realizing that a single word can mean numerous things:

- X is the Roman notation for ten.
- X is the mark of illiterate men.
- X is a ruler removed from the throne.
- X is a quantity wholly unknown.
- X may mean xenon, a furious gas.
- X is a ray of similar class.
- Xmas is Christmas, a season of bliss.
- X in a letter is good for a kiss.
- X is for Xerxes, a monarch renowned.
- X marks the spot where the body was found.

The misinterpretation of words is one of the biggest communication problems we encounter. The following real-life example illustrates the importance of realizing that the meaning of words is in people and not the words themselves. People are the containers of meaning, and words only direct others to what we mean.

A Japanese word, *mokusatsum,* may have changed all our lives. It has two meanings: (1) to ignore, (2) to refrain from comment. The release of a press statement using the second meaning in July, 1945, might have ended the war then. The Emperor was ready to end it, and had the power to do so. The cabinet was preparing to accede to the Potsdam ultimatum of the Allies—surrender or be crushed—but wanted a little more time to discuss the terms. A press release was prepared announcing a policy of *mokusatsum,* with the *no comment* implication. But it got on the foreign wires with the *ignore* implication through a mix-up in translation: "The cabinet *ignores* the demand to surrender." To recall the release would have entailed an unthinkable loss of face. Had the intended meaning been publicized, the cabinet might have backed up the Emperor's decision to surrender. In which event, there might have been no atomic bombs over Hiroshima and Nagasaki, no Russian armies in Manchuria, no Korean war to follow. The lives of tens of thousands of Japanese and American boys might have been saved. One word, misinterpreted.[14]

Incompleteness

Words are in a sense the map of the territory that we wish to share with others. A geographical map serves as a representation of a territory, with many details and facts omitted or distorted. When you compare major landmarks to the map that represents them, they fail to agree in size. On a map a river is a blue line no wider than the hatched black lines of a railroad track. Words, likewise, fail to accurately represent objects, events, feelings, and ideas. It is impossible, in fact, to say everything about anything. We can describe much, but we cannot exhaust all of the events and their minute particularities.

The semanticist would tell us to say, "The map is not the thing." Think for a moment about a map for your city. It probably shows streets, blocks, and outlines of parks. It does not give the position of houses, trees, cars, gravel on streets, or potholes in the road. It is impossible to develop a map that can tell everything about your city.

Just as a map cannot give a truly exhaustive view of a city, language does not give a complete view of reality. As individuals we can never see all there is about our city, and so we cannot describe it as it is but only as we perceive it. Since language and reality never conform, we must mentally practice using *etc.:* There is always more that can be said about anything.

Language barriers arise when we become *intentionally* instead of *extensionally* oriented. People who are intentionally oriented are more absorbed in their own subjective maps of the territory than they are in the territory itself. Intentional orientation is based on personal perception and definition instead of real-world observation. When people are extensionally oriented, they first perceive and inspect the territory, and then they construct verbal maps that correspond to the territory. Verification of facts is important to the extensional person. People who practice this orientation have less tendency to take what others say for granted. When people become extensional in their reactions, they look at and observe the territory and life facts first. Then they construct maps (words) that closely correspond to those facts. Look at an object, close your eyes, and then describe the object. That is intentional meaning. Now put a hand over your mouth and point to the object. That is extensional meaning.

Levels of Abstraction

The human nervous system is incapable of getting all possible details on or about any item. We must abstract some details and omit an infinite number of others. The words we use on various levels of abstraction depend on how easily we can see, understand, and then communicate about the object. A typical ladder of abstraction shows the different levels that emerge as we move from specific details to general information.

Managers must be conscious of abstracting, since any given object or event has multiple levels of meaning. When communicating with others, the manager must mentally define from what abstract level the other person is speaking.

Inference Versus Facts

Often in the process of observing the world we draw inferences before we have all the necessary facts. Inferences are constructed so quickly that we seldom reflect on whether they truthfully represent an object or represent it as we would like for it to be.

Read the following case about Joe Zoe, and then answer the questions following the case without referring back to the story. If the answer is true as it relates to the story, circle *T;* if false, check *F;* if you don't know an answer or need more information, check *?*.

A man and wife had their small house thoroughly redecorated—walls, windows, woodwork. At 5 P.M. the decorators left. The man and wife cleaned up the house, locked up their cabinet that contained silverware, and then went to bed. The next morning, they found a window open, the cabinet open, and all the silverware missing. The police were called and subsequently found a set of fingerprints on the window sill. The fingerprints were sent to police headquarters for identification. A reply from headquarters said that the fingerprints on the window sill exactly matched those of a notorious criminal named Joe Zoe.[15]

Questions About the Story

1. The silverware was stolen. T F ?
2. Joe Zoe took the silverware. T F ?
3. Between the time the house was painted and the window found open, Joe Zoe was in the house. T F ?
4. Joe Zoe left his fingerprints on the window sill. T F ?

Declarative statements of this nature are made on a regular basis in business: "She didn't return the file"; "He didn't complete the work because he's lazy"; "If you would just listen to me, you would understand me." These sentences give no grammatical indication of whether they are factual or inferred. If we do not have the facts to prove these allegations, and we infer the judgment instead, disagreements in communication will follow. There are six basic ways in which we can distinguish between statements of fact and statements of inference:[16]

Factual Statement	*Inference Statement*
1. Made *following* firsthand experience	1. Made *anytime*—before, during, or after experience
2. Made by the observer	2. Made by anyone
3. Must be limited to what one experienced	3. Can go way beyond what is experienced
4. Statements of fact are limited by experience	4. Statements of inference about experience are unlimited
5. Approaches maximum certainty	5. Approaches only a degree of probability
6. Calls for agreement with those involved in the experience	6. Calls forth disagreement with those involved in the experience

In light of the above information, do you want to change your mind on any of the four questions about the Joe Zoe case? Each of the questions should have been answered with a question mark. They could be true or they could be false; but you did not have enough factual information to answer them. Incidentally, this case is based on the famous Marlboro Jewel Case of Scotland Yard. It is regularly used in police training to make officers sensitive to gathering all facts and not jumping to conclusions. When the crime was finally solved, police found that two criminals were involved. Joe Zoe's partner killed him, cut off his hand, committed the theft, and left Joe Zoe's fingerprints at the scene of the crime.

The Shipping Department Case

Assume that you are a new plant manager touring the factory and you pass by the Shipping Department. As you walk by, you see the scene shown in Fig. 5.3. List both the factual and inferential statements you can make about the picture. After you have recorded several statements, discuss the scene and statements with your classmates.

FIGURE 5.3
Source: Irving J. Lee and Laura L. Lee, *Handling Barriers in Communication* (New York: Harper & Row, 1968), p. 15. Copyright © 1956, 1957 by Laura L. Lee. Used by permission of Harper & Row, Publishers, Inc.

Factual Statements	**Inferential Statements**
______________________	______________________
______________________	______________________
______________________	______________________
______________________	______________________

The Shipping Department Case Facts

It may interest you to know the actual details of this case. It's something that really happened in a shipping department. The boy's job was to pack straw in and around some castings to prevent breakage during shipment. One day a new plant superintendent was making a tour of the plant. He observed the young boy whittling on a stick. The superintendent immediately walked up to the boy and fired him. The *inference* was that the boy was wasting time whittling on the job. The *fact* was that the boy had discovered he could do a better job of packing if he tamped the straw down with a sharp stick. And that's what he was doing—sharpening a stick to use for the tamping.[17]

Some inferential statements you could make are: "The young man is whittling wood and not working"; "The employee is lazy"; "The man must not have much to do." We can make several factual statements: "The man is sitting on a box"; "He is whittling wood"; "Boxes are around him"; "A truck is pictured in the doorway"; "The word *straw* is on the barrel."

To avoid drawing inferences, managers should:

1. Realize that all statements about the future are inferential; anything that deals with hopes, predictions, plans, or prophecy is an inference.
2. Realize that anything that cannot be observed—attitudes and motives of others and information we hear secondhand, even though that information may be a fact for the person telling us—is an inference.
3. Realize that factual statements are based on what we see, know, or experience with all our senses.
4. Ask for more data, if we need it to make factual statements.
5. Label our inferences as such, and try to get other people to do the same.

Language Barriers Can Hamper the Global Manager

Thus far, this chapter has examined language from the concept of social semantics and its influence on human interaction and managerial behavior. The discussion has mostly been limited to the American culture. But in our examination of how a manager must effectively deal with global communication issues, the problem of language as a cultural barrier arises. The following section examines this problem from three directions: language as part of the diversity in the American workplace, learning to speak a foreign language, and using translation software.

The Diverse American Workforce

A demographic examination of the American workforce shows that it is rapidly becoming culturally diverse. This will present challenges to managers in the future. Among the largest challenges is the language problem. Jolie Solomon estimates that between now and the year 2000, 88 percent of the workforce growth will come from women, African Americans, and Hispanic or Asian groups. She also estimated that 22 percent of these individuals will be immigrants. In the past, most companies never worried about language issues. It was assumed that English was the language of the workplace. In the future those companies will find that their available labor pool speaks less English than before.

Solomon discussed this new issue in a *Wall Street Journal* article:

> Language is becoming a sticky issue in the workplace. As jobs grow more complex and immigrants make up a rising share of the work force, employers are grappling with some basic questions: Should they hire people with limited English skills? Even if employees speak English when necessary, what happens when they turn to their native tongue among themselves—especially in front of supervisors or customers? And, in a new twist, should employers pay workers a premium if they use language skills with foreign-born customers?[18]

In the past history of American industry, the work that immigrants such as Poles, Greeks, and Hispanics performed required little verbal communication. If a supervisor needed to convey a message, someone was always available to interpret. Today in larger companies most jobs require lots of verbal communication, tighter time requirements, and less supervisor-employee contact. An example comes from a Motorola plant that produces circuit boards. A few years ago, it took several days to manufacture and fill an order. Employees were given assignments and they completed their work in a noncommunicative manner. Today a similar order requires employees to read blueprints and computer instructions individually and to communicate with other employees interpersonally, electronically, and in small groups—and the order is filled in a matter of hours.[19]

Smaller companies, with fewer complex jobs and less diverse workforces, can often accommodate bilingual issues. Pace Foods, Inc. in San Antonio, Texas employs 250 people. Hispanics make up 35 percent of the workforce. Staff meetings are conducted bilingually, and employee handbooks are printed in both English and Spanish.[20]

ETHICS: RIGHT OR WRONG?

The Bilingual Employee

Minda Aguimaldo, a Filipino by birth, had been a nurse in a Los Angeles hospital for ten years. Sara James had been Minda's supervisor at the hospital for one month when she issued a new rule. The rule forbade all the Filipino nurses in Sara's ward from speaking their native Tagalog language. The ban was all-inclusive: in front of patients, in hallways, in the lounges at lunch and on breaks, and even on the telephone.

The ban prompted outrage and concern among minority employees. Minda and the other Filipino nurses wondered why the ban had suddenly been created. After all, the hospital had never before objected to the bilingual nurses speaking in their native tongue and Minda's previous supervisors had never voiced concern. The nurses stressed that Tagalog had never been spoken in front of patients since that was obviously inappropriate. Minda contended that she and her colleagues were more comfortable together at their break time speaking in their native language. Minda also had an elderly mother at home who spoke no English, only Tagalog. Consequently there were times that using Tagalog on the phone was mandatory.

Ms. James responded to the protest by saying that since English was the language used in all areas of the hospital, the use of any other language was simply inappropriate . . . especially since each nurse could speak English well. Minda believed there was more to the ruling. This was supported when she found, in the minutes of a staff meeting, that the issue had been discussed. Ms. James had said, "Use of the Filipino language will not be tolerated. If it happens again, let the head of hospital personnel know." Ms. James denied that such a statement had been made.

The group of Filipino nurses also gathered other comments that told them that Ms. James had passed by a table in the lounge during the nurses' break time and had heard them speaking a foreign language. Then they looked at her, and one of them said something she did not understand. She thought they were swearing at her and she wanted to "get the profanities and cussing eliminated." She also felt that they were trying to hide something and were taking advantage of her because she did not understand the language. She had commented to one of her colleagues, "How can we have teamwork in our division if we all speak a different language? It just isn't right."

Elvia Flores, who is Hispanic and head of the hospital nursing staff, said that she did not approve of the ban. "We should be able to speak whatever," she said. "You cannot say to a person, 'You cannot speak your native language.' That makes very good employees feel like fugitives. I know how they feel because when I came to this country I didn't say anything in school for six years. I was afraid to open my mouth, because I knew that what came out of my mouth would be

Spanish. I remember hiding behind the water fountain or going to the restroom to speak Spanish."

Three days after the ban Minda and the other Filipino nurses were talking about filing a lawsuit against the hospital. Ms. Flores scheduled an immediate meeting with Ms. James and other hospital administrators.

Case Discussion Questions

1. What is the ethical issue in this case?
2. What are the rights of Minda and the other nurses? What rights does the hospital have in relation to employee language?
3. What is your evaluation of how Sara James handled her supervisory role in this case?
4. What alternatives are available for solving the problem in this case?
5. What are the ethical considerations for each of the alternatives?
6. What should the hospital do? What should Minda and the other nurses do?
7. How can the hospital ensure that a situation like this does not happen again?

The Need to Know and Speak Foreign Languages

In the global marketplace one contract can mean the difference between a company's success and survival. The importance of such endeavors means that managers have to be able to communicate with foreign business representatives in negotiating sessions. The smallest of mistakes can be critical.

Traditionally English has been the language of international commerce for over a half century, replacing French and German. This circumstance has forced businesspeople from other countries to learn English. For instance, in Japan students nationwide are required to study English beginning at the seventh-grade level. The results for Japan have been successful. While Japanese business people may not feel comfortable speaking English in important sessions, they arrive in the United States and can travel and function with only minor problems. They can usually read faxes and written reports without any trouble.

Americans, however, have had an insular attitude about learning and comprehending other languages. Often they arrive in a country without being able to say "hello" or order a taxi. Even in the larger international cities, an American businessperson is not guaranteed to be able to find bilingual signs, menus, or translators. "According to Japan's international phone carrier KDD, 40 percent of foreign businesspeople report difficulty in calling in English to make appointments."[21]

Currently only 10 percent of Americans speak a foreign language. Until a few years ago, the only Americans who could speak fluent foreign languages were military decoders and missionaries. One manager points out the danger of this mindset: "(For years we managed in English.) Our message became very diluted. . . . we had to talk very slowly and repeat ourselves a lot. Subtleties got lost. . . . (so did contracts.)"[22] U.S. companies also virtually ignored any foreign language skills their employees possessed. An employee was seldom rewarded for learning a language, and most firms were uninterested in paying for language lessons.

As the global market started developing in the 1980s, a demand was established for Americans who were bilingual. As a result, more and more executives and managers learned Japanese, Spanish, Russian, and other languages. These smart communicators realized that a cheerful *ohayo gozaimasu* (good morning) or *gochisosama deshita* (thank you for the delicious meal), no matter how bad the accent, can help smooth business relationships in Japan. The same is true for every other country. Many Americans who become fluent in a foreign language find it is most useful during the informal social times and during meals. During negotiations, they are more cautious of using the language since they have found that some managers in other countries don't appreciate foreigners who speak their native tongue. As one New York manager put it, "If I speak Japanese, I become an insider, which makes me a threat." But the language gives them a terrific advantage as they listen to what their foreign counterparts are saying in their own language.[23]

Today managers around the world who are training for the global marketplace realize the necessity to learn languages. In Luxembourg, 25 percent of the population is quadrilingual. Japan's economic impact on foreign trade has helped launch a drive in other countries to learn Japanese. The Japanese Language Institute of the Japan Foundation "recently put the number of students studying Japanese at close to a million; the reality is probably at least double that. The great majority of these linguistic pioneers are South Korean (46 percent) and Chinese (29 percent). Among Westerners, Australians are out in front (6 percent), ranking much higher in absolute and per capita terms than Americans or Western Europeans (3 percent and 2 percent, respectively)."[24]

The sacrifice that some are making to learn a language comes from the example of a Russian businessman. He is vice director of a company that trades with Italy, South Korea, and the United States. After two years in business he realized that he could not "be deaf and dumb any more, thus, I began the study of English." The company could afford to hire ten translators, but this person wanted to be the first to read fax messages coming from abroad and to be able to discuss items "with foreign partners *tête-a tête.*" Each morning at 6:45 A.M. his English tutor arrives at his house for a 90-minute lesson that includes phonetics, grammar, and business correspondence. The cost for the lessons is 70 rubles an hour, inexpensive by U.S. standards but enormous in Russia. But upon negotiating his first sale, in English, with a foreign partner, he knew it was worth the cost. "It was a miracle. We understood each other perfectly well."[25]

TRANSLATION AND TRANSLATION SOFTWARE

Companies that do not have bilingual employees require some help in translation. Hiring a translator for written work, or an interpreter for conversations, is a small price to pay for improved understanding between businesspeople who do not speak the same language. The best translators and interpreters realize that translation takes place at both a verbal and cultural level.

Experts in a language understand things like idiomatic expressions, word order, and verb tense. This places important grammatical demands on anyone who is attempting to interpret a language accurately. The importance becomes clear in a typical interpersonal example. An English businesswoman had a French husband with whom she spoke French at home. She complained that she cold never tell her husband, "I went out with a friend for a drink last night," without specifying the sex of the friend. French constraints require that a gender be chosen for every noun, whereas English does not. According to one linguistic expert, "such grammatical demands can have domestic fallout. The lies and ambiguities of one language are not those of another."[26]

Cultural factors are just as critical for interpreters. When American Express was making its entrance into the former Soviet market, it considered using literal translations of its U.S. advertising icons like "privileges" and "Don't leave home without it," until they were told by experts that the Soviets did not have credit card privileges and interpreted the other statements differently. Another example shows how much research must be conducted on the semantics of foreign words before each business item is written, or each presentation made. An American firm was proposing a joint venture with a Russian company. After making a presentation, the Russian negotiators left the room with their lawyer. When they returned, they asked a question about depreciation. In their minds the equipment proposed in the venture could last 100 years. They could not understand why it was to be "depreciated" over a mere five-year period. "That is standard practice in the United States," was the American's reply. The Russian lawyer retorted, "Is this the United States?" At that moment the Americans became aware that the Russians did not understand that the concept of depreciation was an invention of the U.S. tax codes. The Americans mistakenly communicated "what" their company did rather than telling "why" they did it. Luckily, the American's professional interpreter was able to explain the concept in a manner that the Russians could understand. While the interpreter cost the Americans some money, she was able to secure the venture.[27]

When businesses work with regular documents that must be translated into foreign languages, they often look for translation software instead of permanent or part-time translators. Rosemount, Inc. is a Burnsville, Minnesota manufacturer of process control equipment for liquids, ranging from peanut butter to petroleum. Each year they translate more than 4,000 pages of technical information, including illustrations and tables, into French, Russian, and German. They pay human translators for postediting but rely on translation software for the standard work. There are several advantages. First, the documentation does not have to be reformated following each translation. Second, a comprehensive custom dictionary of terms and phrases can be developed. This means that the computer will consistently use the same term, whereas a person may not remember the specific way information was phrased several months earlier. The third advantage is cost. Human translation cost up to $75 per page, while a computer translation averages $10 a page.[28] Translation software has a drawback, however. No translation program is 100 percent accurate. Sometimes errors are made in the idiomatic expressions, word order, verb tense, and in highly technical or legal subject matter.[29] The wise business manager will always have a human translator check every computer translation for accuracy.

SUMMARY

Language affects perception, communication patterns, and interpersonal behavior. This process is called social semantics and is the study of meanings between symbols and their referents.

Word usage is the foundation for accurate communication because words are the primary symbols used by man. Each word has basic, complex characteristics that cause some words to have several meanings or two or more words to have one meaning. Some words have no meaning at all. There are technical and nontechnical words and applications for words and specific regional connotations for words.

Major communication conflicts can result from the way we use words. Conflict is frequently the result when people assume that a word can say all there is to say about an object, or when people associate the word and the thing that word represents as being one and the same. A word in itself is incomplete. The meanings of messages are shared by two or more people when words are added to other words and framed within a context.

Many levels of meanings are available for any particular object. Managers who learn to properly abstract items can use words to approximate an accurate description of objects. Word usage is a particular problem when we infer meaning from objects, events, and statements instead of obtaining all the necessary facts and then interpreting them.

Managers should not take words and the symbolic process for granted. Communication will be accurate only when it is preceded by a great deal of thought and reflection.

KEY WORDS

abstraction
allness
Aristotelian logic
bypassing
doublespeak
extensional orientation
fact
inference
intentional orientation
regionalism
semantics
sign
social semantics
symbol
translation

REVIEW QUESTIONS

1. What is the difference between general semantics and social semantics?
2. What is the precise difference between symbols and signs, and what importance do both play in human communication?
3. Describe the three parts of Aristotelian logic and how they affect language.
4. Describe with examples the six basic characteristics of words.
5. What is the difference between technical and nontechnical words?
6. How does regionalism impact language?
7. Describe how words are constantly in transition.
8. How has the computer impacted word change?
9. What are the five ways that words serve as barriers to communication?
10. Often in arguments and general statements, we base opinions on inferences instead of facts. Give an example of how this occurs and how it can be prevented.
11. Cite a personal example of the "allness" problem and how it interferes with communication.
12. What does it mean when we contend that "the word is not the thing"? How can a person prevent such misconceptions from occurring?
13. How can words hamper the global manager?
14. Describe the impact of word usage on the diversity of the American workforce.
15. Describe the important problems associated with foreign languages and translation in the business world.

EXERCISES

1. In your public or school library conduct a search for material that describes linguistic and semantic problems. The information may be found in stories or articles like the ones used in this chapter or in cartoons. Take the material to your next class, and share it with the instructor and your classmates.
2. Think for a few minutes about the problems that sometimes develop because of word usage or the assumed meaning of the words. Share results of the following instructions with your instructor and classmates.
   - Make a list of problem situations you have been in where misunderstanding occurred because there were two words with one meaning or two meanings for one word.
   - Give some examples where the use of technical words caused problems in understanding something about people.
   - In your travels or experiences you have probably noticed regional differences in word usage. Cite some examples of regional words that can cause misunderstanding.
3. While you are at the library, look up the yearbooks for several encyclopedias. Those yearbooks often list new words that have recently been added to various dictionaries. Make a list of several words that have only recently been officially recognized as dictionary words. Share this information with your instructor and classmates.
4. Collect advertisements that either exhibit word perception problems or that use word perception as an attraction. Share this information with your instructor and classmates.
5. Make a list of technical or jargon words that are used in an activity or job you are associated with. The words should pertain solely to the situation or event and should not be used in everyday conversation. Share the list with your instructor and classmates.

REFERENCES

1. Anatol Rapoport, "What Is Semantics?" in *Et cetera,* 10, 1 (March 1953), International Society for General Semantics. Reprinted by permission.
2. E. Thomas McClanahan, "Typical Talk in the Nation's Capital Speaks Volumes," *Kansas City Star,* October 26, 1990.
3. Don Fabun, *Communication: The Transfer of Meaning* (Beverly Hills, Calif.: Glenco Press, 1968), p. 27.
4. Marilyn B. Bowden, "A Manner of Speaking," *Sky* (July 1991), p. 66.
5. Ibid.
6. Stanley Marcus, "Do We Speak the Same Language?" *Dallas Morning News,* November 27, 1990.
7. Michael W. Miller, "At Many Firms, Employees Speak a Language That's All Their Own," *Wall Street Journal,* December 29, 1987.
8. Jack Anderson, "The Language of Battle Made Simple," *Dallas Morning News,* February 23, 1991.
9. "War's Gobbledygook Gets Dubious Honor," *Dallas Morning News,* November 23, 1991.
10. Alan Gathright, "Doublespeak Becomes a Firing Defense," *Dallas Morning News,* February 2, 1992.
11. David Everett, "Pearl Harbor Day Used in Sony VCR Instructions," *Dallas Morning News,* March 31, 1990.
12. Devern Perry, "The Vocabulary of the Computer," a study conducted through the Information Management Department of Brigham Young University, January 1990.
13. Ibid.
14. Stuart Chase, "Everybody's Talking," in *Power of Words* (New York: Harcourt, Brace & Co., 1953), pp. 4–5.
15. Irving J. Lee and Laura L. Lee, *Handling Barriers in Communication* (New York: Harper & Row, 1957), p. 11. Copyright © 1956, by Laura L. Lee.
16. Ibid., p. 13.
17. Ibid., p. 15.
18. Jolie Solomon, "Firms Grapple with Language Barriers," *Wall Street Journal,* November 7, 1989.
19. Ibid.
20. Ibid.
21. Yukiko Inoue, "The Business of Language," *Business Tokyo* (May 1992), p. 19.
22. Laura Stanley, "Access Japan: The Bilingual Company," *Business Tokyo* (May 1992), p. 41.
23. Inoue, "Business of Language," p. 21.
24. Ibid., p. 19.
25. Alexander Tepliouk, "Russians Batter Language Barriers," *Dallas Morning News,* May 2, 1992.
26. Susan Ludmer-Gliebe, "Translation: Reshaping Language," *Ann Arbor News,* March 29, 1989.
27. John Freivalds, "Soviet Word Games: More than Semantics at Stake," *World Trade* (June/July 1990), p. 26.
28. Eric J. Adams, "Come Again?" *World Trade* (April 1992), pp. 44, 46.
29. Rosalind Resnick, "Language Liberators," *International Business* (December 1991), p. 61.

CHAPTER 6

NONVERBAL COMMUNICATION: AUGMENTING OR CONTRADICTING THE VERBAL MESSAGE

Early in the 1992 U.S. presidential campaign, George Bush's advisors grimaced as he left the Oval Office for a tour of the displays at the National Grocers Association convention. When he spotted some high-tech supermarket checkout equipment, he pointed and acted like a child who had just spotted a new toy. The impression most bystanders received was that he had never seen the likes of such dazzling wonders. His embarrassed advisors quickly rushed him off and could be heard to whisper, "That stuff has been standard equipment for more than a decade."[1] The message from that nonverbal encounter was supported by others during that campaign. In total they carried the thought that the president was out of touch with reality. The impression contributed to the president's defeat.

NONVERBAL COMMUNICATION DEFINED

If someone asked you to list the various ways that a manager communicates, you would probably start your list with several acts associated with words: listening, talking, and writing. These acts are considered *verbal* because they use verbal symbols, or words that stand in reference for facts, ideas, and things. Another form of communication is more predominant than verbal, however.

Nonverbal communication refers to human action and behavior and the corresponding meaning that is attached to behavior. A subordinate may want to say, "Boss, I'm really frustrated and I'd like to talk to you." If the words are hard to express, however, the person will try to send the message by way of gestures, facial expressions, vocal pauses, and body movement. Much nonverbal communication is unconscious or subconscious and can represent a major portion of our mental capacity: We send, receive, and decipher thousands of bits of nonverbal information every day.

The Relationship Between Verbal and Nonverbal Communication

When we communicate with other people, we usually use words. Those words, however, are spoken within a nonverbal context that is more meaningful than mere words alone. Nonverbal behavior relates to verbal behavior in several ways:

1. *Repeating.* A customer asks where an item is located in the store. The employee says, "Aisle 3," and also *points* in that direction.
2. *Contradicting.* Two employees are having a conflict. One says, "I wish you weren't angry." The other quickly responds, "I'm *not* angry," in a loud voice with piercing eyes, a set jaw, and clenched hands.
3. *Complimenting.* A manager praises an employee's performance during an awards ceremony. As the employee walks forward, the manager steps away from the podium, greets the person with a big hug and a warm smile, and says, "I appreciate you and the contribution you have made."
4. *Substituting.* A cashier hurriedly closes a transaction by pushing money into your hand and saying, "Thank you, have a nice day." You don't believe that the person cares whether you have a nice day or not. You say nothing, however, but beam at the person with a sarcastic look that says, "I'm sure you don't mean that."
5. *Accenting.* A sales manager reinforces his positive statements during a motivational talk by pounding the table while telling the sales team, "Let's get out there and do it!"

Why Study Nonverbal Communication?

Although numerous research projects have examined the communication process, no simple formula has been developed for interpreting the specific communicative meaning of behavior. Each act must be examined within its setting and culture. Examining nonverbal communication from a managerial perspective is important for at least six reasons:

1. *No universal communication messages exist.* Each message is created by a unique person, in a unique setting, within a unique cultural background. The more we observe the actions and words of others, the better able we are to understand the messages being sent.
2. *We draw hasty conclusions about the messages sent by others.* As soon as verbal and nonverbal messages are sent, our minds rapidly start the process of deciphering the intended meaning. Without some prior knowledge of nonverbal messages, we draw hasty, and often improper, conclusions.
3. *We grow insensitive to the behavior of others.* When we work side by side with people for a long time, we tend to become insensitive to their words and actions. We ignore messages that are communicated with emotion or feeling. By observing nonverbal behavior, we heighten our sensitivity to others and enrich the communication procedure.
4. *Nonverbal messages are stronger than verbal ones.* When verbal and nonverbal messages clash, the nonverbal is most often accepted. As the words from an old song say, "Your lips are saying no-no, but there's yes-yes in your eyes." Posture, facial expressions, and vocal utterances can outweigh words and help the observer determine the true meaning of a message.
5. *Nonverbal messages clarify verbal messages.* Such things as gestures, movement, and demonstrations help to clarify and reinforce verbal messages. For example, a manager can tell a new employee how a product can be assembled, but the manager can better communicate the process by demonstrating it.
6. *Nonverbal messages are sent more frequently than verbal ones.* According to research conducted by Albert Mehrabian, only 7 percent of the meaning we receive from messages is transmitted through words; 93 percent comes through nonverbal cues (55 percent body, 38 percent voice, and 7 percent words).[2]

Understanding nonverbal communication is critical in business, where a simple misunderstanding can affect employee relations or can make or break a deal. Factor in the expanding global environment, where different languages symbols may be confused or misunderstood, and nonverbal communication becomes even more critical. Not only is it important to understand nonverbal cues, but we must also be sensitive to the variety of standards among corporate and social cultures.

This chapter examines the three major divisions of nonverbal communication: *environmental communication,* including corporate image, time, building design, and room layout; *social communication,* personal space, status, and symbols; and *physical communication,* including gestures, facial expressions, eyes, voice, clothing, and touch. This chapter will also look at Japanese gift giving as an example of nonverbal communication in a different culture and the ethical considerations of the image of Joe Camel.

ENVIRONMENTAL COMMUNICATION

Think about some of the stores where you have shopped and offices you have visited recently. What messages did you receive from those environments? Were some more comfortable and inviting than others? Each territory conveys a message about its occupant. Some are so neat that you feel out of place when you sit down; others are so dirty and messy that you dislike the thought even of having to find a seat, as shown in the following example:

> When customers walk into the showroom at Bill Kummer's cycle shop on Union Avenue just off Business Highway, 42 South, [in Sheboygan, Wisconsin], they have to be struck by one thing—brightness. Chrome, glass and high gloss paint add a sparkle to the showroom floor. "We remodeled our showroom," said Kummer. "We want it to be super clean and comfortable for everyone including the 25 to 40 percent of our customers who are women."
>
> Gone is the grease, clutter and grime usually associated with motorcycle riders. Instead, customers at Bill Kummer's Harley-Davidson, Kawasaki, Suzuki & Ski-Doo find high-tech road and racing machines that glow with polish and class.[3]

Objects in our environment send us a variety of messages. A nicely decorated, clean restaurant sends an inviting message to sit, relax, and enjoy a special moment with friends. A well-designed logo on a piece of advertising sends a message of professionalism. A limousine parked in front of a corporate office usually implies that someone of high status will be picked up or dropped off. A large corner office with windows and nice mahogany furniture also denotes status, whereas a small cubicle with a computer and chair usually indicates a staff position.

Within the environment, image, use of time, territory, and office design all communicate nonverbal messages about the corporate culture.

Image

Environmental communication begins within the organization itself. According to graphic designer Barbara Shimkus, the starting point is corporate image. "What I sell . . . are my ideas. I supervise my projects from the get-go, through printing, to the very end. But often clients are looking for more than just, say a logo and brochure. Often, they're really looking for an image to convey their corporate identity. That's where my ideas come in. In today's marketplace, you can't make it without a good corporate image."[4] The corporate culture described in Chapter 2 embodies the philosophy and emotions of a workplace and develops largely through the nonverbal behavior and customs exhibited over time by top management. The image of this culture is reflected both inside and outside the organization. Inside, it is the norm for doing business. Outside, it is the image of the organization that the public perceives, uses as a reference, and attributes credibility to.

The image of some companies seems to be passive from the beginning. The example of the Disney approach is worth repeating here. Enter any Disney property and you are impressed at once with the immaculate and well-groomed grounds, clear evidence that attention is given to detail. The show business atmosphere designed for young and old alike conveys a message that "this is a fun, exciting and wholesome environment for all to enjoy." Look at each employee and you see neat, clean persons who follow a strict grooming policy. These nonverbal messages are an important part of bringing customers back again and again. That is why Disney is rated at the top of the entertainment service industry.

For some businesses, external environment is instrumental in changing an image. Kevin Jenness, president of Shreve, Crump & Low, an elite Boston jewelry store, describes such a change that forced his company to abandon one of its once-successful locations.

> "The company you keep is important in the jewelry business," Jenness said. "We don't want to be seen next to an inexpensive T-shirt store. When Shreve's moved into the Braintree mall, there were a little better grade of fashion stores in the neighborhood. But over the past five years, the plaza has been "taken over by chain stores," Jenness said. Even the other jewelers at the mall offer discounts. "That's not the kind of image we project. Hanging a 50-percent-off sign on our store every day is anathema to us."[5]

Time

Business is time bound. Consider the workday at a typical automotive plant in the United States. Assembly-line workers must report to the job on time. They punch in on the time clock, work in shifts, and meet specified production quotas that have been determined by time and motion studies. They have a designated lunch hour and two coffee breaks. When they punch out, they hurry to their cars in order to avoid the rush hour traffic jams.

A study conducted by the Hilton Hotel Corporation found that time is viewed and managed differently in the United States between its West Coast and East Coast executives. Over 72 percent of the West Coast respondents said personal goals like vacations and hobbies are among their top priorities, while only 55 percent of the East Coast group placed them that high. Those on the West Coast (48 percent) indicated that they make time for "ideal" weekends, but only 38 percent on the East Coast agreed. Hilton believes that part of the reason for such answers lies in the fact that the temperate climate allows its West Coast executives to spend far more days outside each year. But when they looked deeper, they also found those on the East Coast were burdened with more stress and more easily displayed their anxious behavior to others. When asked whether they often feel stressed "when they don't have enough time," 43 percent of West Coast to 30 percent of East Coast respondents said "yes." The daily schedules of employees on the East Coast seem to allow less personal time; meetings are often held during breakfast, lunch, and dinner. The time factor is often so critical that employees who arrive five minutes late to a meeting are criticized. On the West Coast, however, arriving 5 minutes late often means you are early, and excuses of being an hour late because of a freeway traffic pileup, are accepted without a second thought.[6]

Types of Time

Time in the United States can be viewed from several vantage points.

Business time uses the 24-hour clock and the 365-day calendar; it is vital in the smooth planning and operating of a business.

Relaxed time uses few specific guidelines. A supervisor's saying, "I'll drop by to review those papers in a little while," or "We'll worry about that next week," indicates a relaxed attitude toward time.

Technical time is a precise measurement process used in some businesses, especially manufacturing, where minute time periods are extremely important. For example, brick manufacturing requires that the amount of time that the product remains in the firing, ripening, and drying stages must be noted to the fraction of a second.

As the popularity of time management seminars indicates, time is one of a manager's most valued possessions. To be kept waiting for even a few minutes is frustrating; to be "stood up" for an appointment is outrageous. Managers observe and draw impressions about employees from the way employees use time.

The Value of Time

Different cultures hold different views of time. In Scandinavia, Germany, and Japan, just like on the East Coast of the United States, lateness is discouraged. In Latin America, lateness is common and accepted. The Mexican term *mañana* means either tomorrow or some indefinite time in the future. In business its connotation is often "putting off until tomorrow what could be done today." Still some cultures equate being early with being on time.

Source: AP/Wide World Photos. Reprinted by permission.

An American manager stationed in Riyadh, Saudi Arabia invited a Saudi business colleague and his spouse to his home for dinner. The date he gave was two weeks away. On the same night of the invitation, only one week earlier, the couple arrived. The Americans saw it as a scheduling mixup. By the Saudi standard of temporal flexibility, the guests were on time.

The Arab world takes an entirely different view of time than that held in America. They believe that we cannot control nature or human events by advance planning, clock watching, or discipline. Only Allah has such control and his will cannot be known or foreseen. For this reason, they view time as a continuous flow of events. Past, present, and future all blend together. The Arab expression *inshallah*—"If God is willing"—implies an uncertainty on the part of God. Arabs believe a divine will determines whether deadlines are met and what actions will occur. For instance, a family or religious event might occur a few days before the deadline, thus keeping work from being completed.

In another example, an American manager also stationed in the Middle East was waiting anxiously for work on a project to be completed. As the deadline drew near, he was disturbed to find that the Arab colleague in charge of the project had left town to mediate a family dispute. The American was outraged, not believing that an obligation could be taken so lightly.

The Arab informed him that his obligation to family superseded his obligation to the job. Furthermore, the Arab informed his colleague, his portion of the work would only be done barring *inshallah*s. For the first time the American truly learned the definition of that word.[7]

To prevent miscommunication in our global interactions, we must understand cultural differences in use of time. Rosenfeld and Civikly cite three reasons why time is seen by Americans as one of our most valued possessions.

Time is money. Psychiatrists, lawyers, plumbers, and other independent contractors are paid by the hour. An American's value of time may even supersede his value of money. When asked to donate time to a charitable cause, for example, people frequently back off, offering to donate money, food, or clothes instead.

Time is power. People with busy schedules are perceived as more important than those who have time for social niceties and preliminary chit-chat. The person granted an hour-long meeting with the President of the United States is looked upon as more powerful and important than the person granted only 2 minutes.

Time is status. While the employee must make an appointment to see the employer, the supervisor can "drop in" on the worker without notice or explanation. Status is also communicated by the amount of time a person is kept waiting.[8]

Territory

Humans, like animals, are territorial creatures: We have places and spaces that are uniquely ours. Archie Bunker has "his chair," a mother "her kitchen," a scientist "her laboratory," and a professor "his office." Each designs, maintains, and uses the territory for safety and pleasure and guards and defends it from invasion.

Territorial behavior also pervades business and underlies many nonverbal messages. Usually we consider our work space our territory; it may be a table and chair on an assembly line, a piece of machinery that an individual has run for several years, or the private office that others cannot enter without permission. In organizational territory we arrange the materials we use, place odds and ends where we want them, and generally establish a workplace that is conducive to our mental and physical needs.

Animals growl, hiss, or snarl when their territory has been invaded. Employees do the same. If someone rearranges the parts on an assembly line table, the line worker will probably be distraught. Touching or using machinery without the operator's permission might draw a verbal warning. Opening a door and walking into another's office without first knocking could generate a reprimand. Managers must be sensitive to the territory of others and regard it as an important and privileged place.

FIGURE 6.1 Territorial Claims in the Workplace

We define territory as a place that a person can claim, whether it is an office or a piece of machinery (see Figure 6.1). That place usually remains definable, unchanged, and stationary. In organizations we constantly make reference to territory: "my office," "my chair," "the president's parking space," "the sales territory." We also manipulate this territorial urge to our advantage. Consider the example on page 191.

Design and Arrangement

We are constantly influenced, sometimes without realizing it, by the design and arrangement of the environment. Managers should be familiar with five

Home Field Advantage

In one organization a female manager from the training department agreed to meet with several production managers to discuss her training goals. One of the production managers was her most outspoken opponent and made it clear to others in the organization that "this woman is trying to destroy the management system that the company has successfully established." The meeting was called by the male manager and was to be held in his office.

On the morning of the meeting the trainer called several of the managers who were to attend and asked if they had any objections to meeting in her office—so that she could use the stack of charts she had constructed. Each manager approved of the change in meeting place. The trainer then called her opponent and related that she knew it would be inconvenient to change the arrangements, but would he mind? "Incidentally," she said, "I have touched base with the other managers, and they don't mind at all." The opponent, of course, relented, and the training manager was able to sell her program successfully to all the other managers. Afterward she stated that "having the home field advantage" really paid off.

elements of that environment: building design, office space design, room design, room color, and desk arrangement.

Building Design

According to Alder and Towne, the design of an entire building can shape the type of communication among its inhabitants:

> Architects have learned that the way housing projects are designed will control to a great extent the contact neighbors will have with each other. People who live in apartments near stairways and mailboxes have many more neighbor contacts than do those living in less heavily traveled parts of the building, and tenants generally have more contacts with immediate neighbors than with people even a few doors away. Architects now use this information to design buildings that either encourage communication or increase privacy, and house hunters can use the same knowledge to choose a home that gives them the neighborhood relationships they want.[9]

Architects and builders have long recognized the importance of creating an appealing image in the buildings they construct. Factors like status of the address, ease of access, parking, temperature control and an attractive exterior help draw clients and customers to a location. But some managers never realize that the exterior image of a building is not enough. Office design, functionality, color, and furniture style and arrangement all deliver important nonverbal messages.

Office Space Design

As you look at existing office buildings and also the more contemporary facilities under construction, you probably would never guess that a debate is underway over the design of office space. This debate pits proponents of the conventional office against those who support the open office.

The conventional office has a basic quadrangular configuration and is familiar to everyone. Outer perimeter offices usually have windows. Hall space separates these offices from the inner offices that run parallel to those with windows. Sometimes the center part of the floor is called the "bull pen." Posner describes the pecking order for the conventional office.

- *The perimeter offices are for the honchos.* And if you've got *two* windows, you're really special. This is the senior executive turf. A corner office with windows on two walls is usually claimed by a chief executive officer or a partner.
- *The inner offices are for the junior executives.* No windows, but at least there's a door, and an area you can call your own.
- *The bull pen is for the lower echelon and support personnel.* It's like having your desk in the hallway. No privacy. It's tough to swear or sulk out here, because you are utterly visible.[10]

The open office concept originated in Germany in the 1950s and arrived in the United States in the late 1960s. Instead of enclosed offices it consists of free-form groupings, or work clusters, that fill the space in a way that optimizes the flow of human traffic and work. Proponents claim that this concept establishes a democratic atmosphere and increases communication, flexibility, and even productivity among office personnel.

The open office concept has steadily gained popularity. By the early 1990s, over half the office space in the United States was "open." The majority of this space, however, was utilized by staff members and not by managers. During the 1990s, the many office functions and human needs are being integrated through careful design. Office design is becoming simpler and more modular in order to accommodate evolving technological change. Curvilinear desktops appeal to employees, who are beginning to get more individual control of their workspace with features like below-desk heaters, individual air supplies, task lighting, and music or white-noise controls.[11]

Room Design

Robert Sommer, in his book *Personal Space: The Behavioral Basis for Design,* describes the thought process that underlies the design of restaurants and bars. Patrons tend to stay longer in places with dim lighting, subdued noise, and comfortable seats. An owner who wants to have a fast turnover will need a restaurant with brightly shining lights and little soundproofing.

Furniture also plays a role in how long people will stay in an environment. The Larsen chair, designed for restaurant owners in Copenhagen, is intentionally constructed to be uncomfortable by applying pressure to the back of the occupant who stays in the chair for longer than a few minutes. Makers of expensive automobiles apply the reverse technique. They construct car seats that contour to the driver's back. Some seats even have a lumbar device to prevent back pains caused by long trips.

Room Color

A former political leader once commented that a lifetime of participating in conference meetings convinced him that conferences conducted in cheerful, bright-colored rooms were more successful than those held in duller surroundings.

Research shows that color affects employees and customers both emotionally and psychologically. Colors can be felt as well as merely seen. Red, orange, and yellow create an aggressive exciting and stimulating environment. Studies have shown that people placed in rooms where the floors, walls, ceilings, and furniture are brightly colored have faster heartbeats, higher blood pressure, and accelerated brain activity. Cool colors produced a normal body function in those same areas. Blue is cool, clear, and serene, and has a calming effect. Green is light, fresh, and peaceful.[12]

Desk Arrangements

The two scenes shown in Figure 6.2 are from a typical office. If you had to enter this office, which desk arrangement would make you feel more at ease? Your desk and its size, shape, and position affect the impression that you

(a)

(b)

FIGURE 6.2 Scenes from the Office

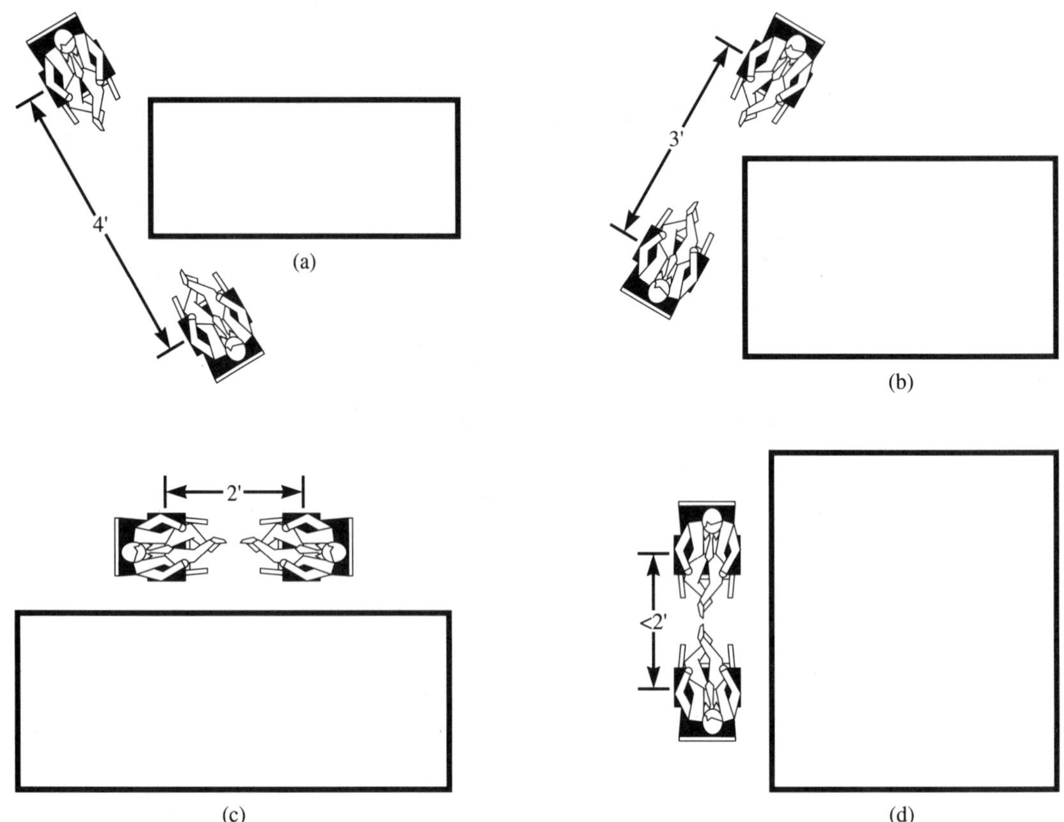

FIGURE 6.3 Four Desk Arrangements
Source: Based on figures in Paul Preston, *Communication for Managers*, p. 127. © 1979, used by permission of Prentice-Hall, Inc., Englewood Cliffs, New Jersey.

make on people and can determine the degree of open communication that takes place in your office.

There are four common desk arrangements (see Figure 6.3). Preston uses illustrations to show the possible participant interaction in each.[13] In the *standard placement* (a) the occupant stays seated behind the desk and controls the office space. The position stresses power and gives the visitor little freedom. Such positioning is sometimes necessary to establish roles as in disciplinary situations.

The *friendly arrangement* (b) removes the desk as a barrier and allows more personal communication. The interaction is still in a social zone, and the occupant still is in full control.

The *back-of-the-desk* (c) position totally removes barriers and places the visitor and occupant on the same level. Usually this arrangement is reserved for those people who share close personal contact.

The *neutral site* (d) is an informal place in the office where the occupant conducts conversation. It can be a couch, lounge, or conference area that is away from the desk. Normally only people with status have this kind of office space available.

Appropriate office arrangements coincide with the purpose of the intended communication. For instance, the standard placement might be inappropriate for giving employees good news but quite appropriate for reprimands. Likewise, a neutral setting can reinforce the goal-setting process or any personal counseling that might be needed. Going to an employee's office can be significant, for it can show recognition of valued performance and encourage interaction.

SOCIAL COMMUNICATION

Working and living environments influence how we communicate and can be examined in terms of how they affect social behavior. Verbal and nonverbal behavior is most easily recognized, understood, and controlled in small groups. This section examines social aspects and nonverbal communication that send important messages: space, status, and symbols.

Space

In the business world, almost everything that people do involves space. Our idea of space synthesizes all human sensory inputs: visual, auditory, kinesthetic, olfactory, and thermal. Each of these constitutes a complex system and at the same time is molded and patterned by culture. Since people grow up in different cultures, they learn to live and operate in different sensory worlds and are often aware of how their world differs from those of people around them. Remember that space is similar to territory but it is also different. Although people establish fixed territories that do not change, their ideas of space are flexible and changing. Edward T. Hall coined the term *proxemics* to refer to the study of human behavior in relation to space[14] and identified four distances most frequently used by Americans in business and social transactions. These distances are culture bound and are determined by an individual's attitudes, feelings, and relationships (see Figure 6.4).

Intimate distance is reserved for people to whom we feel extremely close. This space starts with physical contact and extends out to about 18 inches; it is reserved for lovers embracing and close friends discussing secrets. In business this distance is rarely used, although there are times when

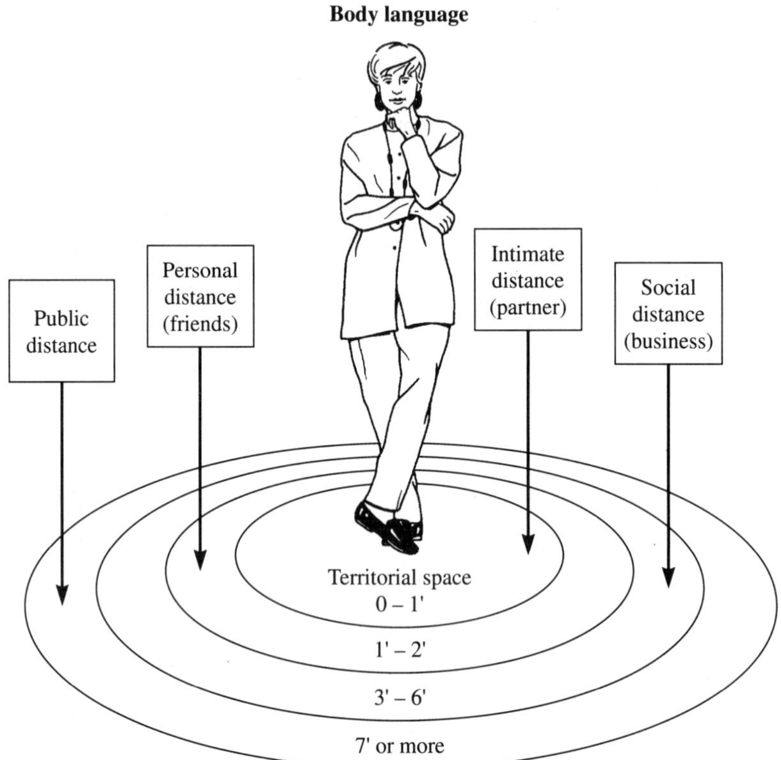

FIGURE 6.4 The Space We Put Between Ourselves and Others
Based on a drawing by Jack Halloran in *Applied Human Relations: An Organizational Approach*, 2nd ed., p. 46. © 1983, used by permission of Prentice-Hall, Inc., Englewood Cliffs, New Jersey. Information for the original drawing was taken from Julius Fast, *Body Language* (New York: M. Evans and Company), © 1970.

thoughts are shared as one person whispers to another. Occasionally a reprimand can be given by a manager speaking softly and directly into the ear of the subordinate (which sounds more like a threat than a reprimand). Handshakes and personal greetings such as hugging or embracing are also observed in business, more frequently in some cultures than in others. Such contact usually occurs within a few seconds and the participants quickly return to a personal or social distance.

Personal distance extends from 1 to 4 feet away from the body. Within that space we entertain casual and friendly relations. This space is often referred to as an invisible bubble that surrounds each person; it is variable in size and can expand or contract according to particular situations.

Social distance, between 4 and 8 feet away from the body, is used for impersonal and businesslike conversations.

Public distance extends from 12 feet to the limits of hearing. This space is used mostly for public speaking because it is not suitable for interpersonal communication.

When individuals invade the personal space of others, adverse reactions can occur. When people are in an elevator, for example, it is common for each person to feel uncomfortable. Since Americans dislike having their personal space invaded, in elevators they become almost inhuman objects. As more and more people crowd into an elevator, less and less space is available. Each person faces forward, folds hands in front, does not make eye contact, watches the floor numbers, doesn't talk to strangers, stops talking to acquaintances and avoids brushing against bodies.

In cramped office situations, desks placed extremely close together induce people to watch others work and to overhear telephone conversations. In those cramped situations even the aisles become subject to property rights. Workers whose desks border the aisle often assume ownership rights to aisle property. One worker described becoming anxious and hostile when neighboring office workers used his wastepaper basket. He felt that his territory was being invaded and that his ownership rights were challenged.

As students, you have perhaps consciously or unconsciously noticed how proxemics plays an important role in your relationships with teachers. Harris found that professors' physical movement toward students affects the students' achievement rates and even career choices. Instructors are more likely to stand closer to, touch, and smile at students they expect to excel, and to be more aloof and cold to students they perceive more negatively. She found that this behavior sets in motion a "self-fulfilling prophecy," the same as with the Pygmalion effect described in Chapter 4. The students who were expected to excel selected seats closer to the teacher, interacted with the teacher more often, and consequently drew more encouragement.[15]

Status

There are many ways to detect status within organizations. Titles, of course, are one of the best, but nonverbal signs and signals also convey messages of power and position. For instance, the use of space says much about the status of individuals.

Fast, in *Body Language,* gives an example of space and distance factors between a boss and visitors. Fast found significance in the time elapsed between knocking at the door and entry:

> The quicker the visitor entered the room, the more status he had. The longer the executive took to answer, the more status he had. . . . How far into the territory the visitor penetrates, and how quickly he does it, in other words how he challenges the personal space of the executive, announces his own status.

> The "big boss" will walk into his "subordinate's" office unannounced. The subordinate will wait outside the boss's office until he is permitted in. If the boss is on the phone, the subordinate may tiptoe off and come back later. If the subordinate is on the phone, the boss will usually assert his status by standing above the subordinate until he murmurs, "Let me call you back," and then gives the boss his full attention.[16]

According to Goldhaber, territory in an organization says three things about the status of individuals who occupy the space:[17]

1. *The higher up you are in the organization, the more and better space you have.* The officers of a company (i.e., president, vice-presidents, and department heads) will have large and attractive offices. Their offices have high-quality furnishings and more windows than subordinates' offices.
2. *The higher up you are in the organization, the better protected your territory is.* A person with high status often is assigned the services of a secretary or assistant. The job of that person is to protect the time of the boss and to filter out individuals that he or she does not want to see.
3. *The higher up you are in the organization, the easier it is to invade the territory of lower-status personnel.* A manager may walk into the office of a subordinate at will, even if the door is closed; the subordinate, however, does not reciprocate.

Symbols

People respond to symbols without realizing it. In fact, some nonverbal symbols are critical to communicating basic messages, and many have been adopted as international symbols (see Figure 6.5).

Logos

Businesses have long recognized that messages can be quickly and accurately transmitted and received through visual symbols. For this reason they invented logos. A *logo* is a symbol that allows easy identification of the company and its products. Businesses hope their logos will be remembered. Two examples show how this strategy has proven successful. NBC spent $1 million on the design of its multicolor peacock logo; Exxon spent $100 million and three years in a joint name and symbol conversion. (Its original name was Standard Oil of New Jersey, and later Esso.)

One survey asked 900 consumers to identify twenty-two nationally advertised logos. The majority of respondents could not name the company or its products for half of the logos. Colonel Sanders of Kentucky Fried Chicken won out, but Nissan Motor Company's Infiniti was recognized by only 29 percent of those surveyed. One message from this example is that logos gain recognition over time. The survey also showed that several logos significantly "downgraded" the image of the company if they were shown minus the company name. Among those downgraded were Prudential Insur-

Toilets

Rail transportation

No smoking

FIGURE 6.5 Symbols

1986

1987

1988

FIGURE 6.6 The Changing Rock of Gibraltar Logo

ance, Continental Corporation's Continental Insurance unit, Green Giant, Merrill Lynch, Land O'Lakes, Rolex Watch, PepsiCo, AT&T, Infiniti, American Express, and Minolta Camera. In each of these cases the company names alone received positive ratings, but the logos got lower ratings when shown alone.[18]

Logos, like the company culture, often change. Prudential Insurance has had nine updates of its rock of Gibraltar design. The original 1896 version displays the rock itself and the company name. In 1984 the company went to a jagged, ultramodern series of striated angles. But the recognition factor fell, and in 1988 the company restored the rock (see Figure 6.6). In Figure 6.7 you can test your knowledge of logos by naming the companies or brands represented by the unnamed symbols. Answers are found on page 218.

FIGURE 6.7 Match the Logo to the Company
Source: Logos are reprinted by permission of the author or copyright holder.

Physical Communication

The social aspects of space, status, and symbols send out nonverbal messages. The most personal, often the most unconscious, but easily the most controllable part of our nonverbal world is physical behavior. This section examines the body, gestures, facial expressions, eye movement, voice, clothing, and touch.

Body

The body is constantly sending messages, such as whether we are happy, sad, angry, or confused. Some characteristics, like height and skin color, remain relatively permanent throughout adulthood. Other factors, like posture and weight, can change. In fact, status has been known to influence a change in the posture of individuals, and posture often can influence the status obtained. Test your understanding of the message conveyed in the following three examples.

1. You are talking to your boss about a salary raise. While you explain the well-justified reasons for the raise, your boss has his head tilted down, his eyes fixed on you, and his mouth cupped in his hand. What message is he sending you?

   a. He plans to approve the raise.
   b. He will not give you the raise.
   c. He is having a hard time making a decision.

2. You are making a presentation to a management group in your company. One member of the audience is only partially listening and continually taps her foot and looks at her watch. What message is she sending to you?

   a. She doesn't believe what you are saying.
   b. She is excited about your content.
   c. She is impatient.

3. You are being interviewed by the president of a company where you hope to work. As you enter the man's office, he grabs your hand and shakes it with both of his hands, motions to a chair, and then pats you on the back. What message is this man sending?

   a. He appreciates your promptness.
   b. He wants to hire you.
   c. He is asserting his status.

The best answer to each of these questions is *C*. Intuitively most of us understand both the subtle and not-so-subtle messages that others send. We also misread nonverbal situations, however, and sometimes other interpretations are correct. The boss in the first example may be confused over the facts that you are conveying but wants to listen to you carefully. In the second example, the woman may have double scheduled two meetings and is feeling pressured to leave one and go to another. Finally, the company president may be a very humble person who simply wants to make you feel comfortable. Three things must be remembered about interpreting signals that the body sends:

1. *A precise meaning cannot always be obtained from body position and movement.* Arms crossed around the chest are usually interpreted to mean the person is closed to interaction with others. Yet nonverbal behavior combined with a verbal explanation and a certain amount of intuition might lead the observer to realize that the other person is physically cold and is attempting to stay warm.

2. *Body language differs from culture to culture.* Every culture has its own body language. Italians talk and move in Italian; British movements differ from those of Americans. Fiorello LaGuardia, a former mayor of New York City, delivered political speeches in Yiddish, Italian, and English and mastered the appropriate gestures for each language group. His gestures were so clear that some people could tell from newsreels which language he was speaking without ever hearing the sound.

3. *Interpretation of body language messages is more accurate when they are received over a period of time and not in one observation.* As we develop work relationships and friendships, we learn to read the nonverbal messages that others send more easily. Anthropologist Ray Birdwhistell conducted a systematic study of human nonverbal communication. *Kinesics,* the name now applied to the study of various movements of the mouth, the eyebrows, and the hands, supports his findings that accurate interpretation of messages is a cumulative process.[19]

Interpretation of messages is often best discovered through the congruence or incongruence of the verbal and nonverbal. *Congruence* occurs when words and actions complement each other. Americans, for example, generally raise their head slightly at the end of spoken statements to which they expect an answer. This is a nonverbal signal to other Americans to give a reply. Response to these signals is intuitive and unconscious.

Incongruence is perhaps best illustrated by the employee who is sitting back in a chair, with arms folded and knees together. Verbally she is telling her employer that she is pleased with the $50-a-month raise she has just received. The nonalert employer would probably accept the employee's seemingly pleased response; but the employer with an awareness of body language might realize that the employee's withdrawn position, folded arms, or shrug of the shoulders indicates complete or partial dissatisfaction.

Gestures

In 1826 Noah Webster, author of *Webster's Dictionary,* wrote a book on speech entitled *Webster's Reader and Speaker.* Webster, one of the first to discuss the importance of nonverbal expression, contended that expressed sentiments should be accompanied with proper tones, looks, and gestures. Facial expressions reveal our inner emotions and passions, while gestures are the movements of our hands and body.

In business settings congruent meaning often is found in situations that call for multiple gestures. When a manager has to discipline a subordinate, the manager's head is held high, the shoulders are pulled back, and eye contact is directed straight at the subordinate. The dominant posture signals: "I am the boss, and I want you to listen." The subordinate's posture signals acceptance or rejection of the manager's power. Acceptance is seen in a submissive pose, with shoulders held down and eyes lowered. The opposite reaction to a reprimand would be a posture that mirrors the supervisor's and says, "I defy you."

Nierenberg and Calero, in *How to Read a Person Like a Book,* offer a complete analysis of nonverbal gestures and behavior in business settings (see Table 6.1).[20]

TABLE 6.1 People-Reading Index

Movement	Description	Possible Meaning
Smiles:		
Simple	Lips together, teeth unexposed	Person is not participating in any outgoing activity, is smiling to himself
Upper	Upper incisors exposed, usually with eye-to-eye contact between individuals	A greeting smile when friends meet or when children greet their parents
Broad	Both upper and lower incisors exposed and eye-to-eye contact seldom occurs	Associated with laughing, commonly seen during play
Holding hands	Two women gently hold each other's hands and with congruous facial expressions communicate their deep sympathy	Woman's expression of sincere feelings to another woman during a crisis
Open hands	Palms up	Sincerety and openness
Crossed arms	Men—arms crossed on chest Women—arms crossed lower on body	Defensiveness, defiance, withdrawal
Leg over chair	Sits with one leg up over chair arm	Indifference or hostility to other person's feelings or needs
Leg kicking	Legs crossed with foot moving in a slight kicking motion	Boredom
Hand to cheek	"The Thinker" position with hand on cheek	Involved in some sort of meditation
Stroking chin	Hand strokes chin, man strokes beard or mustache	In process of making decision
Removing glasses	Very slowly and deliberately takes glasses off and carefully cleans the lenses or puts the earpiece of the frame in the mouth	Procrastination—pausing for thought, gaining time to evaluate
Pinching bridge of nose	Closes eyes, pinches bridge of nose	May signal self-conflict, quandry about a matter
Sideways glance	Often takes a sideways position, body turned away	Associated with distrusting attitude—a gesture of rejection
Hands on hips	Standing—both hands placed on hips Sitting—body leaning forward, one hand on knee	Individual is goal oriented—is ready and able

(continued)

TABLE 6.1 Continued

Movement	Description	Possible Meaning
Leaning back, hands supporting head	Seated, leaning back, one leg crossed in figure-four position, both hands clasped behind head	Gesture of superiority, smugness, and authority
Jingling money in pocket	Jingling coins in pocket	May be much concerned with money or the lack of it
Locked ankles	Ankles crossed tightly, hands may also be clenched	Holding back strong feelings and emotions—apprehension—tension
Tugging ear	Raises hand four to six inches, hand goes to earlobe, gives a subtle pull, then returns to its starting point	An "interrupt gesture"—a signal of a wish to speak
Steepling	Joins finger tips and forms a "church steeple"	Communicates idea speaker is very sure of what he or she is saying

Source: Chart "Body Language" in John W. Drakeford, *Do You Hear Me, Honey?* pp. 56–57. Copyright © 1976 by John W. Drakeford. Used by permission of Harper & Row, Publishers, Inc., New York. Chart condensed from Gerald I. Nierenberg and Henry H. Calero, *How to Read a Person Like a Book* (New York: Pocket Books, 1975).

Cultural Context

Many people assume that gestures mean the same thing everywhere when in fact great cultural differences exist. Common gestures that are used in America carry entirely different meanings in other countries. Let's start with three of the most common American gestures—thumbs up, the victory sign, and the "OK" sign. Each of these gestures can be observed daily in society and business, although the meanings have changed over time.

The thumbs-up gesture seems to have had its start with early pilots, who used it as a sign of "all clear" as they were preparing for takeoff. Later the action communicated the hope that the mission would be successful. Today its use is widespread. Film critics Gene Siskel and Roger Ebert use it to rate movies, the President of the United States uses it as he steps from Air Force One, and General Norman Schwarzkopf used it in his triumphant return from the Persian Gulf War. In Germany, however, thumbs up will order you one beer. In Japan it will get you *five* beers.

Winston Churchill made famous the V-formation of index and middle fingers, using it during World War II as a sign for *victory.* Later the Allied troops adopted it as their own gesture for victory. In the 1960s and 1970s, the symbol was selected by civil rights groups and peace activists who called it the sign of *peace.* Yet this same gesture is considered obscene in England and

Australia if the back of the hand, instead of the palm, is turned outward. Churchill, Margaret Thatcher, and more recently President George Bush offended large numbers when they were photographed displaying the backward victory sign by accident.[21]

Finally, the "OK" sign is a circle formed by the thumb and forefinger with the other three fingers extended. In our culture it usually means perfect or "right on target!" In Japan, however, it is a symbol for money. To the French it means zero; in some Arab countries it is the sign of a curse; and in Germany, Australia, Russia, and Brazil it is an obscene gesture. President Richard Nixon discovered the last interpretation when he displayed a two-handed version of this gesture as he departed a plane in Brazil. To his later embarrassment, a picture of the event appeared in papers throughout the country.

The handshake, which is the initial gesture of friendliness in business, originated as a symbol for peace. People who extended the right hand showed that they had no weapon, were approaching in peace, and were inviting the other person to do the same. Today this symbol is expected and accepted in a variety of ways across cultures. Garrett describes the Western concept of hand shaking. The first 10 seconds, he says, are critical because the other person starts building a perception of whether you are feeling confident, intimidated or comfortable.

> How you shake hands can reveal a lot about you. Do you try to immediately dominate the other person by putting too much pressure into your handshake? Some people actually inflict pain on others with their vicelike grip. Or does your limp, tentative grasp reveal insecurities you are valiantly trying to hide? Not offering your hand to someone who expects it may be interpreted as rude and offensive. At the opposite extreme is the person who may have a high need for approval and compulsively shakes your hand every time he or she sees you.[22]

In India, a person puts his hands together as in prayer and bows. In Germany, a firm one-pump handshake is desirable and a limp one is considered distasteful. In France, however, the limp shake is desired. In southern Europe and Latin America, a handshake with the right hand often takes place while the left hand touches the forearm or elbow. In the Middle East the hand-pumping Western handshake is distasteful and a soft, limp, even moist handshake is preferred. Women in America are often passive about handshakes, but European women shake hands aggressively. In Russia, a handshake is quickly followed by a bear hug and a kiss on the cheek. In the Pacific Rim countries of Japan, Taiwan, South Korea, and China, the handshake occurs slowly, not firmly, and with only one or two pumps. In Japan, however, a simple 15-degree bow from the waist is really preferred, though eye contact should be avoided when bowing.

As a manager preparing to enter the global arena of business, you should study the cultural context of all nonverbal communication. Until the recent

The Embarrassing Hand Gestures

An American manager was sent to Ethiopia to interview nationals for his company's new branch office in that country. Some of the most qualified candidates were the first ones that he interviewed. Later he found that he had offended them without his knowledge by entering the waiting room following each interview and pointing with his finger to the next person in line. In the United States such a gesture is acceptable. In Ethiopia, however, it is reserved for children and as a beckoning signal for dogs. Back at the hotel, his host politely showed that the correct method in Ethiopia would be to extend the arm and hand, hold the hand out with the palm down, and to then close the hand repeatedly. The manager was extremely embarrassed about the actions he honestly considered to be appropriate. . . . Fortunately, his host was able to explain the situation to the nationals and some well-equipped employees were hired.

past, little material to broaden your insight existed, but as the world becomes smaller through expanded communication networks, more and more information is becoming available. By constantly seeking to learn more about the world and its people, you will find it easier to avoid errors like this one made by an American manager.

Facial Expressions

The human face is a valuable instrument of communication; the mouth, eyes, and brow can sensitively convey specific emotions, thoughts, or intentions. The face is the primary way of expressing feelings of anger, joy, fear, sadness, happiness, surprise, concern, worry, embarrassment, contempt, hurt. The face is capable of producing over 250,000 different expressions, even though we use only a few words (for example, smile, grin, frown) to describe general facial expressions.[23]

The face is also one of the most rapid means of conveying meaning. Other nonverbal factors, like gestures or posture, take time to change and use. Facial expressions can be changed instantly, even without detection by the eye. Managers, in fact, sometimes stop a confusing, irrelevant, or undesired message by squinting in a particular way, raising an eyebrow, or setting the jaw. In the business world facial expressions are the first physical conveyors of nonverbal expression.

Although facial expressions are used frequently, the emotions that they express are not always easy to read. The face can convey several emotions simultaneously and is adept at hiding expressions. For example, men are cul-

> **The Misread Facial Expression**
>
> A supervisor observed four subordinates eating lunch together one day and noticed that at least three of the men had cans of beer. Because drinking alcohol was strictly forbidden while on the job, after lunch he called each of the men into his office and fired them. The fourth man, several colleagues argued, was innocent, and although he was eating with the other three, he did not drink. The fourth man was questioned by the supervisor, and, even though no hard evidence against him existed, he was suspended. As the supervisor explained, "He wouldn't look me in the eye. He dodged the question. He had guilt written all over his face."
>
> Later that day, when sharing news of the situation with another supervisor, he learned why the facial expressions had indicated guilt: "You misread the man's 'body language.' What you took for guilt was the man's way of showing respect. He is Puerto Rican, and Puerto Rican culture teaches people not to look into the eyes of those in superior positions. To do so would be disrespectful."

turally taught to act "tough" and sometimes mask feelings of hurt or disappointment. Our cultural programming can lead us astray if we assume that everyone should, and will, act in the same way.

Facial expressions tell us when others are confused. For instance, a manager in a problem-solving meeting may suddenly turn from the podium to the whiteboard to draw a flowchart of the procedure she is discussing. Nonverbal cues from others in the room tell her that the group is confused and needs more information.

Eye Movement

The eye moves an estimated 100,000 times during the average day. It is one of the most expressive parts of the body, and the meanings that can be attached to various eye movements are limitless.

Researchers have found a correlation between the eyes and social space. In the Middle East people hold conversations in small, tight circles. They tend to stand about 2 feet apart (instead of the 5 feet customary for Americans), a distance at which they can see the size of each other's pupils. Because a person's pupils usually dilate when he or she is interested and excited and contract when the person is bored and uninterested, pupil size is used to indicate how one person responds to another. Until recently the factor of pupil size had little bearing in business, but studies have shown that nonverbal messages conveyed by the eyes of models in pictorial advertisements can play an integral role in what is communicated to viewers.

Eye contact customs vary from culture to culture. Americans unconsciously expect business associates to "look them in the eye." They view those who avoid this process suspiciously and perceive them as unfriendly, insecure, untrustworthy, inattentive, and impersonal. To practice "good eye contact" is to show an interest in someone. But too much eye contact can be perceived as dominating, and too little can be perceived as a weakness.

In several other cultures, as in the Puerto Rican example just given, looking someone directly in the eye is not considered proper. The Japanese feel that direct eye contact is intimidating and they also lower their eyes when speaking to a superior as a sign of respect. In school their children are taught to look at a teacher's Adam's apple or tie knot as a nonverbal way of avoiding direct eye contact.[24] Arabs, however, often look each other directly in the eye because they believe "the eyes are the window to the soul." They believe that knowing someone else's heart and soul is an important prerequisite to doing business together. Both Latin American and some African cultures encourage prolonged eye contact, although it is considered disrespectful when practiced by individuals of lower status. In the United States it is considered rude to stare at someone, and individuals acknowledge both the eye contact and comments with head movements and grunts. In England a listener blinks her eyes to let the speaker know that he is being understood.

Voice

Paralinguistic messages relate to voice factors other than words, like tone, inflection, pitch, volume, emphasis, pauses, and general quality. Speech rate or errors in speech like the use of nonwords, "ums," "ahs," or "ers," convey various nonverbal messages like nervousness, anger, or fear. Research supports the belief that the voice is extremely revealing and can register a variety of feelings. What does a voice disclose? A quaking voice reveals nervousness; stridency shows uncertainty; and a smooth, full voice indicates confidence. The way we speak certain words carries many meanings. For example, consider the different meanings conveyed in these sentences by the emphasis of different words.

- *You* did an excellent job on the report. (not just any person, but *you* in particular)
- You *did* an excellent job on the report. (past tense, regarding when you did the report)
- You did an *excellent* job on the report. (not just a good job, but one that was excellent)
- You did an excellent job on the *report.* (not a project or presentation, but a report)

The sensitive manager strives to use a voice that complements and emphasizes the words that he or she speaks.

Clothing

It used to be said that "Clothes make the person"; in some circles the phrase has been changed to "Clothes make or break the person." Books on dress and clothing have emphasized that our clothing influences how the people around us think about us. John Molloy, a clothing consultant for large corporations, was one of the first wardrobe engineers. He combines the elements of psychology, fashion, sociology, and art and teaches salespeople how they should dress to sell more insurance; trial lawyers, to win more cases; and executives, to exert more authority. Molloy believes that the way people dress communicates a variety of messages to others in an organization. In his first book, *Dress for Success,* he describes how types of dress affect corporate executives:

> I showed them [100 executives] five pictures of men neatly dressed in obvious lower-middle-class attire and asked if these men were dressed in proper attire for a young executive. Forty-six said yes, fifty-four said no.
>
> I next showed them five pictures of men dressed in conservative upper-middle-class clothing and asked if they were dressed in proper attire for the young executive. All one hundred said yes.
>
> I asked them whether they thought the men in the upper-middle-class garb would succeed better in corporate life than the men in the lower-middle-class uniform. Eighty-eight said yes, twelve said no.
>
> I asked if they would choose one of the men in the lower-middle-class dress as their assistant. Ninety-two said no, eight said yes.[25]

Malloy's respondents gave their perception of others as a reaction to the clothing those people were wearing. Managers recognize that such judgments are critical, especially in the service sector. For that reason, more and more organizations are requiring employee uniforms. Perhaps you have never given much thought to uniforms. Look around, because they are used in most of the organizations that you frequent daily: fast-food lines, grocery stores, mail service, airlines, retailers, service stations, and even sporting events. The secret to successful uniforms in the 1990s is a sharp modern look that also creates a natural image that both employees and customers feel comfortable with. In fact, organizations have found that employees are happiest in uniforms that express their personality and individuality. According to a Walt Disney spokesperson, "if people feel good about how they look, they'll feel good about how they service their guests."[26]

One service industry, the airlines, give a clear example of how the proper uniform pleases both employees and customers. In the late 1970s, Ralph Lauren designed flight attendant uniforms for TWA. With only minor changes, the same classic uniform is used today. Northwest Airlines had also made use of its uniforms for several years, but in 1992 the company hired Disney Image Maker to design clothing for some 26,000 employees. The cost was about $10 million, but the new businesslike traditional look conveys the message that Northwest is the businessperson's airline.

The known rebel of the industry, Southwest Airlines, take a more casual approach. In the mid-1980s, they changed to "fun wear" uniforms to reinforce their "Fun Fares" slogan. The uniforms fit their image perfectly, according to a company spokesperson. "We say we're the fun airline. Everyone has fun at work and we thought we'd carry that over to the passengers. . . . If you have fun at work, you're happier and you produce better quality work."[27]

The clothing we wear communicates three different things about us. It reveals something about our *emotions* (how we feel affects what we wear, what we wear affects how we feel); it discloses information about our *behavior* (wearing a uniform, for instance, may cause us to act more professionally and even to talk in a different tone); and it *differentiates* us from other people.

Touch

Infants know touch before other senses: The order of sensory development is tactile, auditory, and finally visual. But as we grow older the order of usage reverses: visual, auditory, and tactile. Ashley Montagu, in his book *Touching,* stresses the important need humans have for tactile satisfaction: "[A]dequate tactile satisfaction during infancy and childhood is of fundamental importance for the subsequent healthy behavioral development of the individual."[27]

Psychologist Sidney Jourard studied the amount of physical touching that takes place during exchanges of confidences. He discovered that touching, outside of sexual relationships, occurs on a minimal basis among Americans and English. In fact, both men and women touched mostly the other's hands, arms, and shoulders. According to Jourard, an almost "touch taboo" exists:

> I think it is part of the more general alienation process that characterizes our depersonalizing social system. I think it is related to the same source that underlies the dread of authentic self-disclosure. When people are committed to upward mobility, in competition with their fellows, everyone masquerades, and keeps his real self concealed from the other who is a potential enemy. You keep others at a distance and mystified by withholding disclosure, and by not letting them get close enough to touch, not letting them know how you feel.[29]

Physical contact with other human beings is essential for healthy development. Even in the world of business, touch is an important clue to liking and acceptance. Marketing departments have read the human need for touch, and they have used that knowledge to improve sales.

The importance of touch is often underestimated: A gesture can be used where words are not possible or socially acceptable. For example, in an interview between two men, a simple pat on the back may convey significant emotional support that could not be easily conveyed in words. Touch can also be misunderstood; a female who places her hand on a male's shoulder may be perceived as flirtatious.

Casual touching, such as tapping someone on the chest or back slapping, is acceptable in Latin America, southern Europe, and some Middle East countries. The same touching gestures, however, are seen as extremely offensive in the Far East and northern Europe. When you are unsure of how touch is culturally accepted, it is better to keep your hands to yourself. As managers, we must recognize the impact touch can have, yet we must also be sensitive to the proper time and way to use touch.

A GLOBAL PERSPECTIVE

Gift Giving, Japanese Style

Americans often rely upon products, contacts, and persuasive appeals to establish relationships and gain contracts. Japanese managers operate from a more tradition-bound culture and from a reliance upon stable interpersonal relationships built on mutual trust, understanding, and cooperation. It is within this culture that the Japanese custom of gift giving occurs. The traditional gift, presented at the outset of a meeting between two parties, starts the growth of the important interpersonal relationship.

Gift giving is an important nonverbal expression of friendship, gratitude, and respect in the Japanese business environment. To managers in that culture, the action says much more than words can say. Japanese managers are usually very disappointed if they do not receive gifts.

In Japan gifts are given at some of the same customary times as in Western society: birthdays, weddings, promotions, business openings, in sympathy, and as get-well statements. But they are not given for the American holidays of Christmas, Mother's Day, Father's Day, and Valentine's Day. Two very important Japanese holidays are O-seibo and O-chugen. O-seibo, extending from November 15 through the end of December, compares with the Western Christmas. During this period gifts are exchanged at all levels of business and even from customers to suppliers. O-chugen, a two-week period between June 15 and August 15 (the dates vary from region to region), is a form of Christmas in the summer.

As a manager who is contemplating giving a gift to a Japanese person, you should try to discern that person's tastes and desires before selecting the gift. However, a wide array of items are considered acceptable: special gourmet foods, chocolates, fruits, imported liquors, preserves, cheese, wine, crystal, leather goods, diaries, appointment books, and even American-made golf items. The one thing to keep in mind when selecting the gift is to "buy American."

Wrapping of the gift is special to the Japanese. While Westerners want to see the gift quickly, Japanese regard the care and neatness of the wrap as a statement of the giver's status. Wrap the gift in the finest paper, put the recipient's name and your name as the giver, and then write any brief message that you want to convey. Finally, the wrapped gift should then be placed in an attractive bag.

When presenting the gift, it is customary to hold it in both hands and extend them together to the recipient. This is a nonverbal sign of respect for the receiver and humility of the giver. Never brag about the cost of a gift. Even if it is expensive, it is better to say, "It's a small token," "a mere trifle," or "really nothing at all." You will hear the Japanese use the words *tsumaranaimon* when they present expensive gifts. This is translated to mean "uninteresting" or "a dull thing." One final word of warning about a gift's price: Never give the same-priced gift to people at different levels in a Japanese company.

When you receive a gift, should you open it at that moment? The Japanese custom is to wait and open the gift in private. However, they realize that Americans are not familiar with their customs and like to open the gifts they receive immediately. If you are unsure of what to do, ask permission from the giver to open the gift.

Gift giving is a universal event. But managers entering the globalized world of business take the opportunity to research gift giving in Japan and other countries so that they will know the true message they are sending.[30]

ETHICS: RIGHT OR WRONG?

"Old Joe" Camel

If you manufactured a product that has been proven to kill people, how would you persuasively sell that product to consumers? Advertising specialists say the product would have to appear safe, contain an element of fun and excitement, and be promoted to consumers who had little fear of dying. According to several researchers and consumer advocate groups, the R. J. Reynolds Tobacco company (RJR) has successfully used this approach in marketing its Camel cigarettes to children.

In the past few years, studies have shown a relationship between tobacco and several illnesses including cancer, heart disease, stroke, emphysema, immune deficiencies, and pregnancy disorders. In 1989, the U.S. Surgeon General determined that one of every six deaths was caused by smoking. This included 87 percent of lung cancer deaths, 82 percent of emphysema deaths, 21 percent of heart disease deaths, and 18 percent of stroke deaths. Such findings have led to prohibitions on radio and television advertising; mandatory health warnings on cigarette packages; the banning of smoking in such places as offices; restaurants; and airplanes, and a 1985 plea by the Surgeon General for a "smoke-free society" by the year 2000.[31]

Currently, over 68 million Americans smoke cigarettes and another 15 million use other tobacco products. But sales are declining 3 percent annually since approximately 2 million adult smokers either die or stop smoking yearly.[32] Where will the tobacco companies increase their sales? Critics in the past contended that it had to be the youth market. Now research indicates that children may indeed be the target audience through very successful advertising.

In 1988, RJR created a hip-looking cartoon character named Joe Camel. "Old Joe," as he is affectionately called, is a macho figure who sports sunglasses, is nattily dressed, and is dubbed a "smooth character." He is seen on billboards, phone booths, buses, and on the pages of popular magazines. "Whether he's on the beach or in the bar, straddling his chopper or jamming on the bandstand, (he) is often surrounded by adoring babes."[33] He offers his buyers coupons for T-shirts, baseball caps, and other popular items.

The "Old Joe" advertising campaign is a multimillion-dollar expenditure for RJR, but it has proven to be worth the cost. According to the Coalition of Smoking or Health, in the three years since the campaign's inception, Camel's market share has risen from 4.4 percent to 7.9 percent in the 18- to 24-year-age group. In the under-18 market, however, their sales have jumped from .5 percent to 33 percent. Total sales of Camels are $476 million a year.[34] RJR, of course, has a long-term stake in its marketing plan. Research shows that brand loyalty for cigarettes is higher than for any other major consumer product. About 90 percent of smokers adopt the habit before they are 21 years of age, and once they start, 70 percent remain faithful to one brand.

Several groups have long felt that RJR and other tobacco companies are aiming their advertising at children. In early 1991, a coalition of the American Cancer Society, the American Heart Association, and the American Lung Association petitioned the Federal Trade Commission to ban the Joe Camel campaign, referring to the ads as "one of the most egregious examples in recent history of tobacco advertising that targets children."[35]

In December 1991, the results of three teams of researchers were published in the *Journal of the American Medical Association.* One study came from the Medical College of Georgia. A sample of 229 children, ages 3 to 6, were asked to match twenty-two logo cards with twelve products pictured on a game board. Among the logo cards was: Disney Channel, McDonald's, Domino's Pizza, Coca Cola, Nike, Cheerios, Old Joe, Chevrolet, Ford, Apple, and Kodak. The results showed that while Joe Camel was less familiar to kids than Coke or McDonald's logos, it was more familiar than the Cheerios or Kellogg's cereal logos. Of the 6 year olds, 91 percent matched Joe with a Camel cigarette pack. The same number of respondents matched Mickey Mouse with the Disney Channel.[36]

In another study, conducted at the University of Massachusetts Medical School, 1,055 high-school students from around the country were surveyed and their answers were compared to the answers of 345 adults (21 or older). The findings indicated the children were more likely than the adults to recognize Joe, to know the cigarette brand he represented, and to find the ads appealing. While only 9 percent of the adults smoked Camel, 33 percent of the youth group indicated the Camel loyalty. The researchers ended their journal article with a strong attack on RJR: "Our study provides further evidence that tobacco advertising promotes and maintains nicotine addiction among children and adolescents. A total ban of tobacco advertising and promotions, as part of an effort to protect children from the dangers of tobacco, can be based on sound scientific reasoning."[37]

The third research group, at the University of California Population Studies for Cancer Prevention, confirmed these findings: "We conclude that tobacco advertising, particularly of Camel cigarettes, has been effective in targeting adolescents in the United States. . . . These advertisements appear to influence these prospective new smokers to start smoking the brand that is advertised. . . . Not only is the market share of brands similar to recall of the most advertised brands, but the brands that appear to be aimed the most at adolescents have demonstrated a differential increase in market share in the youngest adolescents over time."[38]

RJR responded to the studies by denying that they targeted children with their ads and were interested in a teenage "start-up" market. Their objectives for spending the millions of dollars in advertising is to encourage adult smokers to switch brands, and to promote brand loyalty. The Tobacco Institute, the industry's Washington advocacy group, said: "Recognition of advertising logos or characters does not automatically translate into purchase of the product. Simply because one sees and recognizes a cigarette ad does not mean that the person will smoke because of the ad."[39]

For three months, RJR stood firm on its advertising, invoked the First Amendment on its rights to free speech, and insisted that its ads did not appeal to children. On March 9, 1992, U.S. Surgeon General Antonia Novello, along with the American Medical Association, asked R. J. Reynolds to stop using its Old Joe cartoon ads. In addition, she called on magazines and retailers to refuse signs and ads bearing Old Joe's likeness. Novello said, "In years past, R. J. Reynolds would have us walk a mile for a Camel. Today it's time that we invite 'Old Joe' himself to take a hike. . . . It's time for the tobacco industry to stop preying on our nation's youth."[40]

While the surgeon general has no enforcement authority and her call for a boycott is sure to be ignored, her voice adds credibility to the growing pressure on RJR. *Advertising Age,* in an editorial titled "Old Joe Must Go," said, "RJR is wrong, and is courting disaster with these ads." Other tobacco industry executives believe "RJR's stubbornness is achieving nothing except drawing the ire—and the attention—of legislators who would be only too willing to ban tobacco advertising altogether."[41]

Case Questions

1. What is the ethical issue in this case?
2. Is the Joe Camel ad campaign aimed at kids?

3. If Joe Camel is memorable, don't the ads lead people to smoke?
4. How do the rights of children who view the ads compare to the First Amendment Rights of RJR?
5. Are tobacco ads in general misleading?
6. What are the nonverbal implications of the Joe Camel case? Are there other products whose nonverbal ads pose ethical questions?

SUMMARY

Nonverbal communication in business can either augment or contradict what we say verbally. Managers therefore must learn to coordinate both their verbal and nonverbal messages and at the same time be sensitive to what their peers, subordinates, and supervisors convey nonverbally.

The three major divisions of nonverbal communication are environmental, social, and physical. *Environmental* aspects of communication include how people select, protect, and utilize territory to their advantage. Building and office space is designed, arranged, and painted with certain objectives in mind. Desk and seating arrangements affect the degree of open or closed communication that occurs within offices. Some cultures value these as a scarce resource, while others do not see it as a constraint.

From a *social* standpoint humans operate within flexible and changing personal space by establishing distances between themselves and others that coincide with the situations they encounter. Work space, job titles, and other nonverbal signs and signals convey status. Symbols, too, such as logos, deliver social messages as they replace words in business.

The most unconscious yet easily controllable part of our nonverbal world lies in *physical* behavior. People constantly send messages with their bodies, facial expressions, gestures, eye movement, voices, and touch. Clothing style, quality, and color convey messages of credibility and class. Physical nonverbal messages combine with environmental and social ones to send many messages on a daily basis. Managers must become sensitive to the way in which these nonverbal messages are used.

KEY WORDS

back-of-the-desk arrangement
business time
congruence
conventional office
environmental communication
friendly desk arrangement
incongruence
intimate distance
kinesics
logo
neutral site desk arrangement
nonverbal communication
open office
personal distance
physical communication
proxemics
public distance
relaxed time
social communication
social distance
space
standard placement desk arrangement
status
technical time
territory

REVIEW QUESTIONS

1. What is the precise difference between verbal and nonverbal communication?
2. Words are spoken within a context of nonverbal communication. Describe the five different ways that nonverbal behavior relates to verbal.
3. One reason for managers to study nonverbal communication is that only 7 percent of the meaning we receive is through words. Tell where the other 93 percent comes from, and list five other reasons for studying nonverbals.
4. Three different divisions of our environment influence us nonverbally. What are they?
5. We often take time for granted, but there are three different types of nonverbal time. Describe them, and also list the three ways we value time.
6. Territory is defined in this chapter as a place that a person can claim, whether it is an office or a piece of machinery. Describe some ways that territory helps messages to be communicated in business.
7. Describe and contrast a conventional and an open office.
8. Name the four different desk arrangements, and tell which ones are the most controlled and the most informal.
9. Name the four different zones of personal space, and describe the distance each covers and the type of communication that occurs in each.
10. How do you describe status within an organization?
11. Why are symbols an important tool for society? Describe their importance.
12. Name the eight ways described in this chapter that we physically communicate with others.
13. We interpret body messages through their congruence or incongruence. What does this mean? 14. Nineteen different gestural movements were listed in Table 6.1. List and describe at least ten of them.
15. According to Birdwhistell, how many different expressions can the face produce?
16. Why is touch between people important?
17. Name the three things clothes communicate about us.

EXERCISES

1. For the next few days observe how you, and people around you, use and abuse time. How much of your time is "relaxed" and how much is "business" related? Do you find yourself mentally employing one type of time when you are physically employing another? In meetings, classes, and at work make a list of how people act nonverbally when they arrive early or late. How do the people who are waiting act?
2. Make an informal survey of the offices where you attend school or work. Examine the waiting rooms, secretarial facilities, managers offices, faculty offices, and other types of public and private space. Keep a list of spaces that are designed for formal and informal use. How many fit the open and conventional office designs? What kind of nonverbal messages did you receive from the designs and the people that work in them? In how many ways were people defending their territory? You may desire to make some simple drawings in order to share this information with your class.
3. In an informal survey make a list of the various colors and color schemes that are used to decorate the walls of your classrooms, administrative buildings, offices, dormitory rooms, and so forth. Did one or two colors dominate? Which colors were they? What kind of feelings did you receive when you examined the different rooms? Did any particular colors give you pleasant or unpleasant feelings? Share your findings with others, and then describe them to your class.
4. Try this simple "invading space" exercise and describe the results to your class. In a library, cafeteria, or other public place pick out a person who is seated alone surrounded by empty chairs.

Sit in the chair closest to the person. Describe his or her response. (You may also wish to explain afterward that you were conducting an experiment.)

5. Make a picture collage with different slogans and symbols that you find in magazines and newspapers. How many of your friends are able to give the names and meanings of the symbols? What kind of nonverbal messages do these symbols denote?
6. Visit a friend, and sit down in his or her favorite chair. Don't offer to move, but note the person's nonverbal actions.
7. Set aside 30 minutes or an hour to observe other people. Select a space where other people are constantly interacting, such as a sidewalk, a student union, a hallway, or the door of a building or cafeteria. Observe the gestures, facial expressions, and body movement that people use. What kinds of meanings do you draw from these behaviors?
8. Design your ideal office space. Compare it with a classmate's and discuss the differences between the two. How would you modify your classmate's? Why?
9. Select a culture different from your own. Find a knowledgeable representative of that culture and set up an interview. Determine nonverbal differences in time, space, status, expressions, physical contact, and voice.

REFERENCES

1. Hugh Sidey, "Time for Some Decorum," *Time* (February 17, 1992), p. 22.
2. Albert Mehrabian, "Communication Without Words," *Psychology Today* (September 1968), pp. 53–55.
3. Rita Wigg, "Changing with the Times and with a Sport's Image," *Sheboygan Press* (January 19, 1992).
4. Tom Walker, "Graphic Designer Shimkus Markets Ideas in Consulting Business," *San Antonio Light,* January 19, 1992.
5. Sue Reinert, "Shreve's Turns Up Nose at Local Mall," *Patriot Ledger,* January 17, 1992.
6. Joan E. Rigdon, "Managers Who Switch Coasts Must Adapt to Different Approaches to Use of Time," *Wall Street Journal,* August 14, 1991, p. B1.
7. Neil Chesanow, "Clocks Without Hands," *Meetings and Conventions* (November 1985), p. 169.
8. Lawrence B. Rosenfeld and Jean M. Civikly, *With Words Unspoken: The Nonverbal Experience* (New York: Holt, Rinehart and Winston, 1976), p. 197.
9. Ron Adler and Neil Towne, *Looking Out/Looking In,* 2nd ed. (New York: Holt, Rinehart and Winston, 1978), p. 276.
10. Mitchell J. Posner, *Executive Essentials* (New York: Avon, 1982), p. 497.
11. Peter Jensen, "The Modern Office: Design," *Vis a Vis* (July 1991), pp. 36, 38, 40.
12. V. Hale Starr, "Your Office Is Your Image," *Legal Assistant Today* (September/October 1988), p. 60.
13. Paul Preston, *Communication for Managers* (Englewood Cliffs, N.J.: Prentice-Hall, 1979), p. 127.
14. Edward T. Hall has conducted extensive research on proxemics, or space. A review of that work can be found in "Proxemics," *Current Anthropology,* 9, 2–3 (1968), pp. 83–108. A more detailed description is contained in Hall's book, *The Hidden Dimension* (Garden City, N.Y.: Doubleday, 1966).
15. Bob Fahey, Jr., "Nonverbal Communication Can Affect Classroom Performance," *U. The National College Newspaper* (October 1991), p. 17.
16. Julius Fast, *Body Language* (New York: M. Evans & Co., 1970), p. 48.
17. Gerald Goldhaber, *Organizational Communication* (Dubuque, Iowa: William C. Brown, 1979), pp. 150–53.
18. Laura Bird, "Eye-Catching Logos All Too Often Leave Fuzzy Images in Minds of Consumers," *Wall Street Journal,* December 5, 1991, p. B1.
19. Ray Birdwhistell, *Kinesics and Context* (Philadelphia: University of Pennsylvania Press, 1970), p. 176.
20. Gerald I. Nierenberg and Henry H. Calero, *How to Read a Person Like a Book* (New York: Pocket Books, 1975).
21. Brett Pauly, "The Thumb: A Handy Device for Digital Communication," *Dallas Morning News,* January 19, 1992, p. 2F.
22. Vena Garrett, "Mastering the Silent Language," *New Business Opportunities* (August 1990), pp. 22, 24.
23. Birdwhistell, *Kinesics and Context,* p. 176.
24. Phillip R. Harris and Robert T. Moran, *Managing Cultural Differences,* 3rd ed. (Houston: Gulf Publishing, 1991), p. 44.
25. John T. Molloy, *Dress for Success* (New York: Peter H. Wyden, 1975), pp. 27–28.

26. Elizabeth Snead, "Classic Styles Keep Workers Timely, United," *USA Today,* July 30, 1991, p. 40.
27. Ibid.
28. Ashley Montagu, *Touching: The Human Significance of the Skin* (New York: Perennial Library, 1971), p. 334.
29. Sidney Jourard, "Out of Touch: The Body Taboo," *New Society* (November 9, 1967), p. 660.
30. Adopted from the following: Sondra Snowdon, "Worldly Gifts and Protocol Tips," *Business Week 1989 Holiday Giving* (Fall 1989), pp. 55–58; "Gift Giving Japanese Style," *Business Week* (Fall 1988), three-page advertisement; Bob Greene, "When in Tokyo," *Business Week* (October 29, 1988), p. 88; Heather Millar, "The Protocol of the Flower," *Sky* (July 1991), pp. 84, 86.
31. George A. Steiner and John F. Steiner, *Business, Government, and Society* (New York: McGraw-Hill, 1991), pp. 589–92.
32. Kathleen Deveny, "Joe Camel Is Also Pied Piper, Research Finds," *Wall Street Journal,* December 11, 1991, p. B1.
33. Geoffrey Cowley, "I'd Toddle a Mile for a Camel," *Time* (December 23, 1991), p. 70.
34. Joanne Lipman, "Surgeon General Says It's High Time Joe Camel Quit," *Wall Street Journal,* March 10, 1992, p. 37.
35. Deveny, "Joe Camel," p. B1.
36. Paul M. Fisher, Meyer P. Schwartz, John W. Richards, Jr., Adam O. Goldstein, and Tina H. Rojas. "Brand Logo Recognition by Children Aged 3 to 6 Years," *Journal of the American Medical Association* (December 11, 1991), p. 3146.
37. Joseph R. DiFranza, John W. Richards, Paul M. Paulman, Nancy Wolf-Gillespie, Christopher Fletcher, Robert D. Jaffe, and David Murray. "RJR Nabisco's Cartoon Camel Promotes Camel Cigarettes to Children," *Journal of the American Medical Association* (December 11, 1989), pp. 3149–3153.
38. John P. Pierce, Elizabeth Gilpin, David M. Burns, Elizabeth Whalen, Bradley Rosbrook, Donald Shopland, and Michael Johnson, "Does Tobacco Advertising Target Young People to Start Smoking?" *Journal of the American Medical Association* (December 11, 1991), pp. 3157–3158.
39. "Cartoon Camel Tied to Smoking by Kids," *Dallas Morning News,* December 11, 1991, p. 12A.
40. "Controversy Over 'Old Joe' Camel Ads," *USA Today,* March 10, 1992.
41. Lipman, "Surgeon General," p. B1.

Answers

The logos on page 200 belong to the following companies:

Prudential Insurance	Continental Airlines	Travelers Insurance
Coca-Cola	Motorola	Hallmark
AT&T	Pepsi	Kentucky Fried Chicken

CHAPTER 7

LISTENING: HEARING AND UNDERSTANDING WHAT PEOPLE REALLY MEAN

Former television news anchor Walter Cronkite was steering his boat into port at Center Harbor, Maine a few years ago. He was amused to see a crowd of people on shore waving their arms at him. He could barely make out their shouts of "Hello, Walter." As his boat sailed closer, the crowd yelled even louder. Cronkite acknowledged the crowd with a tip of his hat, a bow, and a wave. To his surprise the boat jammed aground a few seconds later. As the crowd stood silent, Cronkite realized they had not been yelling his name but instead the words, "Low water . . . low water."[1]

LISTENING

Listening and hearing are not identical. We can hear and not listen, and we can listen and not understand. In fact, listening is made up of four separate stages. The first stage involves hearing, which uses the physical *sensation* of sound waves, is often a passive process, and also uses the usual sensing of nonverbal messages (discussed in Chapter 6). Next, we *interpret* the sounds and sights that we receive, which leads to knowledge and understanding or misunderstanding. Third, we *evaluate* what we hear and decide how to use the information. Finally, we *react* to the entire process.

Listening Dominates Communication Time

According to a folk saying, we are born with two ears and one mouth because we were meant to listen twice as much as we talk. Regrettably, although listening is the first communication skill learned by infants and is the one most used by adolescents and adults, it is also the least-taught skill in the educational process. In the past few years, however, listening has been studied as an important communication skill needed by business professionals. Today it has become the fourth member of the reading/writing/speaking grid.

The first study on listening was conducted in 1926 by Dr. Paul Rankin. He found that people communicate 7 out of every 10 minutes, or 70 percent of their waking time. Studies since then, conducted on blue- and white-collar workers, salespeople, housewives, college students, and others, have increased that figure to between 50 percent and 80 percent of waking hours. As Table 7.1 shows, more time is spent in listening than in any other of the four communication modes.

Since businesspeople spend up to 80 percent of their workday engaged in communication activities, then 6 1/2 hours of an 8-hour workday are spent listening to others. Just think of the many listening situations one en-

TABLE 7.1 Relative Time Spent in the Four Communication Modes

	Listening	Speaking	Reading	Writing
Learned	First	Second	Third	Fourth
Used	Most (45%)	Next most (30%)	Next least (16%)	Least (9%)
Taught	Least	Next least	Next most	Most

Source: This material is from "Your Personal Listening Profile," a brochure prepared by Dr. Lyman K. Steil, President of Communication Development, Inc., St. Paul, Minnesota, for the Sperry Corporation, New York. Reprinted by permission of Dr. Steil and the Sperry Corporation.

counters during a business day: staff meetings, sales meetings, instruction sessions, telephone calls, conversations with superiors, discussions with peers, counseling subordinates, making decisions, and listening to speeches of others.

Since we spend so much time listening, it is crucial that we learn to listen well. This chapter examines reasons for improving our listening, types of poor listeners, ways to improve the skill of listening, the important interpersonal dimensions of listening, and ways to give proper feedback to others.

How Well Do You Listen?

Even though managers spend so much time listening, most listen no better than the average person: "The average person . . . hears only half of what is said, understands only a quarter of that, and remembers even less. . . . Our attention span rarely lasts more than 45 seconds. . . . Most people use only 25 percent of their native ability for listening."[2]

A few years ago, the Sperry Corporation was looking for a new advertising slogan. The old slogan—"Making machines do more so man can do more"—had worked well but lacked the impact that Sperry needed. Through commissioned research studies, Sperry learned that it was different as a company because its employees listened well. These studies led to a long-term advertising campaign centered around the slogan, "We understand how important it is to listen."

Following the campaign's inception, Sperry ran ads on listening like the one in Figure 7.1 in *The New York Times,* the *Wall Street Journal,* other business publications, and on television. More than 90,000 instructional pieces of listening material were sent to Sperry employees, over 10,000 employees attended a company-sponsored listening training program, and hundreds of thousands of listening brochures were mailed to the general public. Sperry showed people, both inside and outside its organization, that listening is an important communication skill.

Thanks to Sperry it is possible to gain insight into how well you listen by answering the questions to three tests that will give you a personal profile of listening behavior. This profile was developed by Dr. Lyman K. Steil, a special consultant to Sperry, and is printed in a Sperry booklet, *Your Personal Listening Profile.*[3] After you complete the tests in Table 7.2, turn to pages 245–246 to see how you compare with others who have completed the profile. There are no right or wrong answers.

In this chapter, we will look at the importance of listening skills in business. You will have an opportunity to assess your listening skills, discover a number of reasons for poor listening skills, and learn how to improve your listening. The chapter will also discuss the importance of effective feedback and how to give feedback.

TABLE 7.2 How Well Do You Listen?

Quiz 1

A. Circle the term that best describes you as a listener:
Superior
Excellent
Above average
Average
Below average
Poor
Terrible

B. On a scale of 0 to 100 (100 = highest), how would you rate yourself as a listener?

____
(0–100)

Quiz 2

How do you think the following people would rate you as a listener?

Your best friend ____________________

Your boss ____________________

A business colleague ____________________

A job subordinate ____________________

Your spouse ____________________

Quiz 3

As a listener, how often do you find yourself engaging in these ten bad listening habits? *First,* check the appropriate columns. *Then* tabulate your score using the key.

	Frequency					
Listening Habit	**Almost Always**	**Usually**	**Some-times**	**Seldom**	**Almost Never**	**Score**
1. Calling the subject uninteresting	___	___	___	___	___	___
2. Criticizing the speaker's delivery or mannerisms	___	___	___	___	___	___
3. Getting over-stimulated by something the speaker says	___	___	___	___	___	___
4. Listening primarily for facts	___	___	___	___	___	___
5. Trying to outline everything	___	___	___	___	___	___
6. Faking attention to the speaker	___	___	___	___	___	___
7. Allowing interfering distractions	___	___	___	___	___	___
8. Avoiding difficult material	___	___	___	___	___	___
9. Letting emotional words arouse personal antagonism	___	___	___	___	___	___

Listening Habit	Frequency					
	Almost Always	Usually	Some-times	Seldom	Almost Never	Score
10. Wasting the advantage of thought speed (day-dreaming)	______	______	______	______	______	______
Total score						______

Key

For every "Almost always" checked, give yourself a score of	2
For every "Usually" checked, give yourself a score of	4
For every "Sometimes" checked, give yourself a score of	6
For every "Seldom" checked, give yourself a score of	8
For every "Almost never" checked, give yourself a score of	10

Source: Dr. Lyman K. Steil, "Your Listening Profile," pp. 3–4.

Listening Skills Can Be Improved

As the findings of Sperry's listening analysis reveal, most people listen poorly. Tests show that the average listener retains only 50 percent of what he or she hears immediately following the remarks. Within twenty-four to forty-eight hours the retention level drops to 25 percent. There are several reasons for this poor showing.

Reasons for Poor Listening

As we listen there are six possible reasons why we do not understand what the sender means: psychological influences, poor listening education, poor perception, drawing inferences, mental gap time and passive versus active listening behavior.

Psychological Influences

As Figure 7.1 shows, language has at least four levels that impact the listening process: the *sound level* at which our ears pick up the speech signal, the *grammatical level* that translates the sound into understanding at the hearer's *meaning level,* and the sender's original *intended meaning level.* In reality, this simple process becomes complicated through misspeaking, mispronunciation, noises distorting sound, and a variety of listener problems. When meaning is not explicit, the listener often infers it. *Phonemic restoration* is an act that uses the basic letter sounds for meaning, like the *b* in bat. It draws from all the levels and hopefully allows a listener to interpret most

THERE'S A LOT MORE TO LISTENING THAN HEARING.

Most of us have perfectly good ears.

So why, then, are we such perfectly awful listeners - listening on the average at a 25% level of efficiency?

The fact is, there's a lot more to listening than hearing.

After we hear something, we must interpret it. Evaluate it. And finally, respond to it. That's listening.

And it's during this complex process that we run into all kinds of trouble.

For example: we prejudge - sometimes even disregard - a speaker based on his appearance or delivery.

We let personal ideas, emotions or prejudices distort what a person has to say.

We ignore subjects we consider too difficult or uninteresting.

And because the brain works four times faster than most people speak, we too often wander into distraction.

Yet as difficult as listening really is, it's the one communication skill we're never really taught.

Well, as a corporation with more than 80,000 employees, we at Sperry are making sure we use our ears to full advantage.

We've set up expanded listening programmes that Sperry personnel from our divisions worldwide can attend. Sales representatives. Sperry Univac computer engineers. Even the Chairman of the Board.

We're convinced that effective listening adds a special dimension to what we can do for our customers. And when you speak to someone from Sperry we think you'll be equally convinced.

It's amazing what more than two good ears can do.

WE UNDERSTAND HOW IMPORTANT IT IS TO LISTEN.

FIGURE 7.1 The Sperry Ad

Source: Sperry Corporation, New York, from *The Economist*, European edition.

of what a speaker is saying, even though the mind often distorts a message through prejudices and hidden agendas.

Lack of Proper Education

As the text of Figure 7.1 explains, we receive little instruction on how to be better listeners and consequently develop poor listening habits and inadequate skills. While most people have taken at least one course in which they were taught to write, read, and speak, few have had a course on listening.

Poor Perception

Each person's perception of the world—of its objects, events, and people—is different. If a listener uses this perceptive filter to preevaluate a speaker, for example, and assumes that the speaker is going to be boring and the topic uninteresting or unimportant, then the listener cannot accurately hear and understand that speaker's words.

Lack of Agreement on the Meaning of Words

Semantic problems can serve as barriers to effective communication (see Chapter 5). Speakers who assume that their words carry meanings that everyone understands are doomed to let technical jargon and company lingo block full understanding by their listeners.

Drawing Inferences

In constructing mental messages, we often *infer* information that is not explicitly stated. Since our minds work in logical steps for problem solving and decision making, we assume that a similar logical sequence occurs in meaning interpretation. A set of simple declarative sentences shows that error. Listeners can hear the following sentences repeated: "The manager's car is in the parking lot," "The parking lot is next to the office building," "The lights in the office building are on," "The manager is in her office." While it is not stated, most listeners infer that "The manager turned on the lights in the office building," even though they could have been turned on automatically or by someone else. Inferring without having all the facts can be dangerous to effective listening.

Gap Time

The mind functions like a high-speed computer that is capable of processing more than 500 words per minute, yet the average person talks at a rate of 140 words per minute. This results in "gap time" on the part of the listener. To fill this empty time, the mind skips to other thoughts at the same time that it listens to a speaker. During your next class meeting, listen for a few minutes and then make a list of the different thoughts that raced in and out of your mind while you were listening to the instructor. This doesn't necessarily happen because the speaker is boring. The process seems to be a psychologically healthy one but also one we can control.

Passive Versus Active Behavior

Because we don't learn proper listening techniques, and because we are lazy about filling our gap time, we develop passive behavior. Passive listeners sit, almost in a trance, and let words and actions pass in and out of their ears and minds. One Sperry executive explained the passive listening response like this: "I think it is one of our basic human tendencies that when someone talks we turn ourselves off. We let his or her mouth move and we try to respond with some non-action kind of comment and we don't want to pick the problem up and work on it."[4]

Gender Differences

The work of Georgetown University linguistics professor Deborah Tannen led her to the conclusion that men and women listen differently, a fact that is exhibited in their conversational styles. Her research shows that conversations between women reveals that they sit facing each other, often leaning in, with strong facial responses, direct eye contact, and encouraging vocal cues like "Yes, yes," "Uh-huh," and "Mmm-hmmm." When men converse, they sit at an angle to each other, assume a more casual posture, maintain little eye contact and facial expression, and expect silence from the other as evidence that listening is really occurring.

When men and women converse together, the difficulties begin. If women interject a word of encouragement, "Yes," men either assume the woman is not listening, or that she is in agreement with what was said. The woman is in reality using the word to show that she is following the conversation. If the woman later voices disagreement or another viewpoint, the man may think that he was misunderstood or misled. Women, on the other hand, interpret that men are not listening if there is an absence of verbal and physical signals (remember that men believe their silence displays attention).

Tannen has found that the roots of such behavior are anchored in the socialization process. Boys learn to use language as a way to assert independence and build status. Girls use it as a way to create intimacy and give support. When this behavior is then displayed in adults, men often feel women do not "get to the point" in conversations, and women feel men have a tendency to lecture. Tannen is quick to assert that neither gender is at fault. It's merely a style difference that men and women need to understand and allow for in conversations.[5]

Descending Order of Efficiency

Problems can occur because of the vertical and horizontal flow of communication in an organization (see Chapter 2). Directors tend to hear 90 percent of what other directors say. But, as Field tells us, less listening takes place as communication descends the organizational ladder:

> A vice president, talked to by a chairman of the board, retains 67% of what the chairman said. A supervisor, chewed out by a VP, remembers about 56% of what he is told. A foreman listening to a manager hears with 30% to 40% efficiency. And a worker, tuned in to a foreman, can be expected to hear only about 20% of what was said.[6]

Poor listening also occurs on the way up the organization ladder. Many senior executives and supervisors are so conditioned to giving orders that they shut themselves off from what subordinates have to say; some are in love with the sound of their own voices. Longenecker and Liverpool emphasize this characteristic of managers: "Most managers are not good listeners because: they are rarely rewarded for listening; listening is sometimes viewed as a passive activity associated with a loss of control or power; the manager's role normally requires him or her to speak more than listen; and speaking is more action-oriented than listening."[7]

Being Paid Not to Listen

In some jobs individuals are paid so much for their technical expertise that they unconsciously try to avoid any required listening sessions. Physicians sometimes fit this mold. A doctor who spends 15 minutes interpreting a nuclear magnetic resonance scan and is paid $500 for the service may not desire to spend 90 minutes on an initial appointment with an older patient that will only pay $100. As Winslow states, patients often do not receive what they need from such doctors.

> Recent health-care research shows that what patients want most from a doctor's appointment is, first, a chance to tell their story and, second, information about their problem and how to solve it. Though patients can also be a barrier to communications, doctors on average interrupt patients within the first 18 seconds of an interview, then spend less than two minutes of a 20-minute session imparting information.
>
> As a result, 60% of patients leave a doctor's office confused about instructions on medication, and more than half of new prescriptions are taken improperly or not at all.[8]

Poor Listening Is Costly

Because we take listening for granted and are passive about this important skill, the value of proper listening is cheapened, and listening mistakes develop that are extremely costly to the organization. Assume that you communicate 80 percent of your workday and that 45 percent of that time is spent in listening activities. Table 7.3 shows what your listening time costs your organization. As the table shows, the organization that employs you is paying a high premium for your listening time. Assume that each employee in the company commits one listening error within the space of a month: A simple $10 listening mistake can cost a company with 100 employees

TABLE 7.3 The Price Tag on Poor Listening

Salary	Cost of Communication Time	Cost of Listening Time
$ 15,000	$12,000	$ 5,400
25,000	20,000	9,000
35,000	28,000	12,600
50,000	40,000	18,000
100,000	80,000	36,000

$1,000; a company with 1,000 employees will pay out $10,000; and an organization with 10,000 employees will lose $100,000. In the United States there are over 100 million workers. A minor $10 listening error by each person would cost $1 billion, and most workers make numerous listening mistakes each week. Listening errors cost money. Most notably, though, they cause the scheduling of new meetings and appointments; loss of orders; reshipping of problem shipments; retyping and recopying letters, memos, and reports; apologizing to customers and trying to repair damaged relationships; and handling countless telephone calls. For physicians, poor listening leads to poor communication between doctors and patients, and that has been proven to be the most common cause of malpractice suits. Much of the unnecessary effort and waste in the examples just cited can be minimized by improving listening skills.

Reasons for Improving Listening Skills

Understanding

Understanding occurs as we hear what others say, observe the way they say it, and relate that information to our own knowledge. The listener, not the speaker, is primarily responsible for the learning that takes place. By clearing the hurdles of ineffective communication (see Chapters 4 and 5) and observing nonverbal behavior (see Chapter 6), listeners can fully understand a speaker's ideas and feelings and can accurately judge the information. Their ability to instruct, supervise, manage, lead, and counsel is enhanced.

Accuracy

Accuracy results when we understand clearly. Accuracy requires that we ask questions when the words and actions that we hear and see are unclear or incomplete. When your boss tells you to be at a meeting with clients on Monday morning at the Holiday Inn in Columbus, you had better know whether she means the Holiday Inn in Columbus, Ohio, or the Holiday Inn in Columbus, Georgia, before you make your travel arrangements.

Coping

Coping is something we all do when, for instance, distracting background noise, unusual accents or dialects, static on the telephone line, or a nonworking microphone interfere with our receiving and comprehending abilities. These distractions can be frustrating at the least and ultimately can distort entire messages. Even highly technical or unfamiliar words can block understanding. Speakers can help their listeners by minimizing these factors. Listeners can improve their listening behavior by practicing and learning to cope with distractions.

Remembering

Remembering what other people say is a hard task for many listeners. We have all been introduced to an important person, only to realize a few minutes later that we didn't retain the person's name. Paper and pencil can be used to record what is said at meetings, but we often need to remember points of discussions when we have nothing to write on. Later in this chapter is an explanation of a method for remembering a speaker's words by the continual mental manipulation of the content of the speech.

Feelings

Feelings are not usually stated in a speaker's words, yet the ideas that speakers verbalize to others are colored by the emotions they feel. If a customer service representative says, "I don't have time to talk with you," to a customer, it could mean that she is busy helping five other people and there are two calls waiting; or the statement could mean that the customer and his problems are a bother to her; or perhaps she is really saying that the customer bores her. Interpreting the "real message" behind what she says requires that you listen to her words and interpret the nonverbal emotions that shape her message. Mastery of both these areas can help you become more sensitive to "totally hearing" others.

Successful Listening Leads to Successful Memory

Middle-age memory lapses can be alarming. But according to memory expert Alan Brown, a few memory changes are a mandatory part of the normal aging process. As people age, both learning and recall slow, and paying attention to people and things requires more effort. Brown acknowledges that most failures occur during listening, the first stage of the three-stage memory process. In stage 1, *sensory memory* allows us to "grab" the information and hold it for a few seconds. Sometimes this step is never completed. During stage 2, *short-term memory* that lasts up to a half minute, the information is shifted to a form that has relevance for the listener. Finally, *long-term memory* takes on two forms: day-to-day experiences and encyclopedic recording. With aging, difficulties sometimes arise in passing information between the three different memory stages.

Brown contends that people who say they have forgotten a name, appointment date, or directions to an office never really got the information in their heads to begin with. They had, he says, a listening breakdown:

> We may have been preoccupied, distracted, or off in our own world when we encountered the information. Even when we do capture the information initially, successful remembering requires that we customize the data in a way that allows our brains to absorb it readily. New memories are fragile. They fade if not attended to. . . . If you are visually oriented, write it down; if you are an auditory person, discuss it with someone; if you are tactile, handle it or use it in a physical way.[9]

Types of Poor Listeners

There are several types of poor listeners in the business environment. As you read the descriptions, decide if you—or anyone you know—fit into one of the categories.

The Faker. This is a pseudo listener—a person who pretends to be doing the real thing. The faker displays head nods that seem to confirm or reject what is being said and adds comments like, "I see," "That's interesting," and "Yeah."

The Continual Talker. This listener never seems to run out of things to say. He takes a stand on every issue, interrupts conversations, and loves to

Goosemyer by parker and wilder

Source: *Goosemyer* by Parker and Wilder. © 1980 Field Enterprises, Inc. Courtesy of Field Newspaper Syndicate.

hear himself talk. If you give this person the opportunity to talk, you may never be able to get another word into the conversation.

The Rapid-Writing Note Taker. This listener thinks it is important to record every word a speaker utters. Unfortunately, she finds herself placing a period at the end of the first point as the speaker introduces the third. She is so involved in the accuracy of note taking that she completely misses the second point.

The Critic. The critic can take any of several forms. This listener calls the subject uninteresting, demeans the speaker's delivery style and lack of supporting ideas, and listens so hard for the facts that he misses the speaker's underlying feelings. A personal bias sometimes arouses his antagonistic emotions.

The "I'm in a Hurry" Listener. This person never slows down long enough to look you in the eyes and finish a conversation. She talks and listens while opening mail, talking to others on the telephone, or shuffling through papers on her desk. Typically the speaker wants to shake this listener out of her busyness and force her to listen. But more often than not, the speaker's typical response is to hurry, finish the words, and walk away.

The "Hand on the Door Knob" Listener. This listener reminds us of physicians, college professors, and many businesspeople. He ordinarily keeps his office door closed. When he decides the talk is over, he gets up from his desk or chair and moves toward the office door. There he stands with his hand on the door knob, nonverbally indicating "Time is up."

The "Make Sure It Is Correct" Listener. She can be found in every office. In meetings and conversations this person listens carefully for facts and is the first to signal when an error has been uttered. While the type of information this person remembers is often important, the method she uses—

interrupting the conversation or making the speaker look bad—can become obnoxious.

The "Finish the Sentence for You" Listener. This person seems to be impatient, is always in a hurry, and feels as though he knows exactly what the speaker will say next. He can be helpful when the speaker is actually stuck and is searching for facts or lost words. But usually he intrudes when a momentary pause is taken or the speaker stops to get her breath.

Supervisors may feel that they know what their subordinates are going to say next. But they must be careful not to program the listening/discussion sessions by constantly finishing another person's sentences. This process can cause a pattern to develop where the subordinate starts talking and will automatically stop mid-sentence to let the superior finish. Needless to say, this can distort good communication relationships.

The "I've Done One Better" Listener. This type of listening is a typical form of one-upmanship. It is a variation of the fish story, where each time the catch is reported the fish grows in length. This listener, in order to obtain psychological strokes, consciously or unconsciously responds to activities and events in the lives of others with, "That reminds me of the time I. . . ." His story, of course, always demonstrates more difficulty, harder trials, worse conditions, and/or better results.

We all fall into the role of poor listener from time to time. But effective listeners work to change their ineffective behavior before it becomes a hard-to-change habit. The next two sections discuss concrete ways to improve your listening skills and your interpersonal listening behavior.

Improve Your Skill as a Listener

Although listening is a seldom-taught skill, it is one that can be improved. To improve your listening, however, you need instruction. By practicing the following six steps on a regular basis, you can improve your listening behavior and your overall communication effectiveness.

Steps for Improving Your Skill

1. *Try to create an interest in the topic.* At the outset of a speech or meeting, when you hear the discussion topic, mentally brainstorm for a few moments and think of all the things that you would like to know about that topic. By starting the listening process with an open mind and a positive attitude, you will find it easier to follow the speaker. Throughout the speech, even if you become disappointed in what is being said, strive to constantly

listen for the positive and interesting information. Ralph Nichols, the forefather of listening improvement instruction, put it this way:

> The key to the whole matter of interest in a topic is the word *use*. Whenever we wish to listen efficiently, we ought to say to ourselves: "What's he saying that I can use? What worthwhile ideas has he? Is he reporting any workable procedures? Anything that I can cash in, or with which I can make myself happier?" Such questions lead us to screen what we are hearing in a continual effort to sort out the elements of personal value. G. K. Chesterton spoke wisely indeed when he said, "There is no such thing as an uninteresting subject; there are only uninteresting people."[10]

2. *Start by constructing your mental outline.* Outlining will be discussed in detail in Chapter 8. For now, remember that listeners need to be aware of the thesis or theme of a talk and the major points that will support the thesis. For instance, a representative from an office product company comes to your office to give a presentation about the purchase of word processing equipment. If the representative is wise, she will research your company and its equipment needs thoroughly before the presentation. Let's assume this takes place. She knows of your needs and your interest. At the start of her presentation she introduces the word processing model that she wants you to consider. (Her thesis will revolve around the model.) Next, she states that her talk will cover four primary areas: the equipment's ability, ease in operation, cost, and the maintenance process.

If you are tuned in at the start, and you will be if you have a vital *interest* in obtaining such equipment, you will start with an empty outline in your mind (Table 7.4). As the representative talks, mentally fill in your outline with her key points (see Table 7.5). By starting with an empty outline you

TABLE 7.4 The Listening Outline

(Thesis)	
(Main point)	
(Main point)	
(Main point)	
(Main point)	

TABLE 7.5 Using the Listening Outline

(Thesis of speech)	The word processing equipment
(Main point)	Capability
(Main point)	Operation ease
(Main point)	Cost
(Main point)	Maintenance

can "actively" participate in the listening process and retain in your mind the speaker's main points after she has finished.

3. *Continually review your mental outline.* Speakers, like listeners, can change their minds and the content of their speeches while they are talking. If you constantly go through a memory review process, you can use your "gap time" for the review and summary process. Remember, the computer in your mind is constantly running. Discipline your mind to work for you by selectively deciding what you will allow it to think.

4. *Use key words in your mental outline.* Remember the pitfalls encountered by the rapid-writing note taker? Don't be guilty of mentally committing that same mistake. Our educational process leads us to feel that we must make extensive notes of everything that is said in speeches. In so doing we fail to discipline our minds and our ears, and, like the note taker, we sometimes miss what is said.

Your mind is capable of handling much more work than you give it. Test it; discipline it; rely on it to work for you. In Table 7.5 only one word or term is entered in each main point division. Using only one word per main point can save you a great deal of work. When you ask yourself, "What kind of capability?" your mind naturally knows you are referring to the machine, and it will in most instances recall several facts that were stated about the machine's capabilities.

5. *Judge between important and unimportant information.* Not everything that the speaker says is important or even relevant. Be critical of the content, but not the person, and attach only the important information to your mental outline.

Our word processing representative described several aspects of operation ease, including ease of entering information into the system, ease of retrieving information from the system, and comfort in using the equipment. All of this information is important. In fact, key words can again be used to enter the ideas into the mind (Table 7.6). Most presentations contain unimportant information that listeners do not need; these are often facts. Don't memorize facts. Facts are meaningless unless you connect them to the talk's main principles and concepts.

6. *Tackle distractions head on.* At times nothing can hinder the act of listening as much as distractions, such as the noise from office or production machines, low-flying aircraft, automobiles, radio and television programs, crying babies, or whispering adults. All of these and more serve to disrupt the meaning of the words we hear and cause us to shift focus to the distraction or the person causing it. Sometimes the shift is necessary. A quick glare at those who are talking, or a polite request to "Please turn down the radio," can eliminate the interference. At other times distractions are not that easily overcome.

Some people listen better when distractions exist. They have learned, usually from first-hand experience, to listen through the disturbance, to hear what is said, and to process and use what they have heard.

Distractions can take forms other than surrounding noise. The accents

TABLE 7.6 The Word Processing Equipment

Capability		
Operation Ease		
E	R	C
N	E	O
T	T	M
E	R	F
R	I	O
I	E	R
N	V	T
G	I	
	N	
	G	

and dialects of the speaker can be a hindrance. Perceptive speakers with distracting problems of this nature usually spend the first few minutes of a talk saying unimportant things to let their listeners adjust to their voice. At other times the distraction may be overly emotional feelings about the topic or the apparent lack of organization. As a listener you must constantly stay flexible and strive to hear the main points of the speaker's message.

Steps for Improving Interpersonal Listening Behavior

Listening with accuracy and understanding in group meetings and speeches is an important skill, but another area that is just as important is interpersonal listening behavior. This type of listening occurs in one-to-one conversations and requires more than hearing and remembering information. It requires that one person attempt to take on a mental and physical understanding of the other—an involvement that is usually missing from large group settings. It goes beyond hearing words to the development of feelings and empathy. The remainder of this chapter explores ways that you can become a better interpersonal listener. Two dimensions, physical and personal, help us go beyond words and achieve greater understanding with others.

Physical Dimensions

Conversations always take place in settings that have limits and usually follow patterns. If you can control these factors, you can drastically improve the listening that occurs between people.

1. *Pick a time and a place that are conducive to listening.* The day is

full of minutes and hours when we can listen. Wise listeners examine the required communication situation and the dynamics of the time and place and make decisions based on the desired outcome.

Some people do their best work early in the mornings. They set up breakfast meetings because their minds work well at 7:00 A.M.; others don't start functioning well until 10:00 A.M. For some, the worst time of the day is immediately following lunch (it is hard to listen on a full stomach) or immediately before closing time (people then are fearful they will have to work late).

The place of the conversation is also important. You may gain power by holding the meeting in your office, but goodwill could be established by going to someone else's office. Some supervisors find it necessary to leave their offices for important counseling sessions because they have no way to transfer telephone calls or their offices are not completely private. Others walk outside the plant doors for meetings, to avoid the roar of plant machinery.

2. *Avoid time restraints.* If you have only a few free minutes, but you know a conversation will take longer, schedule it for another time or date. The other person will probably agree to the rescheduling when you explain that you want enough time to discuss all issues in depth.

3. *Attempt to shut out all distractions.* Tell your secretary to hold your calls, take your telephone off the hook, close your office door, or hang a "Do not disturb" sign outside your door to get the privacy you need.

4. *Arrange your office furniture.* Position the furniture for the best interaction. Chairs should be arranged so that you can look the other person in the eye, convey your attention, and understand his or her nonverbal messages.

Personal Dimensions

After making the necessary physical arrangements, focus your attention on the personal dimensions.

1. *Stop talking.* If you know you listen poorly because you talk too much, stop talking. If your intent is to listen, you can display it best by being completely silent—even if you must bite your tongue. Listening starts *only* when your talking stops.

2. *Prepare yourself for listening.* Realize that true dialogue involves two people. Try to understand your own emotions and feelings so that they will not influence the other person. Try to perceive the other person as he sees himself, and picture yourself as you think he sees you. This will help you project an empathic attitude. But if you are having a hard time listening because other things are on your mind, be honest with the other person and ask to reschedule the discussion time so that you can devote your entire attention to the person and the issue.

3. *Look at the other person.* Sometimes, especially in embarrassing conversations, it is hard to look into the other person's eyes. But a sensitive and caring listener communicates best by looking at the person, instead of

out the window, up at the ceiling, or over the person's shoulder. If looking at the eyes is difficult, look at the hairline, neckline, mouth, or forehead directly above the nose. Eye contact is a nonverbal signal that says, "You have my full attention."

4. *Listen to what is said and what is not said.* Words are important, for they tell us what others are thinking. But counselors and psychotherapists have proven that we sometimes glean more meaning from an encounter from what is not being said. If particular issues are overly repeated, while others are ignored, the wise listener will focus on and ask questions about the area least discussed.

5. *Listen to how something is said.* The nonverbal behavior of a person tells much about the true meaning of his or her message. Wise listeners try to understand any nonverbal behavior that contradicts what is said verbally.

6. *Overcome prejudices.* If you enter a listening situation with an existing prejudice toward the speaker or topic, you will never hear what the other person is saying or trying to say. Listen before you judge. If you still disagree when finished, call in a third person as a negotiator.

7. *Realize that listening is not the same as problem solving.* Some managers don't like to listen because they fear that they will be put on the spot and have to answer questions and solve problems. Listeners do not have to solve other people's problems for them. They can, however, help others as they sort out and make decisions for themselves. A good listener will listen for what the talker is repeating and for what she is ignoring. The listener will mentally put these together and will ask questions aimed at helping the talker arrive at new answers that she can use to solve her own problems.

8. *Actively listen and establish clarity checks.* Active listening restates or paraphrases the speaker's message. It clarifies and obtains accurate facts and gives feedback to the speaker. In "active listening," a clarity check designed by Carl Rogers, a listener responds to a speaker with, "What I heard you say was . . . ," and then gives comments.

For example, a supervisor tells an employee to check on the Blair account, get an update on the production schedule along with cost factors, and order a new machine. Before following the instructions the employee gets a "clarity check": "What you want me to do is check the status and cost of the Blair account and then order the new machine, right?" Wrong! The supervisor really wants her to check the status of the Blair account. The update and the order of the new machine were separate tasks.

Clarity checks are vital when critical decisions must be made, important issues are being examined, or face-to-face communication is not available, as in telephone conversations. One excellent method of obtaining clarity is to send a written memo so that everyone concerned will get the same information.

9. *Ask questions.* Your primary job as a listener is to understand what the other person is saying. Just hearing another's words often does not lead to understanding. But asking questions about what is heard does produce bet-

ter understanding for both participants. Practice asking questions often, but ask them in an open-ended way that produces understanding, not critical defensiveness. Ask questions that focus on who, what, where, when, and how. Here are some examples:

- "Joe, *who* worked with you on the Morris account?"
- "*What* was the status of the account when you took it over?"
- "*Where* do you perceive the present policy is taking us?"
- "*When* do you plan to make the new proposal?"
- "*How* have you been able to complete the project in such a short time period?"

Each of these questions asks for basic information and is stated in a nonthreatening manner. This type of question will provide clarification, improve understanding, and is even helpful for dealing with shy, nervous, and disorganized speakers.

Did you notice that the question "Why?" was omitted? That one word has stopped more conversations than any other. When asked "Why?" we have to immediately stop our train of thought, respond to the question (sometimes in order to defend our actions or beliefs), and then try to work our way back to the original place in the topic. Often the momentary stop causes us to deviate from the original issues and never return. Sensitive listeners use words other than *why* to ask questions and get information from the speaker. If *why* is the only word that will work, try a creative method of asking for the same information. Instead of asking, "Why did you do that?" try, "That's interesting, tell me more about it," or, "I'm interested in hearing the reason for your action."

Robert L. Montgomery, in his book *Listening Made Easy,* illustrates the power of questioning. He tells the story of the late Fred Herman and his unique ability to ask the listener questions:

> Herman was introduced on the Mike Douglas television show one day as "the greatest salesman in the world." What happened next was purely spontaneous; Herman vowed he had no idea what Mike Douglas would ask him.
>
> Douglas began by saying, "Fred, since you're hailed as the No. 1 salesman in the world, sell me something!" Without any hesitation, Fred Herman responded instantly and instinctively with a question. "Mike, what would you want me to sell you?"
>
> Mike Douglas, who is paid a couple of million dollars a year for asking questions, was now on the defensive. Surprised, Douglas paused, looked around and finally answered, "Well, sell me this ash tray."
>
> Fred Herman again spoke instantly, "Why would you want to buy that?" And again, Mike Douglas, surprised and scratching his head, finally answered, "Well, it's new and shapely. Also, it's colorful. And besides, we are in a new studio and don't want it to burn down. And, if course, we want to accommodate guests who smoke."

> At this point, Mike Douglas sat back in his chair, but not for long. Instantly Fred Herman responded, "How much would you pay for the ash tray, Mike?"
>
> Douglas stammered and said, "Well, I haven't bought an ash tray lately, but this one is attractive and large, so I guess I'd pay $18 or $20." And Fred Herman, after asking just three questions, closed the sale by saying, "Well, Mike, I'll let you have the ash tray for $18."[11]

10. *Retain the confidentiality of what you hear.* Occasionally our conversations with peers and subordinates include some disclosing and sharing. This information can be personal and private and is usually discussed under the assumption of confidentiality. While such disclosures are hard to utter, the end result for the listener can be released tensions and frustrations, lowered feelings of pressure, and even warm feelings of established friendship. But such sharing can also make us vulnerable, for the person that we shared the information with possesses, in a very real sense, a part of us. If the conversation session and the shared information are handled wisely, relationships are strengthened, conflicts resolved, and potential trouble often avoided. But if the same information is leaked or gossiped to others, reputations can be ruined and credibility destroyed. A wise listener will try to discern before the conversation whether he or she should listen to, and probe, such topics. If a decision is made to listen, the information should be maintained in strict confidentiality.

11. *Follow up.* All of us have had conversations where personal information was shared but the next time we saw the other person, the previous conversation was never mentioned. In fact, a strange, nonverbal feeling clouded the second meeting. Usually neither person wants to reopen and examine what was previously said. Yet to ignore the time and feelings that were shared is tantamount to saying you are embarrassed about what was said. To avoid this situation, and to keep the lines of communication open, a sensitive listener will follow up with a brief and simple statement. It could sound something like this:

> Say, Fran, I appreciate your sharing your feelings about your work situation last week. I trust everything is OK? We don't have to talk about it, but I just wanted to tell you that if you want to talk again, I'd be happy to listen.

A simple acknowledgement tells Fran that she was not stupid for revealing her problem and that a good listener is available if she should need to talk again.

As these eleven ways to improve interpersonal listening behavior have shown, listening is not an end in itself. Listeners have responsibility to help complete the communication process, which occurs when feedback is shared between two people. The last section of this chapter discusses the use of interpersonal feedback.

Giving and Receiving Interpersonal Feedback

Speakers contribute to better listening on the part of their audience by responding to feedback that they receive and then making immediate adjustments. In an interpersonal setting, listening is enhanced by giving, receiving, and responding to feedback. Wise managers establish written and oral feedback systems that monitor how well employees understand their messages (see Chapter 1). Such systems keep managers from being isolated and bypassed.

In communication, feedback is the reception and consequent response to what a person sees, hears, reads, or feels. We receive feedback through our different senses: seeing, hearing, smelling, touching, and tasting. During communication, we normally respond to what we see and hear.

The study of feedback became popular in the late 1940s during the scientific studies of communication engineering. *Cybernetics* was the term that people like Norbert Wiener used to refer to their feedback research. Early studies examined how systems, like guided missiles, are corrected for accuracy by receiving feedback on how far off course a missile missed its intended target. Such knowledge is vital in technical fields.

In interpersonal communication the knowledge gained by feedback is essential: Feedback tells us when our instructions are misunderstood, how our comments lack necessary relevancy, and how our nonverbal behavior contradicts what we say verbally. For feedback to be helpful to the person receiving it, information must be given clearly, be understood, be accepted, and be usable in making changes to both verbal and nonverbal messages.

Feedback Must Be Given Clearly

As listeners we give both verbal and nonverbal feedback to the speaker. *Nonverbal messages* are communicated through body movement, gestures, and facial expressions. As Table 6.1 on pages 203–204 indicates, messages are sent when we stand, sit, smile, frown, or even look questioningly.

Verbal messages take the form of clarity checks, questions, or sharing of feelings or reactions. Larger and often repeated behavioral patterns can be discussed. When listeners give this type of feedback, speakers can use listeners' reactions as a mirror for observing the consequences of their own behavior: They become aware of what they say and do and how they say and do it. This awareness, if used correctly, can become a behavior modifier.

Feedback Needs to Be Understood

Before individuals can make verbal and behavioral changes based on feedback, they have to understand specifically what they are saying and doing, how they are saying and doing it, and how others feel about what they hear and see. Listeners have this information, but they must be careful not to "dump" it unreservedly on the other person.

Describe behavior. Feedback should describe another's behavior only in terms of what the listener sees and hears and not in relation to what the listener believes the other person is like. Sandra, a manager, was holding a performance appraisal with Ed, a supervisor. Sandra listened to Ed describe his job and then responded, "Ed, I've observed you in staff meetings. You are a motormouth and don't give your people a chance to talk." Ed, of course, was dumbstruck and defensively argued his case. Sandra could have better phrased her comments around Ed's behavior instead of his person: "Ed, I observed your staff meeting today, and you talked a lot and didn't allow comments from the others." Personality traits are difficult or impossible to change; changing behavioral habits is much easier.

Feedback Must Be Accepted

Focus on observations, not inferences. Chapter 4 discussed the danger of acting on inferences rather than observations. Making that distinction is critical for listeners: Describing behavior that we have viewed gives us credibility, but developing inferences based on second-hand knowledge or guesses destroys that credibility, fogs perception of the other person, and can cause inappropriate filtering of what we hear and see.

Cover the "now" instead of the "then." The best time for providing feedback is immediately following an observation or discussion, when the feedback carries more meaning and impact. Focusing on yesterday or some time in the past, instead of now, is unfair and also subjectively distorts the message we want to convey. One of the worst types of poor listeners is the "closet stuffer." This person observes the action and hears the words but builds up ammunition from several episodes before she responds. When she finally shares her feedback, there is too much for the other to hear, much less to utilize.

Feedback Must be Usable in Making Changes

Sharing instead of giving advice. Too often feedback is given because the "release" feels good; this type of feedback usually takes the form of advice. Instead of giving advice, focus on sharing ideas so that others are free to use the information when and if they like.

Give what the other person can use, not what you are capable of giving. We are all capable of continually critiquing others. But the best feedback comes after selectively deciding what will really help the other person to make behavioral changes. Maybe it is a simple word of encouragement, or a point of clarification, or a comment regarding what someone said or how they said it. Thoughtful listeners ask themselves, "If I were that person, what would I need to hear and how would I need to hear it?" Once this question is answered, feedback can then be formulated and communicated.

ETHICS: RIGHT OR WRONG?

Is Your Boss Listening?

At the American Sterling Corporation offices in El Toro, California employees know their phone calls are monitored, but someone occasionally forgets. One young male employee was disciplined when his supervisor found herself on the listening end of a call that he made to his girlfriend to discuss their sex life. "It was very graphic. Of course we turned it off and stopped listening as soon as we realized it was not a 'customer call.'" Needless to say, the employee was embarrassed when the supervisor presented him with a tape of the conversation.[12]

Even as a customer, you can bet that a third or fourth party is often tuned into your conversation. The next time you place an order through almost any catalog company, book a ticket on an airline, talk to a phone company representative, book a rental car or hotel through an 800 number, or place a stock order with your local Shearson Lehman Hutton salesperson, you should realize that someone may be eavesdropping on what you say.

Corporate eavesdropping is on the rise and the confidentiality of employee conversation is being eroded. As new technologies become available, companies have quickly moved to deploy them into the workplace. Employers believe the monitoring process is both legal and necessary to evaluate productivity and service standards. Employees and their supporting trade associations and unions are not as sure that this is true. The practice, however, is now common at catalog, insurance, utility and phone companies, banks, airlines, hotels and telemarketers, and a variety of other organizations.

Monitoring is conducted to determine how many calls can be received or placed in a given period of time, how much time should be given to each caller, and the accuracy of the message being given to the customers. In some companies it is also used to evaluate an employee's performance during a probationary training period.

At the GTE southern California offices the phone operators recently named "monitoring" as the number 1 pressure of their job. A representative of the GTE union, Communication Workers of America (CAW), Local 9510 stated, "Their biggest complaint is they don't know when they're being monitored. . . . The supervisor listening in might not even be in the same building. Or there might be four supervisors listening in at once. Our members have told us that if they could see their supervisor looking at them, they'd feel better. The way it's done now creates a lot of distrust." CAW estimates that supervisors across the nation monitor over 400 million calls a year.[13]

Pacific Bell does let its employees know when a supervisor is listening. They put a light on so operators will know someone is on the other end. "We have employees who don't like it and employees who do. . . . It is the best way of ensuring that good service is getting to the customer."

Employees wonder if such listening is legal and can be done without their knowing. The answer is usually yes. But employees have a friend in some federal and state lawmakers. In four states—California, Florida, Michigan, and Pennsylvania—all parties must consent before calls can be recorded. Nine additional states have introduced bills that would carry the same requirement. As more companies move toward monitoring, it is a given that additional legislation will be proposed.[14]

Case Questions

1. Is there a question of ethics in this case?
2. Whose rights do you believe should prevail, employee or employer?
3. Do you believe employer monitoring behavior impacts the overall quality of listening in the organization? If so, how?
4. How would you feel if you knew a third party was listening when you called for a hotel or plane reservation?
5. Is there a better way for employers to listen to employees?
6. Under what conditions would you approve of monitoring?

A GLOBAL PERSPECTIVE

Listening Hints For Working In Other Countries

In Japan and other countries a primary event that requires more listening than talking is the first meeting. Introductions take on a ritualistic approach. After individuals come together business cards are exchanged and studied. This is followed by several rounds of tea drinking. For Americans this phase is a time to politely listen and to respond to questions while the foreign host will perceptively determine where you fit in your organization and how your job matches their job. First impressions count and the American business person often finds that business is conducted on the basis of perceptive personal judgments and not on a discussion of what seems to make good business sense.[16]

In other countries meetings also begin with small talk . . . "a few minutes in Europe or Japan, but much longer in the Arab world, China, South America or Africa. Personal subjects (family, politics, money, religion) should be avoided, as well as particularly sensitive subjects which vary by country."[17] It is critical that the conversation center on the host country and how things are done there. Foreigners are not only offended, they do not want to listen to how things are done in America or elsewhere.

For the Japanese, silence is an important part of communication. According to Roger Axtell, "Americans abhor silence; those gaps must be filled. But among the Japanese, it is common—even expected—to have periods of silence in which the Japanese businessman contemplates what has been said. The Japanese cannot understand why an American dislikes those quiet moments. As one

Japanese businessman asked, 'Do American business people think and talk at the same time?' "[18]

Copeland and Griggs also have found that the American style of quick communication often offends. "Americans like to think of themselves as friendly. Yet others find us impersonal and rushed. We come on too strong, too fast; we are intimidating to some foreigners. We then fail to fulfill the implicitly promised friendship; we seem phoney."[19]

A second error committed by Americans abroad is the tendency to speak openly and directly regarding whatever they are interested in. This "tell it like it is" approach often offends people in other countries. If the speech rate is too fast, or accents too difficult to understand, many foreigners will pretend to understand you and not admit that they really do not. To help their listening the sensitive speaker will try to prevent what Roger Axtell calls the "deadly sins." The first requires that simple language should always be used instead of idioms, metaphors and jargon that carry little meaning. "Safe as Fort Knox" or "Don't make waves" does not allow for accurate understanding. Words like "y'all" or "caay-yunt" for "can't" will return questioning stares. The rule is say it clearly, say it at a moderate rate, and often repeat the critical lines. "Don't pack too much into one sentence, and pause between sentences. Enunciate clearly and remember *not* to raise your voice."[20]

Axtell recounts an embarrassing situation that occurred during the 1988 Summer Olympics in South Korea. "A T-shirt design innocently created by NBC television workers created a furor. Inspired, perhaps by Michael Jackson, the group had shirts printed with the slang expression 'We're Bad' and a drawing of two boxers in the middle of a South Korean flag. The action was intended to spur on the U.S. Olympic boxers. Instead it created an international incident with the South Koreans. Both the slogan, which was taken literally, and the insensitive use of the Korean flag offended them."[21]

Like the nonverbal example above, other nonverbal behavior can hamper listening between foreign people. Edward T. Hall explained it in the following way, ". . . proper English *listening* behavior includes immobilization of the eyes at a social focal distance, so that either eye gives the appearance of looking straight at the speaker. On the other hand, an American listener will stare at the speaker's eyes, first one, then the other, relieved by frequent glances over the speaker's shoulder. A British anthropologist points out that eye contact during *speaking* differs too. Americans keep your attention by boring into you with eyes and words, while the British keep your attention by looking away while they talk. When their eyes return to yours, it signals they have finished speaking and it is your turn to talk. It seems you can't interrupt people when they are not looking at you."[22]

In China the native listeners often punctuate their spoken words with nods or affirmative grunts. The frequency may be every few words or sentences. The meaning being conveyed is "I have heard you," or "I understand what you are saying." The careful speaker must realize his listeners are not necessarily agreeing or giving their consent.[23]

SUMMARY

Listening is the most used but least taught communication skill. Most people are poor listeners because perception and semantics problems interfere with their accurately hearing what another person says. Add to this physical gap time and passive behavior, and we have a poor listener who costs his company a large amount of money. We can even typecast poor listeners into categories like "the faker" or "the critic." Cultural and gender differences, along with position, further complicate listening efficiency. But there are ways to improve listening.

The skill of listening can be improved by the proper construction of mental outlines. This is accomplished through (1) creating an interest in the topic, (2) constructing your mental outline, (3) continually reviewing your mental outline, (4) using key words in your mental outline, (5) judging between important and unimportant information, and (6) tackling distractions head on. Listening to speeches can be improved by following certain suggestions before, during, and after the speech. In addition, several interpersonal physical and personal dimensions can enhance the ability to listen.

A listener can most effectively communicate through dialogue with others by giving and receiving interpersonal feedback. While the "right way" to exchange feedback may become instinctive after much practice, it will do so only if sensitive behaviors and attitudes are the basis for that practice.

ANSWERS TO CHAPTER TESTS

Profile Analysis of the Sperry Listening Test

This is how other people have responded to the same questions that you answered in Table 7.2 on pages 222–223.

Quiz #1

A. Eighty-five percent of all listeners questioned rate themselves as *Average* or less. Fewer than 5 percent rate themselves as Superior or Excellent.

B. On the 0–100 scale, the extreme range is 10–90; the general range is 35–85; and the *average rating* is 55.

Quiz #2

When comparing the listening *self-ratings* and projected ratings of others, most respondents believe that their best friend would rate them highest as a listener. And that rating would be higher than the one they gave themselves in Quiz #1 . . . where the average was a 55.

How come? We can only guess that best friend status is such an intimate, special kind of relationship that you can't imagine it ever happening unless you *were* a good listener. If you were not, you and he or she wouldn't be best friends to begin with.

Going down the list, people who take this test usually think their bosses would rate them higher than they rated themselves. Now part of that is probably wishful thinking. And part of it is true. We *do* tend to listen to our bosses better . . . whether it's out of respect or fear or whatever doesn't matter.

The grades for colleague and job subordinate work out to be just about the same as the listener rated himself or herself . . . that 55 figure again.

But when you get to spouse . . . husband or wife . . . something really dramatic happens. The score here is significantly lower than the 55 average that previous profile-takers gave themselves. And what's interesting is that the figure goes steadily downhill. While newlyweds tend to rate their spouse at the same high level as their best friend, as the marriage goes on . . . and on . . . the rating falls. So in a household where the couple has been married 50 years, there could be a lot of talk. But maybe nobody is *really* listening.

Quiz #3

The average score is a 62 . . . 7 points higher than the 55 that the average test-taker gave himself or herself in Quiz #1. Which suggests that when listening is broken down into specific areas of competence, we rate ourselves better than we do when listening is considered only as a generality.

Of course, the best way to discover how well you listen is to ask the people to whom you listen most frequently—your spouse, boss, best friend, etc. They'll give you an earful.[24]

Review Questions

1. Name and describe each of the four stages of listening.
2. How does listening compare with how the skills of reading, writing, and speaking are taught and used?
3. This chapter gives six reasons for why we listen poorly. What are they? Which ones do you feel that you can apply to yourself?
4. Name five reasons for improving listening skills. Describe the ones that apply to your own skills.
5. Name the nine types of poor listeners, and give an example of how listening is affected by each type of listener.
6. The skill of listening can be improved. List the six steps for bringing about improvement, and describe what a listener must do, in each step, to be successful.
7. Describe the four ways in which we can arrange the physical dimensions of our interpersonal listening.
8. Eleven methods are available for improving our personal behavior as a listener. Name and describe the methods.
9. Define feedback as a part of the listening process.
10. Explain the seven ways to give and receive interpersonal feedback.
11. How do gender, culture, and position affect listening?
12. How are listening and memory linked, and how does listening improve memory?
13. Distinguish between interpersonal listening and group listening.

Exercises

1. Become aware of the world of sounds that you live in. Find a place where you can listen undisturbed, and for 15 minutes list the different sounds that you hear.
2. Find an article in your daily paper that describes a well-known person. Read the article to a friend, but delete the famous person's name. See if your friend, by listening to the description, can guess the name of the person.
3. For a few minutes consider one or two lectures, speeches, or staff meetings that you have attended recently. Outline the major theme and the supporting points of each. What types of arguments and examples do you remember hear-

ing? How much of that event do you remember? How do your answers compare with the information presented in this chapter?

4. With a friend watch a local or national newscast tonight. Your friend should take notes during the program, but you should not. As soon as the newscast ends, write down an outline of the stories and characters that were covered. Compare this with what your friend recorded. How accurate is your list? Now turn to another station, and exchange the roles of note taker and listener. After the exercise discuss why certain news items and characters were easy to remember while others were difficult.
5. Spend a few minutes reflecting on listening situations you have encountered. Make a list of the words or phrases and the nonverbal behavior that speakers have used that have caused you or others to tune out of the conversation or turn off the speaker. How has such behavior affected how you listen and how you speak and talk to others? Discuss your findings in class or with friends.
6. The three sections of this exercise will demonstrate how the poor listening habits of another affect you.
   a. Divide the class into groups of four or five.
   b. In the following exercises each person in each group should have a turn at talking.
   c. In the first exercise each person should share with the other members the "most exciting" thing that has happened in his or her life. During this short sharing, each of the other small group members should be playing the role of "the faker." They should pretend to be listening but obviously be mentally involved in their own thoughts. They should be polite and should nonverbally behave as if listening.
   d. After all members have finished the exercise, take a few minutes to share the "feelings" the participants had because of the behavior.
   e. Next, go around the room and let each person describe his or her best vacation. Each new respondent should start the discussion with an attitude of "I've done one better."
   f. Again, take time for the group to discuss the feelings regarding the displayed behavior.
   g. Finally, each group member should focus on a problem that he or she has and a way in which he or she would like to change. Each person should be in this discussion. While each hears others describe their problems, he or she should mentally be concentrating on his or her own problems and the possible change.
   h. After this segment, discuss the behavior of group members, the feelings of the participants, and any real-life situations where this same behavior has occurred.
   i. Now bring the entire class together for a few minutes to talk about what has been learned in this series of exercises.
7. Find a picture that has a variety of detail, such as one of buildings, active people, or cars.
   a. Five participants should be selected and brought to the front of the room.
   b. Four are immediately sent outside the room, and the door is closed.
   c. Show the picture to the fifth, and give him or her two or three minutes to study it in detail. Tell this person that he or she will be responsible for describing the picture, in detail, to someone else who in turn will describe it to another.
   d. If extra copies of the picture were made, they can be circulated to all other classmates. This will give people in the audience a chance
      to determine when descriptive changes are made between the real picture and what someone heard and perceived.
   e. After two or three minutes take the picture away, and bring in the first person so that the observer can describe what he or she saw.
   f. The listener then repeats the description to the second outside person, and this process continues until each of the four has heard the description.
   g. After the fourth receives the instructions, he or she should then describe the scene to the entire audience.
   h. The class should take several minutes to analyze where mistakes and listening errors occurred, when major additions or deletions were made in the description, and how close the end product resembled the original.
   i. Spend a few minutes describing real-life situations where similar results have occurred.
8. Divide the class into groups of three. In this

exercise two people will discuss an issue, and the third person will observe the discussion (speaking-listening process). Designate in each group which person will be A, which one B, and which one C.

a. Start the exercise with A and B picking an issue about which each has a different viewpoint. The issue can be one of economic, political, or social importance or one where personal preference is involved.
b. A and B should then proceed to discuss the issue for five or ten minutes. During the discussion C will observe how well listening occurs.
c. In their conversational interaction, A and B should use active listening and clarity checks. Both individuals should also practice giving and receiving feedback. The goal is to understand and clarify the message and not to judge, analyze, or question the person.
d. C's job is to listen and indicate whether clarity checks are observed, see if a more accurate speaking and listening process results, and determine whether better understanding occurred between A and B.

   Each small group should rotate roles so that every individual receives a turn at being the observer.

9. This exercise tests your skills of hearing and remembering.
   a. Ask a friend or classmate to read the following story aloud.
   b. Ask the person to read the story once at a normal rate of speech.
   c. Even though you may be tempted to read it to yourself, please don't. By having someone else read it, you'll have a lot more fun, and you'll learn more from the exercise.
   d. After the story is read, take the test that follows.

The Long-Awaited Day

Harvey Wolff got home at 3:20 P.M., over two hours earlier than usual. The reason? This was July 14, the day when the family would start its annual two-week vacation. Harvey and his wife Carol had mapped out a terrific plan for their twelve-day, 7,500-mile trip.

They would leave their home in Atlanta and drive through to Colorado, where some fishing was in store. From there they would head up to Yellowstone Park, after stopping in Jackson Hole, Wyoming. A drive down the west side of the Teton Mountains would take them through Utah and into California. The kids would love Disneyland. Harvey was looking forward to first seeing San Francisco.

After several days on the West Coast the family would head straight east, back to their home in Georgia.

Carol had things packed in their station wagon. Their two children, Allen, age 10, and Dedra, age 7, were very excited. The children were so eager they even volunteered to help Carol mow the yard, take out the trash, and water the plants that morning while Harvey was at work. That was unusual because they seldom volunteered to help with chores.

When Harvey got home, he changed clothes and gulped down a hamburger and Coke. Carol and the kids had eaten. Harvey wanted to leave soon so that they could drive 240 miles to Shreveport before dark. He quickly drank another Coke.

(continued)

At 4:40 P.M. they pulled out of the driveway but only got two blocks before the girl cried, "I forgot my doll." Harvey turned around and went back. When they left the second time, the kids exclaimed "Oh boy" as they headed down the highway.

Forty miles and one hour and ten minutes later Harvey was about to pull his hair. The kids were starving and "just had to eat." Carol explained that she had fed them only minutes before Harvey got home, but she persuaded him to stop at a roadside café for snacks, just to keep the peace. The name of the place was "The Hungry Man." The children had hamburgers and lemonade. Harvey and Carol had hot dogs, french fries, and coffee. Snack time took forty minutes.

When they piled into the wagon, Carol pulled out comic books for the kids to read. After reading his book Allen pulled out his electronic watch and started playing the tunes. All was peaceful until that happened. His sister complained that she couldn't read with all that noise. Carol didn't like the sound either.

Seventy-five miles from Shreveport, as darkness fell, Harvey thought, "Ah, the same old vacation problems."

Write down the number for the correct answers.

1. The last name of the family was: (a) Harrison (b) Huff (c) Wolff (d) Anderson
2. Harvey got home at: (a) 3:10 (b) 3:20 (c) 3:30 (d) 3:40
3. The vacation started on: (a) July 4 (b) July 14 (c) July 10 (d) July 17
4. The length of the trip would be: (a) 10 days (b) 12 days (c) 14 days (d) 15 days
5. On the trip they would drive: (a) 4,000 miles (b) 5,500 miles (c) 6,000 miles (d) 7,500 miles
6. The family lived in: (a) Atlanta (b) Dallas (c) Montgomery (d) Shreveport
7. The boy's name was: (a) Allen (b) Alvin (c) William (d) Bill
8. The boy's age was: (a) 7 (b) 9 (c) 10 (d) 12
9. The girl's name was: (a) Debby (b) Dedra (c) Patty (d) Sharon
10. The girl's age was: (a) 7 (b) 9 (c) 10 (d) 11
11. What was the first major sight-seeing event scheduled on the trip? (a) Yellowstone Park (b) Jackson Hole (c) Disneyland (d) Colorado
12. The family was driving a: (a) car (b) station wagon (c) Bronco (d) Wagonneer
13. The kids did not help Carol: (a) cut the lawn (b) take out the trash (c) water the lawn (d) water the plants
14. Before leaving Harvey had (a) a hamburger and two Cokes (b) a hotdog and two Cokes (c) two hamburgers and a Coke (d) two hamburgers and two Cokes
15. How far did Harvey want to drive before dark? (a) 140 miles (b) 180 miles (c) 220 miles (d) 240 miles
16. They first pulled out of their driveway at: (a) 4:30 P.M. (b) 4:40 P.M. (c) 4:50 P.M. (d) 5:00 P.M.
17. Before stopping they drove: (a) 1 hour (b) 1 hour 10 minutes (c) 1 1/2 hours (d) 1 hour and 40 minutes
18. The distance they drove before stopping was: (a) 30 miles (b) 40 miles (c) 50 miles (d) 60 miles
19. They arrived at the eating place at: (a) 5:30 P.M. (b) 5:50 P.M. (c) 6:00 P.M. (d) 6:15 P.M.
20. They stopped at a: (a) café (b) truck stop (c) roadside park (d) cafeteria

21. The name of the place was: (a) Country Kitchen (b) Roadside Café (c) Frank's Grill (d) The Hungry Man
22. The children ate: (a) hamburgers (b) hot dogs (c) french fries (d) ice cream
23. The stop took: (a) 30 minutes (b) 40 minutes (c) 45 minutes (d) 50 minutes
24. The children started arguing over: (a) a comic book (b) a game they were playing (c) the boy's watch (d) something to eat
25. How far were they from Shreveport when it got dark? (a) 50 miles (b) 75 miles (c) 85 miles (d) 100 miles

Answers: 1(c), 2(b), 3(b), 4(b), 5(d), 6(a), 7(a), 8(c), 9(b), 10(a), 11(d), 12(b), 13(c), 14(a), 15(d), 16(b), 17(b), 18(b), 19(b), 20(a), 21(d), 22(a), 23(b), 24(c), 25(b).

KEY WORDS

accuracy
active listening
coping
emotions
gap time
interpersonal feedback
interpersonal listening
listening
mental outlining
passive listening
phonemic restoration
remembering
sensory memory
understanding

REFERENCES

1. Don Oldenburg, "From the Word Go, Listening Is a Sometimes Thing." *Chicago Sun-Times,* June 10, 1987, p. 43.
2. Ibid.
3. Dr. Lyman K. Steil, President of Communication Development, Inc., St. Paul, Minnesota, *Your Personal Listening Profile,* a brochure prepared for the Sperry Corporation, New York. Reprinted by permission of Dr. Steil and the Sperry Corporation.
4. John Lewis DiGaetani, "The Sperry Corporation and Listening: An Interview," *Business Horizons* (March/April 1982), p. 36.
5. Deborah Tannen, *That's Not What I Meant!* (New York: Ballantine Books, 1986) and *You Just Don't Understand: Women and Men in Conversation* (New York: William Morrow, 1990).
6. DiGaetani, "Sperry," p. 39.
7. Clinton O. Longenecker and Patrick R. Liverpool, "Making Yourself All Ears," *Management World* (September/October 1988), p. 22.
8. Ron Winslow, "Sometimes, Talk Is the Best Medicine," *Wall Street Journal,* October 5, 1989, p. B1.
9. Adapted from Ann Abbas, "Dedman Memory Expert Says Forgetting Not All Bad, Clears the Clutter," *SMU Forum,* Dallas, Texas, April 1990, p. 2; Alan S. Brown, *How to Increase Your Memory Power* (New York: Scott, Foresman and Company, 1989).
10. Ralph Nichols, "Listening Is a 10-Part Skill," *Nation's Business* (July 1957), pp. 56–57.
11. Robert L. Montgomery, "Are You a Good Listener?" *Nation's Business* (October 1981), pp. 70–71. Excerpted, by permission of the publisher, from *Listening Made Easy,* by Robert L. Montgomery, pp. 70–71. © 1981 by AMACOM, a division of American Management Associations, New York. All rights reserved.
12. Kathy Murray, "Big Brother Isn't Just Watching, He's Listening In on You at Work," *The Sunday Camera* (July 7, 1991), p. 1C.
13. Ibid., p. 3C.
14. Adapted from: Jill Abramson, "Mind What You Say: They're Listening," *Wall Street Journal,* October 25, 1989, p. B1.
16. Roger E. Axtell, editor, *Do's and Taboos Around The World* 2nd ed. (New York: John Wiley & Sons, 1990), p. 20.
17. Ibid., p. 32.
18. Ibid., p. 157.
19. Lennie Copeland and Lewis Griggs, *Going International* (New York: Penguin Books, 1985), p. 15.
20. Ibid., p. 104.
21. Axtell, p. 161.
22. Copeland and Griggs, p. 112.
23. Scott D. Seligman, *Dealing With The Chinese* (New York: Warner Books, 1989), p. 65.
24. Steil, *Listening Profile.*

PART 3

Using Language to Convey Ideas and Achieve Results

Managers rely on their ability to convey meaning by combining language, thought, and action. Employees expect supervisors to be articulate and present expectations in clear, concise, and meaningful terms. As a result, managers are often called on to make presentations about new ideas, plans, projects, or outcomes. They also must be able to put their ideas in writing so that a variety of audiences understand the point of their correspondence and react to meet expectations.

Like any other musical, artistic, or athletic skill, effective presentational speaking can be learned and perfected. Chapter 8 introduces seven steps for presentational speaking that identify specific ways to organize, construct, practice, and perform in a business setting.

Chapter 9 examines the purposes, standard parts, formats, and types of letters and memoranda. Decisions about how and when to use letters and memoranda are determined by the type of message the writer wants to send: good news, bad news, or a communication intended to overcome resistance.

Often written reports help managers solve problems and make decisions by presenting information that informs or persuades. Chapter 10 describes the characteristics of formal and informal reports, basic report parts, and preparatory steps for report writing. The chapter focuses on the inverted report-writing style, a time-saving approach that tells readers at the outset what the writer wants them to know.

Finally, Chapter 11 takes up the editing process of writing. It presents specific techniques for turning average writing into polished, professional prose.

CHAPTER 8

PRESENTATIONAL SPEAKING: MAKING A POSITIVE IMPRESSION

Speakers everywhere watched with empathy as they observed a glitch during the 1992 Academy Awards ceremonies. It reaffirmed Murphy's law that if something can go wrong, it probably will—even in Hollywood, the so-called communications capital of the world. Billy Crystal introduced Hal Roach, the 100-year old film director, for a special award. The Academy applauded the glowing centenarian and he rose to accept their accolades and make a few remarks. As the world looked on, Roach spoke, the Academy strained to hear his words, and the television audience heard nothing. It seems that someone had overlooked the small detail of placing an aisle microphone next to Roach's chair. Crystal made a gracious recovery, however, when he commented that "it seemed apt that Roach's words were inaudible since he had begun his career during the era of silent films."[1]

Three important lessons emerge from this story. First, oral communication is extremely important. As Chapter 6 noted, a manager spends almost two-thirds of each workday in some form of oral communication (meetings, on the phone, one-to-one interactions, and presentations). These formal and informal oral exchanges are vital to business. Hal Roach had something important to say, something others wanted to hear. But the second lesson is that once a person makes a statement, the exact content of that statement is often lost forever. Unlike readers of written reports and letters, who can read and reread the message, listeners have only one chance to take in a speech. Although listeners can often ask questions, they do not have the opportunity to "reread" the speaker's words.

The third lesson is, unfortunately, that in oral communication things can go wrong. Often speakers are inadequately prepared, sometimes because of lack of time to complete the research. Although the amount of actual time a speaker spends in front of an audience is relatively short, innumerable hours must go into research, writing, artwork, and oral rehearsals. Contracts, jobs, bonuses, and individual reputations often ride on presentations. With so much at stake, a manager should strive to make each presentation perfect.

Sometimes things go wrong because the speaker has a personality problem with the listener or has a hidden fear of speaking. Wallenchinsky and Wallace, in *The Book of Lists,* tell us that their survey of 3,000 Americans revealed that giving a speech is the greatest fear most people possess; they fear it even more than dying.[2]

We also know, as in Hal Roach's case, that things can go wrong with presentations because of technology problems. America is a visually sophisticated country, and in this mass media age the medium is part of the message. Audiences base their perceptions of a presenter on the quality of the messages they receive through the verbal and nonverbal exchange. A great speech can be undermined by the poor quality of the accompanying graphics. While the rest of the organizational world has embraced hi-tech tools, many presenters still speak to a group of people using primitive visual aids, or no aids at all. For managers who still struggle with overheads and slides, the new multimedia technique can be complicated, intimidating, and very unfamiliar.

Since we orally present information to others in a variety of ways, we can refer to the process generally as *presentation.* As we talk about presentation making, we will combine our analysis of the traditional speech-making process with the use of technological support. In this way you will learn how managers are more productive when they devote sufficient time and energy to the inception, production, and final presentation of their data and images.

For a presentation to be effective and accomplish its goal, several things must happen. The presenter must have a purpose; the material must be organized in such a way that listeners can understand and follow it; and the material must be presented in such a way that the audience enjoys it and learns from it. If all those things happen, a speaker's initial fear usually becomes satisfaction. If they do not, then the chaos of giving a talk can produce more than fear: it can bring disaster.

A quality presentation requires that we adequately manage six steps: answer initial questions, organize the material, use technology to advantage, construct the presentation, practice what has been developed, and, finally, present the material in the actual performance. This chapter will cover each of these steps in order.

Answering Initial Questions

Asking the questions Why? Who? Where? When? What? and How? in sequence during the opening stages of preparation, you will organize the framework for researching and arranging your material successfully.

Why Give This Presentation?

Each presentation has an occasion for which it is being given. Will the occasion of your talk be a departmental staff meeting, an in-house training session, a small group sales gathering, a one-on-one meeting with an important client, a product promotion meeting, or a banquet entertainment speech? Each occasion is different, and its unique features determine the level of audience enthusiasm, the type of verbal material to use, the potential ways the presentation can be delivered, and your overall purpose for being there.

To Whom Are You Speaking?

The composition of every group is different, and your presentation must be designed for the unique needs of a specific audience. Consider these questions when reviewing your audience:

- What do the listeners know about my topic and the information I can present?
- What is the age level of my audience? You can say and explain things to adults that you might not want to share with children.
- What is the educational level of my listeners? This information can give you insight into their knowledge, attitudes, and value.
- Will the listeners be men or women or both? Ideally, factors of this nature should not make a difference.

- What positions do the listeners occupy? Position reveals information about attitudes, values, types of jobs, and their power to accomplish what you want done.

Where Will Your Presentation Be Given?

Location is important in planning presentations. Big differences exist among office conference rooms, hotel seminar rooms, large auditoriums, and boardrooms. The setting will affect what you will say, how your listeners will hear you, and the outcome of your talk. The differences include factors like seating arrangements, lighting conditions, air control, acoustics, kinds of electronic equipment available, and freedom of movement. Knowing these conditions in advance can help you take steps to overcome many problems and obstacles.

When Will Your Presentation Be Given?

Find out both the date and time of day for your talk. This will help you plan your practice sessions. Several practice presentations should be delivered at the same time of day the speech will be delivered, even if it is 7:00 A.M. or 8:00 P.M. You will have a better understanding of your energy level and the type of adjustments that you will need to make in your physical delivery.

What Is Your Purpose?

Each presentation has a *purpose,* the end result of what the speaker is trying to accomplish. The three common purposes for business presentations are to inform, persuade, and entertain other people.

Inform. Presentations to inform present either new information on a topic or old information presented in a new way. Almost every presentation contains some element of information sharing.

Persuade. A persuasive presentation can also present information, but in addition the speaker will seek to have listeners *accept, believe in,* and *act on* the information.

Entertain. A presentation to entertain is designed to help the audience relax, have fun, and enjoy themselves.

ORGANIZING THE PRESENTATION

After you have answered the initial questions, you can begin to research and construct the presentation.

Researching the Material

The presenter should seek and obtain the information that will help accomplish the purpose of the presentation.

Patterns of organization. Information can come in different sizes and shapes, and the presenter can organize it to maximize the effect he or she wants to make. The facts gleaned about the audience and the occasion, the content of the talk, and the speaker's personality help determine these patterns of organization. As you consider the information you want to relate, make decisions about how you can arrange it for ease of listening and accomplishment of the desired results. Examples of outlines that follow the nine organizational patterns discussed below are located at the end of this book in Appendix B.

Chronological. In this pattern, events are organized according to the time and order of occurrence. This works best for historical information or for describing how something can be accomplished.

Spatial. Sometimes information can be described according to physical location. For instance, a truckers' strike could be described as it starts on the East Coast and gradually moves, through regions, toward the West Coast. Or a company's hierarchy can be explained by "The president is at the top and her three vice presidents are below."

Topical. Some subjects can be naturally divided into subgroups. For example, a manager at Wal-Mart could describe his market position in terms of monthly sales compared to those of Sears, K-Mart, and J. C. Penney.

Sequential. Information described in terms of a series of steps, processes, or procedures requires the sequential method. For instance, you may release the gas pressure by turning the valve two turns; then you wait 5 minutes until the pressure is gone.

Classification. Data can be divided into different categories. For instance, a speech on the top housing markets in the United States could divide its information into major cities and number of housing starts.

Comparative. Use this method when two or more things can be compared. If a manager is viewing several potential training programs for her employees, she may compare them according to cost of travel, cost of tuition, depth of the program, and amount of preparation.

Problem/solution. With this method the problem is usually described along with examples of events or behavior that is a result of the problem. The presenter identifies the various alternatives available and describes each in sufficient detail. The optimal solution is finally offered.

Advantage/disadvantage. A pattern that closely resembles the problem/solution is that of advantage/disadvantage. It is used to show that one or several factors outweigh others. For example, an employer could offer employees the opportunity to tax-shelter some of their earnings. When the personnel representative explains the possibilities at a special meeting, she gives the advantages and disadvantages of a tax shelter over the option of having regular income taxed.

Cause/effect. In this pattern, a problem can be examined from its causes and effects. Usually the causes are examined first, but in some instances the order is reversed. For example, a chemical company might point to required capital expenditures as having a detrimental effect on its quarterly profit.

How Can You Best Present Your Information?

As we have seen, a presenter must decide the best way to communicate information by examining all the patterns of organization just listed through the filter of his or her personal knowledge of the topic. Once a pattern has been selected, the content should then be structured into segments called *verbal supporting material.* After that step is completed, a decision must be made on how to package the material visually.

Verbal Supporting Material. The verbal supporting material used in presentations is important because it helps listeners picture ideas. Verbal support also helps the manager verify, clarify, and amplify points. As you select supporting material, ask yourself several questions:

- Do the particular items really support or explain your contention? Your selection should be relevant, complete, and concise in development and explanation.
- Will each support be accepted by your listeners and help you accomplish the result you are seeking?
- Will the information be interesting?
- Is it motivational?
- Is it too confusing?
- Will the listeners immediately understand it?
- Is it believable?
- Will the audience identify with it?
- Is it factual and reliable?
- Is it really needed?

If you can answer yes to each of these questions, the support that you selected is probably a good one. Some of the most common types of verbal support are comparison, definition, example, illustration, statistic, story, and testimony.

Comparison. A comparison examines the features of one thing in relation to something else. In a business presentation a manager often takes

> The government shattered this majesty (of law) in its assault on junk bond financier Michael Milken. The Milken case demonstrates that prosecutors favor building their case out of court instead of in court. Rather than focusing on trying to convict high profile defendants in court by presenting evidence to a jury of the accused's peers in pursuit of a guilty verdict, the government now prefers to use strong-arm tactics on selected white-collar targets in order to force pre-trial plea bargains. Contemporary government tactics have become so coercive that medieval methods of using branding irons and thumbscrews to obtain confessions through physical torture were mild in comparison to today's psychological torture. Today's induced pleas and settlements are equally as unreliable as measures of culpability.

EXHIBIT 8.1

Source: Paul Craig Roberts, "Takings By the Bureaucracy," a presentation made at the Center for Strategic and International Studies, Bryn Mawr, Pennsylvania, on May 11, 1992, in *Vital Speeches* (October 1, 1992), p. 745. Reprinted by permission.

ideas, events, or products that the listener knows and uses and through comparison presents information that is unknown in hopes of developing both knowledge and acceptance of a new item. In marketing, for example, one product is often compared to another in terms of quality, usage, durability, and price.

Economist Paul Craig Roberts compared the government's past and present pursuit of guilty verdicts in criminal court cases (see Exhibit 8.1).

Definition. Using the definition as a support allows you to give the precise meaning of a word or concept and avoid the possibility of listener misunderstanding. This is especially important if a word has a double meaning or interpretation or if the talk encompasses technical concepts. Avoid an often repeated, "According to Webster . . ." phrase, and think about the possibility of giving your own definition.

Robert H. Edmonds, an economist, decided to use a series of definitions as he explained the difficult concept of inflation. The first two are widely accepted, the third less so. But Edmonds molded that definition into one that he referred to throughout the remainder of his presentation, which also used a cause/effect pattern of organization (see Exhibit 8.2).

Example. Examples are used to give listeners specific information about a general idea. Sometimes they are used to stimulate the mind or the emotions. More often they simply allow listeners to use their imaginations while trying to understand that speaker's thoughts. Examples can take the form of a specific instance, or a hypothetical situation. The former was used by

The most common definition for inflation is too much money chasing too few goods. This is a perfectly good, all-purpose definition. It has the advantage that it emphasizes both money and goods. If money is increased too much, inflation will result. If goods are increased more than money, inflation will lessen. Its major drawback is that it is not particularly useful in trying to limit or control inflation. . . .

A second definition is that inflation is a continuing increase in prices. This refers to prices in general, as expressed by an index of the prices of many commodities, not of any special goods. A rise in the price of oil, for example, does not constitute inflation, nor does an increase in the price of automobiles. Inflation refers to the rise of enough prices so that money clearly has less buying power in general. . . .

A third definition is that inflation is a continuing decrease in the value of money. Although this definition is not as widely recognized as the other two, it is the one I will adopt. My definition is this: Inflation is a continuing decrease in the purchasing power of money, MEASURED by a rising index of prices in general, and CAUSED by an excessive supply of money.

Why is this definition to be preferred?

The answer is simple. BY FOCUSING ON MONEY, WE CAN SOLVE THE PROBLEM. BY FOCUSING ON PRICES, WE CAN'T. Actually, money is the CAUSE and prices are the EFFECT. Understanding money is the only workable approach for ending inflation because money is the central part of the problem.

EXHIBIT 8.2

Source: Robert H. Edmonds, "Appropriate Economics: The Goals of Zero Inflation and Full Employment," a speech delivered at Monterey Peninsula College, Monterey, California, May 17, 1981, in *Vital Speeches* (July 1, 1981), pp. 560–561. Reprinted by permission of the author.

We see the emergence of a worldwide system of research, finance, production and marketing. . . . In 1990, more than 50 percent of U.S. exports and imports were transfers within global corporations.

The Pontiac Le Mans is a good American car. It costs $20,000. Of that, $6,000 goes to the Koreans, $3,500 to the Japanese, $1,500 to the Germans, $800 to Taiwan, $500 to the U.K., $100 to Ireland, and $8,000 to managers in Detroit and lawyers and bankers in New York.

Finance is global and now drives the world economy. We get uptight about the trade deficit, but annual world trade flows come to somewhere around $4 trillion, whereas world financial flows are well over $80 trillion.

EXHIBIT 8.3

Source: William Van Dusen Wishard, "The American Future," a presentation delivered at the Center for Educational Leadership, Lansing, Michigan, June 19, 1992, in *Vital Speeches* (October 15, 1992), p. 21. Reprinted by permission.

William Van Dusen Wishard to describe the emergence of a worldwide system of research, finance, production, and marketing (see Exhibit 8.3).

Illustration. This form of support is really an extended or expanded example. It is used to give impact and clarity to a specific idea. Illustrations serve as a verbal visualization for listeners. They capture the interest and attention of listeners and help clarify information that is often difficult to understand. Illustrations differ from examples because they include a large number of details.

Dale A. Miller, president and CEO of Sandoz Agro, Inc., carefully employed an illustration about failure to use proper safety equipment in his address to the National Association of County Agricultural Agents (see Exhibit 8.4).

> I believe absolutely that when used according to label directions, registered chemical pesticides are safe to the grower and the applicator who uses the chemical, and also to the person who ultimately consumes the farm product.
>
> I believe something else, too:
>
> I believe that not everyone uses chemical pesticides the way that they are supposed to be used.
>
> A reporter for a leading farm magazine recently told one of my employees that every time he goes out on a story where there will be photographs taken, he makes sure to take along goggles and gloves. Not because he needs them, but because he can be fairly certain that the subject of his article won't be using the proper protective equipment—even when they know the ag journalists are coming.
>
> This magazine, and most of the other ag publications, take scrupulous care to show only people who are using proper equipment for the job to be done, proper protection, and proper use and disposal methods. Their aim: to reflect the proper ways; the ideal farmers. However, is this reflection of only the "good stuff" actually doing a disservice to the agricultural industry? What about growers who misapply chemicals? What about improper waste disposal? What about companies that allow misuse of their products? What about sales people who knowingly sell or recommend products for off-label uses?

EXHIBIT 8.4

Source: Dale A. Miller, "Agenda for Tomorrow's Agriculture," a presentation made at the National Association of County Agricultural Agents, Little Rock, Arkansas, August 10, 1992, in *Vital Speeches* (November 1, 1992), p. 57. Reprinted by permission.

I want to spend some time this afternoon looking at the changing role of women in the twenty-first century. In the United States, the role of women has changed dramatically over the last few years. From what I hear, this is happening in Japan as well.

Let's look at some statistics. In 1890, only 5 percent of married women and 20 percent of all women were in the workforce. By 1910, those numbers had risen to 10 percent of married women and 25 percent of all women. In 1950, about 35 percent of American women worked outside the home. By the year 2000, more than 80 percent of women aged 25 to 54 will be in the labor force.

Women are experiencing greater economic gains, greater independence and the enhanced sense of self-worth which comes from making valuable contributions in the work force. Between now and the year 2000, six out of every ten people hired will be women. By the year 2000, 50 percent of our workforce will be female. Businesses will become more and more dependent on the skills of women for their success.

EXHIBIT 8.5
Source: Meyera E. Oberndorf, "The Changing Role of Women in the 21st Century," delivered in Miyazak, Japan, May 26, 1992, in *Vital Speeches* (October 1, 1992), p. 752. Reprinted by permission.

Statistics. Numerical data in presentations are called *statistics.* Statistics are one of the strongest types of support because they help organize the collection and interpretation of information. Statistics can also be misleading. For this reason, ensure that your material comes from reliable and well-known sources, proves exactly what you want it to prove, and is organized in the most easily understandable way. Meyera E. Oberndorf, mayor of Virginia Beach, Virginia, used statistics to help her Japanese audience understand the changing role of women in America (see Exhibit 8.5).

Story. A speaker who wishes to narrate an event or series of events can use the story form of support. A story can be true or fictitious and can be drawn from readings, other speakers, or real-life incidents the speaker has encountered. A problem many speakers have in using stories is to indulge in an overdetailed, rambling narrative. A story can be expertly used in the introduction of a talk and is best employed in a quick, lively manner. David Moore, president of *International Business Magazine,* told an effective anecdote about a Russian wise man in his talk on the confusing arena of international trade (see Exhibit 8.6).

Testimony. The testimony uses the views, opinions, or experiences of someone other than the speaker. Often the material is delivered in the form

There were two men living in a small village in Russia who got into a terrible dispute. They bickered and bickered and fussed and fumed and argued, but could not resolve it. So they decided to talk to the village Sage.

The Sage invited the first man into his home and listened intently to his story. The man told him of the events that had transpired, who had said what and why he felt injured by the situation. When he had finished, the Sage said: "You're absolutely right," and sent him home.

The next night, the second man also recounted the events; who had said what and why *he* felt injured. When he was finished, the Sage responded: "You're absolutely right," and sent him home.

When the second man left, the Sage's wife, who had heard both men's account of the same situation, rebuked the Sage.

"Those men came in here and told you two different stories, and you told them both that they were absolutely right. That's impossible; they can't *both* be absolutely right."

The Sage turned to his wife and said, "You're absolutely right."

The same is frequently true of international trade. You can tell me that we need greater central coordination of our export promotion policies and I have to say, "You're absolutely right." You can tell me we need specific export promotion policies to help exports of, say, advanced technology products, and I have to tell you, "You're absolutely right." And, then in the context of your situation, I'd be absolutely right in agreeing with you.

EXHIBIT 8.6

Source: David Moore, "World Markets: An International Forum for Business Leaders," delivered at the Baltimore World Trade Center in Baltimore, Maryland on September 1, 1992, in *Vital Speeches* (September 1, 1992), p. 684. Reprinted by permission of the author.

of a quotation and in most instances the source is acknowledged. In fact, the strength of this type of support is a result of the status, importance, and authority of the person making the original statement. In Exhibit 8.7, Joel Chaseman, president of Post-Newsweek Stations, Inc., uses a quotation from a recognized historical figure.

As you are putting the finishing touches on your research, one final word of warning: Always, always, acknowledge the sources of your information. Using the words of another as your own is plagiarism. To commit this act on purpose is unethical and illegal. To commit it by error is unprofessional.

What a week this has been for America! Most of us have spent many extra hours watching television just to keep up with it—the inauguration, the hostages, the Super Bowl. This week's events helped me understand how much we take for granted, most of all, that we can react to events together, as a people. Today I'd like to examine that assumption and the challenges to it—present and future, so that the probability of our sharing experience as a nation is preserved without damage to the media which have become so crucial to our viability as a people.

Alexis de Tocqueville said this in 1835:

> Only a newspaper can put the same thought at the same time before a thousand readers. In democratic countries it often happens that a great many men who both want and need to get together cannot do so, for all being very small and lost in the crowd they do not see one another at all and do not know where to find one another. Then a newspaper gives publicity to the feeling or idea that had occurred to them all simultaneously but separately. They all at once aim toward that light, and these wandering spirits, long seeking each other in the dark, at last meet and unite.

EXHIBIT 8.7

Source: Joel Chaseman, "The Media Revolution in America: Television News," a speech delivered at the Town Hall of California in Los Angeles on January 27, 1981, in *Vital Speeches* (April 1, 1981), p. 374. Reprinted by permission.

ETHICS: RIGHT OR WRONG?

The Borrowed Speech

Dr. Joachim Maitre, dean of Boston University's College of Communication since 1987, delivered the commencement address to the college's graduates on May 12, 1991. In the address he quoted almost word for word fifteen paragraphs from an article by PBS film critic Michael Medved without acknowledging his source. Medved's article, "Popular Culture and the War Against Standards," had been printed in the February 1991 issue of *Imprimis*. In the article Medved reported that "ugliness and violence are glorified in film and television, and religion and traditional values are shunned."[3]

As reports of the plagiarism surfaced, Dr. Maitre made no public comment, but colleagues discussed the matter and acknowledged the embarrassment for Boston University. Finally, on July 4, 1991, Dr. Maitre called Medved and offered a "complete apology." He emphasized that his intent was never "to pass off Medved's words as his own."[4] As controversy over the issue continued to brew, Maitre offered his resignation, which was accepted with "deep regret" by university president John Silber. While praising Maitre's work, he emphasized that it is the duty of "all responsible scholars and writers to credit their sources. . . . Failure to do so is unacceptable whether that failure is intentional or not."[5]

Maitre contended that he had originally had every intention to credit Medved's work. He stated his "commencement speech was based on scribbled notes and clippings, not a manuscript, and a written introduction was (prepared and) dedicated to Mr. Medved and *Imprimis.* "Why I failed to read it . . . I cannot explain to anyone's full satisfaction, not even my own. . . . Exhausted from the various events preceding commencement day, I must have slipped into a black hole."[6]

Mr. Medved said he had no plans to take legal action and accepted Dr. Maitre's apology.

Case Questions

1. What is the ethical issue in this case?
2. Why is plagiarism such a bad thing?
3. Did the action merit Dr. Maitre's resignation?
4. What could he have specifically done before the speech to ensure that this situation did not occur?
5. What actions could/should he have taken following the incident to minimize the harmful results?

Visually Packaging Verbal Supporting Material

We commonly refer to items like facts and figures used in presentations as *verbal support.* Often, however, the same material can be made more exciting, presented more clearly, and received by the audience more persuasively if it is visually packaged to fit the audience's needs. The role of each visual is to support the presenter. Visual graphics can help the presenter explain complicated concepts that cannot be explained easily with words. A visual can be a quick, attractive way to present numbers, trends, and relationships. As you consider putting your verbal material into visual form, ask yourself these questions.

- Will the visuals add to or distract from my presentation?
- How difficult are the visuals to produce?

- Will the visuals bring balance and unity to my presentations?
- Will the cost of producing the visuals fit my budget?
- Are the visuals clear? Can they be read?

Graphics like line, bar, pie, and text charts are the most frequently used visuals because they are the simplest ways to illustrate complex data.

Line charts connect data points on a grid. Since they display continuous data from two dimensions, they are excellent for describing trends. Figure 8.1 shows how sales figures (vertical dimension) for a two-year period (horizontal dimension) are displayed for a Biomed product.

Bar charts are similar to line charts because they also compare data size. They differ because the different bars represent changes over time and not a continual movement. Bar charts are the easiest graphic images to understand and they are good at displaying multiple items or issues and complex relationships. They can be created vertically or horizontally, although most display vertically for ease of interpretation.

In Figure 8.2, the *simple bar chart* displays the population of Dallas County, Texas in five-year increments. The *grouped bar chart* compares the pretax earnings of one product to another for the same time period. The *seg-*

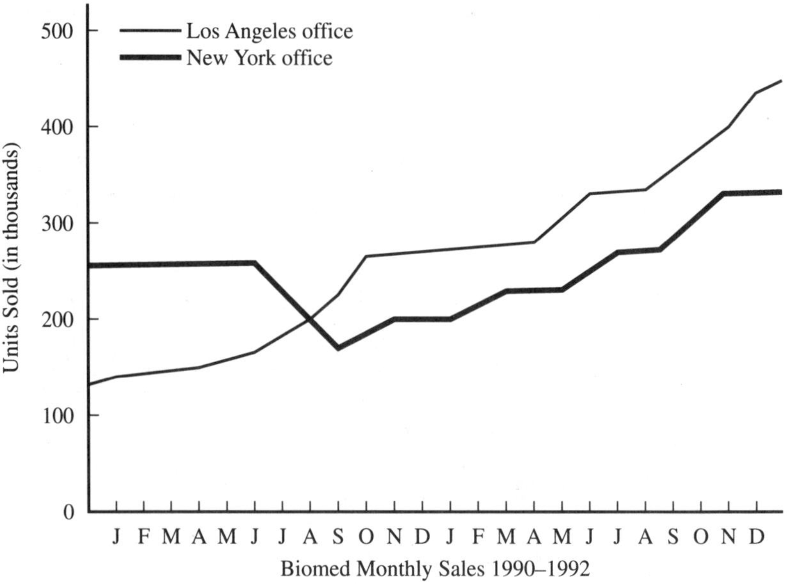

FIGURE 8.1 Line Chart

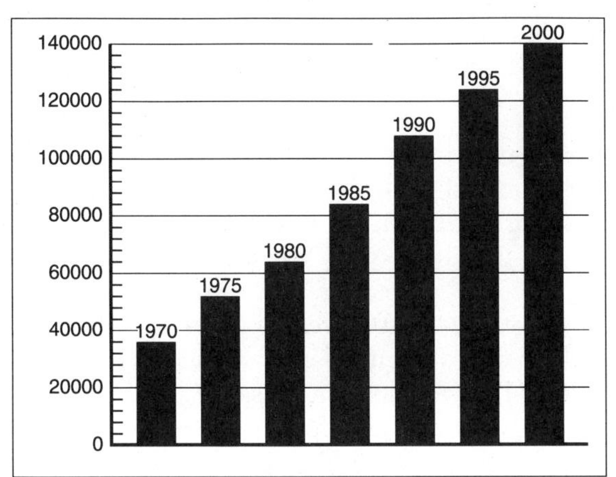

Simple Bar Chart

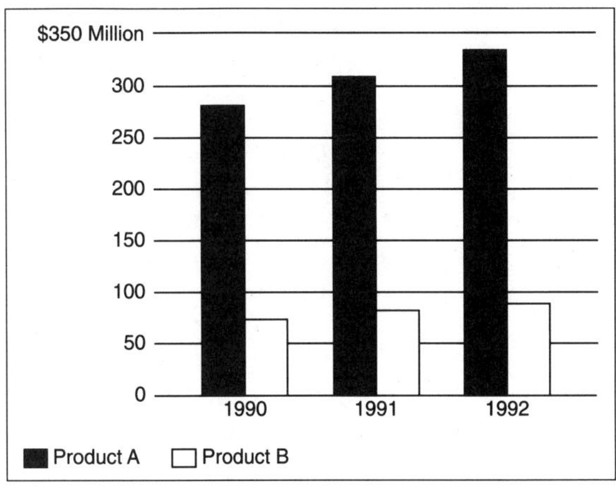

Grouped Bar Chart

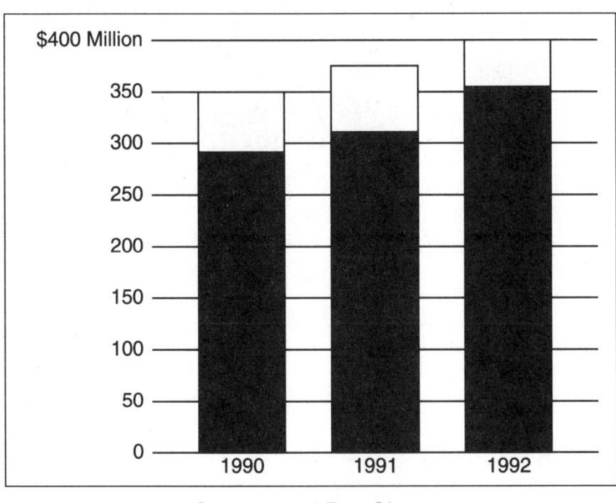

Segmented Bar Chart

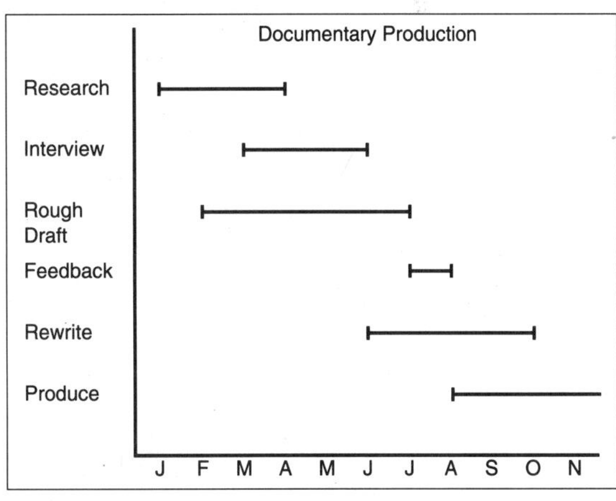

Gantt Chart

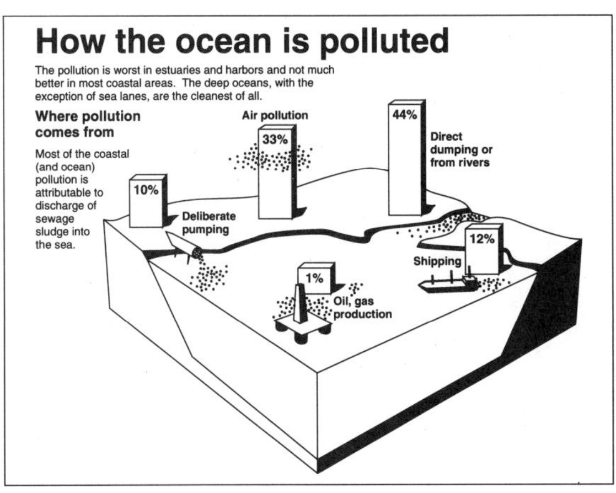

3-D Chart

FIGURE 8.2 Assorted Bar Charts

Source: From "Nations Gather to Examine Earth's Future," *USA Today*, June 2, 1992, p. 4A. Copyright 1992 *USA Today*. Reprinted with permission.

mented bar chart gives the same information but stacks it in single bars. The *3-D chart* visually depicts where the various types of ocean pollution comes from. Finally, the *Gantt chart,* which is used in project management, illustrates how several tasks occur simultaneously without a common starting point.

Pie charts are used to compare values that represent parts of a whole (see Figure 8.3). Segments are often separated from the rest of the pie for special emphasis. *Text charts* support or follow the spoken message (see Figure 8.4). They allow you to present a small amount of information in a short time period; the text supports, but does not overwhelm, the message. Usually text charts are designed with a topic, presented in bold type, and followed by a few words. The main points in the chart can be accentuated with bullets, asterisks, check marks, or other attention getters. Text charts should probably not have more than six lines, with just a few words per line. While text charts can display information both vertically and horizontally, horizontal display is preferred because it allows ease of reading and fits a standard screen.

In the past, managers who wanted to use charts in presentations had to spend long hours producing them by hand. When the first wave of comput-

Healthy Eating Habits of Executives

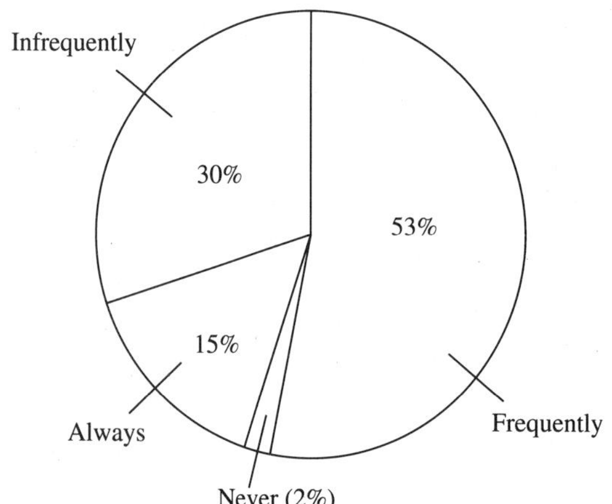

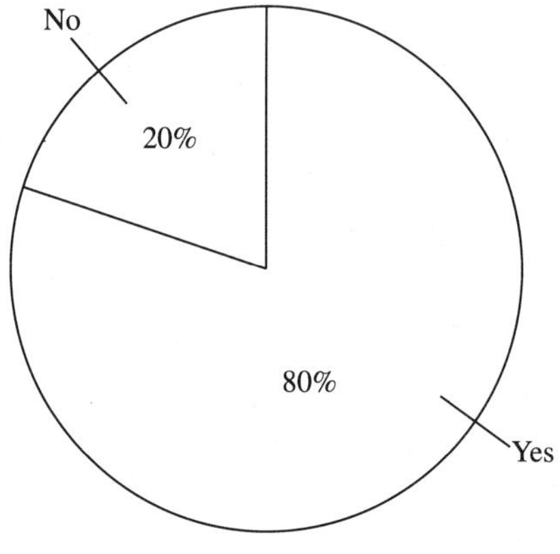

FIGURE 8.3 Pie Chart
Source: Adapted from: "Rocky Road to Staying Fit and Eating Well," *USA Today,* June 9, 1992, p. 13C.

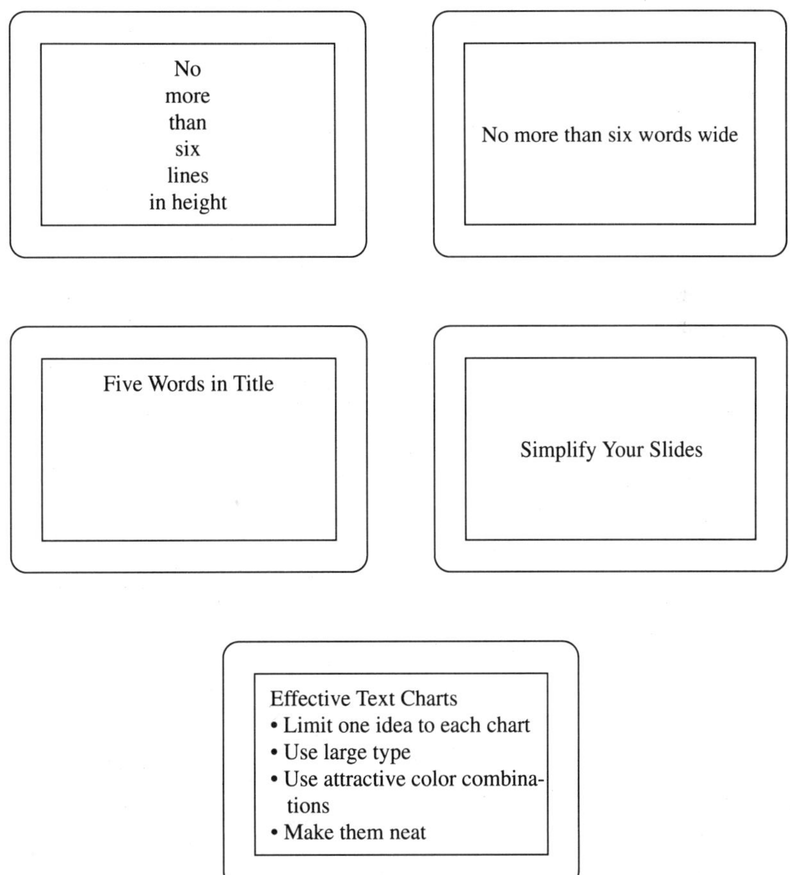

FIGURE 8.4 Text Charts

erized business graphics applications were created, they were slow, cumbersome, and low quality. The new generation of computer software is designed to make graphic preparation easy and exciting both to presenter and audience, as we can see in Figures 8.5 and 8.6. Figure 8.6 combines bar, pie, text chart material, and graphics.

Three levels of software are available. Software at the lower end allows the presenter to create bar charts made from spread sheets. Mid-range packages like Lotus Freelance Plus produce sophisticated charts and graphs but lack other features. At the high end, the more expensive packages like Har-

Close calls

A local three-minute call in the U.S. costs 8 cents — the lowest for all countries questioned in a new survey. Cost of a local three-minute call (in U.S. funds):

United Kingdom 22¢
Australia 18¢
Germany 15¢
France 12¢
Netherlands 9¢

Source: National Utility Service

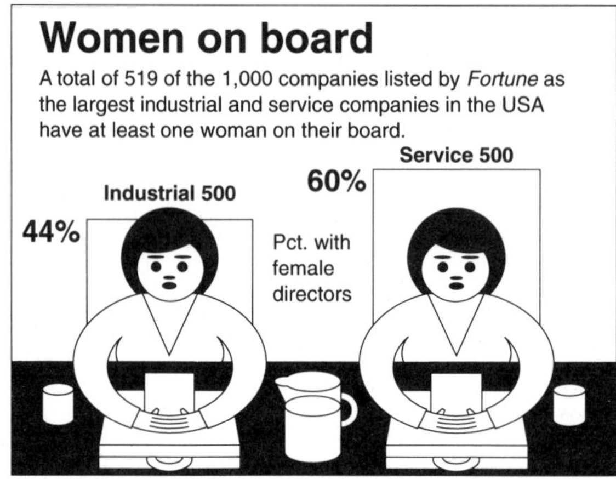

FIGURE 8.5 Vivid Packaging of Ordinary Information in a Variety of Graphics
Source: From "USA Snapshots: A Look at Statistics that Shape the Nation," *USA Today*, June 11, 1992, June 9, 1992, June 8, 1992. Copyright 1992 *USA Today*. Reprinted with permission.

vard Graphics produce high-quality charts and graphs, speaker notes, audience handouts, on-screen slide shows, and special effects like "exploding words," a "screen wipe" and "raining words." Most high-end packages also have a "clip art" library of graphics and help the presenter in organizing and maintaining all graphics elements in the presentation. In addition, they allow the speaker to see on screen exactly what will appear printed out in hard copy.

If you have little experience in using graphics software, you may agree with this flat statement in *PC World:* "The power of currently available

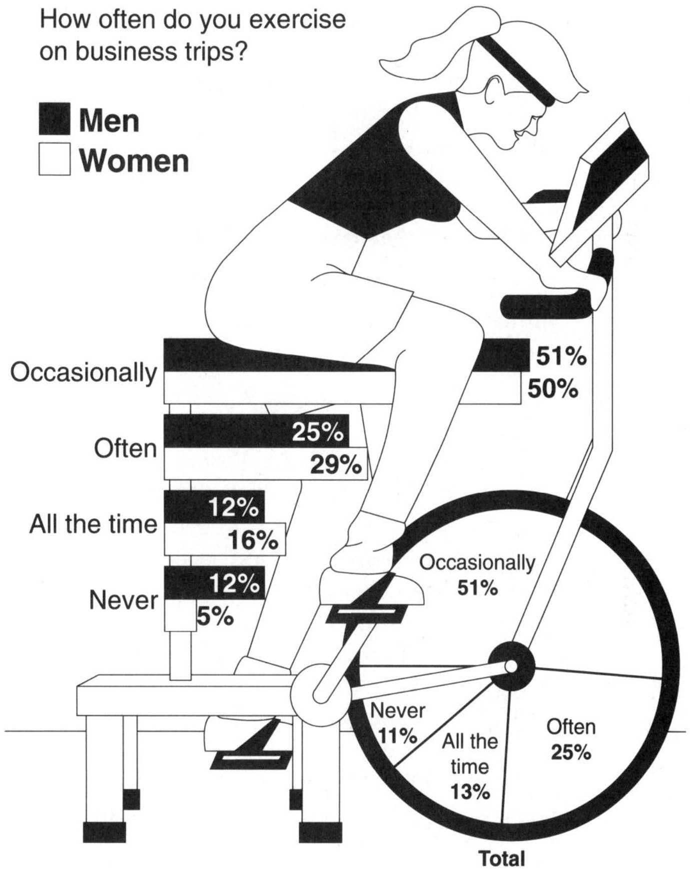

Figure 8.6 An Exciting Combination of Bar, Pie, and Text Charts with a Graphic Example
Source: *USA Today*, June 9, 1992. Copyright 1992 *USA Today*. Reprinted with permission.

graphics software can overwhelm a new user, especially when some packages offer 400 colors and color patterns, then styles of charts and graphs, animation, clip art libraries, and a multitude of type styles and fonts."[7] Keep in mind that the key to good presentation graphics is simplicity. As you develop clean, attractive graphics, you will feel more confident about yourself and your presentation.

USING TECHNOLOGY TO YOUR ADVANTAGE

The design of your visuals of necessity must take into account the equipment you have and will be using for your presentation. High technology has made available to businesses a myriad of electronic presentation devices and environments for their use. We will first consider the electronic meeting options and then the types of equipment most used by presenters.

Electronic Meeting Options

Presenters have four options on when and where presentations can occur: same time, same place; same time, different place; different time, same place; and different time, different place.

1. *Same time, same place.* Presenters and audience members meet together, but instead of listening only to a live speaker, participants watch slide and video images projected on a large display screen, as the speaker makes comments. This format replaces the handouts, transparencies, slides, videos, whiteboards, flip charts, and other visual devices that a speaker would normally use. All information is controlled by computer and displayed on a screen. There are four types of these arrangements.[8]
    a. *Conference room meetings.* One person runs the central display for groups of as many as twenty people. A designated leader updates or informs the participants. This arrangement used in persuasive appeals like board presentations and sales talks.
    b. *Interactive meetings.* Five or ten people meet with no single presenter; each person can convey information or argue a point. This arrangement is good for presenting different options in which individuals vote on plans, figures, or proposals.
    c. *Training centers.* These are usually large rooms in which one or more trainers work with large numbers of participants. Such centers can range from traditional classrooms with simple electronic equipment to completely outfitted computer training labs. Companies use centers of this type for such events as introducing new employees to a company and its policies or procedures, demonstrating new products to target groups or potential customers, and keeping salespeople updated on newproducts.
    d. *Auditoriums.* These range from large hollow shells with lots of chairs (like hotel ballrooms) to mass meeting rooms with elaborate electronic technology. In these more sophisticated arrangements, focus groups evaluate products and stockholders vote for corporate platforms.

2. *Same time, different place.* Many people meet and participate together, even though they are physically separated. This teleconferencing arrangement can consist of either video or audio conferencing.

The video conferencing capabilities of Hewlett Packard allow the company to save travel dollars, make quick decisions, and stay ahead of the competition. Photo courtesy of Hewlett Packard.

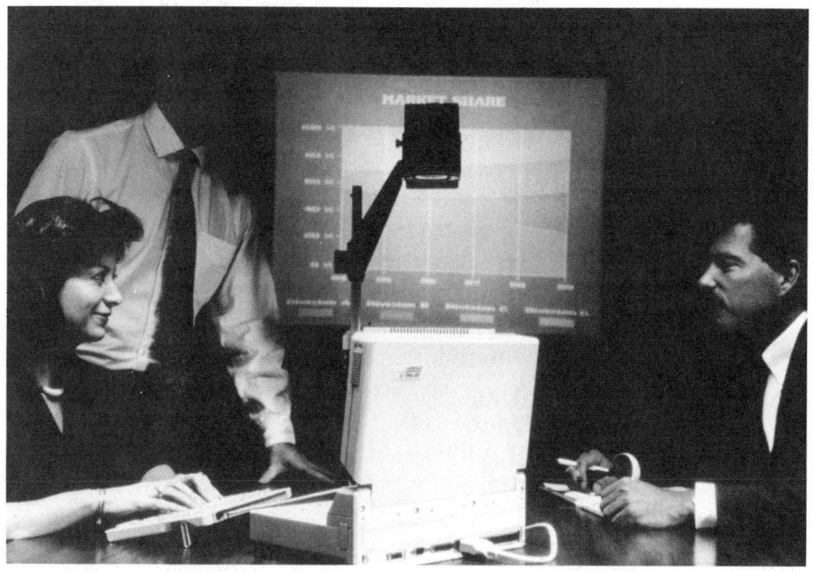

A sales team finalizes a graphics show prior to presenting it to a client. Photo courtesy of Compaq.

a. In *audio conferencing,* participants at several sites can see and hear participants in the originating site but can only respond with audio. The video transmission is one way; the audio two way for interaction. In the past, such conferencing was used extensively for training and high-technology briefings. Use is limited now, but still primarily for the same purposes.
b. *Video conferencing* is live, two-way communication in which people in the originating and receiving sites can see, hear, and interact with each other. The major advantage is that this type of meeting eliminates employee travel time and expense. Video conference meetings are highly structured events where participants keep remarks short and discussion is never open ended. Since each minute is extremely costly, strict time restraints are imposed.

   If companies cannot justify spending the money on outfitting a dedicated video conferencing room in their facilities, they can rent a "public room" from a company like AT&T, MCI, or Sprint. Such rooms will accommodate eight to ten people. The room usually has a large boardroom table, a pair of video screens, a copy stand, a control panel/lecturn combination, and one to four out-of-sight cameras housed in the ceiling and walls. The cameras can zoom to closeups on individuals or the fine print of a document.

   In 1990, the video conferencing market generated revenues of $365 million. It is anticipated that $1.5 billion will be spent on this form of communication by 1995. Three vivid examples bring home the impact of this type of communication activity.[9]

   MAST Industries, the design and procurement division of The Limited, uses video conferencing to link its merchandising buyers and design experts in Andover, Massachusetts and its suppliers in Hong Kong. This allows them to get clothing merchandise into the stores more quickly and cost effectively.

   Bendix/King General Aviation Avionics Division obtained the contract to develop the Traffic Collision Avoidance System (TCAS), to be mandatory on all airliners by 1994. The system's central processing unit is manufactured in Florida, and three other components are designed and made in Kansas. Video conferencing allowed two offices to "meet" face to face frequently and complete their project one year earlier than their competition.

   Video conferencing is also used so that physicians and medical technicians can meet in conferences like "Angioplasty in the 1990s" and observe real-life cardiac catheterizations being performed in hospitals. Those who watch are able to see the procedure in closer detail than if they had actually been in the operating room observing the surgeons.[10]

3. *Different times, same place.* These are "meetings" in staff rooms where electronic messages can be sent and left for people who are not available at the moment of transmission.

4. *Different times, different places.* Computer networks allow people in separate locations to send messages back and forth. These messages can be retrieved or stored for retrieval later.

CONSTRUCTING THE PRESENTATION

As you gather your research material, you must begin constructing it into a logical format in which it can be delivered to your audience. Constructing a presentation is like building a house: when all the unconnected boards are properly put in place, you have a strong and sturdy structure. Likewise, a presentation starts from many single words and independent ideas; when ideas are properly put in place, you have a solid informative or persuasive

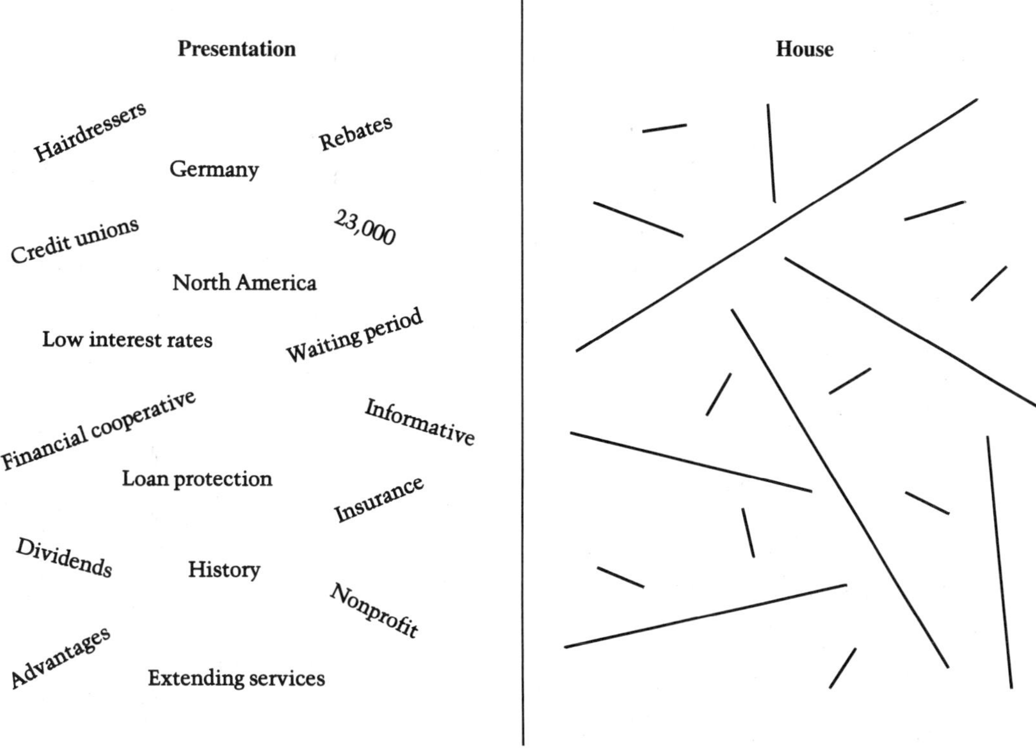

FIGURE 8.7

Presentation	House
Topic: Credit unions	Topic: A simple house

Topic: Credit unions

A. Hairdressers
B. 23,000 credit unions
C. Inform

I. History
   A. Germany
   B. North America

II. What it is
   A. Financial cooperative
   B. Nonprofit institution
   C. Membership open

III. Advantages
   A. Loan policies
   B. Waiting period
   C. Lower interest rate
   D. Some rebates
   E. Dividends
   F. Loan protection
   G. Insurance
   H. Extending services

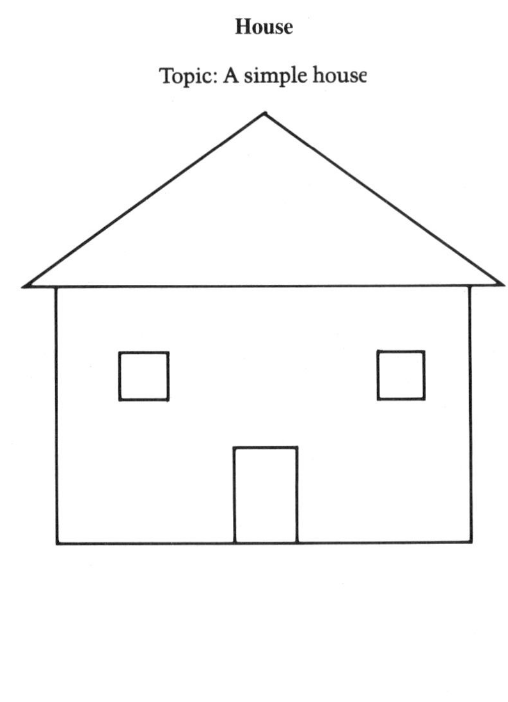

FIGURE 8.8

form. The presentation and the unbuilt house in Figure 8.7 are rough and disorganized. Before the house is suitable for living, a lot of finishing out is required; before the presentation can be delivered, it also needs to be finished out. Figure 8.8 is the completed structure.

The Parts of the Presentation

Organized talks have three main parts, each with a specific function: an introduction, a body, and a conclusion.

The Introduction

First, the *introduction* of a presentation helps the speaker gain the audience's attention. After the opening attention-getting lines, you clearly and specifically connect the topic to your audience. In some way you must assure them that their time and attention will be rewarded. You then develop for your listeners, in some simple form, the main points of your organization. This development serves as the verbal road map that helps your audience listen well and retain the information.

The Body

The *body* of your presentation contains all the information and arguments that you will give the audience. In a presentation to inform, the body consists of the different parts of the topic that together create the whole of that topic. A talk can be divided into any number of parts. The value, however, of the ingredients is in the *balanced integration* of each part. A talk sounds unbalanced when one part is larger than the others. The best method for balancing the presentation is to pick an organizational pattern that corresponds to the topic, information, and results that you want to accomplish.

The Conclusion

The *conclusion* of your talk has three functions. First, you briefly recap the main ideas; this aids the listener in finalizing the mental organizational ladder. Second, you reiterate the importance of the talk to your audience. If you want to encourage listeners to act or behave in a particular way, you should do so here. Third, you end with a cordial, polite statement of goodwill.

The Outline of the Presentation

The organization of a presentation starts with abstract parts that are expanded. When the three main parts are connected, they take the form of the skeleton outline in Exhibit 8.8 on page 278. As you add unique illustrations, examples, and facts, the presentation grows in its strength and beauty. But weak main ideas and insufficient evidence and support can keep you from accomplishing your desired results. Some high-end graphics packages let you create the skeleton outline as you create your graphics. Individual slides can then be copied from one file to another.

The necessary balance starts with a strong *specific purpose statement.* This statement is a simple declarative sentence that describes what a speaker intends to cover and defines the parameters of the presentation. Using the analogy of a tree, the specific purpose would be the tap root, the main root of a tree that securely connects the trunk to the earth. Your presentation should be firmly rooted both in what your audience wants and needs and in what you wish to accomplish—as well as in how your ideas will be presented, the words used, the nonverbal means used to convey the message, and any audiovisual aids that will clarify your message.

As you research and write your material, continually recheck this purpose statement to ensure that each main idea reflects the topic adequately and is a clear division of the balanced topic. If a main idea or a subpoint does not fit the outline, either that idea must be deleted or changed or the topic must be revised.

The Final Outline

Once the construction phase of your presentation is developed, the finishing out of an outline can be accomplished in a simple word or key phrase outline,

Topic: ______________________________

Purpose: ______________________________

Specific purpose: ______________________________

Introduction

A. (Attention getter)
B. (Topic/audience relationship)
C. (Main point outline)

Body

I. Main idea
   A. (Subpoint)
   B. (Subpoint)
      1. (Support)
      2. (Support)

II. Main idea
   A. (Subpoint)
   B. (Subpoint)

III. Main idea
   A. (Subpoint)
      1. (Support)
      2. (Support)
   B. (Subpoint)
   C. (Subpoint)

IV. Main idea
   A. (Subpoint)
   B. (Subpoint)

Conclusion

A. (Recap)
B. (Topic/audience relationship)
C. (Goodwill)

EXHIBIT 8.8 Skeleton Outline

a complete sentence outline, or as manuscript output. You can use these outlines both as practice and to help you in the final presentation. The purpose of the *simple word* or *key phrase outline* is to trigger ideas that are stored in your mind as a result of constructing your material. Exhibit 8.9 gives an example of a key phrase outline.

In the *complete sentence outline* all the main ideas and subpoints are written as complete sentences. The value of this approach is that ideas can be expressed as complete units of thought. There is a danger, however, in using the complete sentence outline to deliver your final presentation. Since we write for the eye, the written sentence is recorded in a way that the mind developed it. We speak, however, for the ear. Consequently, when we first attempt to speak verbatim the words that we have written, those words come out twisted and mispronounced. Thus, the smoothness of the talk is destroyed and the fullness of the original idea is not conveyed.

Manuscripted talks are valuable if you want to read your message word for word and cannot deviate from the text. Heads of state, politicians, and other leaders use this approach to avoid any chance of a slip of the tongue. Most business presenters, however, are better off avoiding a complete sentence outline or manuscript.

Incidentally, please do not attempt to memorize your speech. Practicing until you know major portions by heart is fine, but the time and energy required in memorizing a talk cannot be justified in a productive business environment. Avoiding the temptation to memorize the speech lets you avoid the potential for forgetting a portion and destroying your concentration and credibility. If you rely on key words and forget a point, you can always go on to the next point or make up a new idea out of the many available thoughts in your mind.

The Final Graphics

As you put the finishing touches on your outline, you should also put the finishing touches on the graphics you will be using in your final presentation. The three primary ways in which graphics can be displayed are via transparencies, slides, and graphics shows.

1. *Transparencies and overhead projectors.* Managers who make presentations to small groups of people favor transparencies over slides for several reasons. Transparencies are lightweight, require little storage space, and their content can be added to, removed, and even rearranged. A presenter can write on them at the last minute or even during the presentation. Unlike slides, they can be used in rooms without turning off the lights. Consequently, the speaker can show his or her excitement to the participants, can maintain rapport with them, and they in turn can see the visuals and take notes easily.

When the overhead projectors that transmit transparencies were introduced in the 1940s, they had limited business acceptance because creating visuals for the transparencies was difficult. Today the excellent computer

Introduction

A. Hairdressers in Connecticut do it; barbers in Vermont do it; even Arabian-horse owners in the United States do it.

B. At some point in your lives you will probably be eligible to join a credit union. One out of every 7 Americans today belongs to one of the 23,000 credit unions in the U.S. today.

C. Today, I'm going to talk to you about credit unions, where and how they began, what they are, and the advantages of joining one.

Body

I. History

  A. Started in Germany in 1849, by Friedrich Raiffeisen to help his people.

  B. At time of his death he had started 425 CUs.

  C. 1900—first credit union in North America in Quebec.

  D. 1909—first credit union in the U.S., New Hampshire.

II. What is it?

  A. A financial cooperative organized under state or federal law, by and for people who already have a common bond.

  B. Democratic nonprofit institution with members electing the credit union directors and voting on credit union policies at annual meeting.

  C. Membership is open to everyone in the group.

  D. Every member has an equal vote.

III. Primary advantages of joining

  A. Because loan policies set by directors elected by members, it is easier to get a loan.

  B. Waiting period for a loan is usually less.

  C. Lower interest rate on loans. Maximum is 15 percent by law.

  D. Some of the larger CUs rebate to loan customers at the end of the year. In effect you end up paying 1 to 2 points less interest.

  E. Dividends by law as high as 7 percent on regular savings.

IV. Secondary advantages of joining

  A. CUs provide loan protection insurance.

  B. CUs offer life savings insurance.

C. Credit unions are extending financial services.

1. Financial counseling
2. Consumer education
3. Group travel discounts
4. Auto purchase discounts
5. Home mortgage loans
6. Real estate loans
7. Master Charge—12 percent
8. Share draft—similar to checking
9. Electronic transfer of funds
10. Travel checks and money orders

D. Deposits are insured up to $40,000.

Conclusion
With all the advantages in joining a credit union, you should consider joining when you become eligible. Someday you will need a loan. As the old American saying goes, "In God we trust—all others must pay cash."

EXHIBIT 8.9 The Inside Story of Credit Unions
Source: A speech outline prepared by Theresa Canales-Jud for BA 6114, "Effective Communication," in the Edwin L. Cox School of Business, Southern Methodist University, Dallas, Texas, June 16, 1977. Reprinted by permission.

graphics packages available make producing hard copy for transparencies very easy. With color printers, we now can have full-color transparencies. Even the overhead projector has been transformed. No longer a large boxy unit, it is now a sleek, portable, even collapsable tool.

The latest development in overhead projecting is the creation of the *liquid crystal display panel* (LCD). This panel attaches to the top of an overhead projector and allows text and graphics information from a personal computer to be displayed onto a large wall or screen by using the projector's light source. This tool allows a presenter to use the same material with large audiences that would normally only be possible with small groups.

LCDs work excellently in small work groups where notes and information can be displayed on the screen for brainstorming. Spreadsheet data can be used, manipulated, revised, and even printed at the end for participants. Overhead projection systems allow the presenter to point to or zoom in on data to be emphasized. For small audiences, a direct-view monitor is generally sufficient. For larger audiences, the image will need to increase as the distance between participants and image is increased. A major drawback for some presenters is the high cost of big screen monitors and large overhead projection systems. For critical meetings where overhead projection systems

The "Collaborative Management Room" at the University of Arizona serves as both a training center and interactive meeting facility. It has 24 workstations and can accommodate 60 people. Photo courtesy of the Carl Eller School of Management, College of Business and Public Administration, The University of Arizona, Tucson, Arizona, © Steven Mackler, used by permission.

will be used, a back-up computer should be synchronized to follow the one used by the speaker.[11]

2. *Slides.* The practice of using slides for speaker support has changed little over the years. Technology, however, has brought revolutionary possibilities to slide users. With the new graphics software, any presenter can produce the printed copy for quality slides. Corporations spend an estimated $10 billion on slide making, with many firms spending more than $100,000 each. Slides are popular to use, colorful, compact, easy to transport, simple to project to an audience, and always appear properly positioned on the screen (unlike transparencies, which must be individually adjusted). A presenter can use them to build a logical sequence slide by slide. This keeps the audience from reading ahead.

The major drawback of slides is in the cost of the finished product. Custom slides cost many times more than transparencies, as much as $50–$100 per slide. Finishers are available that can be attached to computers, or the content can be sent by modem to an outside service bureau that produces the slide. The other disadvantage is the requirement of a darkened room. This

The "Emergency Conference Room" in the National Military Command Center is used for large conferences with military and civilian leadership. With six screens, a variety of multimedia presentations can be made in this facility. Photo © Scott Davis/U.S. Department of Defense.

reduces speaker-audience interaction and impacts the ability to take notes.

Slides for business presentations usually have dark backgrounds with light type for ease of reading. For large audiences, the most common tool for presentations is the 35mm slide.[12]

3. *Graphics shows.* Some speakers prefer to use a computer to display visuals while they are making their presentations. This technique is especially useful for software product demonstrations. The technology is the same as that used between computers and overhead projectors, minus the LCD. The major advantage is that the message can be constructed before the presentation and stored on a disc or can be created on the screen as the speaker is talking.

Several drawbacks exist, however. Image quality is not always reliable, the display is sometimes not bright enough for the room, and computer incompatibility often means that the data created and stored on a disk might not run on the computer available to the presenter. Recently a company making a stock offering to the public used the "on-screen presentation" process to describe its offering to financial analysts and potential investors.

They found that normally dry data could be presented in a clear and exciting way so viewers could see company products, the production process, and pictures of key employees.

The Final Notes

As soon as you have finalized your presentation by organizing and writing it, you should convert your ideas to notes that you will use during your delivery. The sooner you start practicing with your notes, the smoother and more complete your final delivery.

Never be afraid to use notes. No audience, whether in a large auditorium or a small boardroom, expects you to remember the organization and main ideas for more than a couple of minutes. Just remember not to signal "distractions" to your listeners.

The key to effective use of notes is in their neatness and unobtrusiveness. Many speakers scribble ideas on large sheets of paper that have been folded and crumpled. Others carry large clipboards that remind the audience of a military drill sergeant. The neater the notes, the easier they are for the speaker to follow and the less distracting for the audience.

In transferring your ideas from the outline to your notes, try using the *key word* approach. If you practice by actually talking through your entire thought, you will find that key words are sufficient. When your eyes see the word, the word will trigger your mind to remember the full ideas you have researched and practiced. In a short talk you should be able to list most of the key words on one or two small cards that can be cupped in the palm of the hand and used undistractingly in front of the audience. Here are some additional hints for effectively using the notes.

1. *Use as few notes as possible.* By listing only key words, you can put even a long speech on two or three cards. Many cards or sheets of paper probably mean that you have filled the cards with complete sentences.
2. *Number your notes.* As soon as you have placed your note cards in proper sequence, number them in case they are dropped or misshuffled before your talk.
3. *List your words lengthwise.* Writing across the narrow portion of the card or paper will facilitate easy viewing and will more closely approximate your original outline.
4. *Avoid dividing lists and complete units of thought onto two different cards.* It is very distracting when a presenter is listing several ideas for the audience and gets to the last one, only to have to shuffle the cards to find it.
5. *Write your key words in outline form.* The visual likeness of your notes and the original outline will psychologically help you remember your ideas.
6. *Use symbols to indicate where electronic aids are used. Never make*

new notes immediately prior to your talk. Occasionally presenters want to replace their worn practice notes with clean new ones prior to their talk. Many have regretted this because the mind remembers the original pattern of words and symbols. The new arrangement is mentally distracting and can cause you to make long pauses and to mispronounce words.

Finalizing Your Audio-Visual Aids

The last construction task, prior to practice sessions, is to put the finishing touches on any audiovisual aids you plan to use. Be sure to eliminate any items that are not completely necessary for clarity and understanding. Have these aids available for practice. Practicing with them will help you eliminate rough edges and ensure that your final performance is smooth and professional.

Practicing the Presentation

For professional speakers, "practice makes perfect." If you work under a time limit that doesn't allow you to perfect a particular task, the end result will probably be less than satisfactory. Some tasks don't have much reward riding on the finish; but sometimes a reputation, a commission, a grade, or a job may rest on the result of a presentation. Future presentations can even be clouded by the negative feedback and response that a speaker receives if he or she fails to live up to personal expectations and those of an audience. Practice and rehearsal are just as important as the organization and construction phase of preparing a presentation.

Athletes, musicians, and professionals in all fields spend countless hours working out routines, smoothing the fine points, and perfecting their skill. The same is true for professional speakers. Excellent speakers are not born; they develop through continual hard work. Speaking is a skill, like any musical or athletic skill, that can be learned and perfected.

Don't Read Your Presentation—Talk It

After you have prepared your notes, start talking through them as if you were telling a friend or colleague what you have developed. Don't fall into the trap of reading your talk. If you do, you'll never trust yourself to leave the written word, and the result will be less effective.

The story is told of a young minister who preached her first sermon in a little country church. When her grandmother, who happened to be present,

Source: By permission of Johnny Hart and Creators Syndicate, Inc.

approached her after the sermon, she asked, "How did I do?" "Well," the grandmother said, "I only saw three things wrong with it. First, you read it. Secondly, you read it poorly. And third, it wasn't worth reading anyhow."

Written material is designed for the eyes to see and easily read. Presentations, when written, sound like other types of written prose. Only after the words have been spoken several times does the content take on a form of its own and sound good to the ear.

Talking your presentation establishes the main ideas firmly in your mind. As you practice, work on clarifying the ideas, not the words. When ideas are understood clearly, the words will usually be there to explain them. By having established the ideas firmly in your mind, you will be able to give attention to other factors that will be present during your final talk.

As you practice, talk the entire speech through from start to finish. Don't leave portions out. If you do, they are liable to be the parts you understand least and need to work on the most. Talk through the entire presentation, including the graphics, at least five to ten times. Three is a must for being able to pronounce the words easily. By six or seven times the smoothness and continuity are established, and by the ninth or tenth time you have major parts firmly remembered. When you are tempted to say you don't have time to practice, remember that a 10-minute talk can be practiced six times in one hour.

Time Your Talk

When you are given a time limit, be courteous and abide by it. As you practice, time yourself and add to or take away information as time allows. A good rule of thumb is to work on missing the allowed time by only 10 percent. For a 5-minute talk, that is 30 seconds; for a one-hour presentation, 6 minutes. Also try to strike a good balance between the introduction, body, and conclusion. The introduction should take about 10 percent of the time, the body 80 or 85 percent, and the conclusion between 5 and 10 percent.

Maintain Good Posture

When you practice, stand straight and tall, just as you will when you deliver the formal talk. Don't sit at your desk or in an easy chair to talk through your material. Practice away from a podium. The proper feel of how you should stand, move, and gesture are best learned by actually standing and having the freedom to move. A tennis player would never practice a serve seated at the end of the tennis court. For a speaker the analogy is just as true because speaking to others involves the whole person: body, mind, and emotions.

As you practice, correct any offensive and distracting mannerisms like leaning on the podium, standing with one leg casually in front of the other, or slouching. A straight stance facilitates breath control, and proper breath control helps you minimize nervousness.

Move—Don't Just Stand There

Polished speakers move with freedom and ease: They look as graceful in front of the audience as an NFL fullback side-stepping tacklers or an actor walking from one side of the stage to another. These speakers know that nervousness produces adrenalin, adrenalin is available for energy, and energy is provided for movement. The last thing a speaker should do is lock himself or herself behind a podium and stand in one place until the speech is over. Also avoid the "fig-leaf" and "parade-rest" positions, where your legs are stiff and your arms are extended downward in front or in back. Lift the hands up above the waist to a "gesture-ready" position. This minimized movement forces the body to contain the nervous energy instead of channeling it into complementary actions. By practicing movement in your rehearsal phase, it will feel natural and will be a habit to follow in the formal presentation.

Gesture Freely

Another physical thing that good speakers do is to gesture naturally. Gestures are made with the arms, hands, and fingers. They add impact to words and turn a dull delivery into an exciting one.

As you rehearse, practice gesturing descriptively to indicate size, shape, design, and other information that can be visually depicted. Make your gestures natural. Avoid using the same ones, in the same way, in the same parts of your talk. At times it is appropriate to build a gesture into a certain part of the presentation as long as it appears natural and spontaneous. As you gain experience as a speaker, attempt to spontaneously feel the hand movement as it complements your words.

Practice Communicating Enthusiasm with Your Face

A speaker's face can show interest, excitement, and enthusiasm, or it can show depression, fear, and nervousness. Practice smiling and delivering nonverbal facial messages to your imaginary audience. Let your facc show your listeners that you want them to listen and that you are drawing feedback from them. When you form the habit of wearing a warm, friendly, confident smile during practice, you will automatically wear the same look during the actual performance. If you don't practice that way, it becomes almost impossible for you to automatically look confident and happy as a speaker.

Eye contact is an extremely important part of your facial expression. As you practice, look at every imaginary person in the audience. When you are in front of the actual group, continue the practice and look at the eyes of each person at least once during the speech. Make each member of the audience feel that you are delivering that talk to him or her.

Develop a Pleasing Vocal Sound

The voice enhances the words we say. It also indicates things about us that we might not want revealed. Through our voice people know when we are tense or relaxed, tired or sleepy, excited or depressed, happy or sad, angry or pleased. The speakers we know and respect for their delivery qualities have many things in common, but their voices are unique. Each sounds different and varies according to several characteristics: pitch, rate, volume, quality, flexibility.

Pitch. Highness or lowness in the vocal tone is produced by the thickness of the vocal cords and the speed at which they vibrate. Pitch is changed by either tightening or relaxing the vocal cords. As you practice using your normal pitch, you will hear your natural sound and know the sound you should have during the actual delivery. If that sound varies during your performance, you can control it to a great extent by breathing deeper, slowing down your rate of speech, and projecting your voice either higher or lower.

Rate. Speech rate is the speed at which you speak. It is a combination of the duration of each word and the pause between words. As we stated in Chapter 7, an average speaker talks at around 150 words per minute. In a formal presentation, however, there is a tendency to talk faster. This is another reason for timing your talk during practice. By establishing a smooth, controlled rate during practice, you are more likely to repeat it during the final performance or at least shift it to a faster or slower rate if needed.

Volume. The loudness of the speaking voice is a combination of force and energy. Most people talk at a normal and pleasing degree of loudness. Occasionally speakers are too soft or too loud. By taping your voice once or twice during rehearsal you will discover if you need to change. Even when they are nervous, speakers generally maintain the same level of loudness during formal talks as in informal conversations. But speakers must occasionally adapt to new requirements, such as when the microphone goes out just before the talk and the auditorium is full of people. Even if you have not practiced with that situation in mind, you can meet the challenge by breathing deeper, slowing your speech down a bit, and directing your words to the back row with added force and clarity of pronunciation.

Enunciation. To enunciate means to clearly and distinctly articulate the words we speak. Again, by listening to an occasional tape of your practice you will hear if you slur certain consonants or syllables or drop letters at the ends of words like saying *comin* or *goin* instead of *coming* and *going.* You can improve your enunciation by speaking those words sharply and distinctly. In the early stages of your rehearsal you may find that certain words are very difficult for you to pronounce. After working on those words, if they still give you problems, look for synonyms you can substitute. Sometimes words that look good to the eye and seem good to the mind are difficult for the tongue to pronounce. Give yourself time to find and practice new words. In the case of proper nouns, foreign words, and other difficult words that you cannot substitute, work on these a hundred times if necessary and then write your own pronunciation shorthand on your notes.

Quality. As you practice, think about the total vocal quality that you want to develop. This is the fullness of your vocal sound and can be enhanced by practicing new vocal techniques like speaking with a foreign accent, using regional dialects, and even reading aloud from books of poetry and prose.

Flexibility. The best thing you can do for your voice is to work on maintaining flexibility. This is the ability to change as needed the rate, pitch, loudness, and quality of your voice. Flexibility to the voice is like spontaneity to the physical presence. It allows you to adapt to whatever conditions exist and to always come out victorious.

Nonwords. A final vocal comment is required. During the past few years Americans have developed a tendency for using vocal nonwords. Some call the utterances "speech tics." They are sayings like *ah, so, and uh, ya know, well,* and *OK?* If you know you have this problem, actively think about what you are saying by picking and choosing each word. Don't worry if the habit is hard to overcome at first. Habits that have been consistently used for years cannot be overcome in mere minutes. But if you keep working at organizing your thoughts, you will gradually overcome the habit. Say only the information that relates to your thoughts, and pause silently between sentences and paragraphs instead of substituting nonsense words while you decide what to say next. A pause is appropriate when looking at your notes and deciding what you want to say next. That is proven to us each time we hear a professional news commentator, politician, or business executive on television or in person. Professional, polished speakers have long ago omitted junky phrasing. You can, too.

The Actual Performance

If you have moved successfully through asking the initial questions, constructing the talk, and practicing your presentation, your final performance will also be successful. This section gives some hints for helping you to make that final performance a smashing success.

Warm Up at Home or Backstage

Anxiety, stress, and nervousness are things that all members of the business world experience at different times. While many good books deal with stress reduction, some simple relaxation exercises will help most speakers displace their prespeech nervousness with controlled energy. Practice the following relaxation sequence regularly so that it will work automatically for you when you make your next presentation. Allow yourself a few extra minutes before you have to talk to stop by the restroom, sit quietly in your car or office, or find a solitary place backstage to run through these exercises.

Deep breathing. Babies breathe the right way. As adults we get the process turned around because we are taught to pull our stomach in and push our chest out. Consequently we use the top third of our lung capacity. Sometimes when we are very nervous we even "forget" to breathe. Shallow breathing tenses up the solar plexus and signals our involuntary nervous system to prepare to fight. This starts the heart beating faster, the blood rushing to our heads, and the horrible feelings we don't want as speakers. Deep breathing, on the other hand, tranquilizes the involuntary system and shuts down the desire to fight or flee. Here's how speakers should practice breathing:

Deep Breathing

1. Push all the air out of your lungs, and clamp your nostrils with your thumb and forefinger.
2. Hold for three or four counts.
3. Release the hold, and without breathing let your lungs fill automatically and deeply with air through your nostrils. You should feel an expansion from the top part of your chest to the upper portion of your groin area.
4. Exhale completely, and try to touch your spine with your abdomen.
5. Inhale again through your nostrils. Stick your abdomen out and fill it first, next your rib cage, and then your chest.
6. Alternate exhaling and inhaling for two or three more times. Be careful to do it slowly and deliberately to avoid hyperventilation.

After doing these exercises, you should feel a calming sensation that is deeply relaxing. Try this sequence the next time you get nervous and especially before a big presentation. It works. When you are talking before the audience and you feel the tightness of the chest that indicates shallow breathing, force your stomach out and the air deeper until you breathe more deeply.

Physical relaxation. While breath control is the starting point for total relaxation, several exercises can help you stay relaxed during your speech. Practice these exercises on a regular basis and run through them prior to your speech:

Physical Relaxation

1. Sit comfortably in a straight-back chair.
2. Tell yourself that it is time to relax, to shut out distractions, and to loosen various tension spots.
3. Start with your head. Alternate between tensing and relaxing the muscles in your scalp, forehead, face, and jaws. Now let the muscles in each of these areas go limp.
4. Move to your neck and shoulder muscles. Focus on those muscles, and force out all the pressure. Let them go limp also.
5. Let the relaxation spread down your arms to your elbows, forearms, wrists, hands, and finally fingers. Tense and relax these muscles, and then let your arms and hands dangle freely beside your body and chair.
6. Focus now on the chest, and do your breathing exercises once or twice until any tightness is gone and your breathing is normal and relaxed.
7. Focus on your spine. As you move down from your shoulders, relax your back muscles, waist, buttocks, thighs, and even knees.
8. Continue on to relax the calves, shins, ankles, feet, and toes.
9. When your entire body has relaxed, you should feel very limp. Continue to sit in your chair for 3 or 4 minutes with your mind free of thought and your body completely relaxed.
10. When you return to the rest of the world, maintain the tranquil feeling, and shut out any attempts by other people or events to interfere with your relaxed state.

Make a Positive Entrance

Arrive early enough at your destination to find out where you will sit, the arrangement of the room, and any unknown obstacles you will have to deal with. When your name is called, walk professionally to the place where you will talk. By avoiding the following "bad entrance" behavior you can add to your credibility as a speaker.

- *The carpet sampler.* This speaker closely checks his path to make sure he doesn't trip over any obstacles. He should have checked earlier so that he could walk boldly to his place.
- *The condemned.* This person's walk nonverbally signals to others that she fears she will be executed as soon as she reaches her speaking place.
- *The ceiling gazer.* This person seems to be looking toward heaven for the words that he will soon give his listeners.
- *The groomer.* This person did not get completely dressed at home and is busy buttoning her jacket, pulling up her skirt, straightening her earrings, or brushing back her hair. An earlier stop by the restroom could have eliminated this display of grooming.
- *The early starter.* This speaker often starts talking as soon as he leaves his seat instead of waiting until he is firmly positioned in his place, fully aware of his listeners, and ready to start.
- *The dizzy dreamer.* As this person gets ready to start talking, her every nonverbal action and movement shouts "total disorganization." All her hard preparation work quickly can be lost if she doesn't regain credibility soon.
- *The steam kettle.* You don't have to ask if this speaker is nervous; you hear it. A slow "Whew" is emitted from his mouth before he catches his breath and starts his opening. By breathing deeply while he is walking toward his place and by slowly taking a deep breath before he starts talking, he could avoid displaying this nervousness to his listeners.

Establish Eye Contact

The sooner you maintain eye contact with your listeners, the sooner you start communicating your credibility and delivering your message.

Work on Warmth and Spontaneity

No one wants to listen to a dull and boring speaker who doesn't seem to enjoy talking to his audience. From the early moments, throughout the talk, and into the final period maintain a warmth that conveys, "I'm really happy and excited to be here with you." Work on spontaneously responding to your listeners' eye contact, their puzzled looks, their nods of agreement, and any unexpected happenings that so often come up in real-life situations. By avoiding the following speaker styles you can convey needed warmth and excitement:

- *The apologizer.* This person minimizes her credibility by telling listeners she is unprepared, didn't have much time to organize her thoughts, is nervous, won't take too much of their time, doesn't know why she was chosen for the talk, or will not try to bore them with facts and figures.
- *"Today I'm going to talk to you about . . ."* Never let this line be the first one out of your mouth. It is important to establish rapport with your audience before you tell them the topics that you will cover.

- *The shy guy.* This speaker looks scared throughout his talk. He never smiles, plays off his audience's responses, or even pretends to be happy. His eyes usually are downcast, as is his countenance.
- *The fidgeter.* Quite the opposite from the shy guy is the speaker who has so much nervous energy that she can't stand still or move smoothly in front of her audience. While some movement is needed and necessary in a speech, undefined and out-of-control movement is a real turn-off to an audience.
- *The magnetic pocket.* Occasionally inserting one hand into the pocket can contribute to a casual and controlled look, but often the "pocket magnet" takes control and doesn't let the hand out of the pocket. A good rule is to try to keep the hands out of the pockets and use them for proper gesturing.
- *The coin jingler.* One reason to keep the hands out of the pockets is to avoid jingling loose change and keys stored there. A good trick is to remove all potentially distracting items from the pockets prior to the talk.
- *The prayer.* Sometimes a speaker takes a stance and holds it throughout the talk. If the stance is one where the hands are folded reverently in front, it can convey an image of praying for help.
- *The walker.* This person absentmindedly walks from side to side, back and forth, or across the room as he talks. There is nothing wrong with walking and moving while talking to your listeners. But do it in a dynamic way where every step and movement looks orchestrated for the hearer.
- *The mumbler.* This speaker has trouble articulating and speaking out. Sometimes she sounds as if she has a mouthful of marbles. If you have this problem, work on clear pronunciation and sharp articulation when you practice.
- *The fumbler.* This speaker seems totally uncoordinated, but he probably has failed to adequately practice. He busily shifts through his notes, occasionally drops items, misplaces transparencies, looks absently at charts that have already been explained, and generally seems to be out of control.

Close Definitively and Cordially

If you have worked hard to create and maintain credibility throughout the talk, you don't want to destroy it at the end. Avoid false endings that send the listeners mentally packing. Maintain to the end a high energy level and also the cordiality that sends to your audience the message "I really enjoyed myself." To ensure that your closing is successful, avoid several pitfalls:

- *Don't hurry home.* Some speakers are so eager to finish and sit down that they either drop their final words or end their talk while walking to their seat. As you put the period on the last word of your talk, continue standing a few seconds to acknowledge nonverbally the ending and wait for applause and possible questions.

- *Avoid the "thank God it's over" look.* Some speakers think that the audience observes them only while they are up front speaking. They consequently sigh, give all sorts of "I'm glad that's over" looks, and immediately destroy the positive image that they worked so hard to create with words and deeds during the presentation. Maintain your professionalism throughout until you reach your seat and even until you are completely out of the presence of anyone in your audience.
- *Don't be an approval seeker.* Closely akin to the last speaker is the one who verbally and nonverbally seeks approval by saying, "Did I really do well?" If you have done your homework and have practiced hard, you will automatically know whether you were excellent, just okay, or terrible. Don't ask for feedback. Wait and let others give it to you.

Before you forget specific events and your subjective recall takes over, find a quiet, secluded place, and review your presentation with the help of the checklist in Exhibit 8.10.

Make a list of things included in this evaluation that you did not do in your speech or prefer to do differently in your next one. Decide to take some self-prescribed steps to ensure that you don't make the same mistakes in your next presentation.

SUMMARY

Oral communication skills are extremely important for managers. A presentation can effectively be delivered if the presenter follows six preparatory steps. The first step is asking the questions Why? Who? Where? When? What? and How? After these questions are answered, the presenter moves to step 2, organizing the presentation, which involves conducting the research, developing the verbal supporting material, and visually packaging that material. This step easily is combined with step 3, using the available technology to your advantage.

Step 4 is constructing the researched material into a logical format that you can follow in delivering it to your audience. Practicing the presentation is step 5 in oral presentation. Specific techniques have been proven successful aids in helping to coordinate memory, physical posture, and clear enunciation. Step 6, the actual performance of an oral presentation, includes such critical elements as making a positive entrance, establishing strong eye contact, projecting warmth and spontaneity, and focusing on a definite and cordial close.

Oral presentations can communicate plans, set the tone of a new organizational direction, or even sell a group on a different approach to goal accomplishment. Whether they are directed at superiors or at a manager's staff, they are a critical component in determining career success.

Did the INTRODUCTION of your presentation:

get the audience's attention at the start? ______

make a connection between your audience and the topic? ______

describe your specific purpose? ______

Did the ORGANIZATION of your presentation:

contain several main ideas? ______

arrange your ideas and information in a "logical pattern"? ______

contain "supporting material" that was clear? ______

contain "supporting material" that was convincing? ______

use smooth transitions? ______

Did the CONCLUSION of your presentation:

briefly summarize the main ideas? ______

briefly restate your specific purpose? ______

move your audience toward desired action? ______

Did you in the DELIVERY:

approach your listeners with confidence? ______

get set before speaking? ______

establish eye contact before speaking? ______

maintain that eye contact throughout the talk? ______

refer only occasionally to your notes? ______

maintain the right degree of excitement and enthusiasm? ______

speak in a spontaneous, relaxed manner and not from memory? ______

avoid speech tics like *ah, you know,* etc.? ______

maintain good posture? ______

use your vocal qualities of pitch, volume, rate, etc., effectively? ______

gesture appropriately? ______

move freely? ______

enunciate clearly? ______

pronounce words correctly? ______

finish speaking before walking away? ______

finish on time? ______

EXHIBIT 8.10

Speaking Through an Interpreter

Successful presentations can sell products, persuade people to make changes in their lives, and help all of us gain understanding. But if audience participants do not speak the same language and each speaker's utterance has to be filtered through an interpreter, the prospects of success may fade.

Maybe you have not experienced this problem before, but in a world where markets are going global and national boundaries and regional alliances are in a constant state of flux, multilingual meetings have become a way of life. "Whether it's a world congress of cardiologists or a board meeting of a multinational company, the multilingual meeting provides . . . a whole set of difficult tasks . . . among them, deciding on the right interpretation format and finding the right personnel and equipment."[13]

At the 1992 Paris Auto Show, Chrysler President Bob Lutz and engineering manager François Castaing adopted a bilingual approach to making presentations and answering questions. In a mixture of French and English they tried to demonstrate that Detroit has to think global in the future. How did it work out? Not as smoothly as they had hoped. "At times the bilingual approach seemed a little confusing to U.S.-born design chief Tom Gale and Jeep head Bernard Robertson, who put on earphones to listen to English translations. . . . At one point, Lutz asked a reporter if he could refer a query to another official. 'Donnez-moi votre question à Tom ou Bernie—Bernie, do you want to take it?' Lutz said."[14]

In planning this kind of program, speakers must decide whether they want *simultaneous* or *consecutive* interpretation and how much they have to spend. In the simultaneous method, the interpreter is usually not seen but interprets at the same time that the speaker is talking. Headphones are often used by the audience. In the consecutive method, speakers must pause after every few points to let the interpreter, who usually stands next to them, respond. Consecutive interpretation is usually a more informal approach and gives the speaker time to pause between interactive responses.

According to one language specialist, "in boardroom discussions . . . consecutive works just fine. But if someone is presenting a lengthy paper, it's annoying. You're breaking the chain of thought to have the interpreter try to catch up. You can only have four or five minutes of speech before the interpreter jumps in. And since only one language is heard at a time, consecutive interpretation is practical only if no more than two languages are used. Cost must also be considered. Simultaneous interpretation is more expensive because of special equipment and the requirement for expert interpreters."[15]

To prepare for using a consecutive interpreter, a speaker should remember seven specific rules.

1. *Look at the person(s) you are addressing.* If you are speaking to the audience, look at them. If you are asking your interpreter a question, then look and speak to him or her. This helps the audience to understand your nonverbal messages.

2. *Slow down your normal speaking pace.* Since an interpreter will be working on small blocks of material, it is necessary to slow down as you are talking and to pause after every few sentences.

3. *Avoid slang, sarcasm, and jokes.* Often material funny to Americans proves to be offensive to people of other nationalities.

4. *Realize that your audience members may understand no English.* Speakers in the past have made that mistake only to find that side comments to the interpreter, or to colleagues who speak the same language, were understood fully by some in the audience.

5. *Graphics help foreign listeners get the message.* The visual material can help an otherwise frustrated listener to better understand the spoken message.

6. *Consider having parts of your message transcribed in both languages and passed out to your audience.*

7. *Say only what is necessary.* Since the interpreter's response doubles the time of your talk, try to cut your material down to only the essentials of what you must say.[16]

Key Words

advantage/disadvantage
audioconferencing
audiovisual aids
bar chart
body
cause/effect
chronological
classification
comparative
comparison
complete sentence outline
conclusion
deep breathing
definition
electronic meeting
enunciation
example
eye contact
facial expression
flexibility
gestures
graphics show
illustration
informative presentation
interactive meeting
interpreter
introduction
key phrase outline
liquid crystal display panel (LCD)
line chart
motivated sequence
patterns of organization
persuasive presentation
physical relaxation
pie chart
pitch
positive entrance
problem/solution
quality
rate
sequential
simple word outline
slide
spatial
statistics
story
testimony
text chart
topical
verbal supporting material
video conferencing
volume

Review Questions

1. One of your first tasks as a speaker is to identify the types of people to whom you will be speaking. Name and describe the five questions you should ask to determine this information.
2. What are two important things to know about the "where" of the presentation?
3. Name the two major purposes for the business presentation, and describe the results of each.
4. As a speaker you can organize your information into nine different patterns. Name and describe each pattern.
5. Speakers use verbal supporting material to verify, clarify, and amplify their contention. Name and describe the seven types of support that were presented in this chapter.
6. What are the different ways in which verbal supporting material can be packaged visually?
7. Describe the different types of electronic meetings.
8. Name and describe the purpose of each of the three parts of all presentations.
9. In this chapter three types of outlines were discussed. Name and describe each type, and tell which one is recommended for general use.
10. Preparation of the final note cards is an important task for the speaker. Explain this chapter's seven hints for effective note usage.
11. You can relieve anxiety before you speak by doing warm-up exercises. Describe the exercises given in this chapter.
12. Describe some of the ways that speakers ineffectually open their talks.
13. Discuss some of the ineffective styles that speakers use that destroy the warmth and spontaneity of their delivery.

Exercises

1. Take a sheet of paper and draw a line from top to bottom down the center of the page. At the top of one side of the page place the word *good,* and on the other side the words *needs work.* Now recall the last presentation that you made and list in the appropriate column each phase of the organization, construction, and practice of the speech. On the back side of the page make a list of ways in which you could improve the items on the *needs work* list. Refer to the list before starting on your next presentation.
2. Using the same presentation that was used in exercise 1, sketch some rough graphics and slides that could have helped you better explain the material in your talk.
3. Attend a special guest presentation on your campus. During and after the presentation, record the following information about the event. Share your findings with other members of your class.
   a. Were the time and the place of the presentation conducive to listening to the speaker?
   b. Did the speaker do her homework in learning who she was speaking to? If not, what changes could she have made?
   c. Were you able to clearly determine the purpose of the presentation?
   d. Which pattern of organization did the speaker use?
   e. Describe at least three different types of verbal supporting material that the speaker used. Were they effective? Were they sufficient? Were they adequately clarifying?
   f. If the speaker used audiovisual aids, were they appropriate and helpful and did they complement the words? If not, tell why.
   g. Describe the speaker's delivery style. Did it add to or distract from her credibility? What about the vocal quality?
   h. In what overall ways was the presentation effective?
   i. In what ways could the presentation have been improved?
4. This chapter has undoubtedly discussed things that you want to change in your presentation making. On a separate sheet of paper, write out

a contract with yourself to improve specific things in the way you speak. Write down the items, list the steps you must take to improve them, and indicate a date by which time you expect to complete the task.

5. Interview a presenter; he or she could be a salesperson, a teacher, a minister, or someone else who regularly talks to large groups of people. Ask that person questions about how he or she organizes, constructs, practices, and actually delivers his or her presentations. Share your findings with your class.
6. Scan the cable channels on your television and see if you can find a speaker who is using an interpreter. What do you observe verbally and nonverbally about the interaction?
7. Review current issues of *Fortune, Forbes,* and *The New York Times.* Make a list of the types of presentational speaking mentioned in articles. Review this list and report on it in class.

REFERENCES

1. Jill Vitiello, "Making Speakers Sparkle," *Meetings and Conventions* (September 1992), p. 183.
2. David Wallechinsky and Irving Wallace, *The Book of Lists* (New York: William Morrow, 1977).
3. "Boston University Dean Apologizes for Plagiarism," *Dallas Morning News,* July 6, 1991, p. 6A.
4. Ibid.
5. "Boston University Dean Quits over Plagiarism," *Dallas Morning News,* July 13, 1991, p. 6A.
6. Ibid.
7. David Benchley, "Presentation Pointers," *PC World* (February 1986), p. 133.
8. Robert Moskowitz, "The Electronic Meeting," *Presentation Products Magazine* (September 1990), pp. 24–26.
9. Michael Allen, "Smile! Here Comes Videoconferencing," *Wall Street Journal,* May 18, 1992, p. R11; Christopher Elias, "Strides in Videoconferencing Keep Executives in the Office," *Insight* (February 29, 1988), pp. 44–45; John Schneidawind, "Cost-conscious Companies Tune in to Video Meetings," *USA Today,* February 22, 1991, p. 4B.
10. Janet Endrijonas, "Face to Face, Place to Place," *Presentation Products Magazine* (May 1991), pp. 23–30.
11. "LCD Panels: Uniting the CPU and OHP," *Presentation Products Magazine* (December 1990), p. 21.
12. John B. Callender, "In-House Slidemaking," *Presentation Products Magazine* (March 1991), pp. 27–33.
13. Ellen Muraslain, "Breaking the Language Barrier," *Meetings & Conventions* (March 1991), p. 47.
14. Micheline Maynard, "Chrysler Executives Use Bilingual Approach," *USA Today,* October 8, 1992.
15. Muraslain, "Language Barrier," p. 48.
16. Marcia Yudkin, "Communicating Through an Interpreter," *The Toastmaster* (July 1989), p. 22.

CHAPTER 9

Written Communication: Preparing Letters and Memoranda

J. Dougals Syp, assistant vice-president of Suburban General Hospital in Norristown, PA, discovered that part of the entrée had been stolen immediately before a luncheon to promote support for the hospital. Syp believed that such behavior warranted a written warning to all hospital employees. On February 10, 1987, he sent the following memo to hospital staff:

> On Wednesday January 27th, twelve (12) crab claws were taken from the Weaver Conference room during the set-up for a luncheon. *THIS IS AN ABSOLUTE DISGRACE!*

The remainder of the memo outlined the consequences that would befall employees who took any hospital food or beverage.

Syp did not anticipate the reaction that his memo caused. Employees posted notes on bulletin boards that poked fun at the tone and content of the message. One message, prepared with cut and pasted letters, read:

Crab claw ransom note. Please be advised that these critters were not stolen they were taken hostage and are being held in Lebanon. Don't contact the police or you may never see your crabs alive again. Leave almost $14.62 in mixed coins in the hospital storeroom.

Other notes advertised the "Save the Crab Claw Foundation," notified employees to report "for urine and stool testing for crabmeat," and announced that the FBI would have trash cans "under survelance (sic)." Amused at first, Syp had all the notes removed by the third day. He unequivocably stated, however, that he would "never again write a memo mentioning crab claws."[1]

Excerpts from Larry Reibstein, "The Next Memo Will Ask Why Workers Have So Much Free Time," *The Wall Street Journal,* February 24, 1987, p. 31. Reprinted by permission of *The Wall Street Journal,*

LETTERS AND MEMORANDA

Writing effective letters ranks among the top abilities of people in business. Adia Personnel Services surveyed 908 personnel executives and found that "despite the increase in office automation, 36% of managers spend three or more hours a day on routine paper work."[2] Letters and memoranda are planned and written each day to summarize agreements, initiate contracts, communicate the time and place of meetings, give instructions to employees, reprimand employees, recognize employee performance, provide information, or just give feedback. After surveying staff and management in a variety of industries, Dianna Booher, author of *Cutting Paperwork in the Corporate Culture,* estimated that in America 30 billion original documents are created each year and that the overwhelming majority of these documents are read only once before they are filed.[3] While the writers of these letters, memos, and reports tend to view themselves as effective communicators, their superiors, peers, and subordinates do not necessarily agree.[4]

Letters and memos are important communication channels. You can accomplish your purpose through these channels by learning when to use them and how to present your message. This chapter examines how to plan your letter or memo so that it focuses on the situation and the receiver.

When to Use Letters and Memoranda

The inexperienced often go to one of two extremes when it comes to written communication. They communicate almost totally in writing or avoid written communication altogether. We know from communication research that the receiver will remember a message longer if it is presented both orally and in writing. This should be a key principle in deciding when to use letters and memoranda. Because written communication is most effective when it is used in conjunction with oral communication, a letter can initiate contact for a face-to-face meeting or act as reinforcement by summarizing a discussion. Before writing, analyze both the situation and the receiver.

The Situation

Ask yourself what you want to accomplish. If your outcome requires a complex explanation, a letter is the wrong communication channel unless you intend to also provide a demonstration of the task or use the letter to set up a meeting (or series of meetings) to explain the process. There are four typical uses of the letter or memorandum:

1. *Daily routine.* Daily routine correspondence includes requesting information, providing information, approving requests, or denying requests. The routine purposes of letters are discussed later in the chapter.
2. *For emphasis.* Sometimes a memo can be a very effective way to give

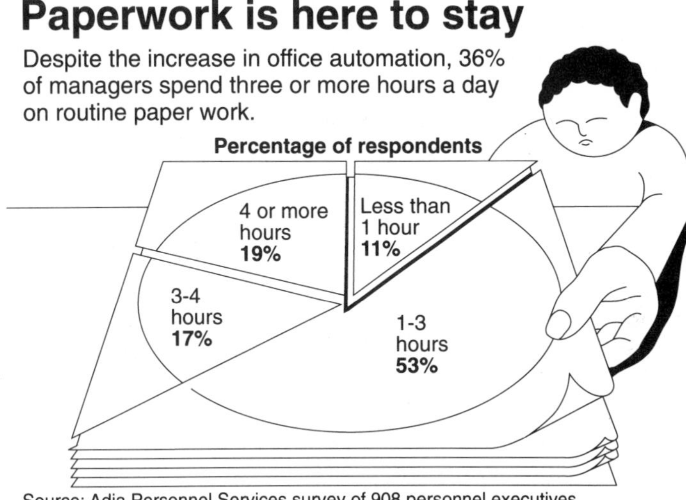

Copyright 1989, *USA Today*. Reprinted with permission.

emphasis. For example, if employees have begun to ignore an organizational policy and are extending the normal coffee break beyond sensible limits, a manager may send a memo to the group members that reminds them of the policy and notes displeasure. While the memo itself provides emphasis, the amount of space devoted to the issue will also communicate how important it is.

3. *For the record.* Managers may participate in activities such as meetings that need to be recorded for future reference. These formal minutes are only one form of memoranda for the record. Others include summaries of discussions that result in recorded agreements or written reprimands.

4. *As a follow-up.* A final purpose for correspondence is to follow up a discussion. Opportunities may be lost because no one acted to follow up a decision to implement an idea. A consultant may lose business because he or she waited to be called and did not send a letter summarizing the plan, fees, and anticipated time frame for the proposed activity. Letters keep the momentum of a situation moving toward the goal by indicating interest, commitment, and action.

The Receiver

Adapt your message to your receiver. What does the reader know about the subject? Consider vocabulary level, educational background, and technical knowledge to determine the words and examples that will be most effective in communicating your message.

How well you know your reader will affect the formality of your letter. You probably would not want to address someone you had never met by that person's first name, yet it would sound stilted to address a friend and fellow worker as "Dear Mr. Smith." The less familiar you are with the other person, the more space you will have to devote to creating common ground in the opening of your letter.

When you communicate face to face, you can observe the receiver's non-verbal reactions to your message as well as reinforce the meaning of your words through your own nonverbal actions. In letters, the words alone must convey your meaning. The words you select are critical and must be aimed at the reader's realm of experience to be effective, especially if a letter is your only channel of communication.

Preparing Letters and Memoranda

Plan Your Message

Before you begin to write, outline what you want to say. Why are you writing? Are you trying to inform or persuade? Do you want the reader to take some action? What basic information does the reader need to get the point? In what order should you place this information? Should the message be sent in a formal letter or as a memo? Get to the point quickly. Do not waste space on trivial, redundant, or superfluous points. Remember, keep your message as brief as possible to increase the probability that the recipient will read the whole thing.

Select Words Carefully

You may have received a letter beginning with the phrase, "This is to inform you that . . . ." The language did not convey warmth or a personal style and delivered an impersonal message, at best. Good letter writing requires a conversational style that avoids stilted conventional jargon. Avoid "rubber-stamp" expressions that depersonalize the letter. Remember that words are symbols that attempt to convey your message. The reader will interpret the words to fit his or her experience. Some words have basically the same definition but very different emotional responses; for example, would you prefer to have your account "reviewed" or "audited"?[5]

If you use technical terms or jargon that are unfamiliar to your readers, much if not all of your message will be lost. Steve Osborne, an advertising specialist, says, "Just because the electro-rectification hypostatic module on your product is a household word in your world, it will cause an immediate, disorienting 'glitch' in the average reader's train of thought, and your mailing will be that much more likely to find itself deep-sixed."[6] Whenever possible, choose the short, simple word over the long or technical term. Your objective is clarity. In using written symbols, you cannot afford to be vague.

Compare the following two sentences:

- Numerous options to augment investment income need to be considered for accumulated income growth.
- You have several options for increasing your retirement assets.

Armadillos at Mile Marker 109

Carmen Medrano, a director in a state department of transportation, knew she had a serious problem that needed immediate attention. Because of the convenience and lower cost, instructions for a variety of jobs were transmitted by electronic mail (E-mail) throughout the state. However, many errors—both costly and dangerous—had occurred. Some employees were forwarding detailed specifications through E-mail before final decisions had been made about the procedures to be followed. Thus, some work was initiated that had to be reversed.

While some errors were "deadly" serious, others were also humorous. One incident involved a highway sign for an armadillo crossing erected in the middle of an elevated highway that crossed 10 miles of swampy terrain. The agency received numerous calls inquiring about the sign; it had become a joke that even made the newspapers with a commentary on the efficiency of the agency.

Medrano investigated and discovered the following: An engineer at the home office frequently used E-mail to correspond with employees in the field. From day to day he would revise his instructions, sometimes totally changing the previous day's message. The constancy, complexity, inconsistency, and length of these messages became frustrating for the crew chief. Since he was accountable for implementing the engineer's instructions, it was his obligation to sort out the important items and execute them in the field. One of these messages stated that there was probably a need for a sign around highway marker 109 to indicate that the area was dangerous because wildlife were often caught on the bridge. The rest of the transmission went into detail about the habitat of armadillos and other animals in the area. The crew chief gave a copy of the transmission to one of the crew members and attempted to explain the instructions. After mulling over the situation for a few minutes, the crew member erected the symbol for an armadillo crossing at mile marker 109.

Medrano's investigation of this and similar errors led directly to the cause: poor written communication skills. Among the many problems she identified were heavy use of acronyms and technical jargon, poorly constructed sentences, incomplete information, and confusing instructions.

The first version was part of a fundraising campaign that went into detail about how a contributor could personally benefit by revising a retirement income plan. The second version eliminates jargon, superfluous words, and vague terms and makes the point. It uses words common to everyday experience and combines these words carefully and simply to achieve the desired objective. The reader can understand precisely the intent of this message.

Identify with Your Reader

Write at a level your reader can easily understand. Attempt to see things from the reader's point of view, and then write your letter to accomplish your purpose with this in mind. "'When I sit in meetings with clients before writing their ads,' says one professional writer, 'I never ask them what they want to say about their product. I ask them to tell me what their potential customers want to hear about the product.'"[7]

Remember that written communication is different from oral communication in that you cannot receive immediate feedback and nonverbal cues. You must anticipate how the reader will interpret word-symbols. Before you communicate, be certain you know all that you want to say. Select expressions that are concrete and appropriate to the reader. Note the difference in specificity between the following two versions of project completion requirements:

- Please complete the project as soon as possible.
- The deadline for completing the project is December 13, 1996.

The expression "as soon as possible" is vague and open to personal interpretation; in the second version, the requirement is concrete. Remember that the recipient of your written communication may have other distracting messages that interfere with reception. Design your message so that it takes multiple interpretations into account.

Use a Positive Tone

Take care to set the appropriate tone. Anger and sarcasm expressed in writing will not accomplish most objectives, nor will they create goodwill. Your choice of words should convey sincerity. Contrast the following approaches to expressing employee disagreement with a company policy change:

- I am concerned about the impact this policy will have on employee morale. Many of our employees consider the requirements a serious invasion of their privacy.
- People will quit rather than work under these conditions.

Attempt to use a positive tone, even when you must say no. Let the reader know that you understand the problem. Provide an explanation that logically presents your position and, whenever possible, provide an alternative solution.

Use the Correct Emphasis

Be sure to put things in their proper perspective by using the correct emphasis. The amount of space you devote to an issue and where you place it on the page suggest its importance to you. Taking two paragraphs to explain why an applicant did not get the job will leave the recipient wondering whether there is more to the message than meets the eye. Putting the most

Who Checks the Form Letters?

Don Bagin reported that his daughter considered transferring from one college to another and wrote a number of schools about their transfer requirements. She received several responses, three personally signed by someone in the admissions office. A fourth letter included a misspelled word and was signed ''Admissions' Staff.''

Since his daughter was not ''impressed by that letter,'' Bagin gave the admissions office a call. While the information about the spelling error was gratefully received, Bagin's suggestion that personally signed letters would make a better impression on prospective students was not appreciated. The person in the admission's office replied: ''Do you realize how long it would take to sign all those letters?'' Of course, the competition obviously found the time and reaped the benefits of this response.[8]

important point last sends a message that it may not be that important to you. To emphasize a point, take a tip from advertising executive David Ogilvy: "Five times as many people read the headline as read the body copy. When you have written your headline, you have spent 80 cents of your dollar."[9]

Proofread

Your message creates an impression about you as an employee. Misspelled words, errors in punctuation, or mistakes in grammar or word usage will reflect on your conscientiousness and ability to communicate. Employers do not overlook these faults. Some high-level supervisors make it a point to circle such errors and either return them to the senders or their supervisors for corrective action. Proofread your work at least three times for possible errors. You may overlook some obvious errors just because you are too involved in the message; therefore, it is always helpful for someone else to proof it for you. Remember, when you sign the correspondence, you take the responsibility for its contents.

Standard Parts of a Letter

Business letters make an impression on their receivers. If the message is neatly presented on high-quality paper, the receiver will conclude that the sender takes pride in his or her work. Use high-quality white bond paper and print with a standard font or have someone prepare the letter for you. Letters usually have six standard parts: heading; receiver's name and address; salutation; body; complimentary close; typed name, title, and signature of the sender.

- *Heading.* The heading tells the reader the address of the sender and when the letter was written. Depending on the format you select, you may place this information at the center of the letter, lined up with the right margin, or typed at the left margin. If you use letterhead, you need only center the date two lines below the address.
- *Receiver's name and address.* The address of the receiver should provide the name, identification, and location of the receiver. Use *Mr., Mrs., Ms.,* or *Miss* unless another title is required. Be exact in using the name of a position or company, and use standard, two-letter postal abbreviations or spell out the name of a state. Type the zip code on the same line as the state.
- *Salutation.* The salutation is a courteous greeting that should include the reader's title. Avoid using impersonal greetings such as *To Whom It May Concern* or *Gentlemen.* Whenever possible, use the title and name of a specific person.
- *Body.* The body of the letter contains the message and answers for the receiver the questions *what, why,* and *who.* It begins two spaces below the salutation and is single-spaced with two spaces between paragraphs.
- *Complimentary close.* The complimentary close brings a letter to a courteous ending. There are a variety of accepted conventional closings, and one should be selected according to the mood you are trying to create. *Sincerely yours* and *Cordially yours* are appropriate for most business situations.
- *Typed name and title and written signature.* The name and title are typed four spaces below the complimentary close, thus allowing space for the written signature.

Basic letter formats can be found in Appendix F.

Basic Letter Formats

Whatever letter format you select, it should have a symmetrical arrangement and be framed by white space or a margin—like a picture within a frame. Appendix F includes examples of the three following standard formats:

- *Modified block style.* The modified block style is the most widely used because it gives the letter a balanced appearance. The beginning of each paragraph is indented, and the date and complimentary close are centered.
- *Block style.* The block style is becoming the preferred style of many organizations because it can be easily and quickly prepared. All lines begin at the left margin, which circumvents the need for setting tabs and indenting paragraphs.
- *AMS style.* The AMS (Administrative Management Society) style uses

the basic block format without the salutation and complimentary close. A subject line is often substituted in caps for the salutation.

Memoranda

Memoranda, more commonly known as memos, are informal messages that can be used to request information, reinforce agreements, clarify previous messages, or deliver short reports about daily problems. While letters are directed to people outside the organization, memos are directed to people inside the organization—boss to boss, boss to subordinate, office to office, and so forth. Typically, the memo uses a standardized form with the words *To, From, Subject,* and *Date* at the top of the page, as in Exhibit 9.1. The sender usually places initials beside his or her name rather than using a signature line.

The content of the memo may be organized in a similar way as the formats for letters and formal reports. Long explanations are rarely necessary because both parties usually have some background about the situation and need only to clarify the specific point of the memo.

Because of the memo's brevity, direct order is commonly used. A summary statement and recommendation are followed by a paragraph that describes the problem and its implications and then presents the facts and analysis. Headings may be used to separate its parts, similar to the formal report. The memo rarely should be more than four pages in length.

Memos are a valuable tool for the manager because they provide a means of recording events for later review, act as documentation, and convey information at the convenience of the receiver. Nevertheless, because of their informality and brevity, memos do not require a lengthy preparation by the sender. While more informality is permissible than in a letter, memos should be complete and courteous.

DATE: November 1, 1994

TO: Charles Rountree, Director
Personnel Services

FROM: Dorothy Jameson, Head
Accounting Department DJ

SUBJECT: Vacant Position

One of our employees has decided to accept a vacant position in another department beginning June 1. Will you please send me a pool of applicants that would be qualified for the accounting clerk III position?

Since we are in the process of preparing the audit for this year's expenditures, the vacancy will pose a problem regarding workload. Can we begin interviewing as soon as possible in order to fill the position on June 1?

I will sincerely appreciate your assistance with this problem. If you need any further information, please give me a call.

EXHIBIT 9.1 A Sample Memorandum

Types of Messages: Direct, Indirect, and Persuasive

You can influence the response of your reader by the way you present your message. If you have good news, there is no reason to "beat around the bush." A direct response is most appropriate. If you have bad news, however, you will want to prepare your reader for it using an indirect approach. If you are trying to elicit a specific response, you will have to persuade the reader by making a case. The following sections of this chapter provide strategies for presenting good or bad news, overcoming resistance, and preparing employee letters and resumes.

Direct Letters: The Good News

When you receive a letter with good news, you don't want to wade through details and explanations. You want the good news first. For example, if you have been selected for a job, the reasons are secondary to the fact that you have the job. *Direct letters* are written to save time and get to the point and include little explanation or background. The basic format of the direct letter is:

1. State the good news;
2. Present explanation and details;
3. Maintain a friendly tone.

Types of letters typically requiring directness are routine inquiries, responses, and acknowledgments.

Inquiries

The *inquiry* seeks information; it is one of the most frequently used letter writing approaches. The letter should get to the point quickly and place the key question in the first line. If the information you seek is more complex, analyze your objective, and prepare a series of questions that will elicit the specific response you desire. Then, start with a general question, and place more specific questions later in the letter.

To encourage a response that will meet your expectations, tailor the message by determining what will motivate the reader to help you. Place general explanatory material following the direct opening sentence, and include questions where needed. Ask the minimum number of questions to get the necessary information.

Be sure to structure your questions carefully. Ask directly for information—don't hint. Itemizing questions adds clarity, as is illustrated in Exhibit 9.2. End your letter with goodwill by expressing your appreciation for the reader's time and assistance, but avoid trite expressions such as "thanking you in advance." Unless you have an unlimited time schedule, include a reasonable time frame for the response. A statement that presents a reason and gives a date is most effective, for example:

> Since I will need this information for a report that must be completed by September 1, may I have your reply by August 29?

Positive Responses

If you are replying favorably to a request, say so in the beginning of your letter. You may want to use a subject line in your letter that identifies the inquiry or refer to the request in the opening statement of your letter. Answer the question as completely as it requires. If you are providing a series of answers, place them in a logical order in the body of the letter.

Sometimes bad news must accompany the good. If so, begin with the good news to emphasize it. Put the bad news in a secondary position in the middle of the letter. Remember also that the amount of space you devote to a topic adds emphasis. You will want to deemphasize the bad news by stating it briefly.

Everyone appreciates a little extra effort on his or her behalf. If you can provide additional information, assistance, or provide another reference, it will benefit your public relations. Exhibit 9.3 is an example of a favorable response to a job reference.

Acknowledgments

An *acknowledgment* lets someone know you have received his or her letter and apprises that person of the status of an order or request. Many organizations use a form letter or postcard as an acknowledgment. An individually

SCC

Salter Chemical Company
2353 Bankston Ave.
Baton Rouge, LA 70810

July 29, 1994

Sales Department
National Communication Institute
1258 Dexter N.
Seattle, WA 98109

Dear Mr. Hurston:

Will you please send me some information concerning the film "The Importance of Effective Written Business Communications"? Our company has a small collection of films, a few of which apply to communication, and we would like to update our collection. I would specifically like responses to the following questions:

1. Will you please provide a summary of the film's contents?
2. What is the rental fee and the cost of purchase?
3. What is the copyright date?
4. What is the length of the film in minutes?
5. We plan to use it to train and instruct supervisory staff. Will it be appropriate for this level audience?

Since my training program proposals for purchasing must be submitted by the end of next month, may I have your reply within two weeks? I appreciate your assistance and look forward to doing business with you and your company.

Sincerely,

Cathy Johnston

Cathy Johnston
Director of Training

EXHIBIT 9.2 An Inquiry

written acknowledgment can convey goodwill and reinforce the relationship between the client and the organization. It should begin with the acknowledgment of the request or order, proceed to establish goodwill, and close with a friendly statement that encourages future business, as in Exhibit 9.4. A checklist of the things to include in a direct letter is found in Table 9.1.

Indirect Letters: The Bad News

Sometimes it is necessary to send letters that contain bad news. Perhaps a very good job candidate was not selected during intense competition for a job. You must present the bad news and maintain goodwill. Such *indirect letters* require a less obvious approach with a buffer statement that delays

B & C

BAKER AND COMPANY
1321 Benton St.
Rockford, IL 61107

April 21, 1994

Mr. Kenneth Cochran
Personnel Director
Welford and Company
320 Napoleon
New Orleans, LA 76143

Dear Mr. Cochran:

Your request for a performance evaluation of John Richardson arrived last Friday. John has worked for us for four years during which time he has demonstrated outstanding qualities of skill, knowledge, and leadership.

His skill and imagination made him our top customer service employee. His helpful, sincere attitude toward customer inquiries has earned only praise from them.

John's superiors commend him for his loyalty and dedication. He rarely leaves the office until he completes his work. In addition he is fast and efficient, evidence of his efforts to maintain good public relations within our company.

As his employer, I could not ask for a better customer-relations worker. Though I am disappointed he is leaving, John has my highest praise and recommendation. His skills and hard work will definitely meet your company's needs. If you need any additional help in evaluating him, please write me again.

Sincerely,

Judy Smythe

Judy Smythe
Office Manager

EXHIBIT 9.3 Positive Response

the bad news and seeks to gain understanding. You might begin your letter with the statement, "We have just completed the review of several outstanding candidates for our vacant position in the accounting department." The buffer should be followed by the details and reasons behind your decision that supports the bad news:

> We have ranked each candidate according to his or her strengths for the job, and selected the top candidate.

Your third step is to announce the bad news as briefly as possible. If you can present an alternative, do so. For example, you may know of another position for which the candidate might apply. Finally, you should try to

S G C

ORDER DEPARTMENT
SELECT GIFT COMPANY
1650 E. 46th St.
Portland, OR 97213

October 30, 1994

Ms. Susan McDaniel
6678 Carroll Lane
Columbus, OH 43204

Dear Ms. McDaniel:

Your Christmas order is on its way to your home and should arrive early next week. United Post Carriers will deliver between 8:00 a.m. and 5:00 p.m., Monday through Friday. If you give them a call at 766-5343, you can specify the delivery time. You will be billed as soon as we have received confirmation that you received the order from the carrier.

We welcome you as a new customer of our product line. You will find the convenience, quality merchandise, and variety an advantage to you in gift selection.

We sincerely appreciate your order and look forward to serving your future select gift needs.

Sincerely,

Michael Conrad, Manager
Sales Department

EXHIBIT 9.4 An Acknowledgment

maintain goodwill by closing in a friendly manner such as, "We appreciate your interest in our firm."

Indirect letters should convince the receiver that you not only gave his or her request or inquiry your attention and an objective review, but that your decision is also unavoidable. The order of items within the indirect letter is:

1. Begin with a buffer statement.
2. Present reasons or details.
3. Present the bad news.
4. Give an alternative if possible.
5. Close in a friendly manner.

Letters that need an indirect approach include letters refusing credit, claims, or requests and should generally follow the outline presented above. The sample letter in Exhibit 9.5 expresses concern and states the refusal in positive language. A checklist of things to include in an indirect letter is found in Table 9.2.

TABLE 9.1 Direct Letter Checklist

Get letter under way quickly.

✓ Place key question in first line, or
✓ Start with a general question and place specific questions later.

Give adequate explanation.

✓ Tailor message to reader.
✓ Place general explanatory material following the direct opening sentence.
✓ Include explanatory material with questions where needed.
✓ Ask the minimum number of questions to get necessary information.

Structure questions carefully.

✓ Ask directly for information; do not hint.
✓ Avoid "loaded" questions.
✓ Word questions carefully to get necessary information.
✓ Itemize questions when necessary.
✓ Vary sentence form and length.

End with goodwill.

✓ Refer to reader's next action.
✓ Avoid trite expressions.

Take care in word choice.

Use correct emphasis.

Source: Adapted from Gretchen N. Vik, Clyde W. Wilkinson, and Dorothy C. M. Wilkinson, *Writing and Speaking in Business*, 10th ed. (Homewood, Ill.: Richard D. Irwin, 1990), p. 89.

Persuasive Letters: Overcoming Resistance and Getting the Desired Response

You will find that there are many occasions when you will have to overcome the resistance of the reader to your objective. In such instances the *persuasive letter* establishes an argument for your position by presenting information that will allow your reader to understand and accept your point of view.

The first step, therefore, is to determine your objective. What outcome do you want from your correspondence? Understanding? Support? Action? Once you have specified the objective, analyze your reader's reaction to it. What objections would he or she have? Put yourself in his or her place and try to see it from his or her point of view. It will probably help to list these objections using education, background, experience, attitudes, and biases as broad categories.

Because you are trying to overcome resistance, an indirect approach that begins with your specific information and supports it with sound reasoning will probably be most effective. You are establishing a case for your argument and thus should direct each piece of evidence at dispelling an objection of your reader. The persuasive letter should have three parts: (1) an attention-

MU

OFFICE OF STUDENT AFFAIRS
THE MIDEASTERN UNIVERSITY
250 Boyd Hall
Bethesda, MD 20016

May 18, 1994

Mr. George Stevens, President
Student Government Association
P.O. Box 11145
Bethesda, MD 20016

Dear Mr. Stevens:

Your interest in the current parking situation on campus indicates a genuine concern about an increasingly complex problem. Certainly, this problem is one that deserves considerable deliberation in attempting to come to a reasonable solution.

A suitable parking system centers on fairness and equality for the student body, faculty, and staff. Faculty and staff must have parking to meet the needs of the school itself. Disabled students present an obvious priority. After careful reexamination of the current parking situation, the members of the review committee feel that equality and fairness may best be preserved by retaining the current system.

Your continuing concern over campus problems will certainly aid in making our campus a better one.

Sincerely yours,

Jeffrey Travers, Chairman
Campus Traffic Committee

EXHIBIT 9.5 A Refused Request

getting opening, (2) the argument, which presents the facts and reasoning, and (3) an action-getting close.

An Attention-Getting Opening

The first paragraph in a persuasive letter must get the receiver's attention and convince her to continue reading. If the first sentence has a negative tone or creates a negative reaction, the reader's perception of the following information will be affected by it. In other words, a negative filter will block or color the remaining information no matter how well it is presented. How would you like to receive a letter with the following opening line?

> I was extremely disappointed to learn that you violated our guidelines for implementing the personnel policies.

While the remainder of this letter may present a reasonable and acceptable explanation of the problem and action to be taken, the reader will probably be too disconcerted by the opening remarks to process it.

TABLE 9.2 Indirect Letter Checklist

Use indirect approach.

✓ Use friendly, neutral talk to establish common ground.
✓ Start with comments that set up the following strategy.

Present the explanation and the refusal.

✓ Give justifying reasons prior to refusal.
✓ Have reasoning flow logically to refusal.
✓ State refusal positively.

Close with a feeling of goodwill.

✓ Use last words to give a forward look.
✓ Show how the reader benefits.

Take care in word choice.

Use correct emphasis.

Avoid critical or patronizing tone.

Source: Adapted from Gretchen N. Vik, Clyde W. Wilkinson, and Dorothy C. M. Wilkinson, *Writing and Speaking in Business*, 10th ed. (Homewood, Ill.: Richard D. Irwin, 1990), p. 126.

The opening should present a buffer statement that establishes common ground and gains attention so that the reader will want to read the rest of the letter. For example:

> We have previously discussed our mutual concern for the effective implementation of the new personnel policies, one area apparently is still not clear and is creating problems for our staff.

This opening establishes mutual objectives and focuses on a specific area for analysis and mutual problem-solving. Neither blame nor a defensive tone has been established.

The Argument

The word *argument* often conjures up thoughts of two parties who fail to agree with each other. Here, however, we will define it to mean a case or the presentation of persuasive appeals that are logical, ethical, or emotional.

The body of the letter should establish your case through a logical presentation of reasoning. Since you are trying to persuade the reader to commit to your objective, choice of words and arrangement of sentences are important. Avoid leading statements or loaded words. Begin with the arguments that will have the greatest effect or success. Use an indirect approach first, presenting evidence that leads to a logical conclusion.

A little surgery can

This company's old letter is a good first start. It's persuasive and has immediacy. All it needs is some additional structure and a little nipping and tucking to make it work even harder.

BEFORE

It's not too late
to lower your
property tax.

1) Dec. 26 Deadline: The town of Plainville just mailed the fiscal 1991 Real Estate Tax Bills. You still have until December 26 to contest your assessed valuation and get an abatement which would lower your taxes.

2) Get an expert: Property owners can obtain abatements on their own, however, the adjustment is usually nominal. For substantial reduction of your property taxes, the services of a professional CPA and real estate tax expert is advised to substantiate your case.

3) No risk contingent fee: My firm, Property Tax Associates, only gets paid if I successfully reduce your property tax. I know what method is currently being used in Plainville to assess your property. I know how similar properties are assessed. And, I can evaluate whether your assessment is taking advantage of the full depreciation deduction to which you are entitled and apply declining value multipliers. In a word, I am a property tax abatement expert and have successfully lowered the property taxes of my clients by thousands of dollars.

4) Free evaluation: I know the Plainville real estate market and can quickly evaluate your current assessment and tax situation, at no obligation to you. I will not take your case if I do not believe I can substantially reduce your real estate taxes. My fee is based on a percentage of your actual tax reduction. So it is in my interest as well, to make sure your taxes are lowered to the full limit of the law.

5) You must act quickly: State law limits the number of days an abatement application can be filed. Call me at (508) 429-2527 for an appointment now, so there will be enough time to properly and legally substantiate your tax reduction request.

PROPERTY TAX ASSOCIATES
ROCCO BEATRICE, CPA, MST, MBA
156 MITCHELL ROAD
HOLLISTON, MA 01746
508 429-2527

A letter with potential . . .

Recommendations:

A. Headline transplant

The old headline telegraphs a strong benefit—but may work better as a subhead, beneath the new headline.

B. Personalization implant

Who are you talking to? With no salutation, this letter doesn't draw readers in.

C. Pace lift

The old letter opens a little slowly and dully. That can be a turnoff to the impatient, indifferent reader.

D. Paragraph liposuction

The old letter has a few oversized paragraphs that look formidable to read. That immediately disinvites the reader.

make a letter better.

A. Headline transplant

The new headline pushes an emotional "hot button" that gets prospects riled up—and ready to act.

B. Personalization implant

A letter with opening personalization enables you to bond one-to-one with the reader. That connection is the same that any sales rep hopes to achieve. And a letter is a sales rep.

C. Pace lift

The new letter opens with a provocative, one-sentence "hook," then quickly hops from point to point.

D. Paragraph liposuction

The new letter keeps paragraphs lean, mean and easy to read.

AFTER

Will You OVERPAY
Your Property Tax
Again This Year?

It's not too late to lower it if you act by the December 26th deadline.

Mr. George Wagner
R-B Electronics
1313 Azure Blvd.
Plainville, MA 01746

Dear Mr. Wagner,

Will you be "nailed" again this year?

Amazingly, six out of every ten property owners overpay on their property taxes . . . and you could be one of them.

But if you act by December 26th—the deadline for contesting your assessed valuation—you can get an abatement that will lower your taxes.

Why you should call Property Tax Associates:

1) Get a larger abatement. You can expect a much larger cut than you could obtain on your own because of our special understanding and knowledge of the abatement process.

2) Pay only if you get a reduction. You don't pay us unless we successfully reduce your tax. And our fee is based on a percentage, so it is in our interest to get your taxes reduced as low as possible.

3) Get a free evaluation. It costs you nothing to learn if you have a chance for an abatement. We know the Plainville real estate market and can quickly evaluate your assessment and tax situation, without obligation.

We've helped many owners like you save thousands on their property taxes. And we can do the same for you.

MAKE NO MISTAKE: The city will not reduce your tax automatically. You must apply by December 26th for a reduction—or overpay again. Call me at (508) 429-2527 today so there is enough time to evaluate and prepare your request.

Sincerely,

Rocco Beatrice
Certified Public Accountant

Potential released

EXHIBIT 9.6 Effective Persuasive Letters: Before and After

Source: Jerry Fisher, "Perfect Pitch," *Entrepreneur* (May 1991), p. 131. Reprinted by permission.

TABLE 9.3 Persuasive Letter Checklist

Start with attention-getting opening.
- ✓ Begin with an attention-getting sentence.
- ✓ Avoid a negative tone.
- ✓ Establish common ground.

Present reasoning in systematic order.
- ✓ Use indirect approach.
- ✓ Avoid overlap and repetition.
- ✓ Establish case through specific information and sound reasoning.
- ✓ Avoid leading statements or loaded words.
- ✓ Begin with arguments that will have greatest impact or success.
- ✓ Label opinions and support them with facts.

End with an action-getting close.
- ✓ Present desired action to the reader.
- ✓ Emphasize benefits of action.
- ✓ Convey friendliness.

Avoid negative language.

Use correct emphasis.

Avoid trite expressions.

Source: Adapted from Clyde W. Wilkinson, Peter B. Clark, and Dorothy C. M. Wilkinson, *Communicating Through Letters and Reports*, (Homewood, Ill.: Richard D. Irwin, 1980), p. 101.

An Action-Getting Close

The argument should bring the reader to a logical close. It is here that you present to the reader the action you desire her to take. State it in the form of a question, emphasizing the positive aspects of the action:

> Since we need to handle personnel grievances at the lowest level possible, will you grant an interview to Ms. James concerning this problem by March 30?

In addition, the close of the persuasive letter should convey goodwill to the reader by emphasizing his or her importance to the effective handling of the situation. The sample letters in Exhibit 9.6 demonstrate the effect of a carefully prepared persuasive letter. A checklist of things to include in a persuasive letter is found in Table 9.3.

Employment Letters and Resumes

One of the most important persuasive letters you will write is the letter of application for a job. Your letter of application and data sheet are reflections of you. In a highly competitive job situation, two equally qualified applicants may very likely be evaluated according to who has submitted the more persuasive letter and set of credentials. Your ability to present yourself will be perceived as a key to your effectiveness in the job.

Before you apply for a position, take a thorough inventory of your assets and abilities, including interests, education, experience, and aptitudes. It may be helpful to write an autobiography recounting the significant things you have done in your lifetime. You should include awards, degrees, extracurricular activities, leadership positions, technical knowledge, interesting courses, part- or full-time jobs, hobbies, training, and military service in chronological order. By preparing an autobiography, you will become aware of your own skills, knowledge, and achievements and can evaluate them in terms of which you enjoyed most and how they relate to the job for which you are applying.

Most employers will request that you submit a resume and a letter of application with references. This information should provide the employer with everything necessary to evaluate your qualifications for the job.

The Resume

Exhibits 9.7 and 9.8 are sample resumes with our comments. While there are many acceptable formats, we recommend one that is simple and allows the recipient to locate information easily. Numerous other styles may be found in your local library's business correspondence section.

Resumes are a concise statement of your job history, education, and personal information. They should give prospective employers a clear picture of your suitability for the job. The resume's appearance, content, and accuracy make first impressions that will allow employers to screen and rank applicants quickly. Target your strengths and make them stand out, but avoid wordiness; keep it brief. Use a style and layout that allow the reader to get to the main points quickly. Use noun phrases with action verbs in parallel form to keep your resume concise and vigorous. A resume of no more than two pages is preferred for most jobs. Balance material on the page. Use bold headings, clear type, appropriate placement, and spacing that contribute to appropriate emphasis and overall visual appeal. Above all, be honest. Do not overstate your achievements, and do not put anything on a resume that is not factual.

A survey of Fortune 500 personnel administrators and business communication instructors conducted by Jules Harcourt and A. C. "Buddy" Krizan found agreement on content preferences: 90 percent of the respondents in both groups ranked name, telephone number, address, degree(s), major, name of college, date of graduation, jobs held, employer, dates of employment, duties, special aptitudes/skills, awards/honors, grade point average, achievements/work experience, and willingness to relocate as preferences.[10] Harcourt and Krizan state:

> The primary thrust of current personnel administrator item preferences is applicant achievement. They are looking for evidences that the applicant has achieved as shown by resume content that includes Grade Point Average, Special Skills, and Work Experience Achievements.[11]

Our sample resumes in Exhibits 9.7 and 9.8 include the following information:

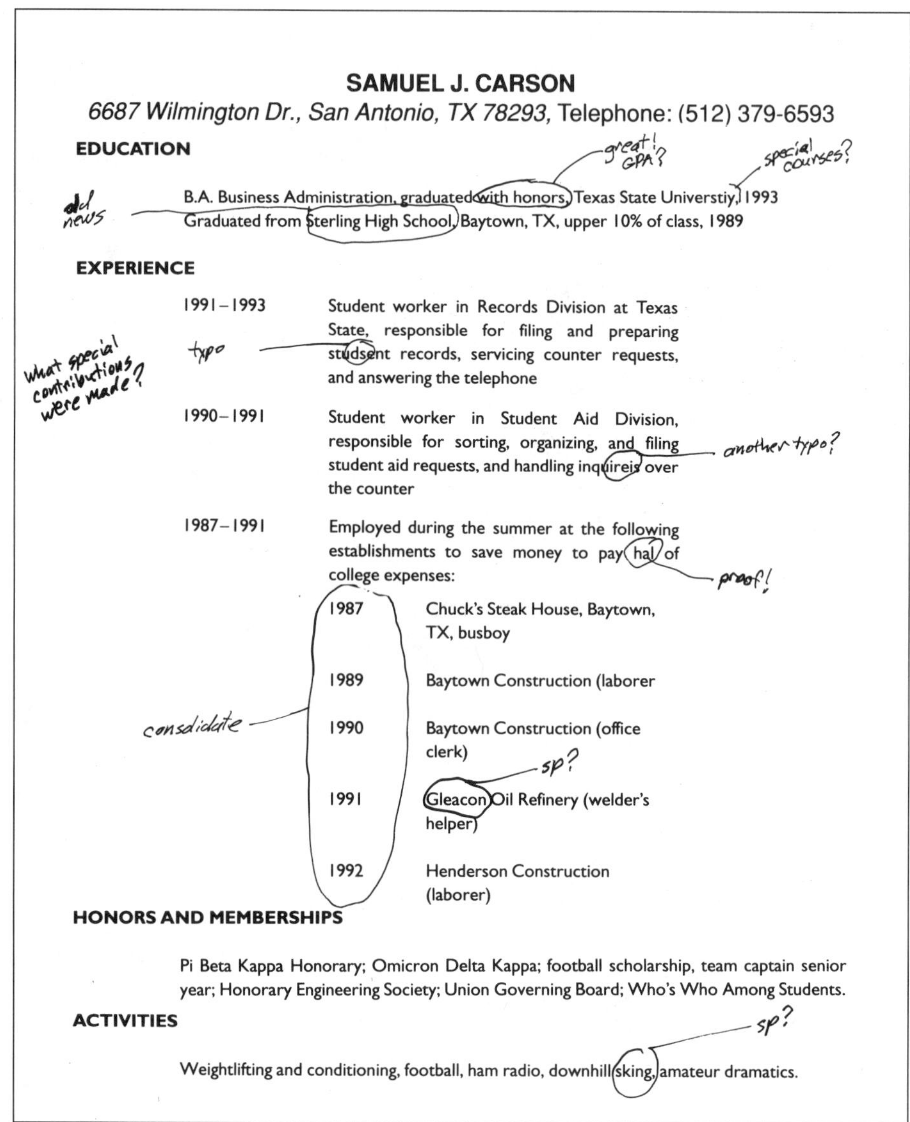

SAMUEL J. CARSON

6687 Wilmington Dr., San Antonio, TX 78293, Telephone: (512) 379-6593

EDUCATION

B.A. Business Administration, graduated with honors, Texas State Universtiy, 1993
Graduated from Sterling High School, Baytown, TX, upper 10% of class, 1989

EXPERIENCE

1991–1993 Student worker in Records Division at Texas State, responsible for filing and preparing studsent records, servicing counter requests, and answering the telephone

1990–1991 Student worker in Student Aid Division, responsible for sorting, organizing, and filing student aid requests, and handling inquireis over the counter

1987–1991 Employed during the summer at the following establishments to save money to pay hal of college expenses:

1987 Chuck's Steak House, Baytown, TX, busboy

1989 Baytown Construction (laborer

1990 Baytown Construction (office clerk)

1991 Gleacon Oil Refinery (welder's helper)

1992 Henderson Construction (laborer)

HONORS AND MEMBERSHIPS

Pi Beta Kappa Honorary; Omicron Delta Kappa; football scholarship, team captain senior year; Honorary Engineering Society; Union Governing Board; Who's Who Among Students.

ACTIVITIES

Weightlifting and conditioning, football, ham radio, downhill sking, amateur dramatics.

EXHIBIT 9.7

1. *Personal Information.* As well as providing your name, preferably in caps and centered at the top of the page, you should provide your address (home and work) and telephone number, and fax number (if you have one). Other personal information can be provided if it is relevant to the job. Because of antidiscrimination laws, most employers do not expect you to provide your race or ethnicity, sex, birthdate, marital status, number of children, weight, or any information on disabilities. Although it is optional, you may wish to provide your short and long-term professional objectives.

Janine C. Baretta

5872 California Ave.
Seattle, WA, 98390
(206) 893-6201

OBJECTIVE: Executive officer in charge of major banking operations at a regional bank

QUALIFICATIONS

Expertise in all aspects of bank operations at a major western regional bank
Specialized knowledge of marketing techniques
Demonstrated strategies for successful branch operations
Extensive personnel management experience

EXPERIENCE

Vice-President, West Coast Bank, Seattle, WA. Responsible for all branch operations, 1990–present.

Director of Marketing, West Coast Bank, Seattle, WA., 1988–1990. Responsible for marketing services of a major west coast bank. Supervised 16 professionals who conducted market research and implemented marketing strategies. Implemented branch marketing campaign that increased customer base by 30% and bank deposits by $4 million. good!

Assistant Director of Marketing, Tacoma Bank of Commerce, Tacoma, WA., 1985–1988. Responsible for market research. Based on my research, the bank implemented new strategies which increased customer deposits by 25%.

EDUCATION

Master of Business Administration, North Carolina State, Raleigh, NC., 1983–1985. 4.0/4.0 grade point average, Master of Business Administration Association.

Bachelor of Arts in Business, Louisiana State University, summa cum laude, 1979–1983. Double major with knowledge of statistical forecasting models, micro and macroeconomic theory, central banking and monetary policy, and international finance. Co-director of team that won first place in national marketing competition. Who's Who Among Students, Beta Gamma Sigma, Omicron Delta Kappa, Phi Kappa Phi.

strong competition

PROFESSIONAL and COMMUNITY ACTIVITIES

National Marketing Association; Chair, Seattle chapter, International Management Association; Seattle Rotary Club; Seattle Chamber of Commerce.

PERSONAL INTERESTS and ACTIVITIES

any experience translating?

International travel, reading and speaking Spanish, tennis, and jogging.

EXHIBIT 9.8

2. *Education.* If you are a recent graduate, education may be your best qualification. Along with the degrees or certifications that you have received, you should also include any special training you have had. Include the field of study, school, and the date you received your degree or certification. Coursework that is particularly relevant to the job can be included. For example, if you are applying for a position that requires some computing expertise, listing courses or seminars in various computer languages would be appropriate. The job for which Samuel Carson is applying (Exhibit 9.7) requires a degree. It is an entry-level, supervisory position. Since Carson has a degree in business and varied, unrelated job experience, he placed education first. To demonstrate that he has an excellent educational record, he noted that he graduated with honors.

3. *Experience.* If your experience is more recent than your education and is relevant to the position for which you are applying, place it first. Include any work experience since you have graduated from high school. Employers are impressed with job experience gained while attending school, no matter what level, since it demonstrates that you have initiative. You can include volunteer work, part-time employment, or temporary jobs. None of Carson's jobs is particularly relevant to the job for which he is applying; however, he has been steadily employed in a variety of positions, a fact that demonstrates his willingness to work. In contrast, Janine Baretta (Exhibit 9.8) has considerable experience and is seeking an upper-level management position. Therefore, she placed her experience first on her resume, and she included more detail about each position.

4. *Affiliations and Cocurricular Activities.* Most employers are looking for indicators that you get along with people, are an effective communicator, have high standards, and have demonstrated leadership skills. This section provides information about accomplishments, activities, and associations. Carson divided this information into two separate headings to distinguish between honors and memberships and general activities. In the section on Honors and Memberships, he demonstrated that he was a high achiever on a variety of levels: in the classroom, outside the classroom, and in his sport. In the section on activities, he provided information about a variety of interests and skills to emphasize that he is well rounded and multitalented. Since Baretta is seeking a professional position where professional and community contact and activities are valued, she has separated these activities from her personal interests and activities.

5. *References.* Professionals in the area of resume writing differ in their opinions about providing references. Many believe that this step is not necessary because employers will let you know if they want you to provide names. Often a job announcement will indicate if you need to provide a list of references as an attachment to your resume. If you are uncertain, you can note on your resume that references will be provided by request.

It is a good idea to have a list of references available. You should ask your references for permission to use their names or to refer people to them. Along with the name, title, organization address, and telephone numbers of your references (home and work), it helps to include your relationship. For example, was the reference a supervisor, subordinate, or coworker?

Depending on the type of job for which you are applying, there may be other major headings you will want to include. Organize these headings in terms of their relevance to the job. Evidence from research on resume content indicates that scholastic standing, work experience, and personal interests are influential factors in evaluation of suitability for a job.[12] If experience is of paramount importance, put it first. It is a good idea to list your credentials in reverse chronological order, beginning with the most current job. Note that our samples have plenty of white space to set off headings, provide readability, and avoid a crowded look.

Exhibit 9.7 is a traditional format, and Exhibit 9.8 is functional. The *traditional format* lists your achievements, experience, and activities in a simple, straightforward manner. A *functional format* highlights your accomplishments and targets a specific job.

Your resume is a reflection of your standards and performance expectations. If it is not carefully prepared, negative conclusions will be made about your capabilities. Cheap paper, poor-quality printing, misspelled words, faulty grammar, and a sloppy format have been the downfall of many job candidates. Give the resume a professional look by having it professionally prepared on a word processor. Studies on resume reproduction conclude that professionals respond negatively to poor-quality resumes even if the credentials are strong.[13] A final caution: Keep your resume updated to reflect your current experience and education. It will have numerous uses (introductions, consulting, recognition, job prospecting) and should be easily accessible. A checklist of things to include in a resume is found in Table 9.4.

Letters of Application

While the resume summarizes your achievements and interests, the *letter of application* requests consideration for a specific job. Since you are trying to convince the reader to hire you, use a persuasive approach. Because the letter of application will make the first impression on the prospective employer, you must be sure that it makes the best possible impression. Standard letter format; high-quality bond paper; and correct spelling, punctuation and grammar are musts. Do not exceed one page; if at all possible, address the letter to an individual.

If a letter of application is solicited, you can directly respond to the solicitation in the opening. State the position for which you are applying and present the reason you are interested in the position. Most employers are also interested in how you learned about the job opening, and they appreciate this information.

Sometimes you can find employment by prospecting for jobs that are not advertised. If you choose this approach, begin with an attention-getting opening that demonstrates knowledge about the organization, as shown in Exhibit 9.9. Do not try to be clever or cute; avoid clichés and contrived

TABLE 9.4 Resume Checklist

Begin with your name.

✓ Center your name at top in capital letters.
✓ Place address, telephone number, and fax number if you have one, in smaller normal type below name.

Place the information that is most important first.

✓ Begin with the experience or education that best prepared you for the desired job.
  1. Include work-related experience since high school. Be sure to include job title, duties, organization, dates of employment, and specific accomplishments. Reverse chronological order puts the emphasis on the most recent job experience.
  2. Provide educational background, including degrees or certificates, field of study, school, date, and courses that specially qualify you for the job. In most cases, grade point averages are desirable on college work only.

✓ List cocurricular activities, honors, and associations that indicate that you are well rounded, that you have leadership skills, and that you have learned how to communicate and work with others.

Provide or offer to provide references.

✓ Give names, addresses, and telephone numbers for each reference..
✓ Indicate how each reference is relevant to your background.

Use a style and layout that make it easy for the reader to get to the main points quickly.

✓ Keep it brief. A resume of no more than two pages is preferred for most jobs.
✓ Use noun phrases with action verbs to keep resume brief and vigourous.
✓ Use headings, type, placement, and spacing that contribute to appropriate emphasis and are visually pleasing.

---

openings. Such approaches can turn employers off rather than gain their attention.

The body of the letter of application should highlight your qualifications for a specific job. Give specific examples of accomplishments that are especially suitable for the position. Remember that employers are looking for indicators that show you communicate and work well with others. Volunteer activities, associations, or avocations that can provide such examples are perfectly acceptable. *Do not summarize information that the reader can easily find in the rèsumé.*

The close of your letter should demonstrate your interest in obtaining an interview to explain your capabilities for the position more fully. Remember that this must be at the convenience of the employer; however, you should provide information on how to contact you and the times and dates you are available as well as expressing appreciation for an opportunity to have an interview.

Thomas L. Vinton
9876 St. James St.
Columbus, OH 42304
(405) 769-0556

February 16, 1994

Mr. Charles Durban
1615 Boynton St.
Columbus, OH 43216

Dear Mr. Durban:

I read with enthusiasm your advertisement for a full-time physical fitness supervisor. If you are looking for someone who has experience using the most modern equipment, who works well with others, and who has extensive knowledge of how to design training programs to meet the needs of the individual athlete, I can be an asset to your new center.

With today's rapidly growing interest in physical fitness, you need an instructor who can apply specific weightlifting programs to specific sports. As a football player at State University, I practiced weightlifting for two years under the supervision of three technically trained strength coaches. In addition to playing football, I also participated on the university baseball team. Other sports in which I have participated include basketball, tennis, skiing, and track.

My knowledge of strength and fitness programs goes beyond my experience with playing the sport. As a part of the coursework I have completed at the university, I studied the identification, analysis, and practices of skills and techniques fundamental to each sport. One of these courses focused on the concepts and current trends in training and conditioning. Another course included planning programs and activities for physical fitness for educational institutions and social agencies.

A physical fitness instructor should be able to work well with people and be interested in fitness in order to encourage others. Athletics has been a major highlight of my life, and I will be able to share this feeling with members of your center.

In order to tell you more about my qualifications for the full-time supervisor you need, may I schedule an interview sometime during the next week? You will discover, I am certain, that I have the qualities you are seeking.

Sincerely,

T L Vinton

Thomas L. Vinton

EXHIBIT 9.9 A Letter of Application

The sample letter in Exhibit 9.9 emphasizes the applicant's strengths as they relate to the position of a physical fitness instructor—knowledge of the latest equipment, accomplishments in a variety of sports, the ability to get along with people, and a proven record in fitness. It begins with an attention-getting opening and ends with a request for an interview. It is also printed on high-quality bond paper. A checklist of things to include in a letter of application is found in Table 9.5.

TABLE 9.5 Application Letter Checklist

Start with an attention-getting opening.

- ✓ If the application has been solicited, open with a direct statement that gives the reason for your letter and mentions the position for which you are applying.
- ✓ If you are prospecting for a job, begin with an attention-getting opening which demonstrates knowledge about the organization.
- ✓ Avoid clichés or contrived openings.

Highlight your qualifications for the desired job.

- ✓ Provide examples of accomplishments that are especially suitable to the position.
- ✓ Emphasize experience or education that best prepared you for the desired job.
- ✓ Do not summarize information that the reader can easily find in the rèsumé. Refer the reader to the rèsumé for more detailed information.

Close with a request for an interview.

- ✓ Request interview at the convenience of the prospective employer.
- ✓ Provide your telephone number and a flexible time frame during which you are available.
- ✓ Express gratitude for an opportunity to be considered for the position.

Use an appropriate letter format.

- ✓ Use headings, type, placement, and spacing that contribute to appropriate emphasis and are visually pleasing.
- ✓ Keep it brief; your letter should be no more than one page.
- ✓ Use action verbs to keep writing vigorous.
- ✓ Eliminate any misspelled words and grammatical errors.
- ✓ If possible, address letter to a person.

A GLOBAL PERSPECTIVE

Tone, Content, and Culture in Translation

> After its brochure was distributed in Japan and brought little response, an American medical-equipment supplier wondered what had gone wrong. He found, too late, that the translator, who had emigrated from Japan before World War II and evidently lost touch with his mother tongue, had written the brochure in *bungotai,* a form of Japanese not used since 1946.[14]

The internationalization of the business community requires demonstrated knowledge of language usage in written correspondence. The results of translation errors can be serious. In one case a freelance translator made such grievous errors that "they cost the client its patent—and a flurry of costly lawsuits ensued."[15]

Cultural differences affect the tone and content of a letter. In English-to-Japanese translations, a "tone of overstated respect" may be expected.

A good translation is seldom produced in a short time. Because of the structure of the Japanese language, translation from English to Japanese is especially time consuming. According to John Bukacek, who administers the Japanese-language division of the American Translators Association, it takes 8 hours to translate 2,000 to 3,500 words from English to Japanese.[16] "American Translators International in Stanford, California, translated a 300-page Japanese financial report in a day and a half using 15 translators."[17] Julie Skur Hill gives the following suggestions for avoiding mistakes in English copy intended for translation into Japanese:[18]

1. Avoid boasting or putting down the competition.
2. Use the appropriate formality when you address the recipient of your correspondence.
3. Unlike the direct approach used for American letters, open with a greeting that demonstrates sincerity and respect.
4. Move from the big picture to the details.
5. Include an explanation of your business, since it may not exist in Japan.

ETHICS: RIGHT OR WRONG?

Lena Guerrero's Credibility Gap

In early September 1992, Lena Guerrero was looking forward to the November elections. As a Democrat and chairwoman of the Texas Railroad Commission, she had a slight lead over her opponent and was expected to become the state's first Hispanic woman to be elected statewide.

Guerrero had spent a decade working in the political trenches. In 1980 she was head of the Texas Women's Political Caucus. A few years later she was elected to the Texas Legislature, and *Texas Monthly* named her as one of the ten best state legislators. In 1991, Texas Governor-elect Ann Richards made Guerrero her first appointee, placing her in an unexpired term on the Texas Railroad Commission, a statewide elected office. The commission regulates the state's oil and gas production, as well as trucking and railroad safety.

Now, however, Guerrero's world was starting to unravel. In a routine background check, her opponent, Republican Barry Williamson, discovered an interesting discrepancy. According to various biographies and campaign literature used by Guerrero for the past ten years, she was an honor graduate of the University of Texas and a member of the scholastic honor society Phi Beta Kappa. But Williamson's campaign discovered that Guerrero had never graduated from the university. They passed this information on to a reporter. On September 11, a reporter from the *Dallas Morning News* called and asked her about the discrepancy. She was surprised and affirmed that she was a graduate and received a diploma. Later that day the reporter checked with the university and found that Guerrero had in fact not graduated, nor was she ever a member of Phi Beta Kappa.

At a news conference on September 12, Lena Guerrero acknowledged that she had not completed her degree and had never graduated. She stated that she entered college as an honors freshman, was honored with an outstanding alumni award in 1991, and did not realize until the question was raised that she was still lacking four hours to graduate with a 120-hour bachelor's degree in journalism. "I went for 12 years, believing fully that I had completed my course work in December of '79. . . . I firmly believed that I was finished." [19] She acknowledged that she was hurt and embarrassed by the revelation. Guerrero stated:

> I have always tried to reflect the accuracy of everything. . . . The bottom line is that I do not believe that anybody has been hurt here but me. And I'm hurt because it was a personal goal. . . . This is not about whether I am qualified to serve on the Railroad Commission, for goodness sakes. . . . The bottom line is that in the last 18 months, I've proven I'm doing a good job. . . . It comes down to this: Barry thinks I lied. And I am saying to you that it was never my intent to deceive anyone on anything.[20]

Bill Cryer, press secretary for Governor Richards, affirmed the governor's support and justified the misstatement in this way: "Ms. Guerrero was working her way through school, and probably in the hurry of finding a job, going to commencement and picking up a diploma (that) was the last thing on her mind. . . . In a political season, you have got to expect things like this to happen. In the real world of what Lena had done and accomplished, that is a very, very small thing." [21]

At another press conference a few days later, Guerrero said she would not release her college transcript and had no intention of resigning her position. She did acknowledge that the Texas Ex-Student's Association had called eighteen months earlier and had told her husband that she lacked a bachelor of journalism degree. At that time, she assumed the association had not looked under her full name. "(My husband) Leo referred that to me while I was on a trip, and I told them to look under Maria E. or Maria Elena. And two days later, I show up at the event. At the event, they hand out the program, and it said, 'BJ 1980.' So Leo and I looked at each other and said, 'Hmmm, they must have found it.' " [22]

Questioned about the listing of the Phi Beta Kappa award, she said she did not know that office and campaign biographies listed her as a society member. On September 15, Williamson produced 1984 and 1985 biographies used by Guerrero when she served in the Texas House. Both listed her affiliation with the honor society. Williamson contended: "This is no innocent mistake. It's a deliberate, calculated case of faking her rèsumé, of embellishing her record to get ahead, no matter the cost to her integrity." He called for Guerrero to release her college transcript. "She said she enrolled in 116 hours. She said, 'I only lacked four hours.' Well, let's see if she only lacked four hours.' " [23]

Reaffirming that she would not release her transcripts, Guerrero said:

> I think if I did that, we play into Barry's strategy and we talk about what classes I took and who I took them from and what I made in them. . . . I have released the most important transcript of all and that's my income tax returns. That's not to show what Leo and I have, but what Leo and I don't have. And what we don't have is interests in any of the regulated industries that I make decisions on every day.[24]

She classified the inaccurate academic distinctions and embellishments by an overly zealous campaign staff and reiterated that "to my knowledge, I never claimed it."[25]

On September 16, Lena Guerrero did release her college transcript. It showed she was a "C" student, had failed five courses (one on the Texas Legislature), and needed nineteen hours to graduate. A representative of the University of Texas stated that journalism students are never awarded the Phi Beta Kappa key. "The scholastic honor society awards its 'keys' only to liberal arts and science majors."[26]

Since Guerrero was appointed to an elective office, she had not filled out the standard Railroad Commission job application that other employees sign. That application states, "A false statement or a dishonest answer to any question may be grounds for cancellation of my application or my dismissal after appointment."[27]

Case Questions

1. What is (are) the ethical issue(s) in this case? What ethical theory would you use to argue this case?
2. Was Guerrero correct in saying that she hurt no one other than herself?
3. What possible solutions are available for solving the case?
4. Which solution is the best?
5. If you were Lena Guerrero, what would you do?
6. How can this case apply to your own life?

SUMMARY

Letters and memos can be effective in accomplishing your goals while maintaining a friendly tone, but they can also create problems. Use them for routine matters, to emphasize the importance of a situation, to record agreements, or as a follow-up to summarize discussions.

Words should be selected carefully, and technical words, acronyms, and jargon should be avoided. Choose the short, simple word over the long or technical term. The objective is clarity. Keep the reader in mind and write at a level that will be easily understood. The tone of the letter should be appropriate and sincere. A positive tone will add to the effectiveness of the message. Your reader will assume that if you devote a lot of space to a point, it is important to you. Put things in the proper perspective by using the correct emphasis.

The format of a letter or memo creates the

first impression on your reader. For memos, which are internal organizational documents, a typical standardized format includes the words "To," "From," "Subject," and "Date" at the top of the page. Give the receiver's name and title; the sender's name and title; a brief statement of the subject of the memo; and the message. While a salutation and a complimentary close are not usually found in a memo, they are needed for a letter.

Letters can convey good or bad news, and your approach will depend upon the action you desire to elicit from the reader. Little explanation or background is needed for good news; use a direct approach and get to the point quickly. For letters with bad news, use the indirect approach: provide reasons or details that will explain the basis for your decision and close with a statement of goodwill. Persuasive letters, including letters prospecting for employment, should have an attention-getting opening, overcome resistance by establishing a case through a logical presentation of reasoning, and end with an action-getting close.

Because international communication often requires written correspondence, it is important to be familiar with the culture, communication styles, and language of the individuals with whom you are corresponding. The style they use is a clue: If they are direct, you can also be direct. If they use a more indirect or formal style, adapt your own style accordingly.

KEY WORDS

acknowledgments
AMS style
argument
block style
body
complimentary close
direct letter
emphasis
for the record
heading
indirect letter
inquiry
jargon
memoranda
modified block style
persuasive letter
positive response
positive tone
resume
routine letter
salutation

REVIEW QUESTIONS

1. List and give examples of some routine purposes for letters.
2. What is meant by the *personal style* of a letter?
3. In what order is a letter presenting good news formatted? Why?
4. In what order is a letter presenting bad news formatted? Why?
5. What is the objective of persuasive letters, and what are the steps involved in writing one?
6. How do letters of application and resumes differ? Why are both important?
7. When are memoranda used? Write five guidelines for preparing memoranda.

EXERCISES

1. Select an advertisement from a magazine, and write a letter to the company requesting more information about its product or service. Submit a copy of the advertisement with your letter for evaluation by the instructor. Use the block format.
2. Request information from a local company about an area that you are researching for a course. The topic may range from biomedical research to nutrition, depending on your interests. Gather as much information as you can—brochures, names of films, videotapes, refer-

ences, cost estimates. Before mailing your letter, have it evaluated by your instructor. Use the modified block format.

3. Review the local classified advertisements for jobs for which you feel you may qualify. Select one, and write the company requesting more information about the position and the company. For example, you may ask for information on the company size, job travel requirements, opportunities for career advancement, working conditions, required skills, and promotional materials. Use the AMS format.
4. Exchange one of the above letters with a classmate, and write a letter of acknowledgment.
5. Write a letter trying to persuade one of your classmates to take on a responsibility, make a contribution to a nonprofit organization, or support a cause. When the class breaks into groups of three to four, exchange letters. Evaluate the letters' effectiveness. Were you persuaded to act? Why or why not? What kind of persuasive appeals were in the letter—logical, emotional, ethical? Which were most effective?
6. Look through some magazines or journals for a sales message in letter form that you feel is effective. Analyze the style, tone, organization, and appeals. Display a copy of the advertisement and present your analysis before the class.
7. Write a sales letter that you feel would convince a white-collar worker to contract a weekly cleaning service. You may want to check with a local firm for the typical services and fees.
8. Write an autobiography that relates your accomplishments, activities, interests, education, and job history in chronological order. Which experiences were most meaningful? Which did you enjoy the most? What would you like to be doing ten years from now? twenty years from now? Now prepare a resume.
9. Review the job announcements at your school or the job listings in a newspaper or trade journal, and select a job for which you qualify. Prepare a letter of application that points out your strengths. Attach your rèsumé, and submit it to your instructor for an evaluation.
10. You have received a job inquiry from an outstanding young woman whom you would like to have on your staff. Because of recent economic difficulties, however, your company has cut down on hiring, and all vacant positions have been temporarily frozen. You are not certain but feel that the position may open up again in three or four months. You would like to hire her then, if it is feasible. Write a response to Jane Jorgenson, 12789 Corby Drive, Baton Rouge, LA 70810, telling her that the accounting division at the National Business Office Supply Company, 43552 Florida Blvd., Baton Rouge, LA 70821, does not have any job openings.
11. You have been asked to accept the chair of the travel committee of the Student Union Activities Council. You are very interested in this committee and, in fact, were chairperson last year. Unfortunately, you are currently involved in several other activities and are beginning to have problems keeping up with your classwork. The president of the council is a good friend of yours who is doing a great job but needs help. She has personally asked you to accept the position for another year as a favor to her. Write a letter to her (Sharon Fitzmorris, P.O. Box 1135, College Station, Your University, State, Zip) refusing the position.
12. You are the supervisor of a group of counselors in the Department of Human Resources in your state. Your counselors carry heavy caseloads and work with disabled teenagers who have difficulty making the transition from adolescence to adulthood. While most of the disabilities are not physically severe and the young people can learn to support themselves, many of these teenagers have severe emotional problems related to their disabilities. Now, you have had an opening on your staff. Because of a tight job market, the number of responses to your advertisement was quite large—sixty-eight applicants. After a very tough screening and interviewing process, you have selected Jason Templeton, who has an M.A. in counseling and five years' experience in a similar position at another agency. You were particularly impressed with his references. Write him a letter stating that he has been selected for the position. His address is 1538 W. Idaho Ave., St. Paul, MN 55108.

REFERENCES

1. Excerpts from article by Larry Reibstein, "The Next Memo Will Ask Why Workers Have So Much Free Time," *Wall Street Journal,* February 24, 1987, p. 31.
2. Elys McLean-Ibrahim, "Paperwork is Here to Stay," *USA Today,* January 9, 1989.
3. Dianna Booher, *Cutting Paperwork in the Corporate Culture* (New York: Facts on File, 1986).
4. Beverly Davenport Sypher and Howard E. Sypher, "Seeing Others as Others See Us: Convergence and Divergence in Assessments of Communication Behavior," *Communication Research* (January 1984), pp. 97–115.
5. Holly Taglier Pederson, "The Business of Communicating," *USAIR* (September 1989), p. 113.
6. Steve Osborne, "Wording Is Everything in Good Mail-Order Copy: Write It Right," *Utah Business* (September, 1988), p. 40.
7. Ibid.
8. Don Bagin, "Do You Check Form Letters?" *Communication Briefings,* 7:6, p. 3.
9. Osborne, "Wording Is Everything," p. 39.
10. Jules Harcourt and A. C. "Buddy" Krizan, "A Comparison of Resume Content Preferences of Fortune 500 Personnel Administrators and Business Communication Instructors," *The Journal of Business Communication,* 26:2 (Spring 1989), p. 181.
11. Ibid., p. 183.
12. Charles P. Bird and Dawn D. Puglisi, "Method of Resume Reproduction and Evaluations of Employment Suitability," *The Journal of Business Communication,* 23:3 (Summer 1986), pp. 31–39.
13. Ibid.
14. Julie Skur Hill, "That's Not What I Said," *Business Tokyo* (August 1990), p. 46.
15. Ibid.
16. Ibid., p. 47.
17. Ibid.
18. Ibid.
19. Christy Hoppe, "Guerrero Admits She Never Received Degree," *Dallas Morning News,* September 12, 1992.
20. Ibid., p. 6.
21. Ibid.
22. Hoppe, "Exes Called Guerrero About Degree Last Year," *Dallas Morning News,* September 16, 1992, pp. 9–16.
23. Hoppe, "Guerrero Says She Won't Open College Records," *Dallas Morning News,* September 15, 1992.
24. Ibid.
25. Richard Estrada, "The Lena Guerrero Issue Is Character, Not Her Grades," *Dallas Morning News,* September 18, 1992, sec. A, p. 21.
26. Hoppe, "Guerrero Admits."
27. Hoppe, "Employees Who Make False Claims."

CHAPTER 10

WRITTEN COMMUNICATION: PREPARING REPORTS

In March, 1991, the Knight Foundation Commission on Intercollegiate Athletics issued a report, ``Keeping Faith with the Student-Athlete: A New Model for Intercollegiate Athletics.'' The commission reviewed nationwide studies of student-athletes' academic performance. They conducted interviews with coaches, legislators, teachers, students, and college administrators; and assessed the need for more rigorous high school preparation. They evaluated the expenditures of college athletic programs. Finally, they urged major reforms in college athletics. Exactly one year later, a follow-up report, *A Solid Start: A Report on Reform Of Intercollegiate Athletics,* included the following statement.

> The public clearly senses that reform is underway. In its report last year, the Knight Commission referred to a Louis Harris poll conducted in 1989 indicating that 78 percent of Americans believed big-time intercollegiate athletics were out of control. A recent follow-up survey indicates that 47 percent of the public now hold that view, a dramatic 31 point decline.

A third report, ``A New Beginning for a New Century,'' found in Appendix C, continues to express optimism, but cautions institutions to maintain vigilance.

Report Writing

The Knight Reports are good examples of the role a written report can play in communicating a message. The first report was to a specific audience for the purpose of informing and persuading. It described past events, presented new information, and made recommendations for the future. The second and third reports updated readers on successes, refined goals, and set new agendas.

The needs and uses for reports vary and include sales projections, interpretations of law to determine compliance requirements, the results of internal audits, recommendations for new policies or procedures, purchasing proposals, and organizational assessments. Reports help managers solve problems and make decisions. They can be formal or informal in form, and they may range from a one-page memo summarizing the responses to a simple telephone survey of prospective customers to thousands of pages, as in the case of the "Report of the Presidential Commission on the Space Shuttle *Challenger* Accident." To be useful, however, reports must be written so that managers can easily understand the problem, logic, and recommendations. Information should be factual, complete, and objective and it should be presented in an organized format.

Report Characteristics

Although writing an organizational report may seem to be a tedious, mundane, or overwhelming process, this is far from the truth. Some reports are routine and can be as simple as computer-printed forms requiring signature verification of personnel activity. Routine reports let the manager know that the organization is meeting basic standards or requirements. Other reports may be one-time activities related to a specific situation. Finally, reports can be vehicles for change and reform in the organization. As demonstrated by the Knight Commission, a carefully prepared report can set new directions, while a progress report can demonstrate whether the project is meeting goals or needs revision.

Report Purposes

Organizations generally use reports for two purposes: informational and analytical.

- *Informational.* This kind of report presents information but avoids making any recommendations. The writer presents material so that the reader is better able to make a decision based on the newly acquired information. Usually no action is required from the reader of an informational report other than simply to read the document. Typical examples of the informational report are progress summaries, status reports, employee procedural manuals, policy statements, and annual reports.

- *Analytical.* The analytical report presents and analyzes facts. From an objective analysis of the facts, the writer offers interpretations, conclusions, and recommendations. The report is organized and written to motivate the reader to act. Examples of this type of report are marketing surveys, workforce evaluations, systems analyses, cost analyses, legal interpretations, and sales proposals.

PRELIMINARIES: PREPARING THE REPORT

Before you begin a report, you need to answer a number of questions.

1. *What is the purpose of the report?* A report is usually the result of a request by management to fulfill some organizational objective. Usually, a written request for a report, known as a *letter of authorization,* precedes the report-writing process. The letter should indicate management's expectations of the report and should always be included with the final report. Are you trying to inform or analyze? Do you need to make recommendations? When is the report due? Sometimes reports are produced on the writer's own initiative. In such cases explaining their purpose and justification will require more attention than it would if the report is requested.

2. *Who will be reading the report?* The person requesting your report probably will not be the only person reading it. Will it be an *internal report* meant for use within the organization, or will it be an *external report* meant for public dissemination? Once information is put in writing, it can be easily copied and distributed for others to review. At this stage you need to question and anticipate the uses of the report. You will need to select a format, choose words, and organize the report to convey information clearly for all your potential readers.

3. *What is the problem?* Your report should include a one-sentence statement of the problem. If you have not defined your problem accurately, it is unlikely that the facts or recommendations will be relevant. Some basic steps in defining a problem and developing the problem statement include writing down the problem, clarifying confusing terms, discovering the problem's symptoms, identifying possible causes, and summarizing the urgency of a solution. If a recommendation is made, you will also need to identify the criteria that need to be met. Are there any cost limitations? Will a solution need to be implemented within a certain time frame? Chapter 13 describes these steps in detail.

4. *What information is needed to fulfill the objectives of the report?* Once you have clearly identified the problem, its causes, and its symptoms, you will need to gather the relevant facts. While some information may be available from the organization's management information system (MIS), you may need to conduct a survey, interview people, observe operations, research laws, review policies or procedures, or review historical records. Be sure to test the credibility of your information: is it first-, second-, or third-hand? Is the source biased? Is the information relevant, representative, documented, and complete?

5. *What does the information tell you?* You will need to organize your data for systematic analysis. The work you have already done in identifying symptoms, causes, and criteria will be very helpful at this point. Did you find any inconsistencies? Did the findings demonstrate that a cause or symptom of the problem could be eliminated? What conclusions did you reach? Based on your analysis, what recommendations do you have?

Say It Clearly

Howard Upton in his article, "Power Up Your Business Writing," emphasizes the need to write as clearly as you speak.[1] Avoid "dull, pretentious gobbledygook." Attempts to use a formal, objective tone can mislead the reader.

Upton tells the following story about a business report he reviewed. The report described the installation of equipment in an electronics plant and included the statement: "There appears to be a reluctance on the part of some employees to adapt to use of the new equipment." Upton interpreted this statement to mean that employees were resisting the idea of change generally. A discussion with the writer of the report dispelled this notion. Apparently the "positioning of the equipment" was the real culprit. The writer explained: "For instance, there's one woman who is under five feet tall," he said, "and she has to stand on tiptoe to reach the control switch on her machine. And there are three left-handed people on the board wiring line who complain the new soldering units are in an awkward location for them."

To be useful, a report must clearly convey the intended message to the reader. In the above situation, Upton concluded *wrongly* that employees were resisting change. In reality the new equipment was awkward for some employees and difficult to use. Had the writer amplified his or her statement with specific examples, the reader would have been able to better understand the problem.

Adapted from Howard Upton, "Power Up Your Business Writing," *Spirit*, in-flight magazine of Southwest Airlines (March 1991), p. 20. Reprinted by permission.

L-S-B

LONE STAR BANK

To: Sam Lewis, Head, Training Department

From: Mary M. Rydesky, Director
Customer Service Department

Date: April 5, 1994

Subject: Development of Programmed Instruction on Punctuation Skills

I would like to work with one of your instructional developers to create a review of punctuation skills for my staff. All sixty-four of my employees must maintain good writing skills because they all prepare memos, reports, and letters to clients. Recently, I've noticed that the correspondence has become difficult to read due to punctuation errors.

Other banks have used letter-writing improvement programs, and I considered importing one. However, they are costly to implement and do not reflect the Lone Star philosophy. My next idea was to develop a program that would accomplish four goals:

- Allow employees to work at a self-determined pace;
- Allow employees to study at home rather than in a scheduled class;
- Reinforce our style of correspondence;
- Minimize costs and time loss.

Programmed instruction seems to meet these goals, but I am not familiar enough with it to develop my own materials. Is there a member of your staff who might assist me?

I will call you on Friday so that we can discuss a timetable for the project. I would like to begin just as soon as you can assign an instructional developer.

mmr: td

EXHIBIT 10.1 Informal Memo Report
Source: Mary M. Rydesky, "Lone Star Bank Memo," prepared for this book.

Report Formality

Since reports are prepared in different sizes, shapes, and levels of formality, it is good to determine what level your report requires before you write.

- *Informal.* An informal report covers less important information, such as routine status and progress reports, trip and expense reports, and minor requests (see Exhibit 10.1). These reports take the form of a letter or memorandum and are usually printed (although they can be handwritten), written on preprinted forms, or sent electronically. The writing style is informal and may address the reader as "you." If copies are needed, they can be made and reproduced inexpensively. The length is usually one or two pages, and the pages are stapled together. The informal report seldom goes outside the organization and usually travels no more than two vertical levels.

- *Semiformal.* This report is longer, typically between two and ten pages, and is typed and reproduced inexpensively (see Exhibit 10.2). The semiformal report usually stays within the organization but is occasionally distributed outward. It travels both horizontally and vertically and reaches several readers at several levels. Although the report is written in a formal style, it is not as detailed or broad as the formal report. The added length often requires several internal headings.
- *Formal.* This is the traditional report that is several pages in length, printed on quality paper, often bound, and implies an official source (see Exhibit 10.3). It presents important information, and thus its readership goes beyond one or two levels. These reports often go to readers outside the organization and are filed or placed on bookshelves for future reference. A long, traditional formal report may be divided into several parts; not all are found in every report, but Exhibit 10.3 shows their preferred sequence.

Parts of a Traditional Formal Report

Formalities

In the opening pages of the formal report the writer places all the information that will help a reader move quickly and clearly to the main text. Each of the opening elements serves a distinct purpose:

- The *transmittal letter* is a cover letter that sends the report to the reader. Any information that might help the reader as he or she prepares to read and understand the report is included.

PROPOSAL FOR IMPROVING WRITTEN COMMUNICATION SKILLS
April 15, 1994

Spelling, dictation, punctuation: All are skills that our Customer Service Staff must have for effective communication through writing. Yet these skills easily become rusty and in need of upgrading. At present, the letters, memos, and reports being prepared by my staff have more errors in punctuation than I think allowable. As a result, these materials are difficult to read.

Improving the writing skills of the sixty-four employees in Customer Service is possible to achieve without spending great sums of money

(continued)

and without taking time away from the job. By developing programmed instruction materials that can be studied at home, we can accomplish the goal of improved written communications at the least cost.

Programmed instruction refers to an educational style in which a sequence for learning is frequently stopped for a test of student understanding. For example, I could insert a question asking you to complete this sentence: "Programmed instruction is an _____ style." By writing in the word "educational," you would reinforce your memory of the definition. By continuing the sequence, you would learn more about the concept.

Programmed instruction is usually developed in a workbook so that each employee may have a copy. It can be studied at one's own pace and is thus more individualized than a classroom presentation that requires all students to absorb material at the same rate. It can be studied alone rather than in the presence of an instructor because it provides the answers immediately following the questions. Later, the workbook can be used as a reference when the employee wants to recall a particular point.

Ann Ford, an instructional developer in our Training Department, has had college coursework in programmed instruction. With her help, I would like to create a workbook to improve the punctuation skills of my staff. If errors decrease, the same technique could be used to upgrade other writing skills. Once the project is approved, Ann will need two weeks to draft the punctuation program. We would then set up conditions for its trial and would submit a timetable for reporting on its effectiveness. Estimated costs for this development and evaluation of materials total $1700.00, or approximately $20.00 per employee. In comparison with other banks, our costs would be low.

Other Banks' Programs	Costs	Methods
Fidelity National	$31.00 per employee	Consultant hired to conduct three-day seminar
Capital Hill	$27.90 per employee	Purchased videocassette/workbook course from XYZ Publishing
Exchange State	$24.25 per employee	Purchased paperback reference texts for each work station
Allied Republic	$24.00 per employee	Presented four one-hour classes to supervisors who were to hold seminars for their employees; used films from the public library

EXHIBIT 10.2 Semiformal Report

Source: Mary M. Rydesky, "Improving Written Communication Skills Proposal," prepared for this book.

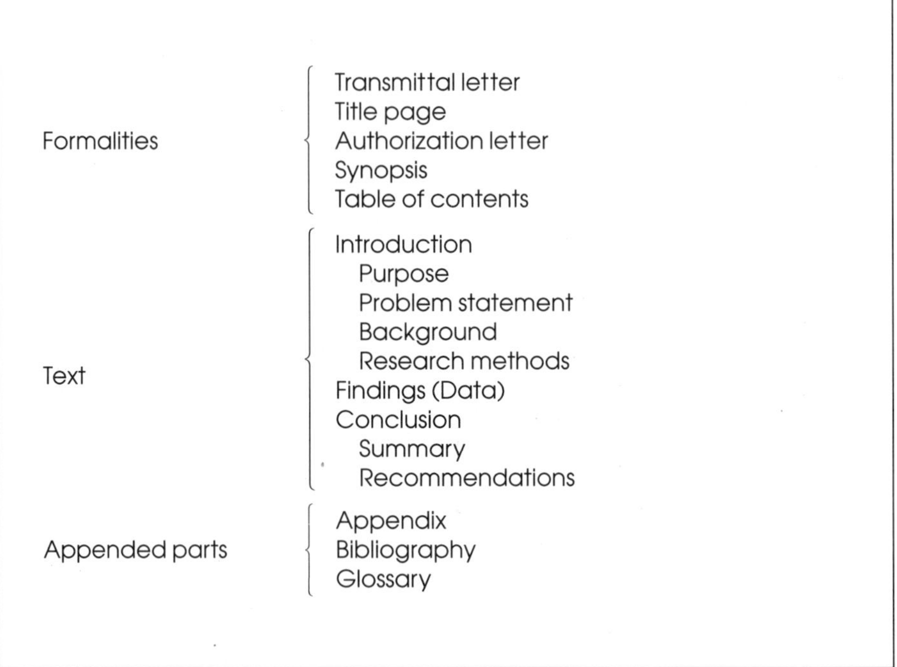

EXHIBIT 10.3 Parts of a Traditional Formal Report

- The *title page* contains the report title, names of the author(s), for whom it was prepared, date of issuance, and any additional source material that might be helpful to the reader.
- The *authorization letter* is a copy of any correspondence sent to the writer that requested or contracted the report.
- The *synopsis* is a short summary or abstract of the report that succinctly capsulizes the text content, problem, research procedures, findings, and recommendations.
- The *table of contents* is an outline of the entire report, from cover to cover, with corresponding page numbers.

Text

Three main parts of the text are normally used:

- The *introduction* presents the background, problem, and research procedure followed in the report.

1. The *purpose* describes why the study was undertaken, its importance, and the significance and impact of the findings.
2. The *problem statement* serves the same purpose as the thesis statement of a speech. Here the writer succinctly states the precise problem under research.
3. The *background* brings the reader up to date with information needed to understand what was researched, investigated, and consequently found.

4. The *research methods* describe data collection, any statistical procedures, and the significance of the findings.

- The *findings (data)* section contains the body of the information discovered.
- The *conclusion* wraps up the heart of the report:

1. The *summary* brings everything together and briefly highlights the report's most important points. Some reports also contain a conclusion section that shows a logical progression from research, to data, to recognizable facts.
2. The *recommendations* section is where the writer makes his request for action.

Appended Parts

Information that appears in tables, charts, or pictures but is not easily placed in the body of the report can go here.

- The *appendix* is for supplementary materials.
- The *bibliography* is where references can be categorized and listed in alphabetical order.
- The *glossary* contains frequently used but often unknown or misunderstood words, along with definitions.

Sample pages from a traditional formal report are included in Appendix B.

Inverted Report Writing

Word processors and dictation equipment are available to help writers commit their ideas to paper, but few aids are available to help readers understand what they're reading. This is especially true when the reader is searching for the hidden meaning of a report that is poorly organized and wordy.

One aid for report readers is the report that is written in an inverted manner. *Inverted reports* begin with the important points instead of concluding with them. Melba Murray calls it the "engineered report writing" style.[2] Only 20 percent of readers reach the most important part of a traditional report, as Figure 10.1 shows, so the inverted style captures 100 percent readership at the start.[3] Four questions to ask before beginning the report are (1) What is the news? (2) Why? (3) How? (4) Now what? When this approach is employed, 100 percent of the readers start with the real facts, of "news," in the report. Because this approach automatically deletes unimportant information, the report is shorter, and most of your readers stay with you to the end.

What Is the News?

The first part of the report presents the primary thing you want the reader to know: "Your answer might be that you've built something, developed it, surveyed it, tested it, analyzed it, read it, proved or disproved it, started or completed it. Perhaps the news is something you've succeeded in doing, failed to

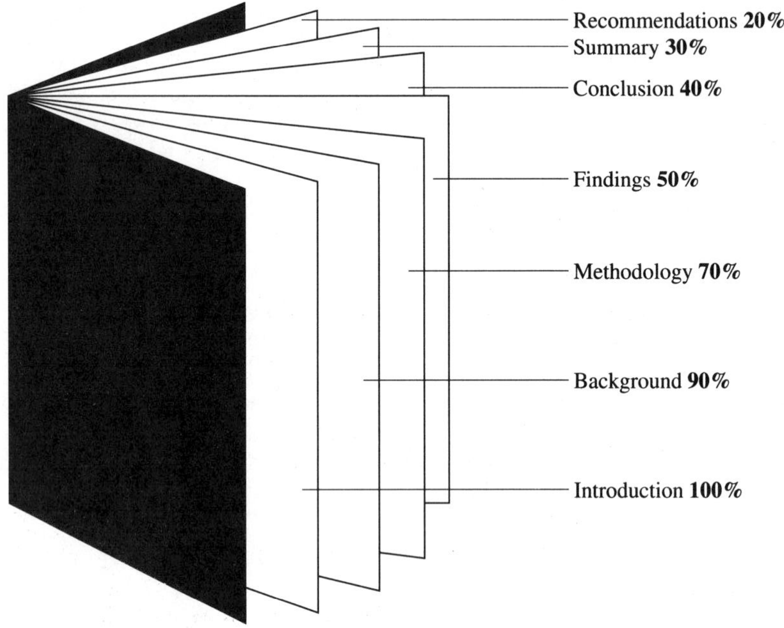

FIGURE 10.1. The Progression and Readership of a Traditional Report

do, or think should be done. It may be a method, a piece of equipment, an idea, a concept, an opinion, or a recommendation for action."[4] Whatever you have to convey, say it quickly, clearly, and briefly. Many reports label this section the Executive Summary.

Why?

Supporting facts or background information should go in this section. If there is something to be gained from a recommendation that you are making, present it here. But present no more than is absolutely necessary for the reader to know.

How?

The "how" takes your reader a step further and describes the way you propose to carry out the "what." In this section you may need to support your position or further develop the major premise.

Now What?

Often by the time you respond to the first three sections you won't need this one. But if you want to reinforce a point, once again propose a particular thing, focus on the urgency of action, or cite specifics, this is the appropriate place.

Exhibit 10.4 displays an internal report for Honeycutt's Honey Corporation. The report is written in the traditional formal report style. Exhibit 10.5 shows the same information in the inverted report mode. Note how the vital information is presented and how succinctly it is covered.

The Impact of Computer Technology

Computers have dramatically changed our options for report preparation and presentation. Software packages can quickly produce professional copy with the same visual appeal as a published book or newspaper. Through networking computer systems that allow different persons to have access to the same information and files, copies can be electronically forwarded to a multitude of receivers, and these same receivers can review and edit them without ever printing a copy.

Word processing packages have a multitude of functions and allow the writer to indent, move, delete, or insert paragraphs, words, sentences, and visuals. Spell-checking functions can search for errors and allow you to insert the corrected word. The thesaurus function lists alternative word choices. The search-and-replace function searches a document and automatically substitutes one word for another. *Grammar and style check* functions compare your work to standard English usage and identify possible errors. *Footnote* functions insert footnotes at the end of the page or notes at the end of the document. *Fonts* (type styles) can be interchanged, enlarged or reduced,

HH
HONEYCUTT'S HONEY, INC.
REPORT

TO: William S. Honeycutt, President

FROM: Martin J. Spears, Vice-President, Sales

DATE: May 12, 1994

SUBJECT: Safety Packaging

Introduction

Purpose. At your request I undertook a comprehensive study of the feasibility and need for devising tamper-resistant packaging for our prod-

(continued)

(continued)

William S. Honeycutt
page 2
May 12, 1994

ucts. This report describes that study, the conclusions it led to, and my recommendations.

Method. The primary method of research was a study of *Business Week, Advertising Age,* the *Wall Street Journal,* and *The New York Times.* Also, at my request our advertising agency, Morris Associates, conducted a marketing survey concerning our product. The methodology and results of that survey are presented in the "Findings" section of this report. Financial data in this report were obtained from records of our Production Department.

Background. Tamper-resistant packaging has been an issue of some concern to the food and drug industry for a decade. This issue was briefly brought to the attention of the public a few years ago when a man was poisoned (not fatally) from a jar of pickles that had been opened prior to purchase. When it became evident the incident was an isolated occurrence, public concern dwindled, and no regulatory or industry-induced action was taken. In August 1982 two people in California were injured by using Murine and Visine A.C. eyedrops spiked with acid. Packaging was not considered a real problem in this incident: because the seals of the products were broken before purchase, it was evident someone tampered with the seals.

The Tylenol scare, however, was a different matter. When seven people in the Chicago area died from cyanide-laced Extra-Strength Tylenol, national media attention focused on the packaging problem, and Johnson & Johnson was forced to take drastic action. The company eventually withdrew all Tylenol from store shelves and announced a national recall of all Tylenol capsules. Johnson & Johnson watched helplessly as its Tylenol share in the pain-killer market dropped precipitously from 35 percent to 6.5 percent.

In November 1982 a national survey revealed 94 percent of Americans knew of the Tylenol tragedy, and even though 90 percent of those people placed no blame on Johnson & Johnson, it was evident the public desired more stringent packaging rules. The government agreed. The Food and Drug Administration established a regulation requiring at least one type of tamper-resistant or tamper-evident seal on all drug packaging.

Even before the ruling, Johnson & Johnson had ordered several $11,000 machines that seal mouths of bottles with an aluminum or plastic wrap. In December 1982, Tylenol returned to store shelves with triple seals: a glued box flap, a tight neck seal, and an inner foil wrap. The seals were estimated to cost 2.4 cents per package.

Findings

Implications. The first obvious result of the Tylenol tragedy is that improper packaging cost Johnson & Johnson a lot of money. It's not that the packaging was unsafe; it's just that the packaging was not tamper-resistant or at least tamper-perceptible. In other words, the fact that Ty-

(continued)

William S. Honeycutt
page 3
May 12, 1994

lenol bottles were susceptible to hidden tampering allowed the tragedy to occur. Johnson & Johnson was not negligent; it was simply not prepared for the eventuality of concealed tampering, and it cost the company dearly.

Recall, replacement, and repackaging of the Tylenol product cost Johnson & Johnson an estimated $100 million. The company's 1982 after-tax income fell by $50 million as a result of the crisis. Perhaps even more revealing, a survey of people who never used Tylenol indicated 80 percent of them would never even try the brand.

Other food and drug manufacturers sat up and took notice of Johnson & Johnson's problems. Kraft, Borden, and Procter & Gamble have implemented various sealing options. Alternatives include plastic "blister" packs, foil wrapping over bottle openings, and plastic bands that shrink tightly to seal lids.

Marketing Survey. The purpose of Morris Associates' survey was to determine what effect consumers' new safety packaging awareness has on their purchase decision and, in particular, if safety seals would make a difference in selling our product. A random telephone survey was taken of the greater metropolitan area. Sample size was 500. Accuracy of these responses as compared to the population as a whole is estimated to be within 3 percent. Results of some of the more important survey questions are listed below:

	Yes	*No*	*Uncertain*
1. Are tamper-resistant seals something you look for when purchasing pain killers and other pharmaceuticals?	77%	17%	6%
2. Are tamper-resistant seals something you look for when purchasing food products?	56%	32%	12%
3. Do you purchase honey at least once every four months?	33%	62%	5%
4. If yes, do you regularly purchase Honeycutt's honey products?	39%	67%	4%
5. Whether or not you use Honeycutt's honey, would you be willing to pay a few cents extra for honey if it had a safety seal around its lid?	55%	32%	13%

The results of this survey are important for two reasons. First, as question 4 indicates, we have a 39 percent share of the local market. This compares favorably to the 32 percent share recorded in last year's survey. Second, as question 5 indicates, safety sealing our product could enhance sales.

Financial Aspects. Our Production Department agrees with me that plastic bands around our jar lids is the most cost-effective method to safety seal our product. Sealing machinery is available in the local area

(continued)

(continued)

William S. Honeycutt
page 4
May 12, 1994

for $9,800, or it can be leased for $1,300 per month for each machine. This machinery could be incorporated at the end of our production line to serve as the final stage of the production process. Three machines would be required, one for each size of jar we pack. The machines are fully automatic and require no additional labor. Production Department estimates that after installation, seals would cost an average of .08 cents per jar.

Additional advertising is necessary to inform the public of our new, responsible packaging. A three-month campaign of newspaper ads, coupons, and store displays would cost $18,400. At the end of this period the effectiveness of the seals could be assessed. Morris Associates recommends retaining our present honey prices during the campaign, evaluating the increase in sales, and then raising prices three or four cents if we decide to go with the program.

Total costs for the three-month campaign with leased machinery would be $30,260. If we buy the machinery immediately, the cost of the campaign without considering depreciation would be $47,960.

Conclusion

Summary. Due to the Tylenol tragedy, the vast majority of the public know what tamper-resistant packaging is and would prefer to have it on all the edible products they buy. A local survey indicates most people would be willing to pay a few cents extra for sealed honey. Because of this opinion, sealing our honey products can provide two distinct advantages. First, there is a good possibility of increased sales. The exact nature of the increase would not be known until after a trial program. Second, sealing our product provides some insurance against the increasing number of lunatics our society seems to be producing. The seals we have in mind would not prevent tampering, but they would make tampering evident to the consumer. Enhancing our image as a responsible, caring food manufacturer can only augment the value of our goodwill and provide positive publicity.

Recommendations. I recommend we proceed with the three month sealing program as soon as possible and begin by renting three sealing machines. Depending on the results, at the end of the three months we can either make a national announcement of our new policy and extend the program to our other regional plants, or if sales drop, we can quietly phase out the program. It is my opinion that the program will succeed, and I recommend we begin allocating funds for the nationwide purchase of sealing machinery.

EXHIBIT 10.4

Source: Timothy Riggins, "Honeycutt's Honey Report," prepared for this book.

HONEYCUTT'S HONEY, INC.
REPORT

TO: William S. Honeycutt, President

FROM: Martin J. Spears, Vice-President, Sales

DATE: May 12, 1994

SUBJECT: Safety Packaging

Based on the research completed, I recommend we initiate a three-month trial program of safety sealing our honey products in the local metropolitan area. With leased machinery, total costs for the project will be $30,260.

Due to the Tylenol tragedy, most Americans prefer tamper-resistant packaging on all the edible products they buy. A local survey we conducted indicates our market share of 39 percent could improve if we safety seal our products, because most people would be willing to pay a few cents extra for sealed honey. This survey and my bibliographical research indicate safety packaging can provide two distinct advantages for us: increased sales and improved goodwill.

While it is almost impossible to prevent tampering, it is fairly simple to seal our products so that tampering is made obvious to the consumer. The most cost-effective method to safety seal our jars is to install plastic bands around the lids. The three-month program would involve placing sealing machines on each of our packing lines, a local advertising campaign, and a final evaluation. If the program is as successful as I envision, we can then proceed with a national program, including the purchase of sealing machines for each assembly line and a national advertising campaign. If the local program is determined not to be cost effective and if public approval is not as high as expected, we can quietly phase out the program.

Because this plan has been discussed and developed with the Marketing, Production, and Finance Departments, it is ready to begin immediately. Please call me if you have any questions about marketing or finance details.

EXHIBIT 10.5
Source: Timothy Riggins, "Honeycutt's Honey Inverted Report," prepared for this book.

or printed in bold or italic. Finally, *computer graphics* can add interest and vitality to your report.

Because of the accessibility, versatility, and ease of computers, most receivers expect reports that are attractive, easy to read, and accurate. Exhibit 10.6 shows a memorandum with effective use of fonts and graphics.

Memorandum

From: Gaylynn Ferreyra *Date:* January 21, 1994
To: Sean Reinhardt
Re: New Procedures for Driver Returns

Executive Summary

After a review of the process for verifying and reporting driver returns, delivery shorts, picking errors, and warehouse damage to determine if the controls are sufficient and the reporting is accurate, it is obvious that the procedures for driver returns are not adequate. The procedural changes listed below, which will be implemented as soon as possible, will strengthen controls over returned product and improve the accuracy of reporting.

Findings

Damage and shorts have been higher than average this year. There also seems to be confusion over what is reported for shorts, damage, and mispicks. This makes it difficult for those responsible for controlling these expenses to take effective action. The table below compares the errors in 1992 to 1993. In every case our total errors have increased. While the total volume of orders also increased by 25 percent, damaged orders, mispicks, and delivery shorts increased by 58 percent, 30 percent, and 69 percent, respectively.

INCREASE IN DRIVER RETURNS

ERRORS	1992	1993	% Increase
Driver returns	1,563	2,277	46
Damage	437	692	58
Mispicks	800	1,043	30
Shorts	326	552	69

Changes in the procedures will give us better physical control over returns, and more accurate reporting of the reasons for invoice adjustments. The next step will be to determine how this information should be summarized or expanded to meet the needs of the managers responsible for controlling shorts, damage, and returns and to reduce these expenses. I will keep you informed of further findings as I continue to review this area.

Procedures

1. Drivers will receive adjustment codes for returns and shorts and training on how the codes should be used. Drivers will initially code all invoice adjustments with the appropriate code.
2. Drivers will place all returned product on the dock in front of their trailers rather than in front of the driver check-in desk.
3. The person responsible for driver check-in will go to each trailer and physically verify all returns. All codes should be verified as correct and

(continued)

Sean Reinhardt
p. 2
Jan. 21, 1994

the Over, Short and Return sheet should be correctly completed. The trailer should be inspected to make sure it is empty.

4. Once checked in, the driver will place returns on one of several carts on the dock. One cart each will be used for frozen and dry returns to stock, damaged product, and mispicks.
5. One person will be assigned to put away returns as they come in from the drivers. This person will start in the early afternoon and work until the night shift starts.
6. For shuttle trucks returning at night, the night supervisor will be responsible for checking in product and assigning a person to restock returns immediately. The operations manager will designate someone to check in trucks returning from Springfield in the morning and any local runs returning early.

Attachment

cc: Whitney Duca
Alberto Talamo

EXHIBIT 10.6

Four suggestions for making your report effective are:

1. *Choose a typeface that is easy to read and helps the reader find the important points.* Most word processing packages offer a variety of typeface choices with the options of italics and boldface. You can also enlarge the font for emphasis or reduce it for notations. Do not use too many fonts or you will detract from the content of your message.

2. *Format your report so that it is visually pleasing and has plenty of white space.* Leave healthy margins on the sides, top, and bottom of each page. Use headings, boldface, underlining, or bullets to reinforce organization and add emphasis, but use them consistently, appropriately, and sparingly. Too much "artistic" effort can distract your reader. You are striving for a professional appearance.

3. *Check spelling, grammar, and word choice.* Inaccuracies of this nature are unacceptable in a written report, and the convenience of software technology to prevent such errors makes them inexcusable.

4. *Include visuals that amplify the report.* Make certain that they have been explained appropriately in the body of the report. Do not use them unless they are necessary to make your point. The following memo report incorporates a table within the findings of the report to emphasize the need for action. Table 10.1 provides a report planning checklist.

TABLE 10.1 Report Planning Checklist

Determine the purpose of the report.

- ✓ Clarify expectations: What is the deadline? What resources will be available? Is it informational or analytical? Do you need to include recommendations?
- ✓ Provide justification for a self-initiated report.

Determine the audience.

- ✓ Tailor report to reader: Is this an internal or external group? What do they know about the problem? Should the report be formal, semiformal, or informal?
- ✓ Use language that is appropriate, clear, and to the point.

Clarify the Problem.

- ✓ Write down the problem.
- ✓ Identify symptoms and causes.
- ✓ List the criteria that must be met by a solution(s).
- ✓ Restate the problem eliminating confusing, redundant, technical, or ambiguous words.

Gather the relevant facts.

- ✓ Determine the history of the problem.
- ✓ Check available data bases (Managment Information System).
- ✓ If needed, conduct additional research through observation, interviews, or surveys.

Analyze the Information.

- ✓ Organize data into logical groupings.
- ✓ Systematically analyze data.
- ✓ Identify inconsistencies.
- ✓ Eliminate causes or symptoms that do not have supporting data.
- ✓ Draw conclusions.
- ✓ List recommendations.

Organize and Write the Report.

- ✓ Begin with the most important points.
- ✓ Provide supporting facts or background information.
- ✓ Include graphics to help clarify information.
- ✓ Describe the steps that need to be taken to fulfill the report recommendations.
- ✓ Include any supporting materials in the appendix.

Edit the report.

- ✓ Check spelling, word choice, punctuation, and grammar.
- ✓ Eliminate "doublespeak."
- ✓ Cite sources.
- ✓ Make the report visually appealing; use current technology.

The Impact of Chinese Formalities

The complex political structure within which Chinese companies must operate greatly influences the amount and type of communication that takes place. The organizational structure in which Chinese managers operate is formal, and daily communication follows prescribed channels. As a result, the Chinese favor formal written reports.

Herbert W. Hildebrant of the University of Michigan found that about 67 percent of the managers in 31 Chinese companies felt formal communication was important. This evaluation dropped to 49 percent for informal communication (telephone conversations or casual meetings).[5] Oral communication is seen as the least important communication skill. In meetings "giving feedback, challenging or questioning others, and interrupting were gentle or nonexistent as compared with U.S. managerial meetings."[6]

The reasons for this formal approach to communication are a reflection of China's linguistic, educational, and political systems. Hildebrant professes that Chinese managers use a formal tone in both written and oral communications: "Overt politeness . . . to the listener/reader is common. Even the heavy use of the second person plural suggests a diminution of the self into a collective consciousness expressed through 'we.'"[7] Honorific titles are always used for persons in positions of authority or leadership.

Chinese teachers are trained in British English. Hildebrant notes: "The more formal tradition of writing . . . continues in the colleges and institutes where British-influenced English language texts perpetuate a more formal tone of business communication than found in U.S. business communication texts."[8]

The Chinese social structure places emphasis on authority. Children are taught to follow the protocol of "who may speak first, who must listen, or who is left speechless."[9] In Chinese classrooms, students record and listen to instructors rather than challenge them. In contrast, American classrooms often have an informal atmosphere that encourages questions and challenging dialog between student and instructor.

The political environment of China also reinforces the formal approach to communication. National policies are set by the Central Committee of the Communist Party of China (CCPC). These policies are communicated "from the National People's Congress to the State Council, to the ministries, the bureaus, the provinces, the autonomous regions, the municipalities, the companies, the factories, the workshops and the party groups."[10] As the written document moves through the appropriate channels, each group may amend or give its stamp of approval. Designated individuals in each of the groups work to make sure that the principles of the Politburo are followed. The formal nature of the document is a reflection of its routing and handling.

Individual business firms are located near the bottom of this hierarchy, and little debate is perceived to be necessary when the document reaches them: the centrally controlled written directive is generally accepted at the operations level. This acceptance decreases the need for discussion or managerial intervention.

ETHICS: RIGHT OR WRONG?

Alton Kosch's Report on the Use of Company Property

Alton Kosch is the new director of Accounting Services at Technical Dynamics, Inc. For ten years he worked for a competitor. Because of his reputation for efficiency, Technical Dynamics lured him away from his employer and made him responsible for reducing overhead costs and increasing net profits. His first goal was to review policies and procedures to determine if they were current and workable. He met with the internal audit staff and directed them to conduct reviews of targeted policies that impact productivity.

One of these reviews involved long-distance telephone charges. Alton was surprised to learn how much money was spent on telephone calls, especially with other forms of telecommunications available at a cheaper rate. In checking, he learned that many employees were assigned charge numbers to conduct official business. After interviewing several employees, however, he found that it had become an acceptable and common practice to use the company charge number for personal calls. Secretaries appeared to follow this practice, using their bosses' numbers.

The procedure for verifying company calls required the persons to whom the numbers were assigned to police the use of their own charge number by signing a computer form that listed the monthly calls in their names. This had become a perfunctory process. The account for the month of December was particularly troubling. Telephone charges are normally higher during December because it is a very active sales month. However, when Alton compared the months of December over the previous five years, it was obvious that the costs during this month were escalating even though sales had not increased a proportional amount. Alton wondered whether the company's lax policy and the habit of calling friends and family during the holiday season was adding to these costs.

Alton soon learned that the telephone was not the only company resource being abused. Copy machines were being used to make personal copies of everything from magazine articles to recipes. Secretaries were using desk computers to earn extra money by typing outside reports during their lunch hours and after hours. Because of the graphic capabilities of the computer software, employees were designing fliers, announcements, invitations, and even Christmas cards and then printing multiple copies on company color printers.

While there was a policy against using company property for personal gain, it was not very explicit, nor was it widely disseminated. Few workers seemed to acknowledge that such a policy existed, or they just didn't care, since it was not being enforced.

Alton found himself caught in a dilemma. He knew this abuse was unethical and had to be stopped if the company was to cut costs. Such behavior would not have been tolerated at the company for which he formerly worked. Alton decided to prepare a report for the vice-president of administration, Geraldine Reinhardt, summarizing his findings and recommending specific actions.

Case Questions

1. What is the ethical problem? How would you address the problem in a report to Vice-President Reinhardt?
2. What facts does Alton need to include in his report?
3. How soon does Alton need to present his findings and recommendations?
4. What format should be used? How should information be organized?

SUMMARY

Reports help managers solve problems and make decisions by presenting information that informs or persuades. The needs and uses vary and determine the formality, length, and writing style of the report. Since reports can be vehicles for change and reform in the organization, they must be carefully researched, organized, and written.

Before beginning a report, the writer needs to answer five questions: What is the purpose of the report? Who reads the report? What is the nature and extent of the problem? What information is needed to fulfill the objectives of the report? And, if it is an analytical report, what does the information tell the reader? The answers to these questions are keys to the success of the report and determine formality, writing style, direction, methodology, organizational structure, and the validity of final recommendations.

Reports can be informal, semiformal, or formal. Informal reports are usually shorter and either routine or less important in content than the other two forms. Semiformal reports are longer than informal reports, more formal in writing style, and also typically internal to the organization.

Formal reports present important information in a traditional, detailed format and often go to readers outside the organization or are used for future reference. Because a formal report is usually circulated on several levels to a wide audience, information in the report is arranged so that readers can move quickly to its various parts. Typical parts include a transmittal letter, a title page, an authorization letter, a synopsis, a table of contents, an introduction, findings, a conclusion and recommendations, and appended parts. To save readers' time and assure that they get the facts or news, we encourage use of an inverted format that places the important facts and recommendations in the first part of the report.

Review Questions

1. What are the purposes and characteristics of written reports?
2. Before beginning a report, the writer must answer five questions. What are the questions and why is each important?
3. Three levels of formality exist in reports. Compare and contrast the different types.
4. The text of a formal report usually consists of three main parts. Name the parts and the information that each should include.
5. What is the inverted report style? How is it helpful for the reader? the writer?
6. Name and describe the four parts of the inverted report style. How does this differ from traditional report styles?

Key Words

analytical reports
appended parts
appendix
authorization letter
background
bibliography
conclusion
findings
formal report
formalities
glossary
informal report
informational reports
introduction
inverted report
news
problem statement
purpose
recommendations
research methods
semiformal report
summary
synopsis
table of contents
title page
transmittal letter

Exercises

1. Find a report that has been prepared for a business. You can find one either at the library, by asking friends, or by calling business colleagues and asking for a sample. When you receive the report, look for its major parts. Are they in the order that this chapter outlined? If not, is there a particular reason for the difference?
2. Read the report that you obtained for exercise 1. As you read, try to determine in which parts your interest wanes or increases. What could the writer have done to better capture your interest?

   Now make some notes on how the report could be rewritten in an inverted style. Use the four questions for the inverted report: *what, why, how,* and *now what?* Would the report topic be better represented by using the inverted style? How many pages do you think could be cut? How much reading time could be saved?
3. Attend a meeting of a civic, professional, leadership, or service organization of which you are not a member. Write a short report about the organization. Include in your report (1) the purpose of the organization, (2) qualifications for membership, (3) primary activities or programs, and (4) the purpose of the meeting that you attended.
4. Your organization, a large chemical company, has been asked by a local service organization to provide speakers for student workshops. You have been asked to investigate the request and prepare a short written report for the director of public relations, Xavier Delacroix, who is also your boss. In your report you are to recommend (1) whether your organization should participate, and (2) if so, who should make the presentations. After talking to the contacts you were given, you find out:
   a. The project is funded by the National Science Foundation, a federal agency, and the local community college. No funds will be provided for your part of the project.
   b. Children in middle school, grades six through eight, will participate. The program is targeting underrepresented groups.
   c. Teachers from the college will provide 75 min-

utes of instruction in mathematics and science every Saturday for the next ten weeks.

d. The project leaders would like your organization to provide role models in careers that require math and science backgrounds and a place where classes can be taught on Saturdays.

e. Speakers will be asked to demonstrate a math or science concept that relates to their field. The teachers will act as consultants.

f. The National Science Foundation will use this as a model project if it is successful.

5. Read the report of the Knight Foundation found in Appendix B. What is the purpose of the report? Write a memo report to your supervisor, the Vice-President of Academic Affairs, that summarizes the implications of this report to your university. (Your institution is a Division I school that fields successful men's and women's sports.)

REFERENCES

1. Howard Upton, "Power Up Your Business Writing," *Spirit* (March, 1991), p. 20.
2. Melba W. Murray, *Engineered Report Writing* (Tulsa: Petroleum Publishing, 1969).
3. Ibid., pp. 26–28.
4. Ibid., p. 26.
5. Herbert W. Hildebrandt, "A Chinese Managerial View of Business Communication," *Management Communication Quarterly,* 2:2 (November, 1988), p. 223.
6. Ibid., p. 229.
7. Ibid., p. 222.
8. Ibid., p. 223.
9. R. H. Solomon, *Mao's Revolution and the Chinese Political Culture* (Berkeley: University of California Press, 1971), p. 49.
10. Ibid., p. 225.

CHAPTER 11

Written Communication: Editing, the Polish that Accomplishes Your Purpose

Walter Johnson won his appeal and will get a retrial because of one wrong word. Enraged when he found condoms in his estranged wife's luggage, Johnson shot her, then buried her in a manure pit behind his house. He attempted suicide by drug overdose when her body was found in April 1987.[1] Johnson's mental history included psychotic episodes and emotional blackouts.

Despite a guilty verdict by the jury, Johnson won the right to another trial because a Sequoyah County (Oklahoma) judge made a mistake while reading instructions to the jury. Jurors were given instructions that "they could find Johnson innocent by reason of insanity if they found that he met two criteria: that Johnson did not understand the nature and consequences of his act, and that he did not know his actions were wrong."[2] One word in the instructions was incorrect. The jury needed only one criterion to find a ruling of innocent by reason of insanity—the judge read outdated instructions that used the word *and* instead of the word *or.*

Because of the error, taxpayers had to pay for another trial. The disappointed judge commented: "Our whole (legal) system is based on words and the usage of words. It can be very critical, but it can also be very frustrating."[3]

Your writing presents an image of you to each person with whom you communicate. To ensure that the image is favorable, make written messages clear, concise, and correct in every detail.

Clarity assumes that the writing has logical development, a well-developed outline, solid sentences, good transitions between the major parts, smooth pace, unity, and cohesion; *conciseness* means that all unnecessary words have been removed; *correctness* means your writing is free of sexism and errors in spelling, punctuation, grammar, and typing. To achieve these, you will need to edit your writing to accomplish your purpose.

Turning Poor Writing into Professional Writing

The Convention Travel Report

Beth Williams graduated from college in May and found a job in the following month. In the first month George Harris, her boss, sent her to a convention so that she could gain some insights into her new profession. When Williams returned, Harris requested a memo from her describing what she had learned.

Williams's grades on college papers had been high; the content was always good, and that, she thought, was the most important consideration. She drafted her thoughts onto paper and gave them to her secretary, who had also just started working, to type.

Read Williams's report (Exhibit 11.1). Circle any errors in grammar, word usage, spelling, and punctuation, and add the number of those errors that you found. Check yourself with the following listing:

- 0–20 errors: You need to refresh your understanding of the rules of grammar, word usage, spelling, and punctuation. Read this chapter very carefully.
- 20–30 errors: You are good at picking out most of the common errors. This chapter will show you how to avoid even more mistakes.
- 30–40 errors: You are very sensitive to the tricky errors that people sometimes overlook. This chapter should serve as a reinforcement for what you already know.
- 40–50 errors: Excellent. You have a superb ability to distinguish between what is right and wrong. Use this chapter as a review to help you polish your writing.

To: George Harris,
Vice President in Charge of Policy

From: Beth Williams,
Government Relations Division

Subject: Convention Report

Sir,

In compliance with your directive to report on the "Government Regulations in the Aerospace Industry" colloquium which I have attended, this memorandum is submitted for your perusal.

The convention discussed three main topics—the DIA's interferance in companies internal security programs, OSHA's noise exposure standards, and the fact that the U.S. Government must inspect the new teflon rivetting technique for quality control purposes and to make sure it meets their requirements. First off, the Fed's position on internal security is full of baloney. They say one hundred and fifty million dollars of microprocessing equipment were stolen last year by spies. And even more was destroyed by espionage! I know our company doesn't have any problems like that, never.

OSHA's decision to impose more strict noise exposure standards could deleteriously impact on our production plans. Their talking about requiring 90 dBh exposure limits, which has me worried; but I don't think we need concern ourselves about it too much at this point in time.

The new rivets is another matter, though. The principle problem with the rivets is that they shear off at high altitudes, so the Govern-ment wants to inspect everyone in the Aerospace Industry to make sure we're doing it right. Federal stress engineers think our men and girls should reinforce their rivets with a steel backing, during air-frame assembly. Otherwise, the affects on high-altitude test flights could be disasterous.

Well, after rivets the discussion was completely finished. For the purpose of quantifying goals and objectives and developing viable alternatives, the convention was a resounding success.

Respectively,

__________number of errors

EXHIBIT 11.1
Source: Timothy Riggins, "Convention Reports," prepared for this book.

A complete list of the errors Williams made in her writing can be found in Appendix C, on pages 633–634, followed by the corrected memo on page 635. Take a few minutes now to review the many errors.

Few professional writers submit the first draft of their work for publication. They realize that rewriting is as important as writing. Some authors rewrite their novels up to ten times and spend as much time rewriting as writing the original draft.

The editing process allows the writer to correct mechanical changes and add professionalism. For example, Franklin D. Roosevelt announced the entry of the United States into World War II by declaring, "Yesterday, December 7, 1941, a date that will live in infamy. . . ." While those words remain in the memories of millions, Roosevelt's original words, before editing, were less memorable. "Yesterday, December 7, 1941, a date that will live in world history. . . ."[4]

The author of "Teaching the Boss to Write" emphasizes that while the biggest problem in writing is hiding the conclusions, other major errors follow: "The most common complaint of managers about the reports they receive is that the conclusions of the writer are either buried or missing altogether. . . . But there is a whole catalog of other sins . . . excessive wordiness, poor grammar and sentence structure, atrocious spelling, and general confusion."[5] Most of these errors can be avoided if the writer takes the time to edit properly.

Three Reasons to Edit

1. *The writer is lazy* and produces vague, unclear, and incorrect copy, and often believes good writing is something that must be excessively pompous and stilted. Consequently this person writes on and on, never getting to the point.

2. *The writer has basic problems in distinguishing between what is right and wrong in writing.* Editing will be harder for this individual. This writer should seek help and have other people check his or her work. This individual should always edit with the help of a dictionary, word speller, and reference manual.

3. *The writer is working under a tight deadline and runs out of time.* This sometimes happens to everyone, but better planning and time management will give the time necessary for thorough editing.

Seven Methods for Reaching Clarity and Conciseness

"Plain English" is becoming a fact in today's business world. A writing consultant recently worked on a major airline's printed materials, rewriting the copy with fewer words and making it easier to read and understand. According to his estimates, the company could have saved over $150,000 a year in paper and printing costs if the material had been written concisely in the first place.

Never let the first draft of your writing leave your office without being edited. Your reputation, your future promotions, and your company's money are at stake.

> Another revealing example is the case of a publisher who produced a book for a group of professionals. He planned to sell the book by direct mail advertising. Although his sales manager wrote a good sales letter, the publisher called in an editorial consultant, who produced a second letter.
>
> The publisher then printed a "split run": half of his mailing was the sales manager's letter; the other half was the consultant's letter. Twenty thousand copies of each were mailed. The result? The edited letter produced *230 percent more* orders than the nonedited letter—at exactly the same cost for the mailing list, the printing, and the mailing.[6]

Work on making your final copy clear, concise, and correct. Remember, it is less expensive to write a good letter or report than a poor one. Vague or ambiguous writing requires further correspondence to clarify the situation. Wordy, meaningless phrases require readers to spend excess time and energy deciphering your thoughts. It is therefore good business and good public relations practice to edit your work by eliminating all useless phrases and unneeded words, using short words and action verbs, and making your writing correct. Edit to help readers understand your message.

Many organizations have learned the value of editing, and sometimes completely rewriting, messages directed to their customers. A major bank, for example, decided to rewrite its consumer loan note, which contained over 360 words and used such cumbersome phrases as "shall become subject to distraint proceedings or any order or process of any court" and "the remedies of the Bank hereunder are cumulative and may be exercised concurrently or separately." The new version of fewer than 100 words comes directly to the point.[7]

> I'll be in default:
> 1. If I don't pay an installment on time; or
> 2. If any other creditor tries by legal process to take any money of mine in your possession.
>
> You can then demand immediate payment of the balance of this note, minus the part of the finance charge which hasn't been earned figured by the rule of 78. You will also have other legal rights, for instance, the right to repossess, sell, and apply security to the payments under this note and any other debts I may then owe you.

As you read your reports and letters looking for errors and shortcomings, look for only one problem at a time. This will make your editing more specific.

AAiming AAt AAccuracy

Failing to check the accuracy of the message can be costly when it comes to advertising. Edited copy can fall short of expectations if *only* spelling, grammar, and punctuation are checked. Just ask American Airlines.

Embroiled in over a year of contract negotiations with the Allied Pilots Association (APA), which represented American's 8,700 pilots, American Airlines published nationwide newspapers ads on January 2, 1991, accusing the "Airline" Pilots Association of disrupting operations and inconveniencing passengers with an illegal "sick-out." The Air Line Pilots Association (ALPA), representing 42,000 pilots and 51 U.S. airlines, demanded an apology in "advertisements of equal size and prominence in the same publications." Robert L. Crandall, chairman of AMR Corp, of which American Airlines is a part, stated that the ads would be rerun identifying the correct pilots' union—namely, Allied.

Threatening legal action, ALPA released the following statement to the press: "We extend our fullest sympathies to our brethren at APA, who are attempting to negotiate with a company that apparently does not even know which union it is dealing with."[8]

1. Eliminate Unneeded Words

The quickest way to achieve clarity and conciseness is to cut the average length of sentences. Readers don't like long sentences, so don't write them. They tire easily when they have to stop and punctuate a long sentence; they lose interest and mentally tune out. Good writing deserves sufficient headings, short paragraphs, and adequate white space on a page. But a piece of writing with all sentences in the fifteen-word range would be terribly dull; a good balance of long, short, and in-between sentences is best.

Years ago, two writers were assigned the task of writing an advertisement for Ivory brand soap. The first wrote:

> The alkaline elements and fats in this product are blended in such a way as to secure the highest quality of saponification, along with the specific gravity that keeps it on top of the water, relieving the bather of the trouble and annoyance of fishing around for it at the bottom of the tub during his ablutions.

The second writer got the contract when he wrote, "It floats!"[9]

Writing frequently does not convey its intended message. The following statements, for instance, were taken from a business memo: "This facility has production capability in the area of a magnitude of 2,000 units per day";

Baby Boomers Demonstrate Verbal Bankruptcy

Paula LaRocque, writing coach at the *Dallas Morning News*, points out that baby boomers are being accused of "shoddy" and "imprecise" language patterns. The boomers—76 million people born between 1946 and 1964—represent over one-third of the U.S. population.

For proof of the boomers' lack of facility with the English language, LaRocque draws from numerous examples, interviews with educators, surveys, and standardized test scores. College entrance examinations began documenting declining verbal skills in 1964, when the first of the baby boomers graduated from high school. These trends continued for eighteen years through 1982, when the last of the boomers graduated. A national survey shows an "increasing number of adults can't decipher the instructions on a medicine bottle or understand recipes, road maps and package labels." Educators continue to blame teaching methodology. Schools are abandoning sight-reading techniques adopted in the 1940s for the old-fashioned, intensive phonics approach.

Perhaps LaRocque's most persuasive examples are anecdotal. Take Dan Quayle's comments on a West Coast earthquake: "The loss of life will be irreplaceable"; or another statement by Quayle on military defense:

> Why wouldn't an enhanced deterrent, a more stable peace, a better prospect to denying the ones who enter conflict in the first place to have a reduction of offensive systems and an introduction to defensive capability. I believe that is the route this country will eventually go.

LaRocque's list of errors seems interminable: unneeded words, jargon, unnatural phrases, trite expressions, lengthy phrases, passive voice, high-calorie words, poor spelling, and poor grammar. A journalist describes subjects "closeted away behind closed doors." A television news anchor describes a plane crash during a "pelting drizzle." A professor depicts images that "elicit a sense of emotive response." One student wants a "change of paste" while another describes a restaurant's enjoyable "hemisphere."[10] Every example emphasizes ineptness with the English language.

Paula LaRocque, "Language's Precarious Condition Can be Traced to Baby Boomer's Education or the Lack of It." *The Dallas Morning News*, May 27, 1990. Reprinted by permission.

"The project will effect a savings in the neighborhood of $40,000 on an annual basis." Regardless of what you think the statements said, the author really meant to say, "The plant can produce 2,000 units a day," and "The project will save about $40,000 a year."

Examine the following groups of words taken from business reports and letters. Those that are "too wordy" can often be changed to simpler alternatives.

Too Wordy	Alternatives
At the present	Now
At your earliest convenience	Soon
Be in a position to	Can
Take action	Act
Hold a meeting	Meet
Study in depth	Study
Consensus of opinion	Consensus
In accordance with	As
Due to the fact that	Because
Until such time as	Until
Basically unaware of	Did not know
The overall plan	The plan
In the amount of	For
In the event that	If
In reference to	About
In order that	So
For the purpose of	To
Despite the fact that	Although

2. Explain Abbreviations and Acronyms

In some professional and highly technical fields, the use of abbreviations and acronyms (pronounceable abbreviations) is widely accepted. Yet be careful to use abbreviations only when they save time and will be understood by the reader. Their use is frequently excessive and confusing. For example, M is code for a thousand in the United States but for a million in England. In the United States 9/12/81 means September 12, 1981, but it means December 9, 1981, in England. If you must use abbreviations like M and MM, be sure to define them the first time they appear in your paper.

An article in the *Dallas Morning News* (see Exhibit 11.2) describes how abbreviations and acronyms have flourished in the military service. The U.S. Army alone has over 10,000 abbreviations ranging from AA for arrival angle to ZTO for zone transportation. A few of the more simple are MICOM (U.S. Army Missile Command), USAREUR (U.S. Army Europe), MACOM (Major Army Command), and SCAMPERS (Standard Corps Army). Some of the more complex, like REPSTACOMBRE, are harder to decipher and show an excessive and confusing tendency. (Incidentally, it stands for "Report EM [enlisted men] on gaining unit morning report in FSA Code 7. The first day of the seventh month for E7–E9 personnel, or the first day of the fifth month for personnel in Grades E6 and below, preceding the expiration of a year's stabilization, EM will be reported in the appropriate FSA code.")

3. Eliminate Jargon

Every profession has established jargon. In some instances it takes the form of abbreviations and acronyms; often the terms are technical and apply only to a specific field. The following examples were used by corporate PR rep-to a supplemental dictionary. If the word is spelled incorrectly, you can edit the document or look up the correct spelling, then replace the word.

Grammar and Style Check. Many new software programs are capable of checking grammar and style. *Parsers* identify each word's range of functions, the order in which words are placed, and the grammatical components of a sentence. Objectionable words or phrases are listed, and a message is sent to the user that describes the grammar or style error.[14] Among the packages available for personal computers are Grammatik (Reference Software), RightWriter (RightSoft), and Correct Grammar (Houghton Mifflin). IBM's Critique is designed for mainframe computers.[15]

Writing Style. A writer's "style" is what sets one work apart from another; William Faulkner, Henry James, and Alice Walker have distinctive writing styles. Style is the force behind readability formulas such as the *Flesch-Kincaid Index* and Gunning's "fog index." Software packages are now available that apply these indexes to written documents to prevent documents, especially those produced by government and public agencies, from being overladen with jargon.[16] These software packages basically count the number of words and syllables to determine sentence difficulty. They also measure *cadence,* or the variation of sentence length and type. Alternating between short and long sentences helps to hold reader interest. Style models that replicate writing styles are also available. Corporate Voice by Scandinavian PC Systems, released in March 1990, allows writers either to choose from fifteen style models or create their own style. The result of these enhancements is that writers can correct 95 percent of their grammatical errors and revise a document so that it incorporates a "model" style.[17]

Document Format. The format of a document can create or destroy its visual appeal and readability. Format options include the ability to set right and left margins, right and left justification of the document on the page, tabs, headers, footers, and page numbering. These can be preset unless the document has special requirements. Most documents set margins at least 1 to 1½ inches from either side of the page. It is standard practice to *justify* the left side—that is, align the text on the left margin. The right side can also be justified, as it is in this textbook. Although right justification is not necessary, it gives a professional look to the page. Headers and footers can be set to provide information about the title, date, source, or page of the document. Tabs allow indenting or the creation of tables or columns.

Graphics. Graphics can amplify a point and add interest to a written document. Many word processing software programs include options to create boxes and insert figures, tables, or texts of any size or placement.

Read this 4 a LARC; it'll just take U a SEC

MIAMI (AP)—The space agency has just published a list of about 3,000 acronyms and abbreviations used in the space shuttle program. So, on a LARC, we thought we'd take a SEC to SCAN and ASSESS the booklet. We hope no one gets MAD.

Many of the abbreviations and acronyms have more than one definition, some as many as 10. For instance, AC can mean Associate Contractor or Aircraft, and CDT means Countdown Time, Central Daylight Time and Command Descriptor Table.

That policy would seem to invite trouble. If someone says, "We have to go ASAP," it could mean "Let's leave As Soon As Possible," or "We should visit the Aerospace Safety Advisory Panel."

If the FAR (Final Acceptance Review) is faulty, a FAR (Failure Analysis Report) might be needed to comply with a FAR (Federal Aviation Regulation).

Other entries might be confused with more everyday affairs. Autoland is not an auto parts store; it stands for Automatic Landing. BARS are not the places to which perplexed aerospace technicians might retreat; it stands for Baseline Accounting and Reporting System.

MAIDS is the Management Automated Information Display System.

If we're not careful, we'll end up in HAL (High Order Assembly Language, or Houston Aerospace Language).

NASA, you know, the National Aeronautics and Space Administration, also sent a glossary to help us understand some fancy space terms.

Like an "Attaching Part" which, we are told, is "an item used to attach assemblies or parts to the equipment or to each other." Or "Multiple Payloads," which are "more than one separate payload carried in the cargo bay."

We admit, though, that we were glad to have some help with "Repair Parts." According to NASA, "Repair Parts" are those "support items that are coded as 'not repairable.'"

LARC, incidentally, stands for the Langley Research Center in Hampton, Va.; SEC for Secondary, Second or Sequential Events Controller; SCAN for Selected Current Space Notice; and ASSESS for Airborne Science Shuttle Experimental System Simulation. MAD can be either Maintenance Analysis Data or Madrid, Spain.

EXHIBIT 11.2
Source: *Dallas Morning News*, Feb. 11, 1977, p. 1. Reprinted by permission of the Associated Press.

resentatives at the Three Mile Island nuclear facility following the near-disaster several years ago.

> *Explosion* became *energetic disassembly.*
> *Fire* became *rapid oxidation.*
> *Plutonium* didn't contaminate things; it became a friendly little substance that *took up residence.*

When asked why the simple became the complex, the PR representatives commented, "We wanted to keep our jobs."

The medical world has a language all its own. *Cephalalgia,* means headache to a doctor. *Pruritus* is itching, and *deglutition* is swallowing. Many professionals believe the use of such words in their trade aids precise speech, but this technical jargon does little to inform readers, alienates them, and masks fuzzy thinking. As you edit, look for the simple, down-to-earth words that will better explain your meaning than the vague abstractions:

Jargon	Down-to-Earth English
Bottom line	Final result
Implement	Carry out
Input	Results
Interface	Discuss, meet, work with
Judgmentally	I think
Meaningful	Real, actual, tangible
Net	Conclusion
Optimum	Best
Proactive	Active
Resultful	Effective, achieve results
Suboptimal	Less than ideal
To impact	To affect, to do to
Viable	Practical, workable

4. Eliminate Unnatural Phrases

The fourth way to attain clarity and conciseness is to avoid unnatural phrases. These often will be eliminated when unneeded words are excised, but sometimes overused and trite expressions tend to linger. The careful editor will cut those words.

Some Phrases to Avoid	Alternatives
As provided by the provisions of your policy	Your policy provides
Attached please find	Here is
In compliance with your request	As requested
The company's present practice is	Our practice is
We do not appear to have received	We haven't received
You will find enclosed herewith	Enclosed is

The above examples represent sloppy thinking and uncritical editing. Business letters and reports, however, are often filled with meaningless clichés and trite or outdated expressions that should be avoided.

Trite Expressions	Alternatives
As per your order	According to your order
At some point in time	At some time
Attached herewith please find	Attached is
At the present writing	Now
Avail yourself of this opportunity	(outdated)
Beg to acknowledge	(never beg)
Behind closed doors	Private
Elicit a sense of	Evoke
Failed to discharge	Did not fulfill
Hand over foot	Fast, brisk, rapid
In conclusion I would state	(say it)
In lieu of	In place of
In other words	(say it the first time)
In view of the fact that	In view of
Massive change	Change
Regarding said order	(outdated)
Skill capabilities	Skills
Stringent standards	Standards
Take stock of	(outdated)
Thanking you in advance	(never thank people in advance)
The bottom line	(outdated)
Very	(overused)

5. Use Small Words

Lack of clarity and conciseness is often caused by the use of large, stiff, polysyllabic words when small words would sound better. Consider using small words if appropriate. They will help your reader to understand your message sooner and will make for concise letters and reports. If a large word expresses the idea best, use it; variety increases understanding and aids pleasurable reading.

Letters

Large Words	Possible Smaller Words
Accomplished	Done
Approximately	About
Currently	Now
Demonstrate	Show
Forwarded	Mailed or sent
Initial	First
Initiate	Start
Investigate	Check
Purchase	Buy
Remunerate	Pay

Reports

Large Words	Possible Smaller Words
Accelerate	Quicken
Accurate	Correct or exact
Alternative	Choice or option
Analyze	Study or understand
Bilateral	Two-sided
Circumspect	Prudent
Corroborate	Support or confirm

Large Words	Possible Smaller Words
Demonstrate	Show
Eliminate	Cut out
Establish	Begin or found
Exterior	Outer or outside
Incorporated	Included
Methodology	Procedure or practice
Modification	Change
Participate	Join or share
Proficiency	Ability
Proximity	Nearness
Quantitative	Numerical or mathematical
Significant	Important
Subjective	Personal or intuitive
Utilize	Use
Voluminous	Large or prolific

6. Use Active Instead of Passive Verbs

Your readers will more likely respond if you treat them like people instead of objects. Do this by writing in the same style as you would talk. In conversations with clients you don't say, "It is recommended"; you say, "I recommend." Here is another example of a passive, impersonal statement that you'll never overhear in a conversation: "Personal endeavors are being made, although the magnitude of their participation is not absolutely identifiable." You may, however, overhear this personal explanation: "People are trying, but we don't know for sure how many or how much."

You may be balking at the first example, especially if the voice of your high school English teacher is alive in your mind with the instruction, "Never start a sentence with *I*." If that bothers you, there are alternatives for substituting active for passive verbs.

We hope you are feeling better.
A representative from your office could contribute so much!

Verbs are the strongest parts of speech, and they are strongest when used in the active voice. Active voice verbs show that their subject is "doing the action." When dull, passive verbs are employed, they act on their subjects.

Passive	Active
The books were inspected by the accountant.	The accountant inspected the books.

The second example is clearly stronger. In the active sentence the one doing the action (accountant) acts, and the verb (inspected) is short and clear. In the passive sentence the word *were* does not help but instead dulls the verb. Thus, the doer of the action takes a role in a prepositional phrase. Look at the difference in strength and clarity when the following active voice sentences are used:

AMERICANMONEYCARD

December 31, 1994

Mr. Alexandro Sorrento
5555 N. Walden Blvd.
San Antonio, TX

RE: Death of Guadalupe Sorrento

Dear Mr. Sorrento:

Thank you for your letter of December 15, 1994. As you requested, the AmericanMoneycard account in your deceased wife's name has been cancelled. Also, all AmericanMoneycards in your possession that were issued in her name should be destroyed. An AmericanMoneycard can be opened in your own name, so an application form is enclosed for you to fill out.

Sincerely,

Warner G. Brumfield, Sr.

EXHIBIT 11.3

Passive	Active
The policy will be enforced by Mr. Jones.	Mr. Jones will enforce the policy.
An improvement in quality has been made.	Quality has improved.
Increases in sales of 15 percent were obtained in July.	In July, sales increased 15 percent.
An executive leadership program was conducted by the Cleveland Chamber of Commerce, and hundreds of people attended.	The Cleveland Chamber of Commerce conducted an executive leadership program attended by hundreds.
Enrollment for the seminar was seventy people.	Seventy people enrolled for the seminar.

A final example in Exhibit 11.3 illustrates how the passive voice impersonalizes a message.

Although the unnecessary use of passive verbs produces weak sentences, sometimes the passive voice has its place. When the *performer's identity is unimportant,* the passive voice can give a sentence its proper emphasis:

Oil is refined in Louisiana.
Productivity is often criticized for its effect on prices.

If the *performer of the action is unknown,* the passive voice may be preferable:

Anonymous calls have been received.
During the last fiscal year, arson has been committed five times.

You can strengthen the verbs in your sentences in four specific ways:

a. *Eliminate impersonal constructions* like *it is, there is, there are,* or *there were.*

Weak:	**Stronger:**
There were repeated delays caused by a malfunctioning machine.	The malfunctioning machine caused repeated delays.

b. *Avoid words which weaken verbs* because they often diminish the strength of your writing, and they take the form of *is, was, to be, have, could,* or *should.*

c. *Pick active verbs instead of nouns or adjectives* when you need a word to express action. When events and activities consistently appear as nouns instead of verbs, writing becomes stiff and colorless.

d. *Use forceful action verbs.* Static verbs like *occur, take place, exist,* or *prevail* should be changed to more forceful ones.

Static:	**Improved:**
Throughout the committee's deliberations an atmosphere of increasing distrust existed.	As the committee deliberated, distrust increased.

While you are concentrating on verbs, consider also the *adjectives* and *adverbs* in your writing. Learn to spot lazy adjectives and adverbs, and replace them with vigorous ones. These six lazy adjectives and adverbs are clichés today because of their overuse:

Very good	*Great* success
Awfully nice	*Richly* deserved
Basically accurate	*Vitally* important

But vigorous adjectives and adverbs, like the following, more sharply define your ideas:

Instantly accepted	Moist handshake
Short meeting	Black coffee
Baffling instruction	Lucid recommendation

7. Use the Readability Index

As a final check of your editing, calculate the readability of your edited copy. Readability indexes have been developed by several contemporary writing authorities. The late Robert Gunning developed the "fog index" (see Table 11.1). Gunning's research focused on such questions as: How long can sentences be, on the average, before they discourage readers? How many long, complex, or abstract words will readers tolerate? The fog index is based on word and sentence length and approximates the number of years of education the reader should have to understand the copy easily. Many compa-

TABLE 11.1 Fog Index

	Read-ability Index	Reading Level	Typical Reading Material
Extremely difficult range	25		Professional journals
	20	Postcollege graduate	No popular magazines
Difficult range	19	College graduate	*Fortune*
	13	College freshman	
Ideal range	12	High school senior	*Time, Newsweek,*
	9		*Wall Street Journal*
Easy Range	8	Eighth grade	*Reader's Digest*
	6	Sixth grade	

Source: From Buff Silveria, "How Fogbound is Your Copy?" *Journal of Organizational Communication* (7:2), 1978.

nies, such as BankAmerica, use a fog index based on several experts' readability measures.

Indexes of this type should not be used as a guide during initial writing; use them instead as a yardstick after you have written. You can find your own readability index by following these steps:

- Count 100 words. If you reach 100 in the middle of a sentence, continue counting to the end of the sentence.
- Count the number of sentences in the 100-word block of copy. Divide the number of words by the number of sentences to get an average sentence length.
- Circle all the words with three or more syllables. Do not include proper nouns, such as people's names, cities, company names, etc., which people will probably understand easily. And do not include simple compound words, even though they're three or more syllables—words such as *bookkeeper, however,* etc. Words that are very common to your industry and that have no easy substitutes, e.g., *underwriting, medicine, computer,* might be included in the simple compound words category.
- Not counting those exceptions, add the "high-calorie" words—those with three or more syllables.
- Divide the total number of words into the total of high-calorie words and multiply by 100. Add that figure and the average sentence length. Multiply the total by .4.[11]

The following example shows the calculated index for a *Wall Street Journal* article:[12]

> John A. Newton had a piece of machinery that didn't produce anything. Now, thanks to government bureaucracy, he has two.
>
> One machine is a $1,200 pollution-control pump that hums away at Mr. Newton's iron foundry. The other is an identical pump that is a backup required by the Ohio Environmental Protection Agency. "Normally, you wouldn't have a spare, $1,200 pump on hand. But they insisted on it," Mr. Newton says.
>
> The spare pump symbolizes for Mr. Newton the endless rules, red tape and regulations that confront his company, Meech Foundry, every day. They consume his time, drain his capital and, he says, drive him crazy with local, state and federal rules about noise, dirty air, pensions, operating permits, labor negotiations, and hiring and firing.

High-calorie words

machinery	symbolizes	bureaucracy	federal
government	regulations	identical	operating
negotiations	pollution control		

- 125 words
- 8 sentences
- Average 15.6 words per sentence
- 8 percent high-calorie words

$$15.6 + 8 = 23.6 \times .4 = 9.44 \text{ fog index}$$

Tests of this nature should not be taken as gospel. Plain English sometimes cannot be measured by formulas. While tests do show how many words are in an average sentence in a piece of writing and how many sentences are in an average paragraph, they do not show whether a consumer contract is grammatical, sensible, or logically organized. It is possible for a piece of writing to test as easy to read but be unintelligible to the reader. As someone once said, "Words often have to be weighed instead of counted."

By taking each of the seven steps to editing, you will produce clear, concise written work that conveys your desired message. Remember to eliminate unneeded words, explain abbreviations and acronyms, eliminate jargon, eliminate unnatural phrases, use small words, use active instead of passive verbs, and use the readability index.

A Final Check for Correctness

The final editing procedure is to check your work for misuse of words, punctuation or grammar errors, and sexist remarks. Such mistakes signal the reader that you have either writing problems or low standards of performance. Correctness is important. The mechanics of writing are the foundation on which creativity rests, and they should be learned early in life. Space in this book does not permit us to cover all the basics; however, an awareness of three common problems will help you avoid them.

Use the Right Word

The editing process should uncover any misused words. Writers know the precise meaning of every word they use. When you are unsure of which word to use, turn to a dictionary or a style manual. Readers do not respect illiteracy.

Correct Spelling and Grammatical Errors

An important part of editing is to proofread your copy for misspellings and grammatical errors. It is embarrassing when a letter or report contains a misspelled word, but costly credibility can be lost when important words or names are not spelled correctly. If errors remain in the final version, the reader, who may be an excellent speller, may question the amount of care and effort you put into your writing. Errors can also drastically change the meaning of your message. A premed student wrote the following instructions for handling a shock patient, but we feel sure he didn't mean what he wrote: "Bleed the wound and rape the victim in a blanket for shock." If you know you are a bad speller, have someone else check your work. Better still, check your words with a dictionary or word speller.

Writing experts have found certain words are more frequently misspelled than others in the business world. The following list includes over 100 of the most frequently misspelled words.

The 100+ Words Most Frequently Misspelled

accommodate	achievement	acquire	all right
among	apparent	argument	arguing
belief*	believe*	beneficial	benefited
bookkeeper	category	coming	comparative
conscious	controversy	controversial	deficit
definitely	definition	define	describe
description	disastrous	effect	embarrass
environment	exaggerate	existence*	existent*
experience	explanation	facsimile	fascinate
government	height	indispensable	interest
irrelevant	irresponsibility	its, it's	judgment
lose	losing	maintenance	led
mere	necessary	occasion*	marriage
occurring	occurrence	opinion	occurred
paid	particular	performance	opportunity
personal	personnel	possession	permissible
practical	precede*	preference	possible
prepare	prevalent	principal	prejudice
privilege*	probably	proceed	principle
professor	profession	prominent	procedure
pursue	questionable	questionnaire	promissory
receive*	receiving*	recommend	quiet
repetition	rhythm	semiannual	referring*
separate*	separation*	shining	sense
studying	succeed	succession	similar*
technique	than	then	surprise
there*	they're*	thorough	their*
transferred	unforeseen	unnecessary	to,* too,* two*
woman	write	writing	villain

*Most frequently misspelled words among the first 100.

Correct Sexist Errors

The word *sexism* originally referred to prejudicial activities against females but now indicates "any arbitrary stereotyping of males and females on the basis of their gender." Today, changing public attitudes toward words such as *man* and *mankind* have led to more widespread use of sex-neutral terms such as *people* and *humankind.* Business and government now encourage the avoidance of sexist language—especially in writing.

Listed here are six areas that effective business writers should be aware of as they edit, in order to avoid traditional sexist terms and attitudes. Your company may not require employees to follow these guidelines completely. Changes in language, however, are becoming an accepted part of business speech and should be incorporated into all business writing. The following suggestions are in line with revisions of the *Dictionary of Occupational Titles* by the U.S. Department of Labor in 1975 to eliminate age and sex connotations.

1. Edit to Eliminate Unnecessary Gender Pronouns.

No	Yes
If credit management is too lax, the seller maximizes sales volume, *but he reduces* the percentage of accounts receivable *he collects.*	If credit management is too lax, the seller maximizes sales volume *but reduces* the percentage of accounts *receivable collected.*

No	Yes
The student should determine which keystrokes *give him the most difficulty* and then practice them.	The student should determine which keystrokes *give the most difficulty* and then practice them.
The bailee has a duty to do only the work agreed on; *he has no right* to use the car *for his own personal purposes.*	The bailee has a duty to do only the work agreed on *and has no right* to use the car *for personal purposes.*

2. Recast into the Plural.

No	Yes
When *an individual* travels by mass transit, *he* is confronted with a user charge.	When *individuals* travel by mass transit, *they are confronted* with a user charge.
Another type of conditional gift is made when the donor expects that *he* may die imminently. *He* may take *his* gifts back if *he* survives or changes *his* mind before *he* dies.	Another type of conditional gift is made when a donor expects to die imminently. *Donors* who survive may take *their* gifts back or change *their* minds before *they* die.
Such participation aids the *student* in developing *his* ability to communicate.	Such participation aids the *students* in developing *their* abilities to communicate.

3. Avoid Using Special Female-Gender Word Forms.

No	Yes
the *girls* or the *ladies* (meaning adult females)	the women
girl, as in, I'll have my girl check that	I'll have my secretary (or my assistant or my associate or the person's name) check that
lady used as a modifier, as in *lady* lawyer	lawyer (when you must modify, use *woman* or *female,* as in: a course on women writers, or the airline's first female pilot)

4. Substitute Alternatives to the Generic Use of the Word *Man*.

No	Yes
man, men, mankind	human(s), human being(s), person(s), people, individuals, humanity, human race, women and men, men and women
men (as in men, machines, money)	labor, human resources
Forty miles an hour, under the conditions described, was faster than an ordinary, *prudent man* would have driven his own car.	Forty miles an hour, under the conditions described, was faster than an ordinary, *prudent person* would have been driving.
By environment we mean simply the sum total of all the resources *available to man* by which he seeks to maintain himself as a species.	By environment we mean simply the sum total of all the available *resources by which people* seek to maintain themselves as a species.

5. Substitute Nonsexist Words for Man Suffixes and Prefixes.

No	Yes
businessman	businessperson, business executive, merchant, industrialist, entrepreneur, manager
businessmen	businesspeople, people in business
chairman	chairperson, moderator, chair, group leader, presiding officer
congressmen	members of Congress, congressional representatives, congressmen and congresswomen
manmade	manufactured, hand-built, handmade, machinemade
manpower	human resources, human energy, work-force personnel
salesmen	salespeople, salespersons, sales agents, sales associates, sales representatives, sales force

No	Yes
spokesmen	representative, spokesperson, advocate, proponent
statesman	political leader, public servant
workmen	workers

6. Use Up-to-Date Occupational Titles.

No	Yes
cameraman	camera operator
deliveryman	delivery driver, delivery clerk, deliverer
draftsman	drafter
foreman	supervisor
maid	houseworker
pressman	press operator
repairman	repairer
salesman	sales agent, sales associate, sales representative, salesperson
serviceman	servicer
stock boy, stock man	stock clerk
yardman	yard worker

A checklist of things to do while editing is found in Table 11.2.

Electronic Editing and Printing Options

Steve Frankel, president of Scandinavian PC Systems of Rockville, Maryland, notes, "Managers and editors who review draft documents now spend as much as 80 percent of their time correcting spelling or grammar mistakes and aligning the writer's style with the organization's standard."[13] In the last ten years, however, software options for editing by computer have increased in sophistication. In addition to checking spelling, providing a thesaurus, formatting, and selecting typefaces, these options allow writers to check their style and grammar usage and insert graphics. Descriptions of some of these editing and printing options follow.

Thesaurus. This option allows you to search for an alternative word by pressing the thesaurus command. Lists of synonyms and antonyms appear on the screen under different definitions or interpretations of the word. You can quickly replace the word or view the document while trying various choices. For example, if you were trying to find the right word to describe a gigantic

TABLE 11.2 Editor's Checklist

Eliminate unneeded words.

✓ Choose simple words rather than wordy phrases.
✓ Avoid long sentences.
✓ Balance long, short, and medium sentences.
✓ Keep paragraphs short.

Explain abbreviations and acronyms.

✓ Use abbreviations and acronyms only when they save time and are understood by the reader.
✓ Define abbreviations the first time they appear.
✓ Write out the words or title and put the acronym in parentheses the first time it is used.

Eliminate jargon.

✓ Avoid technical terms.
✓ Use down-to-earth terms that the reader can understand.

Eliminate unnatural phrases.

✓ Avoid trite expressions and clichés.

Use small words.

✓ Avoid polysyllabic words when small words would sound better.
✓ Alter word length for variety and pleasurable reading.

Prefer active over passive voice.

✓ Eliminate impersonal constructions.
✓ Avoid verb killers: is, was, to be, have, could, or should.
✓ Select active verbs instead of nouns or adjectives.
✓ Use forceful action verbs.

Use a readability index.

Make a final check for correctness.

✓ Check spelling, sexist language, word choice, punctuation, and grammar.
✓ Cite sources correctly.
✓ Make the report visually appealing; use current technology.

hall, you would place the cursor or indicator on the word *gigantic.* A list of words would appear on the screen which might include *enormous, colossal, huge, giant, immense, towering,* or *lofty.* You can then select the word that best fits your meaning by pressing the key corresponding to it.

Spelling Check. Misspelled words create a bad impression and detract from your purpose. Most word processing programs include the ability to check spelling word by word, page by page, or throughout the document. If a word's spelling is correct but it is an unusual word or name, you can skip it or add it

Typefaces. Because many software packages have sophisticated desktop publishing capabilities, writers may select from numerous typefaces. The following three fonts are found in IBM WordPerfect: Courier, CG Times, and Universal. These *fonts* can be printed in bold or italics, and type size can be enlarged or reduced. Most novices are tempted to mix too many types in the same document, producing a hodgepodge effect.

Laser Printers. The best printer choice is a *laser printer,* which operates like a photocopier, inscribing the image on paper with a laser beam and toner. Unlike dot matrix printers, which print out each line, the laser printer produces an entire page at a time. The copy it produces is crisp and camera ready. One caution: For best results, use paper designed for laser printers.

A GLOBAL PERSPECTIVE

Words in Translation

In an article called "Plain English Laws: Symbolic or Real?" Paul R. Timm and Daniel Oswald describe the following situation:

> Distressed after reading a plaintiff's 120-page claim, a British judge ruled the following: in addition to a ten-pound fine and imprisonment, the "warden shall
> 1. cut a hole through the pleading,
> 2. put the plaintiff's head through the hole, and
> 3. lead him round about Westminster Hall while the courts are sitting."[18]

Even though this incident happened in 1566, the point is clear: A communicator should present information clearly and concisely. In the context of global communication, however, these goals are difficult to achieve.

The complexity of global communication is immense. Our world has the capacity to capture information using remote-sensing satellites, VCRs, and videodiscs. This information can then be transported by coaxial or fiber-optic cable, microwave links, communication satellites, laser beams, and modems. If we want, we can store information in memory chips, magnetic film, and microfilm; or we can process it through integrated circuits, sophisticated software packages, and peripherals. Finally, at our request, we can retrieve it on TV, a computer screen, or in laser print copy. Satellites can distribute images of any publication throughout the world.

According to Thomas McCarroll, ideas generate over one-third of the U.S. gross national product.[19] Howard Frederick reports that 575 million copies of news-

papers are published each day, and book production has increased threefold in the last 18 years.[20]

Notwithstanding the miracles of modern communication technologies, however, as few as 15 percent of the world's nations benefit from 90 percent of the world's telecommunications network.[21] Computers are not available to citizens all over the globe. According to Frederick, "ninety-five percent of all computers are in the economically advanced countries. Only 3.5 percent are in Latin America, 1.6 percent in Asia, and .5 percent in Africa."[22] Illiteracy still exists throughout the world in astounding proportions: "60 percent of the population in Africa, 40 percent in Asia, and 25 percent in Latin America."[23]

The diversity of languages also limits our ability to communicate. Scholars are not even certain how many languages exist; estimates range between 2,500 to 7,000 different spoken languages.[24] Twenty percent of the world's population speaks Chinese. The next most popular language, English, is spoken by only 8.3 percent of the world—not exactly a close second. The top ten languages in order are Chinese, English, Hindi, Spanish, Russian, Arabic, Bengali, Portuguese, Malay-Indonesian, and Japanese.[25] Two languages frequently taught in American schools, French and German, rank eleventh and twelfth.

Individuals who know the language of another country and understand its culture will have a distinct advantage over those who do not. Internationally known chef John Folse is a good example. In 1986, when a statewide recession caused business to decline at his restaurant, LaFitte's Landing in Ascension Parish, Louisiana, Folse capitalized on the growing national taste for anything Cajun.[26] After catering a party in New York City, he consummated an international deal with Hilton Hong Kong. Rather than being "home free," his challenges had just begun.

Folse had to overcome international hurdles to maintain the quality of his food. Just a few of these included quick and convenient transportation, appropriate packaging, governmental restrictions, financial transactions, and food preparation. All these challenges had one underlying requirement: the ability to communicate with the people who would affect the quality and reception of his food products. Folse sought help from federal, state, and international agencies; learned basic words in the language; and compiled a "100-word dictionary" that included basic terms to be used in preparing the various dishes. The latter listed words such as *stove, fork, simmer,* and *sauté,* along with the translation and a pronunciation guide.[27] By 1993, Folse was selling services in fourteen countries; he had fed Pope John Paul II and was serving as a consultant to Hilton International.[28]

ETHICS: RIGHT OR WRONG?

DSC's Communication Glitch

DSC Communications produces computer equipment and software to transmit local telephone calls and monitor the efficiency of telecommunications systems. Several major communications companies use DSC products. These computers were installed in five of the seven regional Bell phone companies.

On June 26, July 1, and July 2, 1991, computers began issuing misleading messages in two regions serviced by Bell Atlantic Corp. and Pacific Telesis Group. Millions of residents lost telephone service in Los Angeles, San Francisco, Washington, D.C., Pittsburgh, Maryland, Virginia, and West Virginia.[29]

A week after the massive service disruptions occurred, DSC engineers discovered that a "trigger event" had created information backup at signal transfer points, resulting in massive congestion and network failure. New software was designed and installed to "act as a circuit breaker" to prevent "congestion along the network."[30] A company information release stated, "This provides protection much like a fuse on a power line. . . . It eliminates surges from affecting other elements of the line."[31] Officials could not be reached for comment, and the statement did not identify the cause of the problem or mention whether design flaws existed in the equipment or software.

The Committee on Government Operations of the U.S. House of Representatives and the subcommittee on Government Information, Justice and Agriculture held a hearing on July 9. This joint committee, made up of both panels, is responsible for oversight of the Federal Communications Commission (FCC). The purpose of the meeting was to evaluate the FCC's performance "in assuring phone service to consumers."[32]

During the hearings, DSC officials revealed that minor modifications were made to the software codes in April. Since DSC considered these modifications "minuscule," the company did not run tests of the software and equipment.[33] Frank Perpiglia, vice-president for technology and product development, stated that while other phone companies asked for revisions because of problems that they experienced when tests were run on DSC equipment, the Bell companies did not request revisions, nor did the revisions conform entirely to Bell company rules.[34] When modifications were made, a computer code was omitted, creating "a defect in three or four lines of computer codes. . . . 'Our equipment was without question a major contributor to the disruptions,' Perpiglia told the committee. 'We must be forthright in accepting responsibility for failure.' "[35]

Congressional investigators were still not certain why the breakdowns hit several telephone companies but only two regional Bells. Possible causes included failure of DSC software or equipment, a major system breakdown, a design flaw, or sabotage by a programmed virus.[36] Since all of the outages began about the same time on the same day, the chair of the House telecommunications subcom-

mittee, Edward Markey (D–Mass.), suspected sabotage. Phone company officials admitted this possibility.

During 1991, DSC was experiencing a series of problems including the ending of an exclusive arrangement to supply switching equipment for Motorola Inc. cellular systems. For the quarter ending June 30, 1991, DSC had a loss of $25.7 million.[37] Shortly after the phone network failures, DSC common stock fell.[38] In August DSC announced that it was cutting or laying off 12 percent of its workforce.[39] Chairman James L. Donald stated that DSC had "accelerated efficiency programs" to reduce costs.[40] In the third quarter DSC revenues dropped 24.4 percent. In the first nine months of 1991, DSC lost $100.3 million.[41]

Nelson Palmer, customer operations director, learned what accelerated efficiency programs meant when he arrived at work after completing a quality management seminar sponsored by DSC: his employee badge, which gave access to his office, had been deprogrammed. When he sat down at his desk and tried to access his computer, the screen printed out the words "unauthorized user." Palmer had been terminated.[42]

The day before Thanksgiving, 1991, Bell Communications Research issued a final report on the causes of the service failures on the East and West coasts in June and July. The problem was the result of "a single mistyped character in a line of software programming installed on some of (the) transfer points."[43] Perpiglia stated that when minor program modifications were made "DSC dropped several algorithms." He concluded that foregoing the customary thirteen-week tests "was a huge mistake."[44]

Case Questions

1. Is there a question of ethics in this case?
2. Identify the various stakeholders involved.
3. If you were a DSC equipment user, how would you have interpreted the company's communications during this event?
4. Why did DSC forego the software tests?
5. What were the consequences of the incorrect code?
6. Why did Perpiglia state that DSC made a "huge mistake"?

SUMMARY

Written communications reflect the character of the writer. They should be neat, well organized, easily readable, and acceptably formatted. The editing process allows the writer to correct spelling errors and grammar and stylistic problems as well as adding professionalism to the document's appearance. Properly edited written reports, letters, and memos can be effective tools for achieving action.

Three important reasons to edit are: to

avoid vague, unclear copy; to distinguish between what is right and wrong in writing; or to improve writing that has been produced too hastily. A first draft should never leave your desk without editing.

Effective writing should be clear, concise, and correct. Seven methods for reaching clarity and conciseness are: (1) eliminate unneeded words, (2) explain abbreviations and acronyms, (3) eliminate jargon, (4) eliminate unnatural phrases, (5) use small words, (6) use active instead of passive verbs, and (7) use a readability index. A final check for correctness should make certain that you have used the right word, checked for spelling and grammatical errors, and corrected sexist errors.

Electronic editing and printing options produce high-quality written documents and offer a number of options. Among these are the thesaurus, spell checkers, grammar and style checkers, writing style models, alternative document formats, graphics, variations in typefaces, and laser printing. Because software packages including these editing aids are now accessible to PC users, readers have increased their expectations for document quality.

Well-written, carefully edited copy saves time and money. It also helps your reader understand your message. Wordy, meaningless phrases require the reader to spend excess time and energy deciphering your thoughts. It is therefore good business and good public relations to edit your work.

Key Words

abbreviations
acronyms
active verbs
clarity
conciseness
correctness
edit
fonts
format
grammar
grammar check
high-caloric words
jargon
laser printer
passive verbs
plain English
readability index
sexism
spell check
style
style check
thesaurus
unnatural phrases
unneeded words

Discussion Questions

1. Well-edited writing is based on clarity, conciseness, and correctness. Describe each and its importance to writing.
2. This chapter listed methods by which clarity and conciseness can be achieved in writing. Describe these methods.
3. Explain fully the difference between active and passive verbs.
4. What does a readability index describe, and how is it calculated?
5. What are the three steps in the final check for correctness?
6. Describe how sexism appears in writing, and list three ways that it can be eliminated.
7. Discuss the statement, "Written communication is most effective when it is used in conjunction with oral communication." In your discussion, include a specific example.

EXERCISES

1. Put your learning into practice by rewriting the following "too wordy" statements with only half as many words. Be careful not to change or discard the main thought. Sample answers are in Appendix C on page 635.
   a. In order to keep you informed of the results of the sales meeting held on August 13 to consider ways and means of reducing the cost of the proposed spring sales campaign, we are submitting herewith a brief resume and the procedure outlined for the cost reduction plans.
   b. Memoranda intended for internal distribution should be written just as carefully as those to be distributed outside of the division, and, actually, they serve as an excellent opportunity for developing an individual's proficiency in writing.
2. Rewrite the following passive sentences into the active voice. Answers are in Appendix C on page 636.
   a. A sharp decrease in sales was noted.
   b. The department is dependent on our aid for its success.
   c. It is desired by the president that this problem be brought before the board of directors.
3. Correct the misused words in the following sentences. Answers are in Appendix C on page 636.
   a. We shall be seriously effected by the new corporate policy.
   b. The amount of conventioners who come to New York City varies with the season.
   c. We shall appreciate your advising us of your decision.
   d. The estate was divided between the millionaire's three sons.
   e. Can we have your permission to proceed with the instructions outlined in this letter?
4. Correct the grammatical problems in these sentences. The answers are in Appendix C on page 636.
   a. Divided into two sections, the accountant balances the accounts more readily.
   b. Depreciation accounting is not a system of valuation but of allocation.
   c. To form an opinion as to the collectibility of the accounts, they were reviewed with the credit manager.
   d. This problem can only be alleviated by a change in policy.
   e. Bob Smith's interest and devotion to his work are not to be questioned.
5. Find the misspelled words in the following list. Several of the words qualify. The correct answers are in Appendix C on page 637.

	Correct	Incorrect	Correct Spelling
a. semi-annual			
b. occurrance			
c. facimile			
d. supercede			
e. government			
f. disasterous			
g. proceedure			
h. deficit			
i. permissable			
j. prevalant			
k. irrelevant			
l. questionaire			
m. promissary			
n. preferance			
o. maintainence			

REFERENCES

1. Anthony Thornton, "One Wrong Word Leads to New Trial," *The Daily Oklahoman,* November 16, 1992, November 16, 1992. Copyright, 1992, Oklahoma Publishing Company. Reprinted by permission.
2. Ibid.
3. Ibid., p. 2.
4. M. C. Kirkland, "Effective Writing," *Future* (March/April 1977), p. 50.
5. "Teaching the Boss to Write," *Business Week* (October 25, 1976), pp. 56, 58.
6. Kirkland, "Effective Writing," p. 18.
7. Alan Siegel, "How to Say It in Plain English," *Management Review,* November 1979, p. 15.
8. Bridget O'Brian, "AAnd We'll AAim to AApologize for AAll AAberrant AApologies," *Wall Street Journal,* January 3, 1991.
9. Kirkland, "Effective Writing," p. 18.
10. Paula LaRocque, "Language's Precarious Condition Can Be Traced to Baby Boomers' Education—or Lack of It," *Dallas Morning News,* May 27, 1990.
11. Buff Silveria, "How Fogbound Is Your Copy?" *Journal of Organizational Communication,* 7:2, 1978, p. 5.
12. Ibid., p. 6.
13. Steve Frankel, "Soon Your Computer Will Be Able to Write," *Miami Herald,* May 6, 1990.
14. Ibid.
15. Ibid.
16. Ibid.
17. Ibid.
18. *Milward v. Welden,* 21 Engl Rep. 136 (CH1566), in Paul R. Timm and Daniel Oswald, "Plain English Laws: Symbolic or Real?" *The Journal of Business Communication,* 22:2 (Spring 1985), p. 31.
19. Thomas McCarroll, "What New Age?" *Time* (August 12, 1991), p. 44.
20. Howard H. Frederick, *Global Communication and International Relations* (Belmont, Calif.: Wadsworth, 1992), pp. 64–65.
21. Anne W. Branscomb, "Global Governance of Global Networks," in Anne W. Branscomb, ed., *Toward a Law of Global Communication Networks* (New York: Longman, 1986), p. 6.
22. Frederick, *Global Communication,* p. 76.
23. Ibid., p. 65.
24. Ibid., p. 85.
25. Sidney S. Culbert, "The Principal Languages of the World," *The World Almanac and Book of Facts* (New York: World Almanac, 1990), pp. 808–809.
26. Kelly King Alexander, "A Recipe for Success: A Guide for Doing Business Overseas," *The Greater Baton Route Business Report,* January 16, 1993, p. 17–19.
27. Ibid., p. 20.
28. Ibid., p. 17.
29. John Schneidawind, "Software Flaw Cut Off Phones: DSC Says Computer Codes Were Missing," *USA Today,* July 10, 1991.
30. Jim Mitchell, "DSC Installing New Software," *Dallas Morning News,* July 6, 1991.
31. Ibid.
32. Mitchell, "DSC Installing."
33. Schneidawind, "Software Flaw."
34. Ibid.
35. Edmund L. Andrews, "Computer Maker Says Flaw in System" *The New York Times,* July 10, 1991.
36. Schneidawind, "Software Flaw."
37. Tom Steinert-Threlkeld, "DSC Communications Slicing 12% of Workforce," *Dallas Morning News,* August 3, 1991.
38. Mitchell, "DSC Installing."
39. Steinert-Threlkeld, "DSC Communications."
40. Ibid.
41. Steinert-Threlkeld, "Rumors of DSC's Demise Live on Despite the Company's Rebuttals," *Dallas Morning News,* December 7, 1991.
42. Ibid.
43. Ibid.
44. Andrews, "Computer Maker."

PART 4

COMMUNICATION STRATEGIES FOR THE EFFECTIVE MANAGER

In pursuing organizational missions, managers and employees engage in a variety of activities. Part 4 describes communication strategies for effective teams, leadership, problem resolution, conflict management, meetings, interviewing, or change.

Chapter 12 describes the importance of social interaction in the organization and the characteristics of teams. It also presents a model for effective leadership based upon a situational approach.

Managers must make decisions and resolve problems on a daily basis. Chapter 13 presents a six-step problem-solving and decision-making model. It also describes convergent and divergent thinking and presents creative approaches to generating ideas and selecting solutions. Since solving problems often means managing conflict, Chapter 14 presents an in-depth look at sources, stages, strategies, and forms of intervention designed to reduce conflict and reach consensus.

Chapters 15 and 16 examine two communication activities in which managers frequently engage but rarely receive training: conducting interviews and conducting meetings. Chapter 15 presents the advantages and disadvantages of meetings, and gives suggestions for premeeting planning, meeting facilitation, and postmeeting follow-up. Chapter 16 describes the manager's responsibility as an interviewer along with questioning techniques and guidelines for conducting orientation, counseling, performance appraisal, and disciplinary interviews.

Finally, Chapter 17 examines communication's role in the change process in the organization. The manager is depicted as a change agent with many options for implementing change. The chapter focuses on implementing change through effective communication.

CHAPTER 12

COMMUNICATION STRATEGIES: TEAMWORK AND LEADERSHIP

Tom Huber knew he wanted to be different—he wanted to change the stereotypical idea of what a big company should be. How? He would start his own company with one underlying philosophy: it would be sensitive to the needs of dealers *and* customers—service would come first.

Using his experience gained in working for a company that manufactured and sold custom-made hearing aids, Huber hired six employees who embraced his philosophy. They quickly set about making his company happen. In the first eighteen months, Hearing Technology, Inc. had sales of about $1 million, made a profit, *and* had a growing list of customers.

Orders flowed in as the business grew. Staff increased—and so did turnaround time. Turnaround time on orders extended from three to five to eight days. Dealer calls went unanswered for days. As a result, dealers took business elsewhere. Employees claimed that suggestions never went "up the line"; managers always had a plausible reason why things could not be done. Employees seemed to be at odds with each other and with the goals of the company. According to Huber, "Sometimes it was like being at two different companies." Sales grew and the company continued to make a profit, but the original philosophy somehow was lost in the shuffle—the customer was not getting good service.

Huber and his board took drastic steps to move the company back to his original philosophy. They had two goals: to make any changes necessary to put the customer first and to allow employee participation in decision making. The results were dramatic. Half of the eight key managers left. Weekly team meetings were implemented as incubators for innovative ideas and solutions to long-standing problems. Employees redesigned the way products were built. Some suggestions seemed minute and saved only a few cents; others had greater impact. For example, a team approach for entering new orders allowed inputting orders early in the morning, before the computers slowed down from heavy use. This one idea eliminated chronic delays in entering, and turnaround time dropped to four days. The best part of these changes was that employees were working together and customers were the beneficiaries. Says Huber, "They understand what's needed in a sales and marketing business. They're part of the team."[1]

As organizations have become more complex, so have relationships between managers and employees. During the days of scientific management the manager made all decisions and communicated these decisions to the workers, who performed the tasks. Today the manager must consider government regulations, union contracts, and legal pressures before rendering a decision. In addition, more employees desire to participate in the decision-making process, and computer technology has increased the availability of and access to information analysis. Add fluctuations in the economy, global conflicts, and continually changing personal relationships, and the leader's task begins to resemble what Warren Bennis describes as "a set of conditions that seem to take shape suddenly, like an unscheduled express train looming out of the night."[2]

Earlier chapters defined a manager as someone who "gets things done through others." The manager's goal is to accomplish, bring about, conduct, or direct—and be effective. Bennis carefully distinguishes between the leader and the manager, since they are not necessarily embodied in the same role: "The difference may be summarized as activities of vision and judgment versus activities of efficiency. . . . The leader today is a multidirectional broker who must deal with four estates—his immediate management team, constituencies within his organization, forces outside his organization, and the media."[3] Each area requires effective communication.

Followers have certain expectations of their leaders: to provide resources, give directions, provide compensation, and give information. Leaders also have expectations of their followers: to lend support; cooperate in offering their abilities toward achieving defined goals; and communicate wants, needs, and desires in a constructive manner. In addition, a leader must be concerned with employee motivation; the individual who does not produce or is erratic affects the productivity of others.

What is a group? How does a group become a team? How do managers empower employees and create stimulating work climates? These questions plague every organization. This chapter presents the communication concepts and processes that affect teamwork and leadership. Among the topics covered are the importance of social interaction in the organization, functions and characteristics of teams, styles of leadership, factors that motivate employees, and ways that leaders interact as part of the team in the organization.

The Importance of Social Interaction in the Organization

Although social interaction remains essential within organizations, recent improvements in technology have decreased face-to-face human contact in businesses. In some cases, future technological changes will further decrease this contact. Instead of walking to colleagues' offices, we simply call them on the telephone or send a message to their electronic message center. Communication problems develop when the message is sent through a channel that eliminates the human elements of social contact, nonverbal communication, and listening. Electronic devices such as radio, television, video games, computers, and fax machines have replaced the human element in interaction.

Without face-to-face interaction, communication is enormously impeded. High-level managers recognize this fact and are reluctant to give up face-to-face interaction for the colder mode of sending electronic messages. According to Rosenfield, face-to-face interaction:

1. Encourages meaningful human interaction and participation that can occur only in this kind of contact.
2. Provides individuals an opportunity to expand their world views, improve their problem-solving methods, and discover alternatives they would never know outside the interactive relationship.
3. Facilitates an individual's ability to make commitments to others.
4. Provides a backdrop for understanding the depth and impact of communication: our nonverbal behavior, listening, speaking, and interacting together.[4]

A Team Defined

In today's organizational world, team building is a common buzzword. Why? Aren't groups automatically teams? How groups become teams is the subject of much conjecture and discussion. Teams, like groups, work together to accomplish goals such as winning the NCAA basketball championship or selling the most hamburgers. For the purposes of this text, the terms *team* and *group* frequently will be used interchangeably. However, the two categories differ in some important respects. A *group* is two or more people who interact face to face. A *team* is a group of two or more people who interact over a period of time and share a common purpose. A team meets because of shared goals. As long as the team survives, individual roles and leadership patterns emerge, and communication patterns become established. The nature of business teams means that the duration of some teams is long while that of others is very short.

One of the best ways to explain how groups become teams is to use an analogy of the human hand. A hand is made of four fingers and a thumb. It is a grouping of body parts that performs a variety of functions. When the parts of the hand work together to accomplish a specific task efficiently, they have functioned as a team. Groups in general are important, but in business and industry the team concept has become a focus point for effective communication. In the mid-1960s, Zelko and Dance outlined five trends that contributed to the team phenomenon:

1. The work climate and environment are socially interacting. We have become so specialized in our vocations that we are interdependent; consultations and conferences are an essential part of just doing our jobs.
2. Employees have participative opportunities to express themselves and be heard and to have a voice in matters that concern them. The conference is in a dominant position as a major forum for such opportunities.
3. "Consultative management"—managers consulting with subordinates—relies heavily on the conference setting for drawing out opinions and judgments of members of a work group.
4. A supervisor's reliance on group decision making directly affects the supervisor's use of the conference method.
5. The objectives of democratic management strongly emphasize the group/leader relationship.[5]

The Functions of a Team

Communication experts recognize that "over 90 percent of the Fortune 500 companies use problem-solving and decision-making teams in their daily operations and organizational structure."[6] These teams come in many sizes, shapes, and forms and have a variety of purposes; the common objective of all teams, however, is to reach their goal as quickly and effectively as possible.

Two primary functions of a successful team are *task* and *relationship.* A top executive may decide that some unit heads need to get to know each other better. In such a case, the relationship function is of primary concern to the participants. Other groups have specific goals or tasks that must be completed within a limited period of time; perhaps the organization must comply with federal audit requirements. Here the task function is paramount in importance.

Before we discuss these functions, take a few minutes to complete the questionnaire that appears in Exhibit 12.1. Your answers should relate to a group meeting in which you recently participated. When you finish the questionnaire, add the scores in both columns. The T score is for the task function. The R score is for the relationship function. The highest possible score for the T is 70; the high score for R is 50.

Task

A team's task function is to achieve the goal toward which it is working. In most business interactions all team members focus their attention on the task. The group format is selected in terms of its task and many of the team characteristics (roles, leadership styles, and so forth) are designed to enhance task accomplishment. A high score in the T area indicates that the group is highly task motivated.

Relationship

At the same time that the team works on its task, it must also fulfill another function. The relationship function involves meeting the interpersonal

How to Assess Business Meetings

All managers spend considerable periods of time in business meetings. Rarely do they evaluate in a systematic manner how effective they feel these meetings are. Are they effective or ineffective? The Task/Relationship Index gives you the opportunity to consider one way in which meetings can be assessed. Consider either a specific meeting or a normal work meeting, and allocate a score on the scale below to each of the statements:

1	2	3	4	5
Not at all	Occasionally	A fair amount	A considerable amount	A great deal

	Score T	Score R
a. The meeting helped me understand the job we are doing more clearly.	______	______
b. I learned a lot about people's attitudes during the meeting.		______
c. It was a useful meeting insofar as people got to know each other.		______
d. It was a meeting in which I had to use my knowledge and skills.	______	
e. People built on each other's ideas.		______
f. Ideas were expressed freely.		______
g. The technical content of the discussion was of a high level.	______	
h. People kept to the point and did not waste time.	______	
i. The decision-making process was fair.	______	
j. Each item on the agenda received sufficient time.	______	
k. There was a high degree of honesty and openness in the conversation.		______
l. The acceptability of decisions was high.		______
m. Problems were carefully diagnosed.	______	
n. Creative solutions to problems were developed.	______	
o. Solutions to problems were carefully assessed.	______	
p. Differences of opinion were thoroughly discussed.		______
q. The meeting was well organized.	______	
r. The decision taken was of a high quality.	______	

	Score T	Score R
s. Everyone in the meeting received a fair hearing.		______
t. The purpose of the meeting was clear.	______	
u. Objectives were clearly established during the meeting.	______	
v. I felt satisfied that I had an opportunity to influence the decision taken.		______
w. Time was used to the best advantage.	______	
Totals	______	______

EXHIBIT 12.1
Excerpted, by permission of the publisher, from *How to Assess Your Managerial Style*, by Charles Margerison, pp. 72–74. © 1979 MCB Human Resources Ltd., England. Published in U.S. in 1980 by AMACOM, a division of American Management Associations, New York. All rights reserved.

needs of the team members. When people interact, they must deal with relational factors, e.g., morale, feelings, conflict, cooperation, and communication. The higher the R score for the relationship factor on the questionnaire in Exhibit 12.1, the more your team was focusing on the internal needs of its members.

The longer the team meets, the more attention it requires for its relationship needs. Some committees and other task-oriented groups that have been meeting for long periods of time suddenly find themselves in a meeting where all communication revolves around the participants' social needs and little input is focused on the task. Without realizing it, members are reaching out for interaction with others. At that time some form of social endeavor probably is in order for the group.

Characteristics of Teams

Each group or team has two distinct functions: to accomplish the established task or goals and to maintain internal relationships. As we evaluate teams more closely, we find characteristics that tell us how well the team is functioning and meeting its objectives. According to Fran Tarkenton and Joseph H. Boyett, chairman of the board and vice-president, respectively, of Tarkenton Conn & Co., an Atlanta-based firm that advises large and small business on management and compensation practices, "winning teams" have certain characteristics:

1. They share a common purpose and make sacrifices for the good of the team.
2. They share specific goals—the details that lead to quality and perfection.

3. They keep score and monitor their successes or failures.
4. They share the rewards, are generous with praise, and do not focus on the superstars.
5. Each individual understands his or her role and knows that he or she can always improve through training, practice, planning, and preparation.
6. Every player is involved all the time—emotionally and intellectually.[7]

Goals

In the business world teams form for a reason. All teams have one thing in common, a goal to work toward or a task to accomplish. Team members should be involved in defining the team's mission and goals. Such questions as who is the customer? What does the customer want? How does the customer evaluate success? Who is the competition? What is the competition doing that we are not doing? are keys to determining goals.

Teams monitor general goals by having specific goals that measure critical levels of performance. Specific goals can mean limiting turnaround time to 24 hours, eliminating customer complaints, doubling the number of transactions, or meeting a high-quality standard of product. Teams keep score to determine if they are winning and where they need to improve.

In some teams, members have personal reasons for being a part of the team. If these personal reasons are controlled and channeled toward the common goal, no problems develop. If, however, members try to fulfill their own needs at the cost of team time and energy, opposition erupts and the rest of the members move to pull them back to a position of uniformity.

To save time and energy, the goal should be well defined, the team should have the means to see the goal achieved, and each member should be willing to commit time to the task.

Communication

If ideas are to be fully evaluated, decisions made, and problems solved, communication is necessary. An open, two-way flow of information between all members takes more time than the one-way process, but its results are more fulfilling for all members and the quality and quantity of the information are more useful. Studies of the effect of communication on the quality of team performance show that groups experiencing "low-quality" communication—highly abstract, inconsistent, irrelevant, negative, or facetious statements—also accept low-quality solutions. Groups with "high-quality" solutions were characterized by precise, internally consistent, or positively reinforcing statements and statements emphasizing cooperation and teamwork.[8]

In a winning environment, communication of the mission and common goals plays an indispensible role. To make sure every employee understands the mission, write the mission in two to three sentences and refine it. From this, communicate the heart of the mission in the form of a motto such as, "Details make the difference," "Quality is our first concern," "Customers come first," and post it, write it, talk it, do it.

Share rewards by giving praise and recognition in a meaningful way. Some organizations form clubs or give pins, award certificates, or post pictures to recognize employee performance. The Boeing Company's "Zero Defects" program awarded pins with precious stones to employees who achieved zero defects on the job over a period of time. These are visible testimonies—symbols—to others that the organization recognizes the contributions of the individual as part of the team.

Feedback is another aspect of communicating performance to the team. Tracking several measures of performance that led to achieving the mission and putting this information in a place for all employees to see provides direct feedback on team progress. Regular meetings to discuss progress, share ideas, and participate in decision making allow employees to have some control over the success of the team.

Roles

Each member of a team performs a specific role. The best teams allow members to participate fully. Individuals fill roles that capitalize on their knowledge, skill, experience, needs, and influence. People who are confident in their role generally work well in the group. As discussed earlier, groups have task and relationship functions and perform task and relationship roles to fulfill these group-centered functions. Team members also have individual or self-centered roles that help them satisfy personal needs. These roles include:

Relationship—Positive

1. Shows solidarity, raises others' status, gives help, rewards.
2. Shows tension release, jokes, laughs, shows satisfaction.
3. Shows agreement, shows passive acceptance, understands, concurs, complies.

Task Area—Neutral

1. Gives suggestions, direction, implying autonomy for others.
2. Gives opinion, evaluation, analysis, expresses feelings and wishes.
3. Gives information, orientation, repeats, clarifies, confirms.
4. Asks for information, orientation, repetition, confirmation.
5. Asks for opinion, evaluation, analysis, expression of feeling.
6. Asks for suggestion, direction, possible ways of action.

Relationship—Negative

1. Disagrees, shows passive rejection, formality, withholds help.
2. Shows tension, asks for help, withdraws, defends, or asserts self.
3. Asks for suggestions, direction, possible ways of action.[9]

The team member as leader. Teams are moved toward their goals by contributions from the members and by leadership that organizes those contributions into a workable form. In some informal groups no leadership is needed. But in teams, the leader is usually designated because of position, knowledge, or power. Team leaders initially have power because of their assigned role. They expect and are expected to influence the decision making of the team. They can also negatively affect the team process to the extent that content decisions are made that favor their personal goals.[10] This power can be transient if team members do not fully develop in their leadership.

Team leaders normally do seven things: (1) coordinate team interactions, (2) keep the team on target with the goals and prevent team members from blocking goal attainment, (3) help team members develop the essential mission and goals of the team, (4) make certain all team members have an opportunity to participate in the team's achievements, (5) maintain team harmony and help facilitate conflict resolution, (6) identify areas of group agreement, and (7) remove barriers that impede accomplishment of the team's mission.

Different people can perform different kinds of leadership functions within the group. Informal leaders influence group process and task orientation. These team members often act as group facilitators.

The team member as facilitator. Team *facilitators* help the team move through the process of diagnosing and solving problems that arise as the group seeks to reach its goal. Facilitators are sensitive to the group process, are trusted by the group, are skilled in group dynamics, and are perceptive about problems that endanger group progress. The functions performed by the facilitator include keeping team members aware of progress, monitoring norms to make certain that they are consistent with team goals, keeping tension at a productive level, and making sure everyone gets to participate.[11] Facilitators do not deal with content; they focus specifically on the process. They are time keepers, idea protectors, and idea catalysts. Since facilitators can sometimes be disruptive in pursuing their role, their intervention in the group process must be constructive. When, how often, and what the facilitator elects to focus on become critical decisions.

Dysfunctional roles. Some team members are disruptive. Rather than contributing to the welfare of the team, they become dysfunctional members and sabotage team goals. A *withdrawing* member chooses not to participate. He or she may not want to be a part of the problem/solution and demonstrates these feelings by daydreaming, ignoring participants, coming late to meetings, or leaving early. A *dominating* team member may sidetrack team progress through communication strategies that cite personal experiences *ad nauseam,* argue a point too much, and attempt to force a narrow, opinionated viewpoint on others. A member *competing for leadership* attempts to control the direction of discussion or challenges the leader's credibility. A *hostile* member may use verbal or nonverbal communication strategies that include deflating egos, name calling, or becoming abusive. Finally, the *self-confessing* member uses the group as a personal sounding board to bolster self-confidence and gain support. Some techniques for turning dysfunctional members into functional members include:

1. Recognize contributions and seek feedback.
2. Use a structured approach to group decision making.

3. Designate a specific role that will assist the group in reaching its goals and is do-able by the individual—related to ego, skill, or knowledge.
4. Confront the individual with the problem and ask for feedback and suggestions.
5. Empathize.

Norms

Norms are expectations or rules, agreed on by the group, that govern behavior of group members. While norms are not standardized for every form of behavior, they develop as a group spends time together, and the consequences for violating norms become apparent to all members.

Research shows that norms are established to reduce uncertainty in groups and to encourage conformity by members. Both of these factors lead to increased participation and interaction. A positive side effect also becomes apparent. When norms are in place, even very rigid ones, members are freer with their communication and are more likely to disagree openly than do groups with less cohesion and fewer norms.

According to Litterer, groups bring members into compliance through a four-stage process. In the *education* stage the group introduces important norms. From there the group is involved in *surveillance* to see if the behavior is conforming or deviant. If deviation is observed, a *warning* message is communicated either through verbal or nonverbal means. Finally, *disciplinary* or *rewarding actions* are administered.[12]

In a staff meeting format the sequence might work this way. One member, Ed, had a tendency to always go to meetings unprepared. He neglected to do the necessary research, brought no handouts (which was the norm) and consistently sent the prior week's work to his colleagues two or three weeks late. Ed's colleagues at first stated their displeasure about this behavior in joking ways. When his behavior did not change, they started keeping track of the number of weeks that the behavior persisted. Finally Ed's supervisor read him the riot act, but to no avail. Ten weeks later the group met without Ed and agreed that he should be replaced.

Cohesion

Effective team participation produces another important characteristic—*cohesion.* When this element exists, members feel commitment to each other and the goals of the team. And they establish good, strong communication lines. The more cohesive the team, the more the group communicates, desires social interaction, finds additional goals to pursue, exerts influence over members, adheres to normative behavior, and projects a high degree of member satisfaction. Recent studies confirm that cohesiveness positively influences the amount of information processed.[13]

Nonetheless, cohesion in teams is not easily attained. It takes time. Groups with ongoing interactions can reach a high level of cohesiveness, but there are at least three stages of group development. Individuals must first test and develop personal relationships. Questions such as "Why am I here?"

Koinonia

Curious about the secret to breakthroughs in major scientific discoveries? So was quantum physicist David Bohm. He was particularly intrigued by the fact that noted scientists Einstein and Heisenberg conversed for decades, corresponding and brainstorming, while they exchanged key ideas. Why do some scientists collaborate to solve critical questions while others quarrel over minutiae?

To find the answer, Bohm studied the Athenian philosophers to discover the concept of *koinonia*, Greek for "a spirit of fellowship." Greek philosophers followed the rules of *koinonia* as they debated the great questions of the day. According to Bohm, these ancient rules are essential to teamwork. Trust replaces fear, and information flows freely, "like electricity through a superconductor." MIT management expert Peter Senge describes Bohm's technique in his book *The Fifth Discipline:*

1. Hold regular meetings each week with no agenda. Allow people to express themselves and talk about whatever they wish.
2. Establish dialog by exchanging ideas. Do not try to change the other person's opinion.
3. Suspend critical thinking—try to keep an open mind.
4. Be honest—do not suppress your thinking.

If you follow these four steps, you should reach *koinonia*—respect for your colleagues, a team philosophy, and exciting discoveries.[14]

"Who are these other people?" "Do I really belong here?" and "Do I really want to do this?" must be answered before an individual commits to a team. Once the individual "buys into" the group, conflicts in roles emerge. Unless they are resolved, these "role agendas" can continuously disrupt the group process unless they are resolved. Once roles are clear, team members experience a release of tension and an increase in cohesiveness. Losing a team member is a potential source of trouble. Departure of a member often results in a new role conflict as either a new member becomes part of the group or old members divide the role of the lost team member.

Team *synergy* occurs when a cohesive team matures and allows interdependence of all team members. Such teams have a problem-solving orientation, allow healthy conflict, and are open to criticism and new ideas. Few groups reach this stage of development.

Problem Solving

Effective teams are characterized by their ability to solve problems quickly, efficiently, and accurately. This process is enhanced by strong communication lines and appropriate role behavior. Barriers to success in problem solving can be (1) relational, (2) substantive, or (3) procedural. Many team failures are caused by *interpersonal relations* among group members. Pressure for conformity, use of authority, status differences, personality conflicts, personal goals, and role conflict are a few of the possibilities. *Substantive* barriers occur primarily because of limitations on the information available or how team members use that information to reach a decision. Researchers Hirokawa and Gouran note that "information may be insufficient, incomplete, biased, inaccurate, or of limited relevance."[15] *Procedural* barriers involve the process the team follows to resolve problems. While research has not identified "one best way," team facilitators sometimes apply *group process designs* (GPD) that emphasize group interaction and cooperative action. These techniques address both the task and maintenance functions of the team. Some of these techniques—synectics, the nominal group technique, brainstorming, and forcing techniques—are discussed in Chapter 13.

AVOIDING "GROUPTHINK"

I. L. Janis, in his research on the concept of *groupthink,*[16] identified the characteristics of groups that affect decision making. Groupthink can be defined as extreme concurrence-seeking tendencies in decision-making groups leading to premature consensus.[17] Janis identified five conditions that lead to groupthink: (1) high group cohesiveness, (2) insulation from outside sources of information, (3) lack of methodical procedures for information search and appraisal, (4) directive leadership, and (5) high-stress situations with little hope of finding a solution better than that advocated by the leader.

Additional study of the effect of groupthink on decision making concludes that group cohesiveness is not a factor leading to premature decision making. Highly cohesive groups process more information than groups with low cohesiveness—a key to effective problem resolution. However, directive leadership plays a major role. It negatively influences both the number of solutions proposed and the number of alternatives discussed. In contrast, teams with participative leaders offer more solutions and discuss more alternatives.

In addition to Janis's conditions, studies of the groupthink phenomenon identified seven defective processes that lead to groupthink: (1) incomplete survey of objectives, (2) failure to examine risks of preferred choice solutions, (3) incomplete survey of alternatives, (4) poor information search, (5) selective bias in processing information, (6) failure to re-appraise alternatives, and (7) failure to work out contingency plans.[18]

Repeated research over several decades demonstrates that groups take more risks than individuals acting alone. In a groupthink state, the group has the illusion of invulnerability. This mindset cultivates a "risky shift" wherein extreme confidence and risk taking occur. Group members discard caution and discredit warnings. Members who oppose the group's decisions are stereotyped as ineffectual or inept. The group places direct pressure on members who oppose group agreements. Individuals exercise self-censorship of ideas that contradict the group consensus—and silence *is* considered agreement.[19]

Janis lists numerous historic events attributable to groupthink: Britain's laissez-faire policy toward Hitler before World War II, the unpreparedness of U.S. forces at Pearl Harbor, the Bay of Pigs invasion of Cuba, and the escalation of the Vietnam War. More recent examples include world failure to recognize the impending economic and political collapse of the U.S.S.R. and the space shuttle *Challenger* disaster (see Appendix E).

Leaders who want to avoid groupthink should (1) allow all members to express their opinions before stating their own preferences, (2) encourage discussion of all solutions, (3) emphasize the importance of achieving an optimal solution by exploring all possible information and alternatives, and (4) promote expression of minority viewpoints.[20]

LEADERSHIP CHARACTERISTICS

Attempts to understand how leaders emerge have gone on for centuries. The ancient Greeks concluded that leaders are born, not made—they have natural abilities or talents that allow them to rise to specific situations. Early examples of leaders with the "right traits" are Pompey, Caesar, and Napoleon.

Some of the leadership traits identified by studies have included intelligence, social maturity and breadth, inner motivation and achievement drives, and human relations attitudes.[21] More successful leaders appear to be more informed, less rigid, nonauthoritarian, participative, more agreeable, and less opinionated than less successful leaders.[22] Physical traits of energy, appearance, and height have also been associated with leaders.[23] In a Gallup survey conducted several years ago, 728 chief executives identified the most important traits that people need in order to advance in business. Foremost among these traits were integrity, the ability to get along with others, and industriousness. These same chief executives identified the major failings of subordinates as the inability to understand or work with others and limited points of view.

Generally, the study of traits has not been very successful, since not all leaders possess these traits and many nonleaders do. Researchers have failed to determine how much of each characteristic is necessary to be a successful leader. Most of the traits that have been identified are expected of a person in a position of leadership, and they involve patterns of effective behavior.

LEADERSHIP STYLES

Current studies of leadership focus on leadership styles rather than leadership traits. These studies indicate that different styles—from autocratic to laissez faire—are appropriate in different situations, depending on the people involved. A boss-centered leadership style emphasizes the authority of the manager. For example, a leader may use authority to persuade or coerce employees, present ideas and invite questions, or present a tentative decision subject to change. On the other hand, subordinate-centered leadership occurs when freedom and involvement in decision making lead to a more democratic approach. Robert Tannenbaum and Warren H. Schmidt depict these styles on a continuum of leadership behavior.[24] Figure 12.1 shows the range of behavior and leadership styles associated with each.

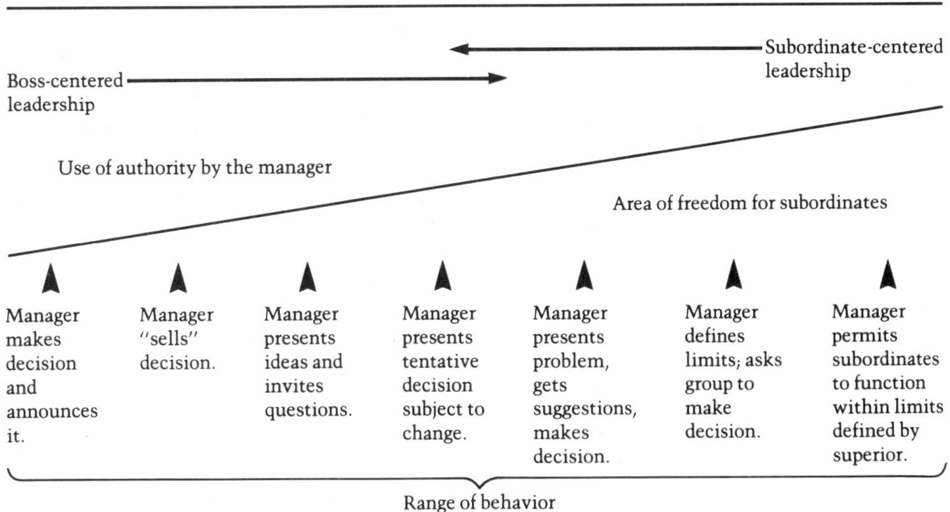

FIGURE 12.1 A Continuum of Leadership Behavior
Source: Robert Tannenbaum and Warren H. Schmidt, "How to Choose a Leadership Pattern," *Harvard Business Review* (May–June 1973), p. 96.

The following discussion describes the leadership styles identified by the Tannenbaum/Schmidt (TS) continuum. A number of well-known leadership theories, associated with each, will also be examined.

Authoritarian

Keenly interested in the way employees responded to their superior's actions, Douglas McGregor formulated his theory X, which identified the characteristics of the autocratic manager. He noted that some managers inspired employees to new levels of productivity and created a climate of support, while others demanded effort, asserted dominance, and alienated employees.[25]

McGregor saw that a very small number of managers act on the assumption that people enjoy being productive and want responsibility. More commonly, managers act on the assumptions that McGregor labeled theory X. The climate of theory X management includes direct supervision; small, distinct tasks without an overall objective; "checking" on workers to ensure that they are following specific instructions; a preponderance of negative rewards and reprimands; communication based on fault finding, criticism, blaming, and accusations; lack of employee input into decision making; and the use of authority or power to silence opposition.

The theory X manager basically demands results and rarely engages in group decision making unless forced to do so. He uses a direct communication style that emphasizes the superior/subordinate relationship, and he frequently reminds you of his position and authority: "I'm the boss, so we'll do it my way."

Democratic

The democratic manager is a positive Pygmalion, as described in Chapter 4. This communicative style includes praising employees for a job well done, delegating projects, clearly outlining expectations, setting high performance standards, minimizing direct orders, using authority to minimize obstacles, and assisting in accomplishing goals. In McGregor's terms, a theory Y manager recognizes and adjusts to personal abilities and encourages growth. Employees' ideas are solicited, particularly about matters concerning their working conditions. The democratic manager keeps employees informed of new developments through staff meetings and team-building techniques in the form of problem-solving conferences. Encouraging employees to advance and develop as well as improve their jobs is a characteristic of the democratic style of leadership.

Participative

According to several theories of leadership, the participative style lies somewhere between the autocratic and democratic leadership approaches. The participative leader invites ideas and usually tries to make constructive use of them, but he maintains control. This leader would stylistically lie right of center in the subordinate-centered range on the TS continuum. A typical scenario might go:

> I have asked you to meet today to discuss the problem we must solve. We have been allotted $X to establish a career center that can be used by all students in the university. You are to determine how this money is to be spent within the following limitations. [Here the manager proceeds to describe these limitations.]

The participative style is more predominant than the democratic style because few managers have full confidence that employees can and will solve problems in the best interest of the organization, without the leader's input and direction. If a theory Y manager goes into an autocratic situation, his staff will need guidelines to follow in learning how to think more freely.

Laissez-faire

Laissez-faire leadership means "leave it alone." Employees offer little input and receive little information from the leader. There is lack of clear performance expectations and minimal direction. Hence, the climate of the organization often becomes chaotic as informal group leaders vie for control and power. Confusion and cliques abound as employees create and follow their own personal goals. An effective leader seeks to change styles depending on the people, task, or situation.

THE SITUATIONAL APPROACH TO LEADERSHIP

A pioneer in research on leader effectiveness, Fred E. Fiedler believed that the work situation would be favorable for the leader if (1) the leader is generally accepted by followers, (2) the task is highly structured, and (3) the leader has position power through formal authority in the organization.[26] If these three dimensions are not positive or have low values, however, the situation will not be favorable. According to Fiedler, the favorableness of the situation combined with leadership style determined leader effectiveness.

Fiedler found that the task-directed or hard-nosed leader was more effective in very favorable and very unfavorable situations. If the situation was only moderately favorable or moderately unfavorable, the more lenient or human relations style of manager was more effective.

Martin Evans and Robert House believed that the same leader can use a variety of styles depending upon the situation.[27] They developed a *path-goal* theory of leadership that relates leadership behavior to employee motivation, satisfaction, and performance. The leadership style that will be most effective is determined by the situation. Thus, leaders must adapt to a dynamic environment, adjusting leadership style according to the people they are leading and the situation in which they find themselves. A leader should use directive leadership with employees who have ambiguous tasks and vague roles. Employees with relatively clear tasks do not like directive leadership. A supportive leadership style has a positive effect on subordinates performing in stressful situations. Finally, the leader should use a participative leadership style if employees have the knowledge and ability to do the task but need the decision-making authority of the leader.

A number of studies isolated task accomplishment and group maintenance or personal relationships as dimensions of leadership behavior.[28] The Ohio State Leadership Studies concentrated on gathering leaders' perceptions of their own styles. The results indicated that managers were not necessarily either task or relationship oriented, but used a combination of task and relationship leadership behaviors. A four-quadrant model, rather than a continuum, was developed to depict the possible combinations of these leadership behaviors.[29]

A Model for Leader Effectiveness

At the Center for Leadership Studies, Paul Hersey and Kenneth H. Blanchard developed a model for leader effectiveness using the concepts presented in the Ohio State studies.[30] Each quadrant is based on the variables of task and relationship and represents one of four basic leadership styles:

1. *High task, low relationship.* The leader clearly defines roles and communicates to group members specific directions concerning what tasks they are assigned, how to complete the tasks, and when the tasks must be completed. This style is most appropriate when employees are new to the job and low in both job and psychological maturity.
2. *High task, high relationship.* The leader remains directive but communicates encouragement through feedback and interaction. This style is used when an employee is low in psychological maturity and high in job maturity.
3. *High relationship, low task.* The leader and subordinate communicate or share decision-making and problem-solving tasks. The employee has the knowledge and the ability to do the task but needs emotional support, which the leader provides.
4. *Low relationship, low task.* The employee has the knowledge and the ability to do the task with minimal interaction with, and communication from, the leader.

These behavior categories are related to the maturity of the employee, both emotionally and in terms of job skills. Thus, the Hersey and Blanchard model differentiates among employees with varying levels of willingness or motivation to do the job as well as varying levels of competency to do it.

Effective leaders are flexible and are comfortable with all four leadership styles. They can move from highly directive behavior to very supportive behavior. As directive leaders, they tell employees what, when, where, and how to do something using structure, control and supervision as tools. A supportive leader lets employees be responsible for their work and depends upon praising, listening, and facilitating. In between these extremes are a number of variations and combinations of styles. Similar to the styles identified by Evans and House, Blanchard describes four styles as:

1. *Commanding.* The commanding leader gives specific directions to subordinates and is highly task oriented. The communication style is direct and specific. Team members are given instructions about roles and goals. Little attention is paid to interaction or relationships.
2. *Prompting.* The leader who uses a prompting style solicits and implements subordinates' ideas, yet maintains decision-making power. Because this leader is high in both task and relationship behavior, the communication style is still somewhat directive. Team members are given information and explanations. Leader solicits suggestions and praises acceptable performance of assigned tasks.
3. *Reinforcing.* The reinforcing leader supports the efforts of subordinates, is approachable, and has genuine concern for people. This style is a combination of high-relationship and low-task behavior. The communication style facilitates participative interaction. This leader listens, encourages, and gives encouraging feedback.
4. *Delegating.* The delegating leader applies achievement-oriented leadership by entrusting responsibility and authority to subordinates. This leader sets challenging goals, has confidence in subordinate's abilities, and expects subordinates to accomplish tasks. This leader presents expectations and gives feedback on results. The style falls in the low task, low relationship area, and communication is minimal.[31]

If leaders must adapt to the people and the situation, it makes sense then that leaders must (1) have the flexibility to use a variety of leadership styles, (2) be able to determine which style is appropriate, and (3) be able to gain agreement with employees about their goals and the style that meets their needs to reach these goals.[32]

Leaders must decide which leadership style to use and when to use it. Individuals develop at different paces depending upon the task. Being too directive or too supportive of team members who do not need this style of leadership can undermine the team's efficiency and effectiveness in reaching its goals. Since teams go through different stages of development and each team member is unique in level of skill, ability, knowledge, and motivation,

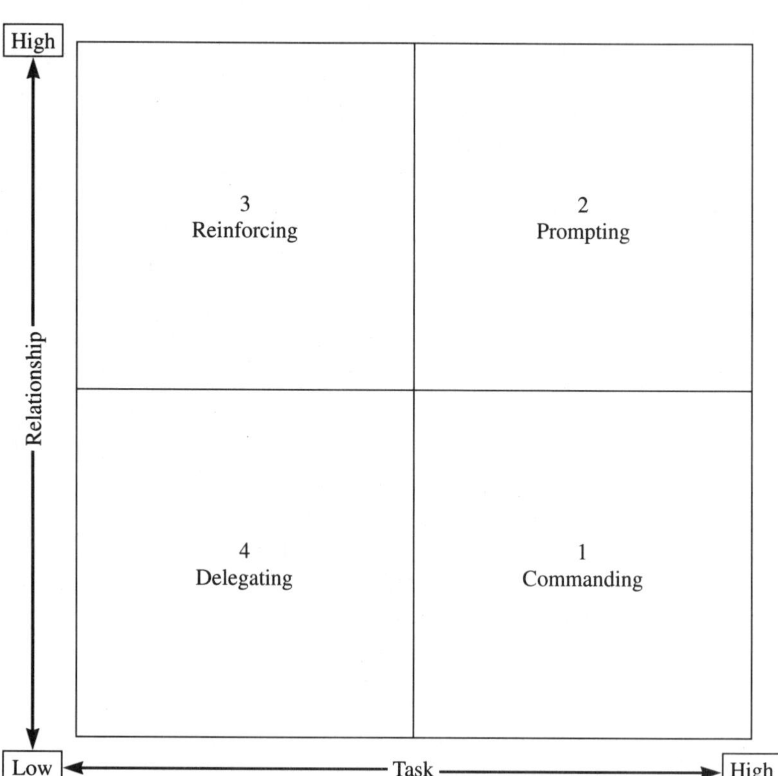

FIGURE 12.2 Situational Leadership: The Four Quadrants
Source: Adapted from Paul Hersey, *Situational Leader* (New York City: Warner Books, Inc. 1984).

leaders must constantly assess the need to adjust their leadership style. The best way to gauge their need for direction or support is to observe reactions and ask for feedback.

Team Building and the Leadership Grid®

In an attempt to measure perception, Robert R. Blake and Jane S. Mouton developed attitude scales to assess perceptions of leader behavior (see Figure 12.3). The Leadership Grid® emphasizes team development rather than individual development. The focus is placed on managerial styles in place of interpersonal relationships. Emphasis is on decision making as a team.

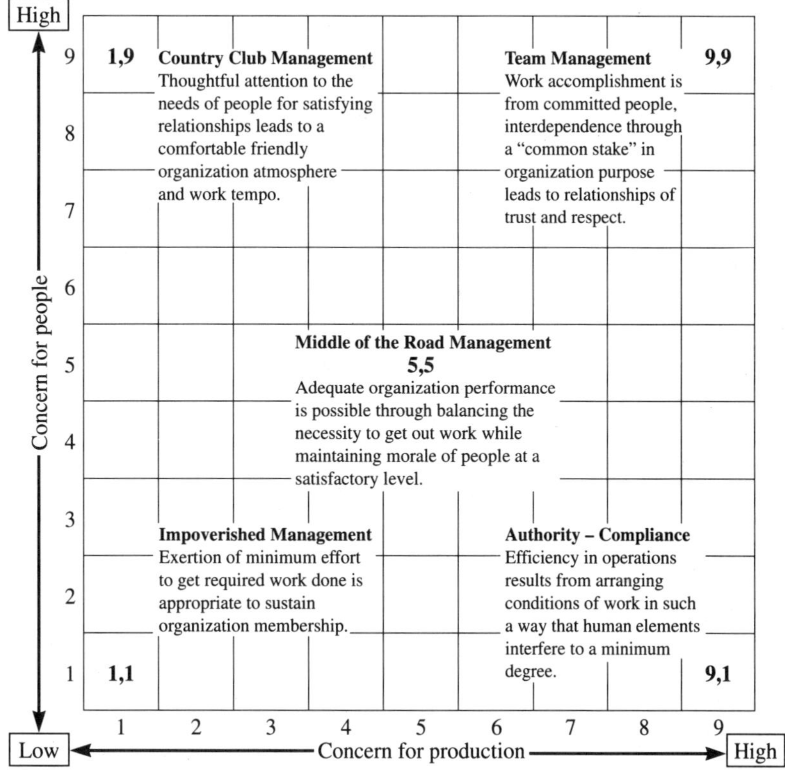

FIGURE 12.3 The Leadership Grid®
Source: The Grid® designation is the property of Scientific Methods, Inc. and is used here with permission.

The grid is set up so that the horizontal axis, numbered 1 through 9, represents concern for productivity. The vertical axis on a 1 through 9 basis represents concern for people. The primary objective is for managers to work for team management, a 9,9 organizational climate, or maximum concern for people and maximum concern for production. Team members apply grid concepts to their own managerial culture. Ground rules and relationships for 9,9 management in individual groups are defined. An attempt is made to build maximum concern for production and maximum concern for people beyond the single work group. Operating tensions are explored with the purpose of going beyond win/lose relationships into problem solving.

The second objective of organizational development is to initiate orga-

Empowering Leaders

Through the Leadership Education and Development (LEAD) program, a partnership between Ford Motor company and the University of Michigan School of Business, Ford managers are experiencing self-empowerment by empowering employees.

LEAD changes the way managers think by breaking old patterns of thinking. Michigan professors and Ford managers work with cross-functional teams to challenge employees with new ideas and create a realistic context. Robert Quinn chairs the Organizational Behavior and Human Resource Management department at the university and is chief developer of LEAD. Quinn structured the program around several management principles: "the hierarchy, which emphasizes measurement, documentation, and information management; the firm, which makes the bottom line the overriding consideration; the 'adhocracy,' a relatively new concept that stresses adaptability, change, innovation, and creativity; and the team, with its emphasis on human resources, development of commitment, and participative decision making."[31]

The results: Ford managers "came in cynical and went out on fire," says Quinn. "Bosses, peers, and subordinates are saying, 'What did you do to this guy?'" Organizational teams are forming within Ford that capitalize on these changes. New networks of managers who have already been through the program are creating "coalitions of empowerment." Says one mid-level manager, "I used to feel other departments such as the computer operations people were the enemy. Now I take the initiative to call and involve them. It works a lot better than blaming them after the fact."[32]

nizational goal setting. Problems involved at this level are important to all groups within the company, such as cost control, union/management relations, safety, promotion policies, and overall profit improvement. Major organizational concerns, in which stakes are real, are attacked. Teams must define and assess the problem and their goals and then put their plan to work.

Finally, a stabilization phase works to support the entire program. Organizational changes are measured and reinforced to withstand pressures that may cause a "slip back" or regression. This phase also serves to evaluate the program's consistency with company goals. Blake had startling results that showed a positive change in every quantitative measure taken after the program had been in effect for one year.

The steps in the Leadership Grid® and its implementation are similar to the organizational development steps of (1) diagnosis, (2) intervention, and

(3) maintenance. In other words, management must first recognize that a problem exists, analyze it, then act to resolve it. The Leadership Grid® provides a systematic method whereby the analysis can occur on an individual group basis as well as an organizational basis. It incorporates an essential quality of team building: recognizing the strengths and weaknesses of each team member and then placing each member in a role that capitalizes on his or her strengths and interests.

A GLOBAL PERSPECTIVE

Leadership at the Moscow Low Voltage Equipment Factory

Success in implementing organizational change and building teams under conditions in the former U.S.S.R. was tenuous at best. But there are a few success stories from the communist era. In 1986, when Yuri Sergeyevich Korolyov was brought in to run the Moscow Low Voltage Equipment Factory, workers had little reason to be concerned about productivity. Ministries told company heads what and how much to produce, but overoptimistic goals set by the ministry were rarely met. Because workers received the same salary regardless of breakdowns and delays, workers ignored basic maintenance procedures.

While the low-tech plant, which produced a variety of devices including washing machines, engines and microwave timers, was a far cry from Western standards, it still had come a long way. Korolyov sought and received permission to turn the company into a worker-owned cooperative. Since workers felt they had a stake in productivity, the plant "stopped losing money, developed a host of new products and raised wages by a colossal 65 percent." Wages surpassed the nationwide average, revenues soared, and the factory posted a profit. "We're more interested in the results of our work now," said Valentine Molakova, one of the 1,600 owner-workers who assembled electronic controls. Creativity was rewarded. One engineer developed a Western-style timer and received a 4,000-ruble bonus. Workers responsible for defective products performed repairs themselves—and lost pay. As a result, more attention was paid to quality work.

As *perestroika* collapsed, President Mikhail Gorbachev lost control, and old-guard communists struggled to prevent change, Korolyov was turning the cooperative into one of a few Soviet shareholding companies. His goals were to make profits and modernize. Because of the collapse of government, components became difficult to get, economic regulations changed almost daily, and the system no longer existed that could coerce suppliers. Even with these difficulties, Korolyov welcomed the new system: "Now everyone is capable of having self-esteem and proving himself."[33]

ETHICS: RIGHT OR WRONG?

The Power Struggle

Maurice Barboza was dedicated to his cause. The idea had come to him while he was researching his own ancestry. He discovered that his white great-great grandfather, John Curtis Gay, died fighting for the Union side during the Civil War. He also discovered that an ancestor of John Curtis Gay had fought in the Revolutionary War. With this evidence in hand, Barboza joined the Sons of the American Revolution and helped his aunt become a member of the DAR.

Further research led to his desire to erect a memorial to all African Americans who served in the revolution. Few memorials in Washington recognized the contributions of this population. A large proportion of African Americans—over 5,000 out of a total of 20,000 regulars and 6,000 militiamen that George Washington recorded under his command in 1776—served during the Revolution. Most Americans know of only one: Crispus Attucks, the war's first casualty in 1770.

Barboza energetically pursued his mission: achieving recognition for all the people who fought for freedom—not just soldiers, but the "wagon drivers, sailors, merchants, blacksmiths, spies, and others." He wanted to accomplish two things: to honor African Americans' contributions and to educate Americans about the African-American historical presence by erecting a memorial in the nation's capital—goals he vigorously sought full-time beginning in 1987. He sold his house and moved into an apartment, which he used as the main office for achieving his goal. After three grueling years of pushing the proposal, he got Congress to approve the design and grant the land. The location was to be between the Lincoln Monument and the Washington Memorial. Efforts to raise money remained—$4 million for the monument and $2 million to maintain it.

Barboza recruited a board of interested and influential individuals. Most had expressed interest in the project, and most were African American. The board was chaired by Margaret Johnston, a long-time friend of Barboza's known for her humanitarian efforts. Other members were Charles Countee, Washington, D.C., Mayor Sharon Pratt Kelly's director of business and economic development; C. Payne Lucas, founder and director of Africare and a former colleague of Johnston's from the Peace Corps; William O. Robinson, dean of the District of Columbia School of Law; Joyce Taylor, management consultant; and Robert H. Frank, former treasurer for the Vietnam Memorial.

Initial fundraising efforts went well. General Motors sponsored a star-studded gala that raised about $250,000. The costs of fundraising and early design work quickly depleted much of the $800,000 that ultimately was raised. Money problems also created tension within the board. An insider noted, "I felt there were board members who were supposed to set up the contacts, and if somebody did not want (Barboza) to be successful, they could do that. I could sense a power struggle going on."

Comments from top executives indicated mixed reactions to fundraising strategies. Alvaro Martens, a Xerox Corp executive, stated, "If you ask corporations for $1,000, they don't pay attention to you. You have to ask them for $10,000 or $100,000." Fundraising consultant Sandy Faurial, who helped raise $10 million for the Vietnam Memorial, summarized Barboza's efforts by describing him as typical of someone engaged in a cause: "They are not good at separating themselves from the cause and so they are uncomfortable with asking people for money, because it feels like it's for themselves. As a result, there was a hesitancy on Maurice's part to go boldly forward, to follow up on contact that were made."

In November 1922, all board members resigned with the exception of Barboza's aunt. A new board was installed consisting of three members, all former military officers. The chair, retired Army general Jerry Ralph Curry, demanded Barboza's resignation. Barboza, who held out until December 1, 1992, set conditions on back pay and disallowed use of his name in any way. "I want them to realize they destroyed this project," he stated. "They cannot continue, they will resign, and leave the project to a group I am trying to put together, and allow us to reorganize. . . . The project is about principles and they don't have any. It's about honesty and everything they've done has been unscrupulous and under the table."

Curry has attempted to broaden Barboza's original idea by including other ethnic groups in the memorial and enlarging the board with "representatives of the Jewish community, the entertainment industry, and . . . some younger people." According to H. Minton Francis, the new president of the foundation, who served in the Nixon and Ford administrations as a deputy assistant secretary of Defense, "The memorial is very much alive. And it is more important than he or me or any one individual."[34]

Case Questions

1. Discuss the concept of cohesion as it relates to this case.
2. What did Barboza mean by his comment, "The project is about principles and they don't have any"?
3. What is the ethical dilemma presented by this case?

SUMMARY

Effective teams develop through effective communication strategies. Teams are important because they (1) encourage interaction and participation, (2) generate more ideas and alternatives (3) facilitate commitment, and (4) develop understanding. Barriers to success of teams in problem solving can be relational, substantive, or procedural.

All teams have task and maintenance functions. A team's task function is to achieve the goal toward which it is working. The maintenance function is to meet the interpersonal needs of the group members. The longer the group meets, the more attention it requires for its maintenance needs.

Effective teams share specific goals, monitor their successes, share rewards, sacrifice for the good of the team, and consist of members who understand their roles and are involved in all aspects of the team's mission. Communication in such teams flows easily between all members and is of a high quality—precise, internally consistent, positively reinforcing, cooperative.

As teams move toward fulfillment of their goals, leadership may emerge from within the group. Some team members may act as facilitators to help the team move through the process of diagnosing a problem. The team leader coordinates team interaction, keeps the team on target, helps team members develop the mission and goals, makes certain all team members participate, maintains team harmony, identifies areas of team agreement, and removes barriers.

Irving L. Janis identified the concept of groupthink, the tendency to agree with the group and accept a premature decision. Since groups take more risks than individuals, leaders should avoid the effect of groupthink by refraining from stating their preferred choices, by encouraging discussion of all possible solutions, by emphasizing the importance of reaching a solution through exploration of all possible information and alternatives, and by fostering free expression of minority viewpoints.

Current studies focus on leadership styles that are appropriate in different situations. A boss-centered leadership style emphasizes the authority of the manager. Subordinate-centered leadership occurs when freedom and involvement in decision making lead to a more democratic approach. Leaders can alter their style to suit the individuals and the situation. Directive leadership is used when subordinates need strong supervision. A coaching style may be necessary if team members need direction and encouragement. Supportive leadership demonstrates concern for people in a high stress situation. Delegating is an appropriate style for mature, knowledgeable, and skilled team members. Leaders must decide when each style is appropriate, be flexible in adjusting leadership styles, and gain agreement from the team members about which style works.

KEY WORDS

autocratic style
coaching
cohesion
communication in groups
delegating
democratic style
diagnosis
directing
dysfunctional role
facilitator
flexible
goals
groupthink
laissez faire
leadership
Leadership Grid®
norms
participative style
problem solving
procedural
relational
relationship function
roles
situational leadership
substantive
supportive
synergy
task function
trait

REVIEW QUESTIONS

1. Why are groups important in the business environment? List the advantages and disadvantages of groups.
2. Describe the task and maintenance group functions. Describe the communication roles for each.

3. What are the characteristics of teams?
4. Define groupthink. What are its symptoms? What can group leaders do to avoid groupthink?
5. What are the barriers to group problem solving?
6. What are some leadership traits? What are the problems with the trait theory of leadership?
7. What are leadership styles? Describe the leadership styles of the following people:
   - The President of the United States
   - A member of the U.S. Senate or House of Representatives
   - The president of your company or university
   - Your immediate boss

EXERCISES

1. Four years ago, you accepted a job with a large accounting firm as a junior member even though you had several years of experience with another small firm. Many of your peers earn several thousand dollars more than you do even though they have less experience. You become acutely aware that you are just as competent, if not more so, than they are. As a matter of fact, you find you are carrying a heavier workload. Because of the promotion policies of the firm, it is not likely that you will ever catch up in salary earnings. How do you feel about this situation? What can you do about it?
2. Lately you've noticed one of your clerks hanging around the coffee pot in your secretary's office, yet her unit is shorthanded and her supervisor, your subordinate, is coping with some personal hardships. Investigating the situation, you find that the clerk (1) has a college degree (2) is earning several thousand dollars less than other employees with degrees in your organization, (3) does not get along with her supervisor, (4) has been involved in numerous interpersonal conflicts with clients and staff members, (5) openly criticizes the organization, and (6) is seeking employment elsewhere. Define the problem. What can you do about it?
3. Keep a journal in which you record the nature of group interaction that occurs each time a group of which you are a member meets. From your entries, identify the developmental stages your group went through. How cohesive was the group? Did the group reach a stage of interdependence in problem solving?
4. In a small group, develop a plan for a tall, self-supporting structure made of 28 blocks (blocks should be approximately 2×2 inches). Limit your planning time to 10 minutes. At the end of this time, you are allowed 40 seconds to build your structure. One team member should make sure that the group follows the time allotted. The structure must stand without support. When you have completed your structure, discuss the team's approach. How did they plan the structure? What role did communication play in contributing to the team's success? What type of leadership emerged? What facilitating functions occurred? How did time constraints affect the team's outcome?

REFERENCES

1. Bruce G. Posner, "Divided We Fall: What Happens When Employees Start Working at Cross-Purposes," *Inc.* (July 1989), pp. 105–106.
2. Warren Bennis, "Leadership: A Beleaguered Species?" in Stewart Ferguson and Sherry Devereaux, eds., *Intercom: Readings in Organizational Communication* (Rochelle Park, N.Y.: Hayden, 1980), p. 159.
3. Ibid., p. 159.
4. Lawrence B. Rosenfield, *Human Interaction in the Small-Group Setting* (Columbus, Ohio: Charles E. Merrill, 1973), p. 7.
5. Harold P. Zelko and Frank E. X. Dance, *Business and Professional Speech Communication* (New York: Holt, Rinehart and Winston, 1965), p. 161.
6. Randy Y. Hirokawa and Dennis S. Gouran, "Facilitation of Group Communication: A Critique of Prior

Research and an Agenda for Future Research," *Management Communication Quarterly* 3:1 (August 1989), p. 71.

7. Fran Tarkenton and Joseph H. Boyett, "The Competitive Edge: Winning Strategies From a Pro," *Entrepreneur* (May 1989), pp. 14–16.
8. Hirokawa and Gouran, "Group Communication," p. 77.
9. R. F. Bales, *Interaction Process Analysis: A Method for the Study of Small Groups* (Reading, Mass.: Addison-Wesley, 1950), p. 59.
10. John (Sam) Keltner, "Facilitation: Catalyst for Group Problem Solving," *Management Communication Quarterly,* 3:1 (August 1989), p. 22.
11. Ibid., p. 23.
12. Joseph Litterer, *The Analysis of Organizations* (New York: John Wiley & Sons, 1967).
13. Carrie R. Leana, "A Partial Test of Janis' Groupthink Model: Effects of Group Cohesiveness and Leader Behavior on Defective Decision," *Journal of Management,* 11:1 (1985), pp. 5–17.
14. Richard Poe, "The Secret to Teamwork: How Koinonia, An Ancient Greek Concept, Can Help You Now," *Success* (June 1991), p. 72. Used with permission.
15. Hirokawa and Gouran, "Group Communication," p. 81.
16. Irving L. Janis, *Victims of Groupthink: A Psychological Study of Policy Decisions and Fiascos* (Boston: Houghton Mifflin, 1971); *Groupthink,* 2d ed. (Boston: Houghton Mifflin, 1982); and *Decision Making: A Psychological Analysis of Conflict, Choice and Commitment* (New York: Macmillan, 1977).
17. Leana, "Partial Test," p. 5–17.
18. Ibid., p. 6.
19. Janis, *Victims of Groupthink,* pp. 197–198.
20. Leana, "Partial Test," p. 10.
21. Keith Davis, *Human Behavior at Work,* 4th ed. (New York: McGraw-Hill, 1972), pp. 103–104.
22. John G. Geier, "A Trait Approach to the Study of Leadership in Small Groups," *Journal of Communication,* 17 (1967), pp. 316–323.
23. Hugh C. Russell, "An Investigation of Leadership Maintenance Behavior," Ph.D. dissertation, Indiana University, 1970.
24. Robert Tannenbaum and Warren H. Schmidt, "How to Choose a Leadership Pattern," *Harvard Business Review* (March/April 1958), p. 96.
25. Douglas McGregor, *The Human Side of Enterprise* (New York: McGraw-Hill, 1960).
26. Fred E. Fiedler, *A Theory of Leadership Effectiveness* (New York: McGraw-Hill, 1967), pp. 142–148.
27. Robert J. House and Terence R. Mitchell, "Path-Goal Theory of Leadership," *Journal of Contemporary Business* (Autumn 1974), pp. 81–97.
28. D. Katz, N. Macoby and Nancy C. Morse, *Productivity, Supervision, and Morale in an Office Situation* (Ann Arbor, Mich.: Survey Research Center, 1950); Dorwin Cartwright and Alvin Zander, eds., *Group Dynamics: Research and Theory,* 2nd ed. (Evanston, Ill.: Row, Peterson and Company, 1960); Roger M. Stogdill and Alvin E. Coons, eds., *Leader Behavior: Its Description and Measurement, Research Monograph No. 88* (Columbus, Ohio: Bureau of Business Research, The Ohio State University, 1957).
29. Paul Hersey and Kenneth H. Blanchard, *Management of Organizational Behavior: Utilizing Human Resources* (Englewood Cliffs, New Jersey: Prentice-Hall, Inc., 1982), p. 89.
30. Paul Hersey and Kenneth H. Blanchard, *Management of Organizational Behavior,* 2d ed. (Englewood Cliffs, N.J.: Prentice-Hall, 1972), pp. 27–87.
31. Adapted from Paul Hersey, *Situational Leader* (New York City: Warner Books, 1984).
32. Ibid.
33. Robert Quinn, *Beyond Rational Management: Mastering the Paradoxes and Competing Demands of High Performance* (Jossey Bass, 1988).
34. "Unique Program Empowers Managers with Leadership Initiative," *Human Capital* (July 1990), pp. 51–52. Reprinted by permission.
35. Steven Greenhouse, "A Rare Success Story in Moscow," *The New York Times* (December 11, 1989).
36. Adapted from an article by Megan Rosenfeld, "He Had a Dream—and Lost It: The founder of a Memorial to Black Patriots is Toppled in Bitter Power Struggle," *The Washington Post National Weekly* (February 8–14, 1993), pp. 10–11. Reprinted by permission.

CHAPTER 13

COMMUNICATION STRATEGIES: EFFECTIVE PROBLEM RESOLUTION

On January 28, 1986, the name Christa McAuliffe became a household word. Early that morning the space shuttle *Challenger* aborted its mission seconds after liftoff in a fiery explosion over the coast of Florida. In that instant the first teacher in space was lost forever. The image of the fatal explosion would be transmitted over and over again on national television, and we would watch a country react in agony to the deaths of McAuliffe and her fellow astronauts.

The direct cause was identified as failure of the "O-ring" seals on the solid rocket booster (SRB). The indirect cause was the result of poorly structured communication and reporting procedures. Some engineers and technicians were almost certain of the cause of the *Challenger* explosion the moment it occurred. Teams had been working on the redesign of the seals and had submitted modifications that were under review. The night before the launch, key personnel advised against the decision to send the *Challenger* on its mission. Their arguments failed to persuade those in charge.

The recommendations of the Presidential Commission on the Space Shuttle *Challenger* Accident, appointed by President Ronald Reagan, went to the heart of the problem: reorganize the entire shuttle management structure to improve accountability, communication, participation, and quality of decision making.[1] The lesson, however, had been an irreparably costly one.

TYPES OF PROBLEM RESOLUTION

In an hour's time a manager may engage in decisions ranging from the investment of millions of dollars to who will be in charge of the office Christmas party. Each time a manager makes a decision, it represents an attempt to resolve a problem. These problems do not often easily identify themselves, but usually other indicators demonstrate that things are not as they should be. A *problem* is the difference between the existing situation and the desired situation, whether it involves something that needs fixing or an opportunity to improve current operations.

Before solving a problem, every manager must first determine who should be involved in the problem-solving process. There are three alternatives: (1) solve the problem alone, (2) involve a group, or (3) hire a consultant. In selecting an alternative, managers aim to maximize the effectiveness of both the quality and acceptance of a solution. Research indicates that creative or independent tasks are best performed by individuals. Tasks that involve integrative functions of the organization or goal setting are more appropriate for groups. Furthermore, if the task is complex, the group problem-solving process is likely to be the most appropriate. However, if the knowledge needed to resolve the problem is not available from those in the group, the manager may need to use an outside resource.

Any decision needs to be weighed considering the following factors:

1. The nature of the problem.
2. How important the acceptance of the decision is to its implementation.
3. The value placed on the quality of the decision.
4. The competency and investment of each person involved, and the role played in implementing the decision.
5. The anticipated operating effectiveness of the group, especially its leadership.[2]

To be an effective leader, a manager must solve problems creatively, efficiently, and effectively. Communication skills play a key role in every phase of problem solving. This chapter focuses on principles and strategies associated with problem solving and decision making, with emphasis on the three approaches to decision making: decisions made by the manager, decisions made by a group, and decisions made with the assistance of a consultant.

Managerial Decision Making

Managers are paid to make decisions and solve problems. Sometimes they have the input of others to help them. Often they must make decisions alone, relying on personal experience and knowledge. This approach involves risk.

If employees fail to understand the decision, disagree with the decision, or do not feel a part of the decision-making process, implementation may fail or cause considerable disruption of the work group. The course of action the manager selects will directly or indirectly affect the organization.[3]

When an employee working on an important project suddenly becomes ill, the manager must quickly decide on a substitute so that the project can be completed. The manager knows staff capabilities, and the staff in turn understands that in a critical situation someone must help with the workload. Little time may be available for discussion or input from group members. The manager may issue a direct command such as, "Vinetta, you'll fill in for Ricardo this week while he is ill." In this situation, acceptance of the decision will probably be high, since the employee understands the constraints: it is an immediate need, it is a temporary assignment, and it is a sympathetic situation. If a decision requires complex procedures and strategies for implementation, the participation of several individuals is usually required, even if the manager has high credibility with subordinates. Lack of

Hurricane Andrew

Hurricane Andrew, which hit the Miami coast of Florida in late August 1992, became the most costly hurricane on record. The damage in Florida was absolute; whole towns were leveled, and the homeless numbered over 250,000. Authorities attributed twenty-four deaths to the effects of Andrew. After devastating Florida, Hurricane Andrew gained strength in the Gulf of Mexico and turned toward Louisiana.[4]

Managers at numerous public and private agencies in Louisiana monitored events in Florida and quickly implemented disaster relief efforts. Red Cross shelters were established for residents in areas targeted for a major hit. Thousands vacated their homes to seek safety and shelter.

How successful were these efforts? While only three lives were lost in Louisiana as a result of the storm, the hurricane damaged homes, crops, and businesses. Power and telephone service were almost nonexistent. Acting on emergency plans, utility crews from other states rushed to Louisiana and reestablished damaged power sources in hospitals and other critical facilities even before the hurricane had fully subsided. However, many residents did not know who to contact or where to go for help. A report prepared by Federal Emergency Management Agency personnel cited lack of an effective communication network and poor planning as causes of slow emergency response in many parts of the state.[5]

adequate information, lack of understanding, or unwillingness to participate will hinder staff implementation of the decision and may lead to disaster.

Less ferocious hurricanes have claimed ten times as many lives as Andrew. Because of technological advances in tracking weather conditions, many lives were saved that in previous years would have been lost. Acquiring accurate information is essential to effective decision making. With new technologies for gathering and analyzing information constantly emerging, it is critical for the manager to stay abreast of the latest developments. Automation has impacted decision making and problem solving on every level. Advanced information systems can provide immediate access to electronic factbooks, artificial intelligence, and multimedia, *smart* databases. *Correct* information is critical to effective planning and personal credibility. Consider the emerging technologies described in the following box.

Artificial Intelligence

Artificial intelligence (AI) systems are designed to accomplish tasks by programming qualitative approaches to problem solving into machines. System design allows the addition or deletion of information or criteria. Thus, a manager can compare options and evaluate a solution before implementing it. AI relies primarily on probability and logical reasoning rather than quantitative calculations. Organizations are rapidly integrating AI into their database management systems in the form of spreadsheets, expert systems, and statistical modeling.

Expert systems, designed for strategic advantage, effectively solve problems by incorporating the problem-solving processes of an expert, using "if . . . then" statements, control strategies, and much specific knowledge (facts, rules, objects). The user inputs the problem statement and receives a response. According to a study by Cooper and Lybrand, "43 percent of the major financial services institutions are using, developing, or actively researching expert systems applications."[6] It has been projected that over half of the top executives will use computers regularly within the decade, even though only 10 to 15 percent use them today.[7]

Executive information systems (EIS) will allow these managers to use both external and internal information to make qualitative and subjective decisions, communicate with employees, and manage their schedules. EIS speeds problem solving and decision making by allowing executives to get immediate answers to questions, monitor productivity, gather information, respond to the marketplace, set up videoconferencing, and customize solutions.

In summary, managers will be confronted with many decisions that require immediate or individual action. The answers to the following questions are keys to effective implementation:

1. Does the manager have the authority to make the decision?
2. Does the manager have time to involve others in the decision?
3. Does the manager have all the information needed to make the decision?
4. Will the decision be accepted by those who must implement it?

Group Decision Making

Group decision making is most effective when the need for acceptance is high or the task is complex. This approach offers numerous advantages. For example, a group represents more knowledge than any one person in the group possesses. The group works together to solve the problem, thus promoting wider understanding and acceptance of ideas and solutions. The differing backgrounds, experiences, and education represented by group members lead to a greater variety of ideas and solutions. Fewer communication problems arise because participants work together to evaluate, analyze, and implement solutions. The solutions are usually solid because the group tests ideas from multiple viewpoints.

The manager may choose to delegate decision making to a committee, voluntary group, or group of specialists. In order to make a decision, several approaches may be used: consensus, compromise, or majority rule.

Consensus

Consensus decision making means that everyone in the group can live with the solution. There is no voting or compromise. Group members are encouraged not to compete internally, since no one wins or loses. Quick, early decisions and agreements are discouraged, and the group is encouraged to challenge and test the ideas of each member. The most important characteristic of the consensus approach is that group members listen and pay attention to what each has to say. Quiet members are encouraged to participate and offer their ideas. When the group reaches the point where each person can say, "Although this may not be everything I want, I can accept and support this decision," then the group has reached consensus.[8]

The consensus group should have a workable number of members. The ideal membership is about five,[9] which gives every member an opportunity to participate in a lively interchange of ideas. If groups get too large, it is difficult to reach agreement and other forms of decision making may be necessary.

Compromise

Each party involved in the decision gives up something or gains something, as in union negotiating or in bartering. The compromise may result in side payments or become coercive in nature. For example, a manager may accept a new title such as assistant director in lieu of an increase in salary.[10]

Majority

When large groups are involved, it is often necessary to resort to majority rule. A vote is taken in which the majority wins and the minority loses. The disadvantages of this form of decision making are that the minority may be a substantial portion of the membership and may attempt to influence or sabotage the majority decision. Since the minority has no power, the majority may disregard the opinion of a fixed or small minority.

The outcome of any decision depends on the *quality* of the decision and the *acceptance* of the decision by the group members. All the forms of decision making discussed thus far hinge on these factors. If the quality of a decision is very poor, then it does not matter how great its acceptance is. Many groups can be very enthusiastic about a decision that has been challenged very little within the group but that may in fact be very weak.

This is also true of the acceptance of a decision. A high-quality decision may be made by a manager or consultant, as in the goal-setting example presented earlier. But if acceptance of the decision by the organization is low, then task effectiveness will be poor.

Assets and Liabilities of Group Decision Making

According to R. F. Maier, the group approach to decision making has both assets and liabilities. As opposed to managerial decisions, the assets of group decisions include more accumulated knowledge, more approaches to solving a problem, increased acceptance of the solution, increased commitment to its implementation, and reduced chances for communication failure. Poorly prepared group and poorly planned group processes can be extremely costly because they can lead to weak solutions. The group can influence or pressure individual members to change. This tendency may work for or against the quality of the solution, depending on the individual.[11]

Risk taking is a more predominant characteristic of groups than of individuals. Group members tend to trust that their combined knowledge and experience provide a sound basis for the decision. As a result, the group may fail to identify areas of weakness. Because the group wants to reach agreement and complete its task successfully, it may jump to conclusions that are not based on appropriate or adequate information. A minority viewpoint may be critical to identifying a solution's weaknesses.

Once a solution has been identified, attempts to persuade participants to agree to it begin regardless of its quality. Such pressure can be applied in many ways. For example, negative or positive comments made by an influential group member can affect the acceptance of a solution whether or not it is the best option. Through persuasion, persistence, or degree of participation, dominant individuals can influence the outcome of the group decision. As Alexander Pope noted in the eighteenth century in *The Rape of the Lock,* "And wretches hang, that jury men may dine."

Maier also points out that group leaders can exert an undue influence on the effectiveness of group decision making. Disagreement can lead to innovation or stifle creativity, depending on how the leader handles the discussion. Conflicting interests may be caused by failure to communicate effectively. The leader needs to ensure that participants agree on the problem and goals before they attempt to agree on a solution.

Group decision making can be an exciting experience that leads to a sense of security and belonging resulting in pleasure and satisfaction to participants. This satisfaction, however, if not handled well, may have harmful effects on group decision making. Irving Janis in his book *Victims of Groupthink* illustrates this point vividly. He describes fiascos in governmental decisions where group pressure decreases the emphasis given to techniques that produce quality decisions. Group members emerge as "mindguards" that protect the cohesiveness of the group. The groups resist contrary information and suppress differing opinions. Several other studies have pointed out that groups may make riskier decisions than any one member might make individually. There is also a tendency to stereotype group members in certain roles such as leaders, followers, or troublemakers.

The Consultation

When neither the manager of the organization nor the subordinates have sufficient knowledge to solve a problem, they must find another resource. That resource may be a *consultant* who specializes in troubleshooting technical problems by defining and analyzing the problem and then implementing the solution. The good consultant understands that acceptance of a solution by the group is critical. A high-quality solution could be proposed but then sabotaged if trust is not established with the group.

Objective consultants can help an organization clearly identify problems, help train employees to deal with these problems, and create a climate that contributes to effective decision making. This is particularly true in union negotiations, when assistance is needed from a third party who is knowledgeable about both the union and company policies and is skilled in communication techniques. Consultants are used to help evaluate organizational structures and technical processes or provide expertise in any area in which the organization lacks knowledge and skill.

Whether a manager chooses to make the decision alone, involve others within the organization, or engage a consultant, he or she will need to follow a process that ensures effective problem solving. Although numerous approaches exist, the six-step model described here is highly effective.

A Six-Step Decision-Making and Problem-Solving Model

The description of problem solving as a process implies that some order of approaching a problem has utility. A process allows agreement about the problem to be achieved through communicating perceptions in an organized manner. *Decision making* includes problem identification, problem analysis, generation of alternatives or solutions, and evaluation and selection of alternatives. *Problem solving* includes all stages of decision making together with implementation and evaluation of the effectiveness of the solution. These six steps are shown in Figure 13.1.

Each manager must be aware that all group members are seldom at the same stage in the problem-solving process. The steps are not necessarily sequential; some may have individually reached steps that others in the group have not yet considered. Individuals or groups can have flashes of insight on any step at any time. Sharing perceptions, knowledge, and hypotheses helps to create understanding and support for the solution.

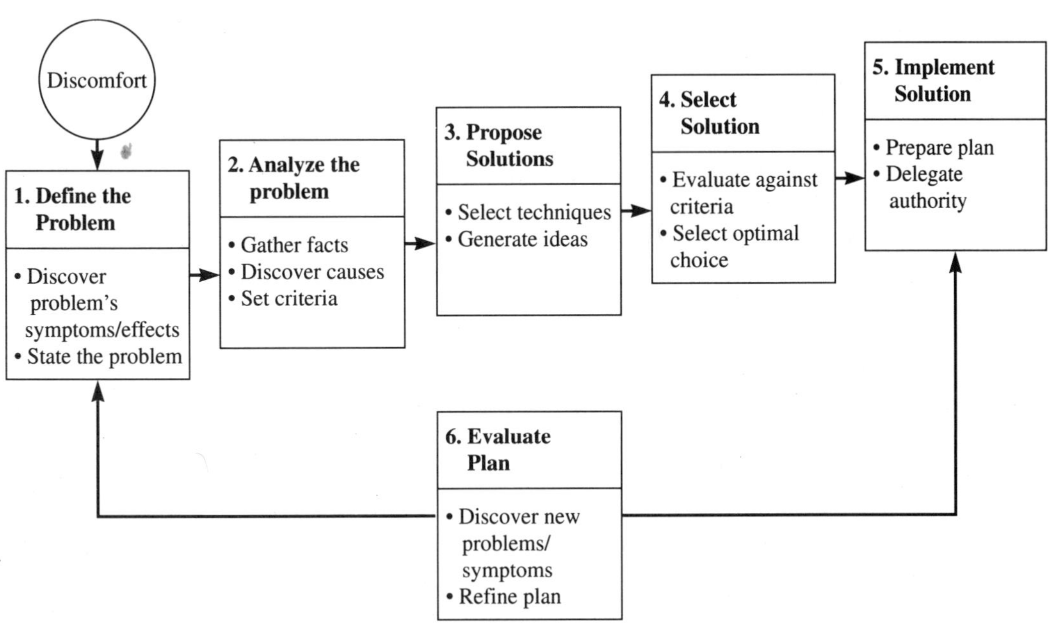

FIGURE 13.1 A Six-Step Problem-Solving Model

Defining the Problem

The most difficult step in decision making is defining the problem. Unless a problem is clearly defined, the manager can end up with a solution that simply deals with an effect rather than the problem itself.

This situation can be likened to a person who is injured and takes an aspirin for pain. The pain may be gone as long as the effects of the aspirin last. However, once the aspirin has worn off the person will experience the pain again. Here, symptoms rather than the cause are being treated. An effective solution eliminates the cause.

Another tendency that interferes with defining a problem effectively is defining the problem in terms of a solution. The manager who cannot meet deadlines for handling the workload and decides to hire more staff has defined the problem in terms of a solution, not in terms of the cause. There should have been many other considerations. For example, are current procedures effective? Are positions clearly defined? Do employees understand their roles? Have goals been clearly communicated to employees? All of these questions focus on causes rather than solutions.

To define a problem effectively, take the following steps:

Write down the problem as you perceive it. Committing your problem to paper helps you discover what it is. You can always go back and revise, adapt, and refine, but writing it down will lead to fuller commitment on your part to follow through.

Clarify any confusing words. Eliminate any jargon used in stating the problem. Obscure terminology should be clearly defined. As you work through this process, you'll find that you also better understand the problem.

Discover the problem's effects or symptoms. What evidence proves there is a problem? What have you observed that tells you things are not as they should be? Problem symptoms or effects are always observable. Examples might be confusion, inability to meet deadlines, unresolved conflict, failure to meet work quotas, poor quality, or incomplete work. A full analysis of the problem's symptoms will give you a better idea of what the causes might be.

Analyze and discover the size of the problem. How serious is it? Is it increasing or decreasing? What are the implications for the future?

Devise a concise statement that summarizes the nature and urgency of the problem. In this statement, indicate how soon a solution must be found. Writing down your problem helps to clarify it. As you define the problem, consider the questions Who? What? When? and Why?

Analyzing the Problem

Once the problem has been clearly stated, gather pertinent facts, identify probable causes, and list criteria.

Gather the facts. Before facts can be gathered, you must determine what information is needed to make a sound decision. Methods for obtaining the information include surveys; face-to-face interviews; observation; library research of laws or decisions; and a review of rules, procedures, or historical files. Some excellent questions to pose in evaluating the usefulness of the information are:

- Is it first-, second-, or thirdhand information?
- Is the source credible? an expert in his or her field? biased?
- Is the information recent? representative? documented?
- Is the information complete?

Discover the causes. The solution must be structured to address the problem's causes. You can observe effects or symptoms of a problem, but you cannot observe the causes. While effects are based on observations, causes are based on inference and probability. For this reason it is necessary to brainstorm all the possible causes of the problem and evaluate them in terms of probability.

Set up criteria for the solution. Problem solving often is defeated because no criteria were established for evaluating a solution. Criteria set the parameters or boundaries for the solution and are the basis on which implementation of the solution will be evaluated. For example, if you fantasize to the limits of your imagination, you may discover an ideal solution. However, if a manager has neither the funds nor the authority to implement the solution, it doesn't matter how effective it is.

Typical criteria involve budget limitations; time limitations; geographical limitations; level of authority; and laws, procedures, or rules that need to be observed. Consider the following questions:

- How urgent is the adoption of a solution?
- Which cause must be eliminated first?
- What rules, laws, or policies must be observed?
- How are the criteria weighed? (Not all criteria are equally important.)

Proposing Solutions

Once the problem has been clearly defined and analyzed, solutions or alternatives should be generated. Two methods discussed later in this chapter are brainstorming and the nominal technique. At this stage it is important to generate as many ideas as possible, reject no ideas, and withhold evaluation. Often a really good solution is overlooked because the manager did not spend enough time on this step. Groups sometimes come to an early agreement on a low-quality solution. The greater the number of ideas, the greater the possibility of a really good solution.

TABLE 13.1 Problem-Solving Grid

Idea Comparison						
Idea	**Criteria and Weights (1 = lowest, 5 = highest)**					
Solution	**Cost = No More Than $1,000/mo**	**Less Than 50 Miles From Home**	**At Least 1,000 sq. ft.**	**At Least 150 sq. ft. of Storage**	**At Least 3 Offices**	**Total**
Location A	5	4	3	5	2	19
Location B	3	5	2	1	5	16
Location C	5	5	1	1	1	13
Location D	3	3	4	4	3	17

Problem: Which location would provide the best site for a new suite of offices?
Solution: Location A meets the most criteria.

Selecting Solutions

Once solutions have been proposed, each solution should be evaluated according to the criteria that have been set. For consistent and objective evaluation, the same criteria need to be applied to all solutions. The solution that most effectively meets all or most of the criteria should be the solution selected.

A grid approach like the one in Table 13.1 can be applied here. On the vertical axis, list your solutions. Horizontally, list your criteria and their weights. Each solution is evaluated against the criteria and a number value is entered in the block. For example, in the first solution above, location A is given 5 on the first criterion, 4 on the second, 3 on the third, 5 on the fourth, and 2 on the fifth. The ratings are added and the totals compared. In this way weak solutions are quickly eliminated.

Implementing the Solution

Many times subordinates participate in problem-solving sessions and committees only to find to their dismay that the solution agreed on by the group is never implemented. One of the primary reasons for this is the lack of a plan. Before problem solving is complete, the group should determine the steps needed to reach its goal. For each step, a timetable should be prepared and a person selected to be responsible for completing the step.

The group should also discuss the obstacles to be faced. For example, what groups or agencies might be hostile to the plan? The group may then determine methods to implement the solution. The overview of chapters takes an in-depth look at this phase of problem solving.

Evaluating the Plan

After implementing the solution, the group should evaluate the results on two levels. First, did the plan meet the goals and objectives set? Second, did the plan eliminate the problem? Once these questions have been answered, the group should determine what new problems have emerged as a result of the plan. At this point, the group can start through the six-step problem-solving model again.

CREATIVE VERSUS ANALYTICAL PROBLEM SOLVING

The average person is either not sensitive to problems, passes them on to others, or ignores them. The more we study an idea, object or situation, the more we notice the details. Once we become more involved in noticing the details, we also become sensitive to whether problems exist. At this point, *problem ideation* begins. Next, we begin to analyze the causes, examine strengths and weaknesses, or identify barriers and obstacles. Throughout the process, two levels of thinking are in conflict—our attempts to be creative and open to possibilities and our attempts to gain order. These two thinking processes—*idea generation* and *idea analysis*—can strengthen the problem-solving process if they are effectively managed and communicated. Idea generation can assist in identifying (1) the problem itself; (2) symptoms and causes of the problem; (3) criteria for solving the problem; (4) facts essential to evaluating the problem, causes and criteria; and (5) solutions. At the same time, idea analysis is helpful in evaluating the relationships between the problem and its symptoms, causes, and solutions.

Divergent and Convergent Thinking

In *The Creative Corporation,* Karl Albrecht describes divergent and convergent thinking:

> In any decision you must first think about the various facts, issues, constraints, and options involved. This is the first phase of your thought process; if you do it well, the second phase will be more effective.

> The second phase, after you have considered the ins and outs of the problem situation, starts when you zero in on a course of action. You make your decision, choose the option you want, and abandon the others. Your mind goes into a very different state during this phase.
>
> This first stage of your thought process is the divergent thinking or *expansion* phase. The second stage is the convergent thinking or *closure* phase. This may seem like a fairly mundane, straight-forward distinction, but I urge you not to pass over it too lightly. It is one of the most important concepts in the entire subject of creative thinking. It is the key to the ability to solve problems and make decisions effectively.[12]

Figure 13.2 divides the six-step problem solving model into the creative and analytical stages. Steps I–III involve *divergent thinking,* wherein idea generation helps in the discovery of problem symptoms, causes, and solutions. We must even be creative in developing the criteria that our solution must meet. Steps IV–VI require *convergent thinking,* the process whereby we analyze and evaluate. We analyze the proposed solutions using the criteria to determine which will be most effective in eliminating the problem's causes. Once a solution is implemented, we again analyze and evaluate the solution to see if it worked.

Right-Brain Versus Left-Brain Activity

A person's cognitive style, or the way the brain processes information, has major implications for problem-solving activities. Ned Hermann of the General Electric Co. Management Development Institute has spent much of his career studying creativity and the activity of the brain. Based on his research, he has concluded that

> the creative individual often takes risks in proposing things that are quite unique, unexpected, or unsettling to the status quo. So, if a climate is to encourage creativity, it must allow people to take risks by removing their fear of being wrong.[13]

Major breakthroughs in brain research have occurred in the last few decades. Clinical cases documented by neurologists, neurosurgeons, psychologists, and speech therapists reinforce findings that damage to the brain's left hemisphere impairs the right side of the body and affects speech, whereas damage to the right hemisphere impairs the left side of the body and disrupts spatial awareness. Severing the connections between these two hemispheres, as has occurred in surgery, results in a total breakdown of communication between the two hemispheres.

The left and right hemispheres have different functions. The left hemisphere is largely responsible for verbal, analytical, symbolic, sequential, and

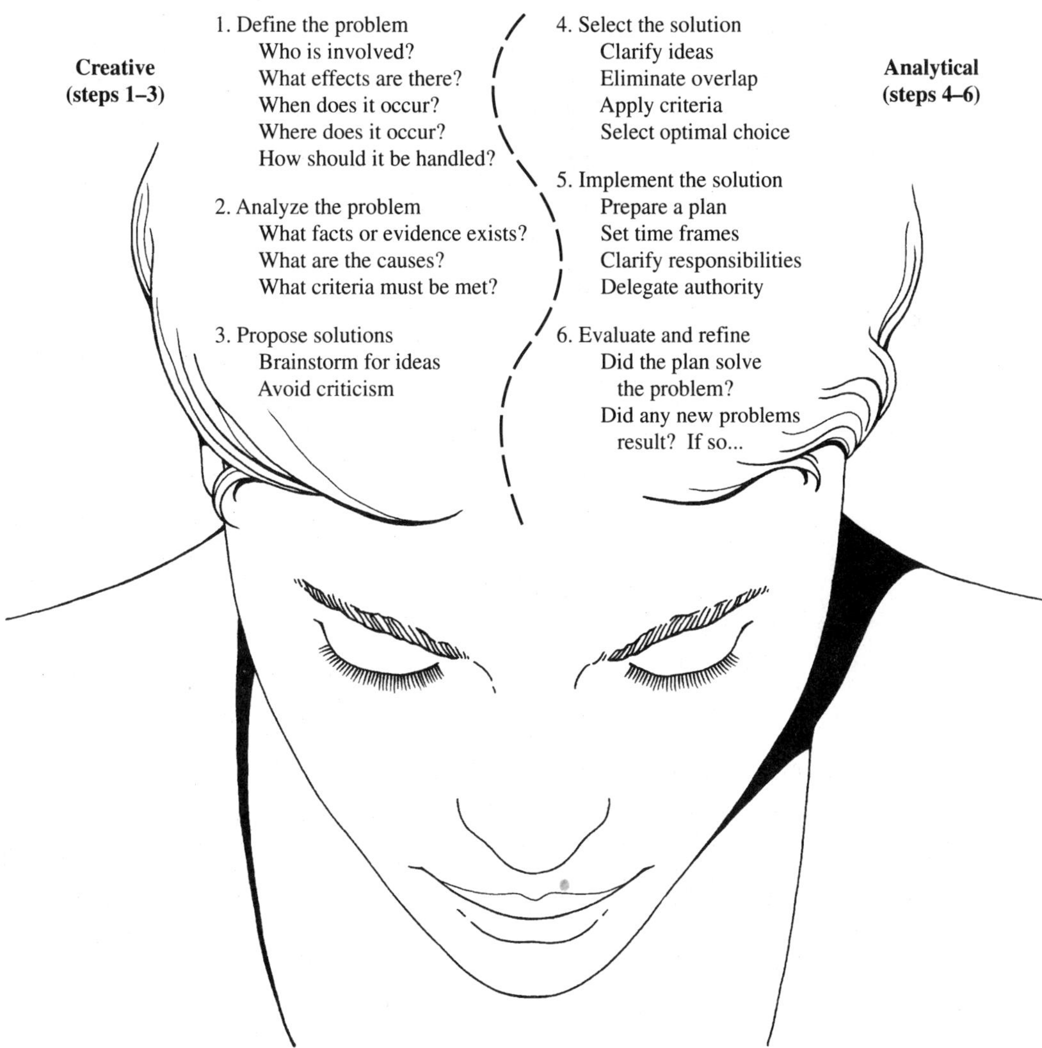

FIGURE 13.2 Problem-Solving Model: The Creative and Analytical Process

logical functions. The right hemisphere is responsible for awareness, orientation, spatial relationships, emotions, and intuition. Springer and Deutch separate these functions as shown in Table 13.2.[14]

Dominance by left or right hemisphere seems to be part of the human condition: We are right- or left- handed, footed, and eyed. The dominance

TABLE 13.2 Brain Hemispheric Dichotomies

Left Hemisphere	Right Hemisphere
Intellect	Intuition
Convergent	Divergent
Intellectual	Sensuous, emotional
Imaginative	Deductive
Rational	Metaphoric, intuitive
Horizontal	Vertical
Discrete	Continuous
Concrete	Abstract
Realistic	Impulsive
Directed	Free
Differential	Existential
Sequential	Multiple
Historical	Timeless
Analytical	Synthetic, holistic
Explicit	Implicit, tacit
Objective	Subjective
Successive	Simultaneous

Source: Sally P. Springer and George Deutsch, *Left Brain, Right Brain* (San Francisco: W. H. Freeman, 1981), p. 186.

pattern also shows in occupational choice. An engineer, dominated by the left-brain functions, is likely to be logical and analytical. An artist, on the other hand, dominated by right-brain functions, is usually oriented to space, shape, and color.

Hermann's study of these functions led him to develop an instrument to measure brain dominance. *The Hermann Learning Profile Survey* has been used to determine if cognitive style and brain lateralization are related to occupational choice.[15] Schkade and Potvin found that an EEG (electroencephalographic) analysis of accountants and artists showed "sharply different hemisphere activity" and supported the validity of Hermann's test.[16] The following example illustrates the effect of brain dominance on group behavior:

The Creative Brain
Ned Hermann

Since the understanding of dominance is critical in applying the new knowledge of brain function, I go to some lengths to demonstrate this when I am able to work directly with people in a group situation. In May

(continued)

THE CREATIVE PROCESS

INTEREST → PREPARATION → INCUBATION →

ILLUMINATION → VERIFICATION → EXPLOITATION

H. Hughes

of this year, I had such an opportunity at a conference called "Brain-streaming: The Art of Whole-Brain Education," sponsored by Syracuse University School of Education. By applying the Hermann Brain Dominance Instrument, I was able to get data on approximately 35 people who were likely to attend the session. By processing this in advance, I was able to create a continuum of this population and from that select five people from each end of the continuum; thus producing two homogeneous groups, one left-brain dominant and one right-brain dominant.

The demonstration was carried out as follows: I displayed the names of the people in Group A and Group B on an overhead projector, and called them up to the front of the auditorium. I did not identify which group was of which dominance. I gave both groups the same assignment—"What work turns you on? What are the common characteristics of the work? Reach a group concensus, make a brief report, be back in 15 minutes." The groups were sent to break-out rooms which were iden-

(continued)

(continued)

tical, with each containing a table and chairs, a flip-chart and felt-pen markers. During the 15-minute interval before their return I teased out of the remaining 150 people in the audience their prediction as to what each group would report and how each group would behave. Precisely at the end of 15 minutes, Group A, the left-brain dominant group, burst into the room, marching in a line with the lead person carrying a flip-chart sheet aloft. They looked triumphant, were smiling and obviously pleased with themselves. I asked them if they had a spokesperson and would that person make a report. The individual with the flip-chart then made the following report:

Group A (Left-Brain Dominant) Presentation

- We read the directions and we got to the task immediately.
- We didn't fiddle around, we didn't have any conversation.
- After we made our lists, we had to list them according to their importance.
- We need to know if we did what we were supposed to do.
- The most important thing which we asterisked and "arrowed," is that our work must be multi-faceted.
- We like to be in control.
- We have a high need for success and recognition.
- We like a structured place.
- We have to have closure.
- We are task oriented.
- We like to see results.
- We are always busy doing something constructive.
- We like to make lists.
- We love to cross things off our lists.
- We love an ordered environment.

Following this report, a comment was made by one of the group that they had actually finished in 13 minutes, but were reluctant to come back early so they took the additional two minutes to prioritize the listing of key characteristics contained on their flip-chart. At this point the right-brained group (B) had not returned and so an emissary was dispatched to get them. When they did return, it was approximately 20 minutes after they had been sent to the break-out room. They drifted in individually—one at a time, and proceeded to meld into the audience, and it was only after a lot of encouragement from me that I got them to assemble up at the front of the room. There were no flip-charts, and there was no obvious spokesperson. After some pleading, one of them volunteered the following report:

(continued)

Group B (Right-Brain Dominant) Presentation

- First of all, we were confused by the word "work."
- We couldn't make a decision.
- Some people mentioned painting, drawing, gardening, and athletics.
- Liking a lot of space.
- Viewing from a whole point of view.
- Seeing the end at the beginning.

Following this report, I asked the Group A people to comment on how they characterized the work that "turned on" the Group B people. Their response was "It seems puzzling to me." The left-brained group then offered gratuitously the comment, "We want you to know that we are glad we are who we are." Then, since the right-brain group had not heard the left-brain report since they had not returned early enough, I asked the left-brain group to recapitulate, and they did so with these key words: Task-oriented, Structured, Closure, Successful, In Control, and Organized.

Whereupon I asked the right-brain group to characterize the work that "turned on" the left-brain group and their response was a simultaneous, unanimous "boring." Now the point of all of this is that people, by reason of the dominance, have different mental processes and different mental preferences, and this affects their choice of work and activities.[17]

Obviously, the input from both left-brain and right-brain dominated individuals is valuable to achieve the best solution to the problem. Since some people learn more effectively by visualizing or relating a problem to individual experience while others can read the problem and analyze facts or numbers, several approaches to presenting the problem should be used. Graphics, tours of a specific problem site, history of the problem, handouts, verbal and nonverbal communication, and opportunities to ask questions may be necessary before all participants completely understand, process, and reach agreement on the problem and its solution.

Applying Creativity to Problem Solving

There is a saying that there are no new problems, just new solutions. Throughout a lifetime an individual learns many ways to do things and when a problem must be solved, applies learned responses, based on these experiences, to new ideas and solutions. Every time we turn the scope on this kaleidoscope of ideas, we view a new combination of colors that is complex and highly creative; all the colors and shapes existed previously, but the turning of the scope created the new arrangement.

Problem Sensitivity

To be a good problem solver, you must first become "problem sensitive"—or aware that things are not as they should be. You must then be willing to take a new look at the world, rearranging experiences and resisting blocks to creativity. The following example illustrates problem sensitivity:

> A student of creative problem solving wanted to practice his creative abilities on a home problem so that his wife could appreciate creative problem solving. He noticed that his wife would remove about three inches from the small end of a ham before baking. His problem sensitivity alerted him to investigate why the end was cut off. His wife didn't know but said her mother taught her to bake ham that way. A subsequent visit disclosed that her mother did it that way because her mother had taught her to remove the end. The grandmother was then contacted to find if she knew why the end was cut off. "Sure," she said. "I didn't have a large enough roaster to take a whole ham."[18]

Blocks to Creativity

In an organizational setting, problem solving is often discouraged. Typical defensive behaviors are placing blame, avoiding the problem, or digressing to other matters. Early and Rutledge outline three basic reasons why problem solving is frustrated in the organization:

1. The individuals assume the problem is bigger than their ability to handle it.
2. Many individuals are not aware of their problem-solving skill.
3. Groups tend to reject solutions before giving them a thorough hearing, reducing the desire of individuals to contribute more solutions.[19]

Specific techniques can enhance creativity and problem-solving ability in an organization. For example, consider the nine-dot problem in Figure 13.3. Many people have struggled with this problem over the years. Inevitably, the problem solver will attempt to stay within the space implied by the nine dots. We have learned throughout our socialization process to follow steps, to stay within the lines, and to deal with problems as neat modules. This training, in fact, acts as a block to creativity. Managers often face the same kinds of blocks within their organizational setting.

Language. Language is one of the primary inhibitors of problem sensitivity. It restricts and directs us with creativity-stifling comments such as "It won't work." "It costs too much." "It will never be accepted." "We tried it," or "Management won't take it."

Culture. Culture is another block to creativity. Beliefs, viewpoints, experience, education, training, lifestyles, and roles all affect problem-solving be-

There are nine dots on this sheet. Without lifting your pencil from the paper, draw four straight connected lines that will go through all nine dots, but through each dot only once.

FIGURE 13.3

havior. Laws, rules, and procedures lay down the social do's and don'ts. From an early age we learn to conform to rules of behavior, whether we're eating at a table or attending a movie. We quickly learn office decorum even though it consists of unwritten rules of behavior.

Emotions. Emotions inhibit our problem-solving abilities. When people are angry or fearful, they're not likely to be openminded and creative, and any attempts they make at problem solving may be futile. At a major hotel a reservation clerk handles irate customers with patience and understanding in attempts to diffuse their anger; the clerk realizes that no agreement can be reached until the customers calm down.

Creative Problem-Solving Traits

Several traits have been associated with creative problem solving: mental *flexibility, fluency* of ideas and associations, and *originality.* Language facility is a key to all three of these traits since it is by means of symbols that you represent your thoughts and communicate your ideas to others. Creative thinkers have the ability to move quickly from the complex to simple, concrete to abstract, or detailed to general. They can also express their thoughts and ideas using symbols that are meaningful to others.

Flexibility. *Flexibility* in thinking depends on proficiency in mental operations. Its vehicles are language, symbols, and feelings. Earlier we mentioned mindleaps, moving from one aspect of a problem to another with flashes of insight. These leaps allow us to move to different ways of thinking, inductive versus deductive, convergent versus divergent, conscious versus unconscious, visual versus structural. Eli Whitney made use of this trait when he was developing his version of the cotton gin. When a cat he was observing tried to catch a chicken through a fence, the cat's claw missed but came away with feathers. This episode led Whitney to conceive of the idea of pulling cotton through a comb.

Fluency. A second trait of creative problem solving is *fluency,* which refers to quantity and recall of ideas and associations. Language facility, not necessarily intelligence, is the most important characteristic of idea generation. Individuals who are limited in language proficiency are also limited in the symbols they can use to represent their thoughts and ideas. Two aspects of language facility are especially important: the ability to move from reality to the abstract and familiarity with different languages. S. I. Hayakawa demonstrated the first ability by means of an abstraction ladder, shown in Figure 13.4. The reality of *Bessie* the cow and the abstract term "wealth" are quite different, but the ability to understand these levels of abstraction allows the individual to visualize the full range of possibilities and choose language that best communicates meaning. The second ability, knowledge of different languages, expands vocabulary and word usage as well as exposes an individual to different ways of structuring thought and expressing ideas.

Originality. *Originality* is the ability to generate the uncommon, the remote, or the clever. Because each person is unique and has the ability to provide an original experience or viewpoint, putting feelings or ideas in one's own words can enlighten or clarify a problem. John James Audubon persisted in drawing birds in ways that suggested movement or activity in their natural habitat. Ornithologists of the time criticized Audubon's approach because he didn't present profiles of birds so that they could be properly studied. Frustrated with the response in America, he traveled to England, where he was immediately declared a genius! Prints from the production of *Birds of America* were suddenly in high demand by the wealthy in Europe and America. Audubon's genius resulted in a successful family enterprise.

Techniques for Generating Ideas

More often than not, people tend to adopt the first idea that seems to get support *whether or not* it is the best idea. A number of techniques have been developed to assist in idea generation using the basic principle that the more ideas that you have to choose from, the better chances there are that you will choose the best idea. We have selected several techniques for you to sample: brainstorming, synectics, forcing, and nominal.

Brainstorming. A number of years ago Alex Osborn came up with a method to encourage the generation of ideas. He called this method *brainstorming.* In brainstorming, four to six group members meet to generate ideas or solutions by contributing on an equal basis. When Sidney Parnes evaluated his technique, he found that groups that had more ideas had better ideas *after screening.* When deferred judgment was applied, groups generated 90 percent more good ideas. His studies also showed that the second half of the ideas generated by the group contained 78 percent more good ideas than the first

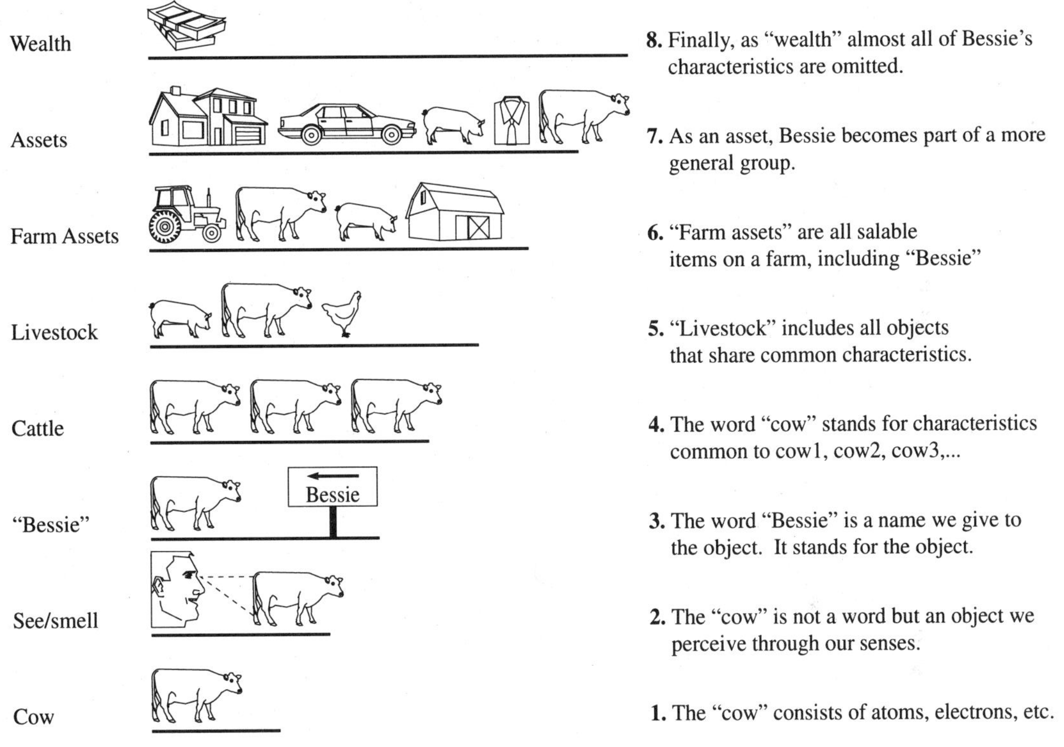

FIGURE 13.4 Abstraction Ladder.
Source: Robert H. McKim, *Thinking Visually: A Strategy Manual for Problem Solving.* Belmont, CA.: Lifetime Learning, 1980, p. 148. Reprinted by permission.

half. Individuals who perform brainstorming use the principle of deferred judgment.[21]

While proposing ideas or solutions, the following rules should be observed:

1. *Criticism is ruled out.* Judgment should be suspended during this step of the process.
2. *Freewheeling is welcome.* The wilder the ideas, the better. It is easier to tame down than to think up.
3. *Quantity is desired.* The greater the number of ideas, the more likelihood of good ideas.
4. *Combination and improvement are sought.* In addition to contributing ideas of their own, group members should suggest ways others' ideas could be turned into better ideas. Two or more ideas may be combined into a still better idea. This method is called hitchhiking.

These rules, when enforced by the group leader, eliminate many of the roadblocks to creative thinking. Ideas will flow much more freely when

The "Silly Putter"

As a bright college student holding a world record for throwing the javelin, Bill Alley was shocked to discover that an injury would keep him from participating in the Olympics. His injury, however, did not hamper his creativity. Using knowledge gained through his engineering degree, Alley developed an aluminum-handled javelin with improved aerodynamics. Because a limited market exists for javelins, Alley put his powers of association to work and visualized the similarities between the handle of the javelin and the handle of a golf putter. He designed a putter with a flexible aluminum handle. When he tested his first batch—4,000 putters—he discovered that his formula did indeed produce flexibility—too much! In his frustration, Alley bent a putter over his knee. His reaction was, "That's exactly what someone does when he misses a putt!" The "Silly Putter" was born and marketed as "a novelty for the temperamental golfer, priced at $19.95." Not only did he sell the original 4,000, he received a total of 6,000 orders![22]

blocks to creativity are removed. The rules should be self-imposed when a person is brainstorming alone.

Synectics. *Synectics* is the process of bringing together previously unrelated elements or making the strange familiar. The process is attributed to W. J. J. Gordon.[23] Usually applied by a group of specifically trained people, it relies heavily on the idea of the metaphor.

The *metaphor* draws an analogy between two objects. Burns's verse, "Her lips are like a red, red rose," is an example of a symbolic analogy. In problem solving, analogy helps us to link a behavior with something with which we are familiar. This eliminates our frustration and confusion in dealing with that behavior. The problem solver may attempt to *personally identify* with the problem being studied. You might imagine, for example, what it would be like to be hunted like an animal.

Another method is the *direct analogy.* In this approach, the problem might be compared with similar objects in nature. We might study the communication systems of whales or porpoises in order to get ideas for developing code systems. Finally, the *fantasy analogy* relies on our ability to use the imagination to create a fantasy solution and then refine it into more practical applications.

Forcing Techniques. Methods designed to help ensure that all possibilities have been exhausted are called *forcing techniques.* They attempt to minimize chance by developing a structure to equalize consideration of all factors. The simplest form is the checklist.

TABLE 13.3 Idea-Stimulating Checklist

Put to other uses?
New ways to use as is?
Other uses if modified?

Adapt?
What else is like this?
What other ideas does this suggest?
Stronger?
Larger?
Plus ingredient?
Multiply?

Minify?
What to subtract?
Eliminate?
Smaller?
Lighter?
Slower?
Split up?
Less frequent?

Reverse?
Opposites?
Turn it backward?
Turn it upside down?
Turn it inside out?

Modify?
Change meaning, color, motion, sound, odor, taste, form, shape?
Other changes?

Magnify
What to add?
Greater frequency?

Substitute?
Who else instead?
What else instead?
Other place?
Other time?

Rearrange?
Other layout?
Other sequence?
Change pace?

Combine?
How about a blend, an assortment?
Combine purposes?
Combine ideas?

Source: Adapted from Alex F. Osborn, *Wake Up Your Mind*, copyright © 1952, 1964 by Alex F. Osborn; copyright renewed © 1980 by Russell and Marion Osborn. Reprinted with the permission of Charles Scribner's Sons, an imprint of Macmillan Publishing Company.

Alex Osborn developed a *checklist* to be used in coordination with the brainstorming technique (see Table 13.3). The list encourages additional ideas by using key words that might trigger associations. For example, the words *adapt, minify, magnify, substitute, rearrange, combine, modify,* and *reverse* help stimulate the problem solver into looking at an idea from a new perspective.[24]

The matrix, which helps the problem solver consider ideas in combination, is the second form of the forcing technique. A matrix should assist in creativity, not act to deter it. A maximum number of ideas should be stimulated by minimum structure. An example of a problem that might require this approach is, "How might Anderson Engineering Company improve productivity in its various subsystems?" In order to exhaust all possibilities, a two-dimensional chart can be developed that lists departments on one of its axes and the *methods* for improving productivity on the other (see Table 13.4). In this example group members would brainstorm using the combination of departments and methods to stimulate ideas. Some solutions for "improving productivity in personnel, using communication" might be:

TABLE 13.4 Matrix Form

Methods / Departments	Coordination	Communication	Goals	Rules and Policies	Procedures	Feedback	Resources	Equipment	Budget	Incentives	Structure	Other		
Personnel														
Engineering														
Marketing														
Design														
Accounting														
Purchasing														
Safety														
Other														

1. Have weekly staff meetings to discuss current staffing needs;
2. Circulate copies of current applications to appropriate department heads;
3. Post job openings on centralized bulletin boards.

Each combination on the grid should stimulate several ideas.

Depending on the complexity of the problem, this grid can be extended into a three-dimensional matrix. However, forcing techniques can become so detailed that the number of considerations becomes overwhelming.

Nominal Technique. The method known as *nominal technique* is often referred to as silent brainstorming. Its main focus is to combine idea generation with equalizing contributions of group members. Many times in group decision making, some members do not take part in active problem solving for a number of reasons. The group star may dominate discussion, preventing other less dominant members from participating. For various reasons, one member may be excluded completely by the rest of the group. Whatever the reason, the group outcome may not reflect everyone's opinion.

To circumvent this problem and still incorporate the idea of brainstorming, Andrew Van de Ven developed the nominal technique.[25] The process combines idea generation and idea analysis in the following steps:

1. *Silent generation of ideas in writing.* Participants individually list all the possible solutions to a problem. This step provides uninterrupted time

Integrative

An *integrative* approach focuses on a series of steps. It stresses goals and values and deemphasizes solutions and win/lose tactics. After extensive research, scholars have defined certain conditions necessary to this approach.[11] They are:

- Freedom from time pressures
- Free interaction of parties
- Shared information
- Limited number of participants
- Positive attitude toward goals
- Trust
- Positive feelings about self (parties are not defensive)
- Understanding of long-range costs
- Specifically stated issues
- Both parties agree on the problems
- Open and specific feedback
- Emphasis on goals and objectives
- Exhaustive search for alternatives
- Consideration of quality
- Involvement
- Questioning attitude
- Flexibility in leadership
- Acceptance of solutions

Individual Styles for Resolving Conflict

Alan C. Filley synthesizes the individual differences in conflict resolution into three styles: "(1) the win-lose battler, who seeks his own goals and is willing to sacrifice the goals of others; (2) the soft or yielding approach, in which one person gives in to the goals of others, even at the cost of his own desires; and (3) the problem solver, who seeks to find an outcome that meets both his own goals and the goals of others."[12] For the battler, winning is important to self-concept; engaging in conflict is a threat to self-esteem. Power plays and dominance are common tactics used to force the opponent to concede to the battler's point of view. Faced with defeat, the win/lose battler must save face, and it is important for future interaction that the opposing party allow the battler to do so.

for participants to think. It also avoids conformity and group pressures, since individuals are working alone.

2. *Round-robin feedback.* After each group member has prepared a list of ideas, the lists are shared with the group. A recorder is selected to list ideas on a piece of newsprint in front of the group. Each member then reads one of the ideas from his or her list, and it is placed on the group list. This process continues with each member reading one idea until all ideas are exhausted.

3. *Discussion of each idea for clarification.* Once all the ideas are on a common list, the group discusses them to ensure that they understand the meaning of each idea. The purpose of this phase is to clarify, elaborate, and evaluate. Ideas should be discussed in sequence, and no items should be eliminated from the list.

4. *Individual ranking of ideas.* At this point the group members again work individually. Each member selects and ranks the ten most important items on the total list. The rankings are then compared, and the group decision is made based on the individual rankings of the group members.

The nominal technique has many advantages. It incorporates brainstorming on an individualized basis and assists in generating more ideas. It tends to equalize contributions by eliminating discussion in the early stages of idea generation and in the critical stage of idea selection. The input of dominant members is limited. Social pressure and conformity are minimized. Participant satisfaction is usually higher than in regular discussion groups; however, this technique can be dissatisfying to strong personalities.

IMPACT OF PERSONALITY TYPES ON PROBLEM SOLVING

Understanding the impact of personality types on problem solving enriches your ability to communicate effectively. In Carl Jung's writings on problem-solving styles, he describes the ways in which people identify a problem, reach a decision, and proceed through the process.[26] Much analysis and research have been conducted to determine the efficacy of Jung's theories.

According to Jung, people gather information to define problems in two ways: by *sensation* or by *intuition.* Most people function using a sensing approach. They stick to the "facts" as they perceive them through their senses of sight, taste, touch, smell, or hearing. Analysis is limited to details which they have observed or accepted as true. These people rely on experience and dislike or avoid uncertainty. This style is appropriate for a stable, routine environment where efficiency is critical. Intuitive types, on the other hand,

Personality Profile: Ross Perot

Ross Perot started Electronic Data Systems in 1962 with $1,000. When EDS went public in 1968, revenues were $7.7 million. Perot pioneered the concepts of computer facilities management, regional data processing centers, and specialization of systems engineers by industry. By the time the company was purchased by GM in 1984, EDS's revenues were $780 million. Perot's estimated wealth in September 1986 was $2.4 billion.

EDS reflected Perot's style—a Puritan work ethic and the motto, "Make it happen." Perot conceives of himself as a leader of people, not a manager of people. He exudes self-confidence. Expecting a high standard of performance from patriotic and loyal employees, he stated, "I'm used to being able to say something once in a whisper, and have committed guys around this country go make it happen."[27]

During the 1992 U.S. presidential campaign, Perot's style became a national focus. Entering the campaign after it became apparent that Arkansas Governor Bill Clinton and President George Bush would be the likely Democrat and Republican nominees, Perot hired some of the best political strategists in the business. Disenchanted voters from both parties found his style attractive. Perot's self-confidence, singlemindedness about the budget, and commitment to force the candidates to deal with economic issues appealed to these voters.

During the 1992 presidential debates, Perot reinforced the image of the man who can get things done. In the debate on October 10, 1992, at Washington University, he stated, "Talk is cheap. Words are plentiful. Deeds are precious. Let's get on with it."

focus on the "big picture." Facts for them are essentially superfluous. They thrive on new challenges, novelty, and change. A dynamic environment capitalizes on their strengths.

Once information is gathered and the problem is identified, Jung observed, people tend to evaluate information by functioning in a *thinking* or *feeling* approach. Thinkers are task oriented and look for a solution that will provide maximum results in solving the problem by eliminating its causes. They are impersonal, logical, organized, conservative, and unemotional. Feelers are more concerned with values and the impact of the solution on people. They are sympathetic, responsive, sensitive, conflict avoiders, and approval seekers.

Jung noted that people proceed through the problem-solving process in different ways. Some are categorized as *judging,* preferring to proceed in a logical, step-by-step sequence. Others are categorized as *perceiving,* avoiding methodical processes and leaping to conclusions. Perceivers are not hindered by doubt or discomfort caused by missing information; rather, they enjoy the challenge of quickly assessing and choosing a course of action. The judging style is effective for problem solving when there is time to work toward an optimal solution; in the face of a crisis, however, the perceiving style will be more effective.

All these styles are appropriate, depending on the type and complexity of the problem. The most important point is to recognize that people have different styles of identifying, analyzing, and approaching a problem.

Many organizations use instruments based on Jung's theories to provide self-assessment for employees. One of the most popular is the *Myers-Briggs Type Indicator* (MBTI)® developed by Isabel Briggs Myers and Katherine Briggs.[28] Many companies use the MBTI® to help their managers better understand their problem-solving styles. The MBTI® uses approximately 100 questions to determine eight preferences in work situations. In addition to the six orientations mentioned previously, two additional orientations, *extravert* and *introvert*, are included. *Extraverts* like to be involved and interact with people. *Introverts* like to work with ideas and need to be encouraged to participate in groups. Table 13.5 describes the effect of the eight preferences. Table 13.6 describes the preferred methods of communication for each preference.

When evaluated by consultants using the MBTI® test, President George Bush was reported to be an "introverted, intuitive, feeling, perceiving type." Bush "tends to undertake too much, then somehow gets it done," says Otto Kroeger, an expert on MBTI®. His strengths are "team-building, persuasion and inspiration." He will listen, quickly assess the situation, make a decision, and act, expecting the team members to work toward the goal or get off the team.[29]

Bush's response to the Iraqi invasion of Kuwait is a good example of this personality type's style. Building an immediate alliance with critical nations through telephone diplomacy, he was able to establish a united front. At home he selected a single expert management team and delegated authority to them to make decisions and handle the crisis. Bush demonstrated that he understood the classic advice given to CEOs in a crisis: "that he understood the crisis, that he was doing something about it, that he was sympathetic to any victims and that he was in charge."[30] His weakness was his inability to articulate his vision to the public. This weakness surfaced during the 1992 presidential campaign, when Bush had trouble explaining to the public his plans for a second term. Although he had a clear domestic policy, he had trouble presenting it. David S. Broder pointed out that in late October, with the election approaching, Bush had "yet to master its main points well enough that they emerge, naturally and convincingly, in his own phrasing during stump speeches and debates."[31]

Understanding your own personality type as well as the personality types of others with whom you engage in problem solving can strengthen all steps in the process. It can also strengthen your ability to communicate effectively in groups because you can recognize the advantages and disadvantages of each other's style.

TABLE 13.5 Personality Types in Work Situations: 1

Effects of Preferences in Work Situations	
Extraversion	*Introversion*
Like variety and action	Like quiet for concentration
Often impatient with long, slow jobs	Tend not to mind working on one project for a long time uninterruptedly
Are interested in the activities of their work and in how other people do it	Are interested in the facts/ideas behind their work
Often act quickly, sometimes without thinking	Like to think a lot before they act, sometimes without acting
When working on a task, find phone calls a welcome diversion	When concentrating on a task, find phone calls intrusive
Develop ideas by discussion	Develop ideas by reflection
Like having people around	Like working alone
Sensing	*Intuition*
Like using experience and standard ways to solve problems	Like solving new complex problems
Enjoy applying what they have already learned	Enjoy learning a new skill more than using it
May distrust and ignore their inspirations	May follow their inspirations, good or bad
Seldom make errors of fact	May make errors of fact
Like to do things with a practical bent	Like to do things with an innovative bent
Like to present the details of their work first	Like to present an overview of their work first
Prefer continuation of what is, with fine tuning	Prefer change, sometimes radical, to continuation of what is
Usually proceed step-by-step	Usually proceed in bursts of energy
Thinking	*Feeling*
Use logical analysis to reach conclusions	Use values to reach conclusions
Can work without harmony	Work best in harmony with others
May hurt people's feelings without knowing it	Enjoy pleasing people, even in unimportant things
Tend to decide impersonally, sometimes paying insufficient attention to people's wishes	Often let decisions be influenced by their own and other people's likes and dislikes
Tend to be firm-minded and can give criticism when appropriate	Tend to be sympathetic and dislike, even avoid, telling people unpleasant things
Look at the principles involved in the situation	Look at the underlying values in the situation
Feel rewarded when job is done well	Feel rewarded when people's needs are met
Judgment	*Perception*
Work best when they can plan their work and follow their plan	Enjoy flexibility in their work
Like to get things settled and finished	Like to leave things open for last-minute changes
May not notice new things that need to be done	May postpone unpleasant tasks that need to be done
Tend to be satisfied once they reach a decision on a thing, situation, or person	Tend to be curious and welcome a new light on a thing, situation, or person
Reach closure by deciding quickly	Postpone decisions while searching for options
Seek structure and schedules	Adapt well to changing situations and feel restricted without change
Use lists to prompt action on specific tasks	Use lists to remind them of all the things they have to do someday

Adapted from *Introduction to Type* by Isabel Briggs Myers.

TABLE 13.6 Personality Types in Work Situations: 2

Preferred Methods of Communication	
Extraversion	*Introversion*
Communicate energy and enthusiasm	Keep energy and enthusiasm inside
Respond quickly without long pauses to think	Like to think before responding
Focus of talk is on people and things in the external environment	Focus is on internal ideas and thoughts
Need to moderate expression	Need to be drawn out
Seek opportunities to communicate in groups	Seek opportunities to communicate one-to-one
Prefer face-to-face over written communication	Prefer written over face-to-face communication
In meetings, like talking out loud before coming to conclusions	In meetings, verbalize already well thought out conclusions
Sensing	*Intuition*
Like evidence (facts, details, and examples) presented first	Like global schemes, with broad issues presented first
Want practical and realistic application shown	Want possible future challenges discussed
Rely on direct experience to provide anecdotes	Rely on insights and imagination to provoke discussion
Use an orderly step-by-step approach in presentations	Use a round-about approach in presentations
Like suggestions to be straightforward and feasible	Like suggestions to be novel and unusual
Refer to a specific example	Refer to a general concept
In meetings, are inclined to follow the agenda	In meetings, are inclined to use the agenda as a starting point
Thinking	*Feeling*
Prefer to be brief and concise	Prefer to be sociable and friendly
Want the pros and cons of each alternative to be listed	Want to know why an alternative is valuable and how it affects people
Can be intellectually critical and objective	Can be interpersonally appreciative
Convinced by cool, impersonal reasoning	Convinced by personal information, enthusiastically delivered
Present goals and objectives first	Present points of agreement first
Consider emotions and feelings as data to weigh	Consider logic and objectivity as data to value
In meetings, seek involvement with tasks	In meetings, seek involvement with people
Judgment	*Perception*
Want to discuss schedules and timetables with tight deadlines	Willing to discuss the schedule but are uncomfortable with tight deadlines
Dislike surprises and want advance warning	Enjoy surprises and like adapting to last-minute changes
Expect others to follow through, and count on it	Expect others to adapt to situational requirements
State their positions and decisions clearly	Present their views as tentative and modifiable
Communicate results and achievements	Communicate options and opportunities
Talk of purpose and direction	Talk of autonomy and flexibility
In meetings, focus on the task to be done	In meetings, focus on the process to be appreciated

Adapted from *Talking in Type* by Jean Kummerow, Center for Applications of Psychological Type, 1985. Reprinted by permission.

A GLOBAL PERSPECTIVE

Asian Empowerment

From the Japanese perspective, the philosophy of "total quality management" means empowering workers to make decisions. Japanese managers at Nissan, Toyota, and Honda encourage front-line employees to discover better ways of doing their work by experimenting with new approaches and measuring and comparing the results. Instead of conceiving their role as making decisions, these managers see their jobs as facilitating and coaching.

One way of emphasizing this change in roles is the elimination of "perks." The companies provide no special parking places, executive cafeterias, private restrooms, expensive private offices, or other trappings that indicate position power and communicate a separation between "workers" and "decision makers." The focus is on *kaiszen,* the Japanese word for constant improvement. Dr. William Byham, a psychologist who has helped screen employees for Japanese-owned firms, describes the Japanese approach as an attempt to instill "an inner motivation that comes from pride in what you are doing." The empowerment of workers is improving quality and efficiency by pushing decision-making down to the lowest level possible. Because of this concept's impact on productivity, it has been adopted by many U.S. companies. The Boeing Co. and Chaparral Steel are just two examples.[32]

ETHICS: RIGHT OR WRONG?

Georgia Haddad's Presidential Challenge

Georgia Haddad had been in a position of leadership in a university for over twenty years. During that time she had worked her way up the administrative ranks to a presidency. She had also learned a lot along the way from experience, strong mentors, and the relevance of her academic background, having earned her Ed.D. at a prestigious private university. Most of Haddad's immediate employees would attest to her knowledge, ability, and leadership skills.

During her many years of leadership, including a presidency at a major state university, Haddad had never encountered major budgetary problems. The financial status of the universities in which she worked had been relatively good. She was an inspirational and charismatic leader and depended on her vice-presidents to manage the day-to-day activities of the institution while she concentrated on image and fundraising activities.

After accepting her current position as president of a medium-sized, private liberal arts college on the East Coast, Haddad established a strategic-planning committee. This committee consisted of twenty-five members with representation from the faculty and administration. After three years, the committee had not reached agreement on the mission of the university. Two different chairs, neither of whom had any training in strategic planning, had attempted to provide leadership. President Haddad did not attend these meetings, stating that "she did not want to stifle discussion."

The president was now faced with a dilemma. Not only was the national economy poor, but her state was suffering high unemployment and a failing tax structure. At the same time institutional costs were increasing and annual giving decreasing. The institution had turned more than once to reserve funds to maintain its current levels of operation. There had been several years without pay increases. Tuition had just been raised and was among the highest among its peer institutions. On the bright side, there was a recent increase in enrollment, and the university still had some money in its reserve accounts. Now, however, the president faced major financial problems if current operations continued.

President Haddad decided to meet with the strategic planning committee and ask it to make a recommendation on how to address the budget problems. The meeting was held in a large, comfortable room, and no time limits were placed on discussion. Representatives from the budget and institutional research offices were present to answer questions. The amount of the fund shortage was translated into the dollar amount of $5.6 million: the university had approximately $2.1 million left in its reserve accounts leaving a $3.5 million shortfall.

A heated dialog ensued. Among the comments made was the following: "If you don't agree about what your business is, how do you know what is essential to your business?" The group as a whole ignored this comment and took the position that current operations that affected teaching, research, and service should be preserved to whatever extent possible, in the hopes that this was a temporary setback, that fundraising would improve, and continued enrollment increases would increase tuition dollars.

At the end of the discussion, the following points of agreement were identified:

1. Student tuition should be raised again to cover at least half of the shortfall.
2. A plan would be put in place to identify and terminate less essential employees.
3. A plan would be put in place to target employees who did not have faculty status for salary cuts or layoffs.
4. No travel or equipment funds would be approved. Faculty were exempt from this agreement since their activities were crucial to the University.

A statement was prepared for faculty, staff, and the press in which the president announced the cut and its impact on the university. The strategies listed above were outlined. A staff member of a critical support unit commented in confidence to her superior, "I guess I feel like a victim."

Case Questions

1. Was concern demonstrated for those whom the decision would affect?
2. Did participants explore the problem as thoroughly as they could or should?
3. Was information distorted, misused, or omitted?
4. Was anything done to diminish anyone's sense of self-worth?

SUMMARY

As a decision maker and problem solver, a manager is concerned with finding the right solutions. The effectiveness of a solution depends on its *quality* and *acceptance.* These two factors plus the *task* must be considered when the manager selects the type of decision making to use: *self, group,* or *consultation.* If the acceptance of the decision is of paramount importance, the group is usually the most effective method of decision making.

Six steps are associated with the problem-solving process: defining the problem, analyzing the problem, proposing solutions, evaluating solutions, implementing solutions, and evaluating the success of the solution. These steps incorporate two stages: creative and analytical. During the creative stage, in which ideas are generated, divergent thinking takes place. This is an expansion stage and affects the first three steps of problem solving. The analytical stage, which is the closure stage and affects the last three steps of problem solving, requires convergent thinking.

Creativity helps generate ideas and is highly dependent on language facility. Several techniques have been developed to stimulate ideas. Brainstorming encourages participation without criticism. Forcing techniques help the group consider as many alternatives as possible. Synectics uses associations to trigger ideas. The nominal technique combines silent brainstorming with group sharing while minimizing group pressures.

Finally, it is important to note that personality types affect group problem solving and decision making because people have differing approaches to identifying problems, reaching decisions, and proceeding through the problem-solving process. For example, sensing people define problems by experience and by sticking to the facts, while intuitive people focus on the "big picture." Thinkers are task oriented, while feelers are concerned about impact on people. Judging types proceed in a logical sequence. Perceivers can act quickly in reaching a decision because they are comfortable with trusting their experience and leaping to conclusions.

Effective problem solving means that the manager must consider the nature of the problem; the importance of the acceptance of the solution; the value placed on the quality of the solution; and the competency, personality types, and operating effectiveness of the people involved. If the desired result is effective communication and implementation of solutions, the keys to success are selecting the appropriate type of decision making—individual, group, or consultant; access to complete and accurate information; and applying creative techniques for idea generation and problem resolution.

Key Words

analytical stage
artificial intelligence
blocks to creativity
brainstorming
consultation
convergent thinking
creative stage
decision making
divergent thinking
forcing techniques
Jung's personality types
nominal technique
problem sensitivity
synectics

Review Questions

1. What factors are important to decision making? What methods can be utilized in decision making?
2. Explain when individuals and when groups can best be used in problem solving and decision making.
3. Describe several methods for generating ideas. What are the advantages of each?
4. List and describe the steps in the problem-solving process.
5. Using Jung's model of personality types, describe the ways in which people identify a problem, reach a decision, and proceed through the problem-solving process.

Exercises

1. Better Jobs, Inc. has five divisions, each of a different type and at a different location. Each division is staffed by employees with different educational levels, ages, and number of years with the company, and also have different assistants.
   a. The employee with two years of college works in the Personnel Department.
   b. The employee with the Ph.D. has Gail for an assistant.
   c. The employee on the Board of Directors has been with the company thirteen years.
   d. The employee with the B.A. degree has been with the company four years.
   e. The employee on the Board of Directors is immediately to the right of Engineering.
   f. The forty-six-year-old employee has Dom for an assistant.
   g. The employee in the Accounting Division is thirty-five years old.
   h. The employee in the middle division has been with the company ten years.
   i. The employee with the B.S. degree works in the first division on the left.
   j. The employee who is twenty-seven years old works in the division next to the employee who has Sue for an assistant.
   k. The employee who is thirty-five years old works in the division next to the division where Jake works as an assistant.
   l. The thirty-two-year-old employee has been with the company five years.
   m. The employee with the M.B.A. degree is fifty-three years old.
   n. The employee with the B.S. degree works next to the Data Processing Division.
   o. The employee in the Accounting Division has been in the company for five years.

   The Problem: Who has Lesley for an assistant? Who has been with the company the least number of years? Divide into groups of four to six students. You have 20 minutes to find the solution to the problem.

a. How did the time limit affect your solution? (How well do you work under pressure?)
b. Whom would you rate as the most logically oriented person in your group?
c. Who were the leaders? Who were the workers?
d. Whom would you rate as the best communicator in your group?

2. Multiquip Corporation, an international manufacturer of multipurpose electronic equipment, received grant assistance to develop a relatively new area of electronics. A new director was hired whose job consisted of full responsibility for the staffing, training, development, and delivery of new electronic equipment. Reporting to him were two research technicians who deal directly with product design, a development lab of six electronic engineers, and one secretary with limited skills.

After several months it became increasingly clear that things were not going well. Feedback about the new director from the other departments was negative, and one superior had strongly recommended firing him. Subordinates and peers were also complaining. Typical remarks were that he "doesn't listen," has "little contact with employees," "does not believe the program will last," and "spends too much time in other departments telling them how to run their business."

Constant deadlines for submitting reports, budget requests, vouchers, purchase requests, personnel forms, and the subsequent red-tape seemed to eat up all of the new director's time. He was also trying to establish guidelines for measuring product effectiveness and proposals for future funding. The specific requirements for completing these items were complex, and everyone on the staff was relatively new. Consequently, much time was spent correcting deletions and serious oversights.

By the end of one year, turnover was high, with three of the six engineers and one technician leaving for other jobs in the company. The director's superior decided to have the director rated by a cross-section of people with whom there was regular contact. All evaluations rated him high on sincerity and initiative. The following is a general rating based on averaging the forms:

Factor	**−1**	**2**	**3**	**4**	**5+**
Capability for job			X		
Leadership qualities		X			
Job performance			X		
Communication skills		X			
Supervisory skills		X			
Attitudes and work habits				X	
Professional development in field					X
Personal qualities					X

Before coming to Multiquip, the new director had supervised product development for a small, regionally oriented firm. His recommendations were very good. Shortly after he left, the firm declared bankruptcy. His educational background included an M.S. in computer engineering from a large state university.

After reading this case, answer the following questions.

a. What is the problem(s)?
b. What are the effects?
c. How soon must a solution be found?
d. What additional facts are needed? How would you get them?
e. What are the probable causes of the problem(s)?
f. Identify the criteria that must be met by the solution(s).

References

1. *Report of the Presidential Commission on the Space Shuttle Challenger Accident,* vols. 1–5 (Washington, D.C.: National Aeronautics and Space Administration, July 14, 1986).
2. J. J. Sherwood and F. M. Hoilman, *Utilizing Human Resources: Individual vs. Group Approaches to Problem Solving and Decision Making,* Institute for Research in the Behavioral, Economic, and Management Sciences, paper no. 621, Purdue University.
3. Harold Koontz, Cyril O'Donnell, and Heinz Weirich, *Management,* 7th ed. (New York: McGraw-Hill, 1980), p. 238.
4. William Booth, "Picking Up Andrew's Pieces," *Washington Post National Weekly Edition* (September 7–13, 1991), p. 11.
5. Edward Pratt, "Report Blames Confusion for Lack of Communication, Planning in Storm," *The Advocate* (September 21, 1992), p. 1B.
6. Daniel Schutzer, *Business Decisions with Computers: New Trends in Technology* (New York: Van Nostrand Reinhold, 1991), p. 40.
7. Schutzer, *Business Decisions,* p. 64.
8. Alan C. Filley, "Conflict Resolution: The Ethic of the Good Loser," in Richard C. Huseman, Cal M. Logue, and Dwight L. Freshley, eds., *Readings in Interpersonal Communication,* 3rd ed. (Boston: Holbrook Press), pp. 248–249.
9. While exact numbers differ, the ideal seems to be five to six members, but no more than eight.
10. Filley, "Conflict Resolution," p. 237.
11. Norman R. F. Maier, "Assets and Liabilities in Group Problem Solving: The Need for an Integrative Function," *Psychological Review,* 74 (1967), pp. 239–249.
12. Karl Albrecht and Steven Albrecht, *The Creative Corporation* (Homewood, Ill.: Dow Jones–Irwin, 1987), p. 90.
13. *G. E. Monogram,* November–December 1980, p. 31.
14. Sally P. Springer and George Deutsch, *Left Brain, Right Brain* (San Francisco: W. H. Freeman, 1981), pp. 185–186.
15. Excerpt from article by W. E. (Ned) Hermann, "The Creative Brain," *Training and Development Journal* (October 1981), pp. 11–16.
16. Lawrence L. Schkade and Alfred R. Potvin, "Cognitive Style, EEG Waveforms and Brain Levels," *Human Systems Management,* 2 (1981), pp. 329–331.
17. Excerpt from article by W. E. (Ned) Hermann, "The Creative Brain," Training and Development Journal (Oct., 1981), pp. 12–13. Reprinted by permission.
18. *Training Manual for Creative Problem Solving* (St. Louis: U.S. Civil Service Commission, St. Louis Regional Training Center, 1980), pp. 3–10.
19. Leigh C. Earley and Pearl B. Rutledge, in J. William Pfeiffer and John E. Jones, eds., *The 1980 Annual Handbook for Group Facilitators* (San Diego, Calif.: University Associates, 1980).
20. Robert H. McKim, *Thinking Visually: A Strategy Manual for Problem Solving* (Belmont, Calif.: Lifetime Learning Publications, 1980), p. 148.
21. Alex Osborn, *Applied Imagination: Principles and Procedures of Creative Thinking* (New York: Charles Scribner, 1953), pp. 300–301.
22. George Gilder, "Guest Column," *Success* (January–February, 1988), p. 82.
23. William J. J. Gordon explains and comments on this theory in Gary A. Davis, ed., *Psychology of Problem Solving* (New York: Basic Books, 1973), pp. 96, 123–124.
24. Osborn, *Applied Imagination.*
25. Andrew Van de Ven, Andre L. Delbecq, and David H. Gustafson, *Group Techniques for Program Planning: A Guide to Nominal Group and Delphi Process* (Glenview, Ill.: Scott, Foresman, 1965), p. 8.
26. Don Hellriegel, John W. Slocum, and Richard W. Woodman, *Organizational Behavior,* 4th ed. (Boulder: West, 1986), pp. 118–125.
27. George Russell, "Need a Rescue? Call Ross," *Time* (December 15, 1986), p. 52.
28. I. B. Myers, *Supplementary Manual, The Myers-Briggs Type Indicator* (Consulting Psychologists Press, 1977).
29. Mindy Fetterman, "Bush Shows Management Savvy in Crisis," *USA Today,* February 8, 1991, p. 1B.
30. Ibid.
31. David S. Broder, "Saving the Best for Too Late," *Washington Post National Weekly Edition* (October 26–November 1, 1992), p. 4.
32. Diana Kunde, "Transplanting Japanese System of Empowered Workers," *Dallas Morning News,* October 16, 1990, p. 3.

CHAPTER 14

COMMUNICATION STRATEGIES: MANAGING CONFLICT

When Theresa Betanzos was promoted to manager of public relations over a group of ten professionals, the outgoing supervisor briefed her on the group. "In a nutshell," he concluded, "having been part of it, you know that the group is very capable, but their productivity won't improve unless a way is found to get rid of John Eckland. I've tried everything in the book with no success. His performance negatively impacts the entire group. He just won't cooperate. Every time the section agrees on assignments, Eckland creates a problem and delays getting the job done. You need to get rid of him."

One thing Betanzos was certain about: the outgoing supervisor had limited communication skills. She had continually needed to "second-guess" him to figure out what was expected of her. Since she had always been someone who worked overtime and was persistent in her objectives, she was able to produce high-quality work consistently.

Betanzos had long known about the problems surrounding Eckland. Personally, she liked him and believed he possessed talent and potential. However, he did have problems performing his job; in fact, Betanzos had often helped him complete a project by volunteering to do some of the work. Eckland's talents seemed to lie in his ability to analyze situations and offer alternative strategies to the one the group had agreed on—a contribution that provoked anger and confusion among other group members. Eckland had an excellent liberal arts education from a fine university. Nevertheless, most of the time he seemed frustrated, and his attitude affected the rest of the group. Betanzos had the gut feeling, though, that Eckland had a streak of solid gold just waiting to be mined.

Immediately after the supervisor left her office, Eckland appeared in the doorway. He wanted to talk about their new relationship. To her utter amazement, he asked to be promoted to assistant director in charge of "strategic planning" with an increase in pay. After a lengthy conversation, she concluded that his own perception of his performance and abilities was miles apart from the previous supervisor's perception.

After much thought, Betanzos negotiated a new job description with Eckland, with no increase in pay, that would place more emphasis on departmental planning efforts and less emphasis on project implementation. One year later, the department received an award from its regional association for outstanding work in the area of public relations. Betanzos knew Eckland had played a critical role in this area and promoted him to assistant director with an increase in pay.

CONFLICT DEFINED

We often suppress conflict for a variety of reasons. Because conflict has been characterized as negative, people shy away from arguing, emotions, and hostility. Conflict sometimes leads to constructive problem solving, however, and can be a positive force. In fact, it places ideas under scrutiny in order to determine their soundness and avoid superficial decisions.

Have you ever participated in a group where everyone came to quick agreement? Was the solution creative or challenging? Did members share common backgrounds and points of view? In other words, was there any testing of beliefs, knowledge, or experience? Be wary when you participate in a group that comes to quick agreement. Early agreement can result in implementation of an unsound idea and the need for further problem-solving activity. Conflict tests ideas. Peter Drucker believes that conflict alone encourages alternatives to a decision and the avoidance of faulty decision making.[1]

Herb Bisno defines conflict as a social interaction between people "involving a struggle over claims to resources, power and status, beliefs, and other preferences and desires."[2] The intensity of the individual's goals can vary from gaining acceptance or securing an advantage to eliminating opponents.[3] Even so, conflict can add to a greater understanding and identification of problems. It can increase alternatives and involvement. Conflict stimulates interest and interaction. Hoffman, Harburg, and Maier observed that conflict encourages creative thinking, commitment, and quality decision-making.[4]

Conflict can also be destructive. When it presents a negative force, it must be managed. Group participants who are not aware of problem-solving skills can use conflict to compete with other members and subvert ideas, resulting in game playing, defense mechanisms, cliques, and hostility. Group participants need to be taught how to use conflict constructively.

This chapter focuses on the source of conflict and ways a manager skillfully handles it through communication. It examines the stages of conflict and the methods that research has identified to reduce conflict. Finally, it presents strategies and steps for resolving conflict.

Sources of Conflict

The American Management Association surveyed 116 chief executive officers on the subject of managing conflict. According to their findings, managers spent about 14 percent of their time managing conflict.[5] Individuals in specific management fields, such as school and hospital administrators, mayors, and city managers, spent as much as half of their time managing conflict.[6] The principal causes of conflict these managers pinpointed included communication breakdowns; poor performance; failure to follow policies

"I've heard this group has had some trouble reaching agreement."

Source: Reprinted with the permission of George Kocar. Illustration originally appeared in *Industry Week,* March 20, 1978, p. 18.

and procedures; competition for scarce resources; misunderstandings about procedures, responsibilities, values, or goals; personality conflicts; and failure to cooperate.

Huseman describes several sources of conflict.[7] Among these are organizational structure, performance measures, ambiguity, goal disagreement, and conflicting reality perceptions. During a series of training sessions on conflict at a major chemical plant in Houston, approximately seventy-five first-line supervisors identified the sources of conflict in their particular work unit. Among the causes listed were multiple direct bosses, unclear instructions, personality conflicts, poor attitude, lack of authority, superiors' lack of experience or understanding, and differing standards of behavior among group members.

The organizational structure can cause problems by pitting departments within the organization against each other. This can be the result of unclear goals or perhaps power building within the unit. When two departments perceive their roles as overlapping or striving for similar outcomes, they may tend to compete with each other.

Performance measures can also be a source of conflict. If these have not been clearly explained to the employee in terms of expectations, the employee will fill in the gaps. Or if the manager bases rewards or punishments on behavior that seems unrelated to the job itself, the employee's behavior will pattern itself to receive the rewards. Consider the following situation.

> My best employee has only one fault. He hangs around the coffee pot for twenty minutes each morning before he begins working. Some of this occurs before the start of business, but most of it is on the clock. The problem is that other employees who are not as productive as my "superstar" hang around the coffee pot, too.
>
> My unit was the best in the division and received special recognition in a nationwide review of agency productivity. The superstar produced about 15 percent more than the average employee in my unit. I use him whenever time and high quality are important factors in the job. He troubleshoots major jobs and trains other employees in the technical aspects of the work. I can't remember his last mistake.
>
> I distributed a memo to all employees reminding them that they are to be at their desks working at 8:00 A.M. Several of these employees are obviously upset, including my superstar. Production is slipping, and my unit is no longer the best in the division.

The supervisor's written communication sent a strong message. By reprimanding the employees for "hanging around the coffee pot," he changed the employees' perception of job expectations: timeliness, not productivity, appeared a priority.

Unclear job roles can create conflict. Competition may result if members of the organization pursue the same goal. Conflict will continue until the job roles are clarified. The following incident is a good example.

> The head of personnel and development at a leading manufacturing firm hired Carlos and Ordell to staff and develop a program for employee rehabilitation. Since this was a relatively new area of emphasis in the company, it was agreed that the two would cooperate by working out their roles and coordinating their activities. As the program grew, it soon became apparent that one of them would be chosen as director. Awareness of this coming opportunity resulted in duplication of effort as Carlos and Ordell competed for attention by performing roles that they perceived would be the key in deciding who would receive the promotion. Rather than discussing their conflicting behavior, they resorted to sabotage, game playing, and isolation. Ordell described Carlos to a friend as "manipulative, self-serving, and untrustworthy."

Carlos and Ordell never clearly understood their roles and how the roles meshed to accomplish organizational goals. At some point early in the conflict, their boss should have stepped in and clarified the relationships.

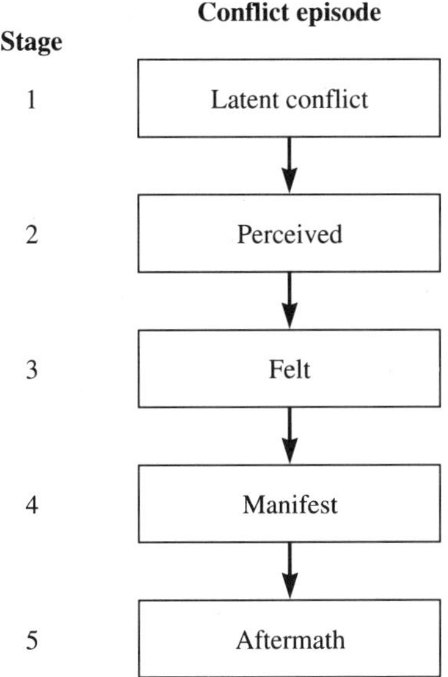

FIGURE 14.1
Adapted from Louis Pondy, "Organizational Conflict: Concepts and Models," *Administrative Science Quarterly*, 12 (Sept. 1967), pp. 299–306.

Conflict, then, can have many sources. To resolve conflict, it is important to identify the source and act to eliminate or minimize its effect. It is also important to identify its stages. Conflict identified and managed early will lead to more positive resolution.

Stages of Conflict

One of the first steps in managing conflict is recognizing it in its early stages. The following situation includes all stages of a *conflict episode* (see Figure 14.1).

> Clara was an auditor. Formerly a college faculty member, she was the first auditor hired on what was to become a five-member auditing team. Accustomed as a teacher to keeping irregular hours, the new 8-to-5 job interfered with her personal schedule. Consequently, she volunteered for as much travel as she could get.
>
> *(continued)*

(continued)

Clara's whereabouts soon became the daily mystery. Since she kept her office door closed, no one could tell if she was in or out. Soon the other auditors and support staff began to complain that Clara was getting privileges not extended to others in the organization. Coworkers' complaints included (1) she arranged trips to coincide with holidays, (2) she "conveniently" worked at home, (3) she exaggerated her travel allowance, and (4) she was never available for meetings or to act as an alternate for other auditors. In short, Clara did not have a workload comparable to others, yet because of her seniority was the highest-paid member of the staff.

The retirement of the department head resulted in promotion of the assistant director and opened a coveted position. Because of her performance, Clara was not considered. This became a major frustration for her. Whenever she was "in," she visited with other staff members and criticized the new director. These visits often gained her support in creating resistance to organizational changes.

The new director attempted to stop the meetings by rearranging the offices. Clara was moved to a location fully visible to the main office and reception area, yet separate from all other auditors.

Clara considered this change in location a challenge. Again, she kept her office door closed. But she held her meetings in a variety of locations outside the office setting. These locations included the lunchroom, the lounge, and the offices of other departments. Thus she foiled the director's plan to curb her visiting.

The director decided to require weekly records from all employees. Each sheet recorded the hours an employee spent on specified activities during the workday. She also issued new regulations for travel, lunch, and work hours. Rising to the occasion, Clara categorized as "other" all time for which she couldn't account and travel came within pennies of the maximum allowed. She arrived at work and left at the specified hours, but because she traveled so much, this became a clouded issue.

Fellow employees' frustration and protestations continued to grow. Finally, the director transferred her to a new position and location with a travel allowance and office 125 miles away.

Conflict-ridden situations similar to Clara's are not uncommon in the modern organization. Typically, the conflict episode, as Pondy describes it, begins with underlying conditions or *latent conflict*.[8] Clara's personal goals differed from those of the organization. Her drive for autonomy and competition with the other auditors for scarce resources (money, position) added to these conditions and increased her frustration.

The second stage occurs when the parties realize that these conditions exist. Pondy calls this stage *perceived conflict.* Once the other auditors began to recognize that Clara received a greater portion of the resources (travel, compensation, free time), this stage was reached.

Felt conflict, the third stage, happens when parties become tense or irritated because of the conditions. This usually results in stage 4, or *manifest conflict.* The auditors' complaints about Clara were overt means of expressing disagreement with her behavior. Auditors also made covert attempts such as keeping track of Clara's whereabouts and checking travel forms. In addition, her boss moved her office and finally relocated her as a means of releasing the tension and eliminating conflict.

The last stage Pondy identifies is *conflict aftermath.* This is the situation that results from the conflict. If the consequences do not resolve the original conditions, they may surface again. The director's attempts to manage the impact of Clara's behavior on other employees did not eliminate the source of conflict. In fact, as we will discuss later, the travel regulations and the use of force to require weekly records aggravated the conflict. The resulting *aftermath* renewed the conflict episode.

Strategies for Resolving Conflict

When two or more persons are in conflict, they often engage in strategies. Strategies can be either outcome directed (who gets what) or goal directed (what would benefit both). After studying conflicting groups, Filley describes three forms of conflict strategies: the win/lose, the lose/lose, and the win/win.[9] Both the win/lose and the lose/lose strategies are outcome directed. The atmosphere is one of victory or defeat. Each party centers on his or her own point of view. Hence, the parties want to achieve specific desired solutions rather than determining mutual goals, values, or motives. The conflict is personalized instead of objective.

Win/Lose

From the time we enter elementary school we learn to compete with our peers. Whether we participate in a spelling bee, a game of softball, or a video game, we strive to win. Rewards are given to the outstanding student, the top 7 percent, or the winning athlete. Winning enters every facet of life.

The drive to win spills over into the organizational environment. For example, in committee or group meetings members can compete with each other for attention and time. Instead of striving to accomplish the organization's goals by selecting the best solution, participants often attempt to make points with the boss or win an argument. Even departments within an

The Ravages of War

History has taught us the disastrous effects of imposing our will on others. One of the best examples is the aftermath of the Allied powers' demands for reparations from Germany after World War I. As the Germans' economy floundered under such great stress, their state of readiness to seek revenge grew. The Allies' attempt to achieve total domination sowed seeds for discontent that would be cultivated by one of the world's most notorious dictators, Adolf Hitler.

Contrast the win/lose approach of the Allied powers with the aftermath of World War II in Japan. Douglas MacArthur was sent to ensure peace and help establish a form of government that would have long-term rather than short-term benefits. American consultants such as W. Edwards Deming worked with the Japanese to develop structures and technologies to improve their standard of living. Today, Japan is a major (and peaceful) competitor in the global marketplace.

organization pit themselves against each other to gain prestige, power, or resources.

A number of problems result from this *win/lose* approach to problem solving. For example, much time may be spent discussing solutions that do not accomplish the goals of the organization. In addition, decisions may be delayed because of the implications of the decision to the winner or to the loser. If opposing forces are equal in power, a deadlock may result. Consequently, no solution will be implemented. People who are not aggressive may withdraw and refuse to participate. Focus of discussion on one or two solutions may prevent the analysis of more and better alternatives. Repeated involvement in win/lose confrontations may decrease or destroy the sensitivity of participants to the problem-solving process. Members may fail to participate in, let alone attend, the committee meeting. Anger may disrupt the meeting, interfere with the desire to understand problems from another point of view, and leave the losers resentful. Resulting solutions may be sabotaged by the losers. The resulting defensiveness of participants will prevent a positive team approach to problem solving.

The characteristics of the win/lose situation include *dominance of power* or *authority,*[10] often referred to as the boss syndrome. The boss asserts his role or position to get the job done. He implies, "You do it because I'm the boss."

A second example of the win/lose situation is ignoring attempts to influence or *giving no support.* For example, if someone poses a particularly controversial idea or one that does not suit your purposes, you give it no support.

Another approach to win/lose is *majority rule* or *vote taking.* There is always a winner and a loser. The loser, or the minority, does not gain anything from the results and frequently undermines the solution.

A final form of win/lose approach is called *railroading.* This is the use of pressure and other tactics to enforce minority opinion. We may coerce a person, or we may apply pressure in some way concerning the person's future with the organization, so that he or she will go along with our point of view.

Lose/Lose

In theory, the *lose/lose* strategy is preferable to win/lose because it entails compromise. In other words, both parties get something, and there is no loser; or conversely, both parties lose something, and no one side gets everything it wants.

Since we are conditioned to "win" from our early years, the idea of compromising or giving up something does not come easily. We have a cultural preoccupation with winning or losing, whatever the arena. From winning the national championship to beating the competition, our society rewards the top performer. To be second best or settle for less than we planned puts us in the position of losing.

Many conflicts will ultimately be resolved through compromise. A seller may ask $100,000 for a house; however, selling it means reducing the price to one that is mutually agreeable to both buyer and seller. The buyer and seller can trade concessions; perhaps the seller will pay the closing costs in exchange for a higher price. In the long run, both parties will be satisfied with the agreement.

If the two parties cannot reach agreement, the solution may require a third-party decision made by an arbitrator, or it may mean resorting to the use of rules. This latter approach frequently occurs when a manager faces a situation in which neither party's position is desirable.

Win/Win

This third form of conflict resolution is the most desirable. All parties agree on the solution, and the solution is not unacceptable to anyone. There are two kinds of *win/win* situations: consensus and integrative.

Consensus

In a *consensus* situation, the focus is on solving the problem rather than on the solution itself. Voting, trading, or averaging do not occur. Conflict is accepted by the parties as healthful toward achieving a high-quality solution. Consensus centers on analyzing the alternatives. Parties do not become polarized because there are a variety of solutions from which to pick to satisfy everyone's needs.

The opposite is true of the obliging or yielding approach. Acceptance, affiliation, and trust are paramount in importance. This approach frequently results in sacrificing personal goals to the goals of the opposition. A problem-solving style integrates the goals of both parties to reach a mutually acceptable solution.

According to studies of interaction between these styles, stalemates occur when win/lose battlers or soft bargainers negotiate with an opponent using their same style. In contrast, problem solvers will reach quick agreement with another problem solver or soft bargainer. As you might expect, the battler wins over the soft bargainer 90 percent of the time and, surprisingly, wins over the problem solver 50 percent of the time.[13]

We all become embroiled in win/lose situations. The important thing is that we recognize the win/lose mode. If the outcome isn't win/lose, it's likely to be lose/lose, or everyone has to give up something. A manager's goals should be that everyone gains.

Recently, an angry student berated several faculty members because he could not schedule the courses he desired for the fall semester. Finally, having lost his temper with the student, a faculty member approached one of the college deans and told her, "This is your job, you take care of it." By this time the student's face was red and the professor was seething. Both the professor and student were ready to come to physical blows. The administrative official immediately sought the assistance of a trained college counselor.

The first approach the counselor used was to remove the student to a quiet area and ask him to explain the problem. The counselor then stated calmly, "I understand why you're upset. I would be, too. You have a scheduling problem, but we can work it out." As the student continued to display his temper, the counselor became even more low key. Recognizing the student needed a cooling off period, he said, "I can help you. We can either sit down now and work things out, or you can come back later. You have to make the decision." While it took a moment for the student to regain his composure, he realized that he was not making any progress by continuing his angry behavior. After working with the counselor for a few minutes, he resolved his problem.

It's difficult for one person to turn around a win/lose confrontation. To do so requires the help of other participants. If you believe a discussion is becoming a win/lose confrontation, try to restate or clarify the group goal. Be sure the goals are clear and understandable. Try to look at things from the other person's point of view. This will provide insight and perhaps uncover problems you previously failed to recognize. Recognize that there is more than one way to solve a problem. Avoid categorical statements such as "there is only one real solution," or "I think that's the best way." Be sure everyone participates in the discussion. If you detect hesitancy or lack of understanding from a group member, encourage questions and expression of point of view. Don't vote. Try to gain agreement by the whole group. Make sure compromises are not superficial agreements. Be alert to loaded language and persuasion. Try to encourage other group members not to use them. Statements such as "Anyone can see that" or "An experienced person would know this" are off limits.

Strategies can be either outcome or goal directed. The win/win strategy is preferable because everyone agrees on the solution. In addition to strategies, however, scholars have also identified several methods for reducing conflict. Used in tandem with the win/win, win/lose, or lose/lose strategies, they can reinforce either an outcome- or goal-directed approach. The following section identifies and defines these methods.

Methods for Reducing Conflict

Pondy's stages of the conflict episode help us better understand how conflict occurs. Strategies such as win/win, lose/lose, and win/lose provide basic approaches to conflict resolution. However, Blake and Mouton studied these strategies and discovered that people frequently employ methods that take the form of withdrawing or avoiding, forcing, smoothing, confronting, or compromising.[14]

1. *Withdrawing.* An individual who uses withdrawal as a method for conflict reduction either retreats or retires from conflict. This action avoids the conflict by disengaging, abandoning, and eliminating the areas of conflict from consideration. Withdrawing as a method of conflict resolution can actually intensify the conflict episode, since frustration and dissatisfaction increase as long as the problem is not addressed and continues to exist. The informal communication network can become active as individuals attempt to cope with the situation. Overt and covert attempts to resolve the underlying problem can result in debilitating organizational behavior.

2. *Forcing.* To force means to exert pressure and may include constraining or compelling action by physical, intellectual, ethical, or moral means. In this situation, the manager uses power and position to achieve the desired response. Forcing can frequently lead to problems with solution implementation, including resistance, sabotage, stonewalling, and other overt and covert actions.

3. *Smoothing.* The individual who uses smoothing as a method attempts to explain or gain understanding of the problem. Typically this approach attempts to minimize what is harsh, crude, offending, or disagreeable; explain

differing points of view; or provide valuable information that may give insight to the situation.

4. *Confronting* (also called *problem solving*). Confronting a problem means recognizing that a problem exists and taking steps to resolve it rather than ignoring or avoiding it. Both parties examine the symptoms, causes, and potential solutions. Participation in the process is important, particularly if the problem is complex and involves many people. Improved acceptance, communication, and implementation of the solution are by-products of this method. (Chapter 13 discusses in detail the steps for problem solving.)

5. *Compromising.* When two parties solve a problem by mutual concession, they compromise. Both parties get something out of the solution. It is rare that both parties involved in conflict resolution can get everything that they want when they want it. An example of compromising is accepting a new title or job redesign rather than an increase in salary.

Studies of these methods indicate that constructive handling of conflict-ridden situations occurs with confronting and smoothing. Withdrawing and forcing have adverse impacts. Compromising has little impact on conflict resolution.

Research findings show that the most effective supervisors used conflict-resolution methods in the following order: (1) confrontation, (2) smoothing, (3) compromise, (4) forcing, and (5) withdrawal. Less effective supervisors applied (1) confrontation, (2) forcing, (3) withdrawal, (4) smoothing, and (5) compromise. Forcing was the least effective means of resolving a conflict-ridden situation.[15]

Once you are in a conflict-ridden situation, you must be able to determine the stage or intensity of the conflict, your strategy, whether it is win/win, lose/lose, or win/lose, and the methods that will help you achieve the desired outcome. Critical to each of these decisions is the form of intervention you will employ. You must ask yourself three questions: Are you directly intervening as a party of the dispute? Are you acting as a mediator between two disputing parties? Is it necessary to have an arbitrator decide the outcome? An affirmative answer to any one of these questions determines the role you will play. The next section explains each form of intervention and when it is appropriate.

FORMS OF INTERVENTION

Three kinds of intervention are possible in a conflict situation: negotiation, mediation, and arbitration. The form of intervention affects the process, roles, and outcome.

Negotiation

BUYER: Nice car. What are you asking for it?

SELLER: Like it? Vintage 1966 Mustang almost in mint condition. I've completely overhauled and restored it inside and out. It would be difficult to part with on any terms, but I'll let you have it for $5,500.

BUYER: Like I said before, nice car, but I'm not willing to go that high. How about $3,500?

SELLER: You can't be serious! Make me a real offer.

BUYER: Looks like it's seen a few accidents and several paint jobs. I'll give you $4,000.

SELLER: Can't do it, but if you give me cash, I'll let you have it for $5,000.

BUYER: I guess you would! $4,500 and that's my final offer.

The bargaining process is a common form of negotiation. Whether you are an engineer, architect, banker, or educator, you will have to work out agreements between superiors, subordinates, or external groups in order to achieve your goals and the goals of the organization. *Negotiation* is the attempt of two parties to reach an agreement or smooth out differences.

Negotiation can occur on two levels. On one level you must decide on the substantive question. In the dialogue above, for example, the substance of the negotiation was the price to be paid for the Mustang: cash or other compensation, and conditions. On another level you must decide what procedure you will follow to negotiate the substance.[16] Each approach you make toward the agreement on cost and conditions results in a response from the other party. This is similar to a chess game, in which each play can affect the next. In fact, each move can determine what direction the game takes or whether play continues.

The process level is particularly important when you are dealing with someone from another culture. In India a 2,000-year-old textbook on statecraft and diplomacy called *Arthasastra* provides negotiation strategies that have had the same impact on the East that Machiavelli's *The Prince* has had in the West.[17] These strategies include *Shaam, Daan, Dand,* and *Bhed.* Basically, *Shaam* means openness or friendliness and begins each negotiation. *Daan* is the "price," or concession, that each party is willing to make. *Dand* is the "stick," or show of power and willingness to use it. *Bhed* is the ability to play the game with cunning. This road map or process provides approaches that can be selected for the appropriate situation. John H. Norton suggests considering the following cultural differences that may affect the process level:

> The tolerance of silence in a conversation, . . . the amount of trust or suspicion toward strangers, respect for age and gender, the number of inches at which the presence of another person becomes uncomfortable, the value of time, . . . the

Shamir Stalls?

After Yitzhak Shamir lost his position as prime minister in Israel, he was reported to have said that he planned to stall peace talks with the Palestinians for a decade with the hope of increasing the number of Jewish settlers in Israeli-occupied territories.[18] According to *Maariv,* an independent Israeli newspaper, Shamir stated, "I would have conducted negotiations on autonomy for ten years and in the meantime we would have reached half a million people."[19] While Shamir's alleged statements confirmed opponents' suspicions, a spokesperson for Shamir denied the accuracy of the report.

meaning of eye contact, competition vs. consensus, the precise meaning of certain gestures, the nature and use of humor.[20]

Overt and Covert Negotiation

During negotiations, participants often resort to overt or covert "power plays."[21] *Overt* activities are not secret; the negotiating party openly communicates its position. They may include cooperative clues, promises, or threats. In contrast, *covert* activities are hidden attempts to manage conflict and subvert or contain the opponent.

Typically, the party in a position of power does not see the need to engage in negotiation. As a result, stronger opponents use covert strategies such as manipulation, disadvantaging (putting the opposition in a weaker position), seduction (offering enticements or largesse), buying influence (paying people off by titles or pay increases), coopting (offering token appointments), emotional extortion (withdrawing support, doing favors, collecting debts), or "divide and conquer" (splitting the opposition). The weaker party may use covert means because it cannot risk an overt approach. Some examples might be passive resistance, concealment, negativism, noncompliance, or stalling.

Bluffing

Bluffing, which can be overt or covert, is directed at creating a perception of power and its use. The use of a bluff is more effective for the short term and often consists of a deliberate lie or misrepresentation of facts. If a bluff involves coercion, outright deception, establishing an unfair advantage, or deliberate harassment, it is considered unethical.[22]

Regardless of an opponent's strength, it's important to remember that manipulative tactics create a good guy/bad guy dichotomy; improperly advantage one side over the other; rely on deceit, rumors, lies, or distortion; and damage the possibility of achieving the one essential ingredient of conflict resolution: trust.[23]

Palm Greasing

It is a common occurrence in some Third World countries to expect to pay a bribe for business. Some agent-distributors accept this as a fact of life and resort to what is commonly called "palm greasing." According to William F. Pendergast, the U.S. Foreign Corrupt Practices Act (FCPA) "prohibits offers, gifts or promises of money to foreign officials to win or keep business."[24] Bribery is a complicated issue that can become extremely costly. For example, for each payment of a bribe you could spend five years in jail and pay "up to $2 million."[25] However, money paid to speed up processing of work is acceptable and not regarded as shady or illegal in many cultures. "It's perfectly all right to pay a clerk to stamp a document faster or a customs agent to hurry with the forms."[26]

Steps for Effective Negotiation

In their book, *Getting to Yes,* Roger Fisher and William Ury describe the soft, hard, and principled bargainers found in Table 14.1.[27] Soft and hard bargainers are *positional bargainers.* Positional bargaining is inefficient and biased in favor of the hard bargainer. Instead of focusing on position, *principled* bargainers "focus on interests, mutually satisfying options, and fair standards."[28] Fisher and Ury offer the following four points:

Read My Lips

When George Bush made the promise, "Read my lips, no new taxes," during his 1988 campaign for President of the United States, he had no idea how much six words in the form of one "sound bite" would return to haunt him. There had been much debate about including the statement in Bush's speech at the Republican National Convention. Some members of his staff believed it irresponsible, given the amount of the deficit. Others believed that Bush needed this kind of tough-guy image to break the perception of a loyal and subservient relationship to Reagan. Thus began a tug-of-war with speechwriter Peggy Noonan and media consultant Roger Ailes on one side and adviser Richard G. Darman on the other.[29]

The debate centered around taking a clear position versus serving the interests of the Republican Party without getting locked into an impossible promise. Bush pollster Robert Teeter advised against a "no tax" stance, but later changed his mind. Arguments intensified around the

(continued)

line, "Read my lips, no new taxes." Every time Darman removed the line from a draft, Noonan restored it. Finally, Noonan, Ailes, and Teeter prevailed.

The six words registered a very positive response with voters. The position was restated in a variety of ways, but it all came out the same: no new taxes. In his 1990 State of the Union address, Bush promised that his spending plan "balances the budget by 1993 with no new taxes."[30] That same year, as part of a budget agreement with Congress, Bush approved a deficit-reduction measure that included raising taxes.

Later, during the 1992 Presidential race, Bush declared that he had made a "mistake" by agreeing to the taxes and directed his ire at a Congress controlled by Democrats. This "mistake" was to be reiterated over and over again by his opponents during the campaign.

1. Do not confuse the people with the problem. Keep them separate.
2. Avoid positional bargaining. Determine underlying interests, then focus on them.
3. Do not select a solution while under pressure. This may limit its creativity and value. Consider as many possibilities as you can.
4. Agree on criteria or standards for measuring the effectiveness of the solution. Insist that objective standards be used.

TABLE 14.1 Bargaining Positions

The Soft Bargainer:
Seeks outcome of mutual agreement; wants to maintain friendly relationship; willing to make concessions; yielding; trusting; takes the initiative and makes offers; willingly discloses minimum needs (the bottom line).
The Hard Bargainer:
Seeks outcome of "victory"; sees other party as opponent or adversary; demands concessions; unyielding; distrusting; "digs into position"; will threaten to get way; misrepresents interests (the bottom line); wants to "win."
The Principled Bargainer:
Seeks outcome based on merits of the situation; focuses on the problem and interests rather than on people and positions; searches for common ground and mutual interests; insists on objective criteria for determining outcomes; avoids a win/lose approach and contests of will.

Source: Adapted from Roger Fisher and William Ury, *Getting to Yes: Negotiating Agreement Without Giving In* (Boston: Houghton Mifflin, 1981).

Nanjing Neighborhood Committees

Mediation has been going on in Eastern cultures for hundreds of years. James A. Wall, Jr., conducted an "exploratory study of 25 practicing mediators in the city of Nanjing, People's Republic of China," located in one of the nation's richest provinces.[31] In this city of about 4 million people, households are grouped into "neighborhood committees" that include about 500 people. Committee members serve in specific roles, including a head, street guards, an assistant for family planning (usually a female), and two to five mediators. The responsibility of the mediators is to resolve conflicts in the streets. Wall interviewed these mediators to determine the type of disputes and the techniques used to resolve them.

Although discussion is frequently used in the West, Chinese rarely talk individually to parties involved in the dispute. This technique is viewed as offensive in China. "Private discussions are not used because almost all social interactions are open to the group and, usually, the public."[32] Wall's study concluded that "more techniques lead to successful mediations." Specifically, the data showed that 147 conflict resolution techniques were used in the twenty-five successful mediations and 116 techniques in the unsuccessful ones. Chinese negotiators did not give up. If one approach did not work, they tried another. Persistence was a basic philosophy.

Mediation and Arbitration

Occasions will arise when two parties are not able to negotiate and reach a solution. In some of these cases the manager may have to intervene to promote reconciliation or to interpret each party's stance to the other. As we saw earlier, mediation is the negotiation of a compromise between hostile or incompatible viewpoints, demands, or attitudes. The mediator acts as a neutral third party to help in the reconciliation process. Consumer protection agencies, for example, act as mediators between customers and retail establishments.

Mediators must determine the problem, gather information necessary for its resolution, get and maintain involvement of the disputing parties, defuse emotions, analyze the complaint and determine alternatives, present these alternatives to the adversaries, and record the outcome. This task is made more difficult because only 45 percent of disputing parties desire a mediator's involvement. If mediation fails to resolve the conflict, arbitration may be necessary.

Arbitration is the hearing and determination of a case in question by a person chosen by the conflicting parties or appointed under a statutory authority. The arbitrator acts as a judge and has power to decide. Small claims courts are a form of arbitration.

While negotiation can occur at any time between two disputing parties, formal mediation and arbitration procedures are usually outlined by organizational policies. Grievance policies and union contracts formally identify the rules and procedures. An employee grievance may begin as a one-to-one problem-solving session between superior and subordinate. If the parties fail to resolve the problems, the subordinate may go to the next step and formally submit a written grievance to the next line of authority. As a mediator, the third party will attempt to resolve the grievance. If this step fails, a formal ruling may be necessary so that the employee can present the grievance to a grievance panel. After hearing the case, the chosen authority will make a decision.

Because of losses accrued in the form of time and productivity when mediation and arbitration are necessary, most organizations encourage conflict resolution through negotiation.

STEPS IN CONFLICT MANAGEMENT

The following steps in conflict management can lead to effective and efficient decision making.

1. **Prepare for conflict.** Be aware that communication leads to conflict resolution. Know your participants. Study them meticulously to determine their opinions about the issue. Encourage them to share their point of view and the reasoning behind it. Remember that awareness of others' perceptions is an aid in conflict resolution.
2. **Defuse emotions.** Sometimes we add to conflict by dealing with a problem while participants are in an emotional state. People cannot be rational and act in a thinking mode when their emotions are overruling their logic. One of the most obvious examples is the child who throws tantrums. A parent cannot reason with such a child. Typical approaches are to send the child to his or her room or to walk away. When the tantrum is over, the parent can gain the child's attention. Sometimes employees also throw tantrums. If a problem-solving approach is tried while the employee or manager is in this state of mind, very little will result. If participants become emotional in a group session, a break is essential. It's important to recognize that all of us become emotional at times and need an opportunity to cool off before proceeding to the business at hand.

   In addition to cooling-off periods, other approaches to defusing emotions are reassuring or smoothing and acceptance. Many of us need to be reassured about our worth and value to the group. Minor anxieties and fears may need some attention and understanding. Simply recognizing that we accept others' point of view and their right to express it is important to group participation. Communication spent in these modes can eliminate hidden agendas and problems during the discussion phase.
3. **Focus on questions that ask why, how, and what.** What seem to be the fundamental difficulties? Are there indications that others are concerned?

Analyze the problem to determine the basic issues. State the problem as a goal or as an obstacle rather than as a solution. Identify obstacles to goal attainment. Depersonalize the problem.

4. **Search jointly for solutions.** Use creative approaches to problem solving, such as nominal techniques or brainstorming. Surveys and interviews can add information that may assist in decision making. Each participant should play a role and have an opportunity to express his or her point of view.
5. **Evaluate solutions in terms of both quality and acceptability.** Parties should not be required to justify personal feelings or preferences. Specific criteria should be agreed on for evaluation and handled one at a time. Avoid expression of self-oriented needs. Avoid voting (unless the group is using a method of parliamentary procedure), averaging, coin flipping, or any form of win/lose agreement. Where necessary, divide the problem into parts that can be handled by subgroups. Resolve feelings of conflict before continuing the problem-solving process.

A GLOBAL PERSPECTIVE

Negotiating Across Cultures

Different cultures require different approaches for resolving conflict. Understanding a particular culture and its politics is fundamental to understanding the communication strategies that work in this setting. Imposing the ethical standards of one culture on another has severe limitations. As Vernon Cronen notes, "morality, social structure, and action are inextricably related."[33]

In an effort to determine cultural effects on approaches to conflict resolution, M. Kamil Kozan investigated conflict management styles in Turkey and Jordan. Using the *Rahim Organizational Conflict Inventory–II,* Kozan's study focused on the following conflict management styles:

- *Dominating* — Forcing, use of power
- *Obliging* — Yielding, conceding to the opposing party
- *Compromising* — Giving up something
- *Avoiding* — Sidestepping the issue
- *Integrating* — Confronting the problem and integrating different viewpoints

Rahim's inventory, used to study U.S. managers, found that they were primarily obliging with superiors, integrating with subordinates, and compromising with peers.[34] While Jordan and Turkey have different heritages, both were moving from a traditional to a modern, industrialized society. Yet Kozan's study found that dominant styles in these two countries differed. Turkish managers were "dominating with subordinates, obliging with superiors, and avoiding with peers."[35] These styles, however, did not hold true for Jordan, where no dominating styles emerged and three out of four managers made decisions without involving subordinates.[36] Ironically, the Jordan culture emphasizes extended discussion and debate and has an aversion to domination.

> This undoubtedly contrasts with popularly held views of Arabs in the West, reinforced largely through media coverage of political conflicts in the region. This is not to imply that conflict was basically played down or smoothed over in Jordanian organizations. Actually, bargaining and compromising were quite widespread. Yet this was done in a style that is essential to doing business in this country. For example, a Western manager who feels pressure for faster results should nevertheless avoid forcing the issue. Deliberate use of power tactics is likely to have adverse effects in this culture. It may also turn the disagreement into a personal issue, making it altogether unmanageable.[37]

Raymond Cohen suggests some of the following lessons for negotiating across cultures:[38]

1. Learn your opponent's culture, language, and history.
2. Get to know the opposition and establish a personal relationship.
3. Recognize that your message may be perceived differently than you intended and that *you* may perceive the opposition's message differently than they intended.
4. Be aware of the nonverbal messages and interpretations of your verbal and nonverbal messages.
5. Recognize that status and face are very important to individuals—avoid anything that may lead to loss of face for your opponent.
6. Do not impose "artificial time constraints."

ETHICS: RIGHT OR WRONG?

Change and Conflict at the South Side Family and Children's Agency
Herb Bisno

The Agency is funded by voluntary contributions, an endowment administered by the granting foundation, client fees, and limited governmental payments for "purchased" services. It is well established in the community and provides a broad range of family and children's services. The staff consists of a director, 25 workers from various of the helping professions, the business manager, and eight support staff.

After a six-month search by a selection committee of the Board of Directors, a replacement was appointed for the long-serving former director, who had died on the job. The new executive came highly recommended as being one of the new breed of sophisticated administrators with a strong orientation toward technical efficiency, economic rationality, and accountability. During the selection process the members of the committee were led to believe that the prospective director believed in "maximum feasible participation" by staff in all aspects of organizational decision making. Upon appointment, the new director was permitted to select a deputy from outside the agency.

Shortly after assuming the position, the director made it quite clear that "maximum feasible participation" implied decision making by the "responsible and the competent." In practice this meant that the basic administrative decisions and policy recommendations to the board would be the prerogative of the executive.

The previous executive committee, consisting of the former director, the three supervisors of the major functional units, the business manager, two elected professional staff, and one elected member of the support staff, was dissolved.

In the place of this executive committee, the director announced the formation of an "Executive Advisory Committee" that would play a "vital role" in the decision-making process. This new advisory committee was to consist of the director, the new hand-picked deputy, the business manager, the three supervisors, and one member of the professional staff selected by the director. The advisory committee would meet at the pleasure of the director. During the first six months of the new director's months of tenure, the committee met twice, both times in the director's large office.

The director informed the supervisors that they would be receiving a salary increase and that they could count on support for their decisions from the "top." It was suggested to the supervisors that they meet monthly with the workers in their respective units and that the workers be encouraged to make suggestions for improving the efficiency of the agency.

It should be noted that these changes in the decision-making process took place in the context of an increasingly conservative social climate.

The professional and support staffs (below the level of supervisor), through their elected spokespersons, expressed objections to the new decision-making procedures, claiming that they were "authoritarian." They requested a meeting to discuss the matter. In response, the director asked the staff to appoint two of its members to attend a meeting at which their concerns would be discussed.

The meeting was held in the board's conference room, with the director in the chair, flanked by the vice president of the board, the deputy director, the business manager, and the three supervisors. The director opened the meeting by expressing pleasure at the attendance by the two staff representatives. This was followed by a statement by the director (with the vice president of the board nodding in apparent agreement) that the previous system has been replaced because that type of so-called industrial democracy was inefficient, inappropriate, and violated the principle that decisions should be made by those most qualified to make them.

The staff representatives then were invited to comment or ask questions. After they finished doing so, a few minutes of general discussion followed, during which all the other participants (except the staff representatives) supported the director. The director then indicated that it was good to have had various views aired and that there was overwhelming support for the new procedures. The director then closed the meeting in a friendly manner, shaking hands with the various participants.

The staff representatives left the meeting convinced that overt resistance would be too risky and probably unsuccessful. At a secret evening meeting of the staff, held in the home of one of them, it was decided that a covert campaign of resistance would be undertaken. This was to include a private meeting with the head of the foundation that provides the endowment, the instigating of a critical letter-writing campaign by members of "client" groups in the community, the leaking of an audio tape (the staff representatives had secretly taped the meeting for a prominent "liberal" member of the board), and a slow-down in work (unofficially reducing the number of clients to be seen). In addition, a friendly newspaper reporter was to be tipped off and given the material for a story.[39]

Case Questions

1. Give examples from this case of stages in Pondy's conflict episode.
2. What strategies were used by management and staff to resolve conflict? How were these strategies communicated?
3. What *covert* "power plays" were used by management? by staff? Discuss the potential consequences of these actions.
4. What should management do now?

SUMMARY

Conflict is a natural phenomenon that can be managed. Since conflict encourages sounder decision making and stimulates interest, it can have a positive effect.

Differing attitudes and perceptions, struggles over power, prestige, or rewards, and unclear roles and expectations can all be causes of conflict. Communication between the differing parties increases cooperation and the likelihood of reaching agreement. To do this, you will need to minimize or eliminate the cause as well as recognize that conflict is a natural and manageable phenomenon. The absence of conflict is not necessarily good, since, as noted earlier, conflict can often have beneficial effects.

Effective management requires an understanding of the conflict episode. Pondy describes a set of underlying conditions which create the first or *latent* stage. The next stage occurs when the parties *perceive* these conditions exist. If the conditions intensify in effect, the *felt* conflict stage begins. If conditions are not resolved, the *manifest conflict* stage surfaces in overt or covert action releasing tension. Finally, *conflict aftermath* is the stage or condition that results from the action taken.

Managers participating in a conflict episode will find several forms of intervention useful. These forms depend on the intensity of the conflict and the policies of the organization. *Negotiation* is direct intervention between two parties who attempt to arrive at a settlement. *Mediation* requires a third-party neutral who interprets the parties to each other and promotes reconciliation. Finally, *arbitration* is the intervention of an appointed authority given the power to decide after hearing the differing complaints. Of these forms of intervention, direct negotiation is least costly in terms of time spent and effect on productivity.

Blake and Mouton identified five methods for reducing conflict: *compromising, confronting* or *problem solving, forcing, smoothing,* and *withdrawing.* Extensive research by Burke indicated the most effective way of handling conflict was *confronting* or *problem solving.* Forcing was ineffective.

An understanding of methods is important, but an understanding of strategies is crucial. Parties engage in strategies that are *outcome directed* (win/lose or lose/lose) or *goal directed* (win/win). The *win/lose* strategy sets an atmosphere of victory or defeat. Preferable to win/lose is the *lose/lose* strategy. Both sides lose something as well as gain something. Finally, the *win/win* strategy focuses on the problem rather than the solution. The solution is acceptable to everyone.

Several steps to conflict resolution can be used as guidelines to effective decision making. The following steps reinforce the win/win strategy:

1. Prepare for conflict.
2. Defuse emotions.
3. Focus on questions that ask why, how, and what.
4. Search jointly for solutions.
5. Evaluate solutions in terms of both quality and acceptability.

The key to managing conflict is an awareness that conflict is healthy and leads to better decision making. If participants accept this principle and apply problem-solving skills, then greater commitment, more creative alternatives, and sounder decisions will more than likely result.

KEY WORDS

arbitration	disadvantaging	mediation	stonewalling
bluffing	emotional extortion	negotiation	win/lose
compromising	felt conflict	overt negotiation	win/lose battler
conflict episode	forcing	perceived conflict	win/win
confronting	integrative	problem solver	withdrawing
consensus	latent conflict	smoothing	
co-opting	lose/lose	soft bargainer	
covert negotiation	manifest conflict	sources of conflict	

REVIEW QUESTIONS

1. Explain how conflict can be both a constructive and destructive process.
2. Describe the different stages of conflict presented by Pondy.
3. The chapter presented three strategies for resolving conflict. Describe each and tell why one is the most desirable.
4. Five methods were listed for reducing conflict. What are the five, and how are they used?
5. Describe the three forms of intervention.

6. Five steps can be helpful in the overall managing of conflict. What are these steps?
7. Give some examples of how cultural differences can affect conflict resolution. How would you prepare to deal with these differences?
8. How does positional bargaining differ from principled bargaining? Give examples of each.
9. What does Kozan's investigation of conflict management styles in Turkey and Jordan teach you about cultural influences on conflict resolution?

EXERCISES

1. With your classmates, discuss the following problem and use Pondy's conflict episode as a guide. What is the source of conflict? Which stage of conflict does the employee describe? To manage the conflict, what should the employee do next?

   I get all the dirty jobs at the office because the foreman knows I won't complain or cause a fuss. I need his recommendation to get out of the division and into a better-paying job. Other people in the section don't have any ambition, so they don't work hard. They would stretch out a job all day if they could. But I want to get ahead.

2. Divide into groups consisting of six to eight participants. Each group should agree on a type of business it would like to represent as the board of directors.
   a. Your employees are listed below [see d]. Diagram a formal organization chart that includes eight positions, and assign each employee a position.
   b. Because of a financial squeeze, your organization must terminate an employee. Decide as a group which employee to terminate.
   c. Select one observer. The role of the observer is to evaluate the group's interaction using the following questions:
   (1) Which participants displayed emotional reactions?
   (2) Which participants asked questions to help clarify general statements?
   (3) What strategies did participants use?
   (4) What methods of reducing conflict did participants use?
   (5) Which participants kept open minds about the ideas of other members of the group?
   d. Your employees have the following backgrounds. Place the position they hold in your organization next to their names.

Position	Name	Education	Age	Years at Company	Current Job Rating*	Marital Status	Children
________	Sam Jones	M.B.A.	52	5	4	D	2
________	Sue Smith	B.S. (Accounting)	35	1	3	M	1
________	Joe Barnes	2 years college	46	10	2	M	5
________	Bill Goode	B.A. (Business)	32	4	3	M	2
________	Gail Beck	High school	25	2	4	M	Pregnant
________	Guy Great	3 years college	21	1	4	S	0
________	Jane Grey	2 years college	37	7	3	D	2
________	Sally Sweet	High school	26	3	3	M	Stepson

*Job ratings are based on a scale from 1 to 5 with 5 the highest rating.

3. With your classmates, describe a recent conflict episode in which you participated. What strategies did participants use? What was the solution? Did it work?

REFERENCES

1. Peter Drucker, *Management: Tasks, Responsibilities, Practices* (New York: Harper & Row, 1973).
2. Herb Bisno, *Managing Conflict* (Newbury Park, Calif.: Sage Publications, 1988), pp. 13–14.
3. Ibid.
4. L. R. Hoffman, E. Harburg, and N. R. F. Maier, "Differences and Disagreements as Factors in Creative Group Problem Solving," *Journal of Abnormal Psychology*, 64 (1962), pp. 206–214.
5. Gordon L. Lippitt, "Managing Conflict in Today's Organizations," *Training and Development Journal* (July 1982), p. 67.
6. Ibid., p. 67.
7. Richard C. Huseman, "Interpersonal Conflict in the Modern Organization," in Richard C. Huseman, Cal M. Logue, and Dwight L. Freshley, eds., *Readings in Interpersonal and Organizational Communication*, 3rd ed. (Boston: Holbrook Press, 1977).
8. Louis Pondy, "Organizational Conflict: Concepts and Models," *Administrative Science Quarterly*, 12 (September 1967), pp. 299–306.
9. Alan C. Filley, "Conflict Resolution: The Ethic of the Good Loser," in Richard C. Huseman, Cal M. Logue, and Dwight L. Freshley, eds., *Readings in Interpersonal and Organizational Communication*, 3rd ed. (Boston: Holbrook Press, 1977).
10. Ibid., p. 236.
11. Ibid., p. 248–249.
12. Filley, "Conflict Resolution," p. 242.
13. L. L. Cummings, D. L. Harnett, and O. J. Stevens, "Risk, Fate, Conciliation and Trust: An International Study of Attitudinal Differences Among Executives," *Academy of Management Journal*, 14:3 (September 1971), pp. 285–304.
14. R. R. Blake, H. A. Shepard, and J. S. Mouton, *Managing Intergroup Conflict in Industry* (Houston, Tex.: Gulf Publishing, 1964).
15. R. J. Burke, "Methods of Resolving Superior-Subordinate Conflict: The Constructive Use of Subordinate Difference and Disagreements," *Organizational Behavior and Human Performance*, 5 (1970), pp. 393–411.
16. Roger Fisher, "Getting to Yes," *Management Review*, (February 1982), p. 19.
17. Deborah Grace Winer, "Winning Words: These Ancient Principles of Negotiation Made the Mehtas Rich," *Success* (November 1988), p. 61.
18. Clyde Haberman, "Shamir Is Said to Admit Plan to Stall Talks 'for 10 Years'," *The New York Times*, June 27, 1992, pp. 1–4.
19. Ibid.
20. John H. Norton, "Practice Makes Perfect in Negotiation Training: Cultural Understanding Is the Key," *World Trade* (February/March 1990), p. 69.
21. Bisno, *Managing Conflict*, p. 10.
22. Bisno, *Managing Conflict*, p. 145.
23. Bisno, *Managing Conflict*, pp. 80–87.
24. "Trade Hotline," *International Business* (November 1991), p. 12.
25. Ibid.
26. Ibid.
27. Fisher, "Getting to Yes," p. 20.
28. Ibid.
29. Bob Woodward, "The Anatomy of a Decision: Six Words that Shaped and May Sink the Bush Presidency," *Washington Post National Weekly Edition*, (October 12–18, 1992), pp. 6–7.
30. Ibid.
31. James A. Wall, Jr., M. Afzalur Rahim, ed., in *Theory and Research in Conflict Management* (New York: Praeger, 1990), pp. 110–117.
32. Ibid.
33. Vernon E. Cronen, Karen Joy Greenberg, ed., in *Conversations on Communications Ethics* (Norwood, N.J.: Ablex Publishing Corporation, 1991), p. 36.
34. M. Kamil Kozan, *Theory and Research in Conflict Management*, pp. 174–187.
35. Ibid., p. 176.
36. Ibid., pp. 180–184.
37. Ibid., p. 186.
38. Raymond Cohen, *Negotiating Across Cultures: Communication Obstacles in International Diplomacy* (Washington, D.C.: U.S. Institute of Peace Press, 1991), pp. 160–161.
39. Herb Bisno, *Managing Conflict*, (Newbury Park, Sage Publications, 1988), pp. 13–14. Reprinted by permission.

CHAPTER 15

Communication Strategies: Making Meetings Work

"**We're meeting managers** to death," says Robert Lefton, president of Psychological Associates, Inc., a St. Louis consulting firm. Harry Thompson, president of GenCorp, Inc.'s reinforced-plastics division agrees: "There are too many of them, with not enough meaning." Lefton's comment was made following a meeting of a large West Coast manufacturing company. Eighteen executives had gathered to discuss major restructuring of the organization. During the meeting these executives sidetracked the agenda to deliberate what to serve at an upcoming office party. Commented Lefton, "I asked the guy sitting next to me to estimate the salaries of the people in the room, and figured out that conversation cost the company $2,200."[1]

The Necessity of Meetings

Meetings are such an inescapable part of business that they are often the butt of organizational jokes: "A meeting is a meeting to decide when the next meeting will be held"; "A meeting comprises a group of the unfit, appointed by the unwilling, to do the unnecessary." Still, the wheels of modern organizations and industry are turned by meetings. A study by Harrison Conference Services and Hofstra University concluded, "Executives spend 25 to 75 percent of their days in meetings and consider about a third of those meetings unproductive."[2]

As one author stated, "The problem is not so much committees in management as it is the management of committees."[3] Members of management and staff of an organization attend meetings daily and weekly. In fact, when we add up the organizations to which we belong (academic, professional, religious, civic, and athletic), we sometimes receive the impression that there are more groups than people in the world. Professional businesspeople attend an average of one meeting a day. The average executive serves on three committees, finds an average of seven fellow executives sitting with him or her on each committee and wishes there were only four others, and meets with each of the committees about every two weeks. In addition to the formal meetings, he or she spends the equivalent of one working day a week in informal conferences and consultation with fellow executives.

Meetings are one of the most effective communication devices used in business. They allow one person or several to give information and ideas to many others in a short period of time. They can be labor and cost effective when used in the right ways.

This chapter examines purposes, types, strengths, weaknesses, and common characteristics of meetings. It concludes with suggestions for what managers should do before, during, and after meetings.

Advantages of Meetings

Meetings have become a regular part of business life for definite reasons.

More involvement. As we discussed in Chapter 12, employees who participate in the decision-making process are committed to team goals.[4] Such involvement ensures that team members are familiar with the problem, the need for change, possible solutions to the problem, and why a particular solution is adopted. Also they become involved personally in the decisions.

Better decisions. There is wisdom in numbers: The decision reached by several people should be better than the decision an individual reaches alone. When responsibilities are shared and completed by several people, more ideas are available during discussion. Also, the presence of several members helps individual members escape the biases that often interfere with decision making.

Quicker completion. When many minds and hands work on a project, the job can be completed more quickly than it could have been with one person.

Disadvantages of Meetings

Although there are definite advantages to having people work in groups, several major limitations must be confronted and resolved.

Time consuming. As Chapter 3 showed, face-to-face communication and interaction are more desirable than one-way communication. It takes longer, however, for two people to talk, work through issues, and make resolutions than it does for one person. When several members are added and the two-way process observed, time requirements are even greater. A Heldrick and Struggles survey of Fortune 500 companies found that 71 percent of chief executives spend over 15 hours per week in meetings.[5] According to Rosenblatt, Cheatham, and Watt, the time issue would not be such a problem if so much time were not wasted:

> Groups waste time in a number of ways: (1) too much time is spent pursuing a single train of thought, with the result that the agenda cannot be completed; (2) members insist on discussing irrelevant points; (3) members spend so much time maintaining group morale and other human relations matters that time does not permit solving the problem assigned to the committee.[6]

Answerable to management. Meetings are only as effective as the decisions they reach and the action steps that they send to management or other groups to implement. If management has endowed the group that meets with the freedom to make decisions that will be carried out, the meeting can accomplish its purpose. If management rediscusses each issue and arrives at its own decisions, the effectiveness of the meeting is minimized. Such a team will "spin its wheels" only a few times before management's behavior reduces morale and incentive to the point of crippling the meeting.

The wrong people attend. Unless the people who have the needed information and the power to make the right decisions attend the meetings, the meeting's effectiveness is limited. A survey by management of the attendees should give a clear picture of the roles represented in the group, who should be replaced, and the types of new members who should be invited.

Expensive. A typical group meeting is a very expensive activity that can cost hundreds of thousands of dollars. For example, if we take the average executive described earlier, we can calculate how much of the company's money is spent weekly on his or her participation in meetings. On a salary of $50,000 per year, each work hour costs $24. Multiplying this by the 15 hours in committee meetings, the cost to the company for this executive attending those meetings is $360 per week. If we multiply that figure by the number of people with whom he or she met and the number of other groups that met on a weekly basis, we see the cost is staggering for the company.

The Weekly Meeting

Until René Grizzard was appointed vice-president of administrative services for Electronic Communication Systems, Inc., little communication took place among the six department directors. The previous vice-president of ECS, John Gray, did not believe in committees or meetings. He communicated with his staff through electronic mail, over the telephone or, when absolutely necessary, one to one. Each unit became autonomous and competed for his attention. Department directors quietly expressed to trusted subordinates their concerns that Gray gave most attention to or cared most about some other department. Consequently, they expressed little interest in cooperating or sharing resources at a time when the company was experiencing a shortfall of funds and cutting back on departmental budgets.

Grizzard realized her first responsibility was to establish a system of communication among the departments. She set up weekly meetings, limited to 50 minutes, during which directors informed each other about their current operations and schedules. Grizzard commented on opportunities or problems, but her main purpose was to motivate the directors and encourage communication and cooperation. She also held individual meetings or scheduled other contacts with the directors. During these exchanges she limited her communication to discussing specific problems, providing guidance, or responding to requests.

By the end of the fourth meeting, the directors were sharing ideas and coordinating their efforts—they were even suggesting ways that their own units could cut costs, share personnel, and contribute resources to the success of another unit's project. At the end of six months, they literally charged out of the room to discuss the implementation of cooperative programs. Best of all, productivity soared and the division received special recognition in a nationwide review of organizational productivity.

The longer the meeting and the greater the number of participants, the more expensive the gathering. For this reason meetings should be held only when the results justify the expense. Before calling a meeting a manager should consider if there is a more time- and cost-saving way of communicating the same information. If a decision is made to go ahead with the meeting, the leader should concentrate on having it highly organized and running it efficiently.

Slow and poorly run. This problem affects the cost problem and arises when the leader and members lack the skills necessary for successful information presentation and discussion.

Types of Meetings

The purposes of meetings in the business world can be best understood by examining the different categories of groups. Meetings may be classified as personal, organizational, and public. Several types are found under each division.

Personal Meetings

Personal meetings are usually informally structured and sometimes have no real purpose. Often the main function is maintaining relationships and interaction among members.

The happening. Occasionally people find themselves in the midst of others. It can occur at a bus stop, in line at the office building snack bar, at cocktail parties, or at the lunch table. There does not have to be a purpose for the meeting, conversation can be shared or unshared, and the individuals can feel either high or low degrees of comfort and involvement.

The conversation group. After an initial happening people may seek out the other individuals and develop friendships or working relationships. If they meet regularly, the conversations can extend from social, non–work-related talk to grapevine gossip and even to some hypothetical ways to solve the organization's problems.

The study group. Participants in a classroom learning situation can develop an informal personal group into a study group. The emphasis is on learning and sharing knowledge with one another and clarifying original thought.

Organizational Meetings: Internal

Organizational meetings are highly task oriented and can consume a large amount of time if they are not structured and run efficiently. The proper conduct of work meetings will be described later in the chapter, after the following introduction to the various types of work groups.

Staff Meeting

One of the most common organizational meetings is the *staff meeting,* which consists of the supervisor and staff of a particular area or division. Since an organization is made up of numerous staff-level groupings, this type of group is often the most visible within a company. The purpose of the meetings, which are usually held weekly, is to make assignments, give instructions to subgroups, disseminate organizational information and policies, examine staff problems, and decide on solutions for these problems. The staff meeting is sometimes the only opportunity for the entire staff to assemble and talk; a tight agenda and effective facilitator are necessary if the group is to progress successfully and not turn into a free-for-all. If a manager uses an open and honest communication process, this meeting can facilitate upward, downward, and horizontal communication within the organization.

Production Meeting

When different departments are involved in work on a common project or in some way contribute to the work being done by others in the organization, they participate in *production meetings.* Either department heads or designated employees attend. The focus of the meeting can be on generating new information that will be sent to other divisions of the company, discussing procedures or instructions, or, more likely, solving budget, production, or work-flow problems.

Advisory Meeting

When a manager or supervisor wants to discuss information, disseminate news, or generate ideas, he or she calls an *advisory meeting.* For example, the IRS may have issued a new reporting procedure that takes effect immediately; the manager of the accounting department calls a special advisory meeting to discuss the proper handling of the procedure within the department. If a manager has received a "rush order," he or she might call together certain key people and lead off the discussion with "I need some input from you . . ." or "Can you tell me what would happen if . . . ?" or "How can we . . . ?"

Committee Meeting

A *committee* is formed when major decisions must be made but a superior either does not want to waste the time of the regular meeting group or knows that the input from several groups is important. Committees consequently consist of members who represent others. The people usually come from various parts of the organization with different information, different views, and different needs. But a committee is heterogeneous in nature, develops a mutual interest in the topic, and can be a "standing," a long-lasting, or a short-lived group.

The very nature of a committee means that it is task oriented and involved in information generation, problem solving, fact finding, or strategic policy-making. Committees are designed as democratic decision-making groups and consequently often use parliamentary procedure.

Quality Circle

The influence of Japanese management techniques on American business led to the growth of quality circles. A *quality circle* consists of five to ten employees who either work together or do work that affects others in the group. The homogeneous group meets regularly to identify, analyze, and solve work-related problems, which can be both task and maintenance related.

Membership is always voluntary, and the groups receive training in time usage and problem-solving techniques before they meet to actually discuss and solve work-related problems.

While problem solving and decision making occur in each of the types of work groups just discussed, this group is designed so that employees can discuss and make job-related decisions on their own without management's input and can then, with management's approval, implement their solutions. This approach has been found to improve morale and generate the most accurate solutions to problems. The groups meet regularly, and solutions can take between three months and a year to accomplish.

Professional Sharing Meeting

Rapid technological changes have prompted more and more businesses to send their technical and professional employees to seminars and professional association meetings. When these employees return, they update others in the organization at a *professional sharing meeting.* Usually the participants are colleagues, have a similar status, or have similar knowledge and skills.

Sales Meeting

For those involved in product sales and marketing, *sales meetings* are held to announce or explain new products, analyze customer acceptance, describe sales aids, and motivate employees. The meeting can focus on the design and production of the product but more often examines aspects of marketing and sales. A sales meeting usually involves a series of individual presentations and the use of multimedia devices.

Organization Meetings: External

Two types of meetings pertain exclusively to the organization and generally reflect on communication activities external to the business.

The Annual Meeting

In public corporations an *annual meeting* is required; most take place in the spring and are attended by the company's officers, the board of directors, and the stockholders. During this meeting stockholders have a rare opportunity to question the officers and directors on matters pertaining to the company. Usually the agendas consist of reelecting the directors, ratifying the appointment of outside accounting firms, approving changes in the company's pension or profit-sharing plans, and authorizing an increase in shares to smooth out stock splits or acquisitions.

Board of Directors' Meeting

The directors of a company are picked because of their knowledge, skills, backgrounds, affiliations, and desires to help run a particular organization. They also have varying tenures and display managerial ability and social consciousness. They are usually generalists, not specialists in the business focus. While a *board of directors* does not directly manage internal (management and staff) affairs, it is legally and ethically responsible for the total enterprise. A board will usually meet between two and four times a year and more often if necessary to make decisions. Meetings can be held in the company boardroom or at different sites. The meeting facilities are usually more attractive than those used for in-company groups.

Board meetings are usually closed to the public, although some members of management and staff are usually present to observe and answer questions. The president of the organization usually chairs the meetings. The chairperson offers no opinions but guides the group according to procedure. Since this group consists of individuals who closely guard their time, it is imperative that those meetings start and end on schedule and are tightly organized around an agenda.

Public Meetings

Public meetings differ from those held within the business because they are presented to an audience that often has no specific affiliation with the organization. Public meetings focus on specific topics, usually informally discussed by a group and projected to the observers, such as a city council zoning hearing. Because of their often large size and their potential for disarray, public meetings require forceful leadership and control of time, a firm agenda, and speakers.

Panel Discussion

When groups are too large to permit each individual to participate, panels of three to five members can be selected to discuss the topic in front of the general audience. Panel members should be well informed on the topic, an agenda should be developed and made known to the panel, and a moderator should control the ebb and flow of the conversation.

The format of each *panel discussion* will be different. Members can present short prepared statements; they can question and discuss the issues among themselves, and they can answer questions from the audience. If time permits, the panel may wish to talk through parts of the discussion in private before speaking to the public.

Symposium

A *symposium* is a structured meeting that involves little interaction among the participants. Three to five persons are again picked because of their expertise, and each presents a short prepared speech or report to the audience. A moderator introduces the program, acknowledges each speaker, and makes transitions between each speech. There is little interaction among the speakers, but the formal presentations can be followed by audience comments or questions directed to individual speakers.

Bland Meetings "Spiced Up" with Computers

New inventions in meeting technology are changing the way companies conduct business. Meeting rooms costing $50,000 to $200,000 provide the ingredients for perfecting the productivity of meetings while avoiding some of the more frustrating human proclivities. Gone are the filibusterers, daydreamers, and blowhards. In their place is a recipe for success. Software packages like VisionQuest by Collaborative Technologies Corp., IBM's TeamFocus, The Facilitator from DiscTech, and OptionFinder by Option Technologies, Inc. have opened new doors to streamline today's competitive environment. Numeric keypads let participants vote secretly on issues, record their thoughts, and generate ideas.

Here is how OptionFinder works. Before the meeting starts, the facilitator sets the agenda and inputs up to fifty-two questions to be answered in the meeting. Participants are given ten-button keypads. "When critical questions are addressed during the meeting, all meeting attendees can respond by making a selection . . . rather than having just the most vocal people answer." The group's opinion is displayed by video projection. Time is not wasted trying to test everyone's opinion, mediating arguments between dominant participants, or collecting and summarizing written comments. Instead, group members can immediately react and explain their responses. Other possibilities for using computers to facilitate meetings include generating and ranking ideas, evaluating the importance of needs, and storing responses and then printing them in various formats.[7]

DiscTech's Facilitator allows a recording secretary to type ideas into a program that literally "dumps" ideas into buckets. The secretary can move ideas from bucket to bucket, subdivide a bucket into two buckets of ideas, or dump a bucket of ideas altogether. Participants can also view ideas in a fishbone diagram. Finally, the minutes can be printed at the end of the meeting.

Using Vision Quest, Marriott employees generated 10,000 ideas in two months. Vice-President Carl DiPietro estimated that using normal problem-solving strategies, the same amount of work would have taken nine to twelve months. Modern technology enables group members to digress less, find areas of agreement more quickly, and be more productive.[8]

Forum

A *forum* is not a meeting in and of itself. It is instead a part of a panel, symposium, or other public presentation where the audience has a chance to interact. Here the audience members participate in the question-and-answer session and provide feedback to the speakers.

PRE-MEETING PLANNING: THE BASIS OF EFFECTIVE MEETINGS

When a meeting runs well you know that preliminary planning played a key role. No one wants to sit through a boring meeting that wastes everyone's time. Everyone who attends a meeting wants to have a reason to be present. Answering a few basic questions prior to a meeting can save you and your organization time and money.

Must You Have a Meeting?

All of us have taken time out of a busy schedule to attend a meeting only to find that our attendance wasn't needed, there was no purpose for the group to meet, the leader wasn't prepared, or the group was meeting because its meetings had become a habit. Before you schedule a meeting as a manager, ask yourself whether the meeting is the best use of everyone's time.

Aronoff, Baskin, Hays, and Davis list several factors that indicate when meetings should and should not be held.[9]

Meetings should be held

1. When issues require that several people be involved.
2. When interaction is needed to spur creativity or critical analysis.
3. When there is time to prepare for and to complete meetings.
4. When participants must act on the decision.
5. When a mutual exchange (feedback) is needed to assure that participants understand.

Meetings should not be held

1. When time pressures prevent adequate preparation.
2. When communication is to be one-way and no participant response is wanted.
3. When the problem is simple and can be handled by one person.
4. When commitment and input from participants are not required.
5. When participants cannot handle the conflict that is usually found in the problem-solving process.

What Is the Meeting's Objective?

Every meeting should have a clear purpose. Determining whether the purpose is to define a problem, seek a solution, share information, or exchange feelings about an issue will help you determine the type of meeting to hold, who should participate, and other important factors.

Every Monday at 7:00 A.M. salespeople at the Wilson Insurance Agency meet for coffee and donuts with agency owner Harold Wilson. The purpose of the meeting is to motivate personnel to achieve higher sales during the week that follows. Employees, however, will tell you that Mr. Wilson uses the same worn-out "positive mental attitude" stories and that they personally would rather sleep in for the extra hour each Monday. Contrast that non-productive meeting with the one held by the Dana Corporation each Friday at 3:00 P.M. The purpose of this social meeting is to relax and share socially, and it has increased productivity.

Who Should Attend the Meeting?

The only participants who should be invited are those whose attendance is really necessary and who can contribute to achieving the goal. Consider the following factors:

1. What resource will each person bring to the group?
2. What is each potential member's knowledge, attitude, and working relationship to the topic and the other members?
3. Is there anything about the future member that will cause him or her to help or hinder goal accomplishment?
4. Will the person's organizational position, title, or status interfere with or help the group as it moves toward the goal?
5. Are there political factions, hidden agendas, or previous hurt feelings that should influence the selection of new members?

How Large Should the Group Be?

Determining who should attend the meeting can help you decide how large the group should be. Other factors include: What is the complexity of the problem? How many people can the meeting facility hold? How much participation do you want from the members? Answers to all these questions will help you make a decision about group size.

Research has shown that most committee meetings have an average of eight members, although most members actually prefer a group size of only five members. One classic study by Slater reinforced the preference for five-member groups:

> Size five emerged clearly . . . as the size group which from the subjects' viewpoint was most effective in dealing with an intellectual task involving the collection and exchange of information about a situation, the coordination, analysis, and evaluation of this information, and a group decision regarding the appropriate administrative action to be taken in the situation.[10]

For each additional member there is less participatory time for all, more possible conflicts, the need for additional interaction, and more people to listen to and speak with.

At What Time Should the Meeting Be Held?

The time you pick for the meeting can have dynamic impact on the outcome. Berko offers some insight into this problem:

> When and where the group meets may have an effect on the decision-making process. Meetings held extremely early or extremely late in the day can cause

> problems. If people feel inconvenienced, they may react negatively, make quick and unfounded decisions, or not participate. The length of a meeting can also have an effect. As time drags on, people get irritated, distracted, and bored. It may be better to have several short meetings than one very long one. It is often wise to have a coffee break during what has become a long session. A simple physical action, such as standing up, can have a positive end result in relieving anxiety and indifference. A leader of a group should watch for such verbal or nonverbal signs as temper flares and fidgeting as possible signs of "it's been too long."[11]

Establishing time limits for the meeting is just as important as determining the right time for the meeting. The meeting should start and end on time, and a limit should be set for the minimum amount of time needed for the meeting.

Where Should the Meeting Be Held?

The place of the meeting can support or hinder the working of the group, and for this reason many companies hold meetings away from the workplace whenever possible. The new location and surroundings contribute to a sense of the importance of the work task, and members benefit from the absence of telephone calls and other interruptions. Likewise, the room itself should be

Shortcuts for Undermining Meetings

- *Don't plan ahead:* Let the juices flow. After all, you've been to hundreds of meetings. You ought to know how to run one by now.
- *Don't tell anyone the purpose of the meeting.* Don't give anyone an opportunity to upstage you.
- *Don't come on time.* You're the boss. Let them know the meeting can't start without you.
- *Don't waste time on logistics.* You can always send someone for additional chairs or materials. If the equipment doesn't work, wing it.
- *Speak softly.* A low voice will demand your listeners' attention and let them know who is boss.
- *Give signals that reinforce your position.* Look at your watch, yawn, interrupt—let participants know you have better things to do.
- *Speak in generalities. Never* discuss details. Remember, you're executive material.
- *Don't* ever *admit you don't know.* Waltz around the question, give an anecdote, or change the topic, but *don't* admit ignorance.
- *Dominate discussion.* Tell long stories that showcase your experience and knowledge.
- *Remember to demonstrate you are "in control."*[12]

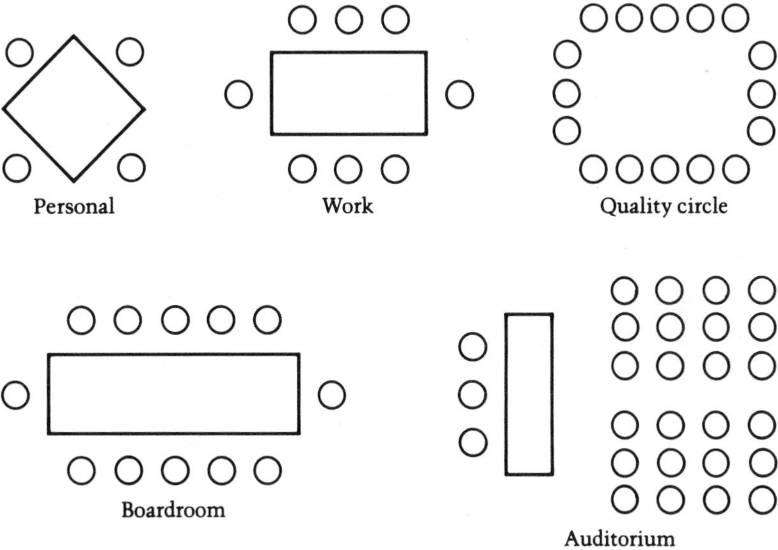

FIGURE 15.1 Seating Arrangements for Various Group Meetings

well lighted, without physical distractions, and have seating to accommodate all those involved. Temperatures should be comfortable.

Because seating arrangements either facilitate or hinder the flow of communication between people, rooms should always be arranged for the type of group using them (see Figure 15.1). Personal groups sit around a table, pull several chairs together in a circle, or find other seating arrangements that work best for study or discussion. Work groups usually use a conference table approach, sometimes with the designated leader at one end. Quality circles usually operate in a large circle of chairs, and sales meetings use a modified auditorium style with the speaker in front of the other members.

At an organizational meeting, directors normally sit around a large, rectangular boardroom table, while annual meetings are best housed in an auditorium setting. Most public meetings also use auditoriums.

What Is the Agenda?

The *agenda* is an outline or master plan for the meeting. It includes the topics to be covered, the order in which they will be covered, additional ideas and suggestions from members, and a designation of who is responsible for what during the meeting. The agenda merely presents factual information to be covered during the meeting. It does not advocate or evaluate any of the ideas or factual material.

Internal Correspondence

From: Jeremy Levy, President
Electronic Communication Systems, Inc. Date: April 26, 1994

To: René Grizzard, Vice-President of Human Resource Development
Barbra Juneau, Vice President of Administrative Services
Thomas Monce, Vice-President of Technology Development
Peggy Scheuermann, Director of Sales
Forrest Washington, Director of Production

Subject: Advisory meeting, Monday, May 20, 1994, 2:00 to 4:00 P.M., Conference Room C.

During the past three years, we have had a high turnover of first-time, first-line supervisors. While ECS has a sizable pool of people to select new supervisors from, we spend many hours training those ones selected to be quality supervisors.

After discussing the problems with each of you individually I have decided to form an advisory board to study the feasibility of establishing a presupervisory training program. This program would be for those key employees who we feel have supervisory potential. It would allow us to examine them early and decide whether they should remain on the supervisory path, and would equip those chosen with the tools they could use to step into the role of supervisor when the time comes.

So that you have an idea of the discussion items that I would like to cover, I am sending you the following agenda:

Agenda Items

1. Feasibility of a presupervisory training program
   a. Pros
   b. Cons

2. Goals of a presupervisory training program
   a. Identification of potential leaders
   b. Development of leadership skills
   c. Retention of employees at supervisory level

3. Goal assessment
   a. Identification of leadership training needs
   b. Transference of leadership skills to the job
   c. Measuring the success of the training program

4. Structure of the program
   a. Objectives
   b. Topics
   c. Instructors
   d. Program length

5. Program Value
   a. Level of skill development
   b. Justification of program in terms of worker productivity
   c. Cost benefits to organization

EXHIBIT 15.1 Meeting Agenda

Whenever possible, an agenda should be prepared before the meeting. If this is not possible, take a few minutes at the start of the meeting to set the agenda before proceeding. Circulating an agenda prior to the meeting will cut down on comments like, "I would be prepared if I had known we were going to discuss this issue." During the actual meeting the agenda helps the leader cut off undesirable ramblings and smoothly bring the group back to the agenda items.

The agenda in Exhibit 15.1 was used by the president of Electronic Communication Systems at an advisory meeting to investigate the feasibility of a presupervisor training program.

The Pre-Meeting Checklist

Arrangements for professional meetings have become big business, and the executive who understands the ropes can save the company thousands of dollars. Planning for major meetings requires a basic understanding of the goals—they will affect the room arrangement, length of the meeting, timing of break, and sequence of activities. A well-run meeting that provides the best possible facilities for each communication event requires the ability to think ahead and coordinate details. Professional meeting planners know that details are critical and approach each event with a system of checklists. Although you should develop your own, Table 15.1 provides one example.

Facilitating the Meeting

A successful meeting requires much advance work, continued efforts throughout the meeting, and a final follow-up and review. The following ideas focus on how to conduct a meeting.

Breaking the Ice

It is important that the members arrive a few minutes early to mingle informally and take care of some social-emotional, or maintenance, needs. This friendliness shows a readiness to cooperate and to work together.

An early arrival will allow the person in charge of the meeting to make sure that the arrangements are in order, enough chairs and miscellaneous items are available, and the chairs and tables are arranged appropriately.

TABLE 15.1 Pre-Meeting Checklist

Determine the purpose of the meeting.

- ✓ Is the meeting necessary?
- ✓ What are the goals of the meeting?

Determine the audience.

- ✓ Who should attend the meeting?
- ✓ What should participants bring with them?
- ✓ How can each person contribute?
- ✓ Are there any "hidden agendas" that may affect the meeting?

Make initial preparations.

- ✓ Have you determined who will be responsible for each part of the meeting or conference?
- ✓ Have you contacted everyone who should attend?
- ✓ Have you chosen a facility and scheduled meeting rooms?
- ✓ Do you have a written facilities agreement with dates, times, and arrangements specified?
- ✓ Have you made lodging arrangements for out-of-town participants? Will they need transportation? Maps?
- ✓ Have you prepared a written agenda? Materials for participants?
- ✓ Have agendas or other materials been mailed to participants?
- ✓ Have you made arrangements for breaks and refreshments?
- ✓ Have the main speakers been selected and contacted? Will they need equipment? Will they need time to rehearse or become familiar with the room?

Prepare the meeting room.

- ✓ Is the room large enough? well ventilated? comfortable?
- ✓ Is the room free of distracting noise, interruptions, sight barriers, etc.?
- ✓ If equipment will be used, are there sufficient/convenient electrical outlets? Is there enough space? Are there enough chairs and tables? Is a lectern or podium needed?
- ✓ Has equipment been checked to see if it works?
- ✓ Are all miscellaneous items in place? (pencils, writing pads, water glasses and pitchers, name cards, etc.)

It is vital that the meeting start on time, thus discouraging rewards for those who arrive late. A short, leader-conducted or self-introductory session at the outset is appropriate, especially when some members do not know others in the group. Explain why any outside visitors are present.

The Leader's Responsibility

The leader not only starts the meeting but is responsible for several other actions. Following the introduction the leader should briefly give any preliminary remarks such as items or announcements not related to the topic, a description of other groups examining the same problem, or a summary of any subgroups working on the current topics under discussion. This short preliminary talk can help the present group stay on target during the discussion. Finally, individual roles, such as note-taker, can be designated by the leader.

All time spent on preparation now gives way to the meeting itself; this is the important activity. While the interaction and functional role behavior of each member are vital, the leader at this point must direct the flow of the meeting, solicit involvement from all participants, keep the group on the track of following the agenda, and reach the final goal.

State the Purpose of the Meeting

The leader should state explicitly the purpose of the meeting and explain the agenda that the group will follow. These remarks should describe the group's task, the impact of the problem on the organization, a review of the problem and its frequency or relation to the group, and any procedures the leader will use at the meeting, such as parliamentary procedure.

Encourage Member Participation

Running a meeting and encouraging member participation are not easy tasks. A leader's style at the start, both verbally and nonverbally, tells the members whether their ideas and input are welcome and respected. As a leader, try to build an atmosphere that is open to honest and frank discussion, but beware also of the controls you place on the group. If you run the meeting too tightly, it might dampen output, group morale, and creative ideas. To let the meeting run too loosely might allow it to flow completely out of control and to accomplish nothing. Some of the ideas advanced by Jack Gibb are pertinent:

- If you appear to be a judge and always evaluate others, they will not talk or participate.
- If you attempt to control the meeting instead of letting it flow in a natural yet productive way, you will receive resistance.
- If the members see you as spontaneous, instead of manipulative, they will trust you and give you more response.
- If you attempt to project yourself into the other person's position instead of remaining neutral and passive to the other's expressed feeling, you will strengthen your leadership position.
- If you maintain a "superior" attitude, others will be closed and unresponsive.
- If you will "keep an open mind" to the different sides of the issues and leave room for member differences, both you and the group will receive less resistance.[13]

Direct the Flow of Communication

One of the best ways to encourage member participation is actively to direct the flow of communication. A leader who helps all members to have vocal input builds a climate of trust, acceptance, and encouragement, as opposed to a climate of intimidation, manipulation, oppression, and resentment. One of the best devices for keeping communication flowing is for the leader to ask questions. Loban offers suggestions for effective use of questioning:

1. Phrase questions to avoid "yes" or "no" answers.
2. Keep questions brief.
3. Use only the most simple words.
4. Use questions with a direct relation to the topic.
5. Use questions that cover a single point.[14]

Use the Agenda and Problem-Solving Mode to Guide the Group

A leader must be open to the flow of ideas presented to the group and realize how those ideas help the group accomplish its goal. Thus, a group leader must constantly practice effective listening. A leader must be able to hear and understand what is said, what is not said, and how something is said. He or she should note when the discussion wanders and help the group get back on course. He or she must ensure that all key points are considered and dealt with and that this takes place in the allotted time frame.

Present the Final Comments

The leader should guide the group to close at the proper time. As this time draws near, he or she may wish to call for a vote or consensus on key issues,

TABLE 15.2 Meeting Facilitator's Checklist

Establish a friendly atmosphere.

✓ Arrive early and check arrangements.
✓ Greet participants before the meeting.
✓ Make certain everyone is introduced.

Direct the flow of the meeting.

✓ Start the meeting on time.
✓ State the purpose of the meeting.
✓ Use the agenda and problem-solving mode to guide the group.
✓ Encourage member participation.
✓ Ask questions to help direct the flow of communication.

Present final comments.

✓ Ask for a consensus or call for a vote on key issues.
✓ Summarize decisions.
✓ Make assignments.

Follow up the meeting.

✓ Summarize agreements, assignments, and deadlines.
✓ Send a written summary to participants.

make assignments for additional out of group action, and finally summarize the key areas discussed and the decisions that were reached. Table 15.2 provides a group facilitator's checklist.

RULES OF PROCEDURE

While most informal personal groups, and some small work groups, run on informal procedures, most formal organizational meetings employ parliamentary procedure. Probably the most recognized set of procedures is found in *Robert's Rules of Order,* which describes how groups should conduct their official meetings and actions.

All members of a group, especially those in leadership positions, should know and be able to apply these rules. Their purpose is to help the group reach its goals, implement the will of the majority ("more than half"), protect the rights of minority members, and expedite business.

This section summarizes the rules of procedure and provides a working knowledge of the rules. Also, a variety of books on the subject should be available at your library or bookstore.

Chairperson

The president or designated leader of a group automatically becomes the presiding officer. If no officer has been designated, the first order of business is to elect a chairperson, from the group, by majority vote.

Order of Business

Most organizations have a prescribed and regular order of business that they follow at each meeting. The order follows this sequence:

1. Call to order
2. Reading, correcting, and approving of minutes
3. Reports from treasurer, standing committees, and boards
4. Reports from special committees
5. Consideration of unfinished business from the previous meeting
6. Consideration of new business
7. Announcements, setting of time and place for next meeting
8. Adjournment

Voting Procedures

Each organization must decide how decisions will be made. Usually motions are made, information is presented, and a vote is taken. The four most common methods for reaching agreement are majority vote, plurality, part-of-the-whole, and consensus:

1. *Majority vote* is the most common form and takes a vote of one more than half of the voting members.

2. *Plurality* means "most," so the item receiving the most votes is the winner. A plurality can be less than a majority.

3. *Part-of-the-whole* is used when a part or percentage of those voting is agreed on as a minimum needed for taking action. Usually 66⅔ percent is the amount selected when groups want more than a majority, but any percentage can be selected as the minimum needed for approval.

4. *Consensus* means "all." For an action to be accepted with this vote, everyone must agree to the proposal. Since the likelihood of everyone agreeing is not great, this method is used only in very important matters.

Motions

1. *Main motions.* Any member can introduce new business by making a motion. This is generally done by saying, "Mr./Ms. Chairman, I move that. . . ." For this business to then be considered, another person must second, or support, the proposal. A second is expressed, "I second the motion." Once a main motion has been introduced, no additional main motion can be considered until the pending motion is processed.

2. *Subsidiary motions* usually help the group dispose of main motions. "The intent may be to remove a motion from consideration by postponing it indefinitely; it may be to refine a motion by amendment or by referring it to committee where it can receive more detailed attention; it may be to postpone a motion definitely or temporarily or to speed a vote by limiting debate or calling for immediate vote."[15]

3. *Incidental motions* arise because of a question on the floor, and thus they take precedent and must be settled before other discussion or votes on pending questions.

4. *Privileged motions* do not relate to the pending question and can interrupt any question on the floor.

The chart in Table 15.3 shows the most frequent motions and the action that can be taken on them.

Following the Meeting

While the main emphasis of a meeting is placed on the preparation and actual meeting itself, the post-meeting period is just as important. During the meeting, decisions were made that now must be carried out. New problems probably also became apparent and new issues were voiced. All of these developments require analysis by the leader and the assigned committees. Within 24 hours after the meeting, a complete set of minutes should be given to each

TABLE 15.3 Frequently Used Parliamentary Motions

Motions	Purpose	Needs Second?	Amend-able?	Debat-able?	Vote Required?	Reconsidered at Same Meeting?	May Interrupt Speaker?
I. *Principal motion*							
1. A main motion	Introduce business	Y*	Y	Y	Majority	N†	N
II. *Subsidiary motions*							
2. Postpone indefinitely	Suppress action	Y	N	Y	Majority	N	N
3. Amend/substitute	Modify a motion	Y	Y	Y	Majority	N	N
4. Refer to committee	Modify a motion	Y	Y	Y	Majority	Y	N
5. Postpone definitely	Defer action	Y	Y	Y	Majority	Y	N
6. Limit/extend debate	Modify freedom of debate	Y	Y	N	Two-thirds	Y	N
7. Call for the previous question	Force immediate vote	Y	N	N	Two-thirds	Y	N
8. Lay on the table	Defer action	Y	N	N	Majority	Y	N
9. Take from table	Consider again	Y	N	N	Majority	Y	N
III. *Incidental motions*							
10. Suspend the rules	Take action contrary to standing rule	Y	N	N	Two-thirds	N	N
11. Modify/withdraw motion	Modify motion	Y	N	N	Majority or unanimous consent	Y	N
12. Divide motion	Modify motion	Y	Y	N	Majority	N	N
13. Object to consideration	Suppress action	N	N	N	Two-thirds	N	Y
14. Raise point of order	Correct parliamentary error	N	N	N	Decision of chair	N	Y
15. Call for division of house	Correct/reverse chair	N	N	N	Majority if chair desires	N	Y
IV. *Privileged motions*							
16. Call for orders of the day	Force consideration of proposed motion	N	N	N	Less than two-thirds negative	N	Y
17. Make matter a special order	Force consideration at specified time	Y	Y	Y	Two-thirds	Y	N
18. Raise question of privilege	Make request during debate	N	N	N	Decision of chair	Y	Y
19. Take a recess	Dismiss meeting for specified length of time	Y	Y	N	Majority	Y	N
20. Adjourn	Dismiss the meeting	Y	N	N	Majority	Y	N

*Y = yes †N = no

group member. Sigband and Bateman have identified three advantages of preparing and distributing the set of minutes.[16]

1. Everyone present will have an identical summary. This should avoid comments like, "I don't remember our discussing that issue."
2. The minutes should clearly list the items demanding action and the name of the person responsible for completing the action. This will eliminate comments like, "I didn't know I was responsible for following up on that."
3. Since the minutes become record, they can be reviewed by those who attended the meeting, those absent, and others who may have need of the information discussed.

An outline and an example of a set of minutes are found in Exhibits 15.2 and 15.3.

Correspondence

From: (Name of leader or coordinator) **Date: (Give date)**

To: (Names of participants and others who should receive summary. List *all* names)

Subject: Meeting Summary

Date of Meeting: ____________ **Times: (Starting and ending)**

Location: ____________

In attendance: (Include names alphabetically by last names of those who attended and those who did not attend.)

Meeting objectives: (State clearly the purpose of the meeting.)

Accomplishments: (Include a brief summary of the business conducted at the meeting. Be sure to include any agreements.)

Assignments: (Include any assignments and deadlines.)

Additional Information: (Add amplifying statements, additional information, or comments.)

Next meeting: (Give the time and place.)

Signature line
____

EXHIBIT 15.2 Standard Outline for Minutes

Minutes of the Advisory Meeting

Date: April 23, 1994

Present: René Grizzard, Barbra Juneau, Thomas Monce, Peggy Scheuermann

Absent: Forrest Washington

Summary:

René Grizzard opened the meeting with a brief background of the current supervisory selection process and the turnover rate for the past three years. She then presented a survey on employee development needs. The majority of the employees surveyed requested training in group leadership and supervisory techniques. A general discussion followed.

Peggy Scheuermann reported on the success of training programs at Fortune 500 companies. The programs with the best results included a total quality management philosophy. A general discussion followed.

Agreements:

The advisory committee concluded that ECS should implement a supervisory training program to develop leadership skills. The program should cultivate a mentor relationship between non-supervisory personnel with leadership potential and current managers. The goal of the advisory committee is to improve both the quality and retention of organizational supervision by:

1. identifying characteristics of potential supervisors
2. developing supervisory and leadership skills
3. providing mentoring relationships with organizational managers

Assignments:

1. Grizzard will investigate the cost of in-house training with a consultant versus outside supervisory training programs.
2. Advisory board members will identify potential leaders in their areas and submit names to HRD.
3. HRD will analyze the level of skill development needed and propose the program structure for review at the next advisory board meeting.

Next Meeting: May 25, 1994, 2:00–4:00 P.M., Conference Room A.

EXHIBIT 15.3 Meeting Agenda

A GLOBAL PERSPECTIVE

Shoudu and the Contract System

Committees can have tremendous power over the operational success of companies. This concept was put to the test at the Shoudu Iron and Steel Co. in China when the contract system was introduced and companies were given more freedom in self-management. In 1987, Shoudu developed a new leadership system that included two bodies: the Workers' Congress or supreme authority, and the Enterprise Committee, a standing committee of the Congress that had the general manager as its head and functions much like the board of directors of an American company. The 1,000 members of the Workers' Congress are elected by the representatives of the branch companies, subsidiaries, and departments. The Congress meets annually and elects the members of the Enterprise Committee, with the exception of the chair, vice-chair, and general manager, who are elected by all workers.

The eleven-member Enterprise Committee consists of managers, workers, and party heads, and as the executive body is authorized to manage critical issues and implement decisions. Reporting to the Enterprise Committee are four subcommittees managed by workers and elected by the Congress. Before important decisions are made, feedback is solicited from the subcommittees and workers. Annual plans, production, and scientific research schedules are debated among workers before they are presented to the Congress for review and approval. The schedule alone may give rise to more than 20,000 suggestions or proposals. After analysis and review, useful ideas are incorporated into the plan. Workers receive feedback on ideas that are rejected, and the general manager is held responsible for the plan's implementation.

The committee system promotes democratic supervision. In speaking about production, Sun Tie, a section chief and member of the Enterprise Committee, said this:

> I know little about the other workshops but I do have a say on what matters in my own steelworks. Leaders respect my views, and I think my presence in the committee has helped to settle some of the difficulties and problems facing workers. The result is that, if something unfavourable happens to a fellow worker, he tends to report it to me and I bring it up in committee meeting. I have a responsibility which I take very seriously.[17]

ETHICS: RIGHT OR WRONG?

ECS and the Flex-Time Project

Electronic Communication Systems was established in 1975 as an electronics manufacturing firm.[18] Most of ECS's income was generated through federal contracts to manufacture equipment for space shuttles. Some of the developments through these programs led ECS to begin producing commercial products, and now at least 75 percent of the company's business comes from the sale of these products.

René Grizzard, ECS's vice-president of human resource development, wanted to update the twenty-year-old management philosophies the company used, and so she pushed for adoption of the total quality management (TQM) concept. Although she met with resistance, she was successful in introducing TQM and the company was beginning to see results. Some administrators, however, were ignoring her successes and literally attempting to sabotage and undermine improvements. Their whole approach to effective management seemed to be territorial; they fought the team approach because it threatened their control. Grizzard was constantly providing quantitative data to underscore the success of the program, most of which they questioned or simply ignored.

Because of their TQM training, ECS employees were working in teams to generate suggestions for improving company efficiency. One of Grizzard's subordinates suggested that the company implement a flex-time schedule. After thorough discussion with her staff, Grizzard decided that the flex-time suggestion would indeed improve productivity, and she drafted a proposal to the company president, Jeremy Levy. Levy was only twenty-nine years old and had held his current position for two years. His father had started the company and was now chairman of the board of directors. Levy held an engineering degree and a master's degree in business administration, both from top-ranked institutions.

After reviewing Grizzard's proposal, he called a meeting of his advisory board which consisted of Grizzard; Barbra Juneau, vice-president of administrative services; Thomas Monce, vice-president of technology development; Peggy Scheuermann, director of sales; and Forrest Washington, director of production (see Exhibit 15.4).

Juneau was new in her position. When the former vice-president of administrative services left ECS to accept the presidency of a rival company, Juneau, because of her outstanding technical skills, college degrees, and ability to work with people, was promoted from a staff position to the vice-presidency. Her only leadership experience had been as a team leader on major administrative projects, a role that called for implementation of new internal accounting or auditing procedures. She was very nervous about her lack of management experience and hesitated to speak up in meetings, especially if she thought she was contradicting one of the other vice-presidents.

Thomas Monce, vice-president of technology development, had been with

Internal correspondence

From: Jeremy Levy, President
Electronic Communication Systems, Inc. Date: July 1, 1994

To: René Grizzard, Vice-President of Human Resource Development
Barbra Juneau, Vice President of Administrative Services
Thomas Monce, Vice-President of Technology Development
Peggy Scheuermann, Director of Sales
Forrest Washington, Director of Production

Subject: Advisory meeting, Monday, July 16, 1994, 2:00 TO 4:00 P.M., Conference Room C.

As a result of our total quality management thrust, René Grizzard has submitted a proposal for flex-time developed by her employees. After reviewing the proposal, I believe that it has potential to dramatically improve efficiency at ECS. For this reason I am asking you to meet with me to assess the proposal.

So that you have an idea of the discussion items that I would like to cover, I am sending you the following agenda:

Agenda Items

1. Feasibility of a flexible time schedule for employees
   a. Pros
   b. Cons
2. Goals of a flexible time schedule
   a. Maintain and improve current quality management objectives
   b. Give flexibility of work time for all employees
   c. Provide cost benefits to ECS

A copy of the proposal is attached.

EXHIBIT 15.4

the company since its beginning and had held his current position since 1975. He was good friends with the president and often played golf with him on Saturdays. The president respected Monce's judgment and often consulted him privately before making a decision.

Peggy Scheuermann, director of sales, came to work for ECS in 1990, after establishing herself over a period of fifteen years as one of the premier sales managers in the business. Bright and creative, she could hold her own with anyone. She was a self-starter who demanded the same exceptional performance from subordinates that she exhibited in her own work life.

Forrest Washington joined the company in 1978 as an engineer. With a degree and outstanding credentials from a premier engineering school, he proved to be quite a catch for ECS. His knowledge and ability had more than once been the key to very profitable ventures. In 1982, Washington was promoted to production supervisor even though he had no training in supervision and no supervisory experience. While he had been an exceptional engineer, he had trouble adjusting to his new position and had to learn his skills on the job. A large government contract in 1989 infused much-needed funds into ECS and significantly increased personnel. At that time, Washington was promoted to director of production with the responsibility of restructuring the various production departments. The TQM program, he felt, was causing problems, some of which seemed to be directly attributable to the new structure.

When Washington received Levy's memo, he was not happy. He already had his hands full adjusting to the TQM stuff, and now Grizzard had to dump something else on ECS. This, he thought, was just another example of how people who had never been on the production "firing line" had no idea of the problems the department faced. Didn't Levy know that production had to meet deadlines and that everyone needed to be available to keep on schedule?

When the meeting was opened at 2 P.M. on July 16, everyone was present except Washington. Levy reminded everyone of the purpose of the meeting, and Grizzard presented the proposal and gave examples of how a flex-time schedule might be adapted for each ECS division. Washington arrived about 10 minutes late, just as Grizzard was asking for questions.

Scheuermann was first to speak: "I think this is a great idea. It will be like a gift from heaven for the sales staff. Trying to keep up with our regular hours and also keep appointments with company representatives often necessitates extensive travel time at night and on weekends. To be honest, many of my staff are wearing out because of the demands we place on them."

Monce also supported the idea, but he wanted some guidelines and restrictions to avoid abuse. He proceeded to outline some guidelines that the group discussed and seemed to agree with. Juneau said nothing for most of the meeting but seemed to nod in agreement with each speaker. She finally commented, "A system to audit employee work hours would probably need to be established." Her comment was incorporated into the guidelines.

Washington was unhappy, and although he said nothing everyone was aware of his feelings. Levy directed the following question to him: "Forrest, you've been unusually quiet. What do you think of the proposal?"

After a long pause, Washington responded, "I have no comment."

Levy adjourned the meeting at 3:25 P.M.

After the meeting, Levy sent the memo in Exhibit 15.6 to the advisory committee.

After the meeting, Washington returned to his office and drafted the memo in Exhibit 15.5 to all production unit heads.

Minutes of the Advisory Meeting

Date: July 17, 1994

Present: René Grizzard, Barbra Juneau, Thomas Monce, Peggy Scheuermann, and Forrest Washington

Summary:

The ECS advisory board met on July 16, 1994 in Conference Room C at 2:00 p.m. to discuss a proposal on flexible time schedules for employees. René Grizzard opened the meeting with a presentation of her proposal for flexible hours.

Agreements:

ECS will introduce flexible hours for all employees to maintain and improve quality management objectives, give flexibility of work time for all employees, and provide cost benefits to ECS.

All divisions will follow these general guidelines for the implementation of flexible hours:

1. Employees can have flexible hours during the week that total more or less than 40 hours.
2. At the end of the month, each employee's cumulative work hours will be audited and must equal a 40-hour week including any sick or annual leave taken.
3. Employees who report to work must do so between 7:30 a.m. and 9:00 a.m. and may leave no sooner than 3:00 p.m. Lunch time should be scheduled between 11:30 a.m. and 1:30 p.m.
4. Employees' schedules must be approved by their main supervisor.
5. Employees must check in and out using the ES-2 system in order to track and audit work hours.

Assignments:

René Grizzard will work with each division to set up the ES-2 system so that the new flexible hours can be implemented by September 1, 1994. Announcements about the new system will be prominently displayed throughout ECS. Each vice-president will discuss the Flex-Time Policy with unit directors to answer any question and get feedback.

Next Meeting: July 30, 1994, 2:00 p.m. to 4:00 p.m., Conference Room C.

EXHIBIT 15.5

Internal Correspondence

From: Forrest Washington, Director of Production   Date: July 17, 1994

To: All Production Unit Heads

Subject: New Flex-Time Policy

Shortly you will receive notification about a new Flex-Time Policy that will be implemented at ECS. While this policy may be appropriate for some divisions of ECS, our production goals cannot be sacrificed for convenience. Thus, our division of ECS will not be implementing this option for production employees.

EXHIBIT 15.6

Case Questions

1. Is there an ethics problem with this case? If so, what is it?
2. Should Levy have known that Washington was opposed to the new policy? What could Levy have done differently during the meeting?
3. Was the policy an "option," as Washington stated in his letter?
4. What was the hidden agenda during the meeting?

SUMMARY

Managers spend considerable time participating in and running meetings. Meetings are important because they allow individuals to share information in a short period of time to achieve mutual goals. During meetings individuals can express their views, expand on ideas, present solutions to problems, and facilitate goal commitments. Some goals may be best accomplished in a meeting, but for other goals a meeting is definitely *not* the context for achieving results. Meetings can be expensive and time consuming. If the wrong people attend, if the group does not follow a planned agenda, or if management does not value the group's decision, the effectiveness of the meeting will be minimal.

Meetings can be personal, organizational, or public. Personal meetings are informal and generally have no real purpose. Organizational meetings can be internal, such as the staff or committee meeting, or external, such as a board of directors' meeting. Public meetings are usually presented to an audience that has no affiliation with the organization.

Attending a meeting that has no discernible purpose is a waste of everyone's time and is costly to the organization. Meetings should not be held unless they require the participation of several people and there is time to prepare for and complete the meeting.

Once a decision to hold a meeting is made, the success of that meeting is affected by the purpose of the meeting, who attends the meeting, the size of the group, the time at which the meeting is scheduled, the location chosen for the meeting, and the agenda. Since meeting arrangements can make or break a meeting, seating, equipment, temperature, and other logistics should all be handled ahead of time. The leader should clearly state the purpose of the meeting, encourage participation, direct the flow of communication, use an agenda, and summarize the group's agreements. Sometimes the leader or chairperson must also be familiar with rules of procedure for formal organizational meetings.

By assessing goals and dynamics before, during, and after each meeting, managers can conduct successful meetings. Their skills as meeting leaders will also constantly improve.

Key Words

advisory meeting
agenda
annual meeting
board of directors meeting
committee meeting
conversation group
forum
happening
minutes
organizational meeting
panel
personal meeting
production meeting
professional sharing meeting
quality circle
Robert's Rules of Procedure
staff meeting
study group
symposium
work group

Review Questions

1. Why are meetings important in the organization?
2. What are the advantages of meetings? What are the disadvantages?
3. Define and give examples of internal versus external organizational meetings.
4. When should meetings be held? When should meetings not be held?
5. For meetings to run smoothly, several questions must be answered before they take place. What are these questions, and why are the answers to them important?
6. What are *Robert's Rules of Procedure,* when are they used, and why are they important?
7. Even when the meeting ends, a manager's communication tasks are not complete. Describe what needs to be done following the meeting.

Exercises

1. In your educational, social, or work experience you have been involved in a variety of meetings. Recall some of those meetings, their purposes, problems, and outcomes. What did the leader do to impede or facilitate the meeting? Meet with a group of three or four other students to describe your experiences.
2. Attend a meeting of a group of which you are a current member. If you are not an active member of a group, seek out groups that will allow you to sit in on their meetings, such as a student or faculty senate meeting or a community forum. After the meeting, use the form in Exhibit 15.7 to analyze the meeting. Speculate on what questions the leader asked before the meeting, critiquing what could have been done more productively during the meeting and also predicting what the leader will do after the meeting.

MEETING OBSERVATION SHEET

1. What was the purpose of the meeting?
2. Was the purpose accomplished?
3. How long did it take?
   just right _____ too long _____ did not finish _____
4. If the purpose of the meeting was not accomplished, what went wrong?
5. List the name of the participants and have each check the degree of satisfaction with the meeting.

Name	Very Unsatisfied	Satisfied	Very Satisfied

6. If you were conducting the meeting, what would you have done differently? Use the Checklists in Exhibits 15.2 and 15.3 as guides for your comments.

EXHIBIT 15.7

REFERENCES

1. Carol Hymowitz, "Executives Face Hidden Agendas and Late Bosses," *Wall Street Journal*, June 21, 1988.
2. Marcy E. Mullins, "USA Snapshots," *USA Today*, August 28, 1989.
3. Rollie Tillman, Jr., "Problems in Review: Committees on Trial," *Harvard Business Review*, 38 (May/June 1960), p. 168.
4. Howard H. Martin, "Communication Setting," in Howard Martin and Kenneth Anderson, eds., *Speech Communication: Analysis and Readings* (Boston: Allyn & Bacon, 1968), pp. 70–71.
5. Julie Stacey, "USA Snapshots," *USA Today*, March 2, 1989.
6. Berhard Rosenblatt, T. Richard Cheatham, and James T. Watt, *Communication in Business* (Englewood Cliffs, N.J.: Prentice-Hall, 1977), pp. 225–226.
7. Morrisa Zimmeth, "Speed Decision Making with Meeting Productivity Software," *Microlife* (March/April 1990), pp. 14–15.
8. William M. Bulkeley, "'Computerizing' Dull Meetings Is Touted as an Antidote to the Mouth that Bored," *Wall Street Journal*, January 28, 1992.

9. Craig E. Aronoff, Otis W. Baskin, Robert W. Hays, and Harold E. Davis, *A Practical Guide to Business and Communication* (St. Paul, Minn.: West, 1981), p. 293.
10. P. E. Slater, "Contrasting Correlates of Group Size," *Sociometry,* 21 (1958), pp. 137–138.
11. Roy M. Berko, Andrew D. Wolvin, and Ray Curtis, *This Business of Communicating* (Dubuque, Iowa: William C. Brown, 1980), p. 146.
12. John Sherman, "How to Make Meetings Even Worse," *Newsday,* Nassau and Suffolk ed., October 6, 1991.
13. J. R. Gibb, *T-Group Theory and Laboratory Methods* (New York: John Wiley & Sons, 1964).
14. Lawrence N. Loban, "Questions: The Answer to Meeting Participation," *Supervision* (January 1972), pp. 11–13.
15. Joseph A. Wagner, *Successful Leadership in Groups and Organizations* (San Francisco: Chandler, 1959), p. 11.
16. Norman B. Sigband and David N. Bateman, *Communicating in Business* (Glenview, Ill.: Scott, Foresman, 1981), p. 382.
17. Zhang Zhiping, "Leadership Established Through a Democratic System," *Beijing Review* (December 18–24, 1989), pp. 26–29.
18. This case was written by Laura Lemoine Lindsay and adapted from "Flex Time," prepared by David Hau, Richard Holden, and Lawrence W. Rohal, in Theodore T. Herbert, *Organizational Behavior: Readings and Cases,* 2nd ed. (New York: Macmillan, 1981), pp. 216–222.

CHAPTER 16

COMMUNICATION STRATEGIES: CONDUCTING INTERVIEWS

Robert Half, founder of Accountemps, "the world's largest temporary personnel service for accounting, bookkeeping, and information systems," frequently funds surveys of corporate executives to find out what they think about critical issues. Not too long ago, Half decided to survey the responses of interviewees "at that moment of truth we have all encountered when applying for a job."[1] The results are fascinating. What follows are some excerpts from the responses of the human resource managers whom he surveyed:

> "Said if he was hired, he'd teach me ballroom dancing at no charge, and started demonstrating."
>
> A man "brought in his five children and cat."
>
> A woman took three cellular phone calls during the interview because she had a "similar business on the side."
>
> Demonstrating her commitment to her pet, a woman "arrived with a snake around her neck. Said she took her pet everywhere."
>
> "Left his dry cleaner tag on his jacket and said he wanted to show he was a clean individual."
>
> "When asked about loyalty, showed a tattoo of his girlfriend's name."[2]

Some of these experiences can jolt even the most experienced manager's ability to apply the techniques of effective interviewing.

Nevertheless, failure to apply good communication skills, whatever the situation, rarely impresses higher administration, especially if the failure involves violating an organizational policy or federal law. You are expected to know both communication techniques and important policy issues and to apply them well.

During the workday a manager talks one on one to a number of employees. In one instance it may be necessary to discuss the reasons an employee is leaving the organization, while in another an employee may be frustrated and need coaching. A third instance may involve reprimanding a problem employee for failing to meet the expectations set by a superior. In addition, the manager may need information to solve a complex problem and thus meet with an expert in order to get essential facts. Finally, the manager may need to conduct a job interview to maintain a fully staffed and effective organization.

This chapter examines each of these interview situations—their contexts and requirements. It examines the role of the manager as an interviewer and provides guidelines for interview preparation and analysis. Several interview approaches using key questioning techniques are presented.

Interviewing is a critical managerial skill and communication activity. Interviews yield information needed to solve problems and make decisions that are essential to an organization's welfare. A manager unskilled in applying interviewing techniques wastes organizational resources. For the purposes of this chapter, an *interview* is defined as interaction between two parties to gain information to accomplish a predetermined purpose. We have selected the word *party* because more than one person may gather information or supply information.[3]

The Manager's Responsibility as an Interviewer

The responsibilities and purposes of an interviewer are fairly clear. First, you must communicate your purpose to the interviewee in understandable terms. Never combine two purposes in one sitting or interview, since your interviewee will be required to spend critical thought-time determining what you want rather than listening to your questions.

Your second responsibility as an interviewer is to prepare for the interview. How will you structure it? Where will you conduct it? Who should be present? What problems should you avoid? Preparation will contribute to an effective interview by (1) avoiding the necessity to reconvene with the other parties, (2) steering clear of questions that are unethical or illegal, and (3) creating the climate most conducive to a positive experience.

Finally, you will want to record the information gathered during the interview. This may require a special form for ranking job candidates, notes that summarize the basic content of the interview, or a memorandum for the record that stipulates the action that will be followed.

Each of these responsibilities needs to be viewed in the context of the primary interview purpose: to conduct a job interview, to orient, to coach, to counsel, to hear a grievance, to appraise performance, to reprimand, or to discover why an employee is leaving the organization. For all of these purposes, however, there are key steps for preparing and conducting the interview.

Preparing for the Interview

Preparing for the interview includes four steps common to all interviewing situations: (1) defining the purpose, (2) deciding who should be involved, (3) analyzing the other party, and (4) planning the interview format or structure.

Defining the Purpose

A clearly defined purpose sets the tone of the interview and helps determine the plan of action. Once you have clarified your purpose, write it down in terms of a goal-directed outcome. For example, "The purpose of this interview is to determine the cause of the production slowdown and agree on a solution that will meet our quota in a specified period of time." Once you have determined your purpose, you will need to decide who can best assist you in reaching your goal.

Determining Who Should Be Involved

While this may seem a rather obvious step, it is one that is often neglected by the most experienced managers. Failure to include the necessary participants in the interviewing process can lead to wasted time and resources. For example, a job applicant may need to interview with several people before the process is complete. To do this, a carefully planned schedule taking into account possible conflicts will need to be prepared. Overlooking a key administrator may create a poor impression and may mean that the applicant will need to return for a second round of interviews.

In order to determine who should be involved in the interview, ask yourself the following questions:

- Who has the knowledge or information needed?
- Who knows the history of the organization that may affect this decision?
- Who will be involved in the implementation of the solution (supervise the employee, meet performance expectations, and so forth)?

Analyzing the Other Party

Each participant in the interview has a point of view based on beliefs, attitudes, experiences, traits, capacities, needs, and aspirations. Your approach will vary depending on the other party's characteristics, awareness of the problem, and willingness to discuss it. For example, if a manager discovered

TABLE 16.1 Problem-Solving and Informational Interview Formats

	Problem Solving		Informative
Opening	Greet interviewee Establish common ground State purpose	*Opening*	Greet interviewee Establish common ground State purpose
Body (in sequence)	Define problem Analyze problem Propose solutions Select solution Agree on action	*Body (as appropriate)*	Seek information Question Reflect Verify Summarize
Close	Provide summary Summarize action to take Make acknowledgments	*Close*	Provide summary Summarize action to take Make acknowledgments

a productivity problem that involved two of her subordinates, she might wish to interview them in order to gain insight. Beth, who is outgoing, competent, secure, and friendly, would probably be easy to approach about the problem. On the other hand, Bob, while competent, has been in his current supervisory position for only three weeks and appears somewhat insecure in the manager's presence. Obviously, the manager's approach with him would be different from that used with Beth. While the manager might follow the same basic format, she would spend more time trying to put Bob at ease.

Planning the Interview Structure or Format

Whether you are conducting an informational or a problem-solving interview, you will follow a basic structure that includes an opening, a body, and a close.

The opening. The opening should accomplish several important steps. First, a greeting establishes contact and sets the tone. Second, common ground should be established by sharing concerns about the need to solve the problem or gain the necessary information. Finally, the purpose should be clearly stated and agreed on.

The body. The body of the interview attempts to accomplish the goal through questioning, explaining, verifying, and summarizing. A problem-solving interview usually follows the problem-solving sequence amplified in the chapter on decision making. The informational interview focuses on drawing out information using both general and specific questions. The problem-solving and informational formats can be compared in Table 16.1.

The close. The interview close should include a summary of the information and agreements that took place during the body of the interview. The intended use of information and any action that needs to be taken should be restated and summarized at this point. Finally, the manager should signal the completion of the process and express appreciation to the participants.

TABLE 16.2 When to Use Closed and Open Interview Questions

Used closed questions if:

- The interviewer seeks measurable facts.
- There is a secure relationship between parties.
- The interviewee is informed and knowledgeable.
- The interviewer has limited time to obtain specific information.
- The interviewee's attitudes are not important.
- The interviewee either cannot or is not willing to discuss answers.

Use open questions if:

- The interviewer seeks to establish supportive climate.
- The interviewee's feelings and attitudes are important.
- The interviewer seeks to clarify the interviewee's point of view.
- The interviewee has an undetermined amount of information on the topic.
- Time is not essential.
- The interviewee is conversant and knowledgeable.

Key Questioning Techniques

An effective exchange of information is often the result of a sequence of carefully structured questions. Questions serve three important functions: to gain information, to encourage participation of the interviewee, and to gain insight about the interviewee's motives, needs, and attitudes.[4] This section discusses several types of questions and the circumstances in which they are used.

Use Closed Questions to Limit Response

Almost every interview encounter will require the use of closed questions. *Closed questions* request specific information and limit the interviewee's freedom of response. Often the question implies the answer or provides a list of options such as, "Did you receive a B.A. or a B.S. degree?" An extreme form of question acts as a problem-solving guide without directing the employee to a solution. The manager may say, "Joe, what do you think is causing the leakage in the main valve?" Thus, the manager encourages Joe to consider the causes and state them in his own terms. We have listed some situations that may call for open versus closed questions in Table 16.2.[5]

Use Probing Questions to Explore

Often the interviewee must be encouraged to discuss a specific topic or encouraged simply to communicate. *Probing questions* direct the interviewee to expand on a response and allow exploration of attitudes and beliefs. While the probe may simply be a verbal response such as "Please continue," it may also be a nonverbal response such as the nod of the head to indicate attentiveness. A thoughtful answer may take as much as six seconds to formulate.[6] Do not try to jump in and fill the silences because it will put you in a controlling mode and set a precedent for future discussion.

Mirror a Response to Encourage Further Discussion

The *mirror question* encourages the interviewee to expand on a response by reflecting back what was just said. For example, a job applicant might say, "I had some difficulty with my last job because my boss was overly concerned with reaching quotas and goals at the expense of the organizational climate." A mirror question that would encourage further discussion might be, "You say you feel your boss was overly concerned with quotas and goals?"

Avoid Leading Questions

You have probably heard the phrase "Don't you think so?" numerous times and may have recognized it for what it was—a *leading question*. The person asking it assumes agreement or at the very least presumes to lead you to the correct response. Leading questions influence the respondent to give a desired response. Frequently used by salespeople to influence clients, leading questions can result in invalid responses. An example might be the manager who attempts to influence opinion at a meeting by stating, "You do agree that this is the right solution to the problem, don't you, John?" Whether or not John agrees, he will probably acquiesce under these circumstances. Vocal emphasis may be all that is needed to state a leading question. Consider the question above phrased as follows, but with heavy emphasis placed on the word "disagree": "Do you *disagree* with this solution, John?"

Sequencing Questions

You will find there are three general approaches to sequencing your questions for an interview. Each of these approaches should be considered depending on the type of interview, the person(s) involved in the interview, and the information you need to gain from the interview.[7]

The Funnel

The *funnel* approach begins with a general question followed by increasingly specific questions. It is the most widely used approach and works best with an interviewee who is well informed about the subject under discussion. An example of the funnel approach might be:

- Question 1: How do you feel about the salary structure at the new plant?
- Question 2: What kind of structure would you recommend?
- Question 3: Why do you feel that this approach is the most effective?
- Question 4: When do you feel it should be implemented?

The Inverted Funnel

The *inverted funnel* sequence begins with a specific question and each question that follows becomes more general in nature. This approach is particularly suited for counseling situations because specific questions encourage discussion at the outset of the interview. As interaction continues, probes and mirror questions motivate the respondent to participate more freely. The following questions exemplify the inverted funnel sequence:

- Question 1: How is the recruitment program proceeding?
- Question 2: Can you pinpoint any specific problems we may be able to solve?
- Question 3: Of these problems, which one will have the greatest effect on our ability to reach our goals?
- Question 4: Can you tell me more about the problem and what you feel needs to be done about it?

The Tunnel

If there is a compressed period of time in which an interview needs to be conducted and the information needed is fairly specific, the *tunnel* sequence is most appropriate. It consists of specific questions requesting specific information and is most frequently used by interviewers to obtain vital information—such as for a loan application or for screening purposes in the emergency room of a hospital. An example of the latter might be:

- Question 1: What is your full name?
- Question 2: Do you have insurance?
- Question 3: Are you employed?
- Question 4: Do you have your own physician?
- Question 5: Are you allergic to any medications?
- Question 6: How are you injured?

Planning the question sequence will save time in the long run by keeping you on the appropriate path toward your goal. In addition you will avoid confusing the interviewee about his or her role and your purpose. An individual who expected to participate in an informational interview but suddenly finds you exploring feelings will question your motives.

Types of Interviews

Each type of interview has a different purpose. To carry out your purpose, you need to prepare for and conduct the interview according to a predetermined plan. Preparation for an interview of a job candidate to assess his or her suitability for a position differs from preparation for orienting a new employee or disciplining an old one. In this section of the chapter, you will learn how to prepare for and conduct employment, orientation, counseling, performance evaluation, and disciplinary interviews.

The Employment Interview

Millions of people participate in employment interviews each year. The decision-making process for the manager in selecting a suitable employee is critical, since placing the wrong person in a position can lead to complex organizational problems in the long run. The astronomical costs of orienting and training new employees in technical positions emphasize the importance of hiring decisions that put the right person in the job. To be effective, the interviewing process must begin with a thorough understanding of (1) the organizational policies and practices and (2) the job requirements.

Preparing for the Employee Interview

Usually, a manager will find the interview only one of a series of decision-making steps that culminate in the selection of the job candidate. First, the nature of the job that has been vacated should be examined. Second, a job description should be prepared and publicized in the appropriate media. Third, a screening process should be agreed upon. Fourth, applications should be reviewed to determine which candidates meet the job requirements. Fifth, interviews should be set up with those candidates who meet the screening requirements. The final selection completes the process.

What Is the Nature of the Job?

Can you imagine hiring a chemist to do office filing? How long do you think such an employee would be motivated and interested in the work? You may feel this is a ridiculous example, but similar errors in judgment occur frequently in employee selection. As a manager, you must identify the personal characteristics associated with effective performance of a job. One method that may help you determine whether the current requirements are realistic is to evaluate the reasons why the previous employee left the position. Was he or she bored and unproductive? If so, why? Perhaps the job itself needs to be redesigned.

Among the things you will be identifying are education, experience, knowledge, skills, interpersonal relations, trustworthiness, and unusual working conditions. Under the law, these are referred to as *bona fide occupational qualifications* (BFOQ) that are necessary to perform the work. Anything of a discriminatory nature—such as sex, age, race, religion, ethnic origin, disability, and veteran status—cannot be part of an employment decision unless the qualification is inherent to the nature of the work (see Table 16.3). For example a bartender must be of legal age; however, age cannot be a consideration for employing a professor as long as he or she meets the qualifications for the position.

Prepare a Job Description

Once you have evaluated the job, prepare a *job description* that clearly outlines the duties, authority, and responsibilities of the position. Be sure to include organizational lines of authority, both upward and downward. To whom does this person report? Who reports to the person in this position?

TABLE 16.3 Employment Interviews: What You Can't Ask

A question is unlawful if it does any of the following:[8]
1. Requests information on date of birth or birthplace
2. Asks information about age, sex, religion, ethnic origin, race, disability, or veteran status unless it is a BFOQ
3. Requests marital status, number or list of dependents by name or age, or the names of relatives other than immediate family
4. Asks about membership in any clubs or organizations
5. Asks if applicant is a naturalized citizen
6. Requests previous name unless requesting a woman's maiden name
7. Requests a photograph or color of hair or eyes
8. Asks if applicant owns home
9. Asks if spouse works

Does he or she have functional authority? If so, over whom? What are the major job functions, and what percentage of effort should be spent on each? For example, a trainer may need to spend 50 percent of his or her effort in the classroom, 30 percent preparing and researching materials, and 20 percent coordinating programs.

The job description will be a valuable tool for advertising the position and clarifying job requirements during the interview session. Before preparing the position description to advertise the job, check with the personnel representative to ascertain appropriate communication channels. Most organizations must advertise a position internally as well as in the local newspaper to allow equal opportunity for employment. In addition it may be necessary to advertise on a larger scope depending on the pool of applicants. For example, if you are trying to hire a college dean, you will probably have to place an advertisement in *The Chronicle of Higher Education* since the applicant pool would include deans from other colleges outside your immediate geographic area. In addition you may need to consider professional journals, trade association newsletters, and local and regional newspapers.

Establish a Procedure for Screening Applicants

To evaluate applicants fairly, an effective screening process should be established. A system whereby applicants' qualifications can be quantitatively measured against job requirements is most effective. A search committee may have to review credentials and select the top three or five candidates in the pool. These candidates may then be interviewed before the final decision is made.

Review Credentials and Screen Applicants

Typically, the candidate's rèsumé and references provide information about educational background, job experience, and work history. These credentials should be reviewed to identify qualifications of each applicant. Following the review, the applicant should be ranked according to agreed-on criteria.

Interview Training at AT&T

To avoid discrimination suits, companies like AT&T have learned that they must document hiring decisions using objective criteria. A 1973 consent order handed down by the Equal Employment Opportunity Commission and the U.S. Department of Labor required AT&T to set up a model program for training employees who would be involved in the selection and hiring process.[10]

To understand the design of AT&T's model program, it is important to first understand the company's three-step interview process. Before AT&T hired a job candidate, the candidate had to complete three levels of interviews. The first interview usually occurred on a college campus. If the graduating student's qualifications matched an opening, AT&T invited the student to a company selection interview. A third, on-site interview was held if the student was interested in the position.[11]

To be qualified to conduct these interviews, AT&T personnel completed a series of highly-structured workshops to prepare them for the selection interview process. Professional instructors worked with trainees in intensive, two-day programs, using role-playing to simulate interview situations. Trainees had an opportunity to both practice the different interview levels and be evaluated.

The first level interview was relatively simple. Instructors taught trainees to keep interviews under 20 minutes, ignore negative or positive behavior and poor communication skills, and document only the answers to their questions.

Modeled on actual experiences, succeeding simulations became more difficult. During the second-level company selection interview, the trainee-interviewer had to sell AT&T to the interviewee and did most of the talking. In the final, on-site interview, there was more of a balance of conversation between the trainee-interviewer and the interviewee.

Ethel C. Glenn and Elliott A. Pood, after researching and critiquing the AT&T recruiting system, raise critical points about the interviewees' communication behavior as part of the interviewing process: 1) interviewers should understand the communication variables that affect perceptions of job candidates, 2) interviewers should be able to separate the communication variables that are important to specific job performance from those that are irrelevant, and 3) interviewers should be able to assess and document communication skills in a legally defensible manner.[12]

The process should follow the Equal Employment Opportunity Commission (EEOC) requirements. Familiarize yourself with *The Supervisor's EEO Handbook: A Guide to Federal Antidiscrimination Laws and Regulations.*[9]

Conducting the Employment Interview

The *employment interview* provides an opportunity to obtain information, explore attitudes, and make observations. The setting should be comfortable and project a positive impression of the organization. One job candidate drove sixty miles to an interview only to be asked to wait in an empty classroom for thirty minutes while a secretary located the department chairman. Her interview lasted fifteen minutes, during which time the chairman received two telephone calls and dismissed her so that he could attend a luncheon appointment. Even though she accepted the job, her negative impression of the chairman affected her interactions with him for many months thereafter.

During the opening moments you should make the interviewee comfortable and create a relaxed atmosphere. Asking the applicant to discuss former work experience is a good place to start, since it is an easy question to answer. As the applicant talks, listen for cues that provide insight into his or her background and attitudes. Questions that ask the applicant to discuss successes and frustrations are especially meaningful. You will also find it helpful to describe the job and explain how it fits into the organization, including salary. The kind of questions the applicant asks you should tell you something about his or her concerns. Problem-solving questions related to the job allow you to evaluate spontaneous reactions and judgment. Finally, when you close the interview, be sure to let the applicant know when he or she can expect to hear from you.

You may wish to use the questions in Table 16.4 as a resource. They are meant simply as a guide and can be used with the employment interview checklist in Table 16.5 to plan an effective strategy. Be sure to allow the interviewee to ask questions as well. Remember that the more you are able to learn about an applicant's background, interests, and interpersonal skills, the better chance you have of finding possible problems that may prevent effective performance on the job. The checklist given in Table 16.5 is meant to aid you in preparing for an employment interview.

The Orientation Interview

The first day on the job makes a lasting impression on the new employee, who has come to work motivated to succeed on the job but lacks the specific information to perform effectively. The overriding question in his or her mind is, "Can I meet the expectations of my boss?" Too often the manager fails to take the time to outline clearly these expectations and provide needed training and resources.

The objective of the *orientation interview* is to acquaint the new employee with the organization, provide information and resources needed to

TABLE 16.4 Employment Interview Questions

1. What is your past work experience?
2. What is your present job?
3. How do you spend most of your time in your present job?
4. Of what successes do you feel particularly proud in your former jobs?
5. What are some of the tasks you find difficult to do? Why?
6. What were some of the things in your past jobs that you particularly disliked?
7. Did your job require you to work frequently with people? Were any of your coworkers difficult to work with?
8. Why are you leaving your present job?
9. What are your personal goals in terms of a career path?
10. How do you measure whether you have been successful in your job?
11. What was your supervisor like?
12. Did you agree with your supervisor's approach to managing the organization?
13. How did you feel your supervisor evaluated your performance?
14. How important is education to your life?
15. In what subjects did you perform best/worst?
16. Did you help finance your education? To what extent?
17. Do you prefer to work on your own or with others?
18. How do you see yourself fitting in with this organization?
19. What contributions can you make to this job?
20. What aspects of your background would you like to strengthen? Why?

TABLE 16.5 Employment Interview Checklist

Establish a friendly atmosphere.

✓ Greet employee and make introductions.
✓ Establish common ground.
✓ State purpose: to interview prospective employee.
✓ Provide an overview of interview process.

Gather as much information as you can.

✓ Begin with topics that are easy to discuss, such as previous experience and interests.
✓ Review the job description and explain the organization's purpose, functions, and structure.
✓ Listen for information that provides insight into job candidate's background and attitudes.
✓ Use probing questions to explore specific areas of interest that relate to the job, particularly weaknesses.
✓ Ask problem-solving questions that allow applicant to respond to situations that may occur on the job.
✓ Avoid questions that refer to age, race, religion, ethnic origin, sex, veteran status, or disability.

Close the interview.

✓ Have applicant summarize understanding of the job.
✓ Clarify any misunderstandings.
✓ Inform applicant when you will make your decision.
✓ Express appreciation for interest in the position.

perform the job, establish a positive attitude between the employer and the employee, and create an atmosphere conducive to productive performance. Obviously, this is a complex task requiring several interviews and much of the organization's staff. Poor or ineffective orientations often result in unmotivated employees and high turnover.

Planning the Orientation

Effective orientation of employees requires effective planning. You will find the following activities helpful in preparing for an employee orientation interview:

- Have a copy of the job description available to give to the employee.
- Make arrangements for essentials such as parking, insurance, and office space during the first few days.
- Have information on company policy, organizational structure, and procedures available for reference and discussion.
- Prepare any materials needed for the performance of the job including telephone equipment, desk, paper, or machinery.
- Arrange for the new employee to meet with key people to assist in training and orientation.
- Have a series of meaningful tasks set up that increase in difficulty and aid in the training process.
- Prepare organizational members for the employee's arrival; a new group member can be threatening. Emphasize that the employee will be a benefit to the organization and in turn to each of them.
- Recognize the importance of social contact in today's high-tech world. Arrange for the employee to meet and eat with others.

Conducting the Orientation Interview

The impression you make as the manager is critical in establishing a climate that will encourage the employee to discuss future problems with you. Do not let a handbook of rules and procedures substitute for a personal orientation. Use this opportunity to clearly express your expectations, but allow personal questions and follow up to see if things are proceeding according to plans.

New employees are wonderful resources for information about the organization. Try to find out what makes them comfortable or uncomfortable in their new work situation. Did the employees have to search for anything? Ask for a comparison of their new experience with experiences at other firms. Have the employees identify major job-related problems in the work area.

A properly oriented employee feels good about his or her job and has the resources and information necessary to meet performance expectations. Just as important, the manager has established a positive impression of an organizational climate that encourages interaction and recognizes the importance of the individual. Table 16.6 provides a checklist for the orientation interview.

TABLE 16.6 Orientation Interview Checklist

Establish a friendly atmosphere.

✓ Greet interviewee.
✓ Establish common ground.
✓ State the purpose of orientation.
✓ Provide an overview of orientation.

Give overview of new position.

✓ Review job description.
✓ Explain organizational structure.
✓ Explain relationship of employee's position within organizational structure.
✓ Explain performance expectations.
✓ Assign specific tasks.
✓ Introduce employee to key people.

Close orientation interview.

✓ Have employee summarize understanding of job.
✓ Clarify any misunderstandings.
✓ Agree on follow-up meetings or other actions.
✓ Acknowledge employee as important part of organization.

The Counseling Interview

At one time or another all managers become involved in giving or receiving help. Different words may be used to describe this process such as counseling, teaching, guiding, training, or coaching; nevertheless, the ultimate goal is to help someone solve problems and face crises. This is a critical role for the manager because (1) it develops employees, (2) it provides insight and understanding, and (3) it promotes a trusting relationship through mutual sharing and problem solving.

Counseling Develops Employees

Problem-sensitive managers who help employees learn the skills to solve their problems will gain by developing a mature, competent workforce. As a helper or counselor, the manager can also coach the subordinate in the skills to identify and solve problems. As the subordinate masters these skills, he or she becomes more mature and increasingly independent of managers, direct supervision, and feedback.

Counseling Provides Insight and Understanding

Many problems can be resolved in their initial stages—before they become crises—if the manager is aware of the causes. The *counseling interview* can be a revealing communication experience during which the manager gains as well as gives insight and information. Learning about a problem early on can lead to less costly solutions and save time and resources.

Counseling Promotes a Trusting Relationship

Finally, the counseling interview can strengthen the trusting relationship between manager and subordinate by helping the receiver understand the problem, receive support, learn new skills, or modify behavior. Counseling involves a dynamic, transactional relationship through face-to-face verbal and nonverbal interaction. Both parties have unique biological and psychological feelings, values, needs, as well as unique perceptions of each other, the situation, their expectations, and their roles. The effective counseling interviewer recognizes that the situation requires the helper to listen, encourage exploration, and establish a trusting relationship.

Preparing for the Counseling Interview

Because of the nature of the counseling interview, you often cannot prepare for a particular situation. Your subordinate may appear in your doorway and request a few minutes of your time for an urgent matter. While it is fairly easy for most of us to give advice based on past experience, most employees will see their problem as unique and your advice as both inappropriate and an attempt to circumvent their problem. Even if the employee seeks your opinion, providing advice will not encourage the development of exploration and problem-solving skills.

Conducting the Counseling Interview

In the role of helper or counselor, your task will be to clarify roles, identify the problem, and determine a course of action.[13]

Clarify roles. You will need to begin the interview by clarifying both your role and that of your subordinate. The first step will be to create an atmosphere that is relaxed, warm, receptive, and sincere in order to get the employee to talk openly. Once you can identify the nature of the problem, you will be able to determine your role. To do this, you will need to answer the following questions:

1. *Can I meet the interviewee's expectations?* Suppose that George has come to you with a complex personal problem that is placing stress on him and affecting his job performance. Can you help him? If the problem requires a professionally trained counselor, the answer to this question may be no, but you can act as a link in getting the employee help, perhaps through the employee assistance program. If the problem does not require professional expertise, however, you may be able to help George gain insight into the problem.
2. *Can I work with the interviewee?* It may be that George needs some information or direction that you can provide, in which case you will want to assist him in solving his problem. If you have time constraints or a personality conflict, you may need to postpone the interview or get assistance.
3. *Do I want to work with the interviewee?* Sometimes employees take advantage of opportunities to be with the boss and actually are capable of handling their problem. Other times you may not want to become involved because of conflicting demands or needs. It is better to be honest with the

interviewee than send crossed messages that may be perceived as lack of interest or concern.

4. *What structure do we need?* The nature of the problem will help you establish the structure or format of the interview. If the problem is complex and requires additional information or the opportunity to practice new skills, you will need to agree on a format that includes several meetings. If, however, all of the information is readily available and both of you have the time, it may be possible to follow the problem-solving steps and select a solution within a limited time frame in one sitting. Before proceeding, you will need to agree on the format.

5. *What do I expect from the interviewee?* A counseling interview is goal directed, whether it is to give empathy or resolve conflict. You as an interviewer have expectations of the interviewee. These expectations may include a change in behavior, such as improved job performance or a better attitude.

Once you have answered these questions, you will have your roles clarified so that both parties will be better able to contribute to a positive outcome.

Identify the problem. During the first phase of the counseling interview, both the interviewer and interviewee engage in problem exploration. The interviewer should be listening for content and feelings and encouraging the interviewee to be concrete—identifying actual events and specific problems. Both parties should agree on the problem and follow the problem-solving steps. The interviewee should describe the symptoms, analyze the facts, and determine the causes. Finally, he or she should explore possible alternative actions and the probable consequences of each. The interviewer should act as a guide in the process and avoid a directive approach.

Determine a course of action. The close of the interview is vital and should not be rushed. The interviewer should summarize the interview by concluding with a statement of the action that is to be taken to eliminate the problem. The interviewee should leave the interview feeling that it has been time well spent and that there is genuine concern about his or her welfare. Nonverbal communication is crucial in conveying sincerity and warmth. This is the time for a warm handshake or caring pat on the back.

Table 16.7 provides a checklist for the counseling interview.

The Performance Appraisal Interview

To achieve output goals, people must both cooperate and coordinate their efforts. They must know what to do, when to do it, and how to do it. It is the job of the manager to determine whether subordinates are performing to meet the goals of the organization. The performance appraisal interview is an essential activity in gauging and improving employee productivity.

Performance appraisal is a test based on the best judgment and opinions of evaluators using definite identifiable criteria that measure the quantity or quality of work or specific requirements. The primary purpose of perfor-

TABLE 16.7 Counseling Interview Checklist

Establish a friendly atmosphere.
✓ Greet employee.
✓ Establish common ground.
✓ State the purpose: to help subordinate solve problem or face crisis.
✓ Clarify roles, expectations.
✓ Explain counseling format.

Provide employee counseling.
✓ Explore the problem and its seriousness.
✓ Use a nondirective approach.
✓ Listen for content and feelings.
✓ Encourage interviewee to be concrete.
✓ Describe symptoms of problem.
✓ Analyze the facts.
✓ Determine the causes.
✓ Explore possible solutions.

Close counseling interview.
✓ Summarize the problem and its seriousness.
✓ Agree on action to be taken.
✓ Convey sincerity and warmth through nonverbal feedback.
✓ Acknowledge value of employee to organization.

mance appraisal is to improve performance. Secondary purposes are to review past performance, set goals for future performance, develop personnel to determine merit, and give recognition.

For its studies of performance, the General Electric Company compared the following approaches to performance appraisal: criticism, praise, and goal setting. Their findings indicated that criticism alone resulted in defensive behavior. If the employee received only praise during the appraisal interview, there was no change in performance. Only the third approach, goal setting, resulted in improved performance. As a result, G.E. developed guidelines for performance appraisal:

1. Emphasize strengths, not weaknesses.
2. Avoid discussing personal characteristics.
3. If you must discuss weaknesses, describe specific behavior and give examples of more acceptable behavior.
4. Concentrate on opportunities for growth.
5. Stress a few important items for growth.
6. Use a reasonable time frame.
7. Focus on an overall objective.[14]

By regularly giving feedback on employee performance, the manager maintains an open climate and avoids the anxiety and fear that precede the yearly evaluation, since the employee has a fairly clear understanding of strengths and weaknesses. The following story emphasizes the frustration employees experience when they don't receive regular feedback on their performance.

Appraisal Frustration

"I've just had my performance evaluation, and all I want to do is *cry!*" Jill lamented to her husband, Gary. "I don't know what my boss expects from me. Take a look for yourself at his comments about my work." Gary took the evaluation form and read the following handwritten comments:

> Jill, you communicate very well with the doctors and patients and have a very warm and caring attitude. I am especially impressed with your willingness to take extra patient loads and perform overtime work. Your judgment and management of your workload are excellent. You have a good attitude and personality and have fit in well with the other staff members.

"I don't get it," Gary responded. "What's wrong with it? He really seems impressed with your performance."

"His comments are fine—but they don't count as much as the criteria. Read further," answered Jill.

As Gary read the rest of the evaluation form he discovered that Jill's supervisor rated her *acceptable* in job skills with the notation, "always completes the job assigned within the time allotted" and "keeps accurate records." Under job knowledge, he marked "needs improvement."

"I realize that my supervisor is a very busy person, but how can someone evaluate my performance without talking to me or giving me a chance to make suggestions or share my ideas? There are lots of things I could do—ways to improve our efficiency that I learned on my old job—and I know they would work here. We used to have some of the very same problems. I've even tried some of them, and the other nurses have picked up on them. Not only that, my supervisor's taking credit for the improvements on our shift. I can't believe that he marked 'needs to improve' job knowledge. I'm more knowledgeable than any of the nurses on my floor. I've only had the job two months, which he acknowledged. "But,' he said, 'I need to be aware of my shortcomings.' Everyone talks about the value of the individual employee. If I'm so valuable to the organization, why don't they listen to me and give me credit for what I've done?"

"Wow! I can't believe the mixed messages you are getting," responded Gary. "I guess I'm lucky that I work for someone who communicates her expectations so that I can understand them."

Preparing for the Performance Appraisal

Managers should take several steps to prepare for the performance appraisal interview. The first of these preparatory steps is to be aware of the typical problems that might hinder your objectivity and effectiveness.

The halo/horns effect. If a person has performed well in one activity, tend to attribute other positive traits to that person, whether or not these traits are actually present. This *halo effect* then affects one's ability to objectively assess actual performance. For example, if Jenny, a secretary, has outstanding technical skills, her boss may assign an outstanding performance rating and overlook or ignore poor interpersonal skills and poor time management. Conversely, if Joe fails in an attempt to perform a task, there may be a tendency to place "horns" on him and assign other negative traits.

Central tendency bias. If a manager is not sure about an employee's performance, he or she may decide to rank the employee as average rather than give a rating that is too high or too low; this *central tendency bias* is a safe position that avoids the need to differentiate or distinguish performance levels. In lieu of central tendency, the manager may have a tendency to give lenient or very critical ratings. This practice should be avoided.

The recency effect. If performance appraisal occurs following an event during which the employee performed exceptionally well or made several critical mistakes, the timing of the event may affect the appraisal, producing the *recency effect.* An effective appraisal should be based on the employee's overall performance during a specific period of time with emphasis placed on the achievement of goals.

The Appraisal Process

To fully prepare for the appraisal, you should review the requirements of the employee's job and the performance goals. Obtain written feedback from the employee concerning his or her perceptions of meeting these requirements and goals. By doing so, you will have some idea of the employee's point of view prior to your interview. Finally, complete the appraisal form, keeping in mind that the interview should allow for employee input and mutual goal setting.

The performance appraisal process itself must be productive. The time and effort expended must be justified by the results obtained. The *appraisal* process should:

1. Allow both the supervisor and subordinate an opportunity to learn about each other's goals, aspirations, and expectations.
2. Give a clear indication of how these expectations are met in specific, measurable terms.
3. Assist in identifying obstacles to productivity that might result from inefficiency, competing goals, or misunderstandings.
4. Identify results, not just activity, and effectiveness rather than effort.
5. Assist in identifying career paths within the organization that allow for growth and development of employees.
6. Provide a clear outline of the performance expectations and how they will be measured.
7. Provide the information needed to effectively administer promotions, raises, and training.

Avoid pitfalls. There are some key pitfalls to guard against in common interview situations. Criticism typically produces defensive behavior and should be specifically related to a particular behavior. Even though you may emphasize employee strengths, praise will not take the sting out of the following criticism. Acceptance of criticism will depend on the employee's newness on the job, the competence of the superior, and the amount of trust and liking developed between the two of them. Minor faults should not be discussed during the annual appraisal. Whatever the deficiencies, the cause should be identified and a plan for improvement agreed on.

In addition, the employee's perception of the job may be different from the superior's, which might make it necessary to clarify job duties and responsibilities as well as the degree of delegated authority. Superior and subordinate may have differing opinions on the best method of performing a task, budgeting time, or setting priorities.

Participate in mutual goal setting. Mutual goal setting is a critical part of the appraisal interview in that it (1) capitalizes on employee strengths, (2) sets standards for improved performance, (3) allows for employee growth and development, (4) establishes priorities, and (5) clarifies organizational goals. The process must be mutual. It must allow the subordinate the opportunity to participate in determining goals and priorities and the best means to accomplish them. It also must allow feedback from the superior that clarifies expectations and performance objectives.

Finally, the employee may be encountering obstacles to performance or problems on the job of which the superior is unaware. Time should be spent in the interview creating a climate that allows the subordinate to express any concerns or frustrations that may not surface in the normal interview process.

Emphasize strengths and capabilities. Appraisal interviews tend to concentrate on changing the employee rather than determining strengths and capabilities. A number of ways to improve performance may prove more appropriate than changing the employee. Be alert for signals indicating that (1) a change or alteration in duties may capitalize on strengths, (2) the employee may need to be transferred to a more suitable position, (3) the manager may need to alter his or her method of supervision and provide more feedback, training, or support.

Eliminate obstacles. Once the manager analyzes the work situation, changes should be initiated to eliminate obstructions. If the employee is not able to perform the job, he or she should be reassigned to a position in the organization in which he or she can perform adequately. Perhaps the employee has the capability but needs technical training or knowledge. It may simply be a matter of providing the necessary supplies or equipment to do the job.

A final note. Note that two factors are at work here: those things the worker can't do as opposed to those things the worker won't do. If the problem is a lack of knowledge, lack of skill, lack of feedback, difficult job requirements, or lack of resources, the worker can't do it. On the other hand, if there are no expectations of reward, the reward is not valued by the employee, or the obstacles to performance are too great, the worker won't do it. Some questions to consider are found in Table 16.8

Remember that the appraisal interview should be the confirmation of interaction and feedback that occurs frequently on the job rather than a yearly gathering of "do's and don'ts." Its primary emphasis should be to evaluate progress and set new goals that capitalize on employee strengths. Do not confuse the appraisal process by introducing a secondary purpose of disciplining employees. The latter is a separate type of interview that should be handled during a different encounter. The checklist in Table 16.9 will provide a guide for planning a performance appraisal interview.

TABLE 16.8 "Can't Do" versus "Won't Do"

1. Is the worker performing properly? If not, analyze the situation.
2. Does the worker understand what to do? If not, provide orientation.
3. Does the worker know how to do the job? If not, provide training.
4. Does the worker try to do the job? If not, evaluate the incentives.
5. Is the worker capable of doing the job? If not, consider job redesign or transfer.
6. Are there psychological problems? If so, can stress and conflict be reduced?
7. Are there health problems? If so, provide the employee assistance.
8. Is the employee's poor performance affecting others? If so, apply progressive discipline.

TABLE 16.9 Performance Appraisal Checklist

Establish a friendly atmosphere.

✓ Greet employee.
✓ Establish common ground.
✓ State the purpose of appraisal.
✓ Provide an overview of appraisal process.

Give overview of new position.

✓ Review job requirements and goals.
✓ Describe important elements of employee's performance.
✓ Allow employee to give observations of performance effectiveness, problems, or obstacles.
✓ Set goals and priorities for future performance expectations.
✓ Determine type of support needed to reach these goals (training, altering of job duties, transfer, change in supervision).

Close performance appraisal interview.

✓ Have employee summarize his/her understanding of job expectations.
✓ Clarify any misunderstandings concerning performance.
✓ Agree on follow-up meetings or other actions.
✓ Acknowledge value of employee to organization and the importance of appraisal process.

The Disciplinary Interview

Top management sets policies, rules, and regulations that must be observed and enforced by line supervisors. Organizations and their members are also subject to state, federal, and international law. As the importance and level of authority increase, the role of the first-line supervisor decreases. Managers can modify behavior through positive reinforcement. Occasionally, however, managers must use force or outward control to correct, mold, or punish unacceptable behavior.

The *disciplinary interview* is probably the most critical interview you will conduct as a manager. Besides the personal stress that both parties usually feel, you must establish a tone and convey a message that is clear and purposeful. When preparing for a disciplinary interview, keep in mind that effective discipline should be appropriate, effective, consistent, immediate, and recorded.

The Disciplinary Action Should Be Appropriate

In most organizations guidelines establish the severity of the action to be taken so that it is appropriate to the offense. For example, it would be inappropriate to fire an employee for being five minutes late to work unless the employee has been consistently or excessively late over a specified period of time.

The Disciplinary Action Should Be Effective

Unless the interview is effective in meeting its objective, unacceptable behavior is likely to continue and perhaps increase in its severity. You must act clearly in the supervisory role as manager to subordinate and explain the problem or describe the rule that has been violated. Once you have done this, tell the employee exactly what is expected in terms of improvement and what assistance you will provide as supervisor. It is important to hear the employee's side of the story so that you may discover obstacles to performance that you can remove. Next, you should explain what will happen if the employee does not meet expectations within a specified period of time. Finally, follow through with your commitment.

The Disciplinary Action Should Be Consistent

You cannot fire one person in your department for coming in late and slap another on the hand for a similar offense without jeopardizing the welfare of the organization. Most organizations use the personnel department as a resource to assist managers in applying discipline. One of the primary concerns is consistency in the application of discipline.

Discipline Should Be Immediate and Private

Whether it is positive or negative, feedback must be immediate to be most effective. An employee may not be aware that he or she is not following the

A Disciplinary Dilemma

Jason Jerrell supervised a department of professional counselors. His employees were highly motivated and performance was rarely a problem until Kevin Windy was added to the staff. Windy had essentially the same background as the other counselors, but he had fewer years of experience.

Six months after Windy's arrival, Jerrell found that he was not developing into as strong a counselor as the others in the department. Windy's monthly client status reports were consistently late. His work was substandard in quantity and quality. Other counselors began to complain to Jerrell because they had to pick up some of Windy's counseling load.

For the first three months, Jerrell assigned this behavior to Windy's newness and inexperience. After the fourth month, Jerrell spoke with Windy in the hall and told him that he needed to meet report deadlines. Windy responded that he took a lot of time with his clients because he wanted to follow the best possible professional standards but agreed to meet the deadlines in the future.

Ever since the discussion in the hall, Windy's attitude has been negative. He consistently takes long lunch breaks, arrives at work late, and leaves work early. Although the last two status reports met the deadlines, they were still poorly prepared. What should Jerrell do?

rules or accepted procedures, and so failure to give immediate feedback will more than likely result in repeated behavior. Feedback can also provide information about the reason for the employee's performance problem. Once the cause is identified, the manager has a number of corrective strategies available, such as training, orienting, counseling, transfer, demotion, suspension, or termination.

Since a corrective interview describes an incorrect or improper behavior of the employee, the manner in which it is conducted can affect the trust relationship between manager and subordinate. It should be conducted in private and out of the range of hearing of other employees.

The Disciplinary Interview Should Be Recorded

Normally, you will want to give an oral warning to an employee on the first offense. Nevertheless, you should document the interview. The employee should be told, however, that the purpose of the interview is an oral reprimand and your written notes are for reference; in contrast, a written reprimand will be permanently placed in the personnel file. Include the following information, and give a copy to the employee:

1. The problem or rule violated
2. Expected performance

3. The disciplinary action taken
4. The time frame in which the behavior must be corrected
5. The consequences of repeated actions

Because of the severity of some disciplinary actions that affect pay—such as suspension, removal, or demotion—employees have the right to judicial due process. Familiarize yourself with the grievance and appeals procedures of the organization, keep accurate records, and meet with personnel and your Equal Employment Opportunity representative before notifying an employee of any adverse action.

Wohlking points out a number of factors that should be considered when disciplining employees:[15]

1. What is the seriousness of the offense?
2. How much time elapsed between offenses?
3. What is the nature and frequency of the offense?
4. What is the employee's work history?
5. Were there extenuating circumstances?
6. What degree of job orientation did the employee receive?
7. What is the history of discipline in the organization?
8. What are the implications for others?
9. Do you have management's backing?

The disciplinary interview is a vital managerial activity. It is important to set a tone that is firm but fair, friendly but instructive. Table 16.10 provides a checklist for the disciplinary interview.

TABLE 16.10 Disciplinary Interview Checklist

Establish a friendly atmosphere.

✓ Greet employee.
✓ Establish common ground.
✓ State the purpose: to resolve a performance problem face to face.
✓ Provide overview of disciplinary interview format.

Apply corrective discipline.

✓ Review the problem and its seriousness.
✓ Allow the employee to give his/her side of problem.
✓ Tell employee what is expected.
✓ Set time frame for improvement.
✓ State consequences if behavior is repeated.
✓ Inform employee of action taken (oral or written reprimand, suspension, termination).

Close disciplinary interview.

✓ Ask employee to summarize understanding of performance expected and action taken.
✓ Clarify misunderstandings concerning performance.
✓ Agree on follow-up actions.
✓ Acknowledge value of employee to organization.

The International Job Search

American employers' expectations of job applicants often conflict with the value systems of other cultures. A. P. Goodman, J. A. Hartt, M. K. Pennington, and K. P. Terrell from the Career Services Office at Catholic University researched the differences in attitudes and values between U.S. employers and those of a cross-section of countries and continents. Among the American managers' expectations of job applicants were (1) self-promotion, (2) directness in communication, (3) self-disclosure, (4) career self-awareness, (5) individual responsibility in finding employment, (6) informality in the interview process, (7) punctuality, (8) effective letters of application and resumes, (9) individual equality, and (10) preparation about the organization.[16] These same expectations, however, create cultural barriers when applied to job applicants from other countries.

Goodman and colleagues cite abundant examples of the conflicting values between American managers and managers from other cultures. While American employers look for assertiveness and confidence, employers from many countries view promoting oneself by discussing one's accomplishments as boastful and self-serving. Since jobs are often allocated by the government or family, voicing long-range career goals may be an indication of disloyalty. Gathering information about the company before the interview is interpreted as inappropriate and indicative of too much independence. Personal interests are disclosed only to friends and family.

It is common practice in the United States to shake hands with a job applicant at the beginning and end of an interview. Actions that express informality such as touching, using a first name, or crossing legs are inappropriate in many other countries. Unlike America, in these countries a younger person defers to an older person and treats that person with respect. Making eye contact with someone of higher status shows disrespect.

Even time can have cultural implications. Many cultures do not consider someone late if he or she arrives anywhere from 15 minutes to two hours from the agreed meeting time. People and relationships are considered far more important than timeliness.

Resumes and letters of application communicate impressions about the job applicant that influence the interview process. These impressions are also culturally biased. Managers' expectations of what the resume should contain and how it is interpreted differ from country to country. For example, extracurricular activities are considered work experience in Denmark and receive much attention. In Germany these activities are disregarded. Latin American countries prefer detailed personal data, including a photograph. Since European countries often use graphologists to interpret handwriting samples, applicants handwrite the cover letter.[17]

The American workforce will become increasingly international in the next century. Effective managers must be aware that their expectations of international applicants must be adapted to the cultural influences that affect and mold behavior. As a first step, you must become familiar with cultural values that bias the interview process.

ETHICS: RIGHT OR WRONG?

Recruiting Advertising Strategies

Maketha Williamson had peaked in her position with Rushdown Advertising in New Orleans. As the firm's top account executive, she was beginning to be bored with Rushdown's market limitations. Thus, Williamson let it be known that she wanted to move to a larger firm in one of the major advertising cities: Chicago, New York, or Los Angeles.

Williamson's work had received national recognition. She was viewed as one of the up-and-coming people in the business, and her impact on the sales and market of Rushdown was well known. Through her initiative and creativity, what was once a "mom-and-pop" firm had become the top advertising firm in New Orleans. Williamson was clever, and her ads demonstrated it. One local beer company had added a number of new blends under her tutelage and captured a major segment of the 21–35-year-old age market. This accomplishment was critical for the company because it needed to turn around a dwindling consumer population and develop a new customer base. The uniqueness of the campaign caught on nationally because of the public's growing experimentation with different beers and acceptance of the small, local producer.

As a result, Williamson's name came to the attention of a major ad agency in Chicago that was always looking for talented individuals for key positions. Jason Paul, the personnel manager, had recently attended a seminar that pointed out the high rate of applicant responses to ads for top jobs. Realizing that the company could get a dozen top-of-the-line candidates, Paul believed that the organization should use a top job opportunity to learn about national marketing strategies. A current publication advised, "You can sort through the best candidates' ideas and choose the cream of the crop and tailor it to your needs." Consequently, knowing that one of the firm's vice-presidents was seriously considering retirement at the end of the next year, Paul lined up a number of outstanding candidates for that position.

To say Paul was impressed with Williamson was an understatement. The more he found out about her, the more interested he became. Williamson had a bachelor's degree in marketing and had won the top award in a national student advertising competition during her senior year at a leading public research university. She then finished her M.B.A. in an accelerated program at a top ten business school, graduating with an A average. Obviously, she had the technical background, a competitive spirit, and proof of her ability. Paul called Williamson and invited her to interview for the vice-presidency. Williamson was pleased and accepted the invitation.

As part of the interviewing process, Paul asked Williamson to review three advertising contracts that the company had in hand and to present her recommendations during a series of interviews. At the end of the third interview, Paul gave Williamson a copy of the organization's structure. For the fourth interview, she was to present a revised structure that would incorporate her management style and strategies as Vice-President of Market Development. At the fifth interview, Williamson gave a 30-minute presentation analyzing the company's competitive position. When this interview was complete, Williamson was told that the company's president, Jerome LaCross, would contact her personally about a job offer.

A week later Williamson found out through an informal network of advertising executives that Paul's company had hired someone else. She felt humiliated and very angry. She had given thousands of dollars of free, expert consulting advice; outlined possible new market opportunities; and provided names of valuable contacts; yet she had not even received the courtesy of a call from Paul letting her know that one of her peers had been selected for the position.[18]

Case Questions

1. What is the ethics problem in this case?
2. What could Williamson have done to protect herself?
3. Does Williamson have any recourse?

SUMMARY

Interviewing is an important means of communication. The interview is the interaction that occurs between two parties who meet to accomplish a predetermined purpose essential to the welfare of the organization. It is the manager's responsibility to understand the interview's purpose, be prepared for it, and record the findings. Key steps include defining the purpose, determining who should be involved, analyzing the other party, and planning the interview structure or format.

Each interview situation follows a basic structure adapted to the specific purpose of the interaction. The opening establishes common ground, sets the tone, and clarifies the purpose. The body of the interview attempts to accomplish the goal through problem-solving or questioning techniques. Finally, the close includes a summary of the information and agreements and acknowledges the value of the encounter.

Effective interviews are often the result of effective questioning. Open and closed questions control the pace and direction of the interview. The nature and sequence of questions should be adapted to fit the situation and the people involved.

The manager's ability to handle the interview effectively—whether it is to counsel, discipline, or appraise performance—establishes his or her credibility with subordinates, develops trust, and encourages growth. Since much of the manager's day is spent in face-to-face information-gathering and problem-solving interviews, interviewing may be the most important of the communication skills.

KEY WORDS

BFOQ
closed questions
counseling interview
disciplinary interview
employment interview
interview
leading questions
mirror questions
open questions
orientation interview
performance appraisal interview
probing questions
sequencing

REVIEW QUESTIONS

1. Why are interview skills important to the manager?
2. Describe a situation in which you were interviewed. What was the purpose of the interview? Did the interviewer dominate discussion or did you? What things did the interviewer do to get you to talk? to maintain control?
3. What are the purposes of performance appraisal? How often should it occur? Share your experiences with this form of interview.
4. What is the role of the manager as a counselor?
5. Why is it important to avoid giving advice?
6. As a manager, why is it important to prepare for the job interview?
7. Barbara is sixty-five years old and has applied for a job on the janitorial staff. The only position open includes as one of the tasks cleaning the men's rest room. Does she fit the bona fide occupational qualifications?
8. Why is it important to discipline employees? When is discipline effective? ineffective? Give an example of each.
9. Describe the elements of a disciplinary interview. Why are they important?
10. Try to recall the first day you went to work on a particular job (part time, full time, or volunteer work). What kind of orientation did you receive? Was it effective or ineffective? Why? If you could have designed an orientation to meet your needs, what would you have included?

EXERCISES

1. Interview someone you have not met before. Spend about 20 minutes finding out what makes the interviewee unique. Be sure to use each other's names as frequently as possible. What techniques did you use, verbal and nonverbal, to get the interviewee to share with you?
2. Interview an expert on one of the communication topics that relate to this course. Follow the interview steps outlined in this chapter: Prepare an outline including sample questions, conduct your interview, and summarize your findings in writing. Present your findings to the class.
3. The way you say something can be more important than what you say. Select four or five words that describe your communication style (such as relaxed, honest, cautious). What styles get you in trouble? What styles do you find offensive?
4. Engage in a problem-solving discussion with someone in which you act as the helper or counselor. The problem can be real or hypothetical. Practice listening and reflecting skills. An observer should summarize the frequency and quality of your responses during the interview as well as the verbal or nonverbal behaviors that encouraged or discouraged the interviewee. Ask the observer to share this information with you at the completion of the interview.
5. Select a job for which you will be acting as an interviewer and prepare a job description. Write a job announcement and list the media in which you would advertise the position. Prepare an interview outline including a list of tentative questions that will help you in the selection process.

6. Prepare a rèsumé and interview for one of the jobs described in question 5. Evaluate the interview.
7. Prepare a plan for orienting the person selected for the position you described.
8. Joe supervises an employee who formerly contributed 100 percent to her organization. She has been punctual, careful, considerate, and helpful to new employees. She is also pursuing a business degree at the nearby community college, is married, and is active socially. Her performance evaluations have been very satisfactory until two months ago when she was not interviewed for a new position. Lately, she has been late for work several times, negligent with accounts and records, sharp with her supervisor, and openly talking about co-workers to cause deliberate friction. Joe has noted the following specific incidents:
   a. The employee is supposed to be on the job at 8:00 A.M. Within the last month she has not reported to the office until 8:30 on six different occasions. Joe has overlooked this since she is an exceptional worker, but the employee continues to be late.
   b. The employee has always regarded her supervisors highly but has begun to talk back to them regularly.
   c. On three occasions she communicated confidential or incorrect information to other staff members, which led to unnecessary confrontations with other employees.
   d. On four occasions the employee lost or misplaced important documents.

   Determine Joe's plan of action and prepare an interview outline. Test your plan by role playing the interview with another class member.

REFERENCES

1. Robert Miller, "Personnel Execs Reveal the Truths about Job Applicants," *Dallas Morning News*, (January 31, 1991). Reprinted by permission.
2. Ibid.
3. Allan D. Frank, *Communication on the Job* (Glenview, Ill.: Scott Foresman, 1982), p. 192.
4. Ibid.
5. Adapted from R. L. Kahn and C. F. Cannell, *The Dynamics of Interviewing* (New York: John Wiley), 1957, pp. 133–143.
6. Raymond Gorden, *Interviewing Strategy, Techniques and Tactics* (Homewood, Ill.: Dorsey, 1969).
7. William J. Seiler, E. Scott Baudhuin, and L. David Schuelke, *Communication in Business and Professional Organizations* (Reading, Mass.: Addison-Wesley, 1982), p. 222; and Allan D. Frank, *Communication on the Job*, pp. 205–206.
8. Patricia Hayes Bradley, *Communications for Business and the Professions*, 2d ed. (Dubuque, Iowa: Wm. C. Brown, 1983), pp. 160–162.
9. "AT&T Discrimination Settlement," *Fair Employment Practices* (Washington, D.C.: The Bureau of National Affairs, Inc., 1978).
10. Ethel C. Glenn and Elliott A. Pood, "Interview Training for Management Recruiters: the AT&T Study," *The Journal of Business Communication*, 17:5 (1980), p. 5.
11. Ibid.
12. "The Supervisor's EEO Handbook: A Guide to Federal Antidiscrimination Laws and Regulations" (New York: Executive Enterprises, 1981).
13. Lawrence M. Brammer, *The Helping Relationship* (Englewood Cliffs, N.J.: Prentice-Hall, 1979), pp. 45–46.
14. The film "Performance Appraisal: The Human Dynamic" by McGraw-Hill, released in 1978, vividly illustrates this research.
15. Wallace Wohlking, "Effective Discipline in Employee Relations," *Personnel Journal* (Sept. 1975), pp. 201–207.
16. A. P. Goodman, J. A. Harrt, M. K. Pennington, K. P. Terrell, "International Students and the Job Search," *Journal of Career Planning & Employment* (Summer 1988).
17. "Finding Employment Overseas: The International Job Search," pamphlet prepared by CareerVision and the University of Virginia (New York: Millicom Media, Inc., 1989), p. 5.
18. This case was written by Laura Lemoine Lindsay based on an article by L. A. Winokur, "Job Seekers Increasingly Find They Are in Demand—As Sources of Free Expertise," *Wall Street Journal*, April 8, 1991.

CHAPTER 17

COMMUNICATION STRATEGIES: MANAGING CHANGE

After forty-three years with the U.S. Navy, Admiral Grace Hopper retired and accepted a position as a consultant for Digital Equipment Corporation. She was seventy-nine years old.

During her naval career, "Amazing Grace" played major roles in the development of naval communication systems. She was credited with being the developer of COBOL as a computer language. Hopper kept a clock in her office with hands that ran backward as the answer to coworkers who said, "We've always done it that way."[1] Here are her comments on change during an interview with *USA Today:*

> HOPPER: Every time I speak, I promise my audience that if, in the next twelve months, any one of them says, "But we've always done it that way," I will instantly materialize beside them (and) haunt them for 24 hours. Human beings have been living in a rapidly changing world. I was born in 1906, and the Wright brothers first flew in 1903. I've seen the entire development of airplanes.
>
> *USA TODAY:* You also know something about the first computer that was built in 1944, don't you?
>
> HOPPER: I was there, a member of the crew. I've watched the whole development of computers. And yet I've heard people

say, "No, I'm a little scared of that," instead of going ahead and doing it. People are allergic to change, and one of the biggest jobs anybody can do in this world is to change people's minds.

USA TODAY: That's rather difficult to do, isn't it?

HOPPER: Do you realize that I watched people who refused to buy refrigerators because the only way to keep lettuce fresh was on ice? You had to have an icebox. I watched people refuse to touch telephones, because they might get a shock. We live in a world of change. And the sooner we accept change and move toward it, the easier it is.[2]

Organizations, like individuals, are constantly changing—through employee turnover, new leadership, economic disaster, regional growth and development, and environmental restrictions.

According to Ellingsworth, "no complex organization can remain healthy and viable for long without the capacity to anticipate, execute, and adapt to change."[3] To change, an organization must have effective communication internally among its members as well as externally with its clients. A surgeon, for example, must be able to give clear instructions to the surgical team as well as be able to explain the purpose and expected outcome of an operation. Change involves communication on all organizational levels and in all forms: group discussion, one-on-one meetings, formal briefings, electronic and voice mail, written proposals, and memoranda.

THE CHANGE STAGE OF PROBLEM RESOLUTION

Effective change management depends on understanding the steps involved in the change process. These steps are, in fact, the implementation stage of problem solving. Chapter 13 described the problem-solving process in both its creative and analytical stages. The first three steps of problem solving are *creative* because they rely heavily on developing ideas rather than on refining or eliminating ideas. The second three steps are *analytical,* because they involve selecting and implementing the ideas, then analyzing the effectiveness of the solution. It is during this second analytical stage that change is implemented.

Often organizations find themselves in crisis situations because they have ignored the need to change for a long time. In the early 1980s, automobile companies in the United States found themselves facing such a crisis. The great demand for energy-efficient vehicles suddenly allowed Japanese imports to capture the market. Even with high tariffs, the Japanese imports thrived. The American public chose their high-quality construction and energy efficiency over the luxurious comforts of domestically produced cars. Because the U.S. auto industry resisted change instead of anticipating and adapting to it, it suffered great losses.

Organizations and individuals must be problem sensitive—that is, they must be able to admit to themselves that a problem exists. Perhaps a better way of stating this is that the members of an organization must be able to *feel* anxiety, pressures, and tension and want to get better. Until individuals and organizations recognize that something is not as it should be, change cannot occur.

In Chapter 13 we described the steps of the problem-solving process that

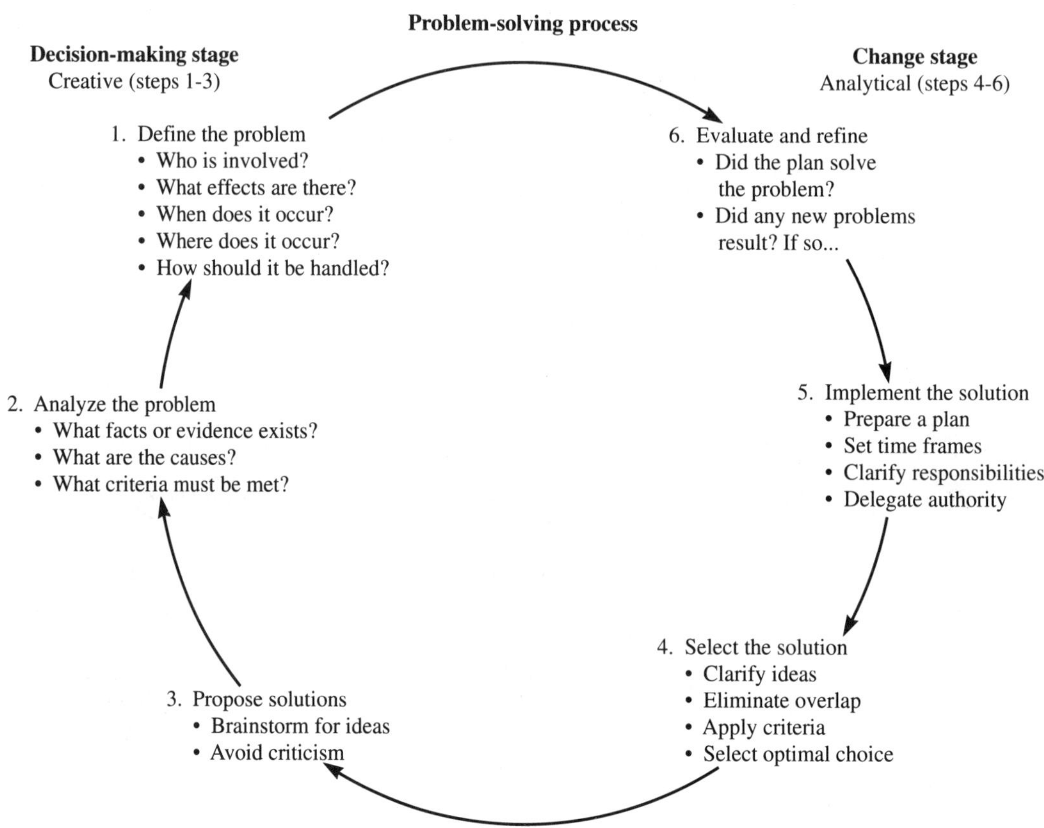

FIGURE 17.1 The Problem-Solving Model Including the Decision-Making (1–3) and Change (4–6) Stages.

resulted in the selection of an effective solution. Once they complete these decision-making steps, many organizations decide that the problem is "solved." In fact, any solution implemented at this stage is incomplete. The most critical step in problem solving is the *change stage,* which comes later. Here the actual plan or strategy unfolds, and the steps for implementation are defined. While effective implementation of change depends on careful attention to all the steps of problem solving, the change stage is vital because it focuses on selecting, implementing, and evaluating the solution (see Figure 17.1).

Selecting, Implementing, and Evaluating a Solution

When those individuals affected by change actively participate in selecting the solution, they have an opportunity to ask questions and clarify misunderstandings about the solution. If individuals involved in implementing the change do not have the opportunity to participate in decision making, someone must fully communicate to them both what the solution will be and the reasons for its adoption. If any reasons that may influence that individual are omitted, he or she may develop resistance. A recent problem-solving meeting illustrates this situation.

At a regular departmental meeting, several faculty members commented that students were registering by computer for courses without discussing their selections with an advisor. The consequences were detrimental to both the students and the university. The question that surfaced from this discussion was, "How do we prevent students from enrolling in courses for which they are not prepared?" Several solutions were proposed, and one was selected. The next day a faculty member who was central to implementing the solution notified the department chair that she had not been in the meeting and found the proposed solution unacceptable. The faculty met again and reviewed the problem. The group discovered that some crucial information had not been given to the absent faculty member about implementation of the proposed solution. Once she heard the group's reasons for adopting it, she was satisfied. Because this faculty member had not been included in the original meeting, more time was spent at the second meeting reexamining much of the information that had been discussed at the first meeting.

The Change Process

Ellingsworth found that people follow a five-step process when changing their attitudes and behavior. The process is based on the research and theories of Everett Rogers and involves the following elements:

1. An innovation (an idea or practice that an individual perceives as new, regardless of how long it has been available).
2. Messages about the innovation, transmitted in some audible or visible form.
3. The passage of time from the first exposure until the innovation is no longer "new."
4. A group of people definable as a social system (by virtue of their common occupation, employment, proximity, formal membership, interest, or anything else that binds them together).
5. Some observable response to the innovation (as messages about it circulate in the social system over time).[4]

Each step in this process relies on *communication* as an integral part of implementing change in the organization. This chapter discusses the nature of the change process and the techniques for facilitating change. We focus on two questions: First, what are the constructive and destructive aspects of change? Second, how can change be effectively implemented? The chapter then explores these questions by examining the change cycle, approaches to change, and the techniques and strategies for facilitating change.

Overcoming Resistance: Why People Fear Change

At every level and in all forms of organizations, people tend to resist change. The present means of operating, or the status quo, is safe and nonthreatening, but change creates inconvenience, uncertainty, and anxiety. The resulting resistance can be witnessed in typical responses such as "It's too much trouble," "We've tried it before," and "What's wrong with the way we do it now?" Some forms of resistance are reduction in output, increased sick leave, strikes, sabotage, political pressure, and fighting. Argyris, having reviewed the results of changes implemented in thirty-two major reorganizations of large companies, found resistant forces existing in all organizations up to three years after changes were announced. He explained why this occurred:

> I believe the reasons for this long delay are embedded in the change strategy typically used by management. . . . The basic strategy has been for the top management to take the responsibility to overcome and outguess the resistance to change. This strategy does tend to succeed because management works very hard, applies pressure, and, if necessary, knocks a few heads together (or eliminates some). However, as we have seen, the strategy creates resisting forces that are costly to the organization's effectiveness, to its long run viability and flexibility, as well as to the people at all levels.[5]

Since management usually participates in both the decision-making and problem-solving processes, the rationale for change is usually clear to managers themselves. Management assumes that other members of the organization will accept its decision-making role and hence its solution without the need for discussion. People, however, resist alterations in their organizational role for a number of reasons:

1. *Disruption of social relationships.* People become comfortable with predictable surroundings and adopt coping behaviors for problem areas. Since their interpersonal relationships fulfill social needs, change disrupts these relationships and causes anxiety.

2. *Threat to roles.* Change in the organizational structure and individual roles may threaten position and recognition. If an individual perceives that the change will result in loss of esteem or recognition, he or she will resist

change. Conversely, increased responsibilities or promotion to higher levels may result in anxiety over the ability to perform new or more complex duties.

3. *Economic loss.* Many individuals fear change because they anticipate a loss of economic security. Since economic changes affect the basic physiological, security, and belonging needs, fear of economic loss creates strong resisting forces.

Uncertainty produces anxiety and results in resistance in 80 percent of the change efforts, yet rarely does change impede employee growth and development. In fact, employees benefit as much or more than the organization, particularly in earning power. Only about 5 percent of those in the workforce actually lose jobs as a result of change. Most reduction occurs through normal turnover and transfers.[6] If management communicates the changes in detail well ahead of time, much anxiety is alleviated and resistance lessened.

THE FORCES OF CHANGE

According to Kurt Lewin change involves opposing forces.[7] In other words, some aspects of a situation work to increase the chances of change, while others work to decrease the chances for change. This is like a tug-of-war. By increasing the strength of positive change forces, change can overcome the resisting forces.

Change forces, which Lewin calls *driving forces,* include any aspects of the situation that increase the willingness to change. Examples include dissatisfaction with the present situation, external pressures, group pressures, anticipation of increased satisfaction, and the power or credibility of the change agent.

Resistance, or *restraining forces* include any aspect of the situation that reduces the willingness to change. These forces include such things as individual preference for the status quo, reluctance to admit a problem exists, fear, ignorance of trends in the environment, or investment in reputation or career. Fear itself is a primary resisting force. Individuals fear losing status because of a change. If a new boss does not regard an individual's capabilities as highly as the previous boss, the individual might become anxious and anticipate that the rewards and career paths may be curtailed. The following incident vividly illustrates the strength of resisting forces.

Resistance to Change: Losing "The Real Thing"

In response to the cola wars, Coca-Cola took drastic steps to counteract the success of Pepsi. Taste tests, even in their own laboratories, reaffirmed the Pepsi taste edge. In addition, the new Pepsi campaign, "The Pepsi Challenge," was affecting market share. To make things even worse, Pepsi's management implemented a $5 million advertising campaign with celebrity Michael Jackson as the centerpiece. Coke executives took drastic steps, replacing their former slogan "The Real Thing" with the "New Coke."[8]

Negative reactions to the announcement on April 23, 1985 were extreme—from hoarding Coca-Cola bottles still on grocery shelves to labeling the new version "Coke for Wimps."[9] Shock waves surfaced inside and outside the company as consumers rebelled and acted out their chagrin. Suddenly a product that had not changed for almost 100 years had been abandoned. For generations of social activity and change, Coke paraphernalia had adorned grocery stores, drugstore counters, and teenage bedrooms. One thing had always remained constant: the Coca-Cola formula and its red and white trademark. Coke was a symbol, a part of the fabric of America. As Lee Bolman and Terrence Deal point out in their book, *Reframing Organizations:*

> The executives of Coca-Cola underestimated the symbolic meaning of their own core product. Symbols create meaning. When a symbol is destroyed or vanishes, people experience emotions that are almost identical to those felt at the passing of a spouse, child, old friend, or pet.[10]

To regain the confidence of traditional consumers as well as regaining market share, the old formula returned to the shelves under the label "Classic Coke." Failure to estimate the resistance to change had provided a costly lesson to the company.

Lewin depicted the restraining and driving forces as shown in Figure 17.2. The line in the center represents equilibrium or the status quo. As long as the restraining forces are equal to the driving forces the organization will maintain the status quo. This state is termed *stationary equilibrium.*

The Three Alternatives

Lewin proposes several options for implementing change: (1) Increase the strength of the driving forces, (2) decrease the strength of the restraining forces, and (3) combine both 1 and 2 above. Several risks are involved in choosing alternatives 1 or 2. If driving forces are increased, there is risk that the old situation may return after pressure is removed. In addition, the use of

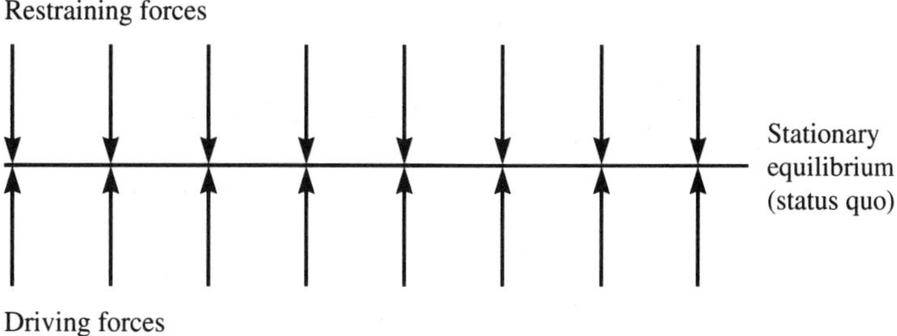

FIGURE 17.2 Driving and Restraining Forces Establishing Equilibrium
Source: Based on model in Kurt Lewin, "Quasi-Stationary Social Equilibria and the Problem of Permanent Change," in W. G. Bemis, K. D. Benne, and R. Chin, eds., *The Planning of Change* (New York: Holt, Rinehart, and Winston, 1969, pp. 235–38).

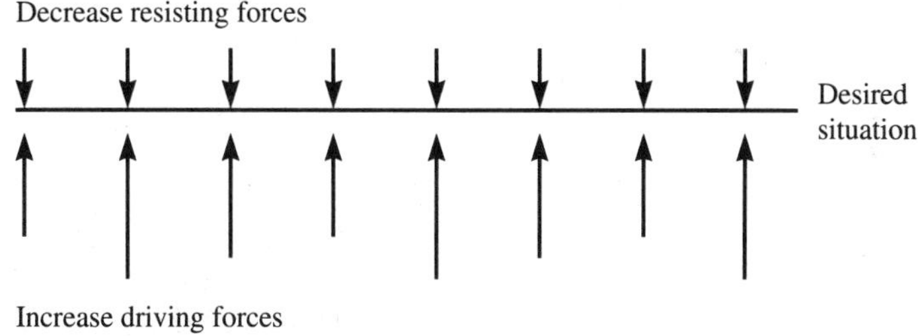

FIGURE 17.3 Kurt Lewin's Third Alternative
Source: Based on model in Lewin, "Social Equilibria."

authority to initiate change may result in counterpressure against change. Alternative 2, decreasing the strength of the restraining forces, may be accomplished by such strategies as increasing participation in problem solving or redistribution of power. The combination of increasing driving forces and decreasing restraining forces allows for the most effective alternative. Figure 17.3 illustrates movement away from the status quo resulting from using the third alternative.

The forces of change and corresponding strategies can be summarized as follows:

I. *Change forces:* any aspect of the situation that increases the willingness to change. These are also called *driving forces* by Lewin. Some examples are:

A. Dissatisfaction with present situation
B. External pressures
C. Group pressure
D. Anticipation of increased satisfaction
E. Power or credibility of change agent

II. *Resistance forces:* any aspect of the situation that reduces the willingness to change. These are also called *restraining forces* by Lewin. Some examples are:
A. Preference for status quo
B. Reluctance to admit problem
C. Ignorance of trends in environment
D. Reputation or career invested in status quo
E. Fear:
1. Of losing status
2. Of devaluing current skill or knowledge
3. Of inability to change
4. Of cost of change
5. Of stress

The Three Phases

The three phases for implementing change, according to Lewin, are the *unfreezing phase,* the *moving phase,* and the *refreezing phase.* Each phase has several strategies (see Table 17.1).

The unfreezing phase involves making present behavior open to change. Ideal conditions for change include openness, honesty, and mutual respect. Anyone affected by the change should be allowed to ask questions to which management honestly responds and through which mutual respect can be gained. Participants usually have a right to know what is going to happen. Resistance by participants may mean something is wrong with the proposed change. The reasons for resistance should be investigated in order to eliminate the causes.

The moving phase identifies and removes interference. Interference consists of forces that impede progress toward change but are not directly con-

TABLE 17.1 Kurt Lewin's Change Model

Unfreezing	→	Moving	→	Refreezing
Recognition of the need for change		Action plan implemented		Change stabilized
Change agent initiates action		Resistance forces removed		Desired behavior reinforced
		Resources provided		Progress monitored
				Revisions made

Source: Adapted from Kurt Lewin, "Frontiers in Group Dynamics," *Human Relations* 1 (1947), pp. 2–42.

60 Seconds with a CEO

Bill Rainey, age forty-seven, is chief executive officer of Exxon's Baton Rouge refinery. Rainey, who received his B.S. in chemical engineering from Auburn University in 1966, is a board member of Mid-Continent Oil and Gas Association, Louisiana Chemical Industry Alliance, and the Louisiana Association of Business and Industry. From a CEO's perspective, here are Rainey's comments on implementing change:

> I've learned over the years, particularly with a large organization, that you spend a lot of time on leadership rather than management. I try to outline the most important things we need to work on and keep everyone focused on that. I involve employees in improving the business. Management often feels like it needs to come up with all the solutions. But employees understand their jobs better than management does and they can devise the best solutions.[11]

cerned with the change. Some examples might be lack of information, lack of resources, lack of necessary skills, and a limited time for implementation of the change. Some methods for removing interference include interacting with the group to clarify information, correcting rumors, and providing training in new or required skills and knowledge, or providing necessary resources.

The last phase, or *refreezing phase,* is an attempt to stabilize the change and prevent reversion to old methods. The period of stability should be longer than the period of change. The manager's role includes refining procedures so that new behaviors become routine—supporting and reinforcing desired behaviors, maintaining stability, providing a positive model of new behavior and attitudes, monitoring progress, revising procedures where necessary, and obtaining support of informal leaders.

The Change Agent's Role

Regardless of organizational title or educational expertise, *change agents* are individuals who work to analyze needs as well as to plan and implement changes. They specialize in overcoming resistance to change, have learned the art of persuasion, and recognize the need to establish credibility. They can develop specific change strategies and tactics to make the change work.

Whether an outside consultant or full-time staff member, the change agent has five key tasks:

1. Establish credibility with the organizational members affected by the change.
2. Gather information necessary for identifying and solving the problem.
3. Establish a supportive environment for change.
4. Implement the approaches necessary to achieve the desired change.
5. Establish procedures for stabilizing, evaluating, and monitoring the change.

Credibility

An employee's typical response in a first encounter with a change agent will be, "Who is this person, and why should I trust him or her?" Credibility is one of the primary keys to persuasion. According to communication experts Seiler, Baudherin, and Schuelke, the change agent will be judged on the following sources of credibility:

1. Competence: knowledge and expertise.
2. Character: trustworthiness, honesty.
3. Composure: confidence, poise.
4. Extroversion: dynamism, personality, outgoingness.
5. Sociability: likability.[12]

An individual achieves credibility through other people's perceptions. In other words, a person may be an expert but may not be perceived as such by others. Certain sources of credibility, such as trustworthiness, may be perceived, while others, such as competence, are not. Finally, one person may perceive credibility where another does not.

Credibility, therefore, varies depending on the receiver, the situation, and the problem. To establish credibility before attempting to implement change, the change agent must have proven credentials and references and be able to establish trust. Personal appearance and enthusiasm are critical.

Fact Gathering

In Chapter 13 we discussed the importance of fact gathering as a part of the problem-solving process. Two points need to be clarified here as they relate to the change agent. First, the change agent must have all the pieces of the puzzle before devising a plan. If a part is missing, the change may not be effective. Jerry Harvey described a consultant who conducted a company-wide organizational development program because morale and productivity were low and conflict between employees had increased. He selected team building as an intervention and skillfully trained all employees. Yet there seemed to be little improvement in productivity. A visiting engineer noticed that the major drive shaft at the main mill was faulty. The company replaced the drive shaft; productivity jumped, and morale improved.[13] While all solutions may not be this simple, this example vividly points out the need for thorough research.

Second, willingness to listen to employees and gain insight into their perceptions of the problem—the process of fact gathering in itself—is important, since it lends credibility to the consultant's role. How many times have you heard someone say, "Nobody asked me; why should I get involved?" Having the opportunity to voice concerns, share information, and express conflicting points of view to a third party result in commitment and participation in the change process.

Supportive Environment

The discussion of team leadership in Chapters 12 and 15 emphasized the importance of participation and commitment. The concept of quality circles is based on these principles. A climate supportive of change encompasses broad agreement on organizational goals, trust between organization members, individual initiative and responsibility, participation in decision making, availability of accurate information on organizational conditions, and openness in organizational communication.

The consultant strives for co-orientation of all employees toward the change goal. To attain co-orientation, or a common belief or point of view, employees must understand the problems necessitating change, the risks generated, the actions and activities required, and their resulting effect on jobs and roles. Employees' participation in the process contributes to recognition of the need for change, better planning, implementation, co-orientation, and positive attitudes. The following questions can help managers determine whether the organization is conducive to change:

1. *Will the organization commit to complete intervention?* We have already pointed out the importance of a thorough investigation of the problem. Consultants must have the support of top management to conduct interviews, review reports, evaluate policies, analyze procedures, and observe behavior in order to determine the most effective intervention. They must also have the freedom to implement broad changes that may range from training to structural reorganization.

2. *Does the organization want a "quick fix"?* Workshops and short courses usually focus on particular techniques or skills and leave it up to the participants to apply the concepts to their jobs. Training often motivates people and reviews or exposes them to principles and concepts that can be applied on the job. If the technique or skill is the cause of a problem, training may be sufficient. In many cases, however, it is aimed at symptoms and becomes a "quick fix" requested by management for selected employees. Training may be only one part of a comprehensive approach to change. Effective change eliminates the cause(s) of the problem and is based on thorough analysis.

3. *Are the contacts in the organization in a position to eliminate change?* There must be commitment and support from top management. Without this support, it won't matter whether the consultant's investigative efforts were thorough or whether the intervention is comprehensive. The plan will probably be put on the shelf. Top management must be exposed to the problem and its effect on the organization. The consultant must keep open lines of communication and, best of all, have top management participate in the change effort.

4. *Will top management participate and encourage participation on all levels of the organization?* Commitment can receive no greater testimony than having employees see their bosses involved and participating with them in all phases of the change effort. Participation of top management is a testimony to commitment and lends authority to the change effort. It also prepares management to fully understand the change and will lend stability to the final stages.

Communication Skills

Persuasion and communication skills are necessary for implementing change. The ability of the change agent to analyze the audience, clarify and communicate purpose, gather information, apply sound problem-solving skills, and plan and act skillfully is critical to each approach. Communication is persuasion. You must choose the argument best suited to the occasion to convince others to act. Organizational communication expert Phillip V. Lewis suggests the following guidelines:

1. *Explain the action to be implemented and the reasons for it.* This will combat rumors and minimize disruptive behavior.
2. *Prepare employees for major changes, and alert them to difficulties.* Sudden changes in the organization may result in fear and anxiety.
3. *Identify informal leaders in the organization, and explain management's objectives.* If top management is supportive, the informal leaders will encourage other group members to be cooperative.
4. *Repeat important information and techniques.* This is the most effective communication technique to increase memory. Repeat information and procedures three to five times.
5. *Allow people time to adjust to the change.* Recognize that conflict is healthy if it airs opinions and ideas that need to be resolved in the long run. Encourage employees who are doing well by recognizing their performance.[14]

Stabilizing, Evaluating, and Monitoring the Change

Employees cannot effectively implement change without understanding their roles, the steps involved in the change, and the time frames attached to these steps. Therefore, it is essential that you think through and communicate the procedures to them along with the means of evaluating and monitoring the change. In addition to knowing what to do, employees will want to know management's expectations. How will the change be evaluated? What factors will indicate that the change worked? Who will determine this? How will employees be evaluated? How will the change be stabilized? Without answers to these questions, the organization is likely to return to the status quo.

The change agent acts as the guide and stabilizing influence in this process. Clear policies and procedures, and a system for program evaluation, are essential to the ongoing success of the change.

Marvin L. Yates: University Change Agent

Located in Baton Rouge, Louisiana, Southern University and A&M College, a land-grant institution, is the largest historically black university in the United States. Southern has provided opportunities through higher education to thousands of African Americans for over 100 years. In 1991, Marvin L. Yates, the new president, embarked on a new and expanded mission.

Yates was known in the university and community as a team player with an imaginative mind. Reared in Memphis, Tennessee, he received a bachelor's degree from Southern University in 1966 and a master's degree in education at Southern in 1967. After earning his doctorate in Urban Education and Administration from the University of Pittsburgh in 1973, he returned to Southern and held a series of administrative positions in his ascent to the presidency.

In his first action as president, Yates collaborated with faculty, staff, and students to establish a plan "focusing on one overall goal—quality in all that we do."[15] In his published agenda, Yates stated, "I have proposed a twelve-point plan of action which will promote the vigorous pursuit of knowledge, bring about an improved image, build a strong foundation, and require measurable results."[16] Yates disseminated the plan in a concise, high-quality publication that presented his vision, listed the twelve points, and described his background and commitment to the institution. But he did not limit himself to the printed word. Yates articulated his vision to both internal and external publics, including the Southern University System Board of Supervisors, the Louisiana Board of Regents, and the 400-member Rotary Club of Baton Rouge.

One year later, on November 11, 1992, President Yates published an update documenting the following accomplishments of the twelve-point plan:[17]

(continued)

(continued)

- Completed and distributed the five-year strategic plan.
- Measurably reduced administrative hurdles and red tape.
- Completed budget hearings on all aspects of the campus, set new budget priorities, and shifted budgetary support.
- Identified five programs as "benchmarks" by which to measure the university's success in increasing program quality.
- Implemented student leadership initiatives.
- Hired several world-class faculty members.
- Conducted continuing professional education activities for the faculty and staff supported through funds provided by the chancellor's office.
- Established a unit to promote a better research climate; made $100,000 available to faculty for seed grants from the chancellor's office.
- Established partnerships with private industry to support academic programs.
- Allocated funds through Title III and the university to support the implementation of a Publications and Graphic Design Office.
- Improved aesthetics of the campus through landscaping.

What had Yates succeeded in doing? He had involved the campus and community in a movement for high-quality education at a time when the state and the nation were experiencing severe budget deficits. He clearly communicated his vision, built the teams, and translated goals and objectives into visible and measurable outcomes. Finally, he communicated those outcomes to let people know what he had accomplished and where he was going.

APPROACHES TO CHANGE

An organization can approach change in a variety of ways. Greiner identified several of the most common methods.

1. *The decree approach:* a unilateral authoritative announcement issued by a powerful person with formal authority.
2. *The replacement approach:* key organizational personnel are replaced with new people who believe in the desired change.
3. *The structural approach:* a change in the organization chart and the subsequent relationship of who is working for whom.
4. *The group decision approach:* emphasizes group participation and agreement on a predetermined course.

5. *The data discussion approach:* change data are presented as a catalyst and clients are urged to discuss the changes.

6. *The group problem-solving approach:* problem identification and problem solving are accomplished through group discussion.[18]

In addition to these approaches, current literature discusses team building, quality circles, the grid approach, and transactional analysis. Some of the latter approaches are actually specialized techniques employing the approaches outlined by Greiner in steps 4, 5, and 6. The following section describes several of these approaches.

The Decree Approach

Decrees are authority decisions made by individuals appointed by the system to act in assigned roles. Presidents, board chairpersons, and department heads have decision-making authority. Those in positions that report to them are bound by their decisions.

Ellingsworth states, and rightly so, that authority is the most rapid and predominant method of decision making. This method, however, is ineffective when individuals who must implement the decision fail to adopt the idea and show commitment; actual implementation may vary or fail. The paradox is that while decisions made by a "boss" or "chief" are efficient, individual decision making allows greater commitment and adaptation to individual needs.

The Replacement Approach

Major changes in staff assignments frequently accompany new administrations. One of the first tasks of a new president or governor is to make appointments in key positions that are politically and strategically critical for implementing the administration's philosophy and policies.

The disadvantage of this approach is the loss of expertise in the layers of personnel at the top of the organizational structure. The new administrators must learn the system, a time-consuming task, before policy can be implemented. Since the new administration's philosophy may mean major changes in personnel or job assignments, it is likely to encounter strong resistance.

The Structural Approach

Earlier in the text we reviewed a variety of organizational structures and the effect of structure on organizational communication. When structure is manipulated, the power to wield positive or negative sanctions is altered. In defining the subordinate's position, the manager also defines the accepted or formally recognized communication channels, role limitations, and sanctions for enforcement.

The New Rule

The Jemison Insurance Company was experiencing many incidents of soliciting during working hours. Many employees brought raffle tickets, candy, popcorn, tickets for school or church activities, and other items to the office and solicited sales.

The abundance of such activities and complaints by other employees encouraged management to institute the following rule: "No soliciting of goods or services will be allowed on company premises unless these goods or services are directly involved with the objectives of the Jemison Insurance Company and have been approved by the Board of Directors. Violation of this rule will result in automatic suspension from work of the division manager and employee(s) involved for a period of three days."

Two weeks after the soliciting rule was put into effect, a supervisor, Jolene Charles, overheard an employee selling golf balls to another employee in the hallway. She recognized both and noted that they were present at the division meeting when the new rule was announced. Both were outstanding employees from one of the best producing units in the company. Reporting them would cost dearly in morale and productivity. A few minutes later, in the restroom, Jolene encountered two more employees selling raffle tickets to support a major community fund drive.

Jolene reported to her supervisor what she had seen and heard. After a lengthy discussion about the new rule and the need to be consistent in its implementation and enforcement, her supervisor directed Jolene to confront each employee and place them on suspension. All four employees became visibly upset but accepted the consequences of their actions.

A week later, Jolene received a note to report to her supervisor. An employee she supervised was reported for passing out personal business cards advertising life insurance. Jolene knew this employee had a part-time job, but since the new rule had been instituted she had not observed him selling insurance during working hours. When her supervisor announced that she would be suspended for three days for allowing soliciting under her supervision, she was shocked. Jolene had never taken home so much as a company pencil. Since she had participated in the new rule's enforcement, it was particularly troubling: Where would this all end? Would the rule really eliminate the problem?

The Restructuring of McGraw-Hill

In 1984, the president of the McGraw-Hill publishing giant, Joseph Dionne, invited Harvard Business School professor Michael Porter to provide guidance on how to improve McGraw-Hill's competitive posture.[19] Dionne had read Porter's bestselling book, *Competitive Strategy,* and was impressed with Porter's ideas. After surveying the situation, Porter proposed a major reorganization of the company's divisions. The traditional book, magazine, and financial services divisions were accordingly transformed into twenty-one "market focus" segments. This restructuring meant that hundreds of employees lost their jobs.

Even with this massive change effort, the results fell well below expectations. "Revenues in 1988 grew only 3.8 percent to $1.8 billion, trailing the rate of inflation. McGraw-Hill is no longer a leader in trade magazine publishing, an industry it once dominated."[20] Ironically, the company made the most money off the divisions that had been least affected by the change efforts.[21] The notion that internal restructuring was the solution to implementing change in market share received resoundingly poor marks.

The Data Discussion Approach

Survey feedback is now a major tool in organizational change. Carefully designed questionnaires gather information from areas needing analysis. Based on the data generated, problems are diagnosed, and plans are developed for their resolution. While the research instrument may be tailored to the organization, many standardized questionnaires are available that include training programs for their use. Most questionnaires provide information on leadership, organizational climate, and worker satisfaction with pay, task, supervisor, or work group. Once the data are collected and analyzed, an external consultant presents and interprets it for the organization using the problem-solving and team-building approaches to diagnose and integrate change.

The Group Decision and Problem-Solving Approaches

The group decision approach relies on participation and consensus in decision making. Benefits are a greater pooling of knowledge and a greater acceptance of the decision by participants, which enhances (1) the quality of the solution and (2) the implementation phase of the desired change. Chapters 12 and 13 provide in-depth coverage of groups, decision making, and problem solving.

Partnering

"Partnering" has become a hot topic in business because it improves the quality, efficiency, and timeliness of product delivery. Essentially, partnering is the long-term commitment of a contractor to be the exclusive provider of products and services. But partners are not chosen lightly. The experiences of Monsanto Agriculture Co. in Luling, Louisiana, 15 miles from New Orleans, provides a good example.

Before selecting a partner, Monsanto formed a partner selection team with representatives from all areas of the company. The team began by developing criteria for selecting a partner, including "technical quality, financial stability and safety and training programs."[22] Monsanto employees then visited the corporate headquarters of three potential partnering companies. According to Monsanto site manager Sonny Hedges, "We wanted to see if they were walking the talk."[23] As a result of this process, Monsanto selected H. B. Zachry Company as their partner.

Instead of former bid procedures, multiple contracts, and the resulting variance in quality, the two companies now focus on shared objectives. The main purpose of the relationship is to improve quality for less cost. And both companies are committed to this goal. Communication of Monsanto's expectations plays a key role. The feedback provided by Zachry's employees is equally important. All parties seem to agree that "partnering" has been an effective change effort.

Team Building

Team building has become a popular approach to facilitating change because it incorporates the process objectives of interpersonal training but maintains a task orientation, making it immediately useful to the organization. Effective for task forces as well as for regular work or family groups, its primary goals are (1) task completion, (2) building interpersonal relations, (3) utilizing effective processes (such as decision making and problem solving), (4) role clarification, and (5) role negotiation.

Quality Circles

Quality control circles were developed in Japan in the early 1960s as voluntary problem-solving groups. Workers met to study and discuss work-related problems. The impact on Japanese quality and productivity has been phenomenal. As a result, the study and transfer of the techniques associated with quality circles became a primary concern of U.S. organizations in the late 1970s and early 1980s.

The quality circle leader is usually a person trained in group participation skills who acts as a focal point for the best interests of the workers as well as the organization. Tasks are delegated to group members to allow information flow and participation in the problem-solving process. Ideas and innovation are encouraged. Final proposals are presented by the group to top management for consideration.

Since the workers who are concerned about the problem actually participate in the problem-solving process, resistance to implementation is minimized and commitment to the solution is enhanced. In addition to feeling involved, these participants usually have the most experience with causes and symptoms that affect the resolution of the problem. Their familiarity with the problem enables them to propose effective solutions that affect the overall productivity of the organization. Japanese organizations such as Sony are strong testimonies to the effectiveness of this approach.

Cultural differences between the United States and Japan have caused a major problem in transferring the quality circle concept to this country, however. Although some U.S. corporations such as IBM share traits with Japanese corporations, the latter more consistently reward leadership, problem-solving, decision-making, and supervisory abilities—all interpersonal skills—than do American corporations. Quality circles themselves do not develop leadership skills, but they rely on these skills for effectiveness.

Quality circles have proved to be a valuable approach to implementing change. However, their success is based on the premise that participants—particularly the group facilitator—have acquired basic knowledge and skills in group decision making, group discussion, leadership, and supervision.

Total Quality Management (TQM)

Total quality management (TQM) was pioneered by W. Edwards Deming in Japan after World War II. Deming emphasized statistical process control (SPC) using a fourteen-point management process leading to quality and productivity. A humanistic approach to organizational change, TQM recognized people as individuals with the ability to make thoughtful contributions to the improvement of all aspects of the organization and its products. With Deming's guidance, Japan successfully changed the quality of its products for Western consumption in five years. Deming became a widely recognized public figure and Japan instituted the annual Deming prize as a token of collective esteem.[24]

Also participating in the development of postwar Japan was Joseph M. Juran, who advocated a quality trilogy: in planning, control, and improvement. His book, *Quality Control Handbook,* became the bible of quality management.[25] It was, however, Philip B. Crosby who brought home to American management the concept of quality as a universal goal.[26] The three basic precepts of total quality management are:[27]

1. All persons have within themselves the ability to be innovative and to pursue excellence.
2. Every member of the organization should have customer satisfaction as his or her goal.
3. Total quality management is accomplished through shared goals, trust, and teamwork facilitated by leaders who focus on constant improvement.

TQM communication strategies emphasize listening, openness, and understanding. Horizontal and vertical communication networks encourage constant feedback from employees and customers. Information about the organization and its effectiveness is accessible, accurate, and timely. Task forces, interdepartmental teams, and focus groups keep communication lines open, breaking down interdepartmental barriers.

Because of the importance of managing change effectively in the global marketplace and also to recognize companies that applied total quality management strategies, the U.S. Congress established the Malcolm Baldrige National Quality Award, administered by the National Institute of Standards and Technology (NIST). (See Chapter 3 for an in-depth discussion of this award.)

Organizational development can be facilitated by any of the approaches reviewed here. Each aims at improving an organization's problem-solving and renewal processes. Regardless of the method chosen, however, any given change should be planned, involve the total organization, emphasize work groups, and have long-range results. The next section explores the strategies for communicating change.

Communicating Change

Earlier we stated that many solutions fail because an action plan for implementation is never developed and communicated to employees. This aspect of change is so critical that numerous techniques have been developed to assist managers in mapping out strategies. Such strategies include preparing action plans, assigning responsibilities, specifying expectations, and clearly delegating authority.

Preparing Action Plans

People become upset or resistant to a specific change when they do not understand the need for it, have no say in deciding what or how to change, or see no benefit to themselves or others from the change. The proposed change simply becomes additional work leading nowhere that may require new skills, additional time, and little reward. Worse, they believe they have been given no opportunity to modify or reject the change. Finally, if the change fails, they believe they will receive the blame.

Before taking action, the change agent should assess receptiveness, gauge resistance, and address individual concerns. Sensitivity to the impact of change on individuals should be identified. What forces will work for or against change? What experience have employees had with change in the organization? Will employees trust management? Will the change affect the organizational or social relationships of groups?

First, employees need to understand the problem that has brought about the necessity for change. Management should describe the larger problem itself as distinct from its symptoms. Next, what are the objectives of the change effort? Specifically, what must be changed to resolve the problem—organizational structure, technology, methodology, resources? What strategies for bringing about this change might be possible—task forces, automation, training? What are the anticipated advantages—market share, quality, profits, rewards? What are the anticipated problems—deadlines, costs, personnel? How will the change be evaluated—what criteria will be used? The exact step-by-step plan for implementation should be prepared in sequence. Each activity necessary for implementing the solution must be identified and arranged in order, from the beginning to the end of the project.

Communicating the plan should involve formal presentations, small group briefings, newsletters, question-and-answer sessions, and suggestions systems. Establishing interdepartmental feedback groups will assist in removing anxiety, gathering suggestions, and answering questions.

Assigning Responsibilities

Clarifying the responsibilities of each person involved in the implementation of the solution is essential. On one hand, competition and rivalry may result when two people see themselves as having similar responsibilities. On the other hand, if assignments are not clarified, employees may assume someone else will take care of it. This assumption leads to costly expenditures for the organization in terms of wasted time and effort. The employee must understand where responsibility starts and stops. Communicating expectations clearly is important, as the following example indicates.

A babysitter for five children ages two to twelve assumed that one week alone with the children while the parents were vacationing would present no problems, since the older children could look after the younger ones. Unfortunately, none of the older children took responsibility for watching the young. Finally, the babysitter assigned one of the older children to assist with care of the two-year-old, and the job was well done. When the children's father heard about the assignment, his response was, "They are just like our ROTC cadets. They can do a heck of a job as long as you assign them a specific task."

Managers should clearly identify responsibilities and delegate authority to assure that all tasks associated with implementing the change are completed. They should review assignments with all team members present to allow questions and clarification as well as to keep the lines of communication open.

Specifying Expectations

A typical error of managers is to tell employees that a solution needs to be implemented "as soon as possible." The letters "ASAP" often appear on documents with no specific date. As we described in Chapter 4, the sender often fails to recognize that words have different meanings for different people. Consequently, many managers are caught empty handed because they failed to communicate specific expectations for completing the task.

"ASAP"

Aimée had been on the job two weeks. This was her first professional position since receiving her master's degree in business administration. She liked her boss but was becoming more and more frustrated with his frequent use of the code "ASAP" to set a time frame. Was she just inexperienced and unable to live up to his expectations? In desperation, she confronted him: "You have given me ten tasks and told me to complete them 'as soon as possible.' At this point my time is precious. By 'as soon as possible,' do you mean 4:30 P.M. today or by the end of the week?" The manager's response was, "Oh, I don't need that for two weeks."

Managers' expectations should be clear and should be discussed with employees. What education, training, or orientation will be required of them? Who will be working with them? How will this affect their current working relationships? What are the expected outcomes and what time lines need to be met? What resources will be provided? What support will you give them? How will their participation in change efforts be individually evaluated?

Delegating Authority

Typically, implementing the solution also involves delegating authority. *Authority* is the right to give orders, set policies, or administer discipline. The ultimate authority in an organization distributes or delegates authority downward in the organizational structure. Usually, managers delegate authority by assigning a subordinate to speak or act as an agent of the organization and manager. Delegation typically occurs on one of five levels. The subordinate receiving delegated authority needs to understand the delegation level in order to determine how to complete the task. The first three steps described below restrict the amount of delegated authority:

Level 1. *Don't do anything unless I say so.* The restraints at this level of delegation are most severe. The manager *tells* the employee exactly what to do.

Level 2. *Give me the information, I'll decide.* At this level the real message is, "Talk to whomever you need, and use your authority to get me the information, but don't express your point of view or act until I decide." This is a safe, low-risk level of delegation.

Level 3. *Do it, but keep me advised.* At this level the supervisor keeps tabs on what is happening, in case intervention may be needed. The message transmitted is, "You can handle it, but I'm still the boss. If someone asks me about the project, I want to have the information." Another version of this level is, "If problems arise, I may need to take over." The resulting thinking and behavior of the subordinate is somewhat of a mind-reading routine. Each action is considered in terms of, "Will the boss approve of this?"

Level 4. *Complete the job, then report to me.* This level of delegation allows the subordinate to use delegated authority to achieve the goal by whatever means are appropriate.

Level 5. *Do the job. The responsibility is yours.* This final level is where true delegation takes place. At all the other levels an assignment has been made. But here the subordinate is held responsible for the outcome.

Once the manager has prepared a plan, set time frames, clarified responsibilities, and determined the level of delegated authority, the next step in the change phase is to evaluate and refine the solution.

Debriefing: Evaluating and Refining the Solution

A manager must ask two key questions to determine the effectiveness of the change: First, does the plan solve the problem? Second, does it result in a new

Deadly Delegation

Dr. René Miles left verbal instructions with the head nurse at the nurses' station not to alter the medication for Kalena Maka without speaking to Dr. Miles first. Several hours later, Kalena began to experience some complications as a result of her recent operation and the medication did not seem to be having the desired effect. Samson Jones, a nurse on the floor with an excellent record, could not reach Dr. Miles. Jones, however, was able to contact Dr. Breen, who was on call and often assisted Dr. Miles. After discussing the condition of the patient over the telephone, Dr. Breen changed the medication.

Shortly thereafter, Kalena had a severe allergic reaction. Jones again contacted Dr. Breen, who immediately came to the hospital and tried to reverse the effects of the reaction with little success. As Kalena slipped into a coma, Jones finally contacted Dr. Miles, who was furious that his instructions had been ignored. Dr. Miles berated Jones and instructed him that in the future he needed to have proper authorization to change medication. Jones responded that he received authorization from Dr. Breen and that he did not know of the instructions, nor could he find any record of them at the nurses' station.

TABLE 17.2 The Change Phase of Problem Solving

Problem Understanding	→	Action	→	Review
Evaluate and select a solution		**Implement the solution**		**Evaluate and refine**
Clarify ideas		Prepare plan		Was the problem solved?
Eliminate overlap		Set time frames		Did any new problems result?
Apply criteria		Clarify responsibilities		
Select optimal choice		Delegate authority		

problem? The first question is crucial. If the problem still exists, the solution was probably aiming at symptoms rather than causes. The problem must be reviewed in order to attempt to identify the true cause, and the problem-solving cycle renewed, as shown in Table 17.2.

Typically, however, when a cause is eliminated, new problems may arise. Depending on how monumental the problems are, the organization may need to act more or less quickly on a resolution. Again, problems need to be identified and the problem-solving process put into action. A *debriefing* is an organizational attempt to review an activity, process, or project to determine if it is effective. If a solution is not effective, new problems are identified. It is important that every member of the team involved in implementing the activity or process be involved in the debriefing so that most problems can be identified and evaluated for their impact on the overall productivity of the organization.

A GLOBAL PERSPECTIVE

The Effects of Globalization on Implementing Change

The decade of the 1990s will be viewed as a time of major international change in the twentieth century. East and West Germany, divided for almost fifty years, engaged in becoming a united republic. The dissolution of the U.S.S.R. began a struggle between keeping autonomy under a new structure or dividing into many nations based on cultural and ethnic heritage. Japan unleashed its newfound power in international marketing and banking. A world economy based on international communication networks became a reality.

Global Change Forces

One day's news, as reported in the June 27, 1992 edition of *The New York Times*, testified to the communication issues surrounding a variety of changes in process throughout the world:

- The United Nations issued an ultimatum to the Serbs to stop fighting within 48 hours or military action would be authorized by the Security Council.
- Boris Yeltsin, President of Russia, "misspoke" when he stated that American prisoners of war might still be alive in Russia.
- European Community leaders issued a statement renouncing the role of a "superstate" and pledging "to curb the power of bureaucrats based at their headquarters."
- The German Parliament adopted a liberalized abortion law after months of debate.
- The United States announced a change in policy and urged negotiation of the return from exile of Haiti's ousted president.
- The Vatican announced that a "universal catechism" guide in many languages would be released for Roman Catholics in six months.
- To provide support for negotiations for democracy, the Bush Administration gave a "high-level" welcome to a Roman Catholic archbishop from Zaire.[28]

The effects of globalization on implementing change in the organization have numerous implications. Because multicultural influences must be considered when more than one country is involved in the change effort, the change agent must understand the full scope of forces that will resist or accelerate the change effort. Environmental pressures, structural relationships, and historical influences all come into play. How large and complex is the organization? How will cultural differences increase communication problems? What political influences will affect decision making? Without answers to these questions, communicating goals and reaching common ground will be impossible.

The rise of Hyundai in the automobile industry, described by David Halberstam in *The Reckoning,* provides a good example of these influences.[29] American automobile manufacturers viewed Korea as just one of many small competitors in the late 1970s and early 1980s. Korea was, however, on an economic rise that would soon create competition for both the United States and the Japanese automotive industries.

Because of its natural resources and dedication to improving its standard of living, Korea observed the successes of its old enemy, Japan, and focused its efforts on becoming a major player in the global market. Combining the concept of a family-owned capitalist company and a state-supported enterprise, Korea spawned Hyundai, a giant conglomerate. Its structure, governmental support, and technology dramatically changed the lifestyles of its employees, unleashing their potential and desire for an improved quality of life.

When auto assembly began in Korea, production of cars was crude and slow, as it had been in Japan initially. Determined and committed managers, however, urged workers to persist and work continually to improve. Recognizing the need to drastically upgrade the quality of its inventory, Hyundai sold stock to Mitsubishi in exchange for technical assistance and modeled its production techniques on those of Japanese companies. To gain a foothold in major international markets, Hyundai struck deals with foreign companies. The ability to take advantage of rapid technological change, communicate goals effectively to the workforce and to the nation, and adapt to a dynamic automotive market turned Hyundai into a formidable competitor. Among Hyundai's accomplishments were securing major construction projects in the Arab world, competing head to head with the Japanese in shipbuilding, becoming a leading exporter of cars to Canada in the 1980s, and successfully entering the U.S. auto market in 1986.

Hyundai's experience exemplifies the effects of globalization on implementing change. By learning the technologies and management approaches of other countries and combining this knowledge with the unique character and culture of the Korean people, Hyundai entered and competed successfully in a global market. In the United States, Hyundai has become a household name almost as familiar to consumers as Nissan or Toyota.

ETHICS: RIGHT OR WRONG?

The NCAA Challenge

During the 1990s, a major change effort was launched in intercollegiate athletics. Abuses in collegiate athletic programs led the Presidents' Council of the National Collegiate Athletic Association (NCAA) to advocate and pass proposals for major campus reform. The report of the Knight Foundation Commission on Intercollegiate Athletics, published in March 1991, proposed a new model for intercollegiate athletics. "Keeping Faith with the Student-Athlete: A New Model for Intercollegiate Athletics" took a year to write and included the advice of over eighty experts.[30] Cochaired by William C. Friday, president of the William R. Kenan, Jr. Fund, and Theodore M. Hesburgh, C.S.C., president emeritus of the University of Notre Dame, a special commission was created to study the problem. Participants included athletic conference commissioners, faculty representatives, athletic directors, senior women administrators, basketball and football coaches, student-athletes, university presidents, attorneys, accrediting agency representatives, professional athletes, broadcasters, and others. The commission was created because of the "expressed concern that abuses in athletics had reached proportions threatening the very integrity of higher education."[31]

In making their case for the need for reform, the commission presented the reversal of ends and means as the root of the problem. "Increasingly, the team, the game, the season, and 'the program'—all intended as expressions of the university's larger purposes—gain ascendancy over the ends that created and nurtured them."[32] They pointed out that nonrevenue and women's sports were overshadowed and secondary to football and basketball. "What remains is, too often, a self-justifying enterprise whose connection with learning is tainted by commercialism and incipient cynicism."[33] Noting that the problems were systemic in the 300 or so major athletic programs, they cited a recent study documenting that "one-half of all Division I-A institutions (the 106 colleges and universities with the most competitive and expensive football programs) were the object of sanctions of varying severity from the NCAA during the 1980s."[34] A U.S. Department of Education study written by Clifford Adelman, "Light and Shadows on College Athletes," found that varsity football and basketball players entered college with poor high school records compared to other groups but graduated at almost the same rate.[35] Athletes, however, took longer to graduate; earned lower grades; took more remedial, introductory, and vocational courses; and completed less demanding academic programs than other students.

Based on their review of these and other data, the commission proposed a structure of reform featuring presidential control with three basic tenets: academic integrity, financial integrity, and independent certification. These tenets, as nationally endorsed values, were the guiding principles communicated throughout the report. Specific objectives include governance of athletics by university presidents with complete authority delegated by boards of trustees, equity in the treatment of intercollegiate sports, controlled involvement with commercial television, commitment to integrity in admission decisions of athletes, commitment to the academic progress and graduation of athletes, reduction of athletic costs, coverage of cost of attendance for the needy athlete, curbing of the independence of athletic foundations and booster clubs, and the annual policy auditing of athletic programs.

In 1992, major shakeups occurred at former powerhouse football schools. The University of Tennessee bought out the remainder of Johnny Major's contract for between $500,000 and $600,000 when Majors resigned after sixteen years of coaching at UT and two back-to-back Southeastern Conference championships in 1989 and 1990.[36] NCAA investigations resulted in nine charges of rules violations at Auburn after Eric Ramsey leveled charges against the Tiger program. At the culmination of a losing season and after years with the university, Auburn's coach, Pat Dye, resigned.[37] Meanwhile, Gene Jelks, an ex-Alabama player, charged that coaches and boosters paid him thousands of dollars to play for the Crimson Tide. He also claimed he received other cash benefits from 1985 through 1989, when he played under Ray Perkins and then Bill Curry.[38] Earlier in 1992, the NCAA suspended Notre Dame linebacker Demetrius DuBose for receiving a $1,300 loan from a booster.[39] But it was at the University of Washington that a star quarterback on what had once been the number one–ranked team in the nation would test the fabric of the Knight report.

Billy Joe Hobert had been a star sophomore quarterback who had led the UW to a Rose Bowl victory, shared the most valuable player honors, and was part of a team that shared the national title.[40] Hobert borrowed $50,000 from a nuclear scientist in Idaho to maintain an expensive lifestyle. The loan became public in a *Seattle Times* story on November 5, 1992.[41] Immediately, UW's athletic director Barbara Hedges stated that there would be an investigation. She pointed out that all freshman athletes receive "an indoctrination on NCAA rules," but this situation could involve an interpretation. Don James, the Huskies coach, was known for his integrity and success. Once he found out about the loan, he suspended Billy Joe from playing, believing that Hobert would be cleared of any wrong.

The NCAA rules were clear: "A student-athlete may not receive preferential treatment, benefits or services (e.g. loans on a deferred payback basis) for his or her athletic reputation or skill or payback potential as a future professional athlete."[42] Since Billy Joe secured the loan without assets, he would have a hard time convincing people that it was not based on future earnings. His father, Terry Hobert, claimed that Billy Joe was reacting to the breakup of his marriage and searching for meaning when he purchased a car, golf clubs, and a stereo; paid off loans on a couple of cars and a couple of guns; and spent the rest on nights out. "It wasn't so wrong, but it was stupid. It wasn't as bad as people are making it out to be. He wasn't into drugs or anything like that."[43] Billy Joe admitted that he did not provide collateral, that the loan did not have a specific payback schedule, and that he had no assets.[44] "I have to say the money I borrowed wasn't the smartest thing I've ever done because I ended up blowing it and now I've got all of these bills and nothing to show for it."[45] Later in the interview, Billy Joe stated, "I just pulled it out and paid cash wherever I went. People must have thought I was the richest guy in town until I stopped showing up at places I had spent the money."[46] Hobert borrowed $25,000 in April, but by May it was gone. He borrowed $10,000 in May and $15,000 in June. Questioned about paying off the loan, Billy Joe responded, "If I become pro, obviously it is going to be easy to pay off. But if I don't, then I'm going to be working a long time to pay off that loan."[47]

The consequence of the loan was that the Huskies might have to forfeit the eight games in which Hobert played in their march to the 1992 Rose Bowl. Pac-10 Commissioner Tom Hansen stated that there had been no forfeitures since the late 1970s.[48] By November 11, 1992, when the university declared him ineligible and notified the NCAA, Billy Joe wished he had hidden the loan.[49] Billy Joe, quarterback coach Jeff Woodruff, and recruiting coordinator Dick Baird all agreed on one thing: all Billy Joe's interactions with them had been vague, "what-if" questions; no specific conversations about the $50,000 in loans had ever been held. Hedges noted that an investigation would follow and center on three issues:[50]

1. Whether the loan was a violation.
2. Whether the coaches knew about the loan before November 4, 1992.
3. Whether the coaches should have known about the loan.

What was at stake? If a player competes illegally in NCAA post-season tournaments, the institution must forfeit whether it knows about the violation or not. The Pac-10 stood to lose the equivalent of $200,000 per school, based on the premise of splitting $3 million from Arizona's appearance in the Fiesta Bowl. If UW had to forfeit and did not go to the Rose Bowl, Arizona would go and no Pac-10 team would play in the Fiesta Bowl. The Huskies might also win an unprecedented third consecutive Rose Bowl championship.[51]

Case Questions

1. Answer the three questions posed to the Pac-10 review committee. Were there any other questions that should have been answered by the committee?
2. Should the University of Washington have forfeited the eight games? Why or why not?
3. Did Billy Joe violate any ethical principles? If so, what were they?
4. What steps should the University of Washington take to initiate change and prevent future problems?

Summary

A variety of forces work to alter the behavior patterns of individuals in the organization. Some forces arouse greater concern than others because of their great effect on the productivity of the organization. All change, however, affects the role of each organization.

Healthy organizations must have the ability to anticipate, execute, and adapt to change. There are ways to marshal the forces of change in order to improve an organization's problem-solving and renewal processes. A thorough understanding of the change phase of problem solving is essential. Participation in the selection of the solution enhances commitment to the implementation of the change. The plan should include specific steps, time frames, assigned duties, and clearly delegated levels of authority. Reviewing and monitoring the change assists in stabilizing the organization and prevents slippage back to the status quo.

Effective change involves the total organization. It is planned, is comprehensive, emphasizes co-orientation of work groups, and requires the participation of a change agent.

The change agent can use a variety of approaches for implementing change and, after a thorough analysis of information, may need to combine several approaches. Finally, success will be based on credibility, effective problem identification, supportive climate, long-range planning, and a system of program evaluation.

Key Words

change agent
change stage
decree approach
delegated authority
driving forces
force field analysis
innovation
moving phase
problem-solving approach
quality circles
refreezing phase
replacement approach
resistance
restraining forces
stationary equilibrium
structural approach
team building
total quality management
unfreezing phase

Review Questions

1. Review the approaches to change presented in this chapter. Which require the least investment of time and effort? Which require the most?
2. Define credibility. Why is it important to the change agent? What are some methods that individuals and organizations use to enhance their credibility? Give examples.
3. When should a company hire an external consultant? When should a company use an internal consultant?
4. Why do people resist change? What can a change agent do to overcome resistance to change? Using Lewin's force field analysis, give a specific example to amplify your answer.
5. What are the basic steps for communicating change? What are the pitfalls of each?
6. How does the change stage differ from the decision-making stage of problem solving? What steps are involved in each stage?
7. How do you determine if an organization is conducive to change? What four questions should you answer?
8. What are some communication skills that the change agent needs to employ when implementing a change? Find an example of a change agent who has used these skills effectively or ineffectively.

Exercises

1. Interview a manager who has employed a professional consultant. Ask the manager to describe the relationship with the consultant, the intervention that the consultant proposed and implemented, and the methods used to stabilize the change.
2. Analyze a major change implemented in your community. Describe the climate that existed at the time the change was initiated. What were the change and resistance forces? What efforts did the change agents make to increase the strength of change forces and to minimize interference? Evaluate the validity of any resistance forces that you identified. What attempts were made to reform behavior and stabilize change?
3. Prepare a detailed change plan for a change that you will implement. Your change can be personal, work related, or community service. Using the force field analysis, analyze change and resistance forces that are presently operating. Identify any interference that you could encounter in attempting to implement your plan. Describe specific steps that you will take to prevent or remove interference. Also, describe specific steps you will take to manage the moving phase and to stabilize the change. Select indicators that you will use to measure the effectiveness of the change.

References

1. "People Shouldn't Be Allergic to Change," *USA Today,* October 3, 1986, p. A11. Copyright 1986, *USA Today.* Reprinted with permission.
2. Ibid.
3. Huber W. Ellingsworth, "Innovation and Change," in James L. Owen, Paul A. Page, and Gordon I. Zimmerman, eds., *Communication in Organizations* (New York: West Publishing, 1976), p. 299.
4. Ibid., p. 299.
5. Chris Argyris, "Today's Problems with Tomorrow's Organizations," *Journal of Management Studies* (Feb. 1967), p. 53.
6. "How to Manage Change," *Applied Management Newsletter* (July 1981), pp. 1–4.
7. Kurt Lewin, "Quasi-Stationary Social Equilibria and the Problem of Permanent Change," in W. G. Bennis, K. D. Benne, and R. Chin, eds., *The Planning of Change* (New York: Holt, Rinehart, and Winston, 1969), pp. 235–38.
8. T. Oliver, *The Real Coke, The Real Story* (New York: Random House, 1986), p. 122.
9. Ibid.
10. Lee G. Bolman and Terrance E. Deal, *Reframing Organizations: Artistry, Choice, and Leadership* (San Francisco: Jossey-Bass, 1991), p. 390.
11. "60 Seconds with a CEO," *Baton Rouge Business Report* (November 17, 1992), p. 17.
12. William J. Seiler, E. Scott Baudherin, and L. David Schuelke, *Communication in Business and the Professions* (Reading, Mass.: Addison-Wesley, 1982), p. 184.
13. William G. Dyer, "Selecting an Intervention for Organization Change," *Training and Development Journal* (April 1981), p. 62.
14. Phillip V. Lewis, *Organizational Communications: The Essence of Effective Management,* 5th ed. (Columbus, Ohio: Grid, 1975), p. 225.
15. "Southern University and A&M College: A People's Institution Serving the State, the Nation, and the World for over 100 Years" (Baton Rouge, LA: Office of the Chancellor, Southern University and A&M College, April 1992). Reprint.
16. Ibid.
17. "Southern University and A&M College: A People's Institution Serving the State, the Nation, and the World for Over 100 Years, Update 1992" (Baton Rouge, LA: Office of the Chancellor, Southern University and A&M College, August 1992).
18. L. E. Greiner, "Organizational Change and Development," Ph.D. dissertation, Harvard University, 1965.
19. A. Beam, "Michael Porter vs. McGraw-Hill," *Boston Globe,* September 20, 1989, p. 40.
20. Ibid.
21. Ibid.
22. Leslie Zganjar, "Partnering Improves Working Relationships," *Baton Rouge Business Report* (November 17, 1992), p. 49.
23. Ibid.
24. W. Edwards Deming, *Out of Crisis* (Cambridge, Mass.: Productivity Press, 1982).
25. Joseph M. Juran, ed., *Quality Control Handbook,* 3d ed. (New York: McGraw-Hill, 1974).

26. Phillip B. Crosby, *Quality Is Free* (New York: New American Library, 1979).
27. Kenneth E. Ebel, *Achieving Excellence in Business: A Practical Guide to the Total Quality Transformation Process* (New York: ASQC Quality Press, 1991), p. 12.
28. "News Summary," *The New York Times,* June 27, 1992.
29. David Halberstam, *The Reckoning* (New York: William Morrow, 1986), pp. 698–706.
30. "Keeping Faith with the Student-Athlete: A New Model for Intercollegiate Athletics, Report of the Knight Foundation Commission on Intercollegiate Athletics" (March 1991), p. v.
31. Ibid.
32. Ibid.
33. Ibid., p. 6.
34. Ibid.
35. Clifford Adelman, "Light and Shadows on College Athletes: College Transcripts and Labor Market History" (Washington, D.C.: U.S. Department of Education, 1990), pp. v–vi.
36. Tom Sharp, "Majors Officially Resigns," *Baton Rouge Advocate,* November 14, 1992, p. D1.
37. Associated Press, "Jelks Meets with NCAA Investigator," *Baton Rouge Advocate,* November 14, 1992, p. D3.
t38. Ibid.
39. Don Borst and Robert Kuwada, "UW's Hobert Is Suspended Over Big Loans," *Tacoma Morning News Tribune,* November 6, 1992, p. B1.
40. Don Borst, "Hobert's Slide Hits Bottom: UW QB's Future is in Doubt," *Tacoma News Tribune,* November 6, 1992, p. C1.
41. Borst and Kuwada, "UW's Hobert Is Suspended," p. 1.
42. Borst and Kuwada, "Hobert's Slide."
43. Ibid., p. 3.
44. Ibid., p. 12.
45. Ibid.
46. Ibid.
47. Ibid.
48. Don Borst, "Hobert Case: UW Forfeitures Still Possibility," *Tacoma News Tribune,* November 7, 1992, p. C1.
49. Don Borst, "Quarterback Wishes He Had Hidden Loan," *Tacoma Morning News Tribune,* November 11, 1992, p. A1.
50. Ibid.
51. Bart Wright, "Forfeit Now or Face Darker Future," *Tacoma News Tribune,* November 11, 1992, p. D1.

PART 5

OVERVIEW OF CHAPTERS

Organizations place extensive demands on managers and employees to communicate effectively. It is the manager's job to accomplish the goals of the organization by communicating and coordinating the tasks of employees, and by eliminating barriers to goal attainment. This section, designed to provide an overview of the material contained in the first four parts, is a chapter-by-chapter synopsis of the subject matter of the text.

Effective Communication as a Management Process

Henry Mintzberg identified three categories of managerial roles: interpersonal, informational, and decisional. Robert Katz added to Mintzberg's work by identifying three skill areas a manager must develop to carry out these roles effectively: knowledge of the job, or *technical skill;* good interpersonal relations, or *human skills;* and the ability to solve problems, or *conceptual skills.* Key to the second and third skill areas is the ability to communicate effectively.

Communication has an extremely powerful and pervasive effect on an organization. Communication is so important in business that even the definition of an organization requires that goals be achieved by a cooperative effort through the use of communication. The *type* of communication used may vary within a given context, but communication itself is the foundation for practicing any and all theories.

The key management theories are classical management theory, human relations theory, systems theory, and contingency theory. Many variables, from context to culture, may determine which theory will be most effective in practice. The most important variable is communication style, and particular styles may be more successful than others within the practice of a given management theory and the dynamics present within a given organization.

Common elements can be identified in any communication situation whether it is two people talking face-to-face or a cable broadcast to thousands. The *source* or *sender* is stimulated by some need, motive, or drive to send a message to a *receiver.* The source must *encode* the message by sorting and selecting symbols through a *channel,* such as a cellular telephone call or written memorandum. The receiver *decodes* the meaning of the *symbols* used by the sender and interprets the *message.* Knowledge, attitudes, experience, sociocultural background, and technology act as filters in giving meaning to the message. Finally, the receiver responds to the message and thereby provides *feedback* to the sender.

During the past few decades the world has become interconnected through a web of communication networks. Today, global communication has become a concern of managers in both large and small companies. The technology of light waves, telephone cables, and communication satellites allows information to be transmitted over great distances very quickly. In the year 2000, managers will be able to communicate with colleagues 10,000 miles away as easily as they can with colleagues in the next office. Learning to use new communication technology is a task that an effective manager must learn quickly.

The Role of Communication in Management

Each organization creates a *culture* with an overall philosophy—a vision for the organization and its product or service. Norms, values, and standards are understood and shared. Common rites and rituals are practiced. Stories and myths describe the company. A climate conveyed through physical arrangements, interpersonal interaction, and communication is created. Both formal and informal communication networks support the organizational culture and play crucial roles. Failure to support, nurture, and audit the effectiveness of these networks can impede the organization in advancing toward its goals.

The Role of Formal Communication in the Organizational Setting

The structure of an organization profoundly affects the formal communication process by dividing work, coordinating activities, distributing authority, and establishing channels of communication. Traditional organizational structures distribute authority and responsibility in a pyramid design. Communication in the formal organizational structure flows downward, horizontally, and upward and is affected by organizational size, complexity, objectives, and growth.

Downward communication flows from top management to subordinates and usually includes goals, policies, directives, job descriptions, instructions, evaluations, and feedback. Poor downward communication occurs when there is lack of growth, lack of clearly defined objectives, failure to audit communication techniques, confusion over the responsibility for communications, and segregation between supervisory and nonsupervisory personnel. Downward communication is improved by establishing clear objectives and making sure that the content of a message is clear.

Upward communication flows from subordinates to superiors and includes reports on activities, resource requests, and feedback. Factors contributing to poor upward communication include the size and structure of the organization, unrealistic assumptions, filtering and distortion, fear of presenting bad news, poor superior/subordinate relations, and information bottlenecks. Upward communication is improved by encouraging feedback, both positive and negative, and by creating an open and receptive climate.

Horizontal communication is lateral or diagonal communication between employees on the same level in an organization. The interaction usually revolves around formal tasks and goals that are vital to the personnel concerned. Horizontal communication assists in work coordination, problem solving, information sharing, and conflict resolution and covers such areas as production, sales, personnel, purchasing, and finance. Horizontal flow also allows subordinates to evaluate and critique their superiors' skills, attitudes, values, personalities, knowledge, and abilities. Horizontal communication is improved by realistic organizational charts, accurate job descriptions, interdepartmental projects, regular meetings for communication, and proper communication techniques. Improvements in technology have resulted in recent organizational design changes that more accurately reflect the formal flow of communication within an organization.

The Role of Informal Communication in the Organizational Setting

The *grapevine* is a type of communication that flows informally within the organization. Also known as the rumor mill, it is a necessary network and is often a good source of information. Informal communication chains can allow managers to predict the extent of the rumor process. Information is spread faster through informal communication networks than formal communication networks. Grapevines and their influence can be controlled, but they cannot be suppressed. Openness in handling problems, disproving rumors, being timely with information, and an effective formal communications system can prevent the grapevine from being destructive. Employees should be educated about its harmful effects.

Informal Communication Chains

The quality of an organization's climate is influenced by the quantity and quality of information that is available and used and by the formal and informal channels through which information is communicated. These communication channels develop into networks that are often referred to as communication loops. *Communication loops* depend on personalities and the working relations of small groups for their existence. Loops are composed of people who are linked by the nature of their organizational tasks. Characteristics of loops are size, transmission technique, immediate or delayed closure, and matching or mismatching of people and information.

The Importance of the Communication Audit

To keep organizational communication healthy and to ensure that the networks operate at top efficiency, employee surveys and communication audits are often used. Three primary audit systems are the OCD audit, the ECCO analysis, and the ICA audit. More recently, the Malcolm Baldrige National Quality Award Criteria also has been used to audit communication within the organization.

POTENTIAL BARRIERS TO AN EFFECTIVE COMMUNICATION PROCESS

Four major elements can limit the development of effective managerial communication skills: people, language, nonverbal behavior, and listening behavior. People take in stimuli through their senses, which act as a filter through which we understand the world. The way that we perceive the events and people around us is the starting point for how we communicate with others. Humans are unique because we can use symbols or words to represent objects, activities, and even abstract events. Symbols, however, can become a barrier to effective communication among people who do not share a common understanding or culture. Nonverbal and listening behavior can either augment or detract from our understanding of what is communicated.

Perception as a Potential Barrier to Effective Communication

Understanding perceptual behavior is the first step in becoming an effective communicator. Because perception is defined as the way we take in information about our world, and because each person gathers information differently, problems arise in the way each individual perceives things and other people. Many of the differences among people can be explained by the programming that occurs during childhood and adolescence. Other differences occur because wants and needs vary from person to person.

Through perception, using all of the five senses, we gain insight and knowledge about the world. Humans rely on sight and sound especially. When we communicate, we put our ideas into words or symbols to which a receiver can attach meaning. Our *references* include experience with past events, present and future expectations, current motivational state, knowledge, and sociocultural background. Misunderstandings in communication often occur because of people's differences in these references.

Our ability to perceive is limited and thus can complicate the communication process. Most objects are composed of elements we never see. In addition, most of our information about the world is gathered secondhand. What we do see is often distorted by our background and position, interfering factors, or another person's interpretation.

Regardless of how hard we try to understand each other and communicate effectively, we often do not see the world in the same way. Many factors influence behavior and create a framework for viewing the world. The traditional employee/manager who grew up during the period 1920 to 1940 and experienced the Great Depression struggled for survival. A work ethic and the "golden rule" contributed to an organizational culture that developed like a family. Many of today's CEOs grew up during this period of influence and use a directive leadership style.

The employee/manager born between 1946 and 1964 during the baby boom era grew up in a period of unprecedented prosperity. This is the first group in the workforce for whom a high school education is the norm and a college education or technical training is expected for high-paying jobs. Finally, the employee/manager in the eighteen-to thirty-year-old range is the best-educated in our nation's history and sees a college degree as a necessity. These individuals are part of a generation who learned most of its facts from television and grew up with high-tech toys.

Perception is subjective and open to a variety of errors. *Stereotyping* results when we oversimplify differences in people and attribute categorical traits to them. In *denial* we try to protect ourselves from people, situations, and ideas that threaten our security. The *halo effect* occurs when our positive perception of specific characteristics or traits of an individual influences our full opinion of that person. *Projection* occurs when people project their own feelings.

A better understanding of our *self-concept* will help us correct perception-based problems. Practicing *self-disclosure,* sharing information about our thoughts and feelings, is also important. Self-discovery and self-disclosure are effective ways to correct perception-based problems. The *Pygmalion effect,* or self-fulfilling prophecy, can condition people to behave the way they are expected to, be it positive or negative.

Finally, as managers, we encourage high performance from our employees by possessing and demonstrating *high expectations* of our own behavior and theirs. Managers prove themselves to be persons of many facets when their expectations of their employees are a key factor in the growth and success of the employees themselves, management, and the organization as a whole.

Word Usage as a Potential Communication Barrier

Language affects perception, communication patterns, and interpersonal behavior. It is the second hurdle one must overcome to be an effective communicator. It focuses on the field of social semantics, evolved from research in linguistics, psychology, and sociology. Language is actually the study of meanings as transmitted by *symbols.* Mankind's superiority and uniqueness have contributed to the availability of a wider range of *signals,* or the ability to use signs to indicate and represent things. Signs can serve as symbols for the past, present, or future.

For humans, communication occurs in two ways—verbally and nonverbally. Nonverbal communication includes environmental signals, social symbols, human gestures, and signs used in the transfer of message and meaning. The symbols most used by humans are *words.* One word can have several meanings; two or more words can describe one thought or feeling. Words can be technical or non-technical, have regional meanings or usages, and their meanings can often change.

Social semanticists have examined problems in the use of words. *Allness* is indicative of people who perceive a portion of what is going on in the world. They are intolerant of other viewpoints and think they know all there is to know about a subject. *Bypassing* occurs when senders and receivers miss each other with the meaning of their words.

Managers must remember that people have meaning, words do not. Words are incomplete. They are in a sense a map of our mental territory that we wish to share with others. People who are *intentionally* oriented first perceive and inspect the real world or territory and then construct a verbal map that corresponds to it.

The human nervous system is incapable of obtaining all the details on or about any problem. Hence, we must *abstract* some details and omit an infinite number of others. The words we use depend on how we conceive and understand an object. We can then decide to communicate our understanding of the real world to others.

In the process of observing our world, we draw *inferences* when we don't have all the necessary facts. *Factual statements* are based on what we observe, know, or experience with our senses. All statements about the future are based on inferences. Anything that cannot be observed is an inference. Inferences should be labeled as such to prevent miscommunication.

Effective managers avoid taking words for granted. Communication is accurate when it is preceded by a great deal of thought and reflection.

Nonverbal Communication: Augmenting or Contradicting the Verbal Message

Nonverbal communication refers to human action and behavior and the corresponding meaning that is attached. Talking and writing are associated with the use of verbal symbols, or words that stand for facts, ideas, or other things. Nonverbal communication, however, includes gestures, facial expressions, vocal pauses, and body movement. These messages are often stronger than the verbal messages and occur more frequently. Nevertheless, we often ignore messages that are communicated nonverbally.

Communication is influenced by the *environment.* Within the environment *time, territory,* and *design and arrangement* contribute to communication messages. Time conveys messages depending upon its vantage point. The value of time can be based upon money, power, or status.

Humans are *territorial* creatures. We design, maintain, and use our territory for our safety and pleasure. The *design and arrangement* of our territory also communicates. Building design, office space design, room design, room color, and desk arrangement all send messages to receivers.

Social aspects of nonverbal communication send important messages concerning space and symbols. *Space,* and its impact on relationships with others, is classified as intimate, personal, social, or public. *Status* is conveyed by factors such as title, body language, assignment of a secretary or an assistant, or the ability of others to invade that space.

Our *physical* behavior also conveys nonverbal messages. Body movement, gestures, facial expressions, eye movement, vocal intonation, clothing, and touch send out messages to others. These messages tell whether we are happy, sad, angry, confused, trustworthy, irritated, organized, or disorganized.

Effective managers coordinate both their verbal and nonverbal messages. They are sensitive to what their peers, subordinates, and supervisors are nonverbally conveying.

Listening: Hearing and Understanding What People Really Mean

Listening is the most used but least taught communication skill. It consumes the majority of our communication time and takes place in staff meetings, sales meetings, training sessions, telephone calls, conversations with superiors, discussions with peers, and counseling.

Listening is composed of four stages: (1) hearing, which uses sound waves and which is often a passive process; (2) interpreting the sounds and sights that we receive; (3) evaluating what we have heard and deciding how to use the information; (4) reacting to the entire process. Most people are poor listeners because perception and semantic problems interfere with their accurate hearing of what another person says. Poor listeners may fake attention or focus on criticizing the speaker. Cultural and gender differences, along with position, further complicate listening efficiency. But there are ways to improve listening.

The skill of listening can be improved by the proper construction of mental outlines. This is accomplished by (1) creating an interest in the topic, (2) constructing a mental outline, (3) continually reviewing the mental outline, (4) using key words in the mental outline, (5) judging between important and unimportant information, and (6) tackling distractions head on. Listening to speeches can be improved by following certain suggestions before, during, and after the speech. In addition, several interpersonal physical and personal dimensions can enhance the ability to listen.

A listener can most effectively communicate through dialogue with others by giving and receiving interpersonal feedback. Feedback is the response to what a person sees, hears, reads, or feels. The knowledge gained from feedback is vital. Effective feedback is clear, understood, accepted, and helpful. It tells us when our instructions are misunderstood, if our comments lack relevance, and whether our behavior contradicts what we say.

Using Language to Convey Ideas and Achieve Results

Managers rely on their ability to convey meaning by combining language, thought, and action. Employees expect supervisors to be articulate and present expectations in clear, concise, and meaningful terms. Managers are often called on to make presentations about new ideas, plans, projects, or outcomes. They also must be able to put their ideas in writing so that a variety of audiences understand the point of their correspondence and react to meet expectations.

Presentational Speaking: Making a Positive Impression

The professional presentation is a vital part of any business. Managers maximize the effectiveness of their presentations by employing seven preparatory steps: (1) answering initial questions about the purpose and occasion of the presentation, (2) organizing the presentation, (3) packaging supporting material visually, (4) using technology effectively, (5) constructing the presentation, (6) practicing the presentation, and (7) giving the actual performance.

The first step asks the questions of why, who, where, when, what, and how. Every group is different, and a presentation needs to be designed for a particular *audience.* The *occasion* assists the speaker in determining the *purpose.* The place, date, and time of the presentation affect how well listeners receive it. To answer the question of why, one must know the purpose of the presentation. The two most common purposes for a business presentation are to *inform* and to *persuade.* A *pattern of organization* is the particular order in which supporting information is presented. The pattern should contribute to ease of listening and accomplishment of desired results. Patterns can be chronological, spatial, topical, sequential, by classification, comparative, problem-solution, advantage-disadvantage, or cause-effect.

Supporting material helps listeners picture the ideas by verifying, clarifying, and amplifying the main points. Useful tools for classification are comparison or definition, providing an example or an illustration, presenting statistics, telling a story, or providing testimony. Visual aids such as charts, graphs, or filmstrips can also help listeners understand and retain the message.

A properly structured speech has three main parts: the *introduction,* the *body,* and a *conclusion.* Each part has a specific function. The *introduction* helps gain the audience's attention. It includes an attention-getting opening, a topic statement, and a preview of the presentation's main points. The *body* contains all of the major arguments and supporting evidence. The *conclusion* recaps the main ideas, emphasizes the message's importance, and ends with a statement of goodwill. Since the effectiveness of an oral presentation relies on the listener's memory of the main points, the speaker must use simple words, key phrases, and signposts to indicate what parts of the presentation are most important.

The best presentations appear spontaneous, no matter how detailed the preparation. Effective speakers know their material well, maintain eye contact with their audiences, add meaning and emphasis through nonverbal communication, and receive feedback from their listeners. Good speakers learn the skill of effective speaking by practice. Like any other musical, artistic, or athletic skill, effective presentational speaking can be learned and perfected.

Written Communication: Preparing Letters and Memoranda

Letters and memos can be effective in accomplishing your goals while maintaining good will; however, they can also create problems. Use them for routine matters, to emphasize the importance of a situation, to record agreements, or as a follow-up to summarize discussions.

Words should be selected carefully, and technical words, acronyms, and jargon should be avoided. Choose the short, simple word over the long or technical term. The objective is clarity. The writer should keep the reader in mind and write at a level that will be easily understood. The tone of the letter should be appropriate and sincere. A positive tone will add to the effectiveness of the message. Your reader will assume that if you devote a lot of space to a point, it is important to you. Put things in the proper perspective by using the correct emphasis.

The format of a letter or memo creates the first impression for your reader. For *memos,* which are internal organizational documents, a typical standardized format includes the words To, From, Subject, and Date at the top of the page. Give the receiver's name and title, the sender's name and title, a brief statement of the subject of the memo, and the message. While a salutation and a complimentary close are not usually found in a memo, they are needed for a letter. Basic letter formats, which have a symmetrical arrangement, are the modified block, block, and AMS styles.

Letters can convey good or bad news, and the writer's approach will depend on the action desired from the reader. Little explanation or background is needed for good news; use a direct approach and get to the point quickly. For letters with bad news, use the indirect approach: provide reasons or details that will explain the basis for your decision and close with a statement of goodwill. *Persuasive* letters, including letters prospecting for employment, should have an attention-getting opening, overcome resistance by establishing a case through a logical presentation of reasoning, and end with an action-getting close.

Because international communication often requires written correspondence, it is important to be familiar with the culture and communication styles of the individuals with whom you are corresponding. The style they use is a clue. If they are direct, you can also be direct. If they use a more indirect or formal style, you need to adapt your style accordingly.

Written Communication: Preparing Reports

Reports help managers solve problems and make decisions by presenting information that informs or persuades. The needs for and uses of reports vary and determine the formality, length, and writing style used. Since reports can be vehicles for change and reform in the organization, they must be carefully researched, organized, and written.

Before beginning a report, the writer needs to answer five questions: What is the purpose of the report? Who reads the report? What is the nature and extent of the problem? What information is needed to fulfill the objectives of the report? And, if it is an analytical report, what does the information tell the reader? The answers to these questions are keys to the success of the report and determine formality, writing style, direction, methodology, organizational structure, and the validity of final recommendations.

Reports can be informal, semiformal, or formal. *Informal reports* are usually shorter and either routine or less important in content than the other two forms. *Semiformal reports* are longer than informal reports, typed, more formal in writing style, and also typically internal to the organization.

Formal reports present important information in a traditional, detailed format and often go to readers outside the organization or are used for future reference. Because a formal report is usually circulated to a wide audience on several organizational levels, information in the report is arranged so that readers can move quickly to its various parts. Typical parts include a transmittal letter, a title page, an authorization letter, a synopsis, a table of contents, an introduction, the findings, the conclusion and recommendations, and appended parts. To save readers' time and assure that they get the facts or news, we encourage use of an inverted format that places the important facts and recommendations in the first part of the report.

Written Communication: Editing, the Polish that Accomplishes Your Purpose

Written communications reflect their writer. They should be neat, well organized, and easily readable, and they should follow an acceptable format. The *editing process* allows the writer to correct spelling errors and grammar and stylistic problems, and also add professionalism to the document's appearance. Properly edited written reports, letters, and memos can be effective tools for achieving action.

Three important reasons to edit are: the writer is lazy and produces vague, unclear copy; the writer cannot distinguish between what is correct and incorrect in writing; or the writer is working under a deadline and runs out of time. A first draft should never be sent without editing. To be effective, it should be clear, concise, and correct. Seven methods for achieving clarity and conciseness are: (1) eliminate unneeded words, (2) explain abbreviations and acronyms, (3) eliminate jargon, (4) eliminate unnatural phrases, (5) use small words, (6) use active instead of passive verbs, and (7) use a readability index. A final check for correctness should make certain that you have used the right word, checked for spelling and grammatical errors, and corrected sexist errors.

Electronic editing and printing options produce high-quality written documents and offer a number of options. Among these options are the thesaurus, spell checkers, grammar and style checkers, writing style models, alternative document formats, graphics, variations in typefaces, and laser printing. Because software packages including these editing aids are now accessible to PC users, readers have increased their expectations for document quality.

Well-written, carefully edited copy saves time and money. It also helps the reader understand your message. Wordy, meaningless phrases require the reader to spend excess time and energy deciphering the writer's thoughts. It is therefore good business and good public relations for managers to edit their work as a matter of course.

Communication Strategies for the Effective Manager

As noted earlier, organizations have missions. In pursuing these missions, managers and employees engage in a variety of activities. Managers must somehow achieve the desired results by communicating the mission to employees. Communication strategies used by the manager involve teamwork, leadership, problem resolution, conflict management, meetings, interviewing, or managing change.

Teamwork and Leadership

Effective teams develop through effective communication strategies. Teams are important because they (1) encourage employee interaction and participation, (2) generate more ideas and alternatives, (3) facilitate commitment, and (4) develop understanding. Barriers to success of teams in problem solving can be *relational, substantive,* or *procedural.*

All teams have task and maintenance functions. A team's *task function* is to achieve the goal toward which it is working. Its *maintenance function* is to meet the interpersonal needs of the group members. The longer the group meets, the more attention it requires for its maintenance needs.

Effective teams share specific goals, monitor their successes, share rewards, sacrifice for the good of the team, and consist of members who understand their roles and are involved in all aspects of the team's mission. Communication in such teams flows easily between all members and is of a high quality—precise, internally consistent, positively reinforcing, and cooperative.

As teams move toward fulfillment of their goals, leadership may emerge from within the group. Some team members may act as facilitators to help the team move through the process of diagnosing a problem. The team leader coordinates team interaction, keeps the team on target, helps team members develop the mission and goals, makes certain all team members participate, maintains team harmony, identifies areas of team agreement, and removes barriers.

Irving L. Janis identified the concept *groupthink,* defined as the tendency to agree with the group and accept a premature decision. Since groups take more risks than individuals, leaders should avoid the effect of groupthink by refraining from stating their preferred choices, by encouraging discussion of all possible solutions, by emphasizing the importance of reaching a solution through explorations of all possible information and alternatives, and by fostering free expression of minority viewpoints.

Current studies focus on leadership styles that are appropriate in different situations. A *boss-centered* leadership style emphasizes the authority of the manager. *Subordinate-centered* leadership occurs when freedom and involvement in decision-making lead to a more democratic approach. Leaders can alter their style to suit the individuals and the situation. *Directive* leadership is used when subordinates need strong supervision. A *coaching* style may be necessary if team members need direction and encouragement. *Supportive* leadership demonstrates concern for people in a high stress situation. *Delegating* is an appropriate style in which leaders pass authority to selected mature, knowledgeable, and skilled team members. Leaders must decide when each style is appropriate, be flexible in adjusting leadership styles, and gain agreement from the team members about which style works.

Effective Problem Resolution

Six steps are associated with the problem-solving process: defining the problem, analyzing the problem, proposing solutions, evaluating solutions, implementing solutions, and evaluating the success of the solution. These steps incorporate two phases: creative and analytical. During the creative phase, ideas are generated and divergent thinking takes place. This is an expansion phase and affects the first three steps of problem solving. The analytical phase requires convergent thinking. It is the closure phase and affects the last three steps of problem solving.

Creativity assists in idea generation and is most dependent on language facility. Several techniques have been developed to stimulate ideas. *Brainstorming* encourages participation without criticism. *Forcing techniques* help the group consider as many alternatives as possible. *Synectics* uses associations to trigger ideas. The *nominal technique* combines silent brainstorming with group sharing while minimizing group pressures.

Finally, it is important to note that personality types affect group problem solving and decision making, because people have differing approaches to identifying problems, reaching decisions, and proceeding through the problem-solving process. For example, *sensing* people define problems through experience and by sticking to the facts while *intuitive* people focus on the "big picture." *Thinkers* are task oriented, while *feelers* are concerned about impact on people. *Judging* types proceed in a logical sequence. *Perceivers* can act quickly in reaching a decision, because they are comfortable with trusting their experience and leaping to conclusions.

To be an effective problem solver, the manager must consider the nature of the problem; the importance of the acceptance of the solution; the value placed on the quality of the solution; and the competency, personality types, and operating effectiveness of the persons involved. If the desired result is effective communication and implementation of solutions, the keys to success are selecting the appropriate type of decision making (individual, group, or consultant); access to complete and accurate information; and applying creative techniques for idea generation and problem resolution.

Managing Conflict

Effective problem resolution often includes resolving conflict. All managers are concerned with finding the right solutions for problems in order to reach organizational goals. Conflict adds to a greater understanding and identification of problems as well as increasing alternatives and involvement. The organizational structure, performance measures, ambiguity of expectations, and conflicting reality perceptions serve as sources of conflict.

If conflict is recognized in the early stages of the conflict episode, it can be managed effectively. A set of underlying conditions creates the first or *latent* stage. The next stage occurs when the parties perceive that these conditions exist. If the conditions intensify in effect, the *felt conflict* stage begins. If conditions are not resolved, the *manifest conflict* stage surfaces in *overt* or *covert action,* releasing tension. Finally, *conflict aftermath* is the stage or condition that results from the action taken.

Strategies for resolving conflict are *outcome directed* (who gets what) or *goal directed* (what would benefit both). Parties engage in strategies that are outcome directed (*win/lose* or *lose/lose*). These strategies set up an atmosphere of victory or defeat. Preferable to win/lose is the lose/lose strategy, in which both sides lose something as well as gain something. Finally, the *win/win* strategy focuses on the problem rather than the solution. This strategy requires a consensus and an approach that stresses goals and values while deemphasizing solutions and win/lose tactics. Individual styles for resolving conflict incorporate these strategies. The *hard bargainer* negotiates to win. The *soft bargainer* values acceptance and trust over the outcome. The *principled bargainer* seeks an outcome suitable to everyone.

Blake and Mouton identified five methods for reducing conflict: compromising, confronting or problem solving, forcing, smoothing, and withdrawing. Extensive research by Burke indicated the most effective way of handling conflict was confronting or problem solving. Forcing was ineffective.

Several forms of intervention are useful in resolving conflict. These forms depend on the intensity of the conflict and the policies of the organization. *Negotiation* is direct intervention between two parties who attempt to arrive at a settlement. Negotiators may resort to overt or covert power plays and bluffing in order to accomplish their goals. *Mediation* requires a third-party neutral who interprets the parties to each other and promotes reconciliation. Finally, *arbitration* is the intervention of an appointed authority given the power to decide after hearing the differing complaints. Of these forms of intervention, direct negotiation is least costly in terms of time spent and effect on productivity.

The key to managing conflict is an awareness that conflict is healthy and leads to better decision making. If participants accept this principle and apply problem-solving skills, then greater commitment, more creative alternatives, and sounder decisions will more than likely result.

Making Meetings Work

Managers spend considerable time participating in and running meetings. Meetings are important because they allow individuals to share information in a short period of time to achieve mutual goals. During meetings individuals can express their views, expand on ideas, present solutions to problems, and facilitate goal commitments. Some goals may be best accomplished in a meeting, but for other goals a meeting is definitely *not* the context for achieving results. Meetings can be expensive and time consuming. If the wrong people attend, if the group does not follow a planned agenda, or if management does not value the group's decision, the effectiveness of the meeting will be minimal.

Meetings can be personal, organizational, or public. *Personal meetings* are informal and generally have no real purpose. *Organizational meetings* can be internal, such as the staff or committee meeting, or external, such as a board of directors' meeting. *Public meetings* are usually presented to an audience that has no affiliation with the organization.

Attending a meeting with no discernible purpose is a waste of everyone's time and is costly to the organization. Meetings should not be held unless they require the participation of several people and there is time to prepare for and complete the meeting.

Once a decision to hold a meeting is made, the success of that meeting is affected by the purpose of the meeting, who attends the meeting, the size of the group, the time at which the meeting is scheduled, the location chosen for the meeting, and the agenda. Since meeting arrangements can make or break a meeting, seating, equipment, temperature, and other logistics should all be handled ahead of time. The leader should clearly state the purpose of the meeting, encourage participation, direct the flow of communication, use an agenda, and summarize the group's agreements. Sometimes the leader or chairperson must also be familiar with rules of procedure for formal organizational meetings.

By assessing goals and dynamics before, during, and after each meeting, managers can conduct successful meetings. Their skills as meeting leaders will also constantly improve.

Conducting Interviews

An *interview* is an interaction between two parties to accomplish a predetermined purpose essential to the welfare of the organization. The manager's responsibility as interviewer is to make sure that the interviewee understands the purpose of the interview. The manager also brings the right parties together and plans the interview structure or format.

Like a speech, the interview includes an *opening* to establish contact and set the tone, a *body* to gain the information necessary, and a *close* that summarizes and indicates when the interview is completed.

Key questioning techniques are essential. *Closed questions* are used to limit response and gain information about attitudes and beliefs. *Mirror questions* help encourage further discussion. Managers should avoid leading questions since such questions assume agreement, or, at the very least, presume to lead the interviewee to a predetermined response.

Managers are involved in several types of interviews, including the *employment interview,* the *orientation interview,* the *counseling interview,* and the *disciplinary interview.* Each of these interview formats requires specific techniques to enhance the effectiveness of the communication situation.

Managing Change

Organizations, like individuals, are in a constant state of change. The change process includes the element of innovation, messages about innovation, the passage of time from the first exposure until the innovation is no longer new, a group of people or social system, and some observable response to the innovation. Communication is an integral part of this change process.

People resist change because it threatens the status quo, bringing with it uncertainty and anxiety. In reality, change is a natural part of the problem-solving process; it is the phase of problem solving where the solution is put in place. Here the actual plan or strategy unfolds, and the steps for implementation are defined. Thus, while effective implementation of change depends on careful attention to all steps of problem solving, the change phase focuses on implementing, evaluating, and refining the solution.

The person or group given the responsibility for implementing the change is called the *change agent. Change forces* include any aspects of the situation which increase willingness to change. *Driving forces* encourage members of the organization to accept the solution. *Restraining forces* include any aspects of the situation that reduce willingness to change. *Alternatives* include increasing the strength of the driving forces, decreasing the strength of the restraining forces, or combining both of these approaches.

An organization can approach change in a variety of ways. The most common approach is the *decree,* a decision made by individuals appointed by the system. This approach may fail because of lack of commitment of those who must implement the decision. The *replacement* approach consists of appointing people in key positions to make politically and strategically critical decisions that conform to the administration's philosophy and policies. Manipulating the *structure* changes the ability of individuals in key positions to wield their power in decision making. The *data discussion* approach is based on generating data, diagnosing problems, and developing plans. *Group decision* and *problem-solving* approaches rely on participation and consensus in decision-making. *Team building, quality circles,* and *total quality management* recognize people as individuals with the ability to make thoughtful contributions to the improvement of all aspects of the organization and its products.

Healthy organizations have the ability to anticipate, execute, and adapt to change. Effective change involves the total organization and is planned, is comprehensive, emphasizes co-orientation of work groups, and requires participation of a change agent. Success of the change is based on the change agent's credibility, effective problem identification, supportive climate, long-range planning, and a system of program evaluation. Many change initiatives fail because they are not communicated effectively. Before taking action, the change agent should have an action plan that gauges resistance and addresses individual concerns. Each person's responsibilities should be made clear. Expectations should be specific and thoroughly discussed. Levels of authority should be delegated so that individuals know what decision-making powers they have. Once the change is implemented, the manager should debrief employees to get feedback for evaluating and refining the change effort.

Managers get things done by communicating their ideas and expectations effectively to others and by receiving feedback. Communication activities consume a majority of each manager's day. Mastering the principles and skills that are fundamental to listening, speaking, writing, and participating in groups can be a key to successful results.

APPENDIX A

DEFINING ETHICAL THEORY

Each chapter in this text contains an ethics case that relates to the chapter content. The material in this appendix is designed to give you an understanding of standard ethical theories that you can use in analyzing the cases. This material originated as chapter 2 in *An Introduction to Ethics for Association Executives.* This manuscript is to be published by the American Society of Association Executives in Washington, D.C. The author, Steven E. Woolley, is manager of the Eastern Region of the United States Chamber of Commerce in New York City. He is also an adjunct faculty member at the City University of New York's Baruch College, where he teaches business ethics. This material is reprinted by permission.

DEFINING ETHICAL THEORY

Steve Woolley

Ethics isn't easy to define. We use the word all the time but seldom stop to think about what it means. The Christian theologian Paul Tillich has as good a definition as I've found anywhere because he helps us understand the relationship between ethics and morality. He says:

> There would be no confusion if, as I now suggest, we defined ethics as the "science of the moral." But this is not a generally accepted definition, the chief reason being that the word "moral," through historical accidents, has received several distorting connotations. Since the eighteenth century, at least in Europe, it has carried the implication of "moralism" in the sense of graceless legalistic ethics. And in the United States, it has, under the influence of Puritanism, taken on a sexual signification: to be "amoral" means to be sexually lawless, or at least to deny conventional sex ethics. Because of these two connotations, one has tried to replace "moral" by "ethical." Were this generally accepted, however, the term "ethical" would soon acquire the connotations of "moral," and there would be no change. Therefore, I recommend that "ethical" be reserved for the *theory* of morals, and that the term "moral" and its derivatives be purged of those associations, and used to describe the moral act itself in its fundamental significance.[1]

Personally, I'd prefer that Tillich had used the word *discipline* rather than *science,* because I think science misleads us. But if ethics is the science of the moral, then what is morality? It really is nothing more than the norms by which the behavior of a person or group of people is judged in terms of its rightness or wrongness, its acceptability or unacceptability. To a certain extent, each culture and subculture has its own norms, and therefore defines morality in its own way.

In view of that, it would be tempting to dismiss morality as the arbitrary whims of whatever group one happened to be in, but as having no real substance. That would be a mistake.

Over the centuries there have been many barriers that have kept members of one culture from recognizing their kinship with the fundamental values of others. Poor transportation, poor communications, mutual ignorance of traditions and languages, and xenophobic suspicions have made cultural differences more obvious than similarities of moral thought. Yet cultures tend to build their definitions around a surprisingly common set of ethical principles. Something like the ten commandments and the golden rule can be found in most any culture. Aberrations, when they occur, have been universally abhorred. The outrages of Hitler, Stalin, and Tojo are, unfortunately, only three examples in recent history, but certainly ones that clearly make the point.

Over the centuries these more or less universal concepts of morality have evolved to a different, if not higher, plane than they once held. For instance, until about 3,000 years ago much of the world found it morally acceptable to engage in child sacrifice. The moral leap that occurred then didn't change everything overnight, but it did set in motion a process of change that could not be stopped. Although human sacrifice has continued in some form as an acceptable practice in some cultures until recently, the weight of moral thinking working against it has prevailed.

Another example, much more recent to our experience, has to do with genocide. There was nothing morally wrong with genocide in most cultures until very recently. The ancient literature, including the Bible, all but praises it. As long as the people being exterminated were them and not us, it was frequently viewed as something akin to vermin eradication. It wasn't hard to get a fairly large number of European-Americans to agree to that exterminating the American Indian was not unreasonable late into the nineteenth century. But the inexorable tide of moral thinking has moved us to a new understanding that is agreed to world wide . . . genocide is wrong. Still practiced perhaps, but wrong and condemned.

So ethics, the science of the moral, has a cultural component, is evolving, is more universal than one might think, and is bold to say some behaviors are right, some are wrong, and much is ambiguous. Because it is a "science," or, to use my word, a discipline, it also leads us systematically through an examination of all its elements, but with special attention given to ambiguity. In this paper, we will try to grapple with many questions of ambiguity and, in so doing, perhaps clear things up a little.

What Do We Know about Ethical Behavior in General?

We are operating with only two pieces of certain knowledge about ethical behavior. First, what is ethical and what is unethical are ambiguous. Part of what makes these categories ambiguous is that most of us are too easily tempted to paint our own political agendas with an inappropriate ethical brush. Let me put it this way: if I feel strongly that my political agenda is the one most supportive of whatever I've defined as social justice, I may feel quite justified in labeling you unethical because you back a competing agenda, which, by definition, is obviously opposed to social justice.

Second, all of us make errors, intentional and accidental, of omission and commission. Therefore it is cynical hypocrisy to be contemptuous of unethical behavior that is simply a reflection of the ordinary failures of human behavior in society. But it is even more inappropriate to excuse such behavior just because it is common.

Even when we factor out that kind of problem, the question of ethics remains ambiguous. It isn't that we can't agree on what is or isn't ethical in concept. That's surprisingly easy to do. It is that situations in which ethical questions arise are seldom easy to understand, nor do they turn on only one question of ethics. Instead, they turn on a multitude of ethical questions. So we find ourselves not only hard pressed to clearly understand the situation, but against it are competing, even conflicting, ethical standards to apply.

It would be useful to stop here for a while and turn to the classical definitions of ethics because, with them in mind, much of this will start to make a lot more sense.

The Traditional View

People who study ethics divide the field into three broad categories: descriptive ethics, normative ethics, and critical or metaethics.[2]

Descriptive Ethics

Descriptive ethics is the discipline of accurately recognizing and describing the nature of the problems being faced and the nature of the ethics applied to its resolution. In leading students through case studies, instructors will ask them to identify the issues (ethical and otherwise) in each case and to identify and describe the positions, values, and reasoning of each of the primary actors in them. It's a descriptive task; they're required to accurately describe the situation. In a sense it's a little like high school biology where, to understand the elements of that earthy science, you first had to be able to describe an amoeba in all its parts.

Descriptive ethics are important. How can you make good decisions about something if you don't clearly understand what it is? Descriptive ethics says, "Before we go any further, let's stop and figure out what's going on here." Now that's just common sense, and it's what we would ordinarily do in most problem solving situations. Yet when it comes to ethical matters, most of us want to get on with things. We don't want to stop here. We want to go right for the answer before we even know enough to ask the right questions. . . . in good business fashion we want to cut right to the bottom line.

If nothing else, descriptive ethics requires us to slow down and rationally evaluate situations so that we have a clear understanding of what the ethical questions are.

Having thus contemplated, we're ready to apply the ethical prescriptions available through normative ethics.

Three Kinds of Normative Ethics

Normative ethics is the discipline of constructing and applying particular value systems to ethical questions. There are different ways different people talk about normative ethics, but Kenneth E. Goodpaster brings them all together nicely by describing utilitarian, contractarianism, and what he calls pluralism.[3]

Utilitarian

Utilitarians got their start with the idea that pleasure was the highest good, and that one should aspire to achieving the greatest pleasure for the greatest number. As time went by, the idea of pleasure faded into something more like negotiating to get the best you can get under the circumstances. At its heart, utilitarian thinking says, "Look, some things may be unfair to a particular individual or group, but as long as it's not me, we have to be concerned about what's good for the country as a whole. What's ethical is what will do the most for the most."

I may have taken some cynical liberties with what the original utilitarians really thought, but that's because I believe modern utilitarianism has sunk to some pretty low levels. It didn't start out quite that way. Utilitarian thinking goes back a long way, but it was given definition by Jeremy Bentham (1748–1832) and John Stewart Mill (1806–1873). Hunter Lewis writes that:

> Bentham began by attacking all deductive systems based on God or a reality beyond this world as "nonsense on stilts" that should be swept away at a glance. The proper course was to stick to this world, not to imagine another, and the most obviously observable fact about this world was that everyone pursued pleasure and avoided pain.[4]

Bentham felt strongly that selfish pleasures were inferior to those bringing pleasure to the public as a whole because, in the end, selfish pleasures were short lived and only resulted in pain generated by conflicts with someone else's selfish pleasure. Therefore, the pleasure to be sought was that which would benefit the public as a whole, and he invented a sort of calculus to compare one pleasure against another to see which ones were more worthy than others.

Utilitarianism had a benevolent foundation and intended to build a society in which the good life was broadly distributed. But in the end it didn't show much regard for any one individual. People, or, more accurately, persons, are likely to be seen as means to an end, that end being the good of the whole, than as ends in themselves.

What is good for the whole may be very unpleasant for some individuals, or even a sizeable minority. That's too bad, and utilitarians would hope those who are disadvantaged would find some solace in knowing that others are much better off for their suffering. As a result, utilitarians can be prone to developing quite an elitist attitude, in which the elite assume extra rights and privileges as their due reward for the burdens of leadership which is rightfully theirs.

Utilitarian thinking has dominated western ethical and political thought for almost 200 years, and it's certainly been a driving force in American thought, especially in business. The idea that the operations of a free market will result in a balance of the greatest good for the greatest number is a distinctly utilitarian one.

Associations in which the membership is seen primarily as a means by which the organization is sustained, and the staff and leadership are provided with enough resources to do what they think best, could be said to be operating from a utilitarian point of view. That could also be true of associations organized to support political views deeply concerned for the improvement of society but for whom individual inequality and suffering are abstractions to be debated rather than issues to be addressed.

The Social Contract

Contractarianists, as Goodpaster calls them, believe in the social contract. Back in high school civics, we learned about Locke, Jefferson and others who said that people should form their governments through social contracts and that if the government violated the contract, the people had the right to change the government. People entered into these social contracts to protect their inalienable rights to certain things. Among them were life, liberty, and the pursuit of happiness. These are individual rights, but they required the collective power of the state to protect them. Our social contract with the state provides that if the state fails to protect and uphold these individual rights, the contract is void.

In modern times their views are best expressed by John Rawls, who says ethics and justice are essentially the same thing, that justice is a matter of fairness, that justice as fairness is established through contracts between a people and their government, and that it can be defined as being based on two principles:

> First, each person is to have an equal right to the most extensive basic liberty compatible with similar liberty for others.
>
> Second, social and economic inequalities are to be arranged so that they are both (a) reasonably expected to be to everyone's advantage, and (b) attached to positions and offices open to all.[5]

What is ethical becomes a question of identifying and protecting rights that extend equally to all people; where there must be some kind of inequality, even the most adversely affected member of society must voluntarily agree to the inequality because, in some very real way, it would make life better for them personally. These collective individual and group agreements comprise the social contract that binds the state together.

If we apply these two principles to an association we might come up with the following.

In an association each member is to have equal access to all rights, benefits, and privileges in a way that, as much as possible, does not interfere with the same rights, benefits and privileges of any other member.

Where there are inequalities in rights, benefits, and privileges, the least privileged member of the association will readily agree that the inequality is a fair one because in some real way it improves the quality of his or her membership. Moreover, the inequalities that do exist are attached to specific offices, not individuals, and the least privileged member has an equal and equitable opportunity to hold one of those offices.

Rawls calls this "justice as fairness," and I think most of us recognize that when associations are habitually run in an unfair way, the rank-and-file members know it and begin to desert the association, plot member-driven revolts, or, at a minimum, give unmotivated grudging support to it.

Now Rawls is not a fan of capitalism, businesses, or business associations, and most association executives would have a hard time with his politics, but it seems to me his basic idea of fairness is a good one. It may not be a question of a rank-and-file member cynically thinking, "Oh, yeah, it's just great that the board took my money to go to Aruba for their February meeting," but more that rank-and-file members will approve of inequalities (perks among others, for instance) as being part of fair, well-understood, intentional, and public decisions about the use of association resources.

Unfairness becomes evident when decisions resulting in inequalities appear to rank-and-file members as being not well understood, irrational, made behind closed doors, and creating benefits for others for which they are unlikely ever to be eligible.

Pluralism (or Duty-Based Ethics)

Goodpaster's final type, pluralism, is the least well defined, and yet one many of us would find most familiar. If utilitarians base their system of values on the greatest good and contractarians base theirs on rights secured by social contracts, pluralists base theirs on duty.

In fact, most observers call this branch of ethics "deontology," from the Greek word *deon,* meaning duty or obligation.

The ten commandments, the Boy Scout pledge, an oath of office are all expressions of ethical value systems based on a sense of duty. In a very real sense, so are commitments to organizational codes of ethics.

But for Goodpaster pluralistic ethics is also expressed by intuitive examination of what common sense or our conscience tells us about what is right or wrong in any given situation. We'll talk more about conscience later, but suffice it to say that whatever else conscience is, it lets us know what our duty is, even when we'd just as soon not hear from it.

Walton coins the term "deonutility" to mean more or less the same thing.[6] That intuitive examination will illuminate our duty, even if our duty will make life difficult for us personally. Going back again in our own history, if Jefferson wrote the contract guaranteeing the right of the people, Washington understood his duty to the people.

The great proponent of duty in modern thinking is Immanuel Kant (1724–1804), who expressed duty in terms of what is called the categorical imperative (a concept borrowed from the Bible). By that he meant duty could be expressed in terms of a law that demanded obedience and from which there could be no exception. To him, and very roughly stated, that law is that each person and all persons must be considered ends unto themself, and never as means. This certainly puts Kant in direct contradiction to Bentham, Mills and the utilitarians, who are perfectly willing to use any given person, or people, as a means to achieve what they see as a greater good for the whole.

Some take issue with Kant because his rule is too inflexible, but there is strong agreement among many of those same people that his core idea is on the right track.

People for whom duty is the highest, though certainly not the only, value, will do their duty regardless of personal cost. From those committed to duty are drawn the saints and moral leaders of humanity. Mahatma Ghandi, Martin Luther King, and Mother Teresa come to our contemporary minds. In them we recognize our highest ideals of what we hope for the future of mankind.

Yet there are others who will make great sacrifices in the name of duty who in fact don't understand duty at all. Fanatics of one brand or another will go to most any extreme in the furtherance of their causes and will lay a claim to duty all the way. But when you apply the acid test of using persons as means or recognizing them as ends, the fanatic always fails. Why is that?

When you treat each and every person as an end and not a means, you have no alternative but to love them. Love then becomes something you do rather than something you feel. There can be no exception; it is the highest and most sacred duty. To love is a categorical imperative that includes the worst and most reviled of humanity as well as those closest and dearest to us. The fanatic can't do that because he or she doesn't love others without exception; they're only means to his or her own ends.

None of us, of course, is capable of such perfect love. The best we can do is approximate it. In fact, we're not overly tolerant of those who come too close to perfect love. It shows up our own selfishness too much, and we have a tendency to martyr people who would do that.

The down side to duty as a driving force is that it can deteriorate into mere legalism. A code of ethics which defines our duty can become just so many rules to be obeyed with little understanding of the intent behind them. Even Kant's categorical imperative can become nothing more than not being unpleasant and generally trying to do nice things for others from time to time, if it isn't too inconvenient. For those familiar with the New Testament, that was the heart of the debate between the temple leaders in Jerusalem and

Jesus of Nazareth. For those not familiar, suffice it to say that the church, as a singular example of a duty-driven institution, has gone through successive periods of sinking into mere legalism, and every couple of hundred years seems to require a reawakening to, and renewal of, its essential duty.

Critical Ethics

The last traditional element of ethics is critical ethics, which from our layperson's point of view could be described as, "Hey, wait a minute, maybe we haven't examined what's under each rock. Let's look at how all these ethical value systems are related and get some new insights." It's a level of abstraction once removed from normative and descriptive ethics, and in a sense, it's what happens when a person with a duty-based value system starts arguing with a person having a rights-based value system.

What's the Point?

So what's the point in all this? Well, if you can keep a mental outline in your head of these three traditional elements of ethics (descriptive, normative and critical), then ethical questions and discussions will start to make more sense. You'll have a structure into which you can slot seemingly random and contrary ideas so they can be addressed in an orderly fashion.

References

1. Paul Tillich, *Morality and Beyond* (New York: Harper & Row, 1963), pp. 21, 22.
2. These categories are drawn largely from Goodpaster. A slightly different approach is taken by Clarence C. Walton in *The Moral Manager* (Cambridge, Mass.: Ballinger, 1988). It is a superb introduction not only to the study of ethics in business, but also to the relation of western philosophy to the contemporary business environment.
3. Much of the following is drawn from Goodpaster, "Some Avenues for Ethical Analysis in General Management," Bulletin 383-007 of the Harvard Business School (Harvard Business School, 1982).
4. Hunter Lewis, *A Question of Values: Six Ways We Make the Personal Choices that Shape Our Lives* (New York: Harper & Row, 1990), p. 226.
5. John Rawls, *A Theory of Justice* (Cambridge, Mass.: The Belknap Press of the Harvard University Press, 1971), p. 60.
6. Clarence C. Walton, *The Moral Manager* (Cambridge, Mass.: Ballinger, 1988), pp. 110–112. Walton, commenting on the works of W. D. Ross, suggests the term "*Deonutility,* defined as the respect for rights and responsibility for consequences."

APPENDIX B

SAMPLE REPORTS

REPORT 1. A MODEL REPORT

Sample Pages from a Model Report

IMPROVING WRITTEN COMMUNICATION

THROUGH PROGRAMMED INSTRUCTION

FINAL REPORT

SUBMITTED TO:

THE BOARD OF EXECUTIVES

PRESENTED BY:

MARY M. RYDESKY

CUSTOMER SERVICE DEPARTMENT

LONE STAR BANK

June 29, 1994

EXHIBIT B.1 Model Report—Title Page

LONE STAR BANK
2000 Commerce Street
Dallas, Texas 75220
214-695-0000

June 29, 1994

The Board of Executives
Lone Star Bank
2000 Commerce Street
Dallas, TX 75220

Enclosed is the final report on an exciting in-company educational program that you authorized in April of this year.

The program, Improving Written Communication Skills: Punctuation Module, has been developed and tested, and the results are presented for your consideration. The program was low cost for Lone Star, took no on-the-job time since it was designed as programmed instruction for home use, and resulted in a significant level of reduced errors in writing.

The report gives a background of the study, describes the method of instruction, and makes recommendations for further development.

Respectfully,

Mary M. Rydesky, Director
Customer Service Department

EXHIBIT B.2 Model Report—Transmittal Letter

SYNOPSIS

This report describes the development and testing of programmed instruction materials for teaching punctuation in the Customer Service Department of Lone Star Bank. The report presents the initial problem, background information that led to the study, the method of research undertaken through testing and training, and the findings of the research after training was performed.

The appendixes contain several items that support and add information to the report: a sample page of instruction, pre- and post-test scores, and selected employee comments on the instruction. The major conclusions drawn from the study are that programmed instruction meets five criteria for Lone Star Bank:

1. It allows employees to work at self-determined paces;
2. It allows employees to study at home rather than on the job;
3. It reinforces learning immediately so that the employee can use each lesson as it is covered, rather than waiting until the course is completed;
4. It reinforces the Lone Star style of correspondence; and
5. It minimizes the costs and time loss while achieving the desired goal of improved performance.

Recommendations for further development are:

1. Transfer Ann Ford to Customer Service so she may develop additional programmed instruction modules.
2. Create modules on dictation skills, spelling, and proofreading during the next six months. Test each module immediately after development.
3. Fund Ann Ford to present Lone Star's Improved Written Communication Skills services at the 1994 American Society for Training and Development annual conference.
4. Fund Rydesky to write an article for *Banking Management.* The article would compare Lone Star's new program with competitors' methods.

EXHIBIT B.3 Model Report—Synopsis

TABLE OF CONTENTS

EXHIBIT B.4 Model Report—Table of Contents

INTRODUCTION

Purpose

This report describes a new training process, programmed instruction, developed and tested at the Lone Star Bank. The report will examine the background of the problem; describe research methods, present the program, Improving Written Communication Skills: Punctuation Module; describe the findings following the training; and make recommendations for future training.

Recommendations

Because the scores indicate that programmed instruction is effective in teaching writing skills, and because Lone Star employees react favorably to this method of instruction, development of additional packages is warranted. Recommendations are:

1. Transfer Ann Ford to Customer Service so she may develop additional programmed instruction modules.

2. Create modules on dictation skills, spelling, and proofreading during the next six months. Test each module immediately after development.

3. Fund Ann Ford to present Lone Star's Improving Written Communication Skills series at the 1994 American Society for Training and Development annual conference.

4. Fund Rydesky to write an article for *Banking Management* magazine. The article would compare Lone Star's new program with competitors' methods.

Problem Statement

The Customer Service Department needed instruction in how to correct punctuation errors. To find the right educational process the department investigated materials and tested a programmed instruction package.

Background

For some time a high incidence of punctuation errors has been noted by the Customer Service Department staff. The director investigated methods used within the banking industry to improve writing skills. They were found to be time consuming and costly to develop or purchase. A comparison of costs was presented in the April 15, 1994, proposal, which is reproduced in Appendix A of this report. While several of the methods resulted in improved writing skills, the costs outweighed the benefits.

Programmed instruction, which is an educational method of presentation that reinforces the student's learning throughout the course, was then investigated. This approach to instruction is organized in a psychologically coherent sequence rather than in a logical sequence. The ideas flow one to another rather than being divided into a logical introduction, body, and summary. Self-instruction and self-testing are incorporated in programmed instruction to decrease reliance on a live instructor in a formal classroom. Because material is presented in small increments punctuated by test questions that require the student to practice the new knowledge, it can be studied during spare moments without compromising the student's attention to the content.

EXHIBIT B.5 Model Report—Text

Source: Mary M. Rydesky, "Lone Star Bank Report," prepared for this book.

Programmed instruction meets five criteria for Lone Star:

1. It allows employees to work at self-determined paces;

2. It allows employees to study at home rather than on the job;

3. It reinforces learning immediately so that the employee can use each lesson as it is covered, rather than waiting until the course is completed;

4. It reinforces the Lone Star style of correspondence;

5. It minimizes the costs and time loss while achieving the desired goal of improved performance.

In addition, the programmed instruction workbooks can be given to the employees to use as reference texts after the initial study period. (A copy of the workbook can be found in Appendix B.)

The methodology for testing was:

1. Customer Service staff was tested on punctuation skills and then divided into two groups of thirty-two. Each group was "matched" by test scores so that neither would be more knowledgeable about punctuation prior to the program.

2. The experimental group used programmed instruction workbooks at home.

3. The control group received a classroom lecture during business hours.

4. Both groups were tested prior to instruction and then again following instruction. (Pre-test and post-test scores were recorded and compared.)

The chronology of the testing was:

May 7, 1994 Pre-tests given; groups assigned.
May 10, 1994 Ford meets with experimental group for a thirty-minute briefing. Employees are asked to complete workbooks at home.
May 11, 1994 Control group receives instruction; lecture takes sixty minutes to deliver.

FINDINGS

As a result of the testing the following findings were revealed:
May 15, 1994 Both groups tested; scores are compared with pre-test scores:

	Pre	Post	Change
A. Experimental group programmed instruction	25.9	34.9	+9.0
B. Control group classroom instruction	25.7	33.2	+7.5

(See Appendix C for complete statistics.) Programmed instruction effects the greater change. Results are subjected to statistical testing; validity is verified.

(continued)

June 10, 1994 Groups are recalled for a surprise retest to see whether retention of information is related to method of presentation.

A. Experimental group	31.3
B. Control group	28.9

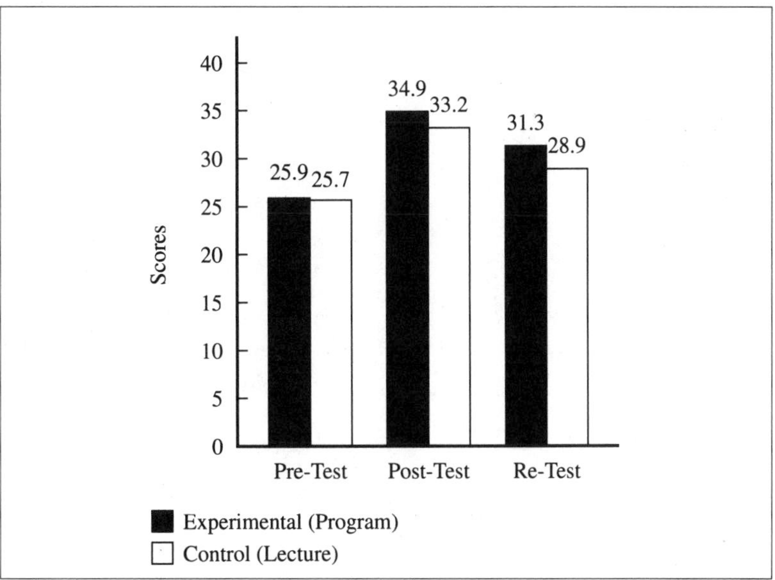

The employees who used the programmed instruction materials retained more knowledge. Employees' comments about programmed instruction are collected.

June 11, 1994 Employees' comments are collated.

A. 98% are favorable and indicate interest in having more programmed instruction materials.

B. 2% disliked doing the study at home.

June 29, 1994 Report of results is submitted to the Committee of Executives. Major recommendation is to continue the development of programmed instruction materials on writing skills.

CONCLUSION

Summary

The programmed method of instruction is by far the most cost effective and beneficial for Lone Star Bank. The greatest contribution of this study is the reduction in errors in correspondence prepared by employees in the Customer Service Department. A comparison of letters written last December with those written in May shows 46% to 75% fewer errors. In addition, fewer letters have been received from customers who request explanations of materials sent to them. If a customer's case can be handled through one piece of correspondence instead of several, the savings for Lone Star are large.

REPORT 2. "A NEW BEGINNING FOR A NEW CENTURY"

Letter Of Transmittal

March 18, 1993

Mr. Lee Hills

Chairman

Board of Trustees

John S. and James L. Knight Foundation

2 South Biscayne Boulevard

Miami, FL 33131

Dear Mr. Hills,

On October 19, 1989, the Trustees of the John S. and James L. Knight Foundation, concerned that abuses in intercollegiate athletics threatened the integrity of higher education, created this Commission and directed it to propose a reform agenda for college sports. Following nearly 18 months of study, involving meetings with more than 90 athletes, educators, coaches, journalists and administrators, we submitted our recommendations in March 1991 in a report entitled Keeping Faith with the Student-Athlete: A New Model for Intercollegiate Athletics.

In that document and its successor, A Solid Start, *issued one year later, the Commission placed less emphasis on specific solutions for discrete abuses in college sports and more on establishing a structure for reform. We suggested what we called the "one-plus-three" model — presidential control directed toward academic integrity, financial integrity and independent certification — a kind of road map to guide academic officials as they grapple with difficult and complex problems in intercollegiate athletics. Our suggestions, confirmed by the*

"A New Beginning for a New Century," Report of the Knight Foundation Commission on Intercollegiate Athletics (March, 1993). Reprinted with permission.

Letter Of Transmittal

initiatives, the leaders of the nation's colleges and universities and the members of the NCAA have put reforms in place over the past three years that, in effect, establish the "one-plus-three" model.

We do not pretend that all of the problems of college sports are behind us. Human nature being what it is, athletics scandal will continue to leave its mark on some institutions. Moreover, the full effect of the reforms recently enacted will not be visible until the end of this decade. We are, however, confident that the "one-plus-three" model promises to curb abuse and offers a framework for addressing other pressing issues in intercollegiate athletics, including burgeoning costs and gender equity.

On behalf of the entire Commission, we express our appreciation to you and the members of the Foundation's board for your staunch support of this undertaking and your confidence in our ability to see it through. We also want to make special acknowledgment of the work of our staff director and his colleagues. Under the skilled leadership of Christopher Morris, the staff and consultants made splendid contributions to our effort.

Respectfully,

William C. Friday
Co-Chairman
President
William R. Kenan, Jr. Fund

Theodore M. Hesburgh, C.S.C.
Co-Chairman
President Emeritus
University of Notre Dame

John Biever

A New Beginning For A New Century

Tempted to believe the battle has been won because the framework is in place, presidents may turn their attention to other demands. That must not be allowed to happen. Optimism about the reforms must be tempered with realism. Reform is not a destination but a race without a finish.

A New Beginning For A New Century

"As our nation approaches a new century," the Knight Foundation Commission observed in 1991, "the demand for reform of intercollegiate athletics has escalated dramatically." Today, that escalating demand is being matched by accelerating reform. College and university presidents, along with the leaders and members of the National Collegiate Athletic Association (NCAA), have taken advantage of a swelling chorus for reform to make a new beginning in college sports. Although barely implemented today, the full effects of recent reforms will be visible as the 21st Century dawns.

The distance college sports have traveled in three short years can be measured by developments in public opinion. In 1989, pollster Louis Harris asked if big-time intercollegiate athletics were out of control. Across the United States, heads nodded in agreement: 78 percent of Americans thought that the situation was out of hand. In 1993, 52 percent of the public continued to agree. This significant 26-point decline represents how far college sports have come. The fact that about half of all Americans remain troubled represents the distance yet to go. Nevertheless, a new air of confidence is measurable and can be seen in other findings of the Harris survey: In 1989, nearly two-thirds of Americans believed state or national legislation was needed to control college sports; less than half feel that way today. Earlier negative views of the NCAA have turned into positive marks for its efforts to control excesses in college sports.

What accounts for the impressive turnaround in perceptions? The improvement is no accident, but a response to the highly visible pace of reform in recent years. Since 1989, college and university presidents, the members of the NCAA, and athletics leaders have addressed a single goal with singular concentration: restoring integrity to the games played in the university's name. They have created a structure of reform that can reshape the conduct, management and accountability of college sports. The new Harris poll tells us the American people are paying attention.

REFORMS OF RECENT YEARS

In 1991, this Commission proposed a new model for intercollegiate athletics, a kind of road map entitled "one-plus-three," in which the "one"— presidential control — would be directed toward the "three"— academic integrity, financial integrity and independent certification.

Such a model, this Commission believed, represented higher education's only real assurance that intercollegiate athletics could be grounded in the primacy of academic values. NCAA legislation in recent years has put this model in place.

These changes promise to reshape dramatically the environment for intercollegiate athletics. In 1989, the NCAA's Presidents Commission was tentative about how best to challenge the *status quo* in intercollegiate athletics. Established in 1984 as a compromise to a more ambitious effort to ensure presidential control of the NCAA, the Commission found itself five years later on the defensive. But by 1993, the Presidents Commission was in firm control of the Association's legislative agenda. Presidents Commission recommendations have dominated three successive NCAA conventions. With majorities of 3-1 or better, the Commission has pushed through preliminary cost reductions, new academic standards and an athletics certification program. Of even greater long-term significance, the 1993 legislation created an NCAA Joint Policy Board, made up of the Association's Administrative Committee and officers of the Presidents Commission, with authority to review the NCAA budget and legislative agenda and to evaluate and supervise the executive director. Presidential leadership is the hallmark of today's NCAA.

In 1989, student-athletes could compete in their first year of college if they had finished high school with a "C" average in 11 core academic subjects, along with combined Scholastic Aptitude Test scores of 700. This weak foundation, combined with lack of attention to academic progress, meant that, five years later, many student-athletes found themselves far short of a college degree. By 1995, eligibility to play in the freshman year will require a 2.5 high school grade point average ("C+" or "B-") in 13 high school academic units.* One year later the 13 units must include four years of English and one year each of algebra and geometry. Meanwhile, graduation rates for student-athletes are published annually and, effective this academic year, student-athletes must demonstrate continuous, satisfactory progress toward graduation: They are now required to meet annual benchmarks in both grades and coursework applicable to a specific degree. Academic integrity is being restored; student-athletes will now be students as well as athletes.

Three years ago, athletics finances were escalating beyond reason. Colleges and universities were in the midst of a kind of athletics arms race: Deficits mounted . . . the costs of grants-in-aid mushroomed . . . athletics budgets ballooned beyond institutional reach . . .

* Under a proposal adopted at the 1992 NCAA convention, initial eligibility requires that, by 1995, high school student-athletes present a 2.5 grade point average (out of a possible 4.0) in 13 core high school units, along with a combined SAT score of 700 (ACT score of 17) in order to compete in their first year of college enrollment. A sliding scale permits a higher aptitude test score to compensate for a lower grade point average, but no student-athlete can compete in the first year with SATs below 700 (ACT below 17), with a high school grade point average below 2.00, *or* with fewer than 13 of the core requirements.

and it was unclear who employed some "power" coaches, since their outside income often dwarfed university compensation. Today, the number of grants-in-aid for men in Divisions I and II of the NCAA has been reduced 10 percent; coaching staffs have been trimmed; athletics budgets are reviewed as part of a new certification process; cost containment is the subject of a major new study; and coaches must have annual written approval from their presidents for all athletically related outside income. Universities have made a start in restoring order to the financial side of the house of athletics.

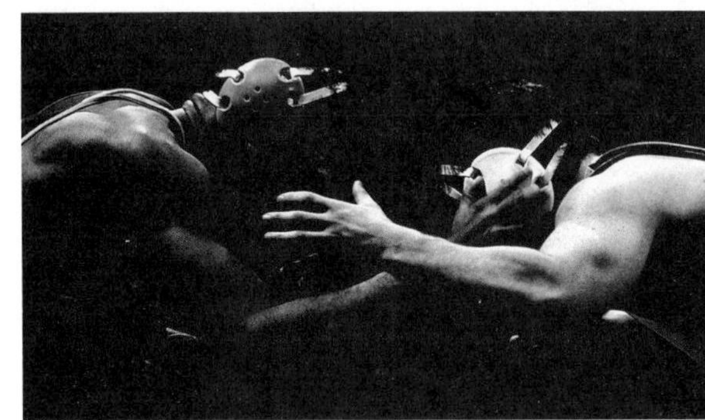

Finally, in 1989, too many big-time athletics programs had succeeded in imposing on universities a great reversal of ends and means. They had, this Commission found, become self-justifying enterprises in which winning-at-all-costs had pushed aside the educational context of athletics competition. Beginning this Fall, each NCAA Division I institution will have to participate in a certification program once every five years. This program requires each institution to examine four key areas — institutional mission, academic integrity, fiscal integrity, and commitment to equity — and (the most important factor) permit an external jury of academic and sports peers to evaluate and verify its findings. The new program promises to align means and ends.

The certification process is the capstone of the reform movement and will remain one of the movement's genuine legacies. Because it involves the entire campus community in a detailed examination of athletics policy issues, certification embodies the standards and values befitting higher education. By calling for regular self-examination of every corner of big-time programs under the bright light of outside peer review, certification should curb abuse before it starts, instead of after the damage has been done.

Meanwhile, on campuses and in conferences across the country, athletics and academic leaders have drawn new energy from the reform movement. Often using the "one-plus-three" model as their lens, presidentially appointed task forces, trustees and athletics boards have examined again the goals and operations of their athletics programs.

CHALLENGES AHEAD

This progress is encouraging, but the struggle for reform is far from won. Winning that struggle is what the "one-plus-three" model is all about. Academic and athletics officials now possess a new framework within which to tackle the many problems of college sports:

- abuses in recruiting, the bane of the college coach's life;
- the compulsion of boosters to meddle in athletics decision-making;
- the search for television revenues and the influence of the entertainment industry on intercollegiate athletics;
- the relationships among high school, junior college, college and professional sports;
- the need to respect the dignity of the young men and women who represent the university on the playing field;
- the obligation to further strengthen academic standards so that the profile of student-athletes matches that of other full-time undergraduates in admissions, academic progress and graduation rates; and
- the imperative to meet the needs of minority student-athletes, particularly those from backgrounds of inner-city or rural poverty.

As this Commission's tenure draws to a close, two great issues, cost containment and gender equity, dominate athletics policy discussions. These are first-order questions, significant problems requiring the best thinking of the nation's university and athletics leaders. Part of their complexity lies in the fact they are intertwined: Costs should not be controlled at the price of rebuffing women's aspirations. Opportunities for women must be provided in the context of controlling outlays for athletics programs that already cost too much. The cost control and equity dilemmas have to be addressed together.

The Cost Explosion. Despite recent modest reductions in athletics expenses, the hard work of cost reduction lies ahead. Quite apart from athletics, American higher education entered the 1990s facing its bleakest financial prospects since World War II. All institutions, including most flagship public and private universities, are in the midst of harrowing financial reductions, often involving staff and faculty layoffs, enrollment ceilings, and the elimination of academic departments. In this environment, athletics programs can expect no special immunity from the financial hardships facing the institutions they represent.

NCAA figures indicate that throughout the 1980s, athletics programs engaged in a financial arms race: Athletics costs grew twice as fast as academic salaries and three times faster than inflation. The urge to be nationally competitive, no matter the expense, assumed its own dynamic. Despite conventional wisdom, about 70 percent of Division I programs now lose money, many of them operating deeply in the red. It seems clear that athletics programs stand in need of the same kind of financial restructuring the larger academic community is already experiencing. On most campuses, athletics operating costs can be reduced substantially. But athletics programs will not disarm unilaterally. The active support of conferences and the NCAA is critical to effective cost control.

Gender Equity. Against the backdrop of the imperative for cost reduction, the unfinished agenda of equity for women also demands attention. Most campuses are struggling to meet the requirements of Title IX of the Education Amendments of 1972, even as case law defining those requirements is being made. In general, according to an NCAA study of gender equity study released in 1992, Title IX regulations call for accommodating the athletics interests of enrolled women, allocating financial assistance in proportion to the number of male and female participants, and making other benefits equivalent. Slowly, often in the face of opposition, opportunity for women to participate in intercollegiate athletics has become a reality.

But the opportunity is not truly equal. On many campuses, fans would be outraged if revenue-generating teams were expected to make do with the resources available to women. Even leaving out of the equation the major revenue-generating sports, football and men's basketball, women's programs generally operate on smaller budgets than men's. No matter the cause, the situation carries with it the threat of continued legal and Congressional scrutiny into whether young women are denied the benefits of participation in college sports.

The equity issue transcends athletics politics because it goes to the heart of what higher education is all about. Colleges and universities advance their intellectual mission by placing a premium on fairness, equality, competition and recognition of merit. These values are as important in the department of athletics as they are in the office of the dean. Keeping faith with student-athletes means keeping faith with women as well as men. The goal to keep in mind is the imperative to create comparable opportunities for participants, whether men or women, while controlling costs.

A PROMISE AND A CHOICE

If that goal is to be reached, the "one-plus-three" model advanced by this Commission will be put to a severe test. Tempted to believe the battle for reform has been won because the framework is in place, presidents may turn their attention to other demands. That must not be allowed to happen. Presidential neglect of these issues is a sure formula for giving ground on the progress already made.

This Commission believes the reforms enacted to date represent some of the most encouraging developments in intercollegiate athletics since the NCAA was established in 1906. But optimism about the reforms and their potential must be tempered with realism. Reform is not a destination but a never-ending process, a race without a finish. That is why the new NCAA certification program is so significant. By requiring presidents, trustees, faculty members, athletics administrators and coaches to examine the integrity of their sports programs every five years, certification keeps the process alive.

Maintaining the momentum for reform is important. The reforms of the last three years remain a promise yet to be kept: They will be implemented fully in 1995-96. This means that not a single student-athlete has yet entered and completed college under these changes. The first student-athletes to do so will graduate, at the earliest, in 1999. The certification program is ready to be launched, but it will not complete a full cycle of all Division I institutions before the 1998-99 school year. Making judgments today about the effects of these changes is premature; their real effects will appear at the end of the decade.

Moreover, no matter how deep-rooted reform is, it cannot transform human nature. Even with the new changes fully in place and working effectively, no one should be surprised when some institutions continue to be embarrassed by revelations about their athletics departments. People in college sports are like people everywhere: Most want to do the right thing; but some will try to skirt the rules, inevitably getting themselves, their associates and their institutions into trouble because, sooner or later, they will ignore the line dividing the acceptable from the unacceptable.

But realism should not give way to pessimism or cynicism. Cynics may dismiss the reform effort, but they do so at their own risk. Something fundamental has changed in college sports. It is perhaps best illustrated by support for the Presidents Commission reform agenda from coaches, athletics directors, conference leaders and faculty representatives. Because not everyone is ready for reform, this support is far from universal; nevertheless, it is impressive.

What has changed fundamentally is the following: The institutional indifference and presidential neglect that led to disturbing patterns of abuse throughout the 1980s have been replaced with a new structure insisting on institutional oversight and depending on presidential leadership backed up by trustee support. The leaders and members of the NCAA now have a framework for meaningful reform if they have the will, the courage and the perseverance to use it.

Along with that framework come new responsibilities. It was once possible for college sports administrators on the one hand, and university presidents and trustees, on the other, to evade responsibility for the difficulties of intercollegiate athletics. Each side could plausibly claim the other possessed the authority to act. That claim no longer holds water. The "one-plus-three" model places authority exactly where it belongs both in the councils of the NCAA and on individual campuses. Presidents today possess the power they need and, with the backing of their trustees, the responsibility to act.

The presidents of the nation's colleges and universities have reached a kind of Rubicon, a point of decision, with regard to their athletics programs. They face a choice about how to proceed, a choice between business as usual and making a new beginning.

Business as usual in college sports will undermine American higher education. It leads inexorably to regulation of intercollegiate athletics by the courts or Congress. That is a consequence no one wants, but many, unwittingly, may invite.

The second choice strengthens American higher education. The Harris poll convincingly demonstrates that the American people respect college sports when they are grounded in the larger mission of the university. As the United States approaches a new century, the new beginning represented by a strong "one-plus-three" model promises to restore higher education's moral claim to the high ground it should occupy.

These choices and their consequences are what is at stake in the athletics reform movement. The final words of the members of the Knight Foundation Commission on Intercollegiate Athletics to the leaders of the nation's colleges and universities are an echo from long ago. In 1929, the Carnegie Foundation for the Advancement of Teaching published a landmark study taking presidents to task for their failure to defend the integrity of higher education. There can be no doubt that presidents today have the opportunity to put that long-standing criticism to rest. A genuine assessment of the value of the current reform movement cannot be made by today's observers. The true test will be applied by historians of the future, because they will ask whether today's presidents employed their power wisely and chose well.

Creed C. Black
President, John S. and James L. Knight Foundation

Douglas S. Dibbert
General Alumni Association, University of North Carolina

John A. DiBiaggio
President, Tufts University

William C. Friday
President Emeritus, University of North Carolina

Thomas K. Hearn, Jr.
President, Wake Forest University

Theodore M. Hesburgh, C.S.C.
President Emeritus, University of Notre Dame

J. Lloyd Huck
Board of Trustees, Pennsylvania State University

Bryce Jordan
President Emeritus, Pennsylvania State University

Richard W. Kazmaier
President, Kazmaier Associates

Donald R. Keough
President, The Coca-Cola Company

Martin A. Massengale
President, University of Nebraska

The Honorable Tom McMillen
Former Member of Congress

Chase N. Peterson
President Emeritus, University of Utah

Jane C. Pfeiffer
Former Chair, National Broadcasting Company

A. Kenneth Pye
President, Southern Methodist University

Richard D. Schultz
Executive Director, National Collegiate Athletic Association

R. Gerald Turner
Chancellor, University of Mississippi

LeRoy T. Walker
President, United States Olympic Committee

James J. Whalen
President, Ithaca College

Charles E. Young
Chancellor, University of California, Los Angeles

The Knight Commission on Intercollegiate Athletics and the John S. and James L. Knight Foundation want to express their appreciation for the contributions of three distinguished educators who resigned from the Commission following their appointment by the President of the United States:

Honorable Lamar Alexander
President of the University of Tennessee
(appointed Secretary of Education by President Bush in December 1990)

Honorable Donna E. Shalala
Chancellor, University of Wisconsin-Madison
(appointed Secretary of Health and Human Services by President Clinton in January 1993)

Honorable Clifton R. Wharton, Jr
Chairman and CEO, TIAA-CREF
(appointed Deputy Secretary of State by President Clinton in January 1993)

Damian Strohmeyer

Statement of Principles

Statement of Principles

Preamble: This institution is committed to a philosophy of firm institutional control of athletics, to the unquestioned academic and financial integrity of our athletics program, and to the accountability of the athletics department to the values and goals befitting higher education. In support of that commitment, the board, officers, faculty and staff of this institution have examined and agreed to the following general principles as a guide to our participation in intercollegiate athletics:

I. The educational values, practices and mission of this institution determine the standards by which we conduct our intercollegiate athletics program.

II. The responsibility and authority for the administration of the athletics department, including all basic policies, personnel and finances, are vested in the president.

III. The welfare, health and safety of student-athletes are primary concerns of athletics administration on this campus. This institution will provide student-athletes with the opportunity for academic experiences as close as possible to the experiences of their classmates.

IV. Every student-athlete — male and female, majority and minority, in all sports — will receive equitable and fair treatment.

V. The admission of student-athletes — including junior college transfers — will be based on their showing reasonable promise of being successful in a course of study leading to an academic degree. That judgment will be made by admissions officials.

VI. Continuing eligibility to participate in intercollegiate athletics will be based on students being able to demonstrate each academic term that they will graduate within five years of their enrolling. Students who do not pass this test will not play.

VII. Student-athletes, in each sport, will be graduated in at least the same proportion as non-athletes who have spent comparable time as full-time students.

VIII. All funds raised and spent in connection with intercollegiate athletics programs will be channeled through the institution's general treasury, not through independent groups, whether internal or external. The athletics department budget will be developed and monitored in accordance with general budgeting procedures on campus.

IX. All athletics-related income from non-university sources for coaches and athletics administrators will be reviewed and approved by the university. In cases where the income involves the university's functions, facilities or name, contracts will be negotiated with the institution.

X. Annual academic and fiscal audits of the athletics program will be conducted. Moreover, this institution intends to seek NCAA certification that its athletics program complies with the principles herein. This institution will promptly correct any deficiencies and will conduct its athletics program in a manner worthy of this distinction.

Acknowledgements

STAFF

Christopher "Kit" Morris
Staff Director

Maureen Devlin
Associate Director

Roger Valdiserri
Executive Assistant to Fr. Hesburgh

Bryan Skelton
Administrative Assistant

CONSULTANTS

Jack Griffin
Hill & Knowlton, New York, N.Y.

Louis Harris
LH Research, New York, N.Y.

James Harvey
Harvey & Associates, Washington, D.C.

Tom Ross
Hill & Knowlton, New York, N.Y.

APPENDIX C

ANSWERS TO EXERCISES IN CHAPTER 11

ANSWERS TO EXERCISES IN CHAPTER 11

The Convention Travel Report Errors (page 361)

1. Sir: There are many different formats for memoranda, but in formal correspondence, a colon should follow *sir,* not a comma. However, since this correspondence follows the standard memo format the word should be omitted.
2. In compliance with: This is an overused expression that can be stated much more succinctly—that is, *as directed* or *as requested.*
3. I have attended: The simple past tense should be used here.
4. Memorandum is submitted: Using the passive voice robs good writing of forcefulness.
5. For your perusal: Another trite expression that should be eliminated. The boss already knows the memorandum was written for him to read.
6. Convention discussed: Things do not discuss; people discuss.
7. Three main topics: Use a colon instead of a dash to introduce a series.
8. DIA's: Acronyms can be very confusing; they should be spelled on first use in a body of writing.
9. Interferance: Misspelled.
10. Companies: This word is the possessive of *companies* and should be followed by an apostrophe. Another way to correct this is to use an *of* phrase rather than an apostrophe, as is shown in the corrected draft.
11. OSHA's: Another unexplained acronym. Although her boss would probably understand, it is better to spell it out the first time.
12. The fact that: This phrase is always unnecessary.
13. Rivetting: Misspelled.
14. For quality control purposes and: "To make sure it meets their requirements" restates "quality control."
15. First off: This phrase is grammatically incorrect and unnecessary.
16. Fed's: The recipient of this report is not the Godfather. Slang has no place in business writing.
17. Full of baloney: Archaic slang is even worse!
18. One hundred and fifty million: Do not use "and" between the parts of a large whole number. Also, when referring to dollars, figures and the "$" sign are preferred (that is, $150,000,000 or $150 million).
19. Were stolen: The subject of this phrase, *equipment,* requires a singular verb.
20. And: Do not begin a sentence with a conjunction.
21. More was destroyed: "More" what? The reference here is unclear.
22. I know: Personal references have no place in formal memoranda. The boss may not care about the opinion of an uninformed junior executive.
23. Never: Double negative.
24. More strict: This comparative expression is unclear. As used, it could mean either more standards or stricter standards.
25. Deleteriously: Use a shorter, more common word if no sense of meaning is lost.

26. Impact on: Unless the writer thinks the standards will physically collide with the plans, she should delete the superfluous one.
27. Their: A common misuse of the intended *they're.* Writing out the contraction can avoid this mistake. Better yet, make the reference clearer as in the corrected example.
28. dBh: An unexplained abbreviation.
29. Has me worried; : The writer injects a personal opinion again. Also, the following conjunction, *but,* requires a comma, not a semicolon.
30. About it: This phrase is unnecessary.
31. To much: This is a common mistake—using a preposition when an adverb is intended. This is also the wrong form of the word *to.*
32. Point in time: Made popular several years ago in the Watergate proceedings, this phrase is ridiculously superfluous.
33. Rivets is: The verb must agree with the subject.
34. Though: When used as conjunction, *though* should introduce a dependent clause.
35. Principle problem: The word *principle* is a noun meaning a fundamental truth, rule of conduct, source, origin. The word *principal* can be a noun or an adjective; as the latter it means chief, leading, highest in rank or importance. *Principal,* the adjective, should be used here.
36. Inspect everyone: The reference of *everyone* is vague and needs to be more defined.
37. Aeorospace Industry: There are three errors here: *aerospace* is misspelled, the words do not need to be capitalized, and *government* should not be hyphenated.
38. We're: By using *we* instead of *they,* the writer shifts her point of view from *everyone* and implies an improper meaning.
39. Our men and girls: These are sexist terms and should be made neutral.
40. Backing, during: This comma is unnecessary.
41. Affects: The noun should be *effects.*
42. Disasterous: Misspelled.
43. Well: Use of *well* in this sense is too informal.
44. After rivets: This is poor construction. The writer means to say "after the subject of rivets was discussed."
45. Completely finished: The word *completely* is superfluous.
46. For the purpose of: Trite expression.
47. Quantifying: Improper use of an impressive-sounding verb.
48. Goals and objectives: Superfluous.
49. Viable alternatives: Overused expression.
50. Resounding success: This is a weak and overused phrase.
51. Respectively: A misused word. The writer means to say *Respectfully.*

To: George Harris,
Vice-President in Charge of Policy

From: Beth Williams, BW
Government Relations Division

Date: 5/5/94

Subject: Convention Report

As directed, I recently attended the convention "Government Regulations in the Aerospace Industry." The discussion involved three main topics: interference of the Defense Intelligence Agency in the internal security programs of companies, noise exposure standards of the Occupational Safety and Health Administration (OSHA), and the U.S. government's quality control inspections of the new Teflon riveting technique.

The federal delegate's presentation on internal security was illuminating. He stated that last year spies stole microprocessing equipment worth $150,000,000. Even more equipment was destroyed by espionage.

OSHA's decision to impose stricter noise exposure standards could severely impact our production plans. OSHA is considering requiring 90 decibels per hour exposure limits, which, according to our production planners, could be a long-range problem for us.

The special rivets are another matter, however. The principal problem with the rivets is that they shear off at high altitudes, so to insure safety the government plans to inspect all companies in the aerospace industry. Federal stress engineers propose our workers reinforce their rivets with a steel backing during airframe assembly. Otherwise, the effects on high-altitude test flights could be disastrous.

The discussion concerning rivets concluded the convention. All the delegates agreed the goal of improving industry relations with the government was achieved.

The Corrected Travel Report Memo
Source: Timothy Riggins.

Eliminate Unneeded Words Exercise (pages 385–386)

Practice 1 (48 words)

In order to keep you informed of the results of the sales meeting held on August 13 to consider ways and means of reducing the cost of the proposed spring sales campaign, we are submitting herewith a brief resume and the procedure outlined for the cost reduction plans.

Sample Answer (21 words)

Here is a resume of plans, drawn at the August 13 meeting, for cutting costs on the proposed spring sales campaign.

Practice 2 (36 words)

Memoranda intended for internal distribution should be written just as carefully as those to be distributed outside of the division, and, actually, they serve as an excellent opportunity for developing an individual's proficiency in writing.

Sample Answer (24 words)

Write memoranda for use within a division as carefully as those sent outside. They give you a good chance to build your writing skill.

Active Voice Exercise (page 385)

1. *(Passive)* A sharp decrease in sales was noted.
   (Active) Sales decreased sharply.
2. *(Passive)* The department is dependent on our aid for its success.
   (Active) The department's success depends on our aid.
3. *(Passive)* It is desired by the president that this problem be brought before the board of directors.
   (Active) The president desires that this problem be brought before the board of directors.

Answers to Misused Words Exercise (page 385)

1. We shall be seriously effected by the new corporate policy.
   The verb should be *affected.* Effect, as a verb, means to bring about. When used as a noun it means result. The word affect means to influence.
2. The amount of conventioners who come to New York City varies with the season.
   The correct word is *number,* which refers to countable units. The word amount refers to general quantity.
3. We shall appreciate your advising us of your decision.
   The proper word is *notifying.* Advising means to give advice.
4. The estate was divided between the millionaire's three sons.
   The correct word is *among,* which refers to three or more units. *Between* is used when referring to only two units.
5. Can we have your permission to proceed with the instructions outlined in this letter?
   The correct word is *may. May* denotes permission, *can* denotes ability.

Answers to Problem Sentences Exercises (page 386)

1. Divided into two sections, the accountant balances the accounts more readily.
   Error: Dangling participle
   Corrected: Divided into two sections, the accounts are more readily balanced by the accountant.
2. Depreciation accounting is not a system of valuation but of allocation.
   Error: Misplaced modifier
   Corrected: Depreciation accounting is a system not of valuation but of allocation.

3. To form an opinion as to the collectibility of the accounts, they were reviewed with the credit manager.
   Error: Dangling infinitive
   Corrected: To form an opinion as to the collectibility of the accounts, we reviewed them with the credit manager.
4. This problem can only be allievated by a change in policy.
   Error: Misplaced modifier
   Corrected: This problem can be alleviated only by a change in policy.
5. Bob Smith's interest and devotion to his work are not to be questioned.
   Error: Omission of a preposition
   Corrected: Bob Smith's interest in and devotion to his work are not to be questioned.

Answers to Spelling Errors Exercise (page 386)

1. semi-annual	incorrect	semiannual
2. occurrance	incorrect	occurrence
3. facimile	incorrect	facsimile
4. supercede	incorrect	supersede
5. government	correct	
6. disasterous	incorrect	disastrous
7. proceedure	incorrect	procedure
8. defecit	incorrect	deficit
9. permissable	incorrect	permissible
10. prevalant	incorrect	prevalent
11. irrelevant	correct	
12. questionaire	incorrect	questionnaire
13. promissary	incorrect	promissory
14. preferance	incorrect	preference
15. maintainence	incorrect	maintenance

APPENDIX D

SAMPLE PRESENTATIONS

This appendix presents eight sample speeches, each with a different pattern of organization (see discussion on pages 257–258 of Chapter 8). All present a variety of types of verbal supporting material (pages 258–264).

Topic: HISTORY OF HBO
Purpose: To inform (chronological pattern)
Specific purpose: To share both the impact HBO has made to the cable industry and the industry challenges it faces in the 1990s.

Introduction

A. Twenty-two years ago television displayed the smallness of our planet with the astronauts' first trip to the moon.
B. A few years later HBO magnified our earth's smallness when it became the first television network to broadcast programming via satellite.
C. This revolutionized the cable TV industry and affected the business plans of many industries.

Body

I. HBO overcame two hurdles in the late 1970s and early 1980s.
   A. The best method of delivering HBO programming
      1. Bicycling programs of film/tape
      2. Microwave transmission
      3. Satellite delivery
   B. The FCC ruled on tightly restricted cable TV programming.
      1. Rules founded on fear
      2. Cable systems could not show movies between three and ten years old.
      3. FCC imposed complex restrictions on televising of sports.
   C. HBO finally freed to carry movies/sports events.

II. HBO programming in mid-1980s
   A. Programming fueled HBO's growth.
      1. Relationships built with top performers
      2. Uncut/original movies offered
   B. The VCR became HBO's new marketing challenge.
      1. Movies drove pay-TV business prior to HBO.
      2. Analyst predicted the VCR would have major impact on pay-TV.
         a. HBO added over 4 million subscribers since 1984.
         b. HBO produced original movies for subscribers.

III. Challenges facing HBO and cable industry in 1990s
   A. Basic cable growth has slowed.
   B. Basic rates have risen.
   C. Competing technologies have emerged.
      1. Direct Broadcast Satellite

(continued)

(continued)

   2. Microwave (MMDS)
   3. Pay-per-view
   4. Multiport
D. Competing industries
   1. Telephone companies allowed to sell cable
   2. Congress approved legislation in 1992
E. Congress/FCC may re-regulate cable rates.

Conclusion

A. HBO is well positioned for the future and will continue to look at innovative ways to market and program for consumers.
   1. Marketing is a primary challenge
   2. Big-event strategy
   3. Image advertising
   4. Retention focus
B. Show image spot

EXHIBIT D.1 Chronological Presentation Format

Source: A presentation outline prepared by Mary Jo Crow in the Edwin L. Cox School of Business, Southern Methodist University, Dallas, Texas.

Topic: DIAMONDS
Purpose: To inform (comparative pattern)
Specific purpose: To explain the different comparisons that must be made when buying a diamond.

Introduction

A. You've heard that diamonds are a girl's best friend. Most women hope to someday have a diamond. Today I am here to tell both you men and women what to consider when buying a diamond.
B. This information is important so you will get the most from your investment.
C. Making comparisons is critical as you consider this important investment.

Body

I. Definition of a diamond: hardest known mineral, formed of crystalline carbon, transparent and colorless, valued as a precious stone.

II. Compare shape and size
   A. Round
   B. Marquis
   C. Pear
   D. Square
   E. Oval
   F. Heart
   G. Large
   H. Small

III. Compare color
   A. Top silver cape
   B. Fine top silver cape
   C. Very fine top silver cape
   D. No color
   E. Blue white

IV. Compare flaws
   A. Bubble
   B. Ice
   C. Hairlike cracks
   D. Feathers
   E. Carbon spots
   F. Clouds

(continued)

(continued)

V. Compare weight
   A. Until 1913, no two countries had exactly the same measure for measuring the weight of diamonds.
   B. A carat weighs exactly one-fifth of a gram, as standardized by the United States. There are 100 points to the carat.

VI. Compare price
   A. Don't be swayed by the "good investment" argument.
   B. Anxiety over debt at the outset of a marriage is one sure hindrance to a good start.
   C. Average-size engagement ring of good quality runs $1,000 and up.

Conclusion

A. I have given you a brief explanation of the five comparisons that should be made when buying a diamond. Remember, the diamond you select must be considered in relation to how much you can spend. Compromises usually must be made. Good luck and happy diamond buying.

EXHIBIT D.2 Comparative Presentation Format

Source: A presentation outline prepared by Julie Jordin in the Edwin L. Cox School of Business, Southern Methodist University, Dallas, Texas.

Topic: THE TRADING OF COMMODITY FUTURES
Purpose: To inform (topical pattern)
Specific purpose: To explain the different positions a trader can take in the futures market.

Introduction

A. I will tell you how to triple your money in a matter of weeks.
B. Commodity futures trading is a speculative investment to some traders. To other traders, it is a hedge against rising prices on the commodity they use in their business.
C. There are three basic positions a trader can take in trading futures.

Body

I. Long position
   A. Definition of *going long*
   B. When to go long
   C. What factors influence a trader to go long
   D. Receiving the commodity

II. Short position
   A. Definition of *going short*
   B. When to go short
   C. What factors influence a trader to go short
   D. Delivering the commodity

III. Hedging
   A. Definition of a *hedge*
   B. Uses of hedging
   C. Receiving the commodity

Conclusion

A. I have described the positions a trader can take in the commodity futures market.
B. It is possible to triple your money in the futures market. However, the odds are far greater that you will not. Unless you are a person who is willing to chance your money at 20 to 1 odds, you should not speculate in the commodity futures market. But if you are willing to take that chance, commodities can be a fast way to get rich.

EXHIBIT D.3 Topical Presentation Format
Source: A presentation outline prepared by Michael Merriman, in the Edwin L. Cox School of Business, Southern Methodist University, Dallas, Texas.

Topic: HAZARDOUS MATERIALS CLASSIFICATION
Purpose: To inform (classification pattern)
Specific purpose: To inform new materials managers how to interpret hazardous material classification using the National Fire Protection Association (NFPA) 704 system.

Introduction

A. Four classifications of hazardous materials:
   1. Extremely hazardous substances
   2. Hazardous substances
   3. Hazardous chemicals
   4. Toxic chemicals
B. Regulations promulgated by government agencies
   1. Environmental Protection Agency (EPA)
   2. Department of Transportation (DOT)
   3. Occupational Safety and Health Administration (OSHA)
C. Three organizations provide information on hazardous materials classification
   1. Department of Transportation (DOT)
   2. Manufacturing Chemists Association (MCA)
   3. National Fire Protection Association (NFPA)
D. With this background in mind, my goal is to inform you on how to recognize, classify, and determine the relative degree of hazard associated with any hazardous material that is labeled in accordance with the NFPA system.

Body

I. The NFPA system was designed for emergency response personnel. Key benefits of the system are:
   A. Label is easily recognized
   B. Classification scheme is logical
   C. This is a simple system to learn and use

II. Hazard recognition
   A. System uses diamond shaped figure
   B. Diamond is subdivided into four quadrants, each representing a different hazard category
   C. Each quadrant has unique color and spatial representation

III. Hazard classification
   A. Health Hazard—Property of material which can directly or indirectly cause injury or incapacitation.
      1. Designated by blue color
      2. Spatial representation—left quadrant

(continued)

B. Fire Hazard—Property of material that supports combustion.
   1. Designated by red color
   2. Spatial representation—top quadrant

C. Reactivity or stability hazard—property of material that can enter into chemical reaction with other stable or unstable materials.
   1. Designated by yellow color
   2. Spatial representation—right quadrant

D. Specific hazards—Unique property of material may cause special problems.
   1. Designated by symbols
   2. Spatial representation-lower quadrant

IV. Hazard determination

A. Each category of hazard is assigned a relative ranking commensurate with the degree of risk associated with a particular compound or element.

B. The relative degree of hazard is based on scale from "zero" to "four" with "zero" little or no hazard while "four" represents a severe hazard.

Conclusion

A. An example utilizing specific hazard field.

B. The NFPA system provides a simple way for inexperienced personnel to become aware of potential degrees of hazards of various materials.

C. For your convenience, I am giving you a wallet size NFPA classification guide.

D. Can I answer any questions?

EXHIBIT D.4 Classification Presentation Format

Source: A presentation outline prepared by Paul Corwin in the Edwin L. Cox School of Business, Southern Methodist University, Dallas, Texas.

Topic: BUILDING A 4-COLOR PRINT ADVERTISEMENT
Purpose: To inform (sequential pattern)
Specific purpose: To describe the information business managers need in discussing the 4 basic steps of ad building preparation, production, printing, and publishing.

Introduction

A. Boardroom scenario: advertising manager asks new MBA a question in "adver-lingo" he doesn't understand. MBA panics.
B. I will tell you how to avoid embarrassment at your first advertising meeting.
C. The 4 P's to building an ad: prepare, produce, print and publish.

Body

I. Prepare the promotion
   A. Client's marketing manager requests an ad or promotion from the agency.
   B. Account executive fills out creative workorder including background and details of the ad.
   C. Creative team (art director and copy writer) develops copy and layout for the ad.
      —Account coordinator then sends copy and layout to client for approval.
   D. When creative is approved account coordinator generates job estimate from 3 sources:
      1. Agency studio manager
      2. Print production coordinator
      3. Art buyer
   E. Final estimate is sent to client for approval.

II. Produce the ad
   A. Art buyer or art director commissions photographer to shoot pictures and send to agency for selection and approval.
   B. Account coordinator builds job jacket and enters it in the studio.
      1. Typesetting sets type.
      2. Proofreader and art director check type for errors.
   C. Mechanical is built.
      1. Camera operator shoots stats of photography and logos to size.
      2. Mechanical artist assembles ad with type and stats.
      3. Mechanical is proofread.
   D. Account coordinator photocopies mechanical and sends to client for approval.

(continued)

IV. Print the ad
   A. Account coordinator attaches a job legend to the mechanical and gives it to the print production manager.
      1. Transparency or slide is sent to color separator for separations to ad size.
         a. Color proof is sent to agency for approval.
      2. Film and mechanical are sent to printer.
         a. Printer sends cromalyn proof back to agency for approval.

V. Publish the ad
   A. Printer sends camera-ready film of finished ad to the publication.
      1. The ad appears in the designated issue of the publication.

Conclusion

   A. Repeat the 4 basic steps to ad building.
   B. You may not be experts or want to work in advertising, but you have all you need to bluff your way through your next meeting.
   C. If nothing more, the audience will never look at an ad the same way again.

EXHIBIT D.5 Sequential Presentation Format

Source: A presentation outline prepared by Amy Landess, in the Edwin L. Cox School of Business, Southern Methodist University, Dallas, Texas.

Topic: MONEY MARKET MUTUAL FUNDS
Purpose: To persuade (advantage/disadvantage pattern)
Specific purpose: To define money market mutual fund investments, to explain how they work, and to list their advantages over regular savings accounts.

Introduction

A. I can tell you how to earn twice as much interest on your savings.
B. The Federal Reserve prohibits your bank from paying you more than 5½% interest on passbook savings.
C. A money market mutual fund can earn you 7% on your savings.

Body

I. Money market mutual fund defined
   A. It is a trust etablished by an investment company.
   B. A mutual fund allows investment in high-yield securities.
   C. It is an old stock market practice for inactive holdings.
   D. A large amount is typically needed for eligibility ($500–$5,000).

II. New interest
   A. Presently seventy-five funds hold approximately $40 billion.
   B. $175 million go into the funds each day.
   C. Even interest of 7.00% cannot keep up with anticipated inflation.

III. Disadvantages
   A. Many money market funds require $5,000 to invest.
   B. Inflation may go above 7%.
   C. The attractiveness of these funds has shifted money out of banks and savings and loans.

IV. Advantages
   A. A current return on your savings as high as 7%.
   B. You invest in high-quality paper and Treasury bills: low risk.
   C. The investor is given exceptional liquidity.

Conclusion

A. If you are looking for an investment with high returns and little or no risk, then I suggest money market mutual funds.

EXHIBIT D.6 Advantage/Disadvantage Presentation Format
Source: A presentation outline prepared by Todd Winter in the Edwin L. Cox School of Business, Southern Methodist University, Dallas, Texas.

Topic: MINIMIZING STRESS
Purpose: To persuade (cause/effect pattern)
Specific purpose: To prove the need for recreation to help minimize stress

Introduction

A. "What is the greatest need of the human mind today?" The answer is "relaxation."
B. Stress is a prevalent problem in our society.
C. I will prove why stress needs to be minimized, how recreation can minimize it, and how to best utilize recreation.

Body

I. Stress needs to be minimized.
   A. Stress is suffered increasingly in our fast-paced modern world.
   B. Excessive stress is a major symptom of neurosis.
   C. Stress can get you into a rut.

II. Recreation helps minimize stress.
   A. *Recreation:* the word means re-creation.
   B. Recreation is a "tactical retreat."
   C. Recreation relaxes you and enables you to have fun.

III. Recreation is best utilized the following ways:
   A. Relearn to play.
   B. Do things you like to do.
   C. Develop work/play contingencies.
   D. Set reasonable goals.

Conclusion

A. I hope you realize that excessive stress is definitely a problem in our fast-paced society and must be curbed.
B. Recreation is one easy and fun way to minimize stress, allowing you to escape work and return to it feeling refreshed and more productive.

EXHIBIT D.7 Cause/Effect Presentation Format
Source: A presentation outline prepared by Diane Reddington, in the Edwin L. Cox School of Business, Southern Methodist University, Dallas, Texas.

Topic:	CHILD CARE AS A BOTTOM LINE FOR BUSINESS
Purpose:	To persuade (group presentation using problem/solution pattern)
Specific Purpose:	To persuade your company to consider voluntarily adding child care benefits and services to your current employment package.
Overriding Objective:	To persuade business executives to take an active role in providing child care benefits for their employees.
Objective 1:	To support and reinforce awareness of child care issues by: addressing demographic changes in the workforce, defining child care considerations, and outlining elements of quality child care programs
Objective 2:	To describe the child care benefits and services available that business can select in implementing a child care plan
Objective 3:	To provide examples of companies with successful child care programs and to explain the early steps in establishing a child care program in business

Person 1 — Introduction

A. Story of supervisor denying emergency leave to employee experiencing child care problems.
B. Employee's options
C. Company's potential options
D. Why child care should be a concern of business
   1. General employer concerns for providing benefits and services
      a. Equity
      b. Applicability
      c. Liability
      d. Cost
   2. Employer has responsibility toward employees' child care needs.
      a. How child care issues affect employers
      b. Employers' methods of treatment
   3. Recent changes in the labor pool
      a. Employers no longer have luxury of unlimited pool.
      b. Employee growth will slow in coming decade.
      c. Women will comprise 65% of the smaller labor pool.
   4. IBM: one company taking action
   5. What about your company?
   6. Overview of presentation

Person 2 — Body

I. Demographic changes in the workplace
   A. Review demographic trends
   B. Present additional facts pertaining to families

(continued)

II. Types of child care considerations
   A. Types of arrangements
   B. Review of child care user statistics
III. Elements of a quality child care program
   A. Elements of quality child care programs
   B. Problems facing employers
   C. The importance of a high-quality child care program
   D. Educational, employment, and societal benefits provided by high-quality programs

Person 3

IV. Child care assisted options and tax benefits available to the employer
   A. Options
      1. Benefits and flexibility programs
      2. Financial assistance
      3. Creating or supporting services
      4. Families with special needs
   B. Tax benefits
      1. Ordinary business expense
      2. Charitable contributions
      3. Tax-exempt organizations
      4. Start-up expense and depreciation
      5. Dependent care expenses

Person 4

V. Examples of successful child care programs
   A. Merck & Co. . . . lowered annual employee turnover
   B. Campbell Soup Co. . . . recruitment
   C. NCNB . . . turnover and recruitment
   D. California utility . . . reduced medical costs, lowered absenteeism, and raised morale
   E. A local law firm . . . employee loyalty raised and job stress lowered

VI. Early steps in providing child care benefits and services
   A. Survey employees regarding child care needs and present uses
   B. Design program that addresses the survey results
   C. Relate child care choice to management objectives
   D. Explore community resources

Conclusion

   A. Child care needs are not employer's sole responsibility.
   B. All sectors of society must share in investment.
   C. Will your company begin the process for providing child care benefits and services?

EXHIBIT D.8 Problem/Solution Presentation Format

Source: A presentation outline prepared by Betty Harris, Paul Corwin, Lewis Cox, and Barbara O'Neal in the Edwin L. Cox School of Business, Southern Methodist University, Dallas, Texas.

APPENDIX E

COMPREHENSIVE CASE

This appendix presents a case that comprehensively covers the theories from each chapter in the text.

This case was prepared by Benjamin Regalado, graduate student, under the supervision of Dr. Robert Rasberry, Edwin L. Cox School of Business, Southern Methodist University, as a basis for class discussion and is not designed to illustrate the effective or ineffective handling of administrative situations.

National Aeronautics and Space Administration: "WHEN MACHINE MEETS MAN: THE SPACE SHUTTLE *CHALLENGER* DISASTER"

January 28, 1986 dawned bright yet crisp on the eastern Florida coast, with soft breezes and a temperature slightly below freezing.

Poised on Cape Canaveral launch pad 39B was the Space Shuttle Challenger, one of the four reusable spacecraft of the United States. Challenger had flown nine times before, and flight 51-L, the 25th shuttle mission, seemed part of the routine.

On board was an all-American crew. Francis R. "Dick" Scobee was commander, already a shuttle mission veteran. Michael Smith, the pilot, was on his first. The three mission specialists, Ellison Onizuka, Judith Resnik and Ronald McNair, each had flown on a shuttle before. Gregory Jarvis and Christa McAuliffe rounded out the crew as payload specialists.

Jarvis was not an astronaut, but a representative of the Hughes Corporation. McAuliffe managed a unique payload—the hopes and dreams of millions of American students. She was neither a scientist nor an engineer, but a teacher from Concord, New Hampshire, selected from 11,000 applicants as the "Teacher in Space." During the mission she would broadcast live to American children lessons on space.

By 8:45 a.m. the crew was secured in the cabin of the orbiter, preparing for the scheduled 9:38 a.m. launch. It was not the first time. Mission 51-L was originally to have launched six days before, but the late launch of Mission 61-C pushed the timetable back to January 25, then 26. Unacceptable weather conditions at the alternative landing site, should the shuttle need to return to earth immediately, delayed the flight until the 27th when, crew on board, heavy crosswinds and a faulty hatch handle forced the fourth postponement.

But despite the cold weather this day seemed perfect. Concern about icing on the launch pad delayed the launch two hours, but at 11:15 a.m. the crew was given a "go" for launch. All prelaunch events proceeded smoothly, and at 11:38 a.m. flight 51-L cleared the launch pad.

The liftoff was glorious, not unlike the flights before it. Steve Nesbitt, a NASA commentator in Houston, narrated the flight from the launch pad through its roll program. Fifty-two seconds into the flight, *Challenger* was told to go "throttle up." Seventy seconds into the flight, Commander Scobee calmly confirmed the flight status.

Three seconds later, ground spectators saw a sudden and puzzling large puff of smoke and vapor from the shuttle, already at 46,000 feet. An instant later, the two solid rocket boosters emerged alone from the smoke and vapor cloud, out of control. *Challenger* could not be seen any-

(continued)

(continued)

where. As the seconds crept by, it became apparent that something very serious had happened.

The space shuttle had exploded.

Space Shuttles Don't Explode

The *Challenger* accident stunned a nation that had come to regard shuttle flights as routine. President Ronald Reagan postponed that evening's planned State of the Union address as the nation mourned its first in-flight space disaster.

A week later, President Reagan appointed the Presidential Commission on the Space Shuttle Challenger Accident to investigate the cause of the disaster. The commission, chaired by former Secretary of State William Rogers, had as members physics and aerospace experts, including Chuck Yeager, the first person to cross the sound barrier in flight, Neil Armstrong, the first person to set foot on the moon, and Sally Ride, the first American woman in space. Four months after the accident, the Commission disclosed the results of its investigation.

Officially, the accident was blamed on a failure of the O-rings on the right solid rocket booster. These slightly larger than a quarter-inch in diameter rubber "rings" were part of a design to keep superheated gases from escaping at the booster assembly joints. The cold launch temperatures had prevented the ring from properly blocking the gases. The pressure of the gases broke the booster away from its bottom attachment to the external fuel tank, and it collided with the external tank at the top. The explosive combination of liquid hydrogen and liquid oxygen blew the external tank apart, and the aerodynamic stresses shattered the orbiter like a plastic toy.

The Commission did not stop at the mechanical cause, however, when it noted contributing causes to the accident. It concluded that the launch decision process was flawed, pressuring for a launch at the possible expense of safety. Many in the system knew about the possibility for O-ring failure. However, other flights had been successful, and any risk seemed minimal. It appeared man had not met his ultimate match in machine—he still had control.

The Proud History of NASA

The National Aeronautics and Space Administration had a long history of triumphs, and in early 1986 some believed it had added another with an operational space shuttle program. Mission 51-L in particular would prove that a common citizen, a teacher whom many Americans could identify with, could go into space. NASA believed it needed to demonstrate that a common citizen could go into space, however, because it desperately needed the attention of the American people.[1]

When President John F. Kennedy challenged NASA in the early 1960s to put a man on the moon by the end of the decade, NASA and the na-

(continued)

tion committed themselves to the task. Five months before 1970 began, the dedication paid off—NASA accomplished its goal. But after the moon shots ended, NASA began to drift. Some argued that no President after Kennedy had an agenda for NASA and for space.[2] At the time of the accident, the agency director was on leave to fight charges of overcharging the government on contracts while he was head of General Dynamics.[3]

It was not as if the shuttle program was a failure. But support began to waver in Congress, where budget cuts were a constant topic, and in the public, which began to perceive shuttle missions as routine. Even television networks, which covered early launches live, now only commented on a launch in the evening newscast.[4] Interest was up for flight 51-L, though, because of the culmination of the Teacher in Space Program.

However, it seemed the shuttle program emphasis, if it ever had a formal one, had changed. Bruce Murray, former director of the NASA Jet Propulsion Laboratory, stated, "The shuttle has become a substitute goal instead of a means of attaining a goal."[5] Ohio Senator John Glenn, who also was the first American in space, remarked on a more global change in NASA, from a "can do" attitude to one of "can't fail."[6]

Attitudes are not formed overnight, but developed over time. The "can't fail" attitude may have resulted from pressures that NASA and others placed on the shuttle program. Although the Commission concluded otherwise, these pressures may, over the long term, have contributed to a launch decision.

To accommodate customers, NASA was willing to change the shuttle manifests, be it for hardware problems, operational constraints, or two members of Congress. In the launch planning cycle, such a change should have forced the cycle to begin again. In some cases it did not, and was even accelerated to meet the launch schedule. Crew simulator training often began after the normal starting point, 11 weeks prior to launch, had passed.

In addition, there was pressure to achieve operational, or routine, status for the shuttle flights. Instead of concentrating on one flight at a time, as NASA had during the moon shots, the same resources were applied over several shuttle flights. The "can't fail" goal of 15 shuttle missions during fiscal 1986 would sacrifice both quality and personnel.

Spare parts often were cannibalized because NASA's inventory was only two-thirds of what it needed to be in operational conditions. Payload safety suffered as well, and it became difficult to analyze and reap the benefits from one flight experience before another was launched.[7]

No matter how things were going inside NASA, the outside world saw a different picture. Public relations had been regarded as one of NASA's strongest areas, but as the shuttle program became routine, the lime-

(continued)

(continued)

light faded. What NASA needed was something to again capture the nation's imagination, and with help from President Reagan, it developed the Teacher in Space Program to keep the shuttle program alive in the mind of the public and Congress.[8] Christa McAuliffe was selected from 11,000 applicants as that teacher.

She was not the first citizen to fly, however. Utah Senator Jake Garn and Florida Representative Bill Nelson had gone before her. However, some astronauts later revealed that they were a "space invalid" or "a pain."[9] Nonetheless, NASA pressed forward to prove that ordinary people could be a part of the shuttle program, and at the same time reap the public relations benefits.

Despite the public relations efforts, NASA did have some difficulties with the media. Delays were met with sarcastic remarks about a "high tech low comedy" or "a flawless liftoff is too much of a challenge" on the nightly network news.[10]

Richard G. Smith, then head of the Kennedy Space Center, said, "Every time there was a delay, the press would say, 'Look, there's another delay . . . here's a bunch of idiots who can't even handle a launch schedule.' You think that doesn't have impact? If you think it doesn't, you're stupid."[11] Although CBS commentator Dan Rather admitted that such remarks may have pressured NASA, he noted that NASA may have paid too much attention to the news and risked people's lives.

When *Challenger* exploded, NASA suddenly slammed the door on the media. Charges flew in the months after the accident that NASA deliberately covered up or failed to quickly pass along damaging information. In its defense, NASA contended it waited so it could release the right information the first time and not fuel rumors or speculations.[12]

However, as difficulties with the media were emerging, communication inside NASA was beginning to crumble.

Management: NASA Style

NASA, headquartered in Washington, D.C., instituted a decentralized management structure to cope with its dual passenger and cargo roles. In the process, however, NASA lost effective control over its three operational arms: the Johnson Space Center in Houston, Texas; the Marshall Space Flight Center in Huntsville, Alabama; and the Kennedy Space Center at Cape Canaveral, Florida. "The centers, in turn, seemed uncertain about their relation to one another. Trying to get a grip on its system, NASA set up elaborate reporting channels that produced reams of paper."[13]

For the shuttle program, these reporting channels consisted of four Review Levels (Exhibit 1). At Level IV, contractors designed and produced the various pieces of the shuttle. At Level III, NASA program managers oversaw the development, testing and launch site delivery of those ele-

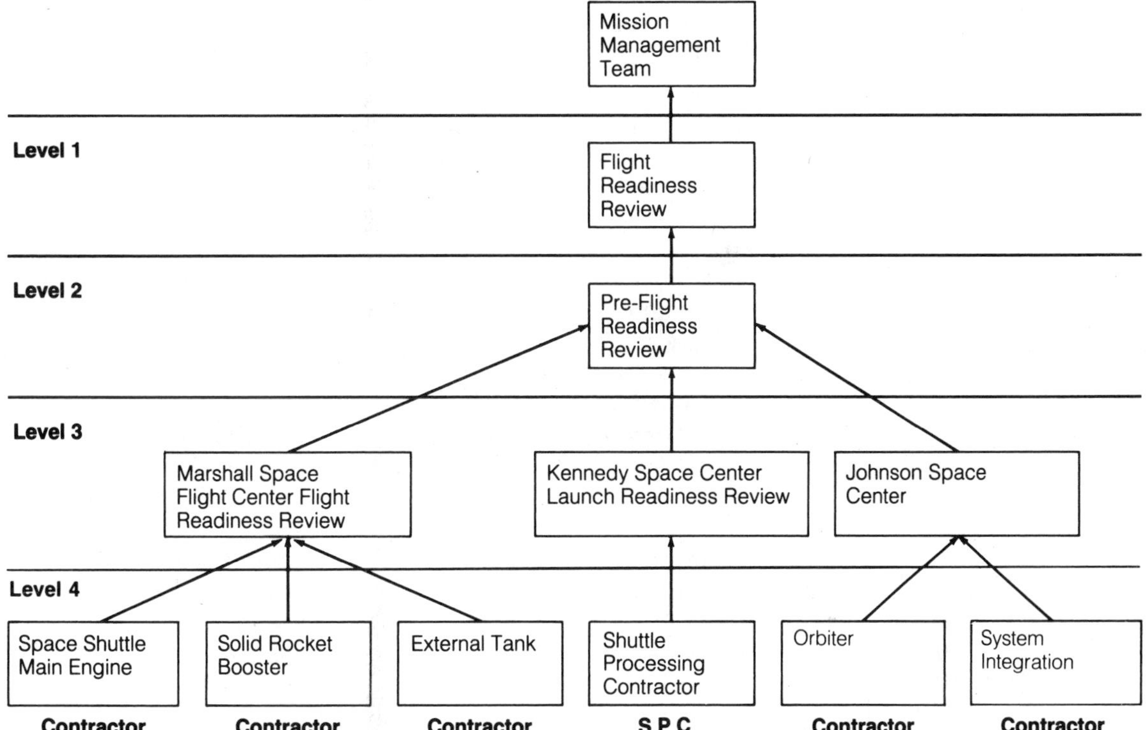

EXHIBIT 1 Readiness Review Levels

Source: *Report of the Presidential Commission on the Space Shuttle Challenger Accident.* Washington, D.C., 1986, p. 83.

(continued)

ments. Level II, the Space Transportation System manager, was responsible for integrating the elements and providing technical advice to Level I, which was responsible for policy, budgetary and top level technical matters. Level I also selected the Mission Management Team, which was responsible for a specific shuttle mission.

Despite the complexity and control problems, NASA believed its communication system worked well and saw no need to change or evaluate it.

Morton Thiokol Wins Big

Morton Thiokol, a Chicago-based aerospace, chemicals and salt company, got a big boost in November, 1973, when it won the shuttle solid rocket boosters contract, beating three major aerospace companies.

(continued)

(continued)

The solid rocket boosters would be the largest ever built, and the contract would be the first monitored by the Marshall Space Flight Center.

Thiokol, as the company was referred to, was selected because it "could do a more economical job . . . in both the development and production phases of the program."[14] This evaluation came despite its rating as fourth in design development and manufacturing. The selection committee did note, however, that the joint design, particularly the use of two O-rings, was "innovative."

An O-ring is a rubber ring running the circumference of the solid rocket booster, slightly larger than a quarter-inch in diameter. It is designed to prevent hot gases generated at liftoff from seeping through the booster assembly joints. The Thiokol design contained two O-rings, each made of several pieces of rubber (not one solid piece as the Titan solid rocket boosters had been), and a bore seal/face seal design which, with an asbestos putty, blocked the escaping gases (Exhibit 2). To accommodate the dual O-rings, the joint was longer, and therefore was more susceptible to bending under pressure.

Thiokol believed that its double O-ring and bore seal/face seal design provided better redundancy (meaning a backup to a primary component in case that component failed) than a double bore seal since there were different manufacturing and assembly tolerances. However, Thiokol, with NASA's approval, later would change the joint design to a double bore seal (Exhibit 2).

Test Results Begin to Raise Concerns

By the mid-1970s solid rocket booster testing was in progress. One important test was the hydroburst, in which highly pressurized water is used to simulate a motor firing. The test results were the first sign of problems to come: in the milliseconds after ignition the joint acted against predictions and opened rather than closed. Thiokol reported the inconsistency to NASA, yet no further tests were scheduled.

NASA, however, was concerned. A September 2, 1977, memo to Glenn Eudy, Chief Engineer of the Solid Rocket Motor Division at Marshall, noted the design allowed an O-ring clearance and may be deficient. Also, an October 21 study by Marshall engineer Leon Ray said the current design was unacceptable.

As an engineer, Ray was at the heart of the evaluation process of the solid rocket booster, but toward the bottom of NASA's complex and long organization chart (Exhibit 3). It would seem impossible to have one end know what the other was doing, even at lower levels. In the shuttle project alone it seemed possible that the engineers could indeed get lost—and disregarded—in the communication shuffle.

To follow through on his study, Ray, through memo by Solid Rocket Motor Branch chief John Q. Miller, told Eudy there were no reasons why the

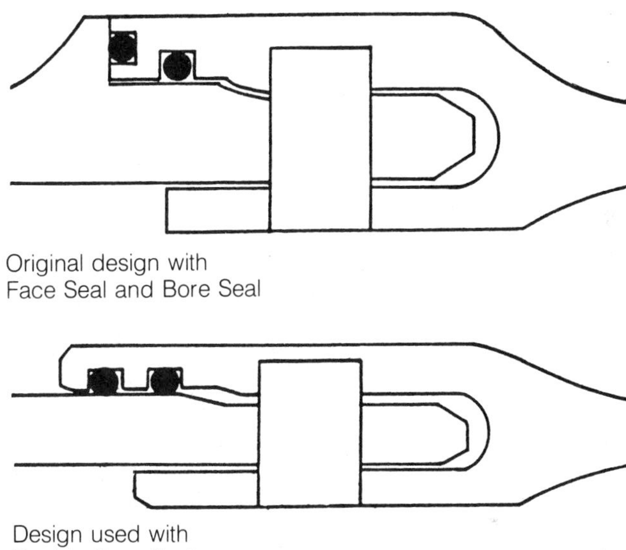

EXHIBIT 2 Double Bore Seal Design

Source: *Report of the Presidential Commission on the Space Shuttle Challenger Accident.* Washington, D.C., 1986, p. 121.

(continued)

seal could not be redesigned to acceptable standards. With no response by a year later, Ray, in January, 1979, again used a memo to Miller to tell Eudy the design was unacceptable.

The next month, after visiting the O-ring subcontractor, Ray for the third time wrote that a new design should be considered. Yet NASA still apparently said or realized nothing, and no records indicated Thiokol had been informed of Ray's concerns. In its March certification review, Thiokol mentioned some leak check failures but did not list them as a problem or failure.

In 1980, a NASA verification and certification committee was impaneled to verify the shuttle system's flight worthiness, including the solid rocket boosters. At the committee's request, NASA performed independent firing tests on the joint. These tests were conducted to the satisfaction of

(continued)

Relevant Organization Charts of NASA and Morton Thiokol

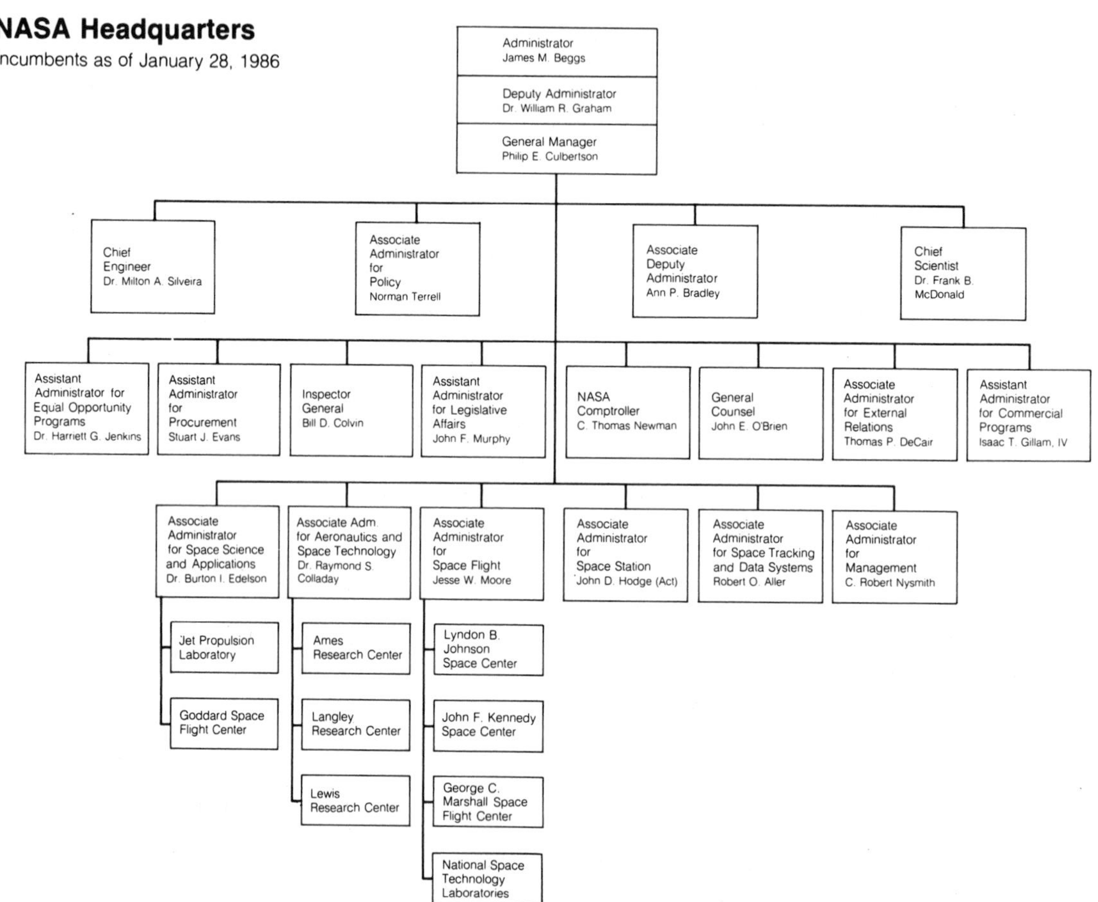

EXHIBIT 3 Relevant Organization Charts of NASA and Morton Thiokol

(continued)

the committee, and were reported out on September 15. On November 1, NASA classified the solid rocket booster joint on the critical items list as Criticality 1R.

Critical Launches, Critical Concerns

There were five criticality classifications that could be given to a shuttle component. Criticality 1 indicated a loss of life and vehicle if that com-

(continued)

Office of Space Flight

Incumbents as of January 28, 1986

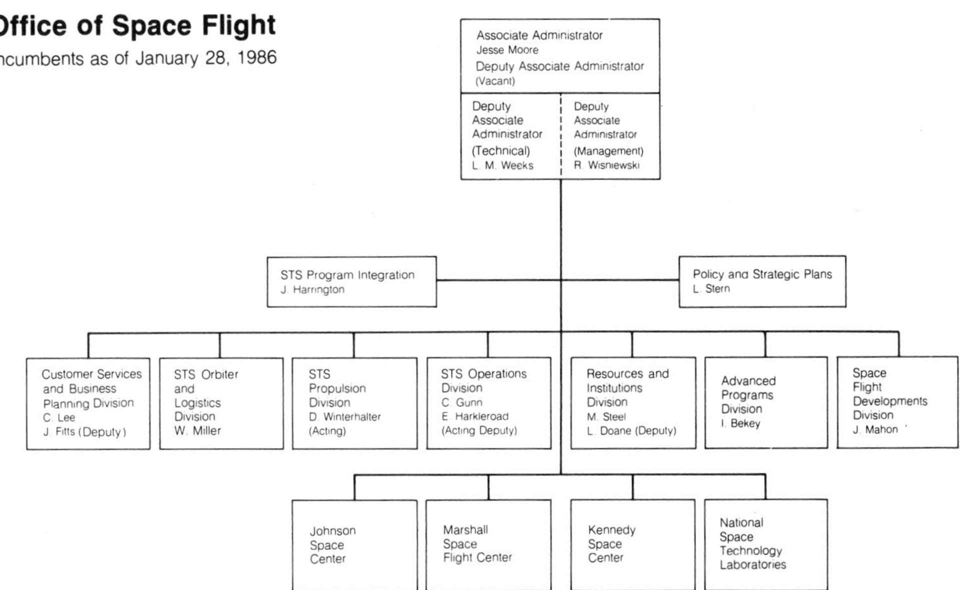

Lyndon B. Johnson Space Center

Incumbents as of January 28, 1986

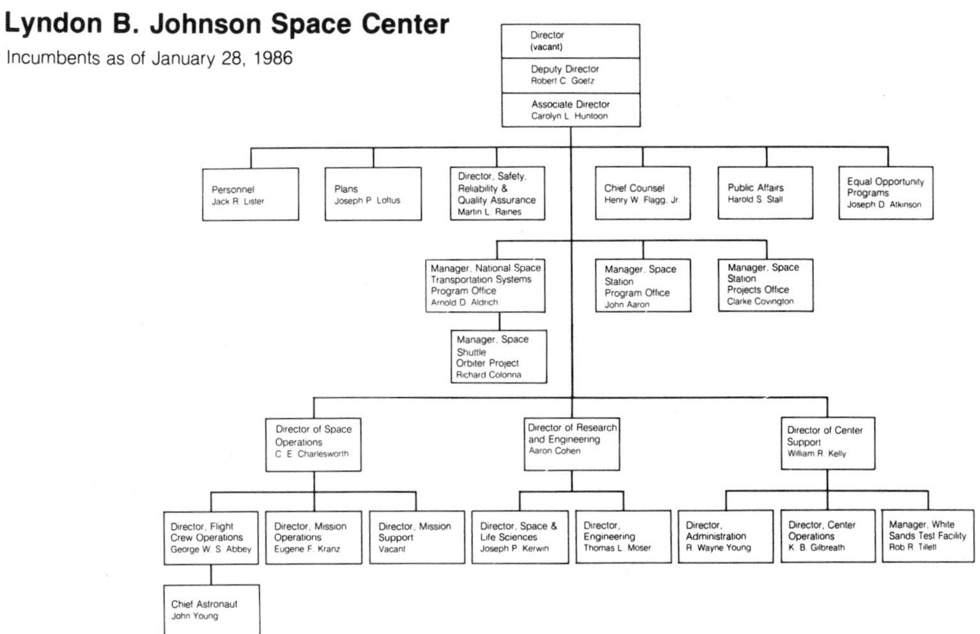

EXHIBIT 3 Relevant Organization Charts of NASA and Morton Thiokol *(continued)*

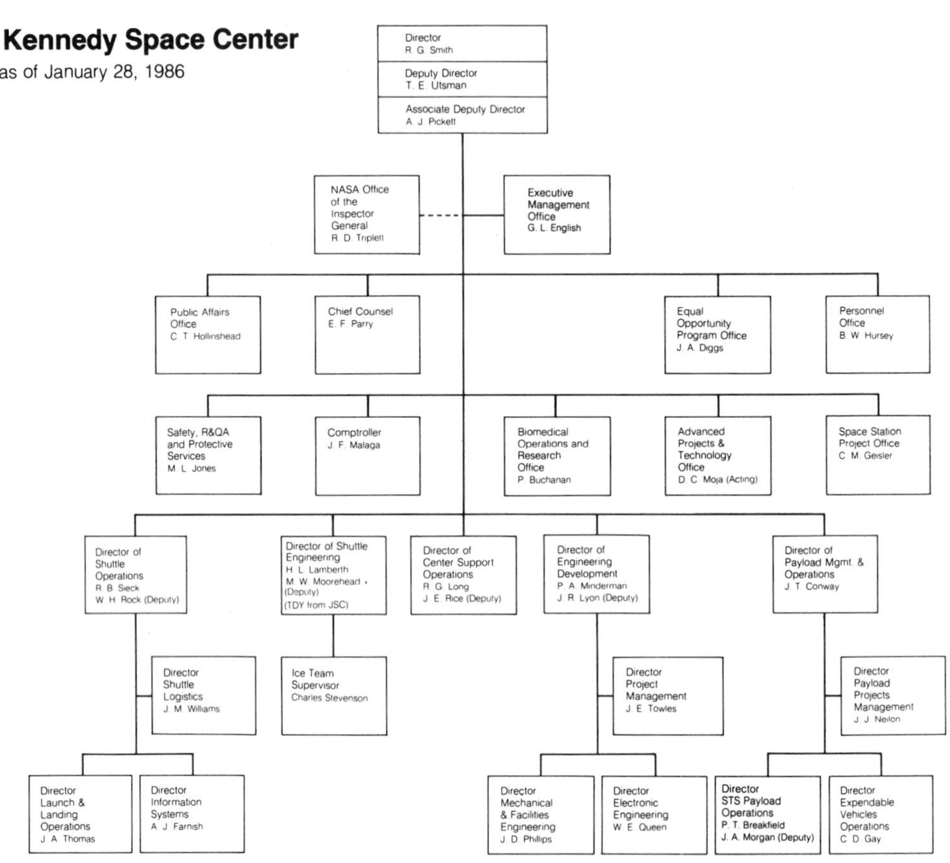

EXHIBIT 3 Relevant Organization Charts of NASA and Morton Thiokol *(continued)*

(continued)

ponent fails. Criticality 2 was a loss of the mission, and Criticality 3 was a catch all for any remaining items. An "R" after Criticality 1 or 2 indicates redundancy, a built back up to the component in case it fails.

For the booster assembly joints, the 1R classification meant a loss of life and mission if both O-rings failed to keep the gases from escaping at the joints. However, as NASA Space Transportation System Manager Arnold Aldrich later said, the language in the Critical Items List report implied the O-rings actually were Criticality 1 since the second O-ring's performance was questionable.

On April 12, 1981, the first of four test flights of the space shuttle Columbia was launched. Columbia reported no problems with the joints. However, the second flight in November, 1981, was the first to have what

George C. Marshall Space Flight Center Organization Charts

Center Organization

Incumbents as of January 28, 1986

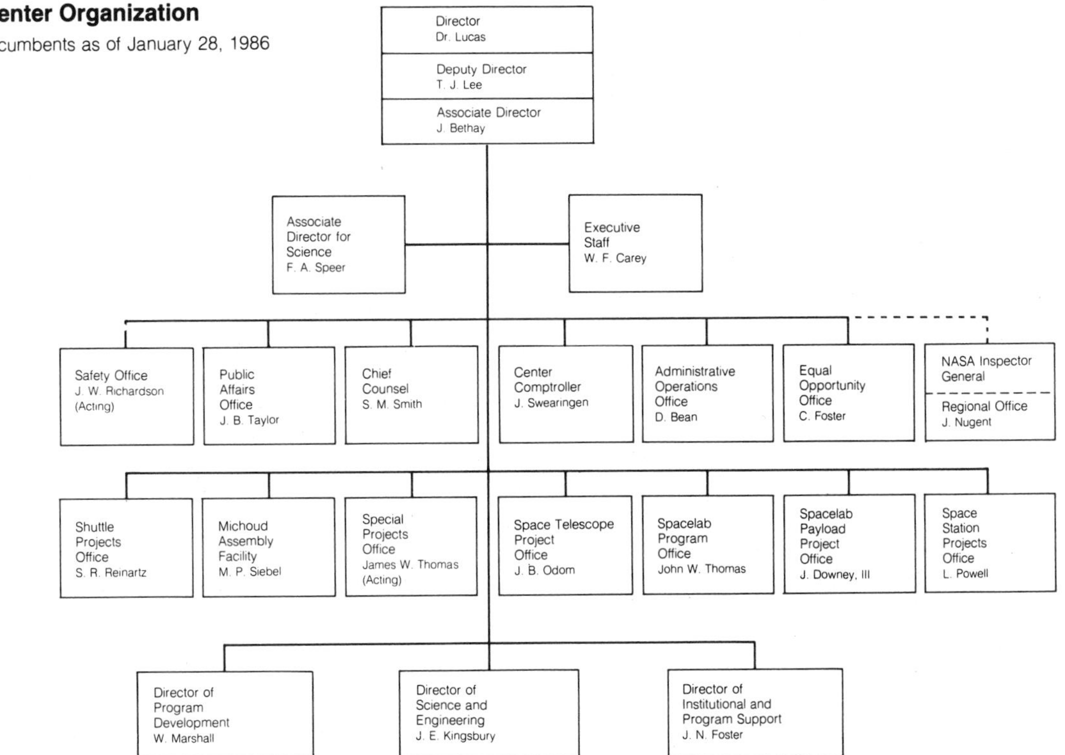

EXHIBIT 3 Relevant Organization Charts of NASA and Morton Thiokol *(continued)*

(continued)

NASA termed an "anomaly" with the O-rings. The asbestos putty had a path created by pressure from the hot gases in it, and the first O-ring had evidence of experiencing heat. The anomaly was not reported to the Level I review of the third flight, however, nor was it assigned a "tracking" number as most problems were.

In December 1982 the Marshall management changed the O-ring rating to Criticality 1. Yet even after being notified of the change, NASA and Thiokol still considered the O-rings as 1R—internal documents after the rating change referred to the O-rings as 1R.

Marshall engineers disagreed with Thiokol hypothesis, and argued for further testing. The dispute between NASA and Thiokol was not resolved,

(continued)

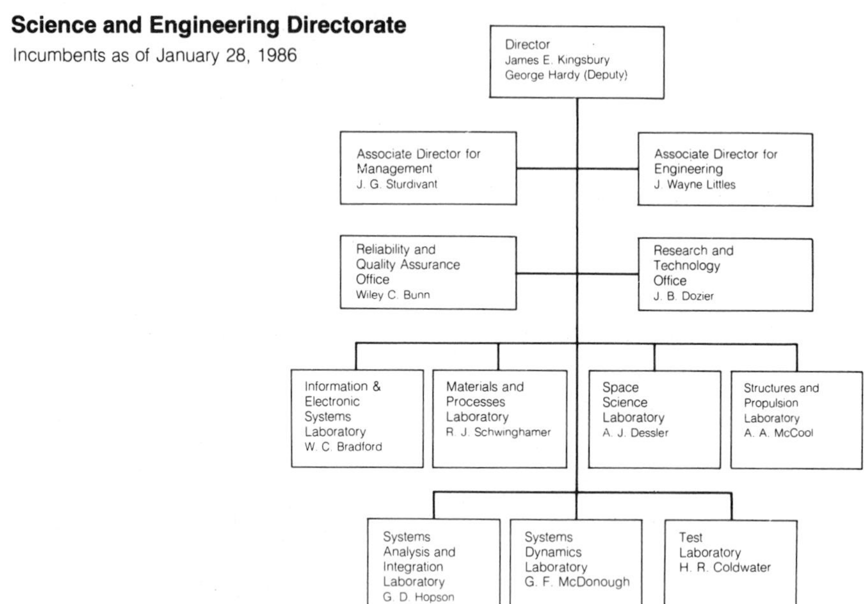

EXHIBIT 3 Relevant Organization Charts of NASA and Morton Thiokol *(continued)*

(continued)

however, and was sent to an independent "referee" for further testing. Marshall management members Dr. Judson Lovingood, Deputy Director of Shuttle Projects, Lawrence Mulloy, Solid Rocket Motor Project Manager, and George Hardy, Deputy Director of Science and Engineering, took the middle road: the joint was redundant in all but worst case situations.

Despite the dispute, the sixth shuttle mission was given a criticality waiver and flew in April, 1983. It appeared that, as Associate Administrator for Space Flight (Technical) Michael Weeks said, "The Solid Rocket Booster was probably one of the least worrisome things we had in the program."[15] This was not surprising. A December count indicated 748 items rated Criticality 1, including 114 on the solid rocket boosters alone. "None was given any priority in urgency, so none stood out as demanding a quick remedy."[16]

An Erosion of Confidence

On February 3, 1984, flight 41-B, the tenth shuttle flight, was launched. Post-flight analysis of the solid rocket boosters indicated for the first time that the primary O-ring had been impinged, or directly hit, by the hot gases and had eroded. Thiokol's response was to point to tests indicat-

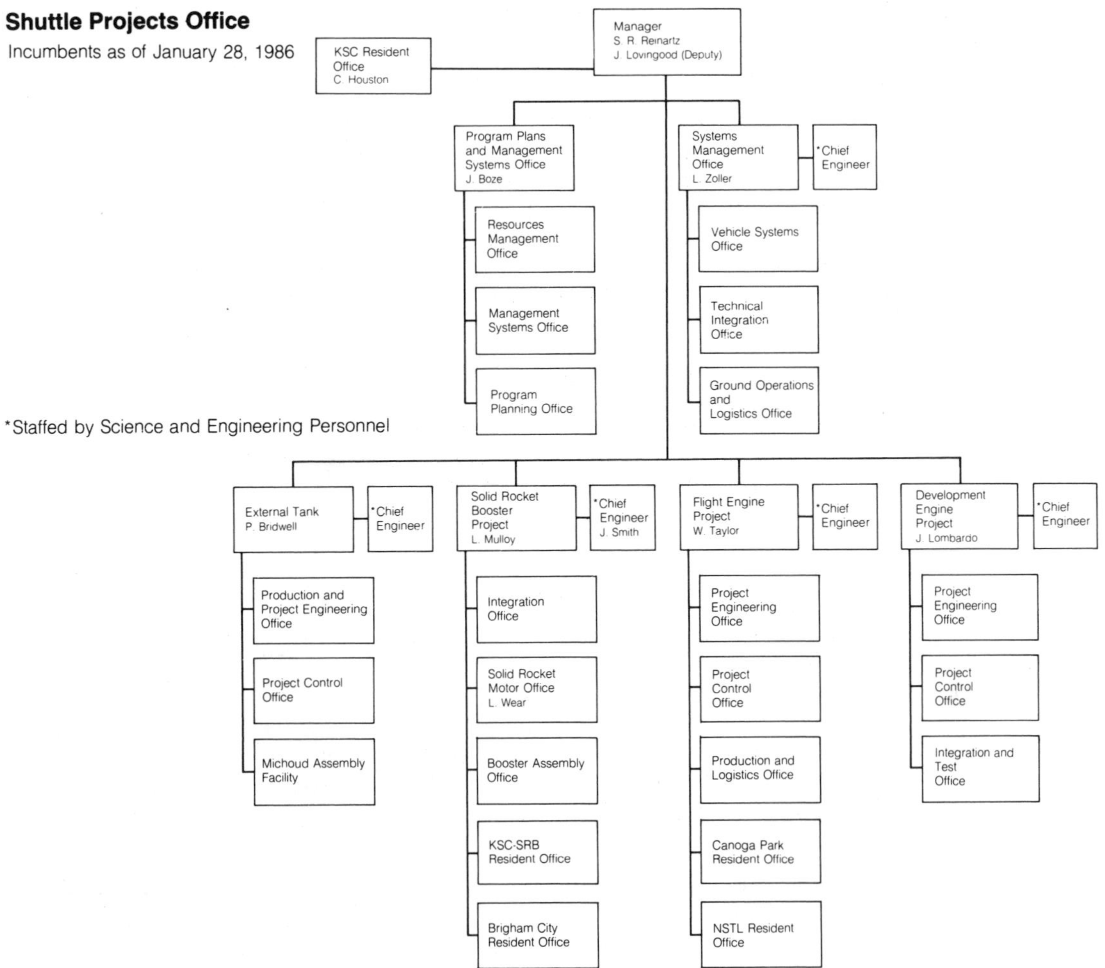

EXHIBIT 3 Relevant Organization Charts of NASA and Morton Thiokol *(continued)*

(continued)

ing the second O-ring seal would not fail. But to NASA engineers the response seemed neither correct nor relevant.

In its Problem Assessment System Report, however, Marshall required no remedial action and did not place a launch constraint on the joint. It seemed that while a possibility of a similar impingement failure recurring existed, it was believed that the O-ring would erode only to a maximum point, which in essence became the maximum level of acceptable error.

(continued)

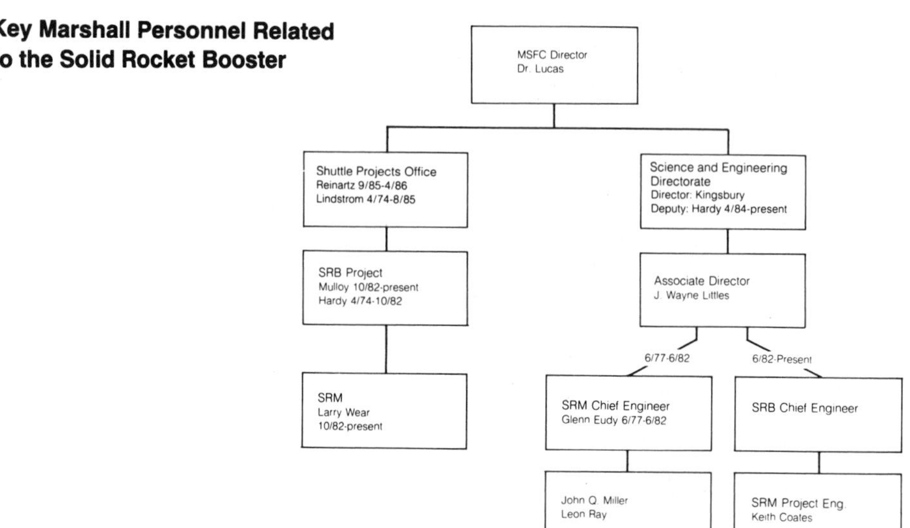

EXHIBIT 3 Relevant Organization Charts of NASA and Morton Thiokol

(continued)

Thiokol kept moving from finding a solution which might require a joint redesign to proving there was safety in the redundancy of the current design. Error might be expected, but it was within safety limits.

NASA went along with the report, and with the thinking behind it. On March 20, the flight 41-C Level I review was briefed on the erosion as a technical issue. The recommendation was to fly "accepting the possibility of some O-ring erosion due to hot gas impingement."[17] Formally, error became acceptable.

(Commission member Richard P. Feynman later called this a "kind of Russian roulette. (The shuttle) flies (with O-ring erosion) and nothing happens. Then it is suggested, therefore, that the risk is no longer so high for the next flights. We can lower our standards a little bit because we got away with it last time."[18])

O-ring damage occurred in subsequent flights with varying degrees of erosion. As from the beginning, Thiokol labeled blow holes (hot gas paths) in the putty as at least a contributing factor in the erosion because they focused the hot gas on the O-ring. Thiokol even conducted tests to prove this.

But Thiokol engineer Brian Russell believed otherwise. In a letter to Robert B. Ebeling dated April 9, 1984, he contended that when the putty leak tests were conducted, the blow holes in the putty were not the re-

(continued)

sult of any failure of the putty itself. Rather, he noted the blow holes had increased as the air pressure used in the leak check tests had increased.

For this reason, NASA asked that Thiokol conduct more tests. This time Thiokol would be slow to respond.

A Cold Start

On January 24, 1985, flight 51-C was launched with the temperature at 53 degrees, the lowest of any launch. This flight had the most serious in the string of "firsts" to date: there was blow-by erosion of the first O-ring and evidence of heat on the second. The first O-ring had failed to seal, and the hot gases had blown by it and also eroded it. This had occurred on flight 41-C, but the second seal had never experienced heat.

NASA engineers and, for the time being, Marshall management raised concern. Lawrence Mulloy, Solid Rocket Booster Program Manager, requested to Solid Rocket Motor office head Larry Wear that O-ring erosion become a part of future flight readiness reviews. Nine days later, on February 8, Thiokol reported there was a concern that the O-ring gas seal could be lost, and the low temperature could have been a factor. But the solution was chillingly similar to those before: while not desirable, it was acceptable.

At the February 21 Level I review of flight 51-D, the erosion was not analyzed as Mulloy had requested. It was referred to once, and once again called acceptable.

However, as a result of the failure on flight 51-C, a test was conducted which indicated there was a high probability that the ability of the O-ring to seal was affected by temperature. But little was done, and joint seal problems continued on the next four flights.

One of those was flight 51-B. The results of its June O-ring analysis of that flight stunned Thiokol. The primary O-ring had failed to hold, and both O-rings had eroded. Immediately after receiving the report, Mulloy put a launch constraint (defined as an unresolved problem with a criticality rating of 1, 1R, 2 or 2R) on the shuttle.

It was perhaps an exercise in futility. Mulloy himself would waive the Level III constraint at each level thereafter.

Efforts from the Engineers

Once the O-ring failure was discovered, the NASA engineer on site at Thiokol's Utah branch informed Associate Administrator for Space Flight Michael Weeks of the problem and noted Thiokol's lack of response to the year-old action item from flight 41-B.

At least one Thiokol engineer was concerned, however. Roger Boisjoly wrote a memo on July 22, noting that Thiokol may lose the solid rocket

(continued)

(continued)

booster contract if a solution to the joint problems was not found quickly. He followed that memo with another to Thiokol Vice President of Engineering Robert K. Lund which stated that an O-ring failure could result in "a catastrophe of the highest order—loss of human life." [19] Boisjoly recommended a task force be put on the problem soon (Exhibit 4).

On August 19, Thiokol briefed NASA on the erosion. The briefing paper noted the critical nature of the problem, yet asserted it was still safe to fly. Still, the following day Thiokol established the task force Boisjoly had called for. However, Thiokol management began to hinder its own engineers by lack of support for the task force.

On October 1, Robert V. Ebeling, Thiokol's solid rocket motor ignition system manager, filed his weekly report with Solid Rocket Motor Project Manager Allen McDonald. The seriousness of the problem was almost too evident: his report literally shouted "HELP!" In the report he outlined the lack of cooperation with the task force, and ended with, "This is a red flag" [20] (Exhibit 5).

It was not red enough. Flight 61-A flew, and blow-by erosion occurred again. The erosion was not reported to the Level I review of flight 61-B, however, and it flew in November.

In December Thiokol stated that the preliminary result of a task force test indicated a need to redesign the test chamber. Ebeling believed Thiokol should solve the problem before shipping any more motors. Unfortunately, he did not voice his concerns to the proper people, because on December 6 shuttle rocket motor project director Brian Russell was asked to request of McDonald that McDonald pursue closure of the O-ring critical problems. To close out a problem, evidence of corrective action to put the problem under control was required.

However, four days later McDonald asked Larry Wear for closure, saying Thiokol planned to work on a solution over the long term. It was as if Thiokol and NASA were gambling on the "acceptability" of the problem.

Up to that time flight readiness reviews had continued without addressing the O-ring difficulties. Despite Mulloy's earlier concerns from flight 51-C about temperature, it was never mentioned in or after February Level I reviews for flight 51-E. Erosion was last discussed in July reviews for flight 51-F. Perceived to be of little risk, it had ceased to be an issue, until January 27, 1986.

Ready to Go . . . Almost

In many respects, *Challenger* was ready to fly. The crew was "rarin' to go." Yet again and again the launch was pushed back. At 12:36 p.m. Eastern Standard Time on January 27, with the crew aboard the orbiter,

(continued)

MORTON THIOKOL, INC. COMPANY PRIVATE

Wasatch Division

Interoffice Memo

31 July 1985
2870:FY86:073

TO: R. K. Lund
Vice President, Engineering

CC: B. C. Brinton, A. J. McDonald, L. H. Sayer, J. R. Kapp

FROM: R. M. Boisjoly
Applied Mechanics - Ext. 3525

SUBJECT: SRM O-Ring Erosion/Potential Failure Criticality

This letter is written to insure that management is fully aware of the seriousness of the current O-Ring erosion problem in the SRM joints from an engineering standpoint.

The mistakenly accepted position on the joint problem was to fly without fear of failure and to run a series of design evaluations which would ultimately lead to a solution or at least a significant reduction of the erosion problem. This position is now drastically changed as a result of the SRM 16A nozzle joint erosion which eroded a secondary O-Ring with the primary O-Ring never sealing.

If the same scenario should occur in a field joint (and it could), then it is a jump ball as to the success or failure of the joint because the secondary O-Ring cannot respond to the clevis opening rate and may not be capable of pressurization. The result would be a catastrophe of the highest order - loss of human life.

An unofficial team (a memo defining the team and its purpose was never published) with leader was formed on 19 July 1985 and was tasked with solving the problem for both the short and long term. This unofficial team is essentially nonexistent at this time. In my opinion, the team must be officially given the responsibility and the authority to execute the work that needs to be done on a non-interference basis (full time assignment until completed).

EXHIBIT 4 Roger Boisjoly's first attempt after STS 51-B (flight 17) to convince his management of the seriousness of the O-ring erosion problem.

Source: *Report of the Presidential Commission on the Space Shuttle Challenger Accident.* Washington, D.C., 1986, p. 249.

MORTON THIOKOL, INC.
Wasatch Division

Interoffice Memo

1 October 1985
E150/RVE-86-47

TO: A. J. McDonald, Director
Solid Rocket Motor Project

FROM: Manager, SRM Ignition System, Final Assembly, Special Projects and Ground Test

CC: B. McDougall, B. Russell, J. McCluskey, D. Cooper, J. Kilminster, B. Brinton, T. O'Grady, B. MacBeth, J. Sutton, J. Elwell, I. Adams, F. Call, J. Lamere, P. Ross, D. Fullmer, E. Bailey, D. Smith, L. Bailey, B. Kuchek, Q. Eskelsen, P. Petty, J. McCall

SUBJECT: Weekly Activity Report
1 October 1985

EXECUTIVE SUMMARY

HELP! The seal task force is constantly being delayed by every possible means. People are quoting policy and systems without work-around. MSFC is correct in stating that we do not know how to run a development program.

GROUND TEST

1. The two (2) GTM center segments were received at T-24 last week. Optical measurements are being taken. Significant work has to be done to clean up the joints. It should be noted that when necessary SICBM takes priority.

2. The DM-6 test report less composite section was released last week.

ELECTRICAL

As a result of the latest engineering analysis of the V-1 case it appears that high stress risers to the case are created by the phenolic DFI housings and fairings. As it presently stands, these will probably have to be modified or removed and if removed will have to be replaced. This could have an impact on the launch schedule.

A. J. McDonald, Director
1 October 1985
E150/RVE-86-47
Page 2

FINAL ASSEMBLY

One SRM 25 and two SRM 26 segments along with two SRM 24 exit cones were completed during this period. Only three segments are presently in work. Availability of igniter components, nozzles and systems tunnel tooling are the present constraining factors in the final assembly area.

IGNITION SYSTEM

1. Engineering is currently rewriting igniter gask-o-seal coating requirements to allow minor flaws and scratches. Bare metal areas will be coated with a thin film of HD-2 grease. Approval is expected within the week.

2. Safe and Arm Device component deliveries is beginning to cause concern. There are five S&A's at KSC on the shelf. Procurement, Program Office representatives visited Consolidated Controls to discuss accelerating scheduled deliveries. CCC has promised 10 A&M's and 30 B-B's no later than 31 October 1985.

O-RINGS AND PUTTY

1. The short stack finally went together after repeated attempts, but one of the o-rings was cut. Efforts to separate the joint were stopped because some do not think they will work. Engineering is designing tools to separate the pieces. The prints should be released tomorrow.

2. The inert segments are at T-24 and are undergoing inspection.

3. The hot flow test rig is in design, which is proving to be difficult. Engineering is planning release of these prints Wednesday or Thursday.

4. Various potential filler materials are on order such as carbon, graphite, quartz, and silica fiber braids; and different putties. They will all be tried in hot flow tests and full scale assembly tests.

5. The allegiance to the o-ring investigation task force is very limited to a group of engineers numbering 8-10. Our assigned people in manufacturing and quality have the desire, but are encumbered with other significant work. Others in manufacturing, quality, procurement who are not involved directly, but whose help we need, are generating plenty of resistance. We are creating more instructional paper than engineering data. We wish we could get action by verbal request but such is not the case. This is a red flag.

Bob
R. V. Ebeling

EXHIBIT 5 In this weekly activity report, Robert Ebeling attempts ("Help!") to draw management attention to the difficulties experienced by the seal task force in getting adequate support, indicating "This is a red flag."

Source: *Report of the Presidential Commission on the Space Shuttle Challenger Accident*. Washington, D.C., 1986, p. 252.

(continued)

the launch was scrubbed for the fourth time. Half an hour later, the launch was rescheduled for 9:38 a.m. the next day.

About 1 p.m., Larry Wear, Marshall Solid Rocket Motor Projects Office Manager, asked Thiokol space booster project manager Boyd Brinton if there were any concerns about the predicted below-freezing temperatures near launch time. Brinton telephoned the Utah headquarters of Thiokol's solid rocket booster program and requested personnel there to

(continued)

determine if there were any weather related concerns. Ignition systems manager Robert Ebeling was notified as well.

By 2:30 p.m. Thiokol engineer Roger Boisjoly had learned of the low temperature predictions. After some discussion between he and Ebeling, Ebeling called Allen McDonald, the Thiokol representative at the Kennedy Space Center, and expressed concern about the performance of the booster joints in the cold weather. McDonald then telephoned Cecil Houston, the Marshall resident manager at Kennedy, who then set up a Level III teleconference between Thiokol, Marshall and Kennedy program managers.

The *Challenger* crew members knew nothing of the discussions taking place. By 2:30 they had been taken off the *Challenger* and back to their quarters to wait for word on the next launch attempt. The crew had little voice in the launch decision anyhow; besides, practically all of the launch-related issues were unknown to them.

The teleconference began at 5:45 p.m. Thiokol engineers related their concerns about the joint performance at the predicted low temperatures to Marshall shuttle projects manager Stanley R. Reinartz at Kennedy and deputy manager Dr. Judson Lovingood at Marshall. The engineers' opinion was to delay the launch until noon or the afternoon, when it would be warmer.

While it appeared a launch decision could be made then, it was not. Rather, the only decision made was to schedule a second teleconference for 8:15 p.m. with more people. Thiokol was asked to transmit facsimiles of its data to all concerned parties.

In a private conversation later, Reinartz told Lovingood that if Thiokol persisted with its recommendation, they should not launch. Lovingood suggested advising Houston-based Level II manager Arnold D. Aldrich of the teleconference and possible recommendation. By 7 p.m. Reinartz had notified several key Marshall people, but he decided not to escalate the concern to Level II and contact Aldrich.

A Second Opinion

The second teleconference began half an hour late with numerous NASA and Thiokol representatives. Thiokol had every point on the solid rocket booster project management hierarchy present. Top Marshall managers were in as well.

Thiokol engineers again presented their case, this time with charts noting blow-by and erosion history, including tests and actual flight data. The worst case of blow-by and erosion to date occurred a year earlier when flight 51-C was launched with the temperature at 53 degrees.

Listening carefully was Robert K. Lund, Thiokol Vice President of Engineering, the man responsible for the engineers. When they finished, Lund

(continued)

(continued)

presented Thiokol's recommendation not to launch until the temperature reached the experience base minimum of 53 degrees (Exhibit 6).

Mulloy then asked Joe Kilminster, Thiokol's space booster program vice president and Mulloy's final authority, for the recommendation. Kilminster was to the point: based on the engineers' recommendations he could not recommend a launch.

It seemed the decision could be made, but then the tables of perspective turned.

Appalling Recommendation

"I'm appalled at your recommendation," George Hardy, NASA's deputy director of science and engineering, reportedly said. However, he said he would not go against it. Mulloy commented dryly if they "can't launch we won't be able to launch until next April."[21]

Discussion was raised about the assertion that the seals were qualified, in tests, from 40 to 90 degrees. While the desired 53 degrees was within this range, Thiokol conceded, 53 degrees was the lowest temperature actually experienced.

Without realizing it, NASA began moving from finding a solution to the O-ring problem to pushing for a launch despite Thiokol's assertion that this time there could be difficulties.

At 10:30 p.m., to sort the facts and opinions, Kilminster asked for a five minute off-line caucus with the Thiokol people. The caucus centered on the launch temperature and the O-rings. Using the evidence of the O-ring failures, Arnold Thompson, supervisor of the rocket motor cases, and staff engineer Boisjoly vigorously opposed the launch.

But it soon became apparent that they were not getting anywhere. At some point in the caucus, Lund was asked to take off his engineering hat and put on his management hat. Symbolically, it demonstrated that

Recommendations:

- O-ring temp must be ≥ 53° F at launch
  Development motors at 47° to 52° F with putty packing and no blow-by SRM 15 (the best simulation) worked at 53° F
- Project ambient conditions (temp & wind) to determine launch time

EXHIBIT 6: Lund Recommendations

Source: *Report of the Presidential Commission on the Space Shuttle Challenger Accident.* Washington, D.C., 1986, p. 107.

(continued)

the recommendation became management's decision. Suddenly, the engineers, perhaps the most knowledgeable about the problem, did not count in the recommendation.

The Decision to Go

Boisjoly left the room defeated. For the first time, the engineers, who usually were asked to prove it was safe to fly, were asked to prove that it was not safe to launch. But absolute proof that the O-rings would fail did not exist.

Thiokol management decided to recommend a launch: the logic was that even if the first seal failed, the second would hold.

The teleconference resumed at 11 p.m. Kilminster read the rationale for the decision, noting that the data were inconclusive, and then officially recommended a launch. Mulloy asked him to send a facsimile of the recommendation in writing and, with no further comments, ended the teleconference at 11:15 (Exhibit 7).

The arguments did not end yet, however. McDonald, who argued the engineers' points at Kennedy while the caucus was taking place in Utah, pressed how NASA could rationalize a launch outside of previous experience limits. Not only were the O-rings a concern, but high winds were sending the booster recovery ships toward shore and, further, the launch pad was icing over.

Finally, trying to make a strong statement, McDonald said he did not want to stand in front of a board of inquiry to explain the decision. Mulloy dismissed the comment, telling him it was not his concern, but his arguments would be passed on in an advisory capacity.

At 11:45 p.m., the facsimile was received at Kennedy. In the meantime, Mulloy and Reinartz called Aldrich, the shuttle system Level II manager, in Houston. They discussed the weather in the Atlantic and the icing concern. But the O-rings concerns, the hours of teleconferencing, were not mentioned. To Mulloy, the Level III issue had been resolved.

A Beautiful Launch Morning

An ice inspection was conducted at 1:35 a.m. A few hours later, Mulloy spoke with William Lucas, Marshall director. While this time Mulloy noted the O-ring discussions of the night before, he showed Lucas the facsimile of the recommendation and said the issue had been laid to rest.

Another ice inspection was completed by 8:45 a.m. By then Lovingood told Jack Lee, deputy director of Marshall, of Thiokol's initial recommendation not to launch. But like Mulloy, he too noted the change in the decision and the facsimile.

By 9 a.m. the crew was secured aboard the *Challenger,* unaware of any of the discussions and concerns of the previous night. While the day

(continued)

MTI ASSESSMENT OF TEMPERATURE CONCERN ON SRM-25 (51L) LAUNCH

- O CALCULATIONS SHOW THAT SRM-25 O-RINGS WILL BE 20° COLDER THAN SRM-15 O-RINGS
- O TEMPERATURE DATA NOT CONCLUSIVE ON PREDICTING PRIMARY O-RING BLOW-BY
- O ENGINEERING ASSESSMENT IS THAT:
  - O COLDER O-RINGS WILL HAVE INCREASED EFFECTIVE DUROMETER ("HARDER")
  - O "HARDER" O-RINGS WILL TAKE LONGER TO "SEAT"
    - O MORE GAS MAY PASS PRIMARY O-RING BEFORE THE PRIMARY SEAL SEATS (RELATIVE TO SRM-15)
      - O DEMONSTRATED SEALING THRESHOLD IS 3 TIMES GREATER THAN 0.038" EROSION EXPERIENCED ON SRM-15
  - O IF THE PRIMARY SEAL DOES NOT SEAT, THE SECONDARY SEAL WILL SEAT
    - O PRESSURE WILL GET TO SECONDARY SEAL BEFORE THE METAL PARTS ROTATE
      - O O-RING PRESSURE LEAK CHECK PLACES SECONDARY SEAL IN OUTBOARD POSITION WHICH MINIMIZES SEALING TIME
- O MTI RECOMMENDS STS-51L LAUNCH PROCEED ON 28 JANUARY 1986
  - O SRM-25 WILL NOT BE SIGNIFICANTLY DIFFERENT FROM SRM-15

JOE C. KILMINSTER, VICE PRESIDENT
SPACE BOOSTER PROGRAMS

MORTON THIOKOL, INC.
Wasatch Division

EXHIBIT 7 January 28 Telefax

Source: *Report of the Presidential Commission on the Space Shuttle Challenger Accident.* Washington, D.C., 1986, p. 97.

(continued)

warmed, Level I and Level II management briefly delayed the launch because of icing. Effects of the cold on O-rings, however, had been forgotten, until 73 seconds after *Challenger* left the launch pad.

A few miles away, spectators watched in disbelief as the horrifying scene unfolded in the Florida sky above them. They hardly noticed it was 36 degrees.

CHRONOLOGY OF EVENTS LEADING TO THE SPACE SHUTTLE *CHALLENGER* DISASTER

November, 1973	Morton Thiokol wins solid rocket booster contract
September 9, 1977	Glenn Eudy (NASA) gives first indication of defective design
October 21, 1977	Leon Ray (NASA) notes the current joint design is unacceptable
January, 1978	Ray argues in memo via John Q. Miller (NASA) to Eudy that there is no reason not to redesign the joint to acceptable standards
January, 1979	With no response, Ray writes again to Eudy
February, 1979	Ray again says redesign should be considered
Throughout 1980	Tests conducted by verification and certification committee
September 15, 1980	Verification and certification committee reports solid rocket motor is satisfactory
November 1, 1980	Joint classified as Criticality 1R
April 12, 1981	First of four test flights launched
November, 1981	Anomaly in O-rings first discovered
December, 1982	Joint criticality classification changed to 1 by Marshall
April, 1983	The sixth flight is launched with a waiver
February, 1984	Flight 41-B (tenth) is launched; first evidence of O-ring impingement noted
March 20, 1984	Review levels are brief on impingement as a technical issue
January 24, 1985	Flight 51-C is launched at the coldest temperature to date; blow-by occurs on first O-ring, second shows evidence of heat
February 7, 1985	Level I review terms erosion "acceptable"
June, 1985	Blow-by of first O-ring and erosion of both discovered from Flight 51-B; launch constraint placed on shuttle
July 22, 1985	Roger Boisjoly (Morton Thiokol) calls for establishment of a task force to find a solution to O-ring problem and avoid "catastrophe of the highest order"

(continued)

(continued)

August 19, 1985	NASA brief on erosion by Morton Thiokol
August 20, 1985	Boisjoly's' task force on O-rings established
October 1, 1985	In his monthly report, Robert Ebeling (Morton Thiokol) notes lack of support for O-ring task force
October 30, 1985	Flight 61-A is launched; erosion reoccurs
November 26, 1985	Review for Flight 61-B does not include a report on the erosion from Flight 61-B
December, 1985	Morton Thiokol reports a need to redesign the test chamber; pursues closure of the issue
January 27, 1986	All times are Eastern Standard Time
12:30 p.m.	Scheduled launch cancelled for third time
1:00	Launch rescheduled for 9:38 a.m., January 28; concerns about launch sought
2:30	Boisjoly learns about predicted low launch temperatures
5:45	First teleconference held; decision made to hold a second teleconference at 8:15 p.m.
8:45	Second teleconference begins; Morton Thiokol engineers recommend delaying launch until temperature reaches at least 53 degrees
10:30	Joseph Kilminster (Morton Thiokol) requests a five minute off-line caucus at Morton Thiokol
10:30–11:00	Morton Thiokol personnel discuss launch recommendation; management overrides engineers and recommend a launch
11:00	Teleconference resumes; decision relayed to Mulloy (NASA) by Kilminster
11:15	Mulloy requests facsimile of Morton Thiokol's recommendation; teleconference ends
11:45	Facsimile received at Kennedy; Lawrence Mulloy and Stanley Reinartz (NASA) call Level II manager Arnold Aldrich (NASA), but do not discuss teleconferences with him
January 28, 1986	All times are Eastern Standard Time
1:35 a.m.	An ice inspection is conducted
7:00	Second ice inspection
8:00	Jack Lee (NASA) informed of Morton Thiokol's recommendation

(continued)

9:00	Crew is aboard *Challenger;* ice conditions discussed by Mission Management Team
10:30	Third ice inspection
11:38	*Challenger* is launched
11:39	*Challenger* explodes

FOOTNOTES

National Aeronautics and Space Administration:
"WHEN MACHINE MEETS MAN:
THE SPACE SHUTTLE *CHALLENGER* DISASTER"

Except as footnoted below, the entire case is based on the following sources:

"Report of the Presidential Commission on the Space Shuttle Challenger Accident," Vol. I (filed with President Ronald Reagan on June 6, 1986).

Manuson, Ed, "They slipped the surly bonds of earth to touch the face of God," *Time*, February 10, 1986.

[1]Moffett, Matt and Laurie McGinley, "NASA, Once a Master of Publicity, Fumbles in Handling Shuttle Crisis," *Wall Street Journal*, February 14, 1986, p. 21.

[2]Magnuson, Ed, "Fixing NASA," *Time*, June 9, 1986, p. 14.

[3]Moffett, p. 21.

[4]Hickey, Neil, "The Challenger Tragedy: It Exposed TV's Failures—as Well as NASA's," *TV Guide*, January 24, 1987, p. 10.

[5]Ibid., p. 17.

[6]Ross, Philip, "Shuttle objectives expected to change," *The Dallas Morning News*, June 6, 1986, p. 11-A.

[7]"Report of the Presidential Commission," p. 174.

[8]Moffett, p. 21.

[9]Magnuson, "Fixing NASA," p. 23.

[10]Ross, p. 3.

[11]Ibid., p. 4.

[12]Ibid., p. 10.

[13]Magnuson, "Fixing NASA," p. 17.

[14]"Report of the Presidential Commission," p. 120.

[15]Ibid., p. 128.

[16]Magnuson, "Fixing NASA," p. 18.

[17]"Report of the Presidential Commission," p. 132.

[18]Ibid., p. 148.

[19]Ibid., p. 139.

[20]Ibid., p. 141.

[21]Ibid., p. 94.

CASE QUESTIONS

Questions relating to "Perceptual Behavior"

1. How did the engineers at Morton Thiokol perceive their role in the launch decision? How did this compare to their actual role?
2. How did three perceptual dimensions play a role in the launch decision?
3. Despite the numerous hours in tests and teleconferencing on the day before the launch, why were the concerns expressed not revealed to Level I?
4. How do NASA's goals relate to the positive Pygmalion concept?
5. How were critical problems perceived by NASA? by Morton Thiokol? by engineers with the administration and the company?
6. What contributes to the perceptual differences between management and the engineers in regard to the importance of the launch?
7. What factors led to NASA's and Thiokol's perception of risk as being acceptable?

Questions relating to "Language Barriers"

1. How did the comments by George Hardy and Lawrence Mulloy affect the interpretation of Morton Thiokol's first launch recommendation?
2. What did the engineers at Morton Thiokol realize about the launch decision?
3. In what possible ways might language have covered up the seriousness of the O-ring and other problems?
4. In relation to the moon shots of the 1970s, what did the shuttle project come to represent to NASA? the "Teacher in Space" idea?
5. What had "criticality" come to mean?

Questions relating to "An Organization's Communication Climate, Flows and Loops"

1. What type of organizational communication network did NASA have? Morton Thiokol? Were they appropriate for the goals of the organizations?
2. Discuss the structure of NASA and Morton Thiokol. How did the structure affect the communication flow between hierarchical lines? between NASA and Thiokol?
3. Is decentralization necessarily bad in large organizations such as NASA? What are some ways to improve the communication patterns at NASA? at Morton Thiokol? Between NASA and contractors?
4. Should the astronauts have known about the pre-launch discussions and debate? the Level II and Level I management?

Questions relating to Culture and Climate

1. Compare the culture of NASA at the time of the moon shots and at the time of the *Challenger* accident. What change, if any, occurred? Why or why not did a change occur?

2. Would the NASA culture be characterized as "strong" or "weak"?
3. How does NASA's size affect its culture? Does a large company have an advantage or disadvantage in establishing a culture?
4. What might be some organizational culture concerns for an organization with large cooperative contracts such as the one between NASA and Morton Thiokol?
5. What might be the reasons that a launch decision was delayed twice?
6. Why had risk with the O-rings and other critical items become acceptable?
7. What organizational culture problems gave rise to a system that generated hundreds of "critical items" and then waivers?
8. Should the astronauts have known about the various criticality ratings, and in particular the pre-launch discussions?

General Questions

1. What would you have done to resolve the communication problem? the ranking of critical items?
2. What role would engineers play in an organization culture that might better suit the development of the shuttle program?

APPENDIX F

LETTER FORMATS

KEYSTONE LTD.
4332 Amherst Ave.
Baton Rouge, LA 70811

February 22, 1994

Ms. B. A. Buckman
Box 1113
Dallas, TX 75275

Dear Ms. Buckman:

This is an example of a semiblock-style letter. Its appearance is balanced because of the indented paragraphs and placement of the date and salutation. It is a traditional style still preferred by many people.

The first line of each paragraph is indented five spaces. The date line and the close begin at the center of the page.

You may desire to use this style for more formal occasions.

Sincerely,
Lynn Harris
Lynn Harris

EXHIBIT F.1 The Modified Block Format

KEYSTONE LTD.
4332 Amherst Ave.
Baton Rouge, LA 70811
(318) 932-7619

February 22, 1994

Ms. B. A. Buckman
Box 1113
Beaumont, TX 77705

Dear Ms. Buckman:

This is an example of a block-style letter, which has become common in many organizations. It is efficient because it saves time and energy for the typist.

The block style has no indentions. All parts of the letter begin at the left margin, including the date, salutation, and signature block.

You will find this a convenient, time-saving format.

Sincerely,

Lynn Harris

Lynn Harris

EXHIBIT F.2 The Block Format

KEYSTONE LTD.
4332 Amherst Ave.
Baton Rouge, LA 70811
(318) 932-7619

February 22, 1994

Ms. B. A. Buckman
Box 1113
Dallas, TX 75275

THE AMS STYLE

This is an example of the AMS style. You'll note the elimination of the salutation and close. There will be times when you will not address your letter to a specific person and the AMS style will be an excellent choice.

As in the block style, all parts of the letter begin at the left margin. It has the same time-saving features with the added simplicity of eliminating the formalities.

Your letter can be direct, yet friendly, with this format. Use it to adapt to your specific letter-writing needs.

LYNN HARRIS

Lynn Harris

EXHIBIT F.3 The AMS Format

INDEX